The Business of Sports

Text and Cases on Strategy and Management

The Business of Sports

Text and Cases on Strategy and Management

George Foster

Stephen A. Greyser

Bill Walsh

Australia · Brazil · Canada · Mexico · Singapore · Spain · United Kingdom · United States

THOMSON

SOUTH-WESTERN

The Business of Sports: Text and Cases on Strategy and Management, 1/e
George Foster, Stephen A. Greyser, and Bill Walsh

VP/Editorial Director:
Jack W. Calhoun

VP/Editor-in-Chief:
David Shaut

Senior Publisher:
Melissa S. Acuña

Senior Acquisitions Editor:
Joe Sabatino

Developmental Editor:
Emma Guttler

Marketing Manager:
Jacquelyn Carrillo

Production Editor:
Amy Hackett

Manager of Technology, Editorial:
Vicky True

Technology Project Editor:
Kristen Meere

Web Coordinator:
Karen Schaffer

Manufacturing Coordinator:
Doug Wilke

Production House:
Interactive Composition Corporation (ICC)

Printer:
West Group
Eagan, MN

Art Director:
Tippy McIntosh

Cover and Internal Designer:
Patti Hudepohl

Library of Congress Control Number: 2005922356

For more information about our products, contact us at:

Thomson Learning
Academic Resource Center

1-800-423-0563

Thomson Higher Education
5191 Natorp Boulevard
Mason, OH 45040
USA

ASIA (including India)
Thomson Learning
5 Shenton Way
#01-01 UIC Building
Singapore 068808

AUSTRALIA/ NEW ZEALAND
Thomson Learning
Australia
102 Dodds Street
Southbank, Victoria 3006
Australia

CANADA
Thomson Nelson
1120 Birchmount Road
Toronto, Ontario
M1K 5G4
Canada

UK/EUROPE/ MIDDLE EAST/ AFRICA
Thomson Learning
High Holborn House
50/51 Bedford Row
London WC1R 4LR
United Kingdom

To our friends and colleagues from the world of sports
who stimulate us and who make the lives of so
many people more interesting, more engaged,
and more enjoyable

To our students who continue to stimulate and motivate
us and who provide solid grounds for being
so optimistic about the future.

To our families who continue to provide much
emotional underpinning to and
love in our lives.

BRIEF CONTENTS

CONTENTS

93   SECTION THREE . . . Clubs

141   SECTION FOUR . . . Players/Athletes and Agents

PREFACE

This book seeks to provide insight into the key decisions made by managers on the business side of sports. We cover many aspects of the sporting landscape to highlight the diverse nature of the decisions involved and the financial and other issues at stake. The book contains an introductory overview section (Section 1) and nine additional sections (Sections 2 through 10) that cover specific topic areas—leagues, clubs, players, college sports, sponsorship, club marketing, broadcasting/media, stadiums, and valuation/profitability.

Organization

Section 1 presents the perspectives underlying "Business of Sports" courses developed at Stanford Business School (taught by George Foster and Bill Walsh) and Harvard Business School (taught by Stephen A. Greyser). These courses have been enthusiastically received, both for their underlying framework of ideas and for the insights provided into the business side of sports. At both Stanford and Harvard, frequent blue-ribbon guests from all the major areas covered in this book have participated in our classes or cotaught with us. These guests have stimulated our thinking as well as provided us with a deeper appreciation of the many varied facets of the business side of sports. This book is much richer for their many insightful contributions to our thinking. A key theme in our teaching is that creative and structured decision making increases the likelihood that preferred outcomes on the business side of sports can be achieved. A second key theme is that many business-of-sports decisions relate to the dual (and related) challenges of (1) growing the sports "revenue pie" in a sustainable and economically viable way and (2) sharing (allocating) that revenue pie among the diverse constituents. These two themes appear continually throughout Sections 2 to 10, as well as Section 1 of this book.

The content of this book was also enriched by the NFL-Stanford Executive Program directed by George Foster and Bill Walsh. The many lecturers and participants in this Executive Program broadened and deepened our knowledge of the many business issues faced by an elite professional sporting league at its many levels.

Supplements

Instructor's Manual (ISBN: 0-324-30350-5) The Instructor's Manual includes extensive case notes prepared by the authors designed to facilitate classroom presentation and utilization.

Website (http://foster.swlearning.com) *The Business of Sports'* website is a comprehensive, resource-rich location for both instructors and students to find pertinent information.

Acknowledgments

There are many people to whom we are indebted. Each of us has had extensive contacts with professionals in the business side of sports over many years. We have learned much from these many interactions, for which we are grateful. As noted previously, a special thanks is due to the many guest speakers who contribute so much to the classroom experience at our respective universities.

The students in our classes are a source of much stimulus and motivation. We have benefited greatly by their high level of interest and their desire to seek a broader and deeper understanding of the business of sports. The hours we spend with them gives us solid ground for being so optimistic about the future. The growing number of our students and our alumni in the many facets of the sports industry is a source of much pride as well as a wonderful resource in our research and teaching.

The Appendix to this book (Information Sources Used) lists the sources of key information and exhibits included in this book. We thank and are very much appreciative of the sources listed in this Appendix. Their diverse coverage enables us to much better convey the rich tapestry of the business aspects of the sporting industry. We strongly encourage readers to visit the websites listed to gain further appreciation of the richness of their coverage of this industry.

The cases included in this book are the result of substantial investment by the Stanford and Harvard case development centers. Some cases are based on "public-record" information while others also include interviews with executives involved in the key aspects of the case. The commitment and time of these executives in the case development added much to the final product included in this book. We are particularly grateful to those organizations that cooperated with us at field sites. Stanford GSB (led by Bob Joss), Stanford Business School Case Writing (led by Margot Sutherland) and the Center for Entrepreneurial Studies (CES— led by Irv Grousbeck, Chuck Holloway, Garth Saloner, and Linda Wells) provided much appreciated resources in both course and case development. We have been blessed by an excellent set of case writers and collaborators at Stanford: Dave Hoyt (six cases); Chris Armstrong (three cases); Chris Boni, Victoria Chang, and Amy Wustefeld (two cases each); and Todd Bello, Tom Covington, Jason Harkness, John Herbert, Ron Johnson, Eric Kroll, Susan Mackenzie, Patrick Molloy, Jake Moskowitz, Alicia Seiger, Steven Sibley, Cecil Smart, and Jessamy Tang (one case each). Paul Reist at the Stanford GSB Library has been an invaluable resource. Harvard Business School case writers and collaborators provided excellent assistance—John A. Clendenin, Kirk Goldman, Wendy Schille, Elizabeth Smyth, Dr. John Teopaco, Natalie Zakarian, Brian Harris, and Mitchell Truwitt.

The manuscript preparation has been superbly managed by Tom Duarte at Stanford University. Original research and data analysis by Chris Armstrong at Stanford enabled the financial aspects of the clubs across multiple leagues to be effectively analyzed and presented. Our assistants Linda Bethel, Tom Duarte, Lauren Margolin, and D.J. Smith (George Foster); Natalie Zakarian, Eileen Hankins, and Luz C. Velazquez (Stephen A. Greyser); and Jane Walsh (Bill Walsh), provided all the professional assistance we could have hoped for (and much more than one could realistically expect).

At Thomson Publishing, we are grateful for the high-quality support and encouragement of Joe Sabatino, Emma Guttler, Amy Hackett, Tippy McIntosh, and Mou Sen Gupta.

The support of our respective families in the journey that underlies the book has been both deep and greatly appreciated.

George Foster

Stephen A. Greyser

Bill Walsh

ABOUT THE
AUTHORS

George Foster is the Wattis Professor of Management at the Graduate School of Business, Stanford University. His teaching and research interests are in the sports management, entrepreneurship, and financial areas. Stanford sports-related courses he teaches include Sports Business Management, Sports Business Finance, and Sports Marketing. Hallmarks of these courses are their focus on a structured and creative approach to sports business issues, the up-to-date content of the material, and the frequent appearance of blue-ribbon guests. Those guests have included league- and club-level management, players and agents from all major professional sports, as well as executives from companies in the sports media, sports marketing/sponsorship, and sports financing areas. He works closely with the Stanford Athletic Department in the recruitment and advising of student athletes.

Foster codirects the NFL-Stanford Executive Program with Bill Walsh. This program brings together front-office and business participants from all NFL clubs and the NFL. Foster interacts extensively with league- and club-level executives from major sports in North America and other parts of the globe. One of his key current interests is the globalization of sports. His ongoing research examines established global sports such as soccer, rugby, cricket, and Formula One, as well as sports aspiring to greatly expand their global footprint (such as basketball, baseball, and football/gridiron). He consults extensively with companies and has served on the Board of Directors of multiple early-stage companies.

Foster has bachelor's and master's degrees in Economics from The University of Sydney and a Ph.D. in Business Administration from Stanford University. He has honorary doctorates from The University of Ghent and The University of Vaasa. He is the author/co-author of 8 books/monographs and over 30 articles.

Stephen A. Greyser is Richard P. Chapman Professor (Marketing/Communications) Emeritus at Harvard Business School (HBS), specializing in brand marketing, advertising/corporate communications, sports management, and nonprofit management. He earned A.B., M.B.A., and D.B.A. degrees at Harvard. His HBS career includes service as a *Harvard Business Review* editor, and later as its Editorial Board chairman. He was also executive director of the Marketing Science Institute, a nonprofit business-supported research center, for eight years.

He is responsible for 15 books and monographs, including *Revealing the Corporation* (2003), is a frequent contributor to professional journals, and has published some 300 Harvard case studies.

Active as a director/trustee, he is past national vice-chairman of PBS, and an overseer of WGBH and the Museum of Fine Arts. He is a director of Opinion Research Corporation, and until sold, Doyle Dane Bernbach, Restaurant Associates, Gruntal, and Tonka. His consulting relationships have included the NBA, NHL, and Boston Red Sox.

He conceived and developed the HBS M.B.A. elective "The Business of Sports," reflecting his lifelong fandom and longtime business involvement in sports. Earlier, he was a sports broadcaster and radio-TV producer. He also served on Harvard's Professional Sports Panel, advising undergraduates considering professional sports careers.

Known as "the Cal Ripken of HBS," in almost 40 years of teaching he has never missed a class.

Bill Walsh is recognized as one of the most innovative and successful football coaches in the history of the game. Among Walsh's achievements as head coach and top executive of the San Francisco 49ers are his three Super Bowl Championships, his election to the Pro Football Hall of Fame, and his development of a 49ers organization that set an NFL record—14 straight seasons of at least 10 wins. Walsh retired from active coaching in the NFL with a career record of 102–63–1, including a play-off record of 10–4. His accomplishments earned Walsh the title "NFL Coach of the Decade" for the 1980s. Two of Walsh's greatest legacies to football, however, are his creation of the widely used "West Coast Offense" and the number of distinguished coaches who worked with or tutored under him. He also twice served as head football coach at Stanford University. Other football programs he has been a member of include University of California at Berkeley, Oakland Raiders, Cincinnati Bengals, and San Diego Chargers.

Walsh coteaches with George Foster the Sports Business Management course at the Graduate School of Business, Stanford University. He codirects the NFL-Stanford Executive Program. He is also special advisor to Ted Leland, the athletic director at Stanford University. In the 1995–2004 period, Stanford Athletics has won the NACDA Director's Cup nine consecutive times, which is emblematic of being a leading college athletic program.

Walsh has bachelor's and master's degrees from San Jose State University. His publication, *Finding the Winning Edge* (1998), is a widely recognized "bible" for coaches seeking to both achieve excellence on the field and have programs and athletes that are ambassadors and role models for the game of football.

SECTION 1... Overviews from Stanford and Harvard

1.1 THE BUSINESS OF SPORTS: A PERSPECTIVE FROM STANFORD

By *George Foster and Bill Walsh*

The sports industry is a major high-profile global industry. Evidence of its elite status abounds. Major sporting events are consistently among the top-rated television programs each year. Major sports figures have global recognition that few business and political leaders attain. Many successful new cable channels are dedicated to sports broadcasting. Rankings of the highest individual income earners invariably include major sports figures.

The business of sports is attracting much interest. Exhibit 1.1-1 presents an overview of the value chain of the sports industry. This book is a comprehensive analysis of strategy and decision making by central participants on the business side of sports. We cover strategic analysis and strategic decisions by leagues, clubs, players, colleges, sponsors and endorsers, marketers, broadcasters, and stadium/arena owners or operators. In many areas, sports has much in common with other businesses. However, there are important areas where the features of the sports industry give rise to distinctively different challenges and opportunities for its managers. Exhibit 1.1-2 is a summary of these areas of commonality and differentiation.

EXHIBIT 1.1-1 VALUE CHAIN ANALYSIS: CREATION AND CAPTURE OF GAINS IN SPORTS

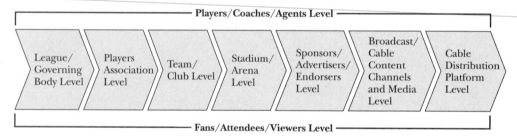

Central Challenges
- Value Creation (Growing the Pie)
- Value Sharing (Dividing the Pie)

EXHIBIT 1.1-2 MANAGING IN THE SPORTS INDUSTRY VIS-À-VIS MANAGING IN OTHER INDUSTRIES

Areas of Commonality	Areas of Differentiation
1. Leadership and Strategy Matters	1. Winning on the Field Central
2. Value Creation and Value Sharing	2. Diverse Owner Objectives
3. Search for Revenue Growth	3. Managing in the Fishbowl
4. Value Chain Encroachment and Fluidity	4. Supporting the Weakest
5. New Product Innovation	5. Handicapping the Strongest
6. Astute and Creative Contracting	6. Revenue Pools and Allocation Rules
7. Quality of the Product Matters	7. Athletes as Business Assets
8. Branding Matters	8. Managing with the "Badly Behaving"
9. Fans and Customers as a Business Pillar	9. Limited Financial Disclosures
10. Globalization	10. Sports and Entertainment Cocktail

Management in the Sports Industry Vis-à-vis Other Industries: Areas of Commonality

1. **Leadership and Strategy Matters.** The sports industry shares with all other industries the importance of having top management exhibit strong leadership and execute well-developed strategies. One aspect of leadership is creating effective coalitions among key participants in the sports value chain presented in Exhibit 1.1-1. This is not always easily achieved. In both the MLB (Major League Baseball) and NHL (National Hockey League), there has been a long history of divergent and entrenched differences between clubs and owners and often between subgroups within the club and owner categories—for example, large-city MLB clubs versus small-city MLB clubs. Throughout many sections and cases in this book, the importance of leadership is reinforced.

2. **Value Creation and Value Sharing as a Major Focus.** Business executives in most industries face the twin challenges of creating value and then sharing (distributing) that value. The sports industry is no different. All the parties listed in Exhibit 1.1-1 can help create (or destroy) value. The change in club valuations over time is an important indicator of value creation. Exhibit 1.1-3 presents the average club valuations across the four major U.S. team sport leagues using estimates from *Forbes* (and a predecessor magazine). Across all four leagues, there is much evidence of value creation. For example, the 1994 and 2003 average club valuations are ($ millions):

	NFL	**MLB**	**NBA**	**NHL**
1994	$160	$110	$113	$ 71
2003	732	295	265	159
Annual Compound Growth Rate	15.2%	9.8%	8.5%	8.1%

EXHIBIT 1.1-3   VALUE CREATION IN MAJOR NORTH AMERICAN SPORTS: CLUB AVERAGE VALUATION INCREASES FOR 1994–2003 BASED ON *FORBES'* ESTIMATES ($ MILLIONS)

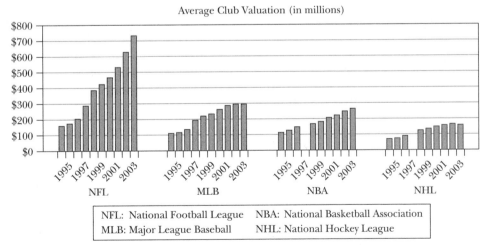

Average Club Valuation (in millions)

NFL: National Football League   NBA: National Basketball Association
MLB: Major League Baseball   NHL: National Hockey League

Source: Calculated from data in annual issues of *Forbes* and, up to 1997, *Financial World.* In 1997, *Forbes* did not make estimates for the NBA and the NHL; Deloitte, *Annual Review of Football Finance* (August 2004).

Associated with this value creation is much debate over value sharing among the key contributors to that creation, for example, owners of clubs, owners of stadiums/arenas, and players.

3. **Relentless Search for Revenue Growth Opportunities.** Business executives in most industries continually pursue opportunities to grow revenues. The sports industry is a leading exemplar of this pursuit. Revenue growth pursuit occurs at multiple levels, including the league, club, player, and broadcast network levels. Exhibit 1.1-4 presents average revenues, player salaries, and profitability across the four major U.S. sports leagues and the English Premier League (EPL). Across all five leagues, revenue growth has been achieved. For example, the 1994 and 2003 average club revenues are ($ millions):

	NFL	**MLB**	**NBA**	**NHL**	**EPL**
1994	$ 62	$ 40	$47	$31	£12
2003	167	129	94	70	62
Annual Compound Growth Rate	9.9%	11.6%	7.0%	8.0%	16.9%

Importantly, it appears that players have shared in this revenue growth in all five leagues. Exhibits 1.1-3 and 1.1-4 highlight how owners (shareholders) in the NFL (National Football League), NBA (National Basketball Association), and EPL have been able to better capture part of this revenue increase than have their counterparts in the MLB and NHL. This issue is explored frequently in this book.

4. **Value Chain Encroachment and Fluidity.** The groups listed in Exhibit 1.1-1 can overlap in their composition. Indeed, one aspect of the relentless search for growth opportunities is the encroachment by parties across parts of the value chain. There are many examples where clubs own or operate their own stadiums/arenas. Increasing interest is being shown by either leagues or clubs to own or operate media level parts of the value chain (such as cable content channels or Internet rights). Examples at the league level are NBA TV and the NFL Network. Examples at the club level are YES Network (linked to New York Yankees) and NESN (linked to Boston Red Sox). This value chain encroachment notion is often called vertical integration. In many industries, it is a widely used means of increasing and broadening the revenue base. There is also fluidity in membership of the value chain groups in the sports industry. Examples are recent sales by media companies of sporting clubs (such as Disney with Anaheim Angels and News Corp. with Los Angeles Dodgers). In some cases, media companies can gain much of the benefit of ownership of a club by astute contracting for club broadcasting rights and avoiding the ownership obligations.

5. **New Product Innovation Fuels Revenue Growth.** Across the major players in the sports value chain, new product innovations are a central part of growth strategies. We can see this at multiple levels. Whole new sporting competitions continue to emerge. The Extreme Football League (XFL) in 2001 was an entirely new league, created by World Wrestling Entertainment and NBC. The Super 12's rugby competition was a league that evolved in the mid-1990s in the Southern Hemisphere, with new teams in Australia, New Zealand, and South Africa. Like new product introductions in other industries, some sporting ventures succeed, but many fail. The last 25 years have showcased many new product innovations that have influenced, and continue to profoundly affect, the sports industry. ESPN, which celebrated its twenty-fifth anniversary in 2004, has transformed television coverage of sports highlights. Fantasy Sports blossomed in the 1990s and is now an important aspect of fan avidity. Electronic sports games, now a multimillion-dollar industry, are also a product of the last 25 years. The central role of new product innovation in fueling revenue growth is common to many industries.

EXHIBIT 1.1-4   FINANCIAL GROWTH IN CLUB REVENUES, PLAYER SALARIES, AND OPERATING PROFITS:
AVERAGE CLUB AMOUNTS FOR 1994–2003 BASED ON *FORBES'* ESTIMATES FOR NFL,
MLB, NBA, AND NHL, AND CLUB DISCLOSURES FOR EPL

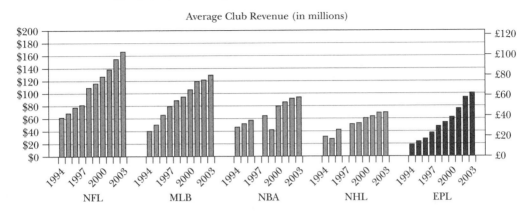

Average Club Revenue (in millions)

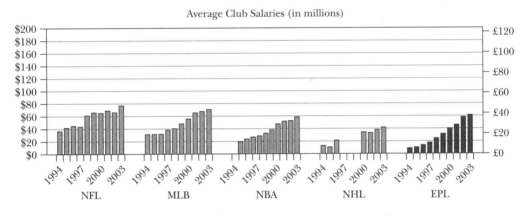

Average Club Salaries (in millions)

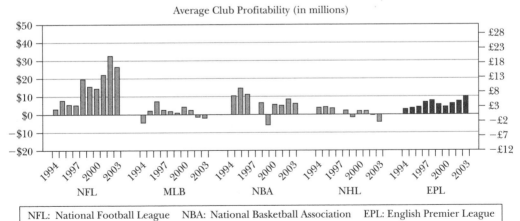

Average Club Profitability (in millions)

NFL: National Football League   NBA: National Basketball Association   EPL: English Premier League
MLB: Major League Baseball   NHL: National Hockey League

Source: Calculated from data in annual issues of *Forbes* and, up to 1997, *Financial World.* In 1997, *Forbes* did not make estimates for the NBA and the NHL; Deloitte, *Annual Review of Football Finance* (August 2004).

6. **Astute and Creative Contracting.** Successful managers in many businesses combine innovative product strategies with contracts that enable them to capture a sizable part of the gains as well as not being exposed to inordinate risks from those strategies. Many contracts in the sporting industry are multiyear. Stadium contracts, player contracts, and television contracts are three examples. One factor differentiating successful participants in the sporting industry is astute and creative contracting. Many clubs have been able to offset part of the high cost of new stadiums by creative contracting in regards to stadium-naming rights and the sale of personal seat licenses (PSLs) to fans. In a related way, participants who struggle on the business field may do so because they are carrying the "excess baggage" of a poor revenue-sharing contract.

The risk-sharing aspects of contracting are of increasing importance. For example, several broadcast and cable television companies have made sizeable write-downs of media rights (such as a U.S. $900 million write-down by News Corp. in 2002) when advertising dollars did not meet the expectation underlying the fixed up-front fees. One consequence has been a "flight to quality" where networks only bid high up-front fees for "high rating–low risk" properties (such as the NFL). An alternative is a move to risk-sharing contracts where both the networks and the league (or club) write contracts where both sides are exposed on the downside and both share in the upside. In the extreme case, networks may be unwilling to bid any up-front fee (such as with the recent Arena Football and NHL national contracts).

7. **Quality of the Product Matters!** Like other industries, delivering a quality product is a key business success determinant in the sports industry. The high priority some leagues give to the "competitive balance" notion is largely driven by the belief that the quality of a sporting event is improved by having the outcome highly uncertain before that event. There are multiple products being provided in the sports industry. The on-field product is central. The XFL, with its brand of "smash-grab" football, failed, in large part, because the quality of the on-field product was "visibly poor." The XFL lasted all but 10 weeks and quickly went from stellar television ratings to minimal ratings. The product in sports includes the fan experience at a stadium, and the quality of the coverage and commentators for those fans not at the stadium.

8. **Branding Matters!** Branding is a major business strategy in many industries, none more so than the sports industry. Branding occurs in multiple areas—examples can be found at the league level, at the club level, at the player level, at the television network level, and at the athlete-endorser company level. For example, leading soccer clubs such as Manchester United and Real Madrid have built global brands that translate into high merchandising revenue as well as high attendances when they play international games in Asia and North America. As with all aspects of brand creation and brand management, not all efforts are successful. Moreover, difficult branding challenges arise in the sporting industry on a regular basis, even to its well-established brands—for example, gambling scandals at the league level, and behavior issues at the player level.

9. **Fans and Customers as a Business Pillar.** Fans of most leading sporting leagues, clubs, or players have deep emotional connections to "their" sport, "their" club, or "their" players. The word *their* is indicative of a deeply felt attachment. Those successful in the sports industry build on this emotional linkage to create sustainable relationships over extended periods (even over generations of families!). Increasingly, there is use of more sophisticated data and analytic tools to nurture and build on these fan resources, for example, the use of customer relationship management (CRM) databases. The determinant of business success at many clubs is often how effectively those clubs have built, retained, and "moneterized" their fan or customer base. This is a common finding across many industries.

Fans as a business pillar are clearly observable at the league level. Leagues differ dramatically in the strength of this pillar. Television ratings are one observable indicator of fan interest. Exhibit 1.1-5 plots broadcast television ratings for selected leagues. It shows ratings for both the regular season and the playoffs/championship games where applicable. The dominant position of the NFL is clearly apparent. NASCAR also has a major fan base that is intensely loyal to its sponsors. Section 8 provides further discussion of television ratings.

EXHIBIT 1.1-5　　U.S. Broadcast Television Ratings for Selected Sports: 2003 (Single Nielsen Ratings Point Represents 1% of the Total Number of Television Households in the U.S.)

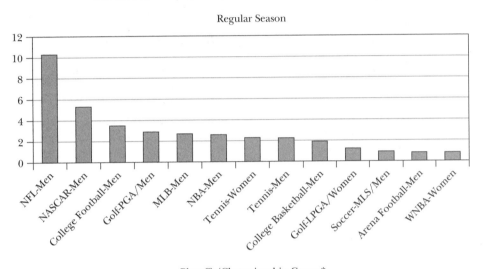

Regular Season

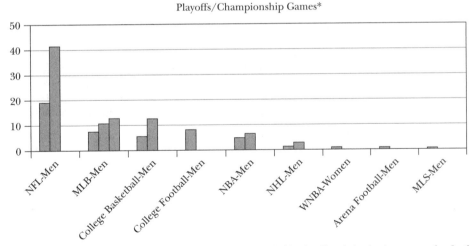

Playoffs/Championship Games*

* Playoffs/Championship Games show separate ratings for different series' in playoffs, culminating in a separate bar for the Super Bowl (NFL), World Series (MLB), College Basketball-Mens Final Game, NBA Finals (NBA), and Stanley Cup Finals (NHL).

Source: Nielsen Television Index Sports Decks, Nielsen Galaxy Explorer.

10. **Globalization.** Across many industries, much effort is being invested in globalization strategies. There are great differences across industries and companies in the success of such strategies. The sporting industry is no different in this respect. There is growing interest in leagues and clubs adopting a global perspective. Translating this global perspective into sustainable business relationships is one of the biggest business opportunities now facing leagues and clubs around the world.

Management in Sports Industry Vis-à-vis Other Industries: Areas of Differentiation

1. **Winning on the Field Central.** After every game in sports, there is a highly public "thumbs up" or "thumbs down" indicator of success. Rarely do other industries have such frequently occurring binary success indicators in the public domain. This aspect affects the front office (business side) of sporting organizations as well as the playing-team side. Senior front office management face the major challenge of building a long-term business culture and focus that can be sustained through the extended periods of limited on-field success that will likely occur in most sporting clubs. Most major front office decisions are affected by either the short-run or long-run on-field success of the club (or athlete).

2. **Diverse Owner Objectives.** Companies in many industries often compete for a similar objective: shareholder wealth maximization. This need not be the case with owners of sporting clubs. Possible objectives that one or more owners in the same league at the same time might pursue are:

- Winning on the field
- Financial gains
- Trophy status of owning a sporting club
- Protecting a community asset

This diversity of owner objectives can create unstable equilibriums unless there are tight constraints on player salaries and other outlays. A small subset of owners with deep pockets and the willingness to incur substantial losses over an extended period can create a lopsided competition. All but a select few may have a realistic chance of winning the championship at the start of the season. Constraints placed on salaries (either salary caps or taxes on above-average salary levels) by some leagues are an attempt to reduce the potential disequilibrium caused by clubs with different objectives or different financial capabilities.

3. **Managing in the Fishbowl.** The media spotlight shines not just on the playing team and its coaches. Front office executives of sporting organizations also live in a fishbowl. Decisions they make are second-guessed and are subject to reevaluation by both informed and uniformed parties on a regular basis. Business executives who have been CEOs or presidents in other industries often cite this aspect as the biggest difference when they transfer to the business side of a sporting organization. Sports business is not for those with thin skins or for those who take public vitriolic attacks on their judgments, and even their integrity, at a deeply personal level.

4. **Supporting the Weakest.** Many industries operate under the Darwinian principle of survival of the fittest. Rarely are attempts made to prop up low-performing companies if there are already a number of viable competitors in the marketplace. This is not the case with major sporting leagues, especially in North America. The player draft that is a feature of

most leagues typically has the poorest performer from the prior year receiving the highest draft pick. Revenue-sharing rules in some leagues aim to infuse extra resources into struggling clubs. The main rationale for seeking to improve the weaker clubs is to promote the leaguewide benefit of a competitive league. There is the danger, however, that poorer-performing clubs will rely more on subsidies from the league and other clubs rather than shift their own capabilities to a more competitive level.

5. **Handicapping the Strongest.** Many successful companies in a broad span of industries are permitted to grow from strength to strength provided they stay within the bands of accepted business norms (such as not abusing dominant market share positions or not adopting predatory pricing). Managers in those industries are given high incentives to be entrepreneurial and win in the marketplace over a sustained period. This is not always so in the sports industry! The competitive balance notion is a key plank on which much of the infrastructure of some sporting leagues is built. So-called sporting dynasties are now viewed in a less accepted manner than business dynasties such as Anheuser Busch in the brewing industry, Intel in the semiconductor industry, or Microsoft in the computer software industry. Where some sporting leagues permit a more open market regime, the results can be telling. Consider Formula 1 racing, which has closely followed the Darwinian model. Concerns are now being raised about the business health of a league where one driver/one team (Michael Shumacher/Ferrari) has achieved intimidating dominance. Shumacher and his team plead guilty to pushing themselves to the limit, both on and off the track. They argue the better solution is for the other drivers and teams to "raise their game," rather than for the Formula 1 league to constrain ("punish") the excellent and skillful innovator. Formula 1 at the league level is currently exploring ways to reduce the competitive imbalance in its sport.

6. **Revenue Pools and Allocation Rules.** Sports executives at multiple levels often live in a world of central and local revenue pools and allocations for distributing or redistributing those revenues. These "pools and rules" are administrative mechanisms whose aim is either to achieve set objectives, typically "competitive balance" at the league level, or to enable clubs in low-revenue situations to be able to meet minimum payrolls. These pools and rules are the result of negotiation between multiple parties, including league administrators, clubs, and player associations. As with most administrative mechanisms, not all consequences can be anticipated. It is important to revisit such mechanisms to examine whether the set of objectives are still appropriate and whether the chosen pools and rules are the best way to attain them.

7. **Athletes as Business Assets.** Many companies proudly proclaim that "people are our most important asset." What differentiates the sporting industry is the high personal profile that individual athletes attain and the emotional attachment many fans feel toward those athletes. While many people admire business leaders, like Jack Welch of General Electric, few people feel any emotional connection to them. The emotional attachment fans have toward athletes in sports provides many commercial opportunities. Endorsement contracts signed by leading athletes have few parallels outside the sporting industry. There is also the opportunity for athletes to help define and personalize club and league brands as well as be role models for youth.

8. **Managing with the "Badly Behaving."** Many high-profile athletes reach success at a relatively early age. These athletes frequently can be exposed to many temptations related to the abuse of alcohol, drugs, and sexual situations, to name but a few. Athletes-behaving-badly stories abound in all forms of the media. Moreover, when serious charges are made (such as murder or rape), trials involving athletes often become media circuses. The risks to all parties—leagues, teams, sponsors, and the athletes themselves—of athletes behaving badly are very high. Resources devoted to efforts to prevent problem situations from

arising are often well spent. However, it is because of the nature of the industry and the media itself that ongoing behaving-badly stories should be anticipated and strategies planned to address them.

9. **Limited Financial Disclosures.** In many industries, detailed audited financial statements are readily available for the major companies. In most parts of the North American sports industry, however, this is not the case. Most clubs are privately owned and the owners rarely place their audited financial statements in the public domain. Individual athletes likewise keep major aspects of their business affairs private. Estimates made by third parties (such as *Forbes*) about the financial side of clubs and athletes are typically the only systematic information in the public domain. In some cases, clubs opportunistically release their financials when it appears in their best interests to do so—for instance, when a club is seeking extra sharing of stadium revenues from a city or when negotiating with a players' association. Not surprisingly, skepticism arises about the validity of reported financial numbers when the only time that information is publicly released it shows a club financially struggling in a negotiation setting where it appears beneficial to show lower rather than higher revenues or profitability.

10. **Sports and Entertainment Cocktail.** The sports industry represents an extreme example of how aspects of the entertainment industry are being incorporated into another industry's presentation or design. The wraparound activities at sporting events (such as cheerleaders) and the music played during stops in a game are all part of the mix of sports and entertainment. However, other aspects of the entertainment industry are of questionable value to sports. Much of the entertainment industry operates with scripted outcomes and the ability to do retakes. A key challenge in the sports and entertainment mix is to make events memorable and high energy and yet retain the fundamental purities of athletic competition and uncertainty of outcome that are the hallmarks of on-the-field sports.

Overview

The text and cases in the following nine sections provide ample illustrations of the above aspects of management across a broad set of sports. We also cover decisions made at multiple levels in the sporting industry—such as the league level, the club level, the player level, the sponsor level, and the stadium-owner level. The chance factor is in all aspects of sports, both on the business side as well as on the playing field. The business side of sports is also like the playing side in that rewards are more likely to go to those who hone their talents, are thorough in their preparation, and who think creatively.

1.2 THE BUSINESS OF SPORTS: A PERSPECTIVE FROM HARVARD

By Stephen A. Greyser

The now multibillion-dollar business of sports has become a pervasive element in our economy and our society. Major business elements of sports regularly move from the sports pages (where the focus is dominantly on competition) to the business pages (often about major sponsorships, ticket price hikes, new types of merchandise, arena/stadium naming deals, etc.), and occasionally to the front page (e.g., strikes/lockouts, threats of franchise transfers, plans for new stadiums, signing of super-star free-agent players, and the like). Also, treatment of sports business has become global, reflected in worldwide coverage of the business dimensions of mega-events such as the Olympics and the World Cup.

Beyond the competition and the playing of the games themselves, the business of sports has grown significantly in both size and financial stakes. Illustratively, there are:

- more professional/collegiate leagues and sports competing for fans' time and money and for marketing/sponsor support

- more big events seeking fan attention, sponsor support, and broadcast exposure

- more broadcast channels and hours providing opportunities for league and team rights fees but requiring company marketing/advertising support

- more opportunities for company/brand sponsorship of leagues/teams/events—"the official (product/service) of the (league/team/event)"—with pressures for more dollars and for measurable return on investment

- more licensed manufactured merchandise (for leagues, teams, colleges, events, players)—plus the memorabilia and autograph industry—and more distribution channels and retail space devoted to it, all competing for consumer purchases

- new financial paradigms for franchises in terms of new stadiums, more revenues from season ticket-holders, and more corporate sponsorships, but with more complex relationships (e.g., team revenue sharing, a more powerful role for players/agents, etc.)

- greater attention to and concern over the business of intercollegiate sports, including conference realignments, broadcast rights fees, and implications for both the "student" and "athlete" dimensions of the players

Along with new challenges for managing within this changing and more complex environment, effective management in the sports industry calls for addressing the traditional needs to attract in-stadium fans, broadcast audiences, and advertisers, and to market merchandise that consumers see as appropriate. Understanding the enlarged landscape for the business of sports calls for recognition of the possible limits to growth in money and/or time on the part of fans, broadcast viewers/listeners, merchandise consumers, and sponsors/advertisers.

The Business of Sports "Model"

Exhibit 1.2-1 offers a model of the world of the business of sports. The model consists of four principal components: Competition ("the game"), Incremental Revenue Sources (beyond tickets), Other Key Elements (such as athletic equipment and fantasy leagues), and the principal source of support for the entire system, Fans.

This is a marketing-based model, reflecting the key role that marketing, promotion, and selling play in the sports management landscape. Hence, many items on the left (Competition) have marketing components that draw from the Revenue Sources on the right.

Unquestionably, the economic success of sports depends on competition. Without effective competition, the opportunity for truly significant revenue will be underfulfilled. Thus, the elements that create and support competition need to be well aligned (e.g., league structure, team management, player relations) in order to generate fan support and the leveraging of revenues from the right-hand side. This creates financial value for all participants, and psychic value for fans.

EXHIBIT 1.2-1   MODEL OF THE BU$INE$$ OF $PORT$

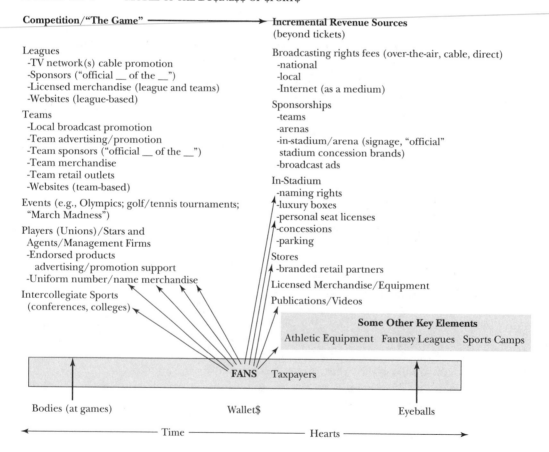

Because many of these areas and components are addressed individually in later chapter essays, the treatment here will focus on the structure of the model and observations about its components.

Competition ("The Game")

There are five major components in this sector of the model.

- **Leagues**—Leagues are the primary organizing entity in the professional sports world, providing the business partnership that connects its teams and conducts competition. Leagues create value through their sport's inherent and/or developed popularity with fans, through the appeal of its players, as well as via marketing partnerships with broadcasters and sponsors ("the official rental car of the NBA").

Broadcast partners and sponsors are principal among the aforementioned leveraged sources (right-hand side of chart). They provide vital "OPM"—other people's money—to support the league/sport and their own interests. For broadcasters, promoting the "league TV package" and its games builds ratings and helps advertisers, some of whom are also league sponsors. For sponsors, their relation with the league and their advertising tied to it are intended to build their own brands and sales. Leagues also market themselves through licensed merchandise (see Licensed Merchandise on page 21).

The four principal North American leagues, plus MLS and the privately owned NASCAR, account for more than $15 billion in annual revenues. Revenues are one obvious measure of league/sport success and tend to parallel other significant ones such as fan favorability and TV ratings. Lest one think that a sport's position with the public is permanent, consider that for decades baseball was indeed America's "national pastime" but now pro football leads, and that NASCAR has vaulted in popularity in recent years as its "footprint" moved beyond the Southeast.

Part of league popularity, and team profitability, lies in its basic economic model. Briefly, the NFL's number one position (in revenues, fan popularity, and TV ratings) is widely considered to rest on its extensive revenue sharing among teams (especially from its huge national TV contract) and its salary cap (actually an aggregate payroll cap) in a collective bargaining agreement that provides players and teams a relatively predictable portion of (defined) team revenues. Occasional very large fees for expansion franchises are shared by existing teams. The NBA has an analogous structure, although unshared local broadcast revenues are more significant for some teams. Baseball shares national TV revenues, but unshared local broadcast revenue is substantial for some (big-market) teams; it has no salary cap, although some revenues are shared from financially stronger teams via a "luxury tax" on high team payrolls. The NHL has revenue sharing, but little national TV revenue to share, and no salary cap; the latter was the major area of contention in the 2004–05 season's work stoppage by the owners. All of the above, plus other elements such as the player draft, affect competitive balance, in turn affecting the likelihood of some teams being able to have reasonable championship aspirations.

- **Teams**—For fans and owners, teams are the heart of competition. Again, marketing-driven team management typically employs broadcast partners (some of which, such as the Yankees' YES Network and the Red Sox NESN, are cable channels corporately owned by the team) and team sponsors ("the official ____ of the ____") to stimulate fandom and generate meaningful revenues. These activities and the use of other people's money mirror the ways leagues promote themselves. Teams also engage in other business activities to increase revenues, such as team retail outlets.

More meaningful to incremental team revenues are revenue sources (right-hand side of Exhibit 1.2-1) leveraged by competitive success, such as luxury boxes and club seats. In addition to yielding much higher per-seat prices than other tickets, these revenues are retained by the teams, because they are not included in "defined" income available for application to player payrolls. The key to a successful revenue structure is to build and maintain a set of committed fans (see page 23). Because of the long MLB season (81 home dates) and the large number of seats, the challenge is particularly difficult in baseball. A critical mass of committed fans allows more vigorous leveraging of the incremental revenue sources (right-hand side).

Except in a few very large cities (e.g., New York, Los Angeles, Chicago), a single team "owns" its territory in its sport. However, most cities have multiple teams across leagues, so there are other teams competing for fans, sponsors, merchandise sales, and media attention.

- **Events**—Some of the biggest and most well-known sports competitions are not conducted in traditional leagues, but are independently organized activities.

The Olympics are the most significant of these, attracting substantial worldwide attention for 2 weeks and 3 weekends every 2 years (alternating summer and winter). The Olympics represent significant business of sports dimensions, notably huge broadcast rights fees (and very large TV audiences) and major sponsorships, treated below.

The World Cup is another quadrennial event of global import and impact, including business-of-sports elements, along with its sister event, the Women's World Cup (held in a different year). The biennial Ryder Cup (golf) captures considerable American and European attention, as well as that of golf enthusiasts worldwide. Other independent events of worldwide salience occur annually, such as the Davis Cup (tennis) and the Boston, London, and New York Marathons.

Individual golf and tennis tournaments (the weekly stops on the tour) are also events, particularly from the standpoint of organizers, who must arrange sponsorship and TV in some instances, and obtain local fan and business support. For the athletes, however, they are part of the tour (analogous to a league), although not all competitors play in each one. For the PGA, for example, national TV and sponsorship exists as for leagues. Tennis has attempted to do the same.

One can consider independent sports events from at least five perspectives other than the competitors': the organizer (typically local), at-venue fans (almost always local), sponsors (sometimes arranged for each event, sometimes by a national or international organizing entity), broadcasting (same as sponsors), and TV viewers (event driven but often followers of a series of events in the sport).

Postseason championship competitions are also events, especially major ones such as in college basketball ("March Madness") and football (bowl games). These are treated in more detail in Intercollegiate Athletics, see page 16. Professional league championships (playoffs) are considered here to be part of league-organized seasons.

As noted below "Players," athletes and/or players are the attraction for paying fans and TV viewers. However, in some instances the event itself is the "draw" (e.g., a championship match where long before the competing teams are known, tickets are purchased, television is scheduled, advertising has been bought, and event-based merchandise has been manufactured).

- **Players (Unions)/Stars and Agents/Management Firms**—There is no competition without players. Players typically are accompanied by Players' Associations (unions) as well as players' agents (and the management firms with which some agents are affiliated). Players are indeed virtually the entire product. People buy tickets to see the *athletes* (or players as a team) perform—not owners or league commissioners.

Star players not only typically improve team performance (in team sports) and ticket sales, but also enhance television ratings and team visibility in the community. The latter occurs through the star's endorsed products (advertised by endorsing firms, often on televised games and programs surrounding them) and through clothing with the star's name and uniform number. Stars in individual sports competition (e.g., Tiger Woods) generate larger at-venue crowds and particularly raise TV ratings. The business value of a star player for teams and leagues is reflected in larger home crowds (especially season ticket sales) and TV ratings, larger road crowds (for other teams' revenue), and higher ratings for league TV games involving the star. Michael Jordan's comeback with Washington is illustrative of all these impacts.

Stars are also the focal point for numerous endorsed products. These products encompass athletic equipment (the largest component) and consumer or business products and services. Many stars also lend public support to causes and foundations. Tiger Woods and Michael Jordan have been notable in building extremely lucrative endorsement portfolios.

Players' Associations in team sports are widely viewed as among the most powerful unions in North America and play a key role in collective bargaining with leagues. Association heads are highly aware that many of their players have very short careers, often less than 5 years. Consequently, as MLBPA's Donald Fehr told me (October 2003), it is important in collective bargaining to avoid mistakes that cannot be reversed until the next agreement, too late to help those players who have left the game or whose talents have passed their point of leverage in free agency by that time.

Players' unions try to gain a bigger piece of the revenue pie for players as a whole by seeking higher percentages of defined revenue in the total player payroll pool, including efforts to expand the revenues eligible for inclusion in the pool, as the NFLPA is said to be seeking in its next contract. (Owners typically resist.) The unions also try to gain earlier free agency for players, as well as salary arbitration eligibility. Each of these has the net effect of providing likely salary increases for the players involved; in free agency, multiple teams (owners) may compete for a player; in arbitration, the player's pay is virtually guaranteed to increase, because both player and team submit a salary offer to the arbitrator. (In baseball, one of the two figures must be selected.)

Union bargaining is supported by what Fehr calls "a credible threat to strike." Baseball has experienced eight work stoppages since 1972 and a near-stoppage in 2002. A potentially crippling blow to hockey (as of this writing) came at the start of the 2004–05 season in a labor dispute that caused a lockout; owners insisted on a salary cap in the wake of what they reported as serious financial travails for more than half the teams. Ten years earlier, the start of the 1994–95 hockey season was delayed more than 3 months by a labor dispute. (Both baseball and hockey suffered in terms of fan support after their 1994 work stoppages.)

Agents work for players in negotiating contracts, especially when players are in free-agent status, and for initial contracts when the sport does not have a scheduled scale for rookies (as the NBA operationally does). Agents too recognize that a player's career is typically short in team sports and most others, except golf. Readers have no doubt followed public statements in negotiations for salary, performance bonuses, signing bonuses, and so on. (The movie role of agent Jerry Maguire reminded its audience of the importance of money, but also of the task agents have of trying to help their athletes in a variety of life experiences.) Regarding off-the-field income for players, agents also are important in facilitating and negotiating endorsements. While relatively few athletes (almost always stars) have significant national or global endorsements, a larger number obtain local-area endorsements and/or speaking/appearance deals with area retail entities such as auto dealers and groups, supermarket chains, restaurant chains, and the like, as well as local corporate meetings.

Major agents often are associated with *management firms,* which in turn have business relationships with TV networks/cable channels and sports sponsors. For stars, or potential stars, financial opportunities can be significant (e.g., made-for-TV golf competitions). In tennis and golf, individual event proprietors may use these firms to help organize their tournament, involving players, TV, sponsorship, and merchandising.

- **Intercollegiate Sports**—Despite its ostensible amateur status—at least insofar as athletes are concerned—intercollegiate sports are truly big businesses. There is wide agreement that relatively few individual college sports make money; examples include major football programs, major men's basketball programs, and hockey (for a few schools). However, revenues off the playing field from the competition on it are substantial and growing, especially television rights fees.

The largest fees are for the National Collegiate Athletic Association (NCAA) basketball championships ("March Madness") and the football Bowl Championship Series. The 4-week basketball competition has not only "branded a month" but is the core that generated a $6 billion 11-year contract for the NCAA through 2013 with CBS. Included are TV, radio, licensing, and other marketing elements for men's and women's basketball (the obviously dominant component), as well as all NCAA championships, except football, where there remains no formal NCAA championship competition. College football's postseason bowl games are also major business-of-sports entities: the Bowl Championship Series multimedia rights contracts with FOX for three bowl games, plus the separate Rose Bowl–ABC deal, constitute more than $100 million in annual fees (2006–09). (Many bowls are now "named" as sponsored events, such as the Nokia Sugar Bowl, although not the oldest one, the Rose Bowl.) Another set of meaningful TV rights fees pertains to conference football championship games (when a conference has at least 12 teams).

Indeed, the world of college athletic conferences generated one of the biggest business-of-sports sagas of 2003 and 2004, when the Atlantic Coast Conference and the Big East fought over realignments in which colleges wanted to and did switch their conference affiliations, impacting significantly on football and basketball. This business dispute involved college presidents and athletic directors, conference officials, and the legal system.

Although not shown on the chart in Exhibit 1.2-1, high school sports are a small but increasingly visible terrain for business initiatives, principally via naming rights for athletic venues, sponsored scoreboards, and signage inside gymnasiums and at playing fields. Observers support (primarily for school budget reasons) or decry (as inappropriate) these echoes of college-level business of sports activity.

Incremental Revenue Sources

Let us now turn to the right-hand side of Exhibit 1.2-1. There are six major incremental revenue sources to be addressed.

- **Broadcasting**—Broadcast revenues have become huge and vital sources of income for leagues, teams, and events. Multiyear, multibillion-dollar rights fees are a key budget component for principal leagues, for the Olympics, and for the NCAA. Rights fees are a major wellspring of "other people's money" for sports properties—both as financial support and in providing partners that promote the entity and its telecasts with their own (additional) resources, principally promotional announcements. (Obviously, it is in the best commercial interest of the broadcast partner to do so.)

In terms of money, for example, the NFL's $17.6 billion current 8-year multinetwork/cable national contract (see case 8.4) yields for each team about $70 million annually in equally shared money. The four principal leagues have been able to sell joint (league package) TV rights for advertiser-supported games since the Sports Broadcasting Act was passed by Congress in 1961. In addition to national television network and cable packages for the principal leagues, NASCAR and other entities, individual teams (except in the NFL) have local TV and radio contracts that in some instances are significant revenue items. In MLB, for example, where local broadcast money is retained by the teams, the New York Yankees gain a competitive financial edge with their large-market rights fees and controlled cable channel (see case 8.3). Beyond these broadcast revenues, a few leagues and other teams have their own cable networks, such as the NFL and the Toronto Maple Leafs. Without live games (part of other national or local contracts), these channels program reviews of the week's games, "classic" games, press conferences, interviews, playing instructional shows, and other content. There are also independent cable channels that treat one sport or type of sport, for example, The Golf Channel and College Sports TV.

The reciprocal of the salience of broadcast revenue for sports is the importance of sports content for TV, especially (of course) for sports-based cable channels. Major sports events are among the most watched individual TV programs every year. The Super Bowl typically attracts the highest ratings, demonstrating its value to the networks (and supporting advertisers) that obtained the rights. Continued reasonably high ratings, in the assessment of broadcast rights owners and advertisers, have led to continued increases in hours of sports on TV.

The absence of sports on TV can also have a big impact. For example, in Canada, the unavailability of hockey during the NHL's 2004 work stoppage meant no nationally televised "Hockey Night in Canada" on Saturday night on the Canadian Broadcasting Company, a tradition for more than 50 years, interrupted previously only in 1994 for a similar owner-player dispute. The impacts of the NHL's absence have also been felt by Canadian cable sports channels and especially by advertisers seeking adult male demographic audiences. The 2004 Canadian situation was not replicated in the United States because of the availability of other professional and college sports (including college hockey for local cable), and the relatively less important role played by the NHL on TV.

The advent of satellite radio networks is projected to add millions of subscriber listeners to broadcasts of leagues, sports news, talk shows, and the like. Sirius has a 7-year contract for all NFL games, and XM has an 11-year deal with MLB. (The firms offer many other channels.)

The *Internet* has become increasingly more significant in the business of sports. Direct e-commerce (e.g., team sales of tickets or season ticket resale programs via the web), sales of memorabilia on eBay, sales of sports information (such as up-to-date game reports), broadcasts of games themselves, fan-engaging chat rooms, and sports gambling are all now elements of Internet sports-based activity. Internet rights are a growing part of negotiated broadcast rights packages or are independently sold or retained by leagues, as the NBA has done. And a very substantial portion of the estimated 15 million Fantasy Sports players (by the Fantasy Sports Trade Association, 2004) make use of the Internet.

With the passage of time and the further growth of computer-active fans in the sports marketplace, the Internet will become more salient for the business of sports.

- **Sponsorships**—The magnitude and ubiquity of sponsorship is a relatively recent phenomenon in sports, yet it has deep roots. The very first formal intercollegiate sports competition in the United States—a crew race between Harvard and Yale on Lake Winnepesaukee (New Hampshire) in 1852—was a sponsored event (!), "presented by" the Boston-based railroad company that took vacationers to the lake and North to Montreal. The scope of sports sponsorship extends across the sports landscape. It too is a huge pool of "OPM" supporting sports entities, providing partners that then spend additional money to promote those entities and their relationship to them.

Here are some illustrations of the breadth and variety of sponsorship:

- sponsored season-long competitions (e.g., NASCAR's Nextel Cup, formerly Winston Cup)
- sponsored individual competitions within a sports event, such as Century 21 for MLB's All-Star Home Run Competition
- sponsored/named football bowl games, pioneered by John Hancock (Sun Bowl) in the mid-1980s
- the major Olympic sponsors, who extend their sponsorship by year-round use of the five-ring symbol in both sports and nonsports contexts, and by substantial additional advertising budgets within the Olympics telecasts themselves
- sponsor relationships, as noted, with leagues, teams, and events ("the official _____ of the _____"), with at-venue signage and advertising on the competition's broadcasts
- sponsorship of league noncompetition initiatives (e.g., Nike's NBA "Basketball League Without Borders" basketball camps on several continents)
- "presenting" sponsorships for specific competitions (e.g., Nextel for the NHL All-Star game, an almost-named competition)
- sponsored scoreboards in arenas and stadiums
- sponsored "crawls" of scores on nightly sports segments of the news and on sports cable channels
- sponsored half-time highlights/scores programs and sponsored pregame programs

Sponsors and potential sponsors are always seeking new opportunities that fit their interests and budget. For example, Verizon became the principal sponsor of "niche" winter sports such as luge. At the team level, many sponsor relationships are with local/regional organizations. Boston-area hospital Beth Israel Deaconess, a Fenway-area neighbor of the Red Sox, is its official health care partner; it supports its sponsorship with banners on utility poles in the area near its main buildings (and those of the Red Sox).

Whether a large-budget or small-budget sponsor, the added costs to support a sponsorship can be proportionately meaningful. This "implementation" is principally via advertising, but it also includes other activities such as retail promotions, at-venue entertainment for business customers, employee events, website displays, and others. Implementation costs are generally estimated at up to three times sponsorship costs to be most effective.

It is important to note (as addressed in several cases) that sponsorship and its associated advertising on telecasts of sponsored competition is not the same as buying advertising on sports programs. The latter is indeed part of financing of the business of sports, but it does not have one key characteristic that sponsorships do, namely what marketers term *cobranding*.

Cobranding, briefly, in this setting means a partnership in identification of the sports property with the sponsor. Each party is appropriately concerned about the value of the relationship. Sponsors pay for the linkage, and the league/team/event is willing to have its name linked with the sponsor firm, that is, lend its own brand equity. The "power of partnership" generates value for both parties. Money and reputation are involved in the relationship. Both elements warrant monitoring for the return on investment to work out.

That sponsorship and advertising have blanketed the sports environment is clearly revealed by watching or listening to sports broadcasts and by attending competition. Indeed, the phenomenon is so much a part of sports (and other parts of life) that it generates its own caricature. A commercial made for the 2004 Olympics juxtaposed competition and commercialism. It began: "In a world of over-commercialization . . ." while synchronized swimmers were shown in performance and opera music was played. The swimmers continued, as did the announcer: "it's nice to take a moment to simply marvel. . . ." A few seconds later: "OK, moment over." This was followed by a VISA message and logo; neither visual nor verbal brand identification had been shown or heard up to that point.

By way of summary, sponsorship is a key revenue component, one that permeates the business of sports. Beyond the sponsors themselves, it impacts on the sponsored sports properties and other sponsored sports settings and on fans/viewers through its omnipresent nature.

- **In-Stadium**—Another significant source of incremental revenue—and in some instances, potentially very large revenue—is from stadiums and arenas. The revenue streams encompass venue naming rights, luxury boxes, personal seat licenses (for proposed new stadiums and arenas), and the traditional concessions (food and drink) and parking income.

Naming rights are a very lucrative revenue area and offer a branding opportunity for the firms involved. Indeed, venues *are* branded entities, offering not only giant billboards in their communities and on television for the corporations involved, but also innumerable mentions in media game reports, schedules, and the like. The price of naming rights can be more than $5 million a year based on the length of the contract, although early arrangements were for far less. For example, Boston's Fleet Center (arena) was named in a 15-year contract for $2 million a year in the mid-1990s, but renegotiation in 2004 by the arena's owners with Bank of America Corporation (which acquired Fleet) was widely reported to be at $6 million per year. The bank subsequently (2005) relinquished its rights and bought out the remaining years.

The most valuable business situations for companies looking at naming opportunities are when the venue is in their headquarters area or when consumer goods/services firms are seeking national visibility. Illustrative of the latter are the Staples Center in Los Angeles (Staples is based in the Boston area) and American Airlines Arena in Miami. A strong combination of the two often occurs—Heinz (Pittsburgh), Gillette (New England Patriots), MCI (Kansas City).

Luxury boxes generate millions of dollars annually through (multiyear) contracts encompassing enclosed preferred seating areas, each with a cluster of seats that often include seating both inside and outside the box itself, and food/beverage service. The value to teams of luxury box revenue is enhanced because in leagues with salary caps these dollars are not part of the revenues eligible for the players' pool. Some teams enhance the income from this source by retaining a box for game-by-game purchase as a special event site for personal or business celebrations.

Personal seat licenses (PSLs) represent a front-end financing mechanism for planned stadiums. Present or prospective season ticket-holders pay a one-time fee—sometimes in the thousands of dollars—for the right to buy season tickets, typically in preferred locations in a new stadium. PSLs were first used by the then new Carolina Panthers for what was then called Ericson Stadium in Charlotte and have occasionally been employed since, especially by NFL teams. The Jets have been reported to be incorporating PSLs into the financial plans for their proposed (as of fall 2004) new Manhattan stadium. Because PSLs can generate $50 to $100 million in cash before construction, it is a very meaningful element in financing new sports venues.

For fans, of course, this constitutes an added fee simply for the right to retain (or purchase) their seats. The seats, of course, they will have to buy each year.

Cash flow from PSLs has grown in importance to teams because taxpayers (beyond fans) have increasingly resisted huge public subsidies for sports arenas that benefit private businesses (teams), in the wake of squeezed public budgets and numerous competing priorities. Thus, the trend has moved to "public-private partnerships," although many owners still seek a significant proportion of public funding. Briefly, as described to me (October 2002) by consultant and author Rick Horrow (who works with NFL and other teams), the major arguments made to advance the public funding component of new sports facilities within public-private partnerships include:

- economic impacts (especially during construction)
- positive effects on urban development (typically as part of a bigger master plan than the sports venue alone)
- attracting out-of-town visitors for multiple days of spending
- helping to convince business to locate in the community
- image enhancement and civic pride for the community

Economists and others often present data to counter the (postconstruction) economic benefits, and state that much of the revenue involved would be spent elsewhere in the community.

Concessions and parking income is an additional per-game revenue stream for stadium/arena owners. In recent years, these per-capita dollars have increased via more extensive food selections, including branded items. Also, especially in new venues, membership clubs for season ticket-holders generate membership fees plus full-meal spending. Money spent at stadiums for food and beverages is significant enough that even teams in sold-out seat situations are concerned when the number of "no shows" increases, such as for late-season games when the team is no longer in contention for the postseason.

- **Stores**—Sporting-goods retailers are another widespread component of the business of sports. These retailers sell equipment, licensed team clothing, and other items through hundreds of branded outlets. The largest, The Sports Authority, has almost 400 outlets accounting for about $2.5 billion in sales in 2003, according to industry association and media sources; six are reported to have sales over $500 million. These are relevant brands themselves.

Many other retail outlets and websites sell licensed souvenir merchandise, sports videos/DVDs, and so on. At sports venues, teams typically have their own retail shops selling their team's (and others') items.

While much of the merchandise sold in these stores is for use in engaging in athletic activity, much is simply for daily use. The latter typically offer fans and consumers the opportunity to "wear their allegiance" to a team or favorite player while going about their daily lives. (See "Licensed Merchandise" below.)

- **Licensed Merchandise/Equipment**—When people buy (for self or gifts), wear, use, and/or display licensed merchandise, they are participating in a significant vehicle for *extending* fandom. Through these acts, one has not only expanded a relationship to the sport, league, or team, but also has activated the relationship financially, off the field.

Licensed merchandise is a huge business, estimated to account for well over $10 billion (wholesale) for items licensed by the principal leagues and NASCAR. Significantly, from these revenues only a portion is represented by the fees/royalties paid to the licensing sports entities by the manufacturers of the equipment, apparel, caps, trading cards, key rings, and so on that are involved. The typical payment is 10% of the wholesale price. The resulting fee revenues that are paid to the league office are divided equally by that league's teams as part of revenue sharing. The leagues normally control the licensing rights; however, in some instances teams that own their stadiums license some stadium-branded items.

Like many nonsports product manufacturers, licensees often have different price/quality levels within their merchandise line. For example, typical licensed team uniform and clothing (e.g., team jackets) product lines have a designated "authentic" category at the top of the line, often promoted as such on league TV games.

The major licensed merchandise/equipment companies have marketing staffs that work on a range of initiatives. A key one is strategy within categories, such as each sport's merchandise. In addition to brand and product category responsibilities, are the challenges of managing relationships with retailers, treated above.

- **Publications/Videos**—Sports publications and videos offer fans another way to bring their fandom home. Leagues and teams publish everything from histories to yearbooks to regular in-season magazines. A spate of books about different sports, teams, and how-to-play guides usually are part of "announcing" the start of each new season, and many are part of media reviews of books and videos. A notable component of team championships is the postseason book and/or video chronicling the road to that year's success. Whether published by leagues, teams, or events, or independently, these items often occupy visible space in the homes of fans.

Some Other Key Elements

Also incorporated into the model are several Other Key Elements of the business of sports. By far the most significant of these is the mega-industry of *athletic equipment,* which both feeds and is fed by growth of participation in sports as well as by consumers' zeal to wear the gear that is emblematic of their favorite teams and athletes. Major branded suppliers, such as Nike, Reebok, Adidas, and others, constitute significant corporate entities. They are involved in marketing partnerships with leagues and teams and pay very large sums for athlete endorsements and even special athlete-branded merchandise lines, such as Nike's Michael Jordan line.

Nike is the industry giant, holding about one-third of worldwide athletic footwear sales in recent years, while spreading its omnipresent "Swoosh" logo on athletes' uniforms, on stores, and in commercials, and its "Just Do It" slogan globally ©. Its legendary founder/leader Phil Knight was able to maintain the brand's marketing and merchandising position into the twenty-first century. (In 2005, he turned over the reins as CEO to William Perez, a globally experienced consumer marketing executive who had been head of S.C. Johnson's consumer products.) Indicative of Nike's global focus is its emphasis on growth in China via aggressive retail store expansion and linkage to Olympic athletes such as gold-medalist hurdler Liu Xiang. Reflecting what I interpreted to be a belief that there are untold millions of people in Nike's potential market, a senior Nike executive once responded to my question about future growth with the phrase "as long as there are two trees," implying the human characteristic of seeking to improve one's competitive ability and performance.

Another athletic equipment giant is Reebok, the number two U.S. manufacturer of athletic footwear. Reebok has also been aggressive in China. The company signed globally recognized NBA star Yao Ming to an estimated $100 million long-term endorsement contract, following the expiration of his earlier Nike deal. Reebok has signage in Chinese at Yao Ming's (Houston Rockets) home arena for visibility in games televised to China. Reebok is also active in other athlete endorsements and league equipment partnerships. Adidas is another major global athletic-shoe firm active in athlete endorsements and sports-based marketing.

Fantasy Leagues are another growing component of the business of sports. Millions of fantasy players, largely via the Internet, become (and stay) involved in the daily and weekly performances of "their" players, and preseason player drafts engage their attention. Participation fees mount, and relationships have developed with the real leagues whose players are the core of fantasy competition.

At the sports participation level, *sports camps* are another component of the business of sports. These encompass, for example, the long-standing youth-oriented training camps (dominantly in summers), full-scale training centers for aspiring quality athletes (such as IMG's in Bradenton, with traditional schooling attached), and adult-oriented spring training weeks with team legends.

Not on the chart, but part of the extended "Other" category are sports-based publications—some of many decades' duration (such as *The Sporting News* and *Sports Illustrated)* and many dedicated to participants and/or followers of specific sports.

Also not explicitly listed are the numerous consumer products and services that sustain the sponsorship of leagues, teams, and events, as noted earlier. A wide range of beers, soft drinks, auto manufacturers, hotel groups, rental car firms, and others are all part of the business of sports.

Fans: Support for the System

Fans are the foundation of the business of sports world. As shown in the model, they support the entire apparatus: with their *bodies* at games; with their *eyeballs* watching on TV; and with their *wallets* for tickets, for cable and pay-per-view fees, and for merchandise, publications, videos, fantasy leagues fees, and equipment, as well as the sponsors' products and services. Whether attending events, watching sports and sports-based TV, or shopping for sports items, fans devote *time* to sports. For most fans, their engagement with sports also embraces their *hearts*.

Building and sustaining a base of "committed fans" is a primary goal of leagues and teams. This encompasses fans' inherent interest in the sport, built on a foundation of the quality and attractiveness of competition, and stimulated by league marketing (including that by broadcast, sponsor, and merchandise partners). Fan interest can derive from one's experiences as a youthful participant and grass-roots exposure (e.g., Little League, Pop Warner), going to games, and watching sports on TV.

As noted earlier, teams work to build a "nation" of committed fans who follow the team (from near and sometimes far) at venues, via TV, via affinity membership (e.g., credit cards), and by buying and/or wearing team items.

Exhibit 1.2-2 shows the "circles of fandom" from core to fringe, and beyond. Greater intensity (among core fans and inner circle) and more people (in all circles) develops with better performance and increased popularity of the team and sport. This is analogous to consumer product usage categories—heavy, medium, light, and nonusage. The focus on fan retention and fan building is consistent with the central tenet of marketing and my own mantra: "Consumers are the alpha and omega [starting point and ending point] of marketing."

A powerful illustration of both increased intensity of fandom (inner circles enlarging) and expansion of fandom (people entering beyond the fringe) occurs when a team truly captures fan enthusiasm. This took place in New England twice in 2004, as the Patriots marched week-by-week to the Super Bowl and later the Red Sox completed their unprobable run to the American League pennant and World Series victory. Legions of people only marginally interested in each became part of a "community of fandom" that transcended sports interest alone. Fan euphoria affected TV viewing, workplace conversation, merchandise sales, and media coverage off the field.

EXHIBIT 1.2-2   Circles of Fandom

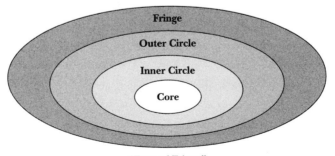

"Beyond Fringe"
(e.g., Community, Event)

There is little doubt that fans love sports competition, particularly live events. Yet the cost of fandom continues to rise. And the cost of the entire business-of-sports system has increased for broadcasters and sponsors as well as for those who own/manage teams, leagues, and events.

Many nonfans, as taxpayers, also provide financial support for sports. As noted in the "Stadium" section, the public portion of spending for sports stadiums and arenas has added billions of dollars to U.S. tax-supported budgets. However, in recent years, the trend has moved toward less public and more private money.

As described at the outset above, there is more and more competition for fan support. Money and time—for attending sports, for watching sports on TV, and for buying sports-related products/services—are being stretched. This leads to a question many (including myself) have asked, namely: "Are there limits for fan support, and have they been reached?" My own answer in recent years has been "yes . . . and now, or very soon." On the whole, however, those of us who shared this view seem to have been incorrect in our assessment. While only time will tell, more games and events, more hours of sports TV, and more merchandise abound. One can only admire fans and their support.

Conclusion

As one considers the overall model, one may ask, "Who owns the business of sports?" Obviously there are many answers—from the leagues, the team owners, and event proprietors who create the opportunity for competition, to the broadcasters and sponsors who significantly finance it, to the players without whom there would be no competition. Undergirding the entire structure, as described, are the fans whose support via tickets, TV viewing, equipment and merchandise purchases, and the like ultimately finance the system. So the most logical answer (to me) is: "All of us who are involved in the competition and the business of sports."

SECTION 2... Leagues[1]

Key Issues

- Value creation and value sharing are two pivotal issues in the business of sports.

- Sporting leagues differ in their adoption of variants of the single-entity ownership model and the distributed club ownership model.

- Competitive balance can be defined at the league level, the game level, and at the national team/all-star team level.

- Multiple mechanisms have been employed to promote competitive balance (albeit with some unintended consequences).

- Revenue sharing is affected by both the size/composition of the revenue pool to be distributed and the allocation rules employed.

Cases

S porting leagues provide the infrastructure within which individual clubs or teams participate. Although individual leagues differ greatly on multiple dimensions, they all share the common belief that some central decision making is imperative for the viability of a league. Illustrative examples of central decision making are:

- Which clubs can compete in the league? What criteria should guide the admission of new clubs?

- What is the structure of the competition? How many games are there? How many teams should advance to the playoff series, if there is to be one?

- What revenues are to be shared among clubs? What revenue allocation rules to be used?

- How to structure relationships with players? Should there be an agreed player-cost-to-revenue formula?

- What media relationships to form? Should television contracts be negotiated at the central league level or should each club have the right to individually negotiate a television contract?

These and many other decisions set the stage in which clubs compete, both on the field and at the business end.

This section outlines some pivotal issues at the league level:

- Decisions relating to the ownership structure of a league

- Decisions about the importance of competitive balance and mechanisms a league can use to promote it

- Decisions about what revenues are centrally collected and how they are distributed

A central theme of this section is that decisions made at the league level greatly affect the total revenue pool of a sport and how that revenue pool is shared among the individual clubs.

Ownership Structure of Leagues

Attempts to form new sporting leagues occur on a regular basis. A new league starts with a clean slate on which to decide the ownership structure. The two ends of the spectrum are the single-entity model and the distributed club ownership model.

Single-Entity Ownership Model: A single group (individual) owns the league and all teams in the league. This single group can be an individual, a group of investors, or even another league. Several examples illustrate this model:

> EXAMPLE 1: ABL (American Basketball League—first game in October 1996; last game in December 1998) and WNBA (Women's National Basketball League—first game in Summer 1997; still operating). Both the ABL and WNBA were professional women's basketball leagues that were structured as a single-entity model. A single entity in both cases owned the league and all clubs in that league. The ABL was owned by a group of investors (and some players who received equity). The WNBA is owned by the NBA.

EXAMPLE 2: XFL (Extreme Football League)—a 50/50 joint venture between the NBC (National Broadcasting Corporation) and WWE (World Wrestling Entertainment). The league and all 10 clubs were owned by the joint venture.

There are multiple advantages of the single-entity model from the owner's perspective:

- Ability to place individual clubs in the preferred cities even where there may not be an investor willing to own a club in one of those cities.

- Ability to assign individual players to teams in such a way as to promote local fan enthusiasm. For example, the WNBA assigned two of its star inaugural signings to clubs close to their college teams. Lisa Leslie, a University of Southern California star, was assigned to the Los Angeles Sparks. Sheryl Swoopes, a Texas Tech star, was assigned to the Houston Comets.

- Ability to promote competitive balance in the league by player assignments (and reassignments). A single entity can assign players such that no club has a disproportionate share of individual stars.

- Ability to constrain player salary escalation. The single-entity model does not have individual clubs within the league bidding against each other for player talent.

The single-entity model provides limited economic incentives to individual clubs. This is a classic problem with highly centralized organizations. Individual clubs that adopt innovative marketing practices or have superior on-field performance find it difficult in most single-entity league models to capture a large share of the benefits.

The single-entity model is frequently found in new start-up leagues. If the league survives, there is often pressure over time to move to a more decentralized model (both in ownership of individual clubs and in decision-making rights). Since 1997, the WNBA has moved away from the single-entity model. Individual WNBA clubs can now be separately bought and sold. Moreover, there is no longer the restriction that only NBA clubs can own a WNBA franchise.

Distributed Club Ownership Model: Here each individual club has its own ownership group. Individual clubs can and do change ownership. Section 10 (Exhibit 10-3) reports 28 recent ownership transactions of sporting clubs in the MLB, NBA, NFL, and NHL.

The NFL illustrates one version of this model. The NFL is a Section 501 tax-exempt organization under the U.S. tax code. Section 501(a) notes that "organizations described in subsection (c) . . . shall be exempt from taxation." Subsection (c) lists the "exempt organizations":

> *Business leagues, chambers of commerce, real estate boards, boards of trade, or professional football leagues (whether or not administering a pension fund for football players), not organized for profit and no part of the net earnings of which inures to the benefit of any private shareholder or individual.*

The NFL, on behalf of its member clubs, collects revenue from multiple sources and distributes these (net of cost) to each of the NFL clubs. Each of the current 32 clubs is a separately owned venture. All except the Green Bay Packers are privately owned and can be sold to a third party (subject to review by the Finance Committee and then voted on by the full league membership).

The NFL club owners play a key role in league decisions via voting on key issues (such as appointment of the commissioner and admission of new clubs) and membership of Standing Committees. Examples of such committees include:

- Finance and related committees (Finance Committee, Audit Committee, and Stadium Committee)
- Business operations (Broadcasting Committee, Business Ventures Committee)

In addition, the NFL has affiliated for-profit entities. Three examples are:

- NFL Enterprises LLC—explores, develops, and operates business opportunities in the areas of satellite broadcasting and new media; includes NFL Network, NFL Sunday Ticket, and NFL.com.
- NFL Properties LLC—NFL's centralized marketing, licensing, corporate sponsorship, and publishing arm; holds rights to market NFL Club's names, symbols, designs, colors, and logos.
- NFL Productions—controls films and video programming and licensing of NFL game footage.

Throughout the year, there are ongoing meetings of these committees, as well as regular meetings between the NFL management and all the owners (or their representatives). Within this distributed club ownership model, there is much scope for leadership and pivotal decision making at the NFL league management level.

Visible Conflicts with Alternative Models: The distributed club ownership model has the greater likelihood that conflicts between various constituents (league versus club; league versus players; club versus club, etc.) will be played out in the public domain or even in high-profile legal cases. One colorful example occurred in a 2004 league (English Rugby Football League) versus club (St. Helens) dispute. St. Helens had a star player (Sean Long) suspended for 3 months by the League when he successfully gambled on a game that St. Helens lost (but he did not play in). Long used private pregame information that St. Helens would be fielding a below-strength team. The gambling suspension ended on Friday, September 17. On September 19, St. Helens was scheduled to play one of its arch-rivals (Bradford). To accommodate a television schedule, the game was moved up to September 17. Was Long eligible to play on the rescheduled date? The League ruled that he was ineligible and that the suspension did not run out until midnight of the seventeenth. St. Helens appealed this decision and undertook legal advice. The League subsequently reversed its initial ruling. The chief executive of St. Helens publicly stated:

> We are pleased that the Rugby Football League have accepted our argument that they were wrong in law and unjust in fact. We are sorry that it took legal correspondence and the threat of legal action at the highest level to change their minds.[2]

It is unlikely that an individual club executive in a single ownership model would make such a public statement, or threaten legal action. Several of the major decisions affecting property rights and business decisions in the distributed ownership league model have come from landmark court rulings—for example, (1) the 1992 *McNeil et al. v. NFL et al.* case, which was central in setting up the current free-agency system in the NFL, and (2) the 1995 Bosman ruling from the European Court of Justice, which allows professional soccer players in Europe to move freely at the end of their contract to another club in Europe.

Constituent groups in sports leagues, such as clubs or players, are not always homogeneous within that league. For example, within MLB, the clubs can have widely diverse interests depending on their being from a large-city market (such as New York) or a small-city market (such as Minneapolis-St. Paul). Player incentives can differ depending on whether the players are rookies or veterans.

Competitive Balance

Competitive balance is a central concern to the administrators of many leagues. Competitive balance on the field can be defined at multiple levels—the league, game, and national team (all-star team) levels. However, a word of caution is in order. The following is but one description of the competitive balance notion and its differing rationales. This is an area where there are strong and diverse viewpoints.

League Level: Competitive balance exists when as broad a set of clubs as possible have a realistic chance at the start of the season of winning the championship or at least making it to the playoffs. Evidence of competitive imbalance at the league level can include:

- One club dominates the number one position over an extended period (a so-called dynasty). An extreme case is the St. George club in the Australian Rugby League—it won every Grand Final for 11 years in a row (1955–65)! The Boston Celtics won 8 NBA Championships in a row from 1958–59 to 1965–69, and 11 of 13 from 1956–57 to 1968–69.

- Domination of the top end of a competition by the same teams occurs over an extended period. Over the 1986–2004 period, only two teams have won the Scottish Premier Soccer League: Glasgow Rangers (13 times) and Glasgow Celtic (6 times).

- Domination of the bottom end of a competition by the same teams occurs over an extended period. For example, in MLB, the following clubs never made it to even the first round of the playoffs in any one of the 10 years from 1994 to 2003: Pittsburgh Pirates (win/loss % of 44.3%), Milwaukee Brewers (44.4%), Detroit Tigers (45.0%), Philadelphia Phillies (46.8%), Montreal Expos (47.6%), Kansas City Royals (48.9%), and Toronto Blue Jays (48.9%). In contrast, the Atlanta Braves (61.2%) and the New York Yankees (60.4%) made it to the playoffs every year during that period.[3]

Game Level: Competitive balance here means that with high probability, the result of a game is not a "given" at the start of the game. Evidence of competitive imbalance includes:

- Large number of games with lopsided results ("blowouts")
- Large number of games where at a very early stage, one side has built a "virtually" unassailable lead

National Team/All-Star Team Level: Being on a national team (such as in soccer) or on an all-star team confers high status. Competitive balance here means that one club does not continuously dominate the composition of this team over an extended period.

Proponents of competitive balance at the league level argue that the uncertainty factor associated with multiple potentially strong teams promotes higher attendance, higher television ratings, and a broader set of sponsors. Fans of many clubs can genuinely believe their club at the start of the season can go "all the way." Having many games with uncertain outcomes right up to the end reduces viewer "turn-off." Having a national or all-star team with players from many clubs adds to the stature of all those clubs, rather than just benefiting a small set of clubs in the league.

Promoting Competitive Balance at League Level

Leagues have used multiple mechanisms in efforts to promote competitive balance. Exhibit 2-1 summarizes some key mechanisms: It is important to not look at these mechanisms in isolation or independent of the ownership model employed in a league. Patchwork solutions based on adjusting a subset of the mechanisms may accentuate rather than improve competitive balance. It is essential to consider that clubs and players have their own incentives and competitive balance of a league may not be high on their priorities.

Player Selection Mechanisms: A draft system where the order in which clubs select eligible players is based on a ranking from worst to best on-field performance from the most recent season will promote competitive balance. Consider a sport such as basketball, where there are relatively few players on a squad. Giving a bottom-performing club first choice of a potential superstar (such as the Cleveland Cavaliers selecting LeBron James in the 2003 draft) can dramatically lift the competitive potential of that club.

In a single-entity league structure, the league management may make supplemental allocation of players outside of a draft to further "assist" low-performing clubs.

Club-Level Mechanisms: Many leagues operate with some form of salary cap. This is a restriction on the maximum amount any club in that league can spend on player payrolls. A

EXHIBIT 2-1   MECHANISMS TO PROMOTE COMPETITIVE BALANCE

1. **Player Selection Mechanism**
   - Draft system based on worst to best on-field performance in prior season
   - Supplemental player assignments (found in some single-entity leagues)
2. **Club Management Mechanisms**
   - Maximum/minimum club salary levels
   - Salary taxes on clubs spending beyond set levels
3. **League-Level Mechanisms**
   - Revenue sharing inversely related to on-field results
   - Revenue sharing inversely related to local revenue base
   - Revenue sharing inversely related to club player payroll
   - Revenue sharing with equal allocations to each club
   - Relegation and promotion of teams (found in many soccer league competitions)
   - Game scheduling such that the number of games perceived to be mismatches is reduced (can occur in leagues where clubs do not play every other club a fixed number of times in a season)

companion requirement is often a minimum salary payroll. The NFL is a high-profile example of a league with a maximum/minimum salary payroll range. The maximum cap on salary payments aims to prevent richer clubs from stacking their teams with a preponderance of the league's talent. The underlying premise is that clubs with higher player payrolls have a higher likelihood of on-field success. Evidence from leagues with no salary caps or no salary taxes strongly supports this premise (see Section 4 for evidence from the NFL, MLB, NBA, NHL, and EPL). The minimum salary payment requirement is motivated by the league's and players' association's desire to have at least a base level of commitment to hiring talented players for each club.

League-Level Mechanisms: League revenue sharing can be an important competitive balance mechanism, depending on both the relative magnitude of centrally collected revenues to total revenues, and the sharing rule adopted. These issues are discussed in the following section, "Revenue Sharing."

Relegation and promotion of teams is another way of increasing the competitiveness of clubs in a league. This is frequently found in professional soccer leagues, where in most countries the elite league has several subleagues where clubs also compete. English soccer has such a structure. The top three leagues are the English Premier League (20 clubs), Division One League (24 clubs), and Division Two League (24 clubs). At the end of each season, the bottom three clubs in the English Premier League are relegated to the Division One League, while the top three in the Division One League are promoted to the Premiership League. Exhibit 2-2 illustrates some movements. This relegation and promotion feature

EXHIBIT 2-2 SURVIVAL OF THE FITTEST IN ENGLISH PREMIER LEAGUE: RELEGATION AND PROMOTION

(Bottom three in Premier League relegated to Division One for next season; Top three in Division One promoted to Premier League for next season)

Premier League		
2000–2001 Season	2001–2002 Season	2002–2003 Season
1. Manchester United	1. Arsenal	1. Manchester United
.	.	.
.	.	.
16. Everton	16. Bolton	16. Aston Villa
17. Derby	17. Sunderland	17. Bolton
18. Manchester City ⎫	18. Ipswich ⎫	18. West Ham ⎫
19. Coventry ⎬ Relegated	19. Derby ⎬ Relegated	19. West Bromwich ⎬ Relegated
20. Bradford ⎭ for 2001–02	20. Leicester ⎭ for 2002–03	20. Sunderland ⎭ for 2003–04

Division One		
2000–2001 Season	2001–2002 Season	2002–2003 Season
1. Fulham ⎫ Promoted	1. Manchester City ⎫ Promoted	1. Portsmouth ⎫ Promoted
2. Blackburn ⎬ for 2001–02	2. West Bromwich ⎬ for 2002–03	2. Leicester City ⎬ for 2003–04
3. Bolton ⎭	3. Birmingham City ⎭	3. Wolverhampton ⎭
4. Preston	4. Wolverhampton	4. Sheffield United
5. Birmingham City	5. Millwall	5. Reading

aims to add stronger teams to the top-tier league and shift the weaker teams to the lower-tier league. It also creates drama (and "life-and-death" experiences!) for fans of clubs at the bottom end of the league ladder near the season end. Over the 10 seasons from 1993–94 to 2002–04, 36 clubs played at least one season in the EPL; only 11 of the 36 had sufficient sustained on-field excellence to remain in the EPL every year of that 10-year period.[4] The relegation and promotion approach requires a series of strong leagues underlying the top-tier league for the promoted clubs to be viable in the top tier. The MLB and NHL come closest in North America to this model with their minor-league infrastructure.

Revenue Sharing

Two central issues in revenue sharing are (1) composition of the revenue pools and (2) the allocation rules by which shared revenues are distributed to individual clubs.

Revenue Pool Composition

A key distinction exists between central revenue pools (revenues directly paid to the league) and local revenue pools (revenues directly paid to the clubs). Where the league is a non-profit organization (e.g., MLB, NBA, NFL, and NHL), all central revenues (net of league costs) are typically distributed to the clubs. Where the league is a for-profit group, the league will often keep a percentage of the central revenue pool. NASCAR, for example, keeps 10 percent of its central television contract money and allocates 65 percent to the tracks and 25 percent to the racing teams. NASCAR is a private-for-profit league that is owned by the France family.

Both the composition and the magnitude of central revenue pools and local revenue pools differ across leagues. For example, the NFL collects all media revenues at the central league level—$2.2 billion per year under the 1998–2005 broadcast contract with ABC/CBS/FOX/ESPN. In contrast, the MLB, NBA, and NHL have media revenues collected at both the central revenue pool and the local revenue pool levels. Sponsorship deals likewise can be at either the league level or the local club level. The NFL has much higher central revenues to total revenues percentage than do the MLB, NBA, or NHL leagues.

Local Revenue Pools and Cross-Subsidization: Clubs do not always keep 100% of the revenues they collect locally. A tradition in many (but not all) leagues is for the home team to share ticket revenues with the away (visiting) club. The NFL, until 2002, operated with a rule whereby the home club kept 60 percent and the away club 40 percent. Since 2002, the NFL has deposited the away-team 40 percent of ticket revenue into a central revenue pool and distributed that pool equally across all 32 clubs. In the approach used until 2002, differences across clubs in their drawing power were reflected in the away-game revenue distributions.

Each MLB club aggregates a broad set of local revenues (local radio and television proceeds, ticket sales, suite rentals, concessions, and parking, minus ballpark expenses) into a single pool. Thirty-four percent of this pool for each club is then contributed to a central revenue pool that is distributed equally to each MLB club.

EXHIBIT 2-3 NFL CENTRALLY SHARED REVENUES OF GREEN BAY PACKERS: 2002–2003 AND 2003–2004

Central Revenues	2002–2003		2003–2004	
	$ (millions)	%	$ (millions)	%
Television Revenues	$ 77.140	50.4%	$ 81.179	45.3%
Other NFL Revenues	4.701	3.1	7.306	4.1
Road Games	10.770	7.0	11.384	6.4
Total	92.612	60.5	99.869	55.8
Local Revenues	60.485	39.5	79.226	44.2
Total Revenues	$153.097	100.0%	$179.095	100.0%

Revenue Sharing and Allocation Rules

The sharing and allocation rule(s) used to distribute pooled revenues can have a dramatic effect on the funds each club has to be competitive on the field. The three main alternatives are:

- Higher allocations to the clubs with low local revenue-generating capability. The MLB allocation rules result in clubs such as the New York Yankees and Boston Red Sox redistributing part of their revenue to lower revenue-drawing clubs such as the Milwaukee Brewers and the Minnesota Twins. This allocation rule reduces both the absolute and relative difference in total revenues across clubs.

- Equal allocation to all clubs in the league. This is the approach adopted by the NFL. This allocation rule reduces the relative difference in total revenues across clubs.

- Allocation rules that favor the higher revenue-generating clubs. The English Premier League allocates its sizable central television revenue contract using a formula in which the better-performing clubs on the field (which also happen to be the highest local revenue-generating clubs) receive the highest allocations. This allocation rule increases the absolute difference in revenues across clubs. (The rationale of the EPL here is to reward successful clubs' performance as opposed to promote competitive balance of clubs in the league. Some observers label the EPL as "raw capitalism" as opposed to the "socialism" they associate with the sharing rules used in North American leagues).

The Green Bay Packers of the NFL publicly releases its financial statements. These provide insight into the relative magnitude of centrally shared revenues to total revenues for a well-known club in the NFL. Exhibit 2-3 presents this information for 2002–03 and 2003–04. Every club in the NFL receives the same central revenues that Green Bay reports: $92.612 million in 2002–03 and $99.869 million for 2003–04. Green Bay had a major stadium redevelopment that was finished before the start of the 2003–04 season. Central shared revenues are more than 55 percent of Green Bay's total revenues in each year.

Major Challenges at League Level

Leadership and strategy at the league level are important factors in understanding the initiatives underway and the challenges being addressed in different leagues. This section briefly highlights some key initiatives and challenges.

Value Creation (Growing the Pie) and Value Sharing: Each league is continually seeking ways to increase revenues from existing sources and create new revenue sources. Exhibit 2-4 presents the annual compound growth rate in revenues, player salaries, operating income, and valuation based on estimates made by *Forbes* and *Financial World* from 1994 to 2003. As a caveat, it is stressed that these are estimates and not based on club-audited numbers. Actual numbers for all clubs are not in the public domain (except for the EPL). Exhibit 2-4 highlights how revenues across all five leagues have increased. Player salaries have also increased over this period. At an aggregate league level, the NFL has experienced the highest growth in operating income and club valuation.

Globalization: Global expansion represents a possible way for the leagues to grow the base of their game, either on or off the field. Soccer is the most global of sports, both in terms of the number of countries with leagues with sizable revenues and in the number of different participants at the youth and adult league levels. The four major North American professional team sports (football, baseball, basketball, and ice hockey) each dominate the global business aspect of their sport. This business domination opens up many challenges in efforts to globally expand their respective sports.

Consider MLB, which has clubs in both the United States and Canada. Its revenue base dwarfs that of leagues on other continents. One consequence is that players from multiple parts of the globe are attracted to play in the MLB and in the North American minor leagues. This provides MLB with the ability to increase its global revenue reach. Demand outside North America for MLB television broadcasts has been fueled by the desire to see locally developed talent play. Japanese interest in MLB games has been increased by the success of Hideki Matsui (New York Yankees) and Ichiro Suzuki (Seattle Mariners). MLB is able to increase its global television revenues by having such players in its leagues.

A major business challenge is how to promote baseball leagues in other countries and the role (if any) of MLB in that development. One option is for MLB to be an investor in new leagues in other countries and to share its business development experience. Another option is for MLB to assist in the development of a World Cup format. World Cups in soccer, rugby, and cricket have generated much additional television revenue and have enabled individual players to attract sponsorship deals for global companies. An individual country professional league body (no matter how powerful) likely will have to accept much less control in decision making when promoting its sport to a broad-based global platform. This is not especially easy

EXHIBIT 2-4   VALUE CREATION AND VALUE SHARING: ANNUAL COMPOUND GROWTH RATES 1994–2003

	Revenues	Player Salaries	Operating Income	Club Valuation
NFL	9.9%	7.4%	21.5%	15.2%
MLB	11.6	11.6	−8.6	9.8
NBA	7.0	11.1	−5.3	8.5
NHL	8.0	14.3	a	8.1
EPL	16.9	19.7	12.1	N/A

a. Not calculated due to absence of positive operating income at the league level in 2003

Source: Calculated from data in annual issues of *Financial World* and *Forbes*; Deloitte, *Annual Review of Football Finance* (August 2004).

to accept for some North American sporting leagues, given the widespread skepticism in the United States of the "benefits" of global bodies such as the United Nations.

Athletes as Role Models: Participants in the sports industry operate in a fishbowl, and none more so than the athletes. All aspects of their behavior are continually under the microscope. "Athletes behaving badly" is a story many members of the media relish running in television, radio, print, and on the Internet. Individual athletes, sporting leagues, and clubs each have high responsibilities in this area. Sporting league administrators can play a leadership role here. Helping develop initiatives that increase personal responsibility of athletes for actions that are at variance with minimal social norms is important. Section 4 further discusses this issue.

Balancing Sports and Entertainment: Fan expectations at sporting events and of sporting stars are continually evolving. Sports networks such as ESPN and FOX Sports push the envelope in seeking "media highlights" that startle, stun, or shock. In some cases, pure sporting achievements fall into this category. In other cases, antics that go beyond the bounds of acceptable sports behavior attract the media and can be replayed ad nauseam. League administrators have the responsibility of setting limits on what behaviors are permissible.

Mega-sporting events are among the most watched media events each year. One challenge for an administrator is deciding what wraparound activities to package with the sporting game itself. Pregame or half-time shows at major sporting events have increasingly been a major part of the publicity the media use to promote interest in the sporting event.

Growing Use of Strategy Analysis

The sports industry attracts many talented executives to its ranks. There is growing use of formal strategy tools in decision making by these executives. Two examples illustrate this point.

National Football League's Game Plan: The NFL, led by its commissioner, Paul Tagliabue, developed a mission and values statement. Exhibit 2-5 presents extracts from the framework the NFL uses to guide its decision making:

> *Our mission and values are rooted in the NFL's history and traditions,*
> *but they also look ahead and challenge us to improve. The framework for*
> *achieving our mission centers on six fundamental elements, which we call*
> *our "strategic constraints." A football team does not take the field without*
> *a game plan. This is our "game plan." It will serve as a foundation for*
> *continuing to build and transform the culture of our evolving organization.*

The NFL economic infrastructure has been strategically designed to combine (1) a high level of revenue certainty at both the league and club level, (2) a balance between revenues and costs at both the league and club level, and (3) a growing pie that players collectively have shared. One manifestation of this strategic design is the strong appreciation in NFL club values over time (see Exhibit 2-4).

EXHIBIT 2-5   NATIONAL FOOTBALL LEAGUE'S GAME PLAN

MISSION AND VALUES

To present the National Football League and its teams at a level that attracts the broadest audience and makes NFL football the best sports entertainment in the world. To achieve our mission, we will consistently challenge ourselves to improve and be guided by these values:

- Integrity
- Performance and Teamwork
- Tradition and Innovation
- Diversity
- Learning

STRATEGIC CONSTANTS

The "Strategic Constants" are the fundamental dynamics that shape our work on a daily basis. We must recognize and understand these "Constants" to achieve our mission.

The Game
Maintain the game of NFL football at the highest level of quality

The Business
Maximize the long-term strength and value of the NFL

Fans & Community
Create compelling experiences that attract and inspire fans domestically and internationally

Partnership & Alliances
Develop successful relationships with partners and allies in media, business, sports and government

The Players
Maintain a strong partnership with the players and the NFL Players Association

The Organization
Create organizational excellence within all league entities

Source: National Football League.

Federation Internationale De Basketball's (FIBA) Scorecards: FIBA is the world governing body for basketball. It is an independent association formed by 212 National Federations of basketball throughout the world. The FIBA Secretary General, Patrick Baumann, has led initiatives to develop a "strategic master plan for the next 4 to 8 years." Exhibit 2-6 shows the relationship between FIBA's vision, mission, long-term objectives, and its scorecards.

EXHIBIT 2-6   FIBA's Vision, Mission, Long-Term Objectives and Scorecards

FIBA'S VISION

The sport of basketball is the core element of FIBA's vision: FIBA believes that sports provide people with values through which they define themselves. Basketball is unique: Fast and precise, mind and body, a sport in which the individual is as powerful as the team.

FIBA'S MISSION

FIBA governs basketball worldwide, making the rules and keeping the sport in line. We make sure basketball is challenging, exciting and fascinating for everyone. FIBA is basketball.

FIBA'S LONG-TERM OBJECTIVES

The development of the sport of basketball is FIBA's raison d'être. Its long-term objectives are geared towards this aim and show a broad range of interests and activities which are grouped into five inter-dependent fields of activity (scorecards).

FIBA SCORECARDS—A BALANCE BETWEEN "SPORT" AND "COMMERCIAL ACTIVITIES"

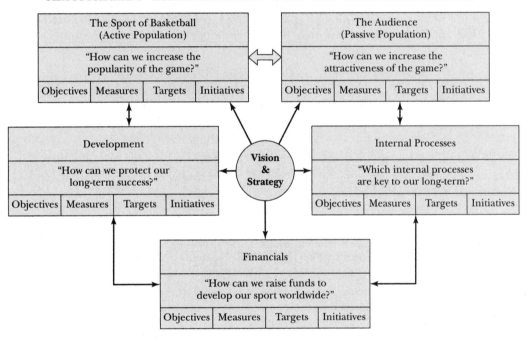

Source: FIBA (Federation Internationale de Basketball), Vision-Strategy-Activities: 2003–2010 (2004).

Exhibits 2-5 and 2-6 both illustrate strategic analysis of the kind employed by leading businesspeople in many industries. A premise of this book is that such strategy analysis will increase the long-term "health" of the sports industry to the benefit of many of its participants, both on and off the field.

Case 2.1 Basketball, Globalization, and the NBA[5]

"It's not the Dream Team!" This was the catch-cry of many press articles describing the U.S. men's basketball team as they prepared for the August 2004 Summer Olympics to be held in Athens, Greece. Such articles also invariably mentioned the U.S. team's poor performance in the FIBA 2002 World Championships—"limped away with a sixth-place finish" illustrated the negative tone of many articles[6]. One upside to such stories was the growing status of basketball outside North America.

Cindy Jones, President of the Sports Management Consulting and Marketing Group (SMCMG), had long-viewed globalization of North American professional sports as a major growth area for SMCMG. Her challenge was to position her firm's consulting such that multiple clients were prepared to pay for advice over an extended period. Basketball was high on Jones' agenda. The sport already was played in many countries and there were active professional leagues in multiple parts of the globe. The high attention given to non-U.S. players in the NBA reinforced her belief that global opportunities warranted serious analysis.

Jones decided to take her five top executives to an off site that would include the FIBA Diamond Ball. The inaugural FIBA Diamond Ball was played in Hong Kong in 2000, just before the Sydney Olympics. The second Diamond Ball would be in Belgrade, (capital of Yugoslavia/Serbia and Montenegro). The competing nations in this pre-Olympic tournament included six of the twelve playing in the Athens Olympics—Angola, Argentina, Australia, Lithuania, People's Republic of China and Yugoslavia/Serbia and Montenegro.

The other six nations competing for the basketball gold medal in Athens were Greece, Italy, New Zealand, Puerto Rico, Spain, and U.S.A.

Jones decided that she would break down possible consulting engagements into two areas:

(a) Growing the sport of basketball globally. Soccer had a global footprint that was the envy of most other sports. While basketball also had an impressive global footprint, many growth opportunities still appeared to exist.

(b) Expanding the NBA brand. The challenge here was to evaluate and prioritize the multiple options facing the NBA.

Her initial focus was to be on men's basketball. Although she was passionate in promoting women's basketball, Jones believed the commercial opportunities for SMCMG in the men's basketball arena dwarfed those in the women's arena (with the exception of youth participation initiatives).

Growing the Sport of Basketball Globally

Basketball has impressive participation and popularity in many parts of the globe. Appendix A discusses FIBA, the international governing body. FIBA was founded in 1932 and is headquartered in Geneva, Switzerland. Jones decided to sketch out multiple areas where growth in the business side of basketball could occur globally. One of her guideposts was examining what was occurring in other professional sports.

1. World-Cup

The pinnacle of professional soccer is the World Cup tournament. Every four years, teams from the 32 qualifying nations compete in a five-week tournament with the final game being the single most watched sporting event for that year. Rugby and cricket also have a four-year World Cup format. These World Cups are a platform for much nationalistic pride and passion. Each of soccer, rugby, and cricket have seen dramatic increases over time in revenues associated with their respective world cups.

Basketball has increased its efforts to have a high-profile World Championship format in which national teams comprised of elite players whose birth/"heritage" qualifies them to represent those countries. FIBA manages this tournament. The 2002 World Championship, held in Indianapolis, U.S.A., was the thirteenth. It was won by Yugoslavia (Serbia and Montenegro) in an 84–77 win over Argentina. The first tournament, held in 1950 in Buenos Aires, was won by the host nation Argentina in a 64–50 win over U.S.A. Up to 1986, FIBA was restricted to amateur athletes. Since 1989 all athletes, both amateur and professional, have been welcomed by FIBA.

Within the United States, the FIBA World Championship is yet to attain status comparable to the World Cups in soccer, rugby or cricket in countries in which those sports had substantial participation or popularity. For each of soccer, rugby, and cricket, elite players almost without exception viewed winning the World Cup as a pinnacle of their sporting achievement. U.S. basketballers, in contrast, have yet to view the FIBA World Championship as having such status. Winning the NBA Final Series is typically the pinnacle of sporting achievement to most professional players.

From a business perspective, building a four-year high-prestige World Cup in basketball had much upside in multiple revenue areas—e.g., television payments, sponsorship, merchandising, and attendance.

2. Olympics

The summer or winter Olympics have included gold medal events for basketball since 1936. The 1992 Summer Olympics in Barcelona is often viewed as the "high-point" in terms of the U.S. profile in Olympic Basketball. The so-called "Dream Team" included a "who's who" of the NBA, including Michael Jordan, Larry Bird, and Magic Johnson. In contrast, in 2004 the U.S. media stressed who had decided not to join the U.S. Olympic team (such as Kobe Bryant, Kevin Garnett, Tracy McGrady and Shaquille O'Neal). While some star U.S. athletes were resting injuries in 2004, most press articles stressed that the invitation to join the U.S. Olympic men's team "isn't so golden anymore."

Olympic gold medals were also awarded in soccer, baseball, and ice hockey. In soccer, the Olympic tournament had tight age restrictions such that most global elite players from the World Cup rarely appeared in Olympic soccer tournaments. Baseball was similar to soccer in that the U.S. Olympic team did not contain many elite Major League Baseball (MLB) players. The Summer Olympics was held in August. Major League Baseball (MLB) in North America did not stop their season to enable elite MLB players to compete in the Olympics. In contrast, the North American National Hockey League (NHL) took a "mid-season" break in 1998 for the Nagano Winter Olympics and in 2002 coinciding with the Salt Lake City Winter Olympics. This break enabled superstar NHL players to represent their countries fight for the Olympic gold medal.

Jones viewed the Olympics as an important stepping-stone to promoting basketball globally. The 1992 Olympics helped showcase major athletes to all parts of the globe. She viewed at least two major opportunities—(a) enabling non-U.S. athletes to promote the game to the world and in particular their own country of origin, and (b) enabling U.S. athletes to promote their talents, their image, and by default the NBA, to a broader audience.

3. Country Against Country Games and Tournaments

Sports such as soccer, rugby, and cricket have a long tradition of country against country national team games. This has not been without conflict or difficulties. For example, the governing global soccer body (FIFA) has tough rules requiring players to play for their country whenever there is a conflict with playing for their club team. Such conflicts rarely arise with North American sports such as football, basketball, baseball, or ice hockey due to the virtual absence of regular country against country games.

Jones wondered about the possibility of a U.S. basketball team taking a European tour at the end of the NBA season. This was a traditional format in rugby and cricket. Elite athletes in these sports attracted endorsement contracts from global companies in part due to the expectation of them playing abroad in high profile country-to-country games.

4. Club-Level Games

On many metrics (attendance, television viewers, and player salaries to name three) the North American NBA dwarfed the other professional basketball leagues. Notwithstanding this, consulting opportunities existed outside North America. The National Basketball League (NBL) in Australia and New Zealand illustrates a non-North American league with a 20-year plus heritage. Currently with 11 teams, the NBL has a cable television contract and multiple sponsors such as Coca-Cola, Fox Sports, Holiday Inn, and Qantas. Each club in the NBL is allowed a maximum of two imports (i.e., Non-Australian or non-New Zealand born players). Most such imports are Americans. The NBL operates with a salary cap at the club level of AUD $736,000 in 2004–2005, a reduction from its 2002–2003 level of $1,050,000. There is also a salary cap on individual players—$175,000 (termed "franchise players"). In July 2003, Rick Burton (then Director of the Warsaw Sports Marketing Program at the University of Oregon) was appointed Commissioner of the NBL. One challenge for the NBL is that its player salaries are well below those of the NBA and below those in European leagues. Highly talented players in the NBL have switched to the NBA or European clubs at different stages in their career.

The NBL faces many battles in expanding its revenue base and in capturing a major percentage of the sports and entertainment spend in Australia and New Zealand. Similar club leagues around the globe frequently were in the same position, if not worse. Most NBL teams in Australia played in relatively modern in-door stadiums whereas many other leagues had few stadiums with 10,000 plus capacity and facilities for corporate entertaining.

Jones viewed each professional league outside the NBA as a consulting opportunity. SMCMG had much experience in giving advice at the North American club level. Their knowledge base was a strong platform to pitch for new business clients abroad.

5. Youth Participation

Basketball and soccer had many advantages over other team sports in promoting youth participation. Both required minimal equipment and had basic rules that could be easily communicated. Sports like gridiron and ice hockey in contrast were more difficult and expensive to develop youth participation. While youth participation in basketball has been growing globally, many commentators believe there was still much upside.

Jones again viewed promoting youth participation as an opportunity for SMCMG. Sponsors could gain a very high profile by underwriting basketball sports camps for kids, by paying coaches to promote the game in schools, and in making equipment (such as balls, clothing, shoes and hoops) available to all children.

GROWING THE NBA BRAND GLOBALLY

The NBA has its roots in professional basketball leagues over many decades. The Basketball Association of America (BAA) was formed in 1946 with 11 charter franchises. During its first two years, the BAA incurred losses due to a bidding war for college players with the rival National Basketball League (NBL). One year later, the BAA merged with the NBL and became the National Basketball Association (NBA).

In 1984 David Stern was appointed the fourth commissioner of the NBA. The league consisted of 23 franchises. In the next 20 years, dramatic increases occurred in player salaries and in the magnitude of television contracts and sponsor deals. In December 2002, Robert Johnson was chosen as owner of the 30th franchise located in Charlotte, North Carolina. Johnson paid a record $300 million franchise fee to enter the NBA.

The NBA's headquarters are in New York, with Stern as its Commissioner. It also has offices in Miami, Toronto, Mexico City, Barcelona, Paris, Tokyo, Hong Kong, Beijing, Shanghai, and Taipei. The NBA is now widely recognized as a global sporting brand. Indeed, in many parts of the globe an association between the sport itself and elite NBA players, is often made. For example, Michael Jordan-labeled apparel and shoes are worn by youth in many countries.

Cindy Jones decided to take a first-cut pass at possible ways to grow the NBA brand globally:

1. Admit Non-U.S. or Non-Canadian Clubs Into the NBA Competition

The closest region geographically for a new club franchise would be one or more NBA clubs based in Mexico, with Mexico City or Monterey the obvious candidates. A more ambitious proposal was to add a third division (NBA Europe) to the current two divisions (NBA East and NBA West). NBA Europe could have four or more clubs from leading European basketball strongholds (such as Croatia or Yugoslavia (Serbia and Montenegro)) or leading European commercial centers (such as London, Madrid, Paris or Rome).

Jones envisioned SMCMG as assisting potential new franchise applicants develop their business plan, promote it to the NBA, and assist in the rollout of those groups that were awarded new NBA franchises.

2. NBA Joint Venture With Other Leagues

Joint venturing is frequently cited as a successful business strategy. Some companies have used the joint-venture model to expand globally—e.g., Starbucks. Jones thought this model was worth at least exploring with the NBA. She wondered whether leagues outside North America would welcome the NBA as a co-branding partner or as equity or joint venture partner e.g., a Latin American/NBA branded league. Would this be attractive to the NBA? She was convinced that the NBA was unwilling to provide cash and other resources to other leagues without having some say in decision-making and being able to limit the potential for the NBA brand to be tarnished. Many professional sporting leagues around the globe had encountered financial problems in the past and had allegations of mismanagement and fraud.

3. Touring NBA Exhibition Games/Club Games

A recent trend in soccer has been the elite club soccer teams playing multiple exhibition games abroad on a regularly scheduled basis. For example, Manchester United made a U.S. tour in July 2004 and played Bayern Munich (July 25th in Chicago), Celtic Rangers (July 28th in Philadelphia), and A.C. Milan (July 31st in East Rutherford, New Jersey). For more than a decade, the NBA and its teams have played a small number of pre-season games in England, France, Israel, and Puerto Rico. In October 2004, the Houston Rockets and the Sacramento Kings had preseason games in Beijing and Shanghai. Jones saw many marketing opportunities in promoting such games. Was it possible to have such games on a regular basis so that sponsors and fans could look forward to them on an ongoing basis?

An extension of this approach is playing a select number of actual season NBA games abroad. For example, the opening 2004 Major League Baseball game featured the New York Yankees (including Hideki Matsui, its Japanese star left-fielder) against the Tampa Bay Devil Rays in Tokyo, Japan. This opening game attracted additional sponsors and much publicity for base-ball, MLB, the Yankees, and the Devil Rays in Tokyo and other parts of Asia. Would the NBA be willing to play a select number of actual NBA games abroad? Jones was convinced she could assist in attracting new sponsors to such games and help grow the NBA revenue pie.

4. Further Promote Non-U.S. Players Participating in the NBA

The growth of international (non-U.S. born) players participating in the NBA has been well reported in the media:

1973–74	2 players from 2 countries
1983–84	8 players from 7 countries
1993–94	24 players from 19 countries
1998–99	38 players from 27 countries
2003–04	73 players from 34 countries

The 2003–2004 NBA season included two-time MVP Tim Duncan (U.S. Virgin Islands—with San Antonio Spurs) and five 2004 All Stars:

- Andrei Kirilenko (Russia—with Utah Jazz)
- Jamaal Magloire (Canada—with New Orleans Hornets)
- Dirk Nowitzki (Germany—with Dallas Mavericks)

- Peja Stojakovic (Serbia and Montenegro—with Sacramento Kings)
- Yao Ming (China—with Houston Rockets)

Jones believed that significant opportunities may exist in using such stars to promote internationally the commercial interests of the NBA. The surge in NBA interest in China when Yao Ming joined the Houston Rockets was a defining event for global sports marketing. Opportunities also existed for increasing non-U.S. sponsors to use these international players to help promote business within the U.S.A.

The 2002–2003 season marked Yao Ming's debut in the NBA. The average NBA away game (road game) attendance was 16,974 per game, down 0.50% from the 2001–2002 season. In contrast, the Houston Rockets led the NBA in average away game attendance increase (8.3%). Other elite players from abroad had the potential to likewise increase domestic revenues for the NBA as well as increasing its international revenues.

Many sports agents and NBA teams were already trawling outside the U.S.A. for the next generation of NBA stars. The quantum difference between NBA salaries and those paid in the leagues of other countries meant the NBA was a magnet attracting many international players. Although historically Jones had focused SMCMG's activities on consulting and marketing activities, she wondered whether adding a player representation division that laser-beamed on identifying and representing international players for North American clubs made economic sense. One of her SMCMG colleagues previously had been a soccer agent in Europe and had represented several Latin American stars. These stars played for European clubs such as Arsenal, Barcelona, Chelsea, Lazio and Real Madrid. He believed there was an opportunity in basketball, but cautioned about the difficulties of dealing with national and club sporting bodies outside the U.S. as well as the frequent allegations of bribery and under-the-table payments.

5. Expanding the Global Media/Broadcast/Internet Coverage of the NBA

There are multiple examples of growing global interest in the NBA:

MEDIA CREDENTIALS: In 1987, the NBA issued 31 media credentials from reporters representing 7 countries for the All-Star Game. For the 2004 All-Star Game, the league issued a record 325 media credentials from 41 countries.

TELEVISION: NBA games and programs were seen in 212 countries in 2004 with broadcasts in more than 42 languages. NBA broadcasts into China in 2004 reached more than 314 million television households.

INTERNET: More than half of the 315 million visits to NBA.com in the 2003–04 NBA season came from fans located outside the U.S.—this was a higher amount of international traffic than any other U.S.-based sports website. NBA.com was the first professional sports league in the U.S. to offer specific international Web destinations for fans. NBA.com's nine international destinations include:

- Brazil (NBA.com/brazil)
- China (NBA.com/china)
- France (NBA.com/france)
- Japan (NBA.com/japan)
- United Kingdom (NBA.com/uk)
- Canada (NBA.com/canada)
- Spain (NBA.com/espanol)
- Germany (NBA.com/germany)
- Taiwan (NBA.com/taiwan)

International television payments were now an important part of NBA revenue mix. The NBA had multiple options going forward. For example, should television stations in other countries pay the NBA a fixed payment each season? This was similar to its North American television revenue model. The alternate was for the NBA to have its own television network that was carried in local language on cable television in each country—NBA-TV England and NBA-TV China. The NBA could receive both a per-subscriber monthly cable fee from each country and advertising revenue much as did ESPN from its overseas cable stations. Jones believed SMCMG had the expertise to negotiate cable television contracts with cable operators in other countries as well as to find advertising partners in those other countries.

Internet rights, although currently small, also was a growth area for the NBA. The NBA could sell its internet rights to live games via third parties (such as Yahoo!) or could have its own internet broadcasts under the NBA brand name. These broadcasts could be tailored for language differences and could focus on players from the country currently playing in the NBA. This was another potential area for SMCMG to play a role.

6. Global Merchandising

The NBA has a roster of international licensees, which provide NBA licensed products to fans in more than 100 countries on six continents. Approximately 20% of the NBA's $3 billion in merchandise sales is generated from outside the United States. The NBA licenses items in categories including apparel, sporting goods, trading cards, school supplies, publishing, home video, home furnishings, electronic games, toys and games, collectibles, and telephone cards. The NBA-Reebok partnership, which tipped off in 2003, marked the first time that one NBA apparel licensee has covered the entire Asia region. The five-year partnership calls for Reebok to design, manufacture, sell and market official NBA jerseys and shorts, caps, practice wear, off-court lifestyle apparel and a range of related accessory items.

7. Marketing Partners

The NBA in 2004 had seven global marketing partners—Adidas; Anheuser-Busch; Coca Cola; Gatorade; LEGO; Nike; and Reebok. One aim was to bring basketball to fans around the globe and to provide these partners co-branding opportunities.

The NBA also has country-specific marketing partners—e.g., in China (Red Bull—official sports/energy drink); in Spain, U.K. and Ireland (MBNA—affinity card); and in Mexico (TelCel—wireless telecom).

MAPPING OUT THE GLOBAL OPPORTUNITIES

Cindy Jones felt both excitement and caution at the many global opportunities in assisting either basketball expanding globally or promoting the NBA brand globally. She was unclear over who might be the major clients that would pay SMCMG for its consulting and marketing advice. While there was no shortage of options in many areas of the world, the ability of individual parties to capture sizable parts of any value they helped create was difficult to "guarantee." Moreover, navigating the complexity of FIBA, national basketball associations, country-specific basketball leagues, as well as player associations in multiple countries would require much thought and negotiating talents. She understood why many sports consulting firms to date had invested minimal resources in global activities. However, SMCMG's success to date had been from leading the band rather than following other people's footsteps. She looked forward to the offsite in Belgrade during the FIBA Diamond Ball. A major goal was to bring greater clarity to SMCMG's new global strategic initiatives in basketball.

APPENDIX A: FIBA

The FIBA.com website is a rich source of information. The following extracts and information is based on that site and two FIBA reports—"FIBA Scorecards 2003–2006" and "Vision-Strategy-Activities 2003–2010."

"The abbreviation 'FIBA' derives from the French 'Federation International de Basketball Amateur.' The Word 'Amateur' was dropped in 1989 after the distinction between Amateurs and Professionals was eliminated. The 'A' in FIBA was however left. This was for reasons of tradition and also because of the 'BA' at the beginning of our sport, Basketball!

Who we are:

- FIBA, the world governing body for basketball, is an independent association formed by 212 National federations of basketball throughout the world.

- FIBA is recognized as the sole competent authority in basketball by the International Olympic Committee (IOC)

- FIBA is a non-profit making organization and, in principle, does not pursue any objective of economic character for its own gains.

- The headquarters of FIBA are established in Geneva, Switzerland. The five zones, each of which has its own office are: FIBA Europe, FIBA Americas, FIBA Asia, FIBA Africa, and FIBA Oceania.

What we do:

- FIBA establishes the Official Basketball Rules, the specifications for equipment and facilities, and all internal executive regulations that must be applied to all international and Olympic competitions, for which FIBA also establishes the system of competition.

- FIBA controls and governs the appointment of international referees.

- FIBA regulates the transfer of players from one country to another.

- FIBA controls and governs all international competitions."

The five global sponsors of FIBA are Adecco, Champion, Molten, Mondo and Zepter.

In May 2003 FIBA announced the backdrop to its strategic plan:

"In recent past and from a global point of view, the sports market has changed very much in contrast to previous decades. The professionalisation of our sports is forcing everyone in this highly competitive market segment to improve constantly in large steps and to act more like a professional market player. A simultaneously downturn of the whole sports and entertainment industry—in conjunction with a huge slump in the world economy—has led to a sharp contraction in overall investment and an increased focus towards the 'premier sports' with regards to rights and events by the media, the sponsors and—as a result—the general public as well."

Basketball, one of the top three Olympic sports and the No. 1 indoor sport worldwide also suffered from this development to a certain extent. Media distribution and revenue for FIBA's events are stalling and the acquisition of new sponsors is a difficult sell—not because of unsatisfactory price/value relationship—but mainly because the product is not top of the mind with media, consumers and targeted commercial partners.

The Secretary General of FIBA (Patrick Baumann) noted, "Rather than speaking about achievements we should speak about the challenges which are ahead of us:

- The right balance between basketball as a business and the integrity of the sport

- The coordination, cooperation and strategy for national team competition and club competition leading to a further growth of the worldwide popularity

- The development programs for high level competition without neglecting the promotion of grass roots basketball

- The improvement of structures, as well as administrative and operational skills on international, regional and national level

In order to be ready for these challenges we have developed in close cooperation with our five continental zones a strategy paper indicating visions, missions, measures and actions.

On five score cards which deal with the sport, the audience, the development, the internal processes and the finances, we have identified the 12 most important goals.

We look forward to working closely with our zones and our 212 national federations to reach the set goals."

FIBA in its "FIBA Scorecards 2003–2006" outlined its 12 goals:

1. Increase the quality of the sport of Basketball in the area of Players, Coaches and Referees

2. Have well organized and efficient National Federations

3. Increase Image, Awareness and Audience at World and Continental Championships

4. Improve Entertainment Value of the Product

5. Attract and Keep Young Players

6. Provide Assistance for Development of Facilities

7. Study the Possibility of New World Events

8. Introduce Worldwide Consistent Standards of Structure and Management

9. Improve Regular and Permanent Communication within the FIBA Family

10. Define Standards of Organization for Different Categories of FIBA Events

11. Harmonise Worldwide Calendar

12. Generate Adequate Financial Resources in Order to Develop Basketball Worldwide within a Balanced Financial Budget

Questions

1. Why is it important to distinguish between (1) globalization options for basketball and (2) globalization options for the NBA?

2. Assume you are an advisor to SMCMG. What do you see as the best business opportunities for SMCMG for:

   a. Growing the sport of basketball globally?

   b. Growing the NBA brand globally?

   The focus here is on SMCMG's consulting and marketing advisory services.

3. What tensions may exist between FIBA and the NBA in their globalization initiatives? How should these tensions be handled?

4. Assume you are in charge of the NBA's globalization initiatives. What are the three most important initiatives? Explain your answer.

CASE 2.2   MAJOR LEAGUE SOCCER 1996–1998: NOW, LATER . . . NEVER?[7]

> *We feel very good about the platform we're at. It's a step-by-step approach where we claw our way up the ladder to being the fifth league. It's important to know who we're not, to have respect for our consumers and cater to their passion for the game. Our main focus is the product because that's what they care about the most.*
>
> —Doug Logan, Major League Soccer Commissioner[8]

In the 1970s, 1980s, and early 1990s the sport of soccer spread across the United States like wildfire. Suburban kids began playing the game as they once did baseball. Soccer camps and recreation leagues sprouted up everywhere. "Just wait ten years and watch professional soccer take off . . . I've been hearing 'ten more years' for about 30 years now," said Dan Counce, General Manager of the MLS Colorado Rapids.[9]

Prior to the emergence of the MLS, which began play in 1996, several leagues tried and failed to take advantage of soccer's enormous popularity in the US. These leagues included the North American Soccer League, The Major Indoor Soccer League, The United States Soccer League, and the American Professional Soccer League. The entrepreneurs behind each league saw huge potential, but failed when they found out that too few people cared about their brand of professional soccer.[10]

League History

MLS had articulated its mission statement for broad dissemination to relevant media, business, and public audiences.

> *Major League Soccer Mission Statement*
>
> *To create a profitable Division I professional outdoor soccer league with players and teams that are competitive on an international level, and to provide affordable family entertainment. MLS brings the spirit and intensity of the world's most popular sport to the United States. Featuring competitive ticket prices and family-oriented promotions such as "Soccer Celebration" at the stadium, MLS appeals to the children who play and the families who support soccer. MLS players are also involved with a variety of community events. In addition, MLS:*
>
> - *Encourages attacking and entertaining soccer with dynamic players and coaches*
> - *Improves the performance of U.S. soccer teams in international competition.[11]*

On December 17, 1993 World Cup USA 1994 Chairman and CEO Alan I. Rothenberg announced the formation of Major League Soccer (MLS). U.S. Soccer previously had promised FIFA (Federation Internationale de Football Association), soccer's international governing body, that it would develop a premier outdoor soccer league in the United States.

Harvard Business School Case No 9-599-023. Copyright 1998 President and Fellows of Harvard College. All rights reserved. For information: permission@hbsp.harvard.edu. This case was prepared by Kirk A. Goldman and Stephen A. Greyser. HBS cases are developed solely for class discussion and do not necessarily illustrate effective or ineffective management.

Shortly after, a bidding process began to determine the cities invited to host MLS teams. The interested communities sold season ticket deposits, established local training facilities, and secured stadium arrangements. New England, Columbus (Ohio), Los Angeles, New York/New Jersey, San Jose, and Washington D.C. were the first cities selected in the Spring of 1994. (Dallas, Denver, Kansas City, and Tampa Bay would be added to the list of inaugural teams early in 1995.)

MLS soon started signing broadcasting and sponsorship contracts. In March 1994, MLS announced that it had a three-year television agreement with ABC Sports and ESPN. ESPN would broadcast 10 games, ESPN2 would show 25 games, and ABC would air the championship game. At an MLS seminar in July, Rothenberg proclaimed that Nike had signed a multi-year sponsorship agreement as an official uniform and footwear supplier and that Mitre would produce the league's official game ball. Over the next few months, MLS added Reebok and Adidas as uniform and footwear suppliers.

That fall, Rothenberg announced the charter investors in MLS. They included Metromedia partners John Kluge and Stuart Subotnick, the Hunt family (headed by sports entrepreneur Lamar Hunt and his son, Clark), LA Soccer Partners, and API Soccer. In the early months of 1995, MLS began signing players. Tab Ramos, a veteran midfielder of the US National Team and the 1994 World Cup, signed as the league's first player on January 3, 1995. Defender Mike Burns, another 1994 U.S. World Cup Team member, signed late in February. On June 6, Mexican goalkeeper Jorge Campos became the first international player to sign with MLS. That same day, MLS named Budweiser its official beer and two more major investors, Phillip Anshutz of Denver and the Kraft Family of New England (owners of the NFL New England Patriots), joined the fold. (**Exhibit 1** shows the investor/operator profile for MLS.)

During the rest of the year, MLS continued to sign stars and sponsorship agreements. By February of 1996, MLS had assigned a total of 40 players to its ten teams. In addition, MLS teams selected a total of 160 players in a sixteen-round draft. The league also joined forces with the USISL (United Systems of Independent Soccer Leagues), in which the USISL would serve as the official minor league to the MLS. Each USISL team would supply players to the MLS team in its region as replacements when they became necessary.

On April 6, 1996, MLS began its first season at San Jose's Spartan Stadium as the San Jose Clash hosted and defeated the Washington D.C. United.

EXHIBIT 1   **MLS INVESTOR/OPERATOR PROFILE FOR 1998**

Team	Investor/Operator
New England Revolution	Kraft family
Columbus Crew	Hunt family
Dallas Burn	League-run
Colorado Rapids	Phillip Anschultz
Kansas City Wizards	Hunt family
Los Angeles Galaxy	LA Soccer Partners
New York/New Jersey MetroStars	John Kluge and Stuart Subotnick
San Jose Clash	League-run
Tampa Bay Mutiny	League-run
D.C. United	George Soros and others
Chicago Fire	Phillip Anschultz
Miami Fusion	Kenneth Horowitz

Compiled from Major League Soccer WWW site (http://www.mlsnet.com).

Single-Entity Structure

New England Revolution operator Jonathan Kraft stated his belief in the MLS product and why it will succeed where others had failed:

> There are people out there willing to invest a lot of money in our product. I think potential investors were very excited about what they saw in our operation. Our single-entity structure [see below] gives people willing to commit tens of millions of dollars the confidence that we are competing against each other on the field. Off the field, we are 100 percent partners in every activity.[12]

"[MLS has] learned from the past," says Craig Tartasky of E. J. Kraus and Associates, a Bethesda, Maryland sports agency. "They've centralized all their salary costs. MLS has done a good job of rolling out and getting attention."[13] The league's centralized structure, called single-entity, maintains ownership of all teams and player contracts. Investors, rather than franchise owners, operate and market teams. MLS adopted this strategy because its founders thought it would "eliminate financial disparities between large and small markets, control player costs, and offer commercial affiliates [i.e., partners] an integrated sponsorship and licensing program."[14]

The single-entity concept adopted by MLS radically altered the ownership concept in American professional sports. "Without single-entity, we would not have been interested," said Stuart Subotnick, co-operator of the New York/New Jersey MetroStars. "That would have been a prescription for failure."[15] In essence, MLS brought the concept of revenue sharing, as developed by the NFL, one step further.

The league has taken on many of the primary responsibilities typically associated with franchises in other sports. The league attracts, signs, and pays players. This allowed the league to establish a competitive balance among its teams. In its first season, MLS set its per team salary cap at $1.13 million for the 20-player roster, and equally distributed the top US and foreign players.[16] For example, it lured most of the US team from the 1994 World Cup as well as international stars such as Carlos Valderrama of Colombia and Roberto Donadoni from Italy and assigned them to Tampa Bay and New York/New Jersey respectively. MLS also paid travel expenses. At least 27 U.S. World Cup and National Team players were on MLS rosters, as well as over 20 international players from Mexico, Central and South America, Africa, and Europe. At least one U.S. World Cup player was on each team.

MLS aggressively pursued and won national marketing agreements with AT&T, Anheuser-Busch, Kellogg, and Nike.[17] These agreements provide the sponsors with access to each team and its venue. Randy Bernstein, the league's executive vice president in charge of marketing, stated:

> Because Major League Soccer [has] a single entity [structure], we are able to package rights to both the league and its 10 teams into one integrated program. We have created an environment where the success of the league as a whole is more important than that of an individual team. We provider marketers the one-stop shopping that they cannot get anyplace else. Our goal at Major League Soccer is to provide sponsors with an

opportunity unique to professional sports. Because of soccer's popularity, we are able to offer social, geographic, or ethnic demographics to our sponsors.[18]

According to MLS, its official sponsors included AT&T, Bandai, Budweiser, Fujifilm, Honda, Mastercard, and Snickers. Its official suppliers were Adidas, Nike, Puma, and Reebok. Corporate partners included All Sport Body Quencher, Kellogg's, Mitre, NAYA Water, TSI Soccer, Umbro, Hewlett-Packard, EDS, and Orlandi Veluta.

MLS also put a great deal of effort into its television arrangements. The league secured agreements with ESPN, ESPN2, Spanish-language Univision, and ABC. In addition, MLS produced all other games itself to sell as prepackaged product to local television stations. Bernstein said, "Teams went out and sold games on TV, to the level that 94 percent of all our games were televised regionally or nationally. We felt that was the key to our marketing."[19]

"Single-entity is the best of both worlds," claimed operator Clark Hunt. "It puts teams on equal footing. But on the other hand, operators have the flexibility to run their own franchise and will drive the league to success through their entrepreneurial skills."[20] In the system, team operators run their clubs as they see fit. They hired their own general managers, front-office staff, and coaches. In addition, they scout, draft, and trade players and market the team locally.[21]

Following the first season, MLS made some changes to allow for a higher level of competition and increased parity among its teams. In an attempt to bring more foreign players to the US, MLS increased its salary cap to $1.3 million per team. Additionally, it increased the number of foreign players per roster to five; from the original number of four.[22] Finally, the league used its power to strengthen the rosters of the Colorado Rapids and New England Revolution, the two teams that failed to make the playoffs in the inaugural season. (In 1997, both the Rapids and the Revolution made the playoffs. The Rapids advanced to the MLS championship game, losing to the United.)

MLS Fans

MLS tried to build its fan base with knowledgeable soccer enthusiasts. Many original MLS cities as well as the expansion city of Miami, have large Hispanic populations. Historically, soccer has dominated the sports culture for Hispanics. MLS also targeted soccer playing youths and fans of the 1994 US World Cup team. Pepsi spokeswoman Alyssa Schaier stated:

Soccer is exploding and it has strongholds in two key areas for us—the youth market and the Hispanic population. There's a strong parallel to how MLS is marketed and how Pepsi is marketed.[23]

Hispanic

In its first year, MLS enjoyed great success drawing Hispanic soccer fans to its games. Bernstein stated:

> *Baseball, football, basketball, and hockey do not do as good a job as they would like to in marketing to the non-Anglo audience. But in particular, the Hispanic fans are not catered to in the United States in professional sports. Major League Soccer caters to the Hispanic fan. How? We bring in top Hispanic players. We market in English and Spanish.*
>
> *Baseball does a pretty good job because they have some Hispanic players. Basketball has no Hispanic players. Football has literally none. Hockey has none. We feel [that] we can really go out and work with that audience and give them what they really want.*[24]

"There is a predisposition (among Hispanic fans) to spend money on soccer before a whole lot of other things," Logan said. "Sunday is church and soccer. It's a cultural thing." MLS appealed to fans who understand the game. Bernstein continued, "This is a world sport. Hispanic Americans are very, very proud. This is their sport. You don't have to teach it to them. You have to give them a good product."

Many Latin American players migrated to the US to play in the MLS. Teams such as the Tampa Bay Mutiny built their fan base on Hispanics and used one of the world's greatest players, midfielder Valderrama, to get there. The Mutiny saw a 177% increase in season ticket sales for the 1997 season.[25] The Los Angeles Galaxy rode Mexican goalkeeper Jorge Campos to the league's highest average attendance (28,916) and a spot in the MLS championship game in 1996. Other teams also depend greatly on the Hispanic market.

"To maximize our market, a Mexican player is what it takes," Dallas Burn President Billy Hicks stated.[26] In 1996, it was estimated that half of the Burn's game attendees were Mexican-Americans. Burn fans followed Hugo Sanchez of Mexico City and came out in droves (35,250 total) for the Cinco de Mayo game at the Cotton Bowl against the Colombus Crew. For 1997, the Burn were not scheduled to have a Mexican player on their active roster until the first two months of the season had passed. Their attendance suffered for those games.[27]

Non-Hispanic

The MLS has also attempted to appeal to all knowledgeable soccer fans. MLS officials wanted to put the best product on the field while still attracting the interest of US fans. MLS officials identified what they considered a fatal flaw of the North American Soccer League (NASL). The NASL had wanted to provide the best product; this meant bringing in rosters full of international players. Many of these stars came from Europe.[28] The American fans did not take to this idea, as Rothenberg explained:

> *That [the NASL] was a foreign dominated league. So while you had some superstars like Pele and Franz Beckenbauer and Johan Cruyff, below that you had almost no Americans and you had a bunch of foreign players that the American public did not relate to. You had mercenaries. They were either on loan or they were just here for the summer and then they were gone, so you could not build any kind of community spirit.*[29]

MLS rules dictated that the rosters of teams must be mostly American. League officials believed that Americans want to see their own on the field. Following the success of the United

States in the 1994 World Cup (which was held in the US), the MLS enlisted many home-grown stars on whom to build its fan base as described above.

Executives thought they could derive a healthy portion of the MLS fan base from America's youth. Soccer has become one of the most popular recreational sports for children. "Youth participation has risen more than 25-fold since the earlier unsuccessful outdoor soccer league—the NASL—was launched in 1975. Now only basketball tops soccer among the under-12 set."[30] According to the Soccer Industry Council of America, 18,098,000 people aged six and older played soccer at least once in 1996. Of that, 74% or 13,410,000 were aged 17 and younger.[31] Logan recognized this and implemented marketing strategies accordingly. He stated, "MLS players are more likely to be seen on MTV than heard on sports talk radio shows."[32] Los Angeles Galaxy midfielder Cobi Jones hosted his own show on the popular cable network. Additionally, the league sponsored many clinics and workshops within youth leagues in each of its markets.

In addition to information on soccer participation by age, the Soccer Industry Council of America 1997 report, *An Overview of the American Soccer Market*, included participation in 1996 by ethnicity, geographic region, and household income. Slightly over 75% of those playing soccer were white, 12.5% Hispanic, and 8% black (3% other). The South represented 29% of participants, with the Northeast, North Central, and West between 23% and 25% each. Regarding annual household income, 36% of players' households were in the $50,000 or more category, split about evenly above and below $75,000; 36% were in households between $25,000 and $49,999, and 28% in those less than $25,000.

MLS 1996

The MLS achieved a great deal in its first season. Soccer critics cited the lack of scoring as the reason many professional leagues previously had failed in the US. Rothenberg and Logan wanted to tailor their league to fit American expectations. In the first season, the league averaged 3.4 goals per game, one goal higher than they had anticipated.[33] Attendance figures also exceeded stated expectations. Midway through the season, MLS senior vice president of business affairs Mark Abbot said:

> *The numbers have been fantastic. Attendance has been about twice as high as we had projected. Our sponsorship and licensing are already both above projections. So, overall, I think we are way ahead of where we thought we were going to be.*[34]

The league averaged over 17,400 paid fans per game. Prior to the season, MLS officials targeted 12,000 fans per game as the league average.[35] These numbers were bolstered by exceptionally high attendance at a few games. At the league opener in San Jose, over 30,000 fans came to Spartan Stadium. In Los Angeles, the Galaxy drew 69,000 at their home opener at the Rose Bowl. Over 78,000 people filled Giants Stadium in East Rutherford, NJ, home of the MetroStars, for the MLS All-Star game. Finally, 42,000 fans paid to see the first MLS Cup championship game at New England's Foxboro Stadium.[36]

The league surpassed its stated expectations in attendance, and lost about $7 million less than the $25 million it had said it expected to lose the first season. Logan did not want the initial success to overinflate his ego. The League was, he said, "an embryonic pilot project with a five-year horizon."[37]

Amid questions of whether or not the MLS had the future viability of the other major leagues, Abbot stated:

> The only way you overcome the psychological barrier is to continue to be successful and show that you have stability. I think we have gone a long way to overcoming those kinds of problems by the successes we have had this year. We have shown that we are a fairly solid organization and that the backing we have is real. We have TV contracts for three years and sponsorship contracts for four years and investors with very, very deep pockets. I think the public and the media know that, and I think they are going to come to believe that we are here to stay.[38]

Logan summarized the first season:

> We did what we said we were going to do. We said we were going to put out on our playing fields high-quality, attractive, aggressive soccer, and we did. We said that people would come, and they did—to the tune of 45% higher than we had thought. We said we would do it prudently. We started out with a sensible business plan and we stuck to it. We said we would put out an honest and affordable product and we have.

> Second, we opened our arms to new Americans and they have responded with glee. Over 40% of our audiences nationwide are ethnic first- or second-generation Americans, mostly Latinos. It's rather interesting on a game-by-game basis to see people who otherwise would not come together to share an experience enter our stadium and—reservedly at first, looking around and saying, "You know, I am not sure these are the people I would hang out with,"—all of a sudden come together during the course of the season for the common purpose of cheering their team.

> We have appealed to the best in the American psyche and we have appealed to it in the following way: We have exemplified tough competition, fair play, access to all, and inclusion of all races, genders, and economic classes.[39]

MLS 1997

> In its first season, the MLS provided an oasis of professional competition for soccer-starved fans. This year, MLS will have to survive on the caliber of its play, not the novelty of its existence.[40]

The Boston Globe columnist Frank Dell'Apa wrote, "The MLS no longer can rely on the feel-good factor, on the fact that the soccer public has been awaiting the establishment of the league, and on the residual effects of World Cup interest. Now, substance is becoming the criteri[on] to attract fans and maintain credibility."[41] Prior to the 1997 season, MLS commissioner Doug Logan predicted league-wide attendance would improve to about 21,000 per game with fewer "peaks and valleys" as the league had experienced in its first season. MLS also faced the reality of World Cup qualifying activity during 1997. The league's best players had commitments to their respective national teams to help the latter earn bids for the 1998 World Cup in France.

In April, just after the season had begun, Logan stated:

> *I am cautiously optimistic we are going to hit our attendance goals. It was very encouraging to see the quality of play on the field. I think the games were significantly better than [at] the start of last season, but also better than they were at mid-season last year. It is going to be a long 33 weeks, but I like what I see so far.*[42]

By October, after the regular season, MLS did not look as spectacular as it had following its first season. "We are where any consumer business is in its second year of operation," said Logan. "There is no such thing as a straight upward line."[43] Both television ratings and attendance had fallen. Regarding the former, television ratings on both ESPN and ESPN2 dropped off compared to 1996. ESPN fell from an average rating of .55 in 1996 to .50 in 1997. ESPN2 drew a .27 rating in 1997 compared to .35 the prior season.

Notwithstanding the falling ratings, the league signed a six-year contract extension with ABC and ESPN. The league expected to receive at least $5 million for the 1998 season and significantly more in future years, depending on advertising revenue. Although the money was an improvement over its prior deal with the networks, the national exposure it would receive had far more value. The agreement meant that a dozen MLS games would be shown on ABC—a network breakthrough for the league—and 35 more on ESPN and ESPN2. The league was also negotiating a new contract with Univision, the Spanish-language network, which already carried an MLS game of the week throughout the first two seasons.[44]

Many of the league's teams suffered from falling attendance. "Even with the numbers of youngsters playing soccer in this country, you have to put on an entertaining product," said Peter Bridgewater, president of the San Jose Clash. "People came to watch soccer the first year and did not enjoy it and did not come back."[45] Despite Bridgewater's claim, the Clash attributed much of their attendance drop, almost 4,000 per game, to their lack of a Mexican national player and a major injury to team star Eric Wynalda.

League-wide attendance dropped by 16%, from 17,416 in 1996 to 14,616 in 1997. The Galaxy, which drew a league-high 28,916 in its first season, fell 29% to a second-best 20,626 per game. Much of this could be attributed to the frequent absence of star players because of national team commitments.[46]

Not every club experienced these problems. The Colorado Rapids, owned by Philip Anschutz, who also owns the NHL Kings and MLS' new Chicago team, the Fire, saw attendance rise by 15%. They enjoyed this increase even though the Rapids finished in fourth place in the Western Conference, four games under .500. The New England Revolution enjoyed a 12.6% jump and led the league with an average of 21,423 fans a game despite finishing two games below .500. The only other team to finish with higher attendance than the previous season was the defending MLS Cup champion D.C. United. Their increase was 9.3%—from an average of 15,281 in 1996 to 16,704 in 1997. (**Exhibit 2** shows MLS attendance for the first two years.)

EXHIBIT 2   MLS Attendance, 1996 and 1997

Team	1996 Average	1997 Average	Change
Los Angeles Galaxy	28,916	20,626	Down 28.6%
New England Revolution	19,025	21,423	Up 12.6%
Tampa Bay Mutiny	11,679	11,333	Down 2.9%
NY/NJ MetroStars	23,898	16,899	Down 29.2%
Columbus Crew	18,950	15,043	Down 20.6%
D.C. United	15,281	16,704	Up 9.3%
Kansas City Wizards	12,901	9,058	Down 29.7%
Colorado Rapids	10,276	11,806	Up 14.8%
San Jose Clash	17,232	13,597	Down 21.0%
Dallas Burn	16,011	9,678	Down 39.5%
League Average	17,416	14,616	Down 16.0%

Source: Compiled from league, team, and media sources.

On the field in 1997, the United dominated the MLS schedule throughout the season, finishing with a 22–11 record and 55 points[47]. Like the Rapids, the United stormed through the playoffs. On Sunday, October 26 a sellout crowd of 57,431 thronged Washington's RFK Stadium to see the Rapids and hometown United face off for the MLS Cup. D.C. set the pace and standard of excellence throughout the MLS season. This game was no different. The United's mix of international and American stars proved once again to be superior as they won their second consecutive MLS Cup.

Following the 1997 season, Logan offered comments about each of the now twelve MLS franchises on topics such as attendance, playing personnel, management, and stadium situations. He noted new or upgraded stadiums in Columbus (the first soccer-specific stadium) and Miami. He recognized superior management (New England, "a real bright spot") and the need for front office restructuring (Kansas City). He cited teams with strong fan support (Colorado, New England, Washington) and declining attendance (NY-NJ and Los Angeles, "the two big markets," as well as Kansas City). He flagged Washington as a "great success story," termed Colorado a franchise where "Cinderella is alive," and praised the new Chicago Fire for selling 1,000 full-season equivalent tickets for 1998 by the end of the 1997 season.[48]

New Issues for the MLS

Although the MLS had hit a few bumps in its road in its second season, league executives thought that overall it had been a very successful year. They saw signs of promise in its attempt to become the fifth major league. However, they recognized that over the next few years they would have to consider several new issues, including stadiums, the relationship of MLS with the NFL and other leagues, and the retention and recruitment of players.

The stadium issue grew as the league solidified its standing. MLS ran into a road block in an effort to persuade those who manage Giants Stadium to convert to grass, although MLS games prior to the NFL season are played on grass. It also failed in negotiation on a lease for the Miami Fusion to play in the Orange Bowl. In frustration, the Fusion were forced to reconstruct a stadium in Ft. Lauderdale. In Columbus, owner Lamar Hunt came up with private money after a bid for a publicly funded stadium for the Columbus Crew failed.

On the other hand, the league was successful in working with investors who own NFL teams. The Revolution, operated by the Kraft family, had a solid year in Foxboro Stadium, home of the Krafts' NFL New England Patriots. Similarly, the Wizards, also owned by the Hunt family, play in Arrowhead stadium, home of their NFL Kansas City Chiefs. The MLS had ongoing discussions with officials in other NFL cities, including Seattle and Pittsburgh, about expansion teams in new facilities.

The primary issue the league faced in 1998 was retention and recruitment of players. Several international stars left the MLS following the 1996 and 1997 seasons. Leonal Alvarez of Columbia and Hugo Sanchez of Mexico left the Dallas Burn after the inaugural 1996 season. After two seasons with the New York/New Jersey MetroStars, Roberto Donadoni chose to return to his home team of AC Milan in Italy. MLS wanted to spend its money wisely in its effort to bring in international players. Logan knew that he could bring the best players in the world to the MLS if he spent millions of dollars as they do in the foreign leagues. He thus far had chosen to develop the American game with primarily US players.

Questions

1. What are the key elements of the basic business model of MLS? What do you think of the MLS mission statement?

2. How did MLS attempt to learn from the NASL experience? What mistakes, if any, made by NASL has MLS worked to avoid? Do you agree with the directions MLS has taken as a result?

3. Why is soccer so popular in other parts of the world, particularly Europe and Latin America, and not so popular in the United States?

4. How would you assess MLS's first season (1996)? How would you assess the 1997 season? Has MLS shown "signs of promise in its attempt to become the fifth major league?"

5. What is your view of each of the three issues articulated in the last section? Is a facility partnership with the NFL a good idea?

6. Do you foresee problems with the single-entity concept? If the league grows, will investors be satisfied with holding only partial control? What about the players' attitude toward single entity?

7. How do you feel about the future of MLS as of now? Can this league be successful long term? What are its key issues/problems? (Use web and bibliographic sources.)

   Note: The former North American Soccer League stated in 1976 five goals for 1985:

   • expansion to 32–40 terms

   • the United States to be the hub of world soccer

   • hosting the World Cup tournament

   • NASL to be the major soccer league in the world, and a major sports league in the United States, on par with others

   • hosting an annual soccer tournament involving other world soccer powers

CASE 2.3 LAUNCHING THE NEW NATIONAL RUGBY LEAGUE SEASON: LOOKING FOR SUNLIGHT THROUGH DARK CLOUDS[49]

On March 2, 2004 the Chief Executive of the National Rugby League (NRL) in Australia was preparing his season launch speech. It was to be given in 24 hours time at a glittering high profile function. Included in the 400 guests were to be the game's superstars, major sponsors, executives from each of its 15 clubs, politicians, and many members of the media. Two weeks ago it was to be a night that the Chief Executive planned to focus on all the great promise the new season held. The previous season had shown increases in crowds, TV ratings, merchandise and sponsorship. The planned lead 30-second commercial was to feature the muscled star athletes in the surf and then coming onto the sand to mix with fans. The background music was the thumping, well-recognized "It's My Game" song of the Hoodoo Gurus. A major target audience for expanding the NRL fan base was women.

The National Rugby League was the governing body for a rugby league competition featuring 15 teams—14 from the eastern Australian States (Broncos, Bulldogs, Cowboys, Dragons, Eels, Knights, Panthers, Rabbitohs, Raiders, Roosters, Sea Eagles, Sharks, Storm and Tigers) and 1 from New Zealand (Warriors).

Rugby League was one of three major "winter" sporting codes played in the Australian March to September time period. The other two codes were the Australian Football League (AFL-Australian Rules) and Rugby Union[50]. The AFL code had made much progress in recent years in broadening its junior ranks to include a highly successful girls competition. Rugby Union had grown in strength in recent years, and in October-November 2003 hosted the high profile Rugby World Cup. This tournament generated over a $40 million profit that the Australian Rugby Union could re-invest into its game at all levels.

Coffs Harbour Visit of Canterbury Bulldogs

The Canterbury Bulldogs were a long-standing Sydney-based NRL club (formed in 1935) with a rich tradition of winning. In 2003, they sold more merchandise than any other team in competition. The Bulldogs had made great progress in attracting a multi-cultural fan base from the many different nationalities living in the Sydney South-Western suburbs. One of its star players was Hazem el Masri, born in Triploi, Lebanon. He was the leading point scorer in the NRL and a wonderful role model for many junior players in all of the league areas. The multi-cultural fan base was an important part of the NRL's growth and marketing strategy base.

As part of the 2004 pre-season, the Canterbury Bulldogs played the Canberra Raiders in the country town of Coffs Harbour on Saturday, February 21st. The Bulldogs players stayed at the Novotel Pacific Bay resort. After the Raiders game, some of the Bulldogs players partied in nightclubs in the town before returning to the resort. The Bulldogs club policy was no women to be allowed in the players' hotel rooms.

On February 24th, reports started to surface of an alleged sexual attack on a 20-year-old woman by up to six players on the Bulldogs. In the subsequent 10 days up to the March 3rd launch of the new NRL season, all sections of the Australian media focused very little on the new season. Rather, the focus initially was on the alleged sexual attack. From the players' side, it was reported that there may have been a sexual encounter but it was of a voluntary kind. Indeed it was also reported that several days prior to the Sunday morning incident a similar encounter may have occurred between multiple Bulldog players and the same female. The media focus then broadened to the issue of whether there was a culture within the rugby league sport that condoned (and even encouraged) encounters between multiple football players and a willing female. One media source reported a comment by an "unnamed player" that became a central part of the media focus. The unnamed player was reported to have said:

> *"It was just a typical night for some of the Canterbury players. Some of the boys love a bun. Gang banging is nothing new for our club or the rugby league."*

All sections of the sport-obsessed Australian media became consumed by taking positions in this rapidly moving set of stories. Talk-back sports radio had many "field-days" with the story. Rumors abounded with many references to other quotes from other "unnamed" persons.

A media journalist reported the following on the Bulldog's coverage:

> *"Nothing sells like sex and sport, they say. And the Bulldogs scandal has proved just how powerful a combination it is for the media. More than 30 talkback callers an hour went to air on Sydney radio 2GB at the height of the story last week. Media Monitors says there were more than 9000 news reports on TV, radio, and in the press. And at f2, John Fairfax Holding's website, traffic figures are double what they would expect for a lead domestic story."*[51]

Past Controversies

Controversy was nothing new for either the NRL or the Bulldogs. The NRL was formed to merge the Australian Rugby League (ARL) competition (featuring 12 teams in 1997) and Super League (featuring 10 teams in 1997). This merger was preceded by several years of infighting between the two leagues. The Bulldogs were one of the first teams to break away from the ARL in 1996 to join the new Super League.

In August 2002, the NRL penalized the Bulldogs 37 competition points for salary cap violations. This penalty shifted them from first to last position and ensured they were excluded from the September-October playoff (finals) games. This was the most extreme action ever taken in the history of the NRL for salary cap violations. A new management team at the Bulldogs was then put in place, with two previous ex-players (both with impeccable off-the-field as well as on-the-field reputations) as Chairman and Chief Executive. The current Chief Executive of the NRL played a strong leadership role in managing the 2002 Bulldog salary cap issue. He received widespread praise and respect from many sections of the rugby league community for his management of this end of season "crisis."

During the debate over the February 24th, 2004, incident references were made to past sexual incidents, involving rugby league players. For example, in 2002, allegations about multiple Cronulla Sharks players being involved in a sexual incident with a woman after a game in Christchurch, New Zealand surfaced. In 2003, allegations were made about several Bulldog players at the same Coffs Harbour hotel. In both cases, police investigated complaints but no charges were laid.

February 24th (Tuesday)	Newspapers report a 20-year-old woman accuses "as many as six Bulldogs" rugby league players of sexually assaulting her at a Coffs Harbour resort. Police said to be investigating the 'incident.' Newspaper article headings include "Woman accuses Bulldogs' players of sexual assault at resort," "Bulldogs' policy is clear: no women at team hotel," and "It's time players learnt something from the same old, sad story."
February 25th (Wednesday)	High-rating radio show broadcasts a "graphic report of the incident." Newspaper article headings include "When will it end," "NRL outrage," and "Sombre atmosphere prevails as Bulldogs put up the business-as-usual sign."
February 26th (Thursday)	Newspaper reports that the Chief Executive of the Bulldogs "made a passionate plea for people not to prejudge the outcome of a police investigation . . . The seriousness of the allegations means that the presumption of innocence needs to be taken into account at all times. Let the police do their job." He "pleaded with sponsors not to abandon the Bulldogs." One potential sponsor "officially informed the club that those talks are now on hold." Newspaper article headings include "League on trial," "Why big fish in a small bowl are well out of their depth," and "Sponsors review commitment."
February 27th (Friday)	Newspapers start to release more graphic and conflicting stories of events. According to "the account given to the police, the woman told the housekeeper six players dragged her into the pool and forced off her clothes." Managers of the players asserted that "their clients were innocent of the allegations." Bulldog officials stated—"We're painted as a club full of rapists and we haven't even had a chance to present any facts." Newspaper article headings include "Sobbing, wet and distressed" and "Dogs are barking about what happened that night."
February 28th (Saturday)	Newspaper reports that "Bulldog players have told their officials the sex was consensual and also occurred earlier in the week." NRL Chief Executive states, "We are very disappointed about it and are very concerned. At the moment, the presumption of innocence must be observed, but I am not saying that significant action will not be considered in the next few weeks." Newspaper article headings include "Shattered and shamed" and "What dogs do."
February 29th (Sunday)	Newspaper reports that the players' "version will shock many readers and, no doubt, provoke an angry reaction from many fans and even the NRL . . . . the players said the woman . . . had sex with eight Bulldogs on the [prior Wednesday] night before their game with Canberra last Saturday at their resort hotel. They said she was encouraging group sex and boasting about it." It also reported that "one player said it was just a typical night for some of the Canterbury players. Some of the boys love a bun. Gang banging is nothing new for our

club or the rugby league." Newspaper article headings include, "Kick in the guts for pin-up boys," "Team is confident that no charges will be laid," and "Bulldogs: grow up or lose contracts."

| March 1st (Monday) | Bulldogs Chief Executive denies any of his players had spoken to the media. NRL Chief Executive reported to say that "the league's investigation into the scandal would be widened to examine comments made in a Sydney newspaper by an unnamed Bulldogs player. I'm disgusted by the comment and make no mistake it will form part of matters being investigated by the NRL." Female journalist reports that "by their actions and statements, [these comments] have dragged down the whole game and, with it, all the hard work done to attract women. Who would want to watch a match where the so-called stars are happy to admit to 'gang-bangs' and refer to women as 'scrags'?" Newspaper article headings include "Victim to recreate ordeal," and "Bulldogs on a tight leash in party town." |

| March 2nd (Tuesday) | Bulldog sponsor Bradly Australia reported it was "unlikely to be renewed following the negative publicity." NRL Chief Executive stated the NRL "was considering introducing its own set of guidelines for clubs involved in away games to ensure there could be no repeat of the Coffs Harbour scandal. At present, clubs organize their own arrangements, with some taking more precautions than others." Bulldogs Chairman reported to have said, "the NRL should trust his [Bulldogs] club to take appropriate action against its players rather than threatening fines and expulsion." NRL Chief Executive stated the NRL had the power to "act against players or clubs, regardless of any in-house punishment . . . I am calling on our clubs and players and particularly the senior people in those organizations to focus on their responsibility as role models in football and the community. It's certainly part of our strategy to appeal to women and children and I certainly understand [if they], as all of us, are horrified by the degrading expressions we've read in the last day or so." Newspaper article headings include, "We will stamp this out: NRL Chief Executive" and "Sponsors find Bulldogs on the nose." |

Questions

1. What issues of concern to the NRL chief executive arise from the events and commentary outlined in the Appendix (Time Line from February 24, 2004 to March 2, 2004)?

2. Who bears responsibility for the negative press outlined in the Appendix?

3. What factors should the NRL chief executive consider in deciding whether and how to address the issues raised by the events and commentary in his March 2 New Season Launch speech?

4. Recommend (1) what the NRL chief executive should include in his March 2 speech and (2) the action steps he should take after his March 2 speech regarding the issues raised arising from the events and commentary outlined in the Appendix.

Case 2.4   CART'S Leadership Challenges: Can It Retain Honda's Engine Sponsorship?[52]

The top management at CART had undergone frequent changes in the 1998 to 2001 period. In December 2001, CART appointed Chris Pook, as its President and CEO. This was its fourth CEO since its IPO in 1998! Pook, as the new CEO could claim to bring a "fresh start" to CART and its relationship with its sponsors. However, it was an open question whether Pook had sufficient time to re-vitalize an increasingly fractured relationship between CART and Honda.

In early 2002, Honda Performance Development considered stopping its program of providing engines for the CART auto racing series (Championship Auto Racing Teams, Inc. NYSE: MPH), and suppling engines to the rival Indy Racing League (IRL) beginning with the 2003 season. Honda's tenure in CART had been highly successful, winning six Drivers' Championships and four Manufacturers' Championships since joining the series in 1994. However, CART's television viewership was falling and the IRL hosted the prestigious Indianapolis 500. An important concern in this decision was engine design. As a transition step, Honda could partner with Ilmor Engineering for the design and development of an IRL engine for the 2003 – 2006 seasons, effectively ceding a race engine design to an outside supplier for the first time in the company's storied motorsports history.

Honda had traditionally used its racing engine program as a central part of its corporate strategy. Its engineers cut their teeth in the competitive world of racing, developing technology that would eventually be used in passenger cars. Honda had sought out the most technologically challenging racing series in order to prove its capabilities and develop its personnel. However, the IRL engine specifications did not have the technical sophistication of CART. Moreover, partnering with Ilmor would dilute the company's ability to develop its own personnel. Should the company switch to the IRL and the attraction of the Indy 500, should it stay with CART, or should it consider other forms of U.S. racing, like the wildly popular NASCAR (National Association for Stock Car Auto Racing)?

An Overview of The Professional Motorsports Landscape in 2002

While there were many professional racing series in 2002, four were of particular relevance to Honda's considerations: Formula 1, CART, IRL, and NASCAR. Each of these four had a sanctioning body that made major decisions that affected other key players (such as race tracks, racing teams, sponsors and broadcasters) in the sport.

Formula 1 (F1) was the premier international autoracing series, with the winning driver acknowledged to be the World Champion. The F1 series consisted of about 16 races (the exact number varied from year to year), with each race held in a different country around the world. The U.S. race, the United States Grand Prix, was held at the Indianapolis Motor Speedway. F1 was an open-wheeled series,[53] with the most technologically advanced cars in the world, as well as the highest budgets. The budget for a top two-car team might run to several hundred million dollars. The F1 series was privately operated, with a strong leader

(Bernie Ecclestone) in control. Honda had supplied engines to F1 from 1983–1992, dominating the series for many of these years.

CART had been the premier open-wheel racing series in the U.S. from its inception in 1979, though it had suffered from competition from the recently-formed IRL. One of CART's unique features was that it raced on many different types of tracks: superspeedways, short ovals, road courses (permanent tracks with both left and right turns), and temporary street courses. This variety of tracks provided a tough test for drivers and teams, as well as interest for fans. CART was less technologically sophisticated than Formula 1, and thus less expensive for competitors, with annual budgets for well-funded two-car teams on the order of $30 million. However, it was more sophisticated than the IRL. While CART had begun as a North American series, it had developed internationally, with races in Mexico, Germany, England, Australia, and Japan. In 2002, CART was publicly owned and traded on the New York Stock Exchange. CART, the IRL, and the competition between the two, is discussed in more detail below.

The Indy Racing League (IRL) began competition in 1996, following a dispute between the owner of the Indianapolis Motor Speedway (IMS) and CART. It was an open-wheeled series that raced solely on oval tracks, with its flagship race being the Indianapolis 500. The IRL used cars that looked similar to those in CART, but were less technically sophisticated and less expensive. The IRL was privately held and run by the owner and president of the IMS, Tony George.

NASCAR (National Association for Stock Car Auto Racing) was the U.S.'s premier stock car racing organization. During the late 1990s and early 2000s, NASCAR eclipsed open-wheel racing in the U.S., due in part to the split between CART and IRL in open wheel racing. The NASCAR season consisted of nearly 40 races, all but two of which were on oval tracks. NASCAR had begun in the South, but had expanded across the U.S., and was very popular in all parts of the country. NASCAR was privately owned and run by the France family, which had owned the organization for several generations.

Each of these organizations had a top-level series that used the organization's most advanced, powerful, and expensive cars, as well as lower-level series that provided supporting races for fans as well as training grounds for drivers and teams.

Motorsports: A Big Business

An old saw in the motorsports business was that "the best way to make a small fortune in racing is to start with a big one." Many team owners spent fortunes on racing, driven by their passion for the sport. Manufacturers have also spent fortunes on motorsports, often in the belief that a great manufacturer had to have a great racing history. Many early manufacturers failed due to their unreasonable commitment to motorsports. However, success on the racetrack could equal success in the marketplace. Ferrari, for example, justified its annual $360 million expenditure in Formula 1 through their passionate fans' association of racing technology with their production cars. The U.S. domestic automakers, once they began providing factory support for NASCAR in the 1960s, realized the value of a strong racing presence, and coined the phrase, "win on Sunday, sell on Monday."

Automobile racing was a big business, comparable in size to the "Big Four" sports in the U.S.: baseball, football, basketball, and hockey. During the 1990s, auto racing was the nation's fastest-growing spectator sport. By 2006, the most successful form of racing in the US, NASCAR, expected annual revenues to top $3.4 billion[54].

Revenues in the auto racing industry came primarily from four main sources: television rights, sponsorship, fan attendance, and merchandising. Sponsorship revenue was the primary source of funding for race teams. This generally came from two types of companies: those who wanted to put their name on the racecar for promotional purposes, and those who provided technical help. In CART, the most important race team sponsors were the engine manufacturers—they provided up to two-thirds of CART's total sponsorship in the form of engines, technical support, and business relationships. Manufacturers did this for two primary reasons: to develop technology and personnel in a highly competitive environment, and to promote their products.

Television was extremely important, as a sponsor's logo might get substantial exposure during the course of a televised race. Engine manufacturers could also receive a substantial amount of commentary during telecasts, providing invaluable validation of the company's technology for the viewing public.

HONDA MOTOR COMPANY

The Honda Motor Company was founded in Japan by Socihirio Honda, who designed and raced cars in the 1920s and 1930s. In 1959 the company entered its first international motorcycle race, seeking to establish the company as a major international manufacturer. By 1961, Honda was a leader in international motorcycle racing, and the company's motorcycle sales increased correspondingly. Honda's next challenge was passenger cars, introducing its first model in 1963. The next year Honda entered Formula 1, building both the car and engine, and winning two races before withdrawing in 1968. In 1983, Honda returned to F1 as an engine supplier. From 1983 through 1992 Honda powered teams won six consecutive Constructor's titles (1986–1991) and five consecutive Driver's titles. During this period, Honda engines dominated F1, and in 1988 won 15 of the 16 races. In late 1992 Honda decided that it had achieved its objective of establishing the company as a major international presence, and withdrew from the series.

The American Honda Motor Company (AHM) was started in 1959, as Honda's first attempt to expand internationally. The company began first with motorcycles. Automobile sales were difficult until the 1970 Clean Air Act imposed emission standards taking effect in 1975. Honda was able to technologically leapfrog over its American competitors with its 1975 Civic, which was the first car to meet the emissions requirements without a catalytic converter. Honda continued to make inroads into the U.S. market. Its Accord model was the top selling car in the U.S. for several years in the 1990s. By the early 2000s, Honda was the largest producer of internal combustion engines in the world, and the eighth-largest auto manufacturer.

Honda and CART

The importance of American Honda to the company's financial performance had been growing with each successive year, and with it the importance of maintaining a competitive advantage over their rivals. Honda's overwhelming success in Formula 1, and the importance of the U.S. market, led the company to consider racing in the U.S. The decision on whether or not to enter CART was made easier due to Honda's F1 experience. At that time, the Indianapolis 500 specification was for a 2.65 liter, V8 turbocharged engine, which utilized technology similar to that found in the 1.5 liter, V6 turbocharged engine that F1 had used until 1988. Discussions began in 1987, and continued until 1991, when the decision was finally reached to enter the U.S. racing arena.

In January of 1993, Honda announced that it would build engines for the CART series, in competition with Ford and Chevrolet. Honda Performance Development (HPD) was started to operate the program. Honda scored its first CART win in 1995, and in 1996 won 11 of 16 races. For six consecutive years (1996–2001), Honda-powered drivers won the CART championship. Honda won the coveted engine manufacturer's championship four times. Much of Honda's success came at the expense of the company's arch-rival, Toyota, which entered the CART series in 1996.

American Honda instituted several different programs to capitalize on their racing success. One was a series of morale-enhancing activities tied to the racing team's success. AHM served cake to all employees on the Monday afternoon following a Honda-powered driver's race win. There were additional benefits, such as Race Days at American Honda's facilities in the U.S. Race Days would consist of a variety of activities. For example, before the Long Beach Grand Prix, there was an autograph session with the Honda-powered drivers for all of the employees at American Honda's headquarters in Torrance, CA. Before the Mid-Ohio race, the Honda-powered drivers toured the Honda factory in Marysville, OH. For the season-ending race in Fontana, CA, the Honda drivers visited the corporate headquarters once again for a question and answer session with AHM employees, as well as a small carnival-style outdoor celebration, complete with the occasional CART driving demonstration by drivers such as the popular champion Alex Zanardi.

An additional benefit was realized through dealer participation in Honda race activities. At every race, American Honda would host between 150 – 250 Honda and Acura dealers. The dealers were treated as VIPs, with pit passes, race day breakfast with the Honda drivers, and access to Honda's hospitality tent. Dealers were also treated to a dealer-specific newsletter outlining Honda's efforts in CART, with numerous references to the connection between Honda's racing and their production cars.

In addition to the exposure that racing gave to its company and products, and its motivational benefits, racing was an important training ground for Honda engineers. The company explained this in an article entitled "Why We Race" on its website, saying:

1. The pressures of racing teach budding Honda engineers many important lessons. First, it challenges them. Forcing them to find new solutions—a better mousetrap, if you will. Racing also demands that you be ready on time. If you don't make the grid, you pack it up and go home. Even making the grid is only a ticket to participate. Racing's hard lesson is that winning is the only standard by which your work is judged.

2. Racing teaches two more important lessons to Honda engineers: teamwork and quick response. When the difference between victory and defeat rests on your shoulders and time is short, you learn the company's logistical system or machining and engineering capabilities pretty quickly. Fortunately, the pipeline for Champ Car engines is shorter; however, racing at Honda still remains the great training ground for our engineers.[55]

CART AND THE IRL

CART's Formation

The CART series was founded in 1979 by a group of team owners dissatisfied with the state of U.S. motorsports. At the time, open wheeled racing in the U.S. was overseen by the United States Auto Club (USAC), which had presided over U.S. racing since 1956. The team owners were concerned about escalating costs, a perceived lack of promotional activities, and a focus solely on the Indianapolis 500. The dissenting team owners were comprised of a group that wanted greater participation in the rule-making and administrative processes, and created a management structure to address this. The resulting organization of CART consisted of team owners as controlling members of the sanctioning body. This structure, however, left questions as to whether CART had the correct incentives when important decisions were made.

USAC was tightly connected with the owners of the Indianapolis Motor Speedway, and retained control of the Indy 500. USAC initially tried to keep CART from participating, but the CART team owners won a lawsuit, which forced USAC to allow them to compete. The Indy 500 was the largest auto race in the world, and a critical race for the CART series, as sponsors were dependent on the exposure that they would receive during the famous "month of May"[56] at Indy. CART and USAC maintained an uneasy peace until 1991, when CART announced its inaugural race in Surfer's Paradise, Australia. Tony George, president of the Indianapolis Motor Speedway (IMS), expressed his belief that CART was losing its focus and getting away from its U.S. and oval track roots. George began to advocate for greater representation within CART. In 1992, CART's Board of Directors was reorganized into a seven-member board, with a non-voting seat for the president of the IMS.

In 1992 Ford began to supply engines to CART teams. Chevrolet had been successfully leveraging their CART success in the marketplace, and Ford began to supply CART teams using a Ford-branded engine built by Cosworth Engineering. In its first year of competition, Ford won 5 of the 16 races, significantly upping the stakes for both manufacturers. Now it wasn't just about winning the most famous race in the world, but instead what company you beat in the process of winning.

THE IRL VERSUS CART

In 1994, the disagreements between CART and USAC/IMS came to a head. For the 1994 Indy 500, Roger Penske, the most well-financed and successful CART owner, teamed with Ilmor Engineering/Mercedes-Benz to exploit USAC's rulebook to develop a non-standard engine solely for Indy that, through a long-overlooked loophole, developed significantly more horsepower than conventional engines. The Penske cars were unbeatable that year, and won the race after dominating qualifying. The fallout was immediate; the USAC rules were quickly changed, and Chevrolet severed its relationship with Penske since it was believed that Penske had shared Chevrolet's engine technology with newcomer Mercedes-Benz.

In addition to Penske's exploitation of the USAC rules, there were additional issues that heightened the antagonism between CART and the IMS. The seven-member Board of Directors proved to be a failure, and it was scrapped in favor of the original structure comprised of all team owners holding at least one of the 24 shares of CART stock. This eliminated Tony George's position within CART, and left him with no voice in the organization.

EXHIBIT 1   CART RACING TEAMS AND DRIVERS, 2002

Team—Engine Provider
Driver (Nationality)

Fernandez Racing—Honda	**Sigma Autosports—Ford-Cosworth**
Adrian Fernandez (Mexico)	Max Papis (Italy)
Shinji Nakano (Japan)	**Target Chip Ganasi Racing—Toyota**
Herdez Competition—Ford-Cosworth	Kenny Brack (Sweden)
Mario Dominguez (Mexico)	Bruno Junqueira (Brazil)
Mo Nunn Racing—Honda	**Team Kool Green—Honda**
Tony Kanaan (Brazil)	Dario Franchitti (Scotland)
Newman/Hass Racing—Toyota	Paul Tracy (Canada)
Cristiano de Matta (Brazil)	**Team Motorola—Honda**
Christian Fittipaldi (Brazil)	Michael Andretti (USA)
Patrick Racing—Toyota	**Team Rahal—Ford-Cosworth**
Townsend Bell (USA)	Michael Jourdain (Mexico)
Players/Forsythe Racing—Ford-Cosworth	Jimmy Vasser (USA)
Patrick Carpentier (Canada)	**Walker Racing—Toyota**
Alex Tagliani (Canada)	Tora Takagi (Japan)
PWR Championship Racing—Toyota	
Scott Dixon (New Zealand)	
Oriol Servia (Spain)	

In 1994, George believed that in order to ensure that the Indianapolis 500 remained a race open to anyone, and one that encouraged close competition, some of its long-standing rules needed to change. The Indy 500 had always encouraged creativity and engineering originality at any cost in the name of winning. George, however, felt that the CART series had become too expensive, with only the richest teams able to remain competitive. He also believed CART was getting away from its roots. He expressed particular concern about the practice of CART team owners recruiting international driving talent (Exhibit 1) and of the increasing number of events held outside the U.S. He announced his intention to start a new open-wheel racing series to compete with CART, named the Indy Racing League, which he would personally control.

The IRL was founded with capital from his family's holdings, (George was the grandson of Tony Hulman, who bought Indy in 1945), and with earnings from events at IMS. Annually, the Indy 500 grossed between $20 and 25 million, and the racetrack as a whole generated between $70 and $100 million.[57]

The IRL plan was to reduce the cost of racing, and conduct all its events on oval tracks. It would reduce costs by limiting engineering innovation and enforcing caps on costs of tires, chassis, and engines. It would also give track promoters incentives to offer at least $1 million in purses, enabling teams to survive based on winnings, without requiring heavy sponsorship. Most importantly, George was gambling that the lure of the Indy 500 would provide a sufficient foundation for his long-term vision of a U.S.-based open-wheel racing circuit[58].

In order to ensure that participants in his new series would be able to compete in the Indy 500, the centerpiece of the IRL schedule, George instituted the "25/8 rule." This rule reserved 25 places in the Indy 500 for full-time IRL participants. Other team owners, such as those in CART, could compete for the eight unreserved spots. With a maximum of only eight possible spots in the race, and the need to purchase new cars and engines built to IRL specifications, participation by CART teams appeared uneconomical. CART teams skipped Indianapolis 500 in 1996, staging a competing race.[59] 1996 was the first year of competition for the IRL, with a three-race season including the Indy 500.[60] The Indy 500 immediately lost some of its prestige and interest, as most of its famous drivers and most successful teams remained with CART and did not participate in the Indy 500. Television ratings on the ABC network for the event fell from 8.4 in 1995 to 6.6 in 1996.[61] Though the 25/8 rule was dropped following the 1997 race, the two leagues did not reconcile, and the Indy 500 remained off the CART schedule.

CART Goes Public

Attempting to succeed without the consistent television coverage and marketing draw of the Indianapolis 500, CART adopted several strategy shifts to create a sustainable business model. In March 1998, Andrew Craig, CART's CEO, led the company in a $73.4 million Initial Public Offering. Most of the shares were bought and held by the Board of Directors, made up mainly of the primary team owners, including Pat Patrick and Derrick Walker. Some of the money raised by CART was spent on the purchase of two smaller support racing series, but most was simply kept in short-term investments. At the end of 2001, CART still had $87.6 million in short-term investments.

Some observers claimed the public company model damaged CART's ability to respond quickly and intelligently to the outside marketplace. They claimed the move decentralized power in CART, which allowed for more bickering between the majority shareholders, and led to slower decision-making. There was also concern about a potential conflict of interest between the board of directors, and the owners of the teams, since they were for the most part the same group of people. It was difficult for the board to make decisions on behalf of the CART series as a whole, because their decisions often conflicted with the best decisions for the success of their individual race teams. This contrasted with the organizations of other major racing series, such as F1, IRL, and NASCAR, which were run in an autocratic manner by powerful individuals who did not own an individual racing team (or teams).

CART also continued its shift in emphasis from being a primarily North American racing circuit to being a more international series. CART increased the number of events outside the US, including Canada, Mexico, Japan, Australia, Germany, England, and Brazil. These events were generally more successful than the American events, as CART's popularity was declining in the U.S. (in part due to the competition with the IRL and CART's lack of participation in the Indy 500 as well as from the growing success of NASCAR).

The consequence of this shift was that the series had a significant international flavor, in terms of drivers, team owners, and sponsors. For example, the Team Players racing team was sponsored by Canada's Imperial Tobacco, and only signed Canadian drivers, as well as wearing the distinctive livery of Players cigarettes, which were unavailable in the U.S. During this international shift, the percentage of American drivers declined rapidly, to less than 20 percent in 2001. The international recognition helped increase the status of the star drivers, with Jacques Villeneuve and Juan Pablo Montoya dominating in CART before moving on to Formula One.

Honda's Dissatisfaction with CART: 2000–2001

In 2000 Team Penske's Gil DeFarran secured Honda's fifth consecutive Drivers' Championship in CART. However, the coveted Manufacturers' Championship was lost to Ford, and Honda was committed to winning it back in 2001. Honda had an all-star driver lineup, with three former CART champions and six other promising contenders. The excitement for the start of the season, however, was tempered by some of CART's management decisions and a series of problems. Some of these included:

Management changes. In June 2000, the CART Board of Directors appointed Bobby Rahal, a team owner and former CART champion as interim CEO. Rahal was not a strong supporter of the engine manufacturers. Rahal's team was supplied by Ford. Rahal was replaced by television executive Joe Heitzler at the end of the 2000 season. However, Heitzler focused more on ways in which CART could make money from television than on addressing the concerns of the engine manufacturers.

Engine rules uncertainties. With the current engine specifications due to expire in 2003, and new engines taking about two years to develop, the manufacturers wanted new rules to be finalized. The manufacturers proposed a rules package, but CART did not make a decision.

When CART did not adopt new high-technology engine rules, the agreement among the manufacturers fell apart. Toyota proposed that it adopt the IRL specifications, in opposition to the positions of Honda and Ford (Mercedes Benz had already left the series). CART, however, continued to delay a decision. In October 2001, CART announced a 3.5 liter, normally aspirated specification (as used by the IRL), but did not provide details. Ford said it had no intention of building an IRL engine, and threatened to leave. The 3.5 liter decision was later rescinded.

Race cancellation. In April 2001, CART cancelled a race at the Texas Motor Speedway due to safety concerns, about two hours before it was to begin. A messy lawsuit followed, ultimately ending with CART paying out millions to track owner Speedway Motorsports, Inc.[62]

Defections to the IRL. In October 2001, Toyota announced its intention to build engines for the IRL in 2003. Shortly after, Roger Penske announced that he would move his team to the IRL, saying that his primary sponsor, Marlboro, wanted to focus on the US, while CART was expanding internationally—an arena that Marlboro addressed by sponsoring a top Formula One team. There were rumors that other CART teams would follow, particularly Ganassi Racing, whose sponsor, Target, wanted to focus its exposure in the United States.

Arbitrary rules changes. Honda's frustration with CART came to a head in June 2001, when without warning, CART made a technical change to an important engine device during the Friday morning practice for the Detroit Grand Prix. The change had supposedly been developed by Toyota, which had been embarrassed by the poor performance of its engines in May at a race in Motegi, Japan. Both Honda and Ford were incensed. One unnamed CART representative succinctly stated, "Great! Now we've figured out a way to piss off the two engine manufacturers who like us!"

The Growth of the IRL

While CART seemed to be accumulating problems, the IRL was developing its series. In its inaugural 1996 season, the new league held only three races, including the Indy 500. By 1997, however, the number was up to ten, which stayed fairly constant until the 2002 season, when the schedule expanded to fifteen races. The television ratings for the early races were dismal, but they steadily improved each year. George was able to leverage the Indy 500 to force television coverage of the rest of the IRL races, and in 1999, the IRL signed a five-year agreement with ABC and ESPN worth a reported $65 million. This deal was expanded in September 2001, and one of the terms of this agreement stipulated that the two partners (ABC and ESPN) would mention the IRL as their exclusive American open-wheel racing series. This exclusivity extended so far as to call CART drivers competing in the 2002 Indy 500 "drivers from another series." With the exception of the Indianapolis 500, fan attendance was often embarrassingly small, and television coverage strove to avoid showing the empty stands.

In 2000, for the first time since 1995, a CART team competed at the Indy 500. The Target Chip Ganassi Racing team brought two drivers, who both qualified well, with one (Juan Montoya) completely dominating the race and handing the IRL a humiliating loss.

The CART invasion of IRL continued in 2001, when Roger Penske returned to Indy in search of his eleventh Indy 500 victory as a team owner, bringing two of his drivers. Ganassi Racing brought three drivers. The disparity in performance was embarrassing for the IRL, as the CART teams and drivers swept the top five spots, with Helio Castroneves winning the event for Team Penske.

After the 2001 season, the defection from CART to the IRL began in earnest, with Toyota announcing it would supply the IRL, and Penske Racing joining the IRL. Other top teams were also rumored to be making the change.

Honda's Decision

In light of its dissatisfaction with CART, and continuing controversy over the engine specification for the 2003 season, Honda considered whether it should follow arch-rival Toyota to the IRL. This decision would be made in early 2002. Honda realized that there was not enough time to successfully design and develop a completely new engine to IRL specifications. To address this, Honda entered into negotiations with Ilmor Engineering, a premier race engine builder with extensive Formula 1 experience, to provide technical assistance for Honda's entry into the IRL. The proposal was to put a Honda badge on an Ilmor engine for the 2003 – 2005 seasons. Beginning in 2006, Honda would supply its own engine, designed and built in-house, as it did in the past.

There was also the issue of intellectual property. Honda spent a considerable sum on research and development for their racing engines. In CART, the manufacturers owned the engines and leased them to the teams. CART's lease program prevented teams from accessing the engine internals, so the company had little risk of losing technology to its competitors. The IRL's rules for buying engines prevented any control of their engine technology once an engine left the facility, and engines were generally tuned and maintained by third-party shops. There was also a risk in working so closely with Ilmor. What would prevent another manufacturer from joining with Ilmor in 2006? There was also a persistent rumor that Toyota was interested in going to NASCAR in 2007, an even lower tech series when compared to the IRL or CART.

There were many questions facing Honda. CART had traditionally used higher technology engines than the IRL, but CART's future engine direction was uncertain. Would CART reverse its announced change to the 3.5 liter, normally aspirated engine? If not, would CART

EXHIBIT 2   COMPARISON OF U.S. AUTORACING SERIES

EXHIBIT 2   Comparison of U.S. Autoracing Series

Motorsports TV Ratings

Broadcast	1996	1997	1998	1999	2000	2001
NASCAR	5.2	5.8	5.7	5.5	5.3	5.9
CART	-	1.7	1.6	1.4	1.3	1.2
IRL	-	-	2.7	2.9	2.2	2.1

Cable	1996	1997	1998	1999	2000	2001
NASCAR	4.0	4.3	4.0	4.1	4.0	3.9
CART	-	1.0	0.8	0.9	0.8	0.5
IRL	-	-	0.6	0.3	0.3	0.5

Broadcast Rights	
NASCAR	$2.4 billion, 8 years, expires 2008 - NBC, Fox
IRL	$65 million, 5 years, expired 2004 - ABC/ESPN; Re-signed through 2007
CART	CART paid $235,000 for each broadcast on CBS

Source: *Street and Smith's Sports Business Journal*, 2002.

use an engine with IRL specifications, or a higher-technology engine more similar to that used in F1? The IRL had a more attractive television package than CART, but attendance at the IRL events was generally very low except for the Indy 500, compared to high attendance at many CART events, particularly street races such as Long Beach and Monterrey, Mexico. (Exhibit 2). The IRL focused on the U.S., while CART was diversifying internationally. The control of each series was also a consideration; CART was indecisive and chaotic, while the IRL was run by a strong, unchallenged, leader.

Should Honda leave CART after the 2002 season for the IRL? How did the trade-offs between the potential marketing exposure from the IRL and Indianapolis 500 compare with the technological benefits of participating in the (historically) most technically sophisticated U.S. racing series, particularly given the issues of working with Ilmor and questions about control over the engine design. Did the U.S. focus of the IRL better meet Honda's needs than international direction of CART? Or should Honda turn to NASCAR, the most popular form of racing in the U.S.?

CART's Leadership Revolving Door

Andrew Craig led CART's IPO in March 1998. In June 2000, CART's Board of Directors appointed Bobby Rahal as interim CEO, a move not welcomed by Honda. In December 2000, Joseph Heitzler was appointed President and CEO. He had been President and Chief Operating Officer of National Mobile Television Productions (since 1998). CART posted as $8.495 million loss for 2001. In December 2001, Chris Pook was appointed President and CEO of CART. Pook was the founder of the Toyota Grand Prix of Long Beach, California. This Grand Prix was one of the premier events on the CART circuit. Pook faced many challenges, including how to retain the Honda engine sponsorship. How could he overcome Honda's growing disenchantment with CART, especially in the light of the IRL's efforts to sign Honda as a key engine sponsor?

EXHIBIT 3   CART Summary Financials ($ millions)

	1997	1998	1999	2000	2001
Revenues					
Sanction Fees	$24.248	$30.444	$35.689	$38.902	$47.226
Sponsorship Revenue	7.221	16.388	19.150	21.063	12.314
Television Revenue	5.604	5.148	5.018	5.501	5.228
Engine Leases, Rebuilds and Wheel Sales	—	2.214	2.054	2.122	1.286
Other Revenue	4.372	8.336	6.865	7.460	4.209
Total Revenues	**41.445**	**62.530**	**68.776**	**75.048**	**70.263**
Expenses					
Race Distributions	28.939	15.183	15.334	15.370	18.599
Race Expenses	6.970	4.818	6.670	9.869	10.618
Admin. & Indirect Expenses	14.295	20.658	20.646	25.275	35.605
Other Expenses	12.517	1.412	1.658	8.324	13.936
Total Expenses	**62.721**	**42.071**	**44.308**	**58.838**	**78.758**
Operating Income	**$(21.276)**	**$20.459**	**$24.468**	**$16.210**	**$(8.495)**
Net Income	**$(17.524)**	**$15.089**	**$18.858**	**$15.153**	**$(0.950)**

	2000	2001
Assets		
Cash and Cash Equivalents	$ 19.504	$ 27.765
Short Term Investments	98.206	87.621
Other Assets	26.391	17.555
Total Assets	**144.101**	**132.941**
Liabilities/Other Obligations	**10.207**	**15.005**
Stockholder's Equity	**133.894**	**117.936**
Liability and Stock Equity	**144.101**	**132.941**

Source: 2001 Annual Report: December 31 Fiscal Year End

Questions

1. Why might CART have experienced frequent management leadership change in the 1998–2001 period?

2. Consider the issues raised in the case from Honda's perspective:

   a. Why does Honda sponsor motor racing in general, and CART in particular?

   b. What factors have led to Honda's growing dissatisfaction with its CART sponsorship?

   c. What factors should Honda have considered in late 2001 in regards to continuing its CART sponsorship?

3. Consider the issues raised in the case from CART's perspective:

   a. What can CART do to make Honda want to retain its CART sponsorship role?

   b. What should CART do if Honda decides to end its CART sponsorship role?

CASE 2.5 WOMEN'S PROFESSIONAL SPORTS, 2004[63]

In summer 2004, as one examined the state of women's professional sports, particularly women's basketball, only one principal league was in operation. The WNBA had begun its eighth season in May. Yet the promising environment that loomed after the 1996 Atlanta Olympics had not led to the successful establishment of women's professional sports in the United States.

In the fall of 1996, the American Basketball League began operations following a September 1995 announcement of its founding. There had been several prior failed efforts to establish women's pro basketball. (See the case, The American Basketball League, on the launch of the ABL.) The following summer (1997) witnessed the start of the WNBA. (See the case, Women's National Basketball Association.) In the fall of 1997, a key question was whether there was enough support for two successful women's leagues, for only one (and if so, which), or for none.

The ABL's second season saw 23% higher attendance, but still at a modest level (4,333 average). For the third season, fewer games were to be televised, and the league was paying the networks (principally FOX SportsNet) for their time. Six weeks into its third season, in December 1998, the ABL announced that it was suspending operations and was filing for bankruptcy. (See the case, The American Basketball League: The Last Chapter.) Media reports later said that debts were over $25 million ($21 million in loans), offset by $1 million in cash.

The WNBA continued its pattern as a summer league, with competition starting in late May during the later stages of the NBA playoffs. Following its single-entity ownership structure, the league owned all its teams, 16 during the 2002 season. However, in October of that year, the league announced that it would be transferring ownership of the teams to the owners of the NBA teams in their cities.[64] In turn, those owners could sell, move, or retain the WNBA franchises. Also, WNBA teams would be allowed to play in non-NBA cities.

By the start of the 2004 season, the WNBA comprised 13 teams. The Connecticut Sun, based at the Mohegan Sun casino in Uncasville, was the only team not in an NBA city. It was, however, in the hotbed of collegiate women's college basketball, near the home of the NCAA women's champion University of Connecticut team.

Television for the WNBA in 2004 was on ABC (the broadcast network of the NBA), ESPN, ESPN2, Oxygen, Telemundo (Hispanic), and NBA-TV. Separately, more than 30 WNBA players were to represent the United States and other countries in the Athens Olympics.[65] This meant additional television exposure and media coverage to broader audiences than those reached by the Saturday afternoon WNBA telecasts on ABC or on evening or Sunday cable telecasts. The monthlong break for the Olympics also meant a split season, with the concluding 3 weeks to be played in September before playoffs extending to mid-October.

Although the WNBA was still in operation, there were no other U.S. women's pro sports leagues. Professional leagues in women's hockey and softball had not materialized, despite continued success at the college and Olympics levels. (In the 2004 Olympics, U.S. women's basketball, softball, and soccer teams all won gold medals.) And the WUSA (women's pro soccer league) had suspended operations in mid-September 2003, disappointing fans (and players) who thought that the impending Women's World Cup competition would serve to boost interest in the sport and the league.

CASE 2.6 WOMEN'S PROFESSIONAL BASKETBALL AND THE AMERICAN BASKETBALL LEAGUE[66]

At the 1992 Barcelona Olympics, the United States men's basketball "Dream Team" captured a gold medal and a worldwide audience. The team consisted virtually entirely of NBA players, who dominated the competition. In contrast, the women's team came home with a bronze medal and a feeling of failure. They had not taken full advantage of an opportunity to promote women's basketball in the U.S.[67] In 1992, the U.S. Olympic basketball teams (men's and women's) had thirteen corporate sponsors, including Kraft USA, McDonald's Corp., Converse, Visa USA, and Quaker Oats. As a group, these companies had paid an estimated $40 million for media advertising announcing their involvement with USA Basketball.

In the aftermath of the women's team experience in the 1992 Olympic Games, USA Basketball (the entity responsible for U.S. international basketball competition) put together the first full-time dedicated women's national team. These women would play a 52-game exhibition schedule in 1995–96 that would take them more than 100,000 miles to four continents in the 10 months that led up to the Atlanta Olympic Games.[68] Having lined up corporate sponsors, USA Basketball then asked America's best women players to make the year-long commitment. When USA Basketball announced the formation of its women's national team, organization president C.M. Newton (Director of Athletics, University of Kentucky) made sure coach Tara VanDerveer, on leave from Stanford University, knew what was expected. "He told me this was not about bronze, and it wasn't about silver; it was only about gold," VanDerveer said.[69]

Title IX and Women's Basketball

The timing of the U.S. women's national team coincided with almost 25 years of growth for women in sports aided by Title IX. Passed by Congress in 1972, Title IX was a key factor furthering women's participation in sports. It required equal opportunity and equal facilities for men's and women's sports. Many scholarships also were in place, and colleges competed in recruiting top high school players. Girls who became Blue Chip Players—a group of the top 100 high school basketball players in the U.S.—were often aggressively recruited by colleges and given scholarships.[70]

Title IX stipulated that "no person in the U.S. shall, on the basis of sex be excluded from participation in, or denied the benefits of, or be subjected to discrimination under any educational program or activity receiving federal aid."[71] For intercollegiate athletics, Title IX looked at the accommodation of athletic interests and abilities and the programs that supported these activities. (See **Exhibit 1.**)

Visibility for Women's Amateur Basketball

In 1995, a 35–0 University of Connecticut basketball team and star Rebecca Lobo drew unprecedented regional and national attention for the sport. The 1995 NCAA Women's Final Four was sold out at Minneapolis. Further, its ratings on CBS had beaten the regular-season

Harvard Business School Case No 9-599-031. Copyright 1999 President and Fellows of Harvard College. All rights reserved. For information: permission@hbsp.harvard.edu. This case was prepared by Natalie Zakarian under the supervision of Stephen A. Greyser. HBS cases are developed solely for class discussion and do not necessarily illustrate effective or ineffective management.

EXHIBIT 1   TITLE IX CRITERIA

Category	Description
Equipment and Supplies	Quality, suitability, quantity, availability, maintenance, replacement
Scheduling of Games and Practice Times	Number of competitive events per sport, number and length of practice opportunities, opportunities to engage in available pre-season and post-season competition
Travel and Per Diem Allowances	Modes of transportation, housing furnished during travel, length of stay before and after competitive events, per diem allowances and dining arrangements
Opportunity to receive Coaching, Assignment and Compensation	Availability, assignment and compensation of full time coaches, assistants, graduate assistants
Locker Rooms, Practice and Competitive Facilities	Quality, availability, exclusivity of use, maintenance and preparation of facilities
Medical and Training Facilities and Services	Quality and availability of medical personnel, athletic trainers, weight and conditioning facilities, training facilities; and health, accident and injury insurance coverage
Recruitment of Student-Athletes	Opportunities for coaches or other personnel to recruit; whether financial and other resources are equivalently adequate; and treatment of prospective student-athletes

Source: From the Internet, Title IX

NBA game in its Sunday afternoon time slot. After winning the 1995 NCAA title in front of a 500-member media contingent, the University of Connecticut team was welcomed home by 8,000 fans.[72] Subsequently, during the 1995–96 season ESPN televised 25 NCAA tournament games. The 1996 Final Four was telecast live on Friday and Sunday in prime time, instead of on consecutive days as it had been on CBS. The Friday semi-final games had a 2.5 and 2.0 rating (a 5 and 4 share) respectively. The Sunday final game had the highest cable TV rating in history for a women's game, and was ESPN's second highest-rated basketball game—men's or women's.[73] The rating was 3.7, a 6 share, reaching 2 1/2 million homes.

The 1996 Women's National Team

In October 1995, the USA Basketball's Women's National Team undertook its 1996 Olympics training with a 26-city tour competing against NCAA teams and international opponents. In its tour, twenty of its victories came in a three-month schedule with the top NCAA women's teams, games which the National Team won by an average of 46.2 points.

Backed by a multi-million dollar promotional campaign, the team enjoyed big crowds in their exhibition games. The team went on to post a pre-Olympic 52–0 record. Its games sparked interest in the sport with many promotional appearances in the course of the tour, and national television commercials with the marketing partners.[74]

The Olympics

The national tour leading up to the games had provided the sport with a big boost in awareness. In ten months of play, the team had a perfect 60–0 record; the last eight wins came in Olympic play. Women's basketball games at the summer 1996 Olympics showed great drawing power. The Australia-Korea women's game in the Georgia Dome drew 25,000 people on a Sunday night.[75] At the final game for the gold medal, a crowd of more than 38,000 watched the U.S. Olympic team roll past Brazil, 111–87.[76]

The USA-Brazil women's gold-medal game on August 4, 1996 carried by NBC had a 15.5 rating and a 3.3 share. That translated to 14,818,000 homes tuned in from 6:30 p.m. to 8:30 p.m. Eastern time.[77] Through the course of the Olympics, many fans and viewers found the women's basketball competition, especially the US Team, more interesting than the men's competition. The latter again was dominated by the NBA superstars on the U.S. team.

Women's Professional Basketball

Fan interest in women's basketball had not always been so strong. Between 1976—when women's basketball first became an Olympic event—and 1991, no less than six women's pro leagues tried to get off the ground. The National Women's Basketball Association and the Continental Basketball Association never made it to the opening day tip-off. The Women's Professional Basketball League achieved a little more success, playing three seasons before folding in 1981. Even that league's most successful franchise, the Chicago Hustle, lost a total of $718,000 during its three-year run.[78]

The WPBL was made up of eight teams and lasted from 1979–1981 before going on hiatus for one year. Upon its return in 1983 it collapsed after a one-year run. Former coach of men's basketball at Rice University, Don Knodel, was coach of the WPBL Houston franchise. The problem, Knodel said, was lack of capital. Another factor was the strength and skill of women players. Women players today [1996] are bigger and better than players were in the WPBL. "[Today] they can do so many things that the men can do, so long as they don't have to get up in the air," Knodel said.[79]

The American Basketball League

According to its founders, the American Basketball League (ABL) was created to showcase the women who play the game and give them a distinct identity. Co-founders Steve Hams, Anne Cribbs, and Gary Cavalli raised $4 million in startup capital and announced the formation of the ABL on September 26, 1995.

Hams launched the effort to establish a women's professional league in 1994. It resulted from his lifelong enthusiasm for sports and his involvement with his daughter's developing basketball career. Anne Cribbs had been a member of the USA's swimming teams for the 1959 Pan American Games and 1960 Olympic Games. She won a gold medal in the 400-meter relay in Rome (1960). Since 1991 she had been responsible for managing and generating sponsorships for major national and international events including World Cup '94.

Cavalli had been Associate Athletic Director and Sports Information Director at Stanford from 1974–1982. As president of Cavalli & Cribbs he had over 15 years experience in sports-related public relations, marketing, TV production, and event management.

Before the ABL's 1996–97 inaugural season began, ABL CEO Gary Cavalli from the league office in San Jose, California said, "We think we have the right plan. We're playing at the right time of the year. We've got seventy-five percent of the top players. Women's basketball is a great sport, and if we present it right, we'll do well."[80] Atlanta general manager Debbie Miller-Palmore said, "Our stance is that we're just trying to help promote women's basketball."

The national tryouts for the ABL were May 28–June 1, 1996. The trials drew more than 500 applicants. Some 80 to 100 players were to be drafted. A final 44 would be selected to join the 35 high-profile players already signed.[81]

The inaugural season began October 18, 1996. When play started, the ABL had recruited seven members of the 1996 U.S. gold medal Olympic team, including starters Dawn Staley and Nikki McCray. The ABL had also recruited Katie Smith, an All-Star from Ohio State and Tonya Edwards, an All-Star shooting guard from Tennessee.[82] Former NCAA stars Jennifer Rizzotti (University of Connecticut) and Dana Johnson (Tennessee) had also been recruited.[83] The ABL had signed Reebok as the official uniform supplier to four teams—San Jose, Atlanta, the New England Blizzard, and the Denver XPlosion. This had given the League the opportunity to sign many players under the Reebok umbrella— Jennifer Azzi (San Jose), Saudia Roundtree (Atlanta), Shelley Sheltz (Denver), Sheri Sam (San Jose), Carolyn Jones (New England), Stacey Lovelace (Atlanta), and Edna Campbell (Denver).

Players in the ABL could earn between $40,000 and $125,000 for 40 games. This was said to be comparable at the high end to an NBA minimum salary for 82 games. Players also owned 10% of the league. The ABL avoided the three largest markets, New York, Los Angeles, and Chicago. Most of its franchises were located near the top women's collegiate basketball schools in the country. Teams for 1996–7 were based in San Jose, California; Seattle; Portland, Oregon; Denver; Atlanta; Columbus, Ohio; Richmond, Virginia; and Hartford-Springfield, Massachusetts. These cities had small arenas in mid-size communities where women's college basketball teams had drawn strong fan support. (See **Exhibit 2** for information on arena capacities.) University of Connecticut players proved to be a huge reason why New England led the league in attendance during the 1996–97 season. Attendance at college games had gone over the 5 million mark in the 1995–96 season.

At the end of its first season the ABL said that its losses were $4–5 million. Richmond accounted for about $600,000 of the loss. It averaged 3,139 fans (in an arena seating over 9,000) for 20 regular-season home dates. In the fourth game of playoff competition with a 2–1 advantage in a best of 5 series, Richmond drew only 4,826 fans in a home game. The franchise would be moved to Philadelphia, by far the largest ABL market, for the 1997–98 season.[84]

The regular 40-game ABL schedule ran from mid-October through late February. The season concluded with a five-game championship series in early March. The ABL had drawn an average of 3,536 fans per game during the regular season and 4,200 per game in February. Average game attendance ranged from 5,008 for New England (playing in Hartford and Springfield Mass.) to 2,682 for Columbus. Portland and Colorado drew over 4,100 per game;

EXHIBIT 2   COMPARISON OF ARENA CAPACITIES (ABL VS. WNBA)

ABL	Arena	Capacity	WNBA	Arena	Capacity
New England	Hartford Civic Center	15,418	Phoenix	America West	19,023
	Springfield Civic Center	8,712	New York	Madison Sq.	19,763
Portland	Memorial Coliseum	10,934	Houston	Summit	16,661
Colorado	Denver Coliseum	9,300	L.A.	Sports Arena	16,021
	McNichols Arena	14,500		Forum	17,505
Richmond	Robins Center (Univ.)	9,171	Charlotte	Coliseum	23,698
	Richmond Coliseum	11,992	Cleveland	Gund Arena	20,562
Seattle	Mercer Arena	4,623	Sacramento	Arco Arena	17,317
San Jose	San Jose Event Center	4,550	Utah	Delta Center	19,911
Atlanta	Morehouse Olympic Arena	5,700			
Columbus	Battelle Hall	6,313			

Source: Compiled from ABL and NBA Home Pages

Seattle, San Jose, and Richmond about 3,100; and Atlanta 2,780. (In contrast, in its inaugural season in the summer of 1997, the WNBA's average attendance was 9,669. Phoenix and New York were both over 13,000, with others ranging from 9,700 to 7,600. WNBA teams played in NBA arenas.)[85]

The ABL All Star Game on December 15 had drawn 6,400 fans. At the end of its first season the ABL estimated that 60% of the people who came to the games and watched them on TV were women.

For its initial season, the ABL's television package was a game of the week on Sunday night on SportsChannel (cable) plus playoff coverage. SportsChannel carried 20 games. In addition, the cable channel BET (Black Entertainment Television) aired eight games. The ABL was unable to secure agreements for games on national broadcast television. The ABL enlisted companies such as Reebok, Nissan, Lady Footlocker, Phoenix Home Life Mutual Insurance, Baden Sports, and First USA Bank as corporate sponsors.[86] For example, Reebok provided uniforms and sneakers for four of the teams in 1996–7, and produced licensed jerseys, hats, and T-shirts.

The Founding of the WNBA

Rick Welts, president of NBA Properties, the NBA's marketing and licensing arm, had first talked about a women's basketball league with Commissioner David Stern in the mid-1980s. Ten years later Welts saw everything come together in a way he said could never have been planned.[87] The WNBA announced the formation of the WNBA on April 24, 1996—following the ABL playoffs, and seven months after the ABL had announced it was forming a women's basketball league. On August 7, 1996 Valerie Ackerman was named President of the WNBA.

A separate case (on the WNBA) chronicles the background of the WNBA's founding, its basic business concept, some of the key research information used by the NBA in launching it, and other related information.

CASE 2.7 WOMEN'S NATIONAL BASKETBALL ASSOCIATION (WNBA)[88]

Many observers considered 1996 (and 1997) to be The Year(s) of the Woman in Sports. Many women and women's teams excelled in the Atlanta Olympics, and several new professional women's sports leagues were being launched or explored. The latter included the American Basketball League (which completed its initial regular season in February 1997), the Women's National Basketball Association, Women's Professional Fastpitch (softball), a women's professional soccer league, and a women's professional hockey league. Of these, many observers considered the Women's National Basketball Association to be the one most likely to succeed.

In April 1996 the NBA Board of Governors approved the concept of the Women's National Basketball Association, to start play in the summer of 1997. During the ensuing months, the NBA moved forward with the tasks of signing players for the single entity enterprise, selecting cities for the teams, attracting marketing partners, arranging for television broadcasts, and developing a staff under the leadership of President Valerie Ackerman—all in preparation for a June 1997 start for the WNBA.

Women's basketball had a long history in the U.S. as a collegiate and amateur game; the first inter-collegiate competition was in 1896 (between Stanford and Berkeley). In 1924, the International Women's Sports Federation was formed, and included basketball in its competition. Widely regarded as the most significant event for female participation in amateur sports was the 1972 passage by Congress of Title IX, which banned discrimination on the basis of one's sex as to participation in educational programs/activities (including sports) receiving Federal funding. This led to substantial increases in financial support for school and collegiate women's sports over the succeeding years.

More recently, several abortive efforts had been undertaken to initiate women's professional leagues, beginning in 1978 with the Women's Basketball League, which lasted three seasons. Other leagues subsequently started, in part based on interest kindled by Olympic gold medals by the U.S. women's team in 1984 and 1988. In a lengthy pre-Olympics tour in 1995–6, the U.S. women's team compiled a 52–0 record against college and international opponents prior to winning the gold medal in the Atlanta games.

An extensive set of press releases (described in **Exhibit 1**) chronicled the NBA Board's approval of the WNBA concept; NBC Sports' announcement of coverage of WNBA games; the announcement of ESPN/Lifetime regarding weeknight WNBA television coverage; the naming of Valerie Ackerman as WNBA president; the announcement of eight cities as initial WNBA franchises; a statement of the Women's Sports Foundation about the WNBA; the announcement of four marketing partners for the WNBA; the naming of the eight teams; the initial team player assignments; and the announcement of three more international players. (Many more press releases were issued.)

The WNBA positioning statement (2 pages) **(Exhibit 2)** included the pre-inaugural objectives, key relevant background factors favoring the enterprise, information on TV exposure of women's basketball, positive indicators for the WNBA, the target audiences for the WNBA, and the "core thought" regarding pre-launch WNBA communications. The articulation of target audiences and communications points was informed by custom research undertaken in summer 1996 by the NBA. As described below, excerpts from the research report appear as **Exhibit 3.**

Harvard Business School Case No 9-599-032. Copyright 1999 President and Fellows of Harvard College. All rights reserved. For information: permission@hbsp.harvard.edu. This case was prepared by Stephen A. Greyser. HBS cases are developed solely for class discussion and do not necessarily illustrate effective or ineffective management.

WNBA Research Overview

The accompanying excerpts from a longer research report represented some central findings about prospective fan interest in the WNBA. The information was based on a national study of 1000 people (age 7–55) conducted for the NBA in mid-1996 (prior to the Atlanta Olympics).

Almost half the respondents expressed some interest in women's pro basketball (very and somewhat, compared to uncertain and none) in the context of NBA involvement. Of those "very interested" (about one-third of those interested), slightly over half were female, slightly less than half were male.

The initial two charts show first the percentage of avid WNBA fans ("very interested in attending or watching on TV") who were also avid fans of the NBA and other women's and men's sports. Next one sees the percentages of all basketball fans (and male and female, separately) who said they are interested in the WNBA. The following chart shows interest in the WNBA among core fans by age and gender. Major reasons for interest among avid WNBA fans are shown next, followed by a demographic fan segmentation of avid WNBA fans.

With respect to television viewing, the next chart shows how people intending to view WNBA telecasts expected to watch them—alone or with others.

In terms of WNBA player recognition, other research (post-Olympics) showed that three star players had meaningful name recognition among sports fans age 12 and above. These were Rebecca Lobo, Sheryl Swoopes, and Lisa Leslie—all of whom achieved aided recognition scores in the 28%–33% range.

EXHIBIT 1   INFORMATION EXCERPTED FROM NEWS RELEASES FROM THE NBA AND WNBA

April 24, 1996—The NBA Board of Governors approved the concept of the WNBA, to begin play as a summer league in 1997. Commissioner David Stern said: "We believe that significant network and sponsor opportunities exist to create a foundation on which to build a league."

The league will work as a "single entity" with the players contracting with the league. The teams will operate the franchises under operating agreements with the league. Player assignments will be based on territorial competition and a draft. Players could play in Europe or other leagues during the WNBA off season.

Teams will be in cities with existing NBA teams and arenas. The 10-week season is planned to have 25–30 games, followed by playoffs.

In the press conference, many comments were made about the momentum building for women's basketball at the college level and increased participation by young and teenage girls.

June 27—NBC Sports announced live weekly full-season coverage of the WNBA on Saturday afternoons. [NBC had been the NBA's broadcast network partner since the 1990–91 season. In 1995–96, regular season NBA ratings had been 5.3 (14 share), the highest since 1988–89. The NBA's 1996 Finals had the second-highest rating in history, 16.7 (31 share).]

July 16—WNBA regular season games will be televised in prime-time by ESPN and Lifetime Television. One live weeknight game will be telecast on each cable channel. The two channels also will jointly televise a playoff semifinal doubleheader.

"Collective marketing and branding expertise" was cited as an important element of the partnership, including Lifetime's strong identity as "Television for Women" and ESPN's strongest male demographic on cable. These would combine to provide "the most extensive coverage ever of any professional sports league in its first season," according to the NBA.

August 7—Val Ackerman was named WNBA president. She had joined the NBA in 1988, and had managed NBA relations with a variety of basketball organizations, including the Basketball Hall of Fame, FIBA (the worldwide basketball federation), and USA basketball. Ackerman was a Virginia graduate, where she was a four-year basketball starter, and earned a law degree at UCLA following a season of professional play in France.

October 30—The WNBA announced eight cities for its inaugural season in summer 1997. Teams will play in Charlotte, Cleveland, Houston, and New York (Eastern Conference) and Los Angeles, Phoenix, Sacramento, and Utah (Western Conference).

Cited in the press release was the combination of state-of-the art buildings, proven management in professional basketball, and some major media markets.

A timetable for a sequence of events for the winter and spring of 1997 was also announced, including the release dates of the WNBA schedule, the team names and logos, the draft, etc. Information was also released on the ball size (same as for women's high school and college competition), the 3-point line (same as college), the length of games (same as college), and the shot clock (30 seconds). Two stars of the Olympic gold medal team were also named as WNBA players, "with additional player announcements expected."

Fall 1996—The Women's Sport Foundation "applauds the WNBA's efforts in providing sports opportunities for women," in a press conference citing the role of the Olympics in bringing women's sports to the forefront.

[The Foundation, founded in 1974 by Billie Jean King and supported by champion female athletes, "seeks to create an educated public that encourages females' participation and supports gender equality in sport."]

December 19—The WNBA announced its first four marketing partners—Lee Jeans, Bud Light, Champion (apparel), and Spalding. Spalding will supply and market the official WNBA basketball. They all signed three-year marketing agreements. Each was given category exclusivity for sponsorship and WNBA television. The press release noted that "the long-term marketing commitments . . . represent a crucial component in the successful launch of the WNBA."

Each partnership included advertising in every WNBA national telecast and in each team's local telecasts, exclusive promotional rights to the WNBA logo and team logos, on-court signage in every WNBA arena, and player appearances in every WNBA team market.

February 14, 1997—The names and logos for all eight teams were displayed for the first time. Some names were selected to tie in with the existing NBA franchise in the same market, such as the Sacramento Monarchs (Kings), Utah Starzz (Jazz), and Houston Comets (Rockets). Others were linked to a key characteristic of their city or state, such as the New York Liberty and Cleveland Rockers. Team colors were similar or identical to those of the NBA team, "ensuring immediate fan recognition."

January 22—The first sixteen WNBA players and their team assignments were announced, including eleven members of past or 1996 gold medal Olympic teams.

February 3—Three additional "premier international players" signed to play in the WNBA. They had competed for Brazil, France, and Japan. Already announced among the first sixteen players were stars from Russia and Australia.

EXHIBIT 2   WNBA POSITIONING STATEMENT

CORE THOUGHT:

All league, team and partner communications prior to the WNBA launch should incorporate the following core thought:

If you love basketball competition, you must see the WNBA, because the games feature...

- tremendous play
- intense competition
- inspiring role models
- NBA-style in-arena experience

OBJECTIVE:

Prior to the WNBA's inaugural game on **June 21, 1997,** our league-wide goal will be to generate broad knowledge of, and enthusiasm for, the WNBA, its teams and its players.

BACKGROUND:

- Increasing number of women and girls around the world are playing basketball. The International Basketball Federation estimates that there are currently 250 million active basketball players worldwide, of whom at least 1/3 (or more than 80 million) are female.

- On a global basis, basketball is the most popular sport among female teens.

- In the U.S., over 9.2 million females of all ages play basketball on a regular basis (a 30% increase over the last 6 years), and basketball is now the leading participatory sport for girls at the high school level.

- In 1995/96, over 5 million people atended NCAA women's basketball games (+140% vs. 1986).

TELEVISION EXPOSURE:

- The 1996 Olympic women's basketball gold medal game (featuring the U.S. against defending world championship Brazil) generated a 15.5 television rating.

- The 1996 NCAA championship game on ESPN generated a record 3.7 rating, making it the second-highest rated college basketball game (men's or women's) on ESPN since 1993.

- ESPN expanded its coverage of NCAA women's basketball to over 120 hours in 1995/96 (triple the coverage from the preceding year).

POSITIVE INDICATORS FOR THE WNBA:

- *Best Basketball in the World*—The WNBA will feature the most exciting and highest level of women's basketball in the world.

- *Significant Television Coverage* - Each week during the season, three games will be telecast live and in prime-time—one each by NBC, ESPN and Lifetime—for a total of 34 national broadcasts.

- *NBA-Style Entertainment*—WNBA games will take place in NBA arenas and will provide fans with the same type of exciting game entertainment they experience at NBA games.

- *Top Management*—The WNBA teams will be managed by NBA teams, who have a proven track record in managing and presenting professional basketball.

TARGET AUDIENCE:

Based on market research conducted by the WNBA, the following groups have been identified as critical target groups for the league:

- **Sports fans,** including: (a) men 20 to 39, who are big sports fans and watch sports on television as often as possible; (b) big fans of NBA and men's college basketball; and (c) fans of women's college basketball (both male and female).

- **Kids 7 to 17,** who enjoy playing and watching basketball and who will drive the interest of their families.

- **Active women, 18 to 34,** who enjoy sports, who may have once played basketball, (and hence have a special appreciation for the game) and/or who are excited about the recent growth of women's sports.

- **Relatives and friends of basketball players,** who follow the exploits of their friends and family members and will be drawn to the WNBA through these associations.

EXHIBIT 3   Excerpts from NBA Research Report

WNBA Fans Are Basketball Fans

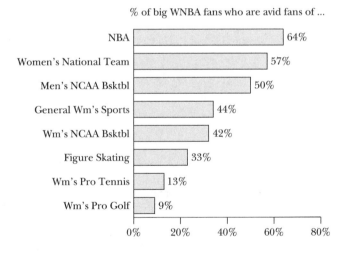

% of big WNBA fans who are avid fans of ...

- 64% of avid WNBA fans are big NBA fans.

- Big WNBA fans are avid fans of the sport of basketball; Four of the top five sports interests of WNBA fans are basketball-specific.

EXHIBIT 3   *(continued)*

Basketball Fans Are WNBA Fans

% of total basketball fans
interested in the WNBA ...

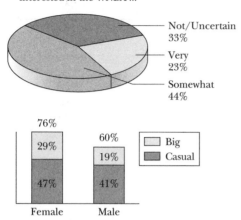

Not/Uncertain
33%

Very
23%

Somewhat
44%

• Two-thirds (67%) of all basketball fans have some interest in the WNBA.

• Female basketball fans express a higher rate of interest in the WNBA than their male counterpart, particularly among those who are "very interested." 76% of female basketball fans are interested in the WNBA vs. 60% of male basketball fans.

76%		
29%	60%	☐ Big
	19%	◼ Casual
47%	41%	
Female	Male	

WNBA Demographics

WNBA avidity by age

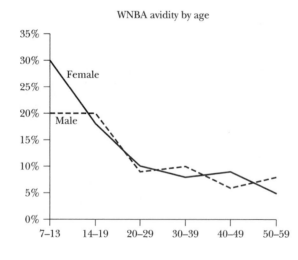

Female

Male

• WNBA interest among core fans skews young 30% of girls 7–13 and 20% of boys 7–13 are *"very interested"* in the WNBA.

• Approximately 20% of the traditional Teen age group (12–17) is *"very interested"* in the WNBA.

• The average age of the core WNBA fan is 26 years old.

WNBA Fans Are Basketball Fans

"Major Reasons" for big WNBA fan interest

Good Role Model Potential	86%
Women Needed a Pro League	81%
Top Quality Athletes Performing	79%
Athleticism	78%
Curiosity about New League	75%
Close Competition	68%
Star Draw of Certain Players	68%
NBA Involvement	65%

WNBA Fan Segments

(Groups are not mutually exclusive meaning a respondent can exist in more than one group)

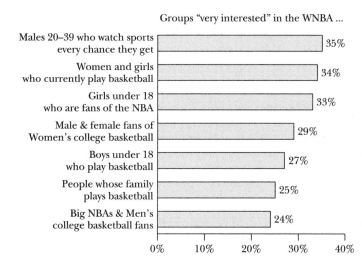

Groups "very interested" in the WNBA ...

Males 20–39 who watch sports every chance they get	35%
Women and girls who currently play basketball	34%
Girls under 18 who are fans of the NBA	33%
Male & female fans of Women's college basketball	29%
Boys under 18 who play basketball	27%
People whose family plays basketball	25%
Big NBAs & Men's college basketball fans	24%

• *"Avid Male Sports Fans (20–39)," "Female Basketball Players,"* and *"Female NBA Fans Under 18"* are statistically tied among groups expressing the greatest interest in the WNBA. At least one-third of each group is "very interested" in the WNBA.

WNBA Viewing Experience

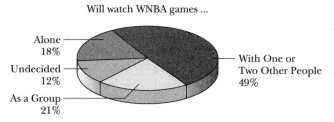

Will watch WNBA games ...

- Alone 18%
- Undecided 12%
- As a Group 21%
- With One or Two Other People 49%

• Viewing a WNBA broadcast will be a communal experience. 70% of Big WNBA fans intend to watch games with someone else.

• Females are sure to be among the viewing groups, as a greater percentage of fans plan to watch televised WNBA games with mostly female friends/family (28%) than male friends/family (25%).

(Chart not shown)

CASE 2.8   THE AMERICAN BASKETBALL LEAGUE: THE LAST CHAPTER[89]

On December 22, 1998, the American Basketball League (ABL) announced that it was suspending operations. Officers planned to file Chapter 11 bankruptcy and liquidate the league. The announcement came as a shock to players and fans alike. The ABL was only six weeks into its third season. The league had experienced expansion (from eight to ten teams for 1998–99), shifted and folded franchises, the signing of collegiate stars and a "name" coach (former Celtics coach K.C. Jones), and an attendance high of over 15,000 (1998).

Attendance

During its second season (1997–98) ABL attendance had increased 23% over its first year to 4,333 attendees per game. Some games attracted more than 10,000 spectators. During the second season, each team played 40 games, followed by a best 3-of-5 championship series. Games took place in relatively small arenas which held an average of 8,900.[90] Prior to the start of the 1997–98 season, the league had expanded from 8 to 9 teams. Between the 1997–98 and 1998–99 seasons, two teams folded, and two expansion franchises were created. The league started its third and final season with nine teams.

Television Broadcasts

During its first season, the ABL's television coverage was modest. Of the 176 games played over the course of the 20-week season, 28 games were shown on cable television—20 on Fox SportsNet and eight on Black Entertainment Television. "We need to be on TV at a predictable time. . . . Fans who are not in team markets need to know where we are," said Ann Cribbs, vice president of corporate and community development at the ABL. "We have fans who write us and say, 'We get together every Sunday night to watch your games. Sometimes we can find you and sometimes we can't.'"[91]

For 1998–99, CBS had contracted with the league to broadcast two championship series games, and Fox SportsNet was scheduled to show 16 games during the regular season. The latter were to be shown live once a week. The league paid the networks to appear on television.[92] "This year we offered millions of dollars to the TV networks for air time, but couldn't obtain adequate coverage," ABL co-founder and CEO Gary Cavalli said.[93]

Sponsors

By its third season, the ABL had attracted a number of sponsors. These included Reebok, Lady Footlocker, Phoenix Home Life Mutual, Nissan, First USA Bank, and licensed merchandise manufacturer Baden Sports. Sponsors also contributed to the teams by making cash payments and donating equipment and merchandise.

Harvard Business School Case No 9-599-109. Copyright 1999 President and Fellows of Harvard College. All rights reserved. For information: permission@hbsp.harvard.edu. This case was prepared by Stephen A. Greyser and Elizabeth E. Smyth. HBS cases are developed solely for class discussion and do not necessarily illustrate effective or ineffective management.

WNBA

While the ABL had continued its efforts to build its fan base and television viewership, the National Basketball Association was forming a strong "league of their own"—the Women's National Basketball Association (WNBA). (For information on the founding of the WNBA, see HBS Case No. 599-032, "Women's National Basketball Association.") The league initially consisted of eight teams, each of which played 28 games over the summer months. Games were held in large NBA arenas that seated an average of 19,300, although seats in some arenas were screened off to create the atmosphere of a smaller venue. Attendance during the first season (1997) averaged 9,804 per game, and increased 12% to 10,869 per game during the 1998 season. NBC, ESPN, and Lifetime had contracts with the WNBA to televise one live regular season game each per week (a total of 30 games). Among them, all playoff games (3 in 1997 and 8 in 1998) were televised. League sponsors included Nike, Bud Light, Champion, GM, Lee jeans, Sears, and Spalding.

Reflections

In response to the ABL shut-down, Fox spokesperson Vince Wladika said "It's a shame. The ABL provided us with high-quality women's programming, both nationally and regionally."[94] WNBA President Val Ackerman said, "this is an unfortunate setback for the women's sports movement. We applaud the great effort and passion of the ABL's players and all the league and team personnel who labored so hard to start and sustain a league."[95]

"A lot of us realized that the ABL was a risky venture, but I believed in what the ABL was about," said former Stanford standout Kate Starbird, who played for the Seattle Reign. "This summer, I was a little scared, but I really believed we'd play out the season. It was a shock today to get the phone call that we wouldn't be playing anymore."[96]

In a statement, Cavalli said: "This is a sad day for our fans, employees, players, and coaches, and for women's basketball in general. We gave it our best shot, we fought the good fight, and we had a good run. But we were unable to obtain the television exposure and sponsorship support needed to make the league viable long term."[97]

Questions for Cases 2.5 Through 2.8

1. What conditions favored 1997 and immediately beyond for women's professional sports? Why were they not factors earlier? To what extent do you see this (even now) as more hope than reality?

2. Regarding women's professional basketball, how would you describe the ABL's core strategy (basic business model) and its principal differentiators? From the vantage point of fall 1997, what are your opinions as to the ABL's likely success? What factors are central?

3. How would you describe the WNBA's core strategy (basic business model) and its principal differentiators? How similar or different are they from the ABL's? From the vantage point of fall 1997, what are your opinions as to the WNBA's likely success? What factors are central?

4. Do you believe that both the ABL and WNBA can be successful? Only one (if so, which one)? Neither? Why? How predictive of long-term success is the first season?

5. What do you think of the major target audiences and major appeals as articulated by the WNBA? How would you build fans? How important are stars?

6. How important are men as WNBA game attendees or TV viewers? How will men and women likely see the caliber of play in the WNBA (and ABL)—as tops in its genre (women's basketball) or second tier (basketball)?

7. In light of the ABL's failure, what additional observations do you have about women's professional basketball?

8. What observations do you have about the progress and position of the WNBA as it prepares to enter the coming season? Address the effect(s) of the fall 2002 franchise "de-coupling" between the NBA parent teams(s) and WNBA franchise(s).

9. More broadly, what are your views on the current climate for women's professional sports in the United States, especially since the suspension of the WUSA (soccer) following its 2003 season?

10. Assess the effects of Title IX on the prospects for growth in women's professional sports, and its impact on the growth of girls' and women's participation in school and college sports.

Footnotes

1 This section was written by George Foster.

2 "Long Cleared to Play." Sporting Life.com (September 11, 2004).

3 There were playoffs in 9 of the 10 years from 1994–2003. There were no postseason playoffs in 1994 because of a players' strike.

4 The 11 are Arsenal, Aston Villa, Chelsea, Everton, Leeds (relegated for 2004–05 season), Liverpool, Manchester United, Newcastle, Southampton, Tottenham, and West Ham (relegated for 2003–04 season).

5 This case was written by Eric Kroll, Cecil Smart, and George Foster. The assistance of the NBA and FIBA is gratefully acknowledged. NBA documents ("NBA: A Global Game") and FIBA documents ("Vision—Strategy—Activities 2003–2010) were very helpful.

6 See J. A. Adande. "Dream Theme is Way Over." *Los Angeles Times* (August 2, 2004).

7 Research Associate Kirk A. Goldman and Professor Stephen A. Greyser prepared this case. HBS cases are developed solely as the basis for class discussion. Cases are not intended to serve as endorsements, sources of primary data, or illustrations of effective or ineffective management.

8 Alex Yannis. "Second season ended on up note." *The New York Times*, October 28, 1997.

9   Rick Morrissey. "A league waits for its popularity to kick in." *Sacramento Bee*, April 30, 1997.

10 Morrissey. *Sacramento Bee*, April 30, 1997.

11 Excerpts from MLS League Structure information material.

12 Gus Martins. "MLS attending to business." *The Boston Herald*, April 29, 1997.

13 Brian Trusdell. "Scoring points." *Sales and Marketing Management*, October 1996.

14 Greg Pesky. "Heading for the pros." *Sporting Goods Business*, April 1994.

15 Roscoe Nance. "MLS investors say ownership setup a big draw." *USA Today*, November 25, 1994.

16 Grahame Jones. "Like a phoenix rising." *Los Angeles Times*, April 5, 1996.

17 David Leonhardt. "Is Major League Soccer using its head?" *Business Week*, January 29, 1996.

18 Dan Herbst. "Soccer gets another kick." *IAC PROMT*, January 1997.

19 Trusdell. *Sales and Marketing Management*, October 1996.

20 Nance. "Single-entity structure requires sharing." *USA Today*, November 25, 1994.

21 Nance. "MLS investors say ownership set up was a big draw." *USA Today*, November 25, 1994.

22 Alex Yannis. "MLS set to build on first-year success." *The New York Times*, March 23, 1997.

23 Herbst. *IAC PROMT*, January 1997.

24 Morrissey. *Sacramento Bee*, April 30, 1997.

25 Jody Meacham. "Attendance goal a longshot." *The Record*, May 4, 1997.

26 Meacham. *The Record*, May 4, 1997.

27 Meacham. *The Record*, May 4, 1997.

28 Morrissey. *Sacramento Bee*, April 30, 1997.

29 Jones. *Los Angeles Times*, April 5, 1996.

30 Herbst. *IAC PROMT*, January 1997.

31 1997 National Soccer Participation Survey by the Soccer Industry Council of America.

32 James Zoltak. "Major League Soccer's Logan: sport now has leg up in U.S." *Amusement Business*, February 24, 1997.

33 Zoltak. *Amusement Business*, February 24, 1997.

34 Grahame Jones. "Getting their piece of the pie." *Los Angeles Times*, July 27, 1996.

35 Zoltak. *Amusement Business*, February 24, 1997.

36 Zoltak. *Amusement Business*, February 24, 1997.

37 Yannis. *The New York Times*, March 23, 1997.

38 Jones. *Los Angeles Times*, July 27, 1996.

39 Grahame Jones. "Major League Soccer surpasses its goals." *Los Angeles Times*, October 22, 1996.

40 Jere Longman. "For MLS, survival depends on quality." *The New York Times*, April 1, 1997.

41 Frank Dell'Apa. "Novelty subsiding, MLS must offer substance." *The Boston Globe*, April 1, 1997.

42 Longman. *The New York Times*, April 1, 1997.

43 W. D. Murray. "Soccer slumped in second season." *The Daily News of Los Angeles*, November 2, 1997.

44 Grahame Jones. "Does sport of future have a future in United States?" *Los Angeles Times*, October 26, 1997.

45 Murray. *The Daily News of Los Angeles*, November 2, 1997.

46 Jones. *Los Angeles Times*, October 26, 1997.

47 MLS awards three points for each win and one point for every shoot-out win. Four United victories came via shoot-outs.

48 Jerry Langdon. "MLS'Logan confident about sponsor support." *USA Today*, October 28, 1997.

[49] This case was written by George Foster. It draws on press articles in the *Sydney Morning Herald, Sun-Herald, Daily Telegraph,* and *Sunday Telegraph. Journalists of articles were Sean Berry, Lee Glendinning, Jessica Halloran, Les Kennedy, S. MacLean, Jacquelin Magnay, Steve Mascord, Roy Masters, Juan-Carlo Tomas, Brad Walter,* and *Danny Weidler.*

[50] Both Rugby Union and Rugby League had their roots in England's Rugby School. Rugby League was a breakaway code from union with 13 players (as opposed to 15 players in union). It was founded in the North English counties of Lancashire and Yorkshire in 1895. Rugby League players were paid as opposed to the amateur status of union players at that time. A similar breakaway from union occurred with the formation of Australian Rugby League in 1908.

[51] S. MacLean. "Dogged by the Press Pack." the *Australian* (March 11, 2004).

[52] Tom Covington and Jake Moskowitz prepared this case under the supervision of George Foster and David Hoyt.

[53] Open-wheel racing cars are single-seat cars with exposed wheels designed specifically for racing. While professional racing "stock cars" are specially made for racing, they appear externally similar to passenger cars, with wheels enclosed by fenders.

[54] Paul Kagan Associates, industry analyst.

[55] http://www.hondaracing.com/hpd/why.html (October 1, 2003).

[56] The entire month of May was dedicated to preparations for the Indy 500, with such events as practice, qualifying, Bump Day, Carburetion Day, and of course, the race itself.

[57] Jim Allen. "Once Race Series Get Going, They Pay for Themselves." *Street & Smith's SportsBusiness Journal* (May 6, 2002).

[58] Staff. "IRL Finally Feeling Momentum." *Street & Smith's SportsBusiness Journal* (October 22, 2001).

[59] This was called a lockout by CART supporters and a boycott by supporters of the IRL.

[60] Jonathon Ingram. "Selling in NASCAR's Shadow." *Street & Smith's SportsBusiness Journal* (May 22, 2000).

[61] Indy Racing League.

[62] Daniel Kaplan. "Battered CART Shifts Its Hopes to New Strategy." *Street & Smith's SportsBusiness Journal* (May 6, 2002).

[63] This case was written by Stephen A. Greyser.

[64] Peter May and Jason Devaney, "Changing WNBA Landscape," *The Boston Globe,* October 9, 2002.

[65] Letter from WNBA President Valerie Ackerman to Stephen A. Greyser, May 19, 2004.

[66] Natalie Zakarian prepared this case under the supervision of Professor Stephen A. Greyser. This case was developed from published sources. HBS cases are developed solely as the basis for class discussion. Cases are not intended to serve as endorsements, sources of primary data, or illustrations of effective or ineffective management.

[67] Doug Carlson, *The Tampa Tribune,* "Respect at Last; Women's Basketball is Poised to Enter a New Era of Popularity," November 14, 1995.

[68] Mick Elliott, *The Tampa Tribune,* "Gone with the Win; U.S. Women Grab Final Piece of Gold," August 5, 1996.

[69] W.H. Stickney, Jr., *The Houston Chronicle,* "ABL Presents a League of Their Own; Finally the Timing Appears Right," October 13, 1996.

[70] Lou Ann Ruark, *Tulsa World,* "A Whole New Ball Game," January 19, 1997.

[71] From the Internet, Title IX

[72] Doug Carlson, *The Tampa Tribune,* "Respect at Last; Women's Basketball is poised to Enter a new Era of Popularity," November 14, 1995.

[73] W.H. Stickney, Jr., *The Houston Chronicle,* "ABL Presents a League of Their Own; Finally the Timing Appears Right," October 13, 1996.

[74] J.A. Adande, *The Washington Post,* "For Dream Team III, It's Business as Usual; Women Hope to Rebound from Disappointing '92," July 19, 1996.

[75] Kelli Anderson, *Sports Illustrated,* "Try, Try, Again; Women's Pro Basketball an Oft-Failed Idea is Back with Two Very Different Leagues," October 16, 1996.

[76] W.H. Stickney, Jr., *The Houston Chronicle,* "ABL Presents a League of Their Own; Finally the Timing Appears Right," October 13, 1996.

[77] Ibid.

[78] Daniel Green, *Working Woman,* "Toss Up," April 1997.

[79] W.H. Stickney, Jr., *The Houston Chronicle,* "ABL Presents a League of Their Own; Finally the Timing Appears Right," October 13, 1996.

[80] Peter Schmuck, *The Baltimore Sun,* "The ABL and the WNBA Have Different Philosophies but a Common Goal: To Make the Women's Pro Sport a Major-League Success," February 2, 1997.

[81] Celeste E. Whittaker, *The Atlanta Journal and Constitution,* "ABL Promises Women Players a Proleague of Their Own," May 4, 1996.

[82] Lori Riley, *The Hartford Courant,* "A Year Older, League's Still 'Got Players'," October 10, 1997.

[83] Bruce Berlet, *The Hartford Courant,* "They're Taking the Next Step," July 25, 1996.

[84] Vic Dorr, Jr. *The Richmond Times Dispatch,* "TV or Not TV? That Was the ABL Question; The Business Needs Philadelphia Market," July 17, 1997.

[85] *The Boston Globe,* August 30, 1997 and league information.

[86] Amy Shipley and Karl Hente. *The Washington Post,* "Women's Pro Leagues Battle for Position," May 4, 1997.

[87] Andy Bernstein, *Sporting Goods Business,* "The SGB Interview: Rick Welts," November 1996.

[88] Professor Stephen A. Greyser prepared this case. HBS cases are developed solely as the basis for class discussion. Cases are not intended to serve as endorsements, sources of primary data, or illustrations of effective or ineffective management.

Copyright © 1998 President and Fellows of Harvard College. To order copies or request permission to reproduce materials, call 1-800-545-7685, write Harvard Business School Publishing, Boston, MA 02163, or go to http://www.hbsp.harvard.edu. No part of this publication may be reproduced, stored in a retrieval system, used in a spreadsheet, or transmitted in any form or by any means–electronic, mechanical, photocopying, recording, or otherwise–without the permission of Harvard Business School.

[89] Professor Stephen A. Greyser and Research Associate Elizabeth E. Smyth prepared this case. HBS cases are developed solely as the basis for class discussion. Cases are not intended to serve as endorsements, sources of primary data, or illustrations of effective or ineffective management.

Copyright © 1998 President and Fellows of Harvard College. To order copies or request permission to reproduce materials, call 1-800-545-7685, write Harvard Business School Publishing, Boston, MA 02163, or go to http://www.hbsp.harvard.edu. No part of this publication may be reproduced, stored in a retrieval system, used in a spreadsheet, or transmitted in any form or by any means–electronic, mechanical, photocopying, recording, or otherwise–without the permission of Harvard Business School.

[90] "How the leagues differ," http://www.southflorida.digitalcity.com/DCSports.

[91] Maricris G. Briones, *Marketing News,* July 6, 1998.

[92] Richard Sandomir, "Pro Basketball; Too Few Dollars, No Real Exposure," *The New York Times*, December 23, 1998.

[93] Richard Sandomir, "Pro Basketball; Too Few Dollars, No Real Exposure," *The New York Times*, December 23, 1998.

[94] Ibid.

[95] Amy Shipley, "ABL Says It Is Bankrupt and Shuts Down," *The Washington Post*, December 23, 1998.

[96] Susan Slusser, "American Basketball League Folds," *The San Francisco Chronicle*, December 23, 1998.

[97] Associated Press, "ABL Folds During Third Season," ESPN website, http://www.espn.com.

SECTION 3... Clubs[1]

Key Issues

- Dramatic differences exist across clubs in their revenues. These differences can reflect differences in off-field "endowed assets"(such as stadium status and local television contracts) and business management ability as well as on-field performance.

- Clubs differ in the priorities they give to winning on the field, financial gains, trophy status of ownership/management, and enhancing a community asset.

- Factors affecting the business priorities of a club include the objectives of the ownership, financial capacity, the "endowed assets," and the general league infrastructure.

- "Success" in club ownership and operation encompasses a range of management and entrepreneurial skills off-the-field as well on-field coaching and playing skills.

- Decisions to "retire"or trade marquee players (sometimes called "franchise royalty") have an important business dimension as well as on on-field performance dimension.

Cases

Club management makes many decisions in a sporting club that impact both on-field performance and business aspects such as financials, brand value, and sponsorship contracts. This section highlights some key decisions that impact how clubs create value and how much of that value they are able to capture for themselves.

Within a single league, major differences exist across clubs in key financial variables. Exhibit 3-1 plots 2003 revenues for clubs in five leagues. Summary data are (in $ millions):

	Average	Highest Club	Lowest Club	Ratio of Highest to Lowest
NFL	$167	$245 (Washington)	$131 (Arizona)	1.87
MLB	129	238 (NY Yankees)	81 (Montreal)	2.94
NBA	94	160 (NY Knicks)	63 (Memphis)	2.54
NHL	70	131 (NY Rangers)	43 (Phoenix)	3.05
EPL	62	£175 (Man. United)	£28 (West Bromwich)	6.25

Such dramatic differences, even while controlling for differences due to league-based factors, highlight the pivotal importance of decisions made at the club level and how clubs differ in their "endowed" assets.

Owners and Managers

The equity owners of a sporting club, in most cases, have the decision rights to appoint the top management group and to determine the level of authority of that group. Equity owners are very heterogonous on multiple dimensions. One difference is the composition of the equity group. Three possible models are:

Single Owner/Private Investor Model: This individual is often independently wealthy, having either inherited wealth or had prior successful investments. For example, Mark Cuban, owner of the Dallas Mavericks in the NBA since 2000, accumulated wealth via his cofounding of MicroSolutions (sold to CompuServe) and cofounding of Broadcast.com (sold to Yahoo!). This single investor can decide to play a very active role in club decision-making, or adopt a very hands-off approach in which, after selecting key managers, he becomes a passive investor. These are two ends of the spectrum. Moreover, an owner may start at one end of the spectrum and change over time (either formally or informally).

Multiple Owners/Private Investment Syndicate Model: A group of individuals pool their resources to acquire ownership of a club. For example, the Boston Celtics of the NBA were purchased in 2002 for $360 million by Boston Basketball Partners, LP (BBP). BBP is a privately held investment syndicate with a four-member managing board, consisting of H. Irving Grousbeck, Wyc Grousbeck, Steve Pagliuca, and The Abbey Group, represented by Robert Epstein. BBP also has other founding investors who have a more restricted set of decision rights with respect to management of the Celtics. An investment syndicate document will frequently outline the decision rights of different investors. In some cases, the syndicate will be led by a dominant individual who may appear to operate similar to a single owner/private investor model. However, the other investors can always seek arbitration or

EXHIBIT 3-1 *Forbes'* Estimates of 2003 Revenues of NFL, MLB, NBA, and NHL Clubs ($ millions) and Reported 2002 Revenues of EPL Clubs (£ millions)

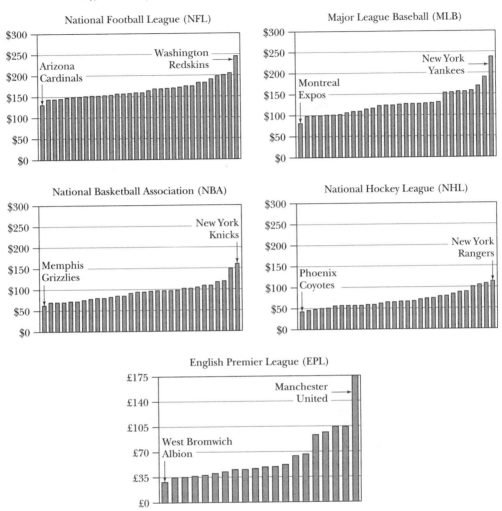

Source: *Forbes* magazine and club documents; Deloitte, *Annual Review of Football Finance* (August 2004).

take legal action if they believe improper actions are being taken by the dominant member of the syndicate.

Multiple Owners/Publicly Traded Corporation Model: This model is most often found in professional soccer leagues. Manchester United, one of the leading soccer clubs in the world, is a publicly owned company whose shares are traded on the London Stock Exchange. Many other leading soccer clubs in the world are also publicly traded—for example, Arsenal and Newcastle in England, Celtic and Rangers in Scotland, Roma and Jurventus in Italy, and Borussia Dortmund in Germany. A publicly traded company has a Board of Directors that has the responsibility to appoint the senior management group. These board members are elected via individual shareholding voting.[2]

Clubs as Publicly Traded Corporations

Multiple leagues differ in their use of the equity ownership models. The NFL has a combination of individual private investors and private investment syndicates. It now prohibits the publicly traded ownership model. The Green Bay Packers is a publicly traded company, having been "grandfathered" as an exception to the NFL prohibition of this ownership model. Exhibit 3-2 presents a 5-year summary of Green Bay's financials over the 1999/2000 to 2003/2004 period. These financials provide insight into the magnitude of key line items in a major sporting club. Green Bay in 2003–04 ranked tenth in terms of revenues for the 32 teams in the NFL. Its stadium renovation was finished for the start of the 2003 NFL season. The surge in local revenues for 2003–04 reflects the greater revenue-generating opportunities with the renovated stadium. Although Green Bay is publicly traded, it has restrictions that many other public companies do not. For example, there are "anti-takeover" provisions (and NFL ownership provisions) that effectively insulate it from a hostile third party wanting to gain a back-door entrance into NFL ownership.

EXHIBIT 3-2 GREEN BAY PACKERS FINANCIALS: 1999/2000 TO 2003/2004 ($ MILLIONS)

	1999/2000	2000/2001	2001/2002	2002/2003	2003/2004
National Revenues					
Television Revenues	$61.005	$67.685	$69.402	$77.140	$81.179
Other NFL Revenues/ NFL Properties	4.161	3.978	5.291	4.702	7.306
Road Games	9.396	9.415	10.199	10.770	11.384
Total National	74.562	81.078	84.892	92.612	99.869
Local Revenues					
Home Games (net)	14.582	16.739	17.837	20.497	26.538
Private Box Income	5.794	5.794	7.632	10.532	10.484
Marketing Revenue	8.058	8.689	9.066	10.548	14.137
Pro-Shop Revenue			6.212	11.148	15.382
Atrium Revenue	—			0	3.051
Local Media			2.936	3.424	3.721
Concessions/Parking (net)	5.819	5.651	3.105	3.973	4.519
Other			0.234	0.363	1.394
Total Local	34.253	36.873	47.112	60.485	79.226
Total Revenues	108.815	117.951	132.004	153.097	179.095
Operating Costs					
Player Costs	76.639	76.934	78.838	77.636	96.097
Team Expenses			14.828	15.650	17.184
Marketing Expenses			2.809	2.966	3.910
Pro-Shop Expenses	32.596	38.247	4.789	7.871	10.668
General and Administrative			12.384	17.061	15.338
Other			15.079	8.714	6.753
Total Operating Costs	109.235	115.181	128.736	129.898	149.950
Profit from Operations	$(0.420)	$2.770	$3.268	$23.199	$29.145
Revenues Rank in NFL	16	18	20	10	10

Source: Annual Reports of Green Bay Packers

Several arguments are put forward by those opposing use of the publicly traded ownership model in professional sports:

- Club objectives. Sporting clubs may pursue dominant objectives other than value enhancement/shareholders' profit maximization that most publicly traded capital markets expect (see the following section, Objectives of Sporting Clubs).

- Ownership "integrity." Leagues may prefer to exclude from club ownership individuals with unsavory backgrounds, gambling associations, and the like. Publicly traded stock exchanges rarely impose such criteria when deciding whether to register new investors in a company.

- Perceived likelihood of ownership instability. Takeovers and mergers are always a possibility for publicly traded companies. There is a belief by some that managers may take short-run actions to reduce the likelihood of a takeover that are not in the best interests of the long-term health and competitiveness of a sporting league.

- Required financial disclosures for a publicly traded company viewed as excessive. Many private investors in sporting clubs oppose third parties knowing details of their financial dealings. Having a subset of investors with publicly traded securities would indirectly focus much attention on the financial status of some intensely private and powerful club owners.

The Boston Celtics of the NBA had publicly traded stock until its acquisition in 2002 by the privately held Boston Basketball Partners. Several individual clubs in the MLB, NBA, and NHL are or have been owned by larger publicly traded corporations (typically media companies). Current examples include Comcast (Philadelphia 76ers and Flyers), Cablevision (New York Rangers and New York Knicks), and Time Warner (Atlanta Braves). Prior examples include Disney (Anaheim Angels), News Corp. (Lost Angeles Dodgers), and Time Warner (Atlanta Hawks and Atlanta Thrashers). Note that the annual reports of these media companies do not provide the detailed financial breakdowns found in "pure" publicly traded sporting clubs such as the Green Bay Packers.

Objectives of Sporting Clubs

Equity owners of sporting clubs can differ in their objectives. These include:

Winning on the Field: In a search for one or more championships, an owner may be willing to incur sizable losses with little likelihood of being able to recoup them (either through subsequent profitability or franchise appreciation).

Financial Gains: An owner may view a sporting club as similar to many other business investments. Each major outlay has to be justified using financial criteria such as discounted cash flow, internal rate of returns, or payback. In some sporting franchises, asset appreciation (also called asset build) rather than operating income is the major source of financial gains. Section 1 (Exhibit 1.1-2) highlights the increases in average sporting club values (as assessed by *Forbes*) over a 10-year-plus investment horizon. Average valuations (in millions) of clubs in recent years are:

	1994	1996	1998	2000	2002	2003
NFL	$160	$205	$385	$466	$628	$733
MLB	110	134	220	262	294	295
NBA	113	148	N/A	207	248	265
NHL	71	90	N/A	148	164	159

In many cases, owners have incurred operating losses that would need to be offset against asset appreciation when computing total financial returns.

"Trophy Status" of Being a Sporting Club Owner Without the "Win at All Financial Cost" Objective: The status and prestige of owning a major sporting club is very alluring to some individuals. However, some such owners are unwilling to continually fund losses in an attempt to become dominant on the field. Several investment groups specifically aim to be at least cash-flow neutral. They view owning the club as providing a "fun and challenging life experience" but seek to avoid continual drains on their personal wealth by the club perennially losing money.

Retain or Enhance a Community Asset: One motivation for wealthy individuals purchasing a team is to keep a club from moving to another city. A related objective is to transform a club that has been languishing or has had little community support. For example, Arthur Blank's purchase of the Atlanta Falcons of the NFL was in part motivated by his desire for Atlanta to have a club that the community was enthusiastic about and make it "the pride of the city." Blank, a cofounder of Home Depot, has invested large amounts of his wealth in promoting multiple community interests in Atlanta—for example, via donations to the Atlanta International Museum of Art and Design. His active ownership of the Falcons is part of this larger mission for the Atlanta community.

Organization Structure Issues

Sporting clubs typically distinguish between the playing team side and the business side:

Playing Team Side: Includes coaching, general manager, player personnel, scouting, training, and medical personnel, as well as the players themselves. It also often includes people involved in equipment management for the players and video/technology activities related to the on-field game.

Business Side: Includes the senior business management team, and functional areas such as marketing, sponsorship, ticketing, and stadium operations, as well as accounting, finance, human resources, legal, and media/public relations.

Exhibit 3-3 illustrates nonplayer headcount in selected MLB, NBA, NFL, and NHL clubs. Headcount comparisons across clubs are affected by what activities are managed by a club. A club with stadium management responsibilities will have additional head count vis-à-vis a

EXHIBIT 3-3   SPORTING CLUB (NONPLAYER) HEADCOUNT COMPOSITION: EXAMPLES FROM INDIVIDUAL CLUBS

General Areas	National Football League (NFL)		Major League Baseball (MLB)		National Basketball Association (NBA)		National Hockey League (NHL)	
	Carolina Panthers	New England Patriots	Chicago White Sox	San Francisco Giants	Houston Rockets	Seattle Sonics	Dallas Stars	San Jose Sharks
Playing Team (On-Field) Side								
Coaching Staff[1]	18	19	8	9	5	5	4	4
Personnel/Scouting[2]	13	20	4	6	6	4	13	10
Strength and Conditioners[3]	3	4	5	3	4	1	2	4
General Management/Others[4]	13	7	22	7	8	7	10	15
	47	50	35	25	23	17	25	33
Business Side								
Marketing/Sales[5]	23	48	36	70	59	56	55	26
Communications[6]	14	26	31	17	16	15	12	10
Operations/Facilities[7]	45	57	46	19	23	12	15	30
Accounting/Legal/H.R.[8]	8	17	18	18	27	9	25	11
General Management/Others[9]	16	23	14	22	5	9	9	16
	106	171	145	146	130	101	116	93
Total	153	221	180	171	153	118	141	126

1. Coaching Staff: Includes Head Coach and Assistant Coaches

2. Personnel/Scouting: Includes Player Personnel, Salary Cap Management, Scouting

3. Strength and Conditioners: Includes Trainers, Physiotherapists

4. General Mgt. and Others: Includes General Management on Team Side, Equipment Managers, Internal Medical, Team Travel, Video and IT for Team.

5. Marketing/Sales: Includes Consumer Marketing, Ticketing, Premium Seating, Season Ticket Holders, Client Relations, Corporate Marketing, Sponsorships, Suite Sales, Guest Relations, Fan Loyalty, Merchandising, Retailing

6. Communications: Includes Public Affairs, Community Relations, Media Relations, Alumni Coordination, Game Day Broadcasting, Home-Game Statistical Crew

7. Operations and Facilities: Includes Stadium and Arena Management, Ground Operations, Security, Travel, Training Facility Ground Management

8. Accounting/Legal/H.R.: Includes Accounting and Finance, Legal, Human Resources

9. Other: Includes Executive Staff, Administrators and Assistants, Information Technology, Government Relations, League Officers

Source: Media guides/websites of clubs.

comparable club playing in a stadium managed by a city authority. Moreover, the "endowed assets" of a club (such as strength of local fan base) can affect headcount. A club that can consistently sell out its arena before the start of a season (such as the Detroit Red Wings of the NHL) may have less need for headcount in ticket marketing than a club that struggles to have a sellout for any game in the season.

Exhibit 3-4 shows an illustrative generic organization structure for a sporting club. There is no blueprint that each club follows. Much depends on the preferences and personalities of four key players in a club: owner, general manager, CEO/president, and coach. Carmen Policy, a CEO/president of two NFL clubs, observed major differences across clubs in the organization of responsibilities for key on-field decisions such as the hiring of the coach, top-draft selections, and player salaries. He distinguished among four basic models:

- Ownership centric—The owner takes the lead on such decisions.

- CEO centric—The owner defers to the CEO, who chooses to take the lead on such decisions.

- General manager centric—The GM is allowed the responsibility and chooses to take the lead rather than delegate it to the coach.

- Coach centric—The coach takes the central role in decisions on draft selections and player salaries.

Scarcity of talent is one key factor guiding which model is chosen. Individual coaches, as part of their contract when hired, may require sizable say in areas beyond the week-to-week on-field game planning. For example, some strong-willed high-profile coaches have demanded that the coach and general manager roles be combined as their own responsibilities. However, even here there is fluidity. A coach who "demands" the responsibilities that in other clubs are assumed by a separate general manager may find his power base eroded if the club has an extended sequence of losses on the field.

EXHIBIT 3-4   ILLUSTRATIVE ORGANIZATION STRUCTURE/REPORTING RELATIONSHIPS FOR SPORTING CLUB

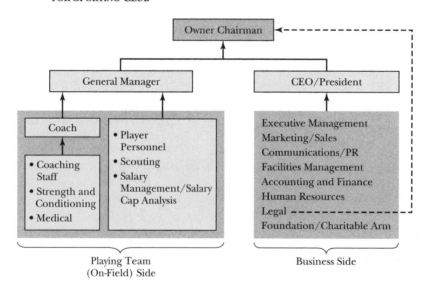

EXHIBIT 3-5 **BUSINESS STRATEGY OF MANCHESTER UNITED**

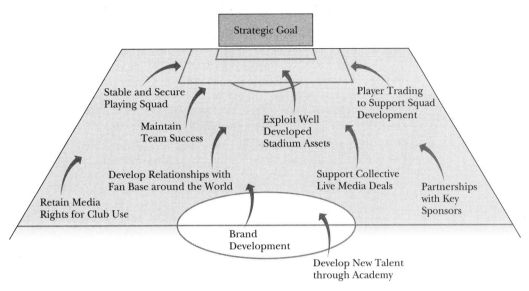

Not just team tactics … a business strategy

Just as the right team tactics are necessary for success on the pitch, so the right business strategies are required to achieve growth in operating profits across our three main revenue sources: match day receipts, sales of media rights, and commercial income.

Source: Extract from Manchester United's *Annual Report,* 2002.

Exhibit 3-5 is an extract from Manchester United's *Annual Report.* It is an excellent presentation of linking the playing team side and the business side of a club in a strategic business framework.

Assessing Business Priorities of Clubs

The business priorities of a club are a function of multiple factors, including:

1. Objective(s) of owner. Earlier we outlined possible goals of club owners, for example, winning on the field, financial gains, trophy ownership status, and building a community asset. Which objective or set of objectives is being pursued will dramatically affect business priorities.

2. Owner's financial capacity and financial willingness to commit resources to club. Owners differ greatly in this area. Some owners require their club to be "cash-flow positive" each year, which can greatly constrain a management team if many other owners are not operating with this constraint.

3. League infrastructure. League infrastructure can greatly affect the business priorities of clubs in different leagues. Consider player salary management. Leagues that have no restrictions on salaries (such as the EPL) make player acquisition decisions a function of financial capacity. In contrast, where there is a "hard" salary cap (such as in the NFL), club managers have the more complex task of juggling the multiyear planning of staying within that cap.

4. Club's endowed assets. As a result of prior decisions and their outcomes, clubs differ in key areas that affect business priorities. Two illustrative examples are:

a. Stadium situation. Some clubs play in modern state-of-the-art revenue-generating stadiums while other clubs struggle in "economically obsolete" facilities. This greatly impacts business priorities. The Minnesota Twins of the MLB and the Minnesota Vikings of the NFL share the outmoded Metrodome. Solving their "stadium situation" is pivotal for the Twins and Vikings to prevent their already large revenue gap with other clubs in their respective leagues from growing even larger.

b. Brand value. An elite set of clubs have stellar brands while others struggle with brands that evoke little emotional connection from their fans.

Managers seek to leverage their key endowed assets while strengthening areas where they are weak.

5. Controllability in a given time frame. One edict of effective managers is to "focus on issues that you can affect." Small-market teams in the MLB and NHL have an economic disadvantage, given that locally negotiated television rights differ so dramatically—for example, the local media revenues of the New York Yankees (largest television market) are more than eight times those of the Milwaukee Brewers (32nd largest television market). In the short run, even astute television contracting by the Brewers can do little to sizably reduce this gap. However, the Brewers can affect other elements of local revenue, for example, ticket sales and concession revenues.

Business Aspects of Player-Related Decisions

Business management skills are central in both the playing team side and the business side. The decision by some leagues to introduce salary caps has added another area of club management where financial skills as well as on-field player evaluation skills are important on the playing team side. The NFL's salary cap per club is (in $ millions):

1994	1997	2000	2002	2004
$34.6	$41.5	$62.2	$71.1	$80.6

Each club now employs a "capologist" whose function is to work with the complex set of rules to compute the multiyear implications of different player contracts for the club's ability to stay within the abovementioned caps. Note that the caps are maximums. There is also a required minimum that clubs must spend on salaries.

The vast majority of player acquisition and retention decisions are made within the playing team side of a sporting club. They typically will involve the general manager, the director of player personnel, and possibly the coach. In a few cases, the business-related stakes of some player-related decisions are so high that input from a broader set of club management may be included in the decision.

One such class of decisions relates to aging "marquee players" (sometimes called franchise royalty). Should they be traded, or should they be "prodded" to take a graceful retirement? Many clubs face such decisions. A high-profile example is the San Francisco 49ers of the

EXHIBIT 3-6   DECISION TO KEEP, TRADE, OR RETIRE MARQUEE PLAYERS IN THEIR TWILIGHT: BILL WALSH'S PERSPECTIVE OF FACTORS FOR SPORTING CLUBS TO CONSIDER

1. Options available to replace athlete.
2. Financial capacity to continue paying veteran: salary cap issues, and impact on other negotiations.
3. Expected future performance of athlete.
4. Health risks for athlete.
5. Willingness of other teams to offer inducements to trade.
6. Impact on franchise's reputation of trading athlete. Is athlete "franchise-royalty"?
7. What do key decision makers want: Player? Player's Family? Owner? Management? Coach?

NFL. Under coach Bill Walsh, the 49ers won three Super Bowls in the 1980s (1982, 1985, 1989). Subsequently, they won two additional Super Bowls in the 1990s (1990, 1995) under coach George Seifert. No other NFL club has won five Super Bowls in such a short period.[3] An elite number of 49er players became household names, such as Roger Craig, Randy Cross, Ronnie Lott, Joe Montana, Jerry Rice, and Steve Young. Many viewed these players as the heart and soul of the team. In each case, decisions had to be made by the 49er organization regarding salary and health. Exhibit 3-6 outlines factors Bill Walsh recommends be considered by the club. From a club's perspective, once a decision has been made that an acceptable salary offer will not be made, retirement is the preferred outcome. This enables the club to gracefully exit the player without the fan's alienation being stoked by that player appearing on a competing team. Not surprisingly, many players resist "forced retirement." Montana ended up being traded to the Kansas City Chiefs, while Craig, Lott, and Rice were each traded to the Raiders. In each of the Montana, Craig, Lott, and Rice cases, fan anger at the 49er management was expressed in many parts of the media.

Working with the Media—An Essential Aspect of Club Management

Effective club management is facilitated by clubs having productive relationships with the media. Exhibit 3-7 illustrates some guidelines Bill Walsh recommends be used for media interactions. Resources invested in developing media skills across all areas of a sporting club are typically well justified. This includes management and coaches on the playing team side, the business side, and the players themselves. Players' associations can play a role in assisting players to develop media skills. Clubs also have high responsibilities here. The media can latch onto ill-considered comments by players to create distractions and community relations problems for a club. For example, the San Francisco 49ers ran into such problems when a player made the following homophobic comment: "I don't want any faggots on my team. I know this might not be what people want to hear, but that's a punk. I don't want any faggots in this locker room." There is only downside from such comments. All representatives of a club have to be disciplined in their interactions with the media.[4]

EXHIBIT 3-7   B ILL W ALSH ' S G UIDELINES FOR I NCREASING THE L IKELIHOOD T HAT M EDIA I NTERVIEWS W ILL M EET Y OUR "N EEDS AND E XPECTATIONS "

- Set and adhere to specific time constraints in personal interviews (e.g., 5-10-15 minutes, etc.). Let the media know why your interview will have a time limit.

- Have an understanding of the subject, which will be covered in one-on-one interviews.

- Keep in mind that it never pays to be confrontational. Be calm. Soften hard questions with your responses. Control your emotions—the interviewer may know how to trigger them.

- Don't forget that while honest, direct responses are important, you are not required to provide distinct personal feelings, strategies or contingencies.

- Have specific information at hand or available. Back up assertions with facts, statistics, and even relevant personal experiences. Be careful of making careless observations using unsubstantiated numbers or names.

- Change or shift the subject if you are asked a provocative question (i.e., answering another question is one possible step you can take).

- Don't forget that humor can be reported as sober, serious remarks. Any humor you use should be far afield of serious exchange. While light, engaging humor can naturally soften intense, critical exchanges, its use can be a double-edged sword.

- Don't expound, as a general rule, on a particular subject outside a straightforward response. Pontificating often results in overstatement and careless observations. Keep in mind that media will seldom forget or overlook such comments.

- Don't repeat a negative question. If you do, it then can be (mistakenly) reported as having been initiated by you. It can also serve as an admission of something to which you don't want to be associated.

Source: B. Walsh, B. Billick, and J. Peterson, *Finding the Winning Edge* (Champaign, IL: Sports Publishing, 1998, pp. 387–388).

CASE 3.1 NFL CLUB BUSINESS MANAGEMENT: ASSESSING PRIORITY DIFFERENCES ACROSS 3 CLUBS[5]

Cindy Jones, President of the Sports Management Consulting Group (SMCG) had just accepted an offer to chair a debate at the next World Sporting Congress to be held in New York in July 2004. The debate topic was "Business Management Priorities Facing National Football League (NFL) Clubs" for the coming 2004 and 2005 seasons. The focus was to be on priorities of Presidents and the business staff of NFL teams. Jones was thrilled to receive the invitation. The session would be highly attended. It was a golden opportunity for her to make a positive impression on many people who might be future clients of SMCG. To provide a cross section of issues, she selected the three following NFL clubs, in alphabetical order:

- Arizona Cardinals
- Houston Texans
- San Francisco 49ers

Jones was determined to be "more than fully prepared" for the debate. Her first task was to make her own assessment on what were the top three business management priorities each club faced. Then she wanted to understand why clubs may differ in both the rankings of these individual priorities and in the specific ones included.

Collecting Background Information

One challenge Jones faced was the lack of published financial information on individual clubs. Most clubs did not publicly report detailed financial information. Forbes'[6] estimated 2002 revenues for the 32 NFL clubs ranged from $227 million for the Washington Redskins (1st) to $126 million for the Arizona Cardinals (32nd)—the Houston Texans had estimated revenues of $193 million (3rd) and San Francisco 49ers $142 million (22nd). The Forbes estimate of 2002 operating income ranged from $87.8 million for the Washington Redskins (1st) to $0.4 million for Atlanta Falcons (32nd)—Houston Texans was $47.8 million (5th), San Francisco 49ers was $16.0 million (24th) and Arizona Cardinals was $12.8 million (28th). Forbes' 2003 club valuations ranged from $952 million for Washington Redskins (1st) to $505 million for the Arizona Cardinals (32nd)—Houston Texans 2003 value was $791 million (3rd) and San Francisco 49ers was $568 million (24th). Exhibit 1 offers comparable local market data such as market size, population, and number of other professional sports teams in the market for each of the three clubs.

Jones gathered information from public sources such as newspapers, magazines, and the Internet. She was well aware that these sources might not be complete or timely. Indeed, one of her own challenges was that some information in public sources she examined was wrong but not corrected by the clubs. Her sense was that some of the data in Exhibit 1 is approximate at best.

Another challenge facing Jones was that the ranking of business management priorities was a function of the chosen objective. Clubs appeared to differ on what was their primary objective(s). She decided she would initially consider separate rankings of business management

EXHIBIT 1   LOCAL MARKET INFORMATION

	Arizona Cardinals			Houston Texans			San Francisco 49ers		
Market Size	15			7			4		
Population*	2,718,300			4,055,300			5,951,800		
Other Teams									
NFL							Oakland Raiders		
MLB	AZ Diamondbacks			Houston Astros			San Francisco Giants		
MLB							Oakland Athletics		
NBA	Phoenix Suns			Houston Rockets			Golden State Warriors		
NHL	Phoenix Coyotes						San Jose Sharks		
Record**	Win	-	Loss	Win	-	Loss	Win	-	Loss
2003	4	-	12	5	-	11	7	-	9
2002	5	-	11	2	-	14	10	-	6
2001	7	-	9	N/A			12	-	4
2000	3	-	13	N/A			6	-	10
1999	6	-	10	N/A			4	-	12
1998	9	-	7	N/A			12	-	4
Stadium—Year Built	New Construction To Be Ready for 2006 Season			2002			1960		

*Source: Arbitron. Market Ranks: Fall 2002. Metro P12+ Population.

**Source: NFL.com, Past NFL Standings.

priorities for several possible objectives (including club winning-on-the-field; club being financially successful; and, club enhancing fan support and loyalty).

Arizona Cardinals

The Arizona Cardinals are owned by William Bidwill. Bidwill has been associated with sports management since his youth. His father was a "prominent Chicago sports figure and member of the Pro Football Hall of Fame . . . and purchased the team in 1932."[7] The club has been owned and operated by the Bidwill family since then and William became the sole owner in 1972.[8] Although the official website indicates there are several Vice Presidents within the organization, it appears that Michael Bidwill is overseeing the day to day management of the team with Rod Graves and Ron Minegar primarily responsible for the football and business operations, respectively, of the club.[9]

The Cardinals moved from St. Louis to Phoenix, Arizona in 1988. They were immediately faced with several challenges. They were promised a new stadium when they left St. Louis but it took 13 years and significant political maneuvering to get approval for one. "They weren't winners (and) . . . they fell victim to another Arizona phenomenon—the displaced fan."[10] While in St. Louis, the team won the NFC East Division Championship in 1974 and 1975 but for the majority of the years, the team had a losing record. Since moving to the Phoenix area, the Cardinals have struggled and only produced one winning season after being in Arizona for sixteen years.[11]

The management team has spent 13 years trying to get a new stadium funded with public and private money. The public passed Proposition 302 in November 2000, which initiated the steps for a public revenue stream to support a new multi-purpose stadium in Glendale,

Arizona. However, a series of judicial actions delayed progress for nearly two years. The Tourism and Sports Authority (TSA) and the Cardinals broke ground on a new stadium on March 18, 2003. The Cardinals will first play there at the start of the 2006 NFL season. The new stadium will have a total of 63,000 permanent seats including the 88 luxury suites, and 7,000 club seats.[12] The capacity can be expanded to 73,000.

In an interview on ESPN, Michael Bidwill, Vice President and General Counsel, states that the lack of revenue directly affects the management's ability to put together a winning team. He attributes the lack of revenue to not having a new stadium.

> *"That's what this is about. It's about winning. It's about getting good players on the field and getting good players on the team and going out and competing for those in the free agency market and retaining our own quality free agents. And that, as you see, takes big signing bonuses, which are generated by the revenues off of these stadiums."*[13]

In 2003, Forbes estimated Cardinal revenues to be $126 million (32nd out of 32), operating income to be $12.8 million (28th), and valuation to be $505 million (32nd).[14] The club has struggled to create significant interest in game attendance. The team played at Sun Devil Stadium which has a capacity of 73,014 seats, 68 luxury suites, and 5,000 Club Seats. But the average attendance, in 2002, was only 40,910, or 56%, the lowest number of seats sold and lowest sellout percentage in the league.[15] The low attendance figures translate into low revenue from concessions and parking. The current stadium is owned by Arizona State University and there are no naming rights associated with it.

The City of Glendale created a presentation where they stated they believed the new stadium should provide financial benefits to the region, stimulate economic and job growth regionally, promote positive fan experiences, create positive national exposure from a dual point sports and entertainment destination with the adjacent Coyotes Arena, and provide a venue for youth sports and non-football and cultural activities.[16]

In the same ESPN program, Andrew Zimbalist, Sports Economist, Smith College, drew a very different conclusion. He states "there's no evidence . . . that new facilities bring economic growth to an area."[17] He continues to counter Bidwill's belief that a new stadium will generate incremental operating income and improve the team's performance on the field. He notes that there is a disproportionate percentage of the Phoenix population that are "displaced northerners . . . (and) are fans of northern teams."[18] Passion and loyalty for one's local sports are often developed in the formative years, early in life. Prior to 1988, Arizona did not have a professional football team so those adults that grew up in Arizona and are still living there do not have strong ties to the local team. Dan Bickley, of The Arizona Republic, is of similar opinion: "Arizonans have long been castigated for a general lack of passion toward their athletic teams. There is great negative energy within our midst."[19] Natives to Arizona do not necessary have strong, emotional ties to the Cardinals so demand for tickets may be lower and corporate sponsorship dollars may get diluted from multiple new stadiums in Phoenix and multiple sports teams.

The 2003 Season continued the on-field struggles of the Cardinals, ending with a 4–12 record. After the Cardinals suffered their 12th consecutive road loss, Head Coach Dave McGinnis was quoted as saying, "I'm in shock." In January 2004, the Cardinals named Dennis Green as their new Head Coach under a five-year contract. Green came with a strong winning record, including 10 seasons with the Minnesota Vikings—1992–2001 with a 101–70 (0.591) record.

Houston Texans

The Houston Texans' ownership group is led by Robert McNair. McNair was primarily in the energy business. He founded Cogen Technologies, the largest privately owned cogeneration company in the world, which was sold in 1999. In addition to the Houston Texans, he is the senior executive, founder, and/or owner of The McNair Group, an investment portfolio group, Palmetto Partners, Ltd., a private investment company, the McNair Foundation, and Cogene Biotech Ventures, a biotechnology capital fund. McNair is ranked 149 on Forbes' 2002 list of richest Americans.

The Houston Texans are the most recent addition to the National Football League. McNair's quest to own a National Football League club really progressed after McNair's and Chuck Watson's efforts to bring an expansion hockey club to Houston was unsuccessful in 1997. McNair formed Houston NFL Holdings to bring an NFL club to Houston. On October 6, 1999, the NFL owners voted to award an NFL franchise to Houston NFL Holdings for $700 million. The first playing season for the club was the 2002 NFL season. Prior NFL history in the city was the Houston Oilers, who played there from 1960 to 1996. In 1997 the Oilers moved to Tennessee.

Being a new club, Houston NFL Holdings had much to do but the fun and excitement was just beginning. Within two years, the Houston Texans would be playing their first NFL game. The ownership group had to prioritize their tasks but also had to be able to handle working simultaneously toward multiple goals. They needed to assemble an on-field team, develop a brand, build a stadium, hire a management team, and more.

The 12 months following the NFL's announcement to award an expansion franchise to Houston were action packed. McNair's group hired a general manager, conducted market research to ascertain the team image and fan expectations, selected a team logo and team colors, broke ground on a new stadium, and sold the naming rights. The Houston Texans' official website indicates the milestones and timing on reaching each of these milestones.

Where do the Texans start?

The first significant hire by Houston NFL was Charley Casserly, Executive Vice President/General Manager. Casserly was general manager for the Washington Redskins and spent 20 years there. He left the Redskins in September 1999, shortly after Daniel Snyder acquired them. Casserly joined Houston NFL Holdings in January 2000, just 3 months after McNair knew he was getting an expansion team. McNair had to build a team and he needed someone with experience to assemble it.

Casserly needed to determine a strategy to build the team. Two recent NFL expansion teams, Carolina Panthers and Jacksonville Jaguars, both saw success in the early years. However, they took different approach. "The Texans' head coach is Dom Capers, who went through a similar process as the first head coach in Carolina in 1995. (Tampa Bay Buccaneers' Assistant General Manager John) Idzik thinks the NFL landscape, particularly as it applies to the salary cap, is different seven years later and will lead to a different strategy for Capers' team this time around. 'When Dom was at Carolina, they drafted a certain way and Jacksonville kind of went a different way—younger, less expensive,' said Idzik."[20] Carolina built through free agency and acquired high priced, experienced players and as the players got older, they were not able to sustain their success. Carolina recorded a 12–4 record and went to the NFC Championship game in their second season, 1996, but have not posted a winning record since then. The Jaguars also reached the playoffs in their second season and continued to reach the playoffs for the next three seasons. Their sustained success is attributed to growing through youth.

Casserly had the 2001 draft, the expansion draft, and free agency to acquire players and build a team in less than 2 year. The team signed their first players to contracts on December 29, 2001 and held their first off-season work out on March 25, 2002. This gave them less than 6 months to prepare for their first official game. Being an expansion team, they are perceived by some to be at an inherent disadvantage in developing a winning team:

> *"A team needs time to jell. Especially when the team's task requires a high level of collaboration among teammates, it is important to keep team composition stable long enough that teammates can learn not to work together and how to combine their efforts into a coherent whole . . . Researchers Berman, Down, and Hill analyzed the records of all teams in the NBA from 1980 to 1994, to see if there was a relationship between team performance and team members' 'shared experience,' based on the average length of time team members worked together. Berman and his colleagues found a significant effect: the more stable a team's membership was, the more likely the team would win."*[21]

The Pittsburgh Steelers in the 1970s won four Super Bowls within six years and won two in back to back years. They had superior offensive and defensive talent but also a group of players and a head coach that had played together during their dominant years: Lynn Swann, Terry Bradshaw, Franco Harris, John Stallworth, Mike Webster, Jack Ham, Mel Blount, Joe Greene, and Jack Lambert. "Free agency, coupled with a cap on salaries makes it nearly impossible to assemble a team of superstars and keep it together year after year," (New York Giants General Manager Ernie) Accorsi said. "The days are probably over when a Chick Noll could draft eight future Hall of Famers out of college and keep enough of them around to win six divisional crowns and four Super Bowls for the Steelers in the 1970s . . . 'It drives us crazy—you'd like to keep everybody, but you can't.'"[22]

In their first season (2002), the Texans posted a 2–14 record, including a debut home game win over the Dallas Cowboys. The Houston Press believed the team "exceeded expectations" in their first year. One journalist, however, noted they are "now officially on the hot seat to turn the still-raw Texans into a playoff contender, and I don't mean someday, off in the distant future, I mean now."[23] In their second season, Houston posted a 5–11 record. Running back Domanick Davis was named 2003 NFL Rookie of the Year. On February 1, 2004, Reliant Stadium hosted Super Bowl XXXVIII, in which New England defeated Carolina 32–29.

Creating a new brand takes time. Prior to the Texans, Houston had an NFL club, the Houston Oilers. However, the new club would not benefit from an association with the Oilers because the Oilers' owner, Bud Adams "was turning off so many fans in the Oilers' dying days."[24] The new club had to start from the beginning. One month after the league awarded Houston a club, McNair started forty focus groups to study the fan expectations and team image and introduced a "transition" logo until the official team name and logo were finalized. On September 6, 2001, they announced the team's name, logo, and colors. Fortunately, "football is king in Texas"[25] so establishing interest was not a challenge. Creating a passionate, loyal, fan base in a two years time was the challenge.

McNair is committed to running the Texans as a business and is seeking financial rewards. With a $700 million purchase price, the management team has a quite a task. Other than Charley Casserly, key players on the management team include Steve Patterson, Senior Vice President and Chief Development Officer, Scott Schwinger, Senior Vice President, Treasurer, and Chief Financial Officer, Suzie Thomas, Senior Vice President, General Counsel and Chief Administrative Officer, and Jamey Rootes, Senior Vice President and Chief Sales & Marketing Officer.[26] Patterson played the key role in ensuring the new stadium was built and ready for the Texans first game. Rootes then had the opportunity to generate revenue from naming rights, luxury suite sales, club seats, regular ticket sales, and corporate sponsorships. Within the first 12 months of club formation, the naming rights were sold for $300 million, a record deal.[27] The club has been able to sellout the entire 2002 and 2003 regular NFL seasons. It has many other fans on its paid wait list.[28] In 2003, Forbes estimated their revenues be $193 million (3rd out of 32), operating income to be $47.6 million (5th), and valuation to be $791 million (3rd).

San Francisco 49ers

The San Francisco 49ers are part of The DeBartolo Corporation's portfolio. Denise DeBartolo York serves as the Chairman.[29] The DeBartolo Corporation officially received full ownership of the club in 2001. However, she and her husband John York "took charge of the team in 1998"[30] from her brother Eddie DeBartolo Jr. The DeBartolo Corporation currently owns Louisiana Downs, a thoroughbred racetrack, and has equity interest in computer software and healthcare ventures. The corporation evolved from The Edward J. DeBartolo Corporation (EJDC). EJDC generated significant wealth from shopping mall development and management.[31]

DeBartolo York acquired first hand experience in managing a professional sports team and working with leagues when EJDC owned the Pittsburgh Penguins professional hockey team. She served as President for three years, including the 1990–1991 NHL season when the Penguins won their first Stanley Cup and was instrumental in Pittsburgh hosting the NHL All-Star Game in 1990.[32] John York, Denise DeBartolo York's husband, serves as President, The DeBartolo Corporation, and "is the fundamental source providing oversight between the company's home office in Youngstown, OH and the 49ers in San Francisco."[33]

The 49ers have a rich history for developing great players and great success. The 1950s' teams produced Pro Football Hall of Famers Y.A. Tittle, Joe Perry, Hugh McElhenny, and John Henry Johnson.[34] After Eddie DeBartolo Jr. acquired the team in 1977 and brought in Bill Walsh as head coach, they produced "professional sports' winningest franchise over the next fifteen years."[35] The team proceeded to be the first team to win five Super Bowls. They share the most Super Bowl wins record with the Dallas Cowboys.[36] During DeBartolo Jr.'s tenure, the organization earned a reputation for class in the community with their extensive community outreach programs.

Big shoes to fill

With the ownership transfer from DeBartolo Jr. to DeBartolo York, the new management team would like to maintain the high level of on field success and positive brand image. However, the team's earlier success appeared to come at a cost. Eddie DeBartolo Jr. had a strong desire to win but earned a reputation for poor fiscal responsibility. Pro Football Weekly's Joel Buchsbaum said "the bottom line just didn't seem to matter to him as long as it was (enough) wins and (not too many losses.)[37] Allegations were made that the 49ers prior management, in the late 1990s, violated the salary cap provisions of the NFL Collective Bargaining Agreement. The NFL and the 49ers reached a settlement.[38] The settlement of the alleged salary cap violations put the team at a disadvantage because of the loss in draft picks in 2001 and 2002 and the financial obligations the team faced.[39] Despite these challenges, the 49ers reached the playoffs in both the 2001 and 2002 NFL seasons.

The current ownership is reputed to believe strongly in fiscal responsibility. To illustrate the point, a local San Francisco area columnist wrote they have "taken a solemn vow of fiscal responsibility."[40] To illustrate the point, they hired a general manager, Terry Donahue, who has "preached and delivered on his promises (of) fiscal responsibility."[41] Insiders have reported that previously the operating budget was never critical in operations. Developing and adhering to a budget and revised forecasts were not common practices within the 49ers organization prior to new management. With increased attention to financial matters, there is focus on revenue generation and operating expenses. In 2003, Forbes estimated their revenues to be $142 million (22nd out of 32), operating profit to be $16.00 million (24th), and valuation to be $568 million (24th). The club has been able to increase revenue through sponsorship sales and maintain a high level with their local pre-season television and radio rights. The team has had over 90% sellout every year except one year between 1993–2000.[42] In 2002, they averaged 69,734 fans per game, 97% sellout, but they do not have club seats at their stadium and only have 89 luxury suites to sell.[43] They increased their ticket prices from $50 to $58 per ticket in 2002. The 16% increase in ticket price places them 9th in average ticket price.[44] Unlike many clubs, the 49ers charge the same price for all seats in the stadium.

Getting a new stadium has been a high priority for the club for many years. Their current lease with the City of San Francisco extends through 2008.[45] In 1997, the public passed two referendums that would contribute up to $100 million to build an entertainment complex including a new stadium.[46] But costs escalating far above the original $325 million estimate caused the team to put the project on hold in 1998.[47] Another setback came when their naming rights agreement with 3Com ended in 2002 and then the City of San Francisco's Board of Supervisors made selling the naming rights to the city's public stadium even more difficult. The San Francisco Examiner and San Francisco Business Times published articles about the city's position and the impact their views would have on the ability to build a new stadium.

> *"The Board of Supervisors backhanded the San Francisco 49ers on Monday, rejecting a naming rights deal for Candlestick Park that would have brought in a fat paycheck for the team and The City's Rec and Parks Department. 'We do not need to prostitute ourselves at the feet of NFL franchises,' Supervisor Tony Hall said. 'It may not be a perfect stadium, but it's our Candlestick.'"[48]*

> *"The Board of Supervisors' refusal to hand off to the 49ers the right to sell Candlestick's naming rights — and a related move by Supervisor Matt*

Gonzalez to bar corporate monikers on city-owned structures—effectively blocks a new stadium ... 'Without naming rights, there cannot be a new stadium,' Harris (President, San Francisco 49ers) said." [49]

The importance of getting a new stadium has been evident for many years. Former 49ers President Larry Thrailkill had indicated in 1998 that they were interested in hiring "a top executive solely to oversee the stadium project." [50] The San Francisco Examiner reported, "The Niners have the absolute worst stadium in the NFL, bar none. They hired Peter Harris as team president . . . for the sole purpose of getting a stadium built. Unfortunately for their 49ers faithful, this subject has become dormant . . . Mr. Harris, from all accounts, appears to be a capable, nice man, but the red tape he is dealing with must be unbearable." [51] Six years later, in 2004, the 49ers still do not have a new stadium in the works. San Francisco Mayor Willie Brown believes "the Niners aren't focused on a stadium." [52]

The San Francisco 49ers cultivated an image of class and dignity during the 1980s and early 1990s. [53] The team was represented well by players such as Brent Jones, Ronnie Lott, Joe Montana, Steve Young, and many others. Maintaining a positive brand image is a day-to-day challenge. The club has faced multiple public relations issues in recent years including the departure of former head coach, Steve Mariucci, and the fines levied on Terrell Owens. General opinion was divided on the need and reason for Mariucci's firing but the common perception was that the ownership did not handle the firing well. The 49ers also had endured the public relations challenges caused by Terrell Owens' antics. He "is the guy who spiked the ball on the star in the middle of the field at Texas Stadium, infuriating the Dallas Cowboys two seasons ago. He did the Sharpie thing and grabbed pom-poms to join the cheerleaders after scores this season." The club was also involved with some controversy surrounding a derogatory remark running back Garrison Hearst made after a game about homosexuals. The "Hearst episode mushroomed into a national issue and a hot topic on talk shows." [54]

In 2003, Dennis Erickson succeeded Mariucci as Head Coach. He had been coach at Oregon State (1999–2002 with a 31–17 record). His prior NFL Head Coach experience was with Seattle Seahawks (1995–1998 with a 31–33 record). The 49ers went 7–9 for the 2003 season. In the post 2003 period, there were much publicized departures of well-known players, including:

- February 26th, 2004—released Derrick Deese (12 year veteran offensive linesman) and Garrison Hearst (11 year veteran running back).

- March 1st, 2004—released Jeff Garcia (quarterback).

- March 4th, 2004—traded Terrell Owens (wide receiver). Initially traded to Baltimore Ravens. Subsequently traded to Philadelphia Eagles.

Salary cap challenges were cited as a major factor in many of these decisions. General Manager Terry Donahue commented (March 24th) that:

"When I look back I believe the roughest part is behind us. It's traumatic losing our players. Traumatic losing Jeff Garcia, or Garrison (Hearst) or Tai (Streets) or Jason (Webster). Yet at the same time, we were able to keep some very promising, young players and we feel very good about that".

"We have a clear vision as to where we are going. It isn't easy to get there. There is a lot of criticism, second guessing and everybody thinks they know how to do it better. The reality of it is that we need to have the courage to

stay the course. We have a plan and we need to stick with the plan. We need to hang in there and finish it".

"We knew full well that when we made the decisions we made there was going to be some rough sea ahead. This was not going to be just a smooth sail. When we come out of it on the other end, we're going to be a healthier, much more stable organization. We're not going to have to deal constantly with what we've been dealing with since 1999. And we're very close to getting there."

Questions

1. Cindy Jones seeks your advice. She asks you to separately consider for each club the top three business management priorities for each of four possible objectives (three objectives she thinks may be important and a fourth additional one you think should also be considered):

   a. *Objective 1*: Club winning on the field

   b. *Objective 2*: Club being financially successful

   c. *Objective 3*: Club enhancing fan support and loyalty

   d. *Objective 4*: Your recommended additional objective

   What is your recommended additional objective? Explain how your four objectives might differ from each other. Explain your choice. Within the three teams considered, how might there be differences in objectives?

2. What factors should a team consider in determining the top three business management priorities for a given objective?

3. For each of the three teams and any three of the objectives (two of objectives 1, 2, and 3 and your objective 4), outline with justifications and explanations your three business management priorities. [Note: Some business management priorities may be the same entry across the teams.]

4. What conclusions can you draw about sports business management at the club level from your answers to the above questions?

CASE 3.2   COLORADO CRUSH AND THE ARENA FOOTBALL LEAGUE[55]

I was enormously impressed by the Colorado Crush. I think that this is arguably one of the strongest ownership groups in all of sports. You have got the NFL owner. You have got the NFL legend. You have got the landlord. They all work together to make this thing go. Yet despite that prestige as an ownership group, it's one of those situations where in each season in the Arena Football League it's just that your resume doesn't get it done.

— David Baker, Commissioner of the AFL, June 19, 2003.

The Arena Football League kicked-off before 8,257 spectators on February 26, 1987, with a showcase game between the Chicago Bruisers and the Miami Vise. The four-team league included the Chicago Bruisers, the Pittsburgh Gladiators, the Denver Dynamite and the Washington Commandos. In its inaugural season, average attendance was 11,279 per game and by the league's tenth anniversary, attendance had surpassed one million for the season.

Since 1987, the number of teams in the AFL has varied from four to nineteen, with sixteen participating in the 2003 season. In 2000, as an endorsement of the AFL's success, "arenafootball2" (af2) was created to serve smaller market cities. Fifteen teams played in af2's inaugural season and by 2003, the league had expanded to 28 teams.

A high scoring, fast paced game, arena football was played by squads of eight players competing on a 50-by-28 1/3-yard field surrounded by padded hockey boards. The games were typically played on converted fields in indoor basketball or hockey facilities. The average ticket price for an AFL game in 2003 was $22, compared to $50 for the National Football League (NFL). Contributing to the lower ticket price were the greatly reduced salaries of AFL players compared with those in the NFL. The typical AFL player earned $40,000 per year[56] compared to $1.1 million for the typical NFL player.

Players

AFL players and managers had a relatively harmonious relationship. In December 2002, the league signed a critical (from the league's perspective) 10-year collective bargaining agreement that included revenue sharing and a salary cap of $1.643 million per team.[57] The majority of the players were former Division 1 college/NFL players.

The AFL benefited from the NFL success of two of its former quarterbacks—Kurt Warner (St. Louis Rams) and Tommy Maddox (Pittsburg Steelers). Commissioner Baker commented on the myth that AFL players weren't as talented as their NFL counterparts in his State of the League speech. Baker said, "One of the great myths here is that these guys aren't that good as athletes. Kurt Warner said on NBC that the fact of the matter is [AFL players] are better athletes than I have seen in the NFL."

Commissioner Baker

In 1995, David Baker, a former real estate lawyer and politician, and the owner of the Anaheim Piranhas was attending his first owners meeting. He gave a passionate speech on civility. The next day AFL team owners voted him league president. Eighteen months later they recommended he become Commissioner. As Commissioner, one of Baker's first moves was to established the Fan's Bill of Rights. Two examples from the eleven rights are:

- We believe that every Fan is entitled to a total entertainment experience at an affordable cost for all members of the family from the time they arrive at the arena to the time they depart.

- We believe that every Fan is entitled to interact with and have access to players and coaches for autographs and conversation in recognition of their support at every game.

Shortly after he took over the post, Baker met with NFL commissioner Paul Tagliabue. Subsequent to that meeting, the NFL bylaws were changed so that no team owners could purchase an interest in another football team unless it was an arena club within that owner's NFL market. As a result of the new bylaw, over a three-year period, Baker was able to recruit NFL owners so that by 2003, nine NFL owners had stakes in AFL teams.[58] Baker also relocated teams to larger cities and deftly pushed out lightweight owners from the AFL's small market past. Under Baker's reign, NFL ownership and improved team capitalization raised the average franchise value from $400,000 in 1995 to $12 million in 2002[59], and several franchises relocated to larger cities.[60]

Baker was a firm believer in the possibility that the league could provide an enjoyable experience for both fans and players, while at the same time offering a good investment opportunity for owners. Baker commented:

> *[Professional sports can be perceived as] a bunch of greedy owners employing a bunch of spoiled, wealthy athletes, and the fan should be happy just to be in the building. Our goal is to be the most fan-friendly league in the world, and that's not totally altruistic, anyone who is good at business will tell you that pleasing the customer also benefits you as a company.*[61]

Under Baker's rein, power shifted from individual teams to the league's headquarters. Baker was well respected as Commissioner, and league owners welcomed the stronger Commissioner's Office.

NBC Contract

Perhaps the biggest victory in 2002 in the AFL was the contract the league announced with NBC in March. NBC decided to look to the AFL to fill a scheduling hole (around 90 hours of programming from January to June) created when the network lost its contract with the NBA. NBC looked at alternatives, including Formula 1 auto racing, lacrosse, tennis, and short-track speed skating, but executives were most interested in replacing the NBA with a regular sports series based on a new model—no upfront rights fee, cost certainty and long term exclusivity.

NBC's road to reorganizing its professional sports contracts started in 1998, when the network declined to bid $450 million a year for continued rights to its NFL package. In the summer of 2000, Major League Baseball officials proposed that NBC and Fox pay $300 million a year each to renew deals—triple what they were paying. NBC passed. The NBA was the last to fall. NBC had broadcast the league since 1990, but when losses reached $200 million for the 2001 season, the network offered around 20% less than it was paying when negotiations began that fall. As the negotiations began to stall, Cable TV moved in, along with ABC, and soon NBC was out of the NBA. NBC executives claimed that dropping the leagues avoided at least $1.5 billion in losses.[62]

Neal Pilson, President of Pilson Communications and former President of CBS Sports, negotiated the NBC contract on behalf of the AFL. Pilson recalled how the AFL took advantage of the NBA's departure:

> *The morning after the NBA left NBC, I was in [NBC Sports Chairman] Dick Ebersol's office. I told him I had a property that could fill the time periods occupied by the NBA. I had previously brought the Arena Football League to their attention but they had never expressed much interest. After losing the NBA, I think they saw Arena Football as an opportunity to program the time periods and maintain full employment for their staff. It was a revolutionary agreement.*

NBC offered the AFL a slot on the condition that the league waive a rights fee and grant NBC options to broadcast the games in perpetuity. Under the agreement, NBC would recoup the first $10.1 million in advertising revenues to cover its production and promotion costs, the next $3 million would go to the AFL, additional revenue would be split 50/50 between NBC and the AFL. AFL team owners also agreed to give NBC 5% of any proceeds exceeding $12 million that were acquired in the sale of a franchise.[63] NBC agreed to broadcast up to five games throughout the country, which for the most part, occurred between 3 pm and 6 pm on Sunday afternoons.

The NBC contract was undoubtedly a major coup for the AFL (two major owners purchased teams as a result of the news) but the AFL wasn't the only beneficiary. NBC was coming off a rocky five-year period during which it had lost rights to the NFL, MLB and the NBA, and an embarrassing venture in the XFL (which resulted in a $50 million loss). In defense of comparing the AFL and the XFL, Pilson commented, "The investment in the XFL was over $100 million. The AFL is nowhere near that level. And furthermore, the XFL was a true start-up, the AFL has been around for 18 years."[64]

As part of its contract with NBC, the AFL, which had been telecast on ESPN for all but two years of its existence, moved its season start from April to February to accommodate the network's schedule. Despite its recent troubles, NBC Sports President Ken Schanzer was optimistic on the eve of the AFL 2003 season opening weekend. Schanzer announced:

> *What we're doing this weekend is beginning to build a new sports property in American television. We intend to be patient as that product builds. We believe that an audience will come to this game. Every time there's been spring football, there's been an appetite for it. The XFL demonstrated that. If you have the right brand of football, there's going to be an audience for it.[65]*

The network broadcast 56 AFL games between February and June 2003. Both the AFL and NBC turned a small profit for the 2003 season, but ratings were relatively low, 1.5 to 2.0, despite modest ratings projections. For example, an AFL game competing with the LA Lakers v. San Antonio Spurs playoff game drew a rating of 0.9, while the basketball game drew a rating of 7.0 (one rating point = 1 million households).[66] Under the NBC agreement, if the AFL reached certain ratings and advertising triggers, the network would extend the two-year agreement to six.[67] By mid-April 2003, the AFL hired an outside PR firm to help boost awareness based on its ten-week average rating of 1.33, and a season low of 1.0 in late March.[68]

EXHIBIT 1   AFL 2002–2003 AVERAGE HOME GAME SEASON ATTENDANCE

Team	2002 Season Avg.	2003 Season Avg.	Arena Capacity %	2003/2002 Attendance Change % +/−
Colorado Crush	NA	17,427	101.3%	NA
Chicago Rush	9,301	13,898	86.9%	49.4%
San Jose SaberCats	13,493	13,532	96.4%	0.3%
Los Angeles Avengers	12,398	13,220	82.1%	6.6%
Arizona Rattlers	13,597	13,028	79.8%	−4.2%
Dallas Desperados	13,603	12,949	78.8%	−4.8%
Tampa Bay Storm	12,462	12,463	88.8%	0.0%
Orlando Predators	12,308	12,205	73.5%	−0.8%
Indiana Firebirds	10,086	11,623	72.4%	15.2%
New York Dragons	9,140	10,463	87.4%	14.5%
Las Vegas Gladiators	5,656	9,791	61.7%	73.1%
Grand Rapids Rampage	9,918	9,675	91.3%	−2.5%
Georgia Force	7,070	9,126	81.5%	29.1%
Detroit Fury	6,636	8,489	57.3%	27.9%
Buffalo Destroyers	7,251	7,622	41.3%	5.1%
Carolina Cobras	9,417	6,843	56.0%	−27.3%
AFL AVERAGE	**9,957**	**11,397**	**76.6%**	**14.5%**

Source: Published May 22, 2003 in *The Sports Business Daily*

Note: The AFL had 17 Sellouts in the 2003 season compared to four in 2002. The Colorado Crush recorded sellouts in all eight of their home games.

Despite its modest TV ratings, the 2003 AFL season was a success by other measures (see Exhibit 1). Attendance was up 14.5%, merchandise sales up 38%, and website traffic was up 88% relative to the 2002 season.[69] New high profile sponsors came on board for the 2003 season, including Gatorade and Nike.

During his "State of the AFL" speech delivered on June 19, 2003, Commissioner Baker took a long-term view with respect to the league's television ratings:

> Our interest is what our ratings are going to be in year 5. We think we had a great year in terms of integrity as a product and in terms of credibility as a broadcast. We have had 60 million people watch Arena Football this year. Now, for us, that is significantly more than a whole lot of other sports that have much more maturity on network television. This is the first year where we were on network television every week. Our advertisers all liked it. We lost one advertiser this year and it was a company that withdrew all of their advertising at the outbreak of the war.

During the speech, Baker emphasized his confidence in the league by mentioning plans for AFL's expansion. He announced:

> I anticipate that we'll have about two teams to add every year for the next three years. And that is significant expansion in addition to all of af2 expansion that has the potential to take place at a time when other leagues are contracting or not expanding at all. We have already got teams that are admitted for Nashville, Washington, and San Francisco, and all of

> *those are NFL owners that are already admitted and due to come on-line over the next couple of years. In addition to that, we're looking at markets like Boston, Columbus, St. Louis, Philadelphia, all of which have expressed an interest.*

According to the Sports Business Journal, the AFL was looking to expand its television presence by negotiating regional cable coverage in time for the 2005 season. The league was reported to be in talks with multiple carriers, including Fox Sports Net. Such a deal would enable the league to broadcast many more games than in the 2003 season and give the league an opportunity to promote its games on NBC.[70]

Investment considerations

While an owner of an NFL team can expect a guaranteed revenue stream of $130 million to $200 million, according to Pilson, "the owner of an AFL team has no guaranteed revenue stream at all." He continued, "There is a world of difference between AFL and NFL ownership." Ownership in the AFL, he explained, was based on asset appreciation. According to Pilson, "profitability" depends on the owner's expectations:

> *Ownership in any professional league is to some extent financially focused. The AFL is dealing with some teams losing in the area of $1.5 to $2 million, some are close to break-even, and a few are profitable. But if you were in the league eight years ago, when your team was worth $0.5 million, now you might expect to sell your team for $12 – 15 million, so you are willing to incur annual losses if your asset has appreciated over eight years to that extent.*

CRUSH HISTORY

In 2001, Commissioner Baker approached John Elway[71] about purchasing an AFL franchise in the Denver, Colorado market. Elway was intrigued by the league because of its player accessibility and its younger fan base, but he wasn't ready to invest. Stan Kroenke, who owned Denver's NHL team, the Colorado Avalanche, and its NBA team, the Denver Nuggets, as well as the 20,000 seat arena, the PepsiCenter, in which both teams played their home games, was also aware of the Denver franchise opportunity. Arena Football would add 8 to 9 events per year at the PepsiCenter during the regular season and possibly more with playoffs.

Michael Young[72], who had been working with Pat Bowlen, owner of the Denver Broncos on corporate partnerships and marketing, recalled the genesis of the unlikely partnership:

> *I was in an NFL marketing meeting listening to a presentation about competing products and the AFL caught my attention. Denver is an extremely strong sports market, one of the top three in the country. So if arena football is something that has an opportunity, there is no question it would do well in Denver. If somebody else brought a franchise to Denver, they could talk about how the AFL is more affordable and has more access to players, in contrast to the high and mighty NFL. I decided if there is going to be an AFL team in town, Pat Bowlen should have a hand in it in order to control the message.*

Bowlen agreed with Young's analysis but insisted on one condition. According to Young, Bowlen said, "the only way I'm going to do this is if John Elway is involved." When Young approached Elway a few days later, the timing couldn't have been better. Kroenke had recently stopped by Elway's office to let Elway know that he was seriously considering putting together an AFL team and he wanted Elway to be a part of it. Elway suggested that they all come together. Young, who represented the Bronco's interest, was initially uncomfortable with the idea. Kroenke Sports teams competed for marketing dollars and ticket sales with the Broncos. There was not animosity per se, but executives at the two organizations weren't exactly best friends either.

Structure of the Syndicate

Young described the formation of the partnership:

> After long discussions and a lot of research and salesmanship, we agreed on a formula where each partner put in equal amounts of money and each partner brought an asset to the table that could be measured, so that everyone contributed equally. Kroenke brought the PepsiCenter facility, the operational staff, and corporate sales. The Broncos brought our season ticket holder list, which is around 30,000 people, and our waiting list, which averages 12,000 to 13,000 people. The Broncos also brought the ability to market inside our games and on the team's website, as well as access to the Bronco's corporate sponsors and partners. Elway was the engine. He brought the sex appeal and a face to a faceless organization.

The three investors agreed to move forward and conducted due diligence in preparation of their investment. But after reviewing the final pro formas, everyone balked. The numbers predicted that the team would lose $2 million per year. The owner group had faith in the potential for an AFL team in Denver, but they realized that success was not entirely under their control—the league would have to build the AFL brand in order for their investment to make financial sense. The NBC deal was the missing link. Young recalled, "We heard about the NBC deal and thought, there it is, there are the millions of dollars that we need to brand the league to bring awareness to the league outside of the city of Denver. That's when we said, okay, we're back in."

On June 20, 2002, Kroenke, Elway, and Bowlen announced their purchase of the Denver AFL franchise. The trio took advantage of Commissioner Baker's limited time offer to NFL owners—act now and secure an AFL franchise for a guaranteed price of $4 million. Young commented, "David Baker is the reason why the AFL is still here. We exercised our option on his special deal. We were the first to take advantage of it. And we thought we'd make some people on the fence think that there was something to this offer."

The three owners shared a 33 1/3% stake in the franchise. As part of the purchase, the AFL granted Elway, Bowlen and Kroenke permission to launch an af2 franchise in Colorado Springs as early as 2004. For the 2003 season, Elway was President and Chief Executive Officer; Michael Young, Bowlen's owner representative, was Executive Vice President of Development; and Ron Sally[73], Kroenke's owner representative, was Chief Operating Officer. After the 2003 season, Sally was named President and Elway kept his title as CEO.

At the time of the announcement, Elway was quoted with an enthusiastic endorsement of the league's prospects. Elway said, "Only about 30% of people in the U.S. know what Arena Football is. I was talking to Ken Schanzer a few days ago and he said, 'I guarantee you that 90% of people will know what the Arena Football League is by the time we kickoff next year.' "[74]

The Market

With so many sports franchises in the Denver area, the Crush was looking to create a new market of sports fans rather than stealing market share from other teams. This plan was especially important to Kroenke, who in addition to the Avalanche, Nuggets, and Crush, had an ownership stake in the NLL CO Mammoth. Kroenke Sports President Don Elliman commented on the concern of over saturating the Denver market, "It forced us to think about the price point that we could charge. We were convinced that with both lacrosse and arena football, we'd be talking about a different fan base."[75]

NFL fans in the Denver market had to compete for limited and relatively expensive tickets to attend games. By bringing an AFL franchise to the market, the owners believed they were increasing accessibility for football fans. Market demographics were shifting and younger viewers, often referred to as "Generation Y," were not watching football on TV. Generation Y viewers were well suited for the AFL. The typical Generation Y viewer had a shorter attention span and a desire to see quicker, faster, and different types of entertainment. Sally commented, "When a 12-year-old kid goes to an NFL game, he or she may be bored. It's a long game and there are dozens of stoppages in play, particularly if the game is televised." The Crush viewed penetration into the Generation Y market as a means to build a loyal fan base for the AFL as well as increasing the long-term viability of the NFL.

Pre-season challenges

The NBC deal moved the 2003 season up by 75 days. For most teams, that meant fewer days for advanced ticket sales, but for Colorado, the shift meant that the owner group had six months between the time they announced their purchase and the team's first kickoff. Sally remembered learning about the accelerated season start:

> In August, the Commissioner gave us a good news/bad news message: the NBC deal is finalized (good news) and the season is going to start the first weekend in February (bad news). Consequently, our preparations for our inaugural season became a runaway freight train. At the time, we didn't have a name, a logo, uniforms, and more importantly, we didn't have a field, helmets, footballs, or players. During a speech around that time, I said, "all we have at this point to tell you guys is that we know we're going to play on February 2."

The team name was decided in a name-the-team contest, which received more than 9,000 entries. But every other decision for creating a team was up to the owners, and the clock was ticking. The idea was to leverage the resources of Kroenke Sports and the Denver Broncos' organization. Young recalled the challenges associated with that plan:

> We had all these resources available to us, but it doesn't help when you have to ask these people who have other jobs to drop everything because we have a

pressing timeline. We only had two full time Crush employees. Everybody else was a shared resource. It took a lot of charm, begging, and promises to get people to focus on us rather than the things they got paid to do.

In developing its logo and colors, Elway, Sally and Young wanted to present an edgy image, one that would appeal to Generation Y. They also wanted to use the colors of the teams that were involved in the ownership group—the Broncos, the Nuggets, and the Avalanche. Sally described the vision for the team's logo, "We wanted something that would be traditional but would have flash, be a little bit edgy, something that was easy to duplicate, not too busy, and clean." The team's logo and merchandise were very well received. The Crush earned two top ranks in its inaugural season—the first AFL team since 1995 to sell out every game and the highest merchandise sales for an expansion team.

On the field

The team played in Kroenke's PepsiCenter, which hosted more than 200 sporting events, concerts and special events every year. In addition to the Crush, the area was home to the Colorado Avalanche (NHL), the Denver Nuggets (NBA), and the Colorado Mammoth (National Lacrosse League, NLL). It was possible to have three of the four teams playing at home in the same week, and on rare occasions, two of the teams would play home games on the same day. The arena had different seating maps for each sport and a fifth map for concert events.

On the field, the Crush's 2003 inaugural season was disappointing. The team finished with a 2–14 record, and no wins at the PepsiCenter. However, it sold out crowds for every home game.[76] (See Exhibit 2.) When the season concluded, the Crush fired its head coach,

EXHIBIT 2   COLORADO CRUSH 2003 INAUGURAL SEASON SCHEDULE AND RESULTS

Date	Result	TV	Radio	Opponent
February				
Sun, Feb 2	L 40–44	NBC	AM-850	Georgia Force at home
Fri, Feb 7	L 55–57		AM-760	Grand Rapids Rampage at home
Sun, Feb 16	L 53–59	NBC	AM-760	Los Angeles Avengers at home
Sat, Feb 22	L 40–80		AM-760	San Jose SaberCats away
March				
Sun, Mar 2	W 38–35	NBC	AM-760	Indiana Firebirds away
Fri, Mar 7	L 55–73		AM-760	Dallas Desperados away
Sun, Mar 16	L 45–72	NBC	AM-760	Arizona Rattlers away
Sun, Mar 23	L 56–71		AM-760	Detroit Fury at home
Sun, Mar 30	L 52–61		AM-760	New York Dragons away
April				
Sat, Apr 5	L 34–68		AM-760	Las Vegas Gladiators away
Sun, Apr 13	L 58–76	NBC	AM-760	Chicago Rush at home
Sun, Apr 20	W 49–45	NBC	AM-760	Tampa Bay Storm away
Sun, Apr 27	L 49–65		AM-760	San Jose SaberCats at home
May				
Sun, May 4	L 42–48		AM-760	Orlando Predators at home
Sun, May 10	L 34–45		AM-760	Los Angeles Avengers away
Sun, May 18	L 48–59		AM-760	Arizona Rattlers at home

Bob Beers, who had been an NFL scout for many years with the Denver Broncos but had no prior experience with the AFL. Beers' two assistant coaches were also let go.

Sally explained, "We underestimated the sophistication and complexity of the game. We knew it was different, but we didn't recognize the depth of the differences. We believed that having exposure to an NFL team would translate very easily to the AFL, but we learned a very valuable lesson."

Young expanded on the differences between AFL and NFL football:

> We had a lot of NFL experience and we thought if anything, arena football should be a lot easier than NFL football. But the strategies and the game clock management in the AFL are three to four times more difficult than the NFL. There are more scenarios that can play out, from substitutions to offensive/defensive specialists, to all sorts of different things that can happen at the end of the game. That's where Beers fell short. It's not something you can learn in a year or two. We lost a lot of games because we didn't know how to manage the clock or we didn't know how to game strategize.

In July 2003, just months after firing Beers, the Crush announced Mike Dailey as its new head coach. Unlike Beers, Dailey had AFL experience as the head coach of the Indiana Firebirds, where he compiled a 63–46 overall record in seven seasons. Dailey led the Firebirds to five playoff appearances, three division championships and an ArenaBowl championship in 1999, when he also earned AFL Coach of the Year honors.[77]

Despite the team's 2–14 record, Commissioner Baker was optimistic about the Crush's long-term viability. When asked to comment on the Crush after his State of the AFL speech in 2003, Baker remarked, "If you look up winner in the dictionary, it's got John Elway's picture next to it. If the people in Denver can give them some time, there's going to be an ArenaBowl party in Colorado within the next 4–5 years."

Challenges Ahead

As of mid-January 2004, season ticket sales for the 2004 season were approximately 700 seats behind the pace of sales for the 2003 season. The team was planning to launch its major ad campaign to push ticket sales, which had held off until the Broncos' season concluded.

In addition to ticket sales, the Crush owners were keeping a watchful eye on ways to improve the NBC television ratings. The ownership group was appreciative of NBC for giving the league a national platform and believed that the network was instrumental in attracting NFL owners to AFL teams and thus was critical to enabling the longevity of the league. Some AFL observers however, felt that NBC could have done more to deliver the promotions on the network and outside of the network to drive viewers to NBC on Sunday afternoons.

Young was seeking ways to increase television exposure for the Crush beyond its NBC national broadcasts. He was on the verge of securing a deal with Comcast, which was starting a local basic cable channel, Channel 5, devoted entirely to local programming. Ideally, the local cable channel would cover every Crush game that was not being broadcast on NBC.

Pilson commented on the many challenges facing the Crush at the start of its second season:

> *The Crush will have to maintain the expectation that their games are fun and enjoyable. That should not be a problem. They also have to demonstrate a reasonable prospect for winning football games and this is harder to do in a very competitive league. The Crush survived a 2–14 record in year one because of the strength of everything else they did. A less capable management team would have had great difficulty in moving ahead to year two. But the Crush kept the loyalty of their fans, laid the groundwork for a more successful team in year two and the promise is there for significant improvement.*

Questions

1. What value attributes do the three parties in the Colorado Crush syndicate bring to the table?

2. What are the challenges facing the start-up management team of the new Denver AFL franchise in June 2002?

3. Evaluate the progress made by the Colorado Crush as of January 2004. What major challenges does it still face?

4. Evaluate the financial attractiveness of owning a franchise in the Arena Football League as of January 2004.

CASE 3.3 LIFE AS A MINOR LEAGUE CEO: FRANK BURKE AND THE CHATTANOOGA LOOKOUTS[78]

At 11 p.m. on August 30, 1997, Frank Burke, President and General Manager of the Southern League's Chattanooga Lookouts, sluggishly walked into his office at historic Engel Stadium. It was after a game in which the Memphis Chicks had defeated the Lookouts 5–1 in front of a capacity crowd of over 7,000 fans and the famous San Diego Chicken. Frank looked over at his padded wall, which originally had been part of the outfield wall at the former Fulton County Stadium in Atlanta, which was the home of the Atlanta Braves for 31 seasons ending in 1996. Almost reflexively, he leaped up and bounced against his prized possession, pretending to be an outfielder snaring a fly ball which should have cleared the wall for a home run. Reinvigorated, Frank was now ready for the last two games of the season.

As was typical for Burke, he had his hand in just about everything at the stadium except the actual game. After getting his office work done early, before the game, Frank had collected money in the parking lot and flipped hamburgers and hot dogs out in the left field picnic area. During the game he greeted fans and helped out in the concession stand. Frank had dutifully followed a similar routine during every home game of the season. Although their on-the-field record did not show it, the Lookouts thus far had experienced a very successful season.

Historical Background

Frank Burke

J. Frank Burke grew up in Detroit, Michigan, the son of a "serious baseball fan." His father, Daniel, earned an MBA from Harvard in 1955. Daniel spent the early years of his career with General Foods Corporation before venturing into broadcasting. He became President and Chief Operating Officer of Capital Cities Broadcasting in 1972. After a merger with the American Broadcasting Company (ABC Television), Burke remained as President and COO. In 1990, the elder Burke became President and Chief Executive Officer of Capital Cities/ABC. Just after his 1994 retirement, he fulfilled a long time dream with his purchase of an expansion franchise in the minor leagues; this franchise eventually became the Portland Sea Dogs of the AA Eastern League. The younger Burke reflected:

> In 1968, when I was seven years old, I went to 55 Detroit Tigers home games. The Tigers won the World Series that year in seven games. My dad was running WJR (the flagship station of the Tigers network) at the time. At the games, it was mostly myself, my dad, and my older brother. We got to sit in the press box.
>
> I remember four or five times when my older brother couldn't go. I had that two or three hours of my father's undivided attention. That's very hard to come by with a busy father.

After playing baseball at Middlebury College in Vermont, Frank took a job at ABC Sports. He was an assistant to the producer of ABC's Olympic Unit, working at both the 1984 Winter

Harvard Business School Case No 9-599-029. Copyright 1999 President and Fellows of Harvard College. All rights reserved. For information: permission@hbsp.harvard.edu. This case was prepared by Kirk A. Goldman and Stephen A. Greyser. HBS cases are developed solely for class discussion and do not necessarily illustrate effective or ineffective management.

Games in Sarajevo, Yugoslavia and the 1984 Summer Games in Los Angeles. After the Olympics, he worked on ABC productions of CFA College Football, Wide World of Sports, and the Professional Bowling Tour. In 1985, just after ABC's merger with Capital Cities, he left to pursue an MBA at Harvard. After his 1987 graduation, Burke joined General Mills. By 1990, he was the Marketing Manager of Children's Fruit Snacks. He stated:

> I was very frustrated at General Mills with the length of time it took to do things. I was working on a new product and they told me, "We can have this on the market in fifteen months." I said, "In fifteen months, who knows whether anyone will want it?"

In 1990, Burke left General Mills, and, with his wife Susan, purchased a group of radio stations in Maine.

> We bought the radio stations, which were a real struggle. However, they taught us a lot about small business. I really liked the immediacy of it. When we did something, we could see the change right away. Now, when I do something at the ballpark, or cause something to be done, I see the results of it very, very quickly.

Burke later said:

> My father told me, when I was at the radio station, that I was doing something he never had the nerve to do. He always worked for big companies. I really like making decisions and living with them. I found large corporations carefully designed to make sure I did not screw up too badly. It just was not for me. I never felt that I wanted my boss's job. I did not think he had enough responsibility.

In 1994, Burke decided on yet another career change. Frank and his father had tried to purchase the AAA Maine Guides during the Fall of 1986. Although this bid failed, he kept his hopes alive. He resumed the search for his own minor-league baseball team. In late 1994, Burke started selling off the radio stations and closed in on his purchase of the AA Chattanooga Lookouts.

> My father's team in Portland was off-the-charts successful. We knew that the level of success achieved in Portland would not likely happen in a second franchise. But, what we saw in Chattanooga was a place with a strong heritage and unbelievable amounts of potential, none of which was being realized.

Minor League Baseball and the Southern League

Minor League Baseball is made up of four primary levels—Rookie League, A, AA, and AAA.[79] The National Association of Professional Baseball Leagues oversees all of Minor League Baseball. NAPBL was formed in 1901, the same year as American League, to represent the interests of professional clubs that were not members of either the National or American

League. Burke proclaimed:

> *The difference between AA and AAA is much smaller than the difference*
> *between A and AA. AAA is more of a holding tank [for the major*
> *leagues]. AA is where they separate the prospects from the suspects.*

The AA level is made up of three leagues, the Texas, Eastern, and Southern Leagues. Originally established in 1885, the current incarnation of the Southern League started in 1964 as the successor to the AA South Atlantic League. The Southern League was the first minor league to use the three-umpire system (rather than two). Salaries typically are between $1,200 and $1,500 per month during the season. If a particular player is a "hot shot" or a veteran who can teach, he might earn $3,500 per month. Southern League players frequently jump directly to the Major Leagues, skipping the AAA level. Burke continued:

> *In AA, the travel is the hardest because they travel by bus. The cities have*
> *to be a certain size to support an AA franchise, so they tend to be further*
> *apart than are the cities in an A league. AAA is all airplane. Because A is*
> *smaller cities which are closer together, travel by bus is practical. We have a*
> *lot of restrictions on traveling. The team cannot play a night game after*
> *the players have traveled 200 miles. They cannot play the next day if they*
> *have traveled 500 miles. In fact, (NBA superstar) Michael Jordan bought*
> *a special bus for the Birmingham Barons during his year there so he did*
> *not have to sit so close to the guy in front of him.*

The Southern League's ten teams, located in five southern states, are organized in two five-team divisions. Each team plays a 140-game split season: 70 games per half. Each team plays a home and road series against every team in both halves of the season. If a game is rained out, then it must be made up in that homestand or during the next visit to the other team if it is within that half. Otherwise, it is not made up. First-half division winners play their division's second-half winners in a best-of-five series. (If one team wins both halves, it plays the team with the next best overall record.) The divisional playoff winners then meet in a best-of-five series for the league championship. (See **Exhibits 1** and **2** for information on the Southern League.)

EXHIBIT 1   MAJOR LEAGUE AFFILIATION AND STADIUM INFORMATION—SOUTHERN LEAGUE, 1998

Club	Affiliation	Stadium	Capacity
Birmingham Barons	Chicago White Sox	Hoover Metro	10,800
Carolina Mudcats	Pittsburgh Pirates	Five County	6,000
Chattanooga Lookouts	Cincinnati Reds	Joe Engel	7,500
Greenville Braves	Atlanta Braves	Greenville Municipal	7,027
Huntsville Stars	Oakland Athletics	Davis Municipal	10,000
Jacksonville Suns	Detroit Tigers	Wolfson Park	8,200
Knoxville Smokies	Toronto Blue Jays	Bill Meyer	6,412
West Tenn. Diamond Jaxx	Chicago Cubs	N/A	N/A
Orlando Rays	Seattle Mariners	Tinker Field	5,104
Mobile Bay Bears	San Diego Padres	Hank Aaron	6,000

Orlando, previously the Cubs affiliate, switched to the Mariners in 1998. The Cubs took over the former Memphis franchise, the Diamond Jaxx, in 1998.

Source: Chattanooga Lookouts

EXHIBIT 2   **1997 SOUTHERN LEAGUE ATTENDANCE FIGURES**

Club	Total Attendance	Openings	Average Attendance	1996 Attendance
Mobile, AL[a]	332,639	69	4,821	N/A
Birmingham, AL	302,144	68	4,443	296,131
Huntsville, AL	285,580	66	4,327	255,139
Carolina (Raleigh), NC	265,219	66	4,018	278,361
Greenville, SC	254,049	68	3,736	230,124
Chattanooga, TN	228,391	65	3,514	227,885
Jacksonville, FL	238,238	68	3,504	219,947
Orlando, FL	147,241	64	2,301	175,399
Knoxville, TN	138,389	66	2,097	142,537
Memphis, TN[b]	113,183	58	1,951	197,084

[a]The Mobile franchise played in Wilmington, NC in 1996.

[b]The Memphis franchise moved to Jackson, TN for the 1998 season because Memphis became an AAA expansion city.

Source: Chattanooga Lookouts

Chattanooga Lookouts

One of professional baseball's oldest teams, the Lookouts were founded in 1885. The Lookouts joined the Southern League at its inception for their inaugural year. The Lookouts got their name from Lookout Mountain, site of the Civil War "Battle Above the Clouds." In 1929, Engel Stadium, named after former Lookout owner Joe Engel, was built on East 3rd Street in Chattanooga. During his tenure, Engel used unique promotional events to draw fans. He once gave away a house at a Lookouts game. In 1931, Engel signed the first woman to a baseball contract; 17-year-old Jackie Mitchell appeared in one exhibition game against the Yankees.[80] For a time, the Lookouts shared Engel Stadium with a Negro League team, the Chattanooga Choo-Choos. National Baseball Hall of Fame members who played in Chattanooga include Kiki Cuyler, Clark Griffith, Burleigh Grimes, Rogers Hornsby, Ferguson Jenkins, Harmon Killebrew, Willie Mays, and Satchel Paige. (See **Exhibit 3** for a view of Engel Stadium.)

The franchise left the city of Chattanooga in the late 1960s due to floundering attendance. New owners moved a different franchise to Chattanooga to play in Engel Stadium in 1978. This team assumed the Lookouts' name. Since their return to Chattanooga, the Lookouts have had several different ownership groups. The owner who sold the team to Burke in 1995 was a real estate speculator from Chicago. He had sued the city and county over renovations to Engel Stadium in 1989. In addition to new box seats and a concessions concourse, the city had renovated the playing field. The wrong material had been used in the subsurface draining system, causing the field to flood whenever it rained. The owner won a $500,000 award, but lost local government support as a result.

The Purchase and Burke's Analysis of the Situation

On February 1, 1995, Frank and Daniel Burke, and Charles Eshbach announced their agreement to purchase the Chattanooga Lookouts. (Although the exact price was not announced, estimates were in the range of $3.5–4.5 million.) Many of the franchise's employees'

EXHIBIT 3   J<small>OE</small> E<small>NGEL</small> S<small>TADIUM</small>

paychecks bounced that same day, ending the tenure of the prior owner with a bang. On March 24, less than twenty days before the Lookouts' home opener, Burke and his partners closed on the purchase. He stated:

> *When we purchased the team, I knew that many of its operations were in disarray. Attendance figures had been a figment of the prior owner's imagination. Engel Stadium was dirty and a terrible place to watch a baseball game. Many suppliers refused to do business with the team. Finally, most promotional activity was based upon free tickets, giveaway items, and bartered media.*

Although he left the General Manager in place for the 1995 season, Burke saw several challenges he personally needed to undertake to turn the wayward franchise around.

Make the ballpark less forbidding. Engel Stadium was dirty, poorly lit, and out-of-date. Although the listed seating capacity was 7,500, in fact there were only 6,000 seats. Prior owners had done little to maintain what was left of the stadium. Poor relations with the city left neither side with an incentive to improve on the stadium's facilities. Burke improved concessions, occasionally serving hot dogs himself. He replaced the lights in the concourse so people could see the food they were buying. He added lights to the parking lot for safety. The Lookouts introduced two mascots, "Louie the Lookout" and "The Trash Monster." A shower was placed in centerfield as had been done at Wrigley Field (home of the Chicago Cubs) in order to cool fans off during the heat of the summer. Additionally, he added the now-famous Home Run Train, which emerges, smoke churning and whistle blaring, when Lookouts players hit home runs.

Reverse the team's negative credit problems. The prior owner had milked the team for cash, refused to pay bills, and continually bounced checks. Burke had to establish himself and the Lookouts as credible with both the city and suppliers. He set a positive precedent by paying over $150,000 for new stadium lights himself, which brought Engel Stadium back up to league standards. By fronting this money, Burke immediately became popular with the city and county governments. He also made himself a fixture at the ballpark, making sure people saw him as a "hands-on" owner.

Increase the entertainment value, not ticket prices. In Burke's view, previous management had cheapened the value of Lookouts tickets. As a result, Burke believed that he could not even consider a price hike. Instead, he made season tickets a bargain, emphasized the picnic areas which include food with the price of a ticket, and worked to make Engel Stadium a fun place to see a baseball game. Children had the opportunity to dump their garbage in the Trash Monster's belly and get autographs from Lookouts players before, after, and sometimes during games. Burke made it his mission to find out what the fans wanted and committed himself to giving it to them.

Communicate the changes to fans. Burke's impression was that prior to his ownership the Lookouts had a black eye in the community. Fans went to games to get something other than baseball. Players came to Chattanooga to be a step closer to the major leagues. Burke worked to connect personally with both the fans and the players. His face became so well known around Chattanooga that he won the 1997 King Bubba at the Bubba and Belle Ball, a local community service event.

Establish the value of product. The prior owner had given away so many tickets over the years that Burke believed they had lost their value and that people went to games only for the giveaways and promotional goods, not for the game itself. A baseball purist, Burke was eager to change this behavior. Between 1995 and 1996, he cut out 40,000 free tickets. He wanted to entertain his fans with the game and its atmosphere. He emphasized the picnic areas and added mascots, changing regular games into family events.

Making the Changes

Burke believed that prior ownership had built its fan base on the wrong principles. He stated:

> They believed in giving things away, and I believe that entertainment is what we give away. We still give stuff away, but we cut out all the things I was embarrassed about that first year. I never thought the people who came just for the cheap giveaways were there for the right reasons. They were not there to spend time with their families. They were not there to watch baseball. They were not there to enjoy a night out in the summer. They were there to get something cheap and meaningless and then turn around and leave.

Burke immediately started making changes during that first season. He watched and learned. For the second homestand, he added the lights in the concession area. For the third, lights were added to the parking lot because people said they felt unsafe. Burke commented, "People walked into the park [after the changes] saying that it was unbelievable." He continued:

> I even dressed up in the Trash Monster costume one night. The kids followed it around everywhere. I was stunned by how many of them asked me for my autograph. It was great.

"We put in a 21-foot long train that spouts real smoke. It comes out from behind a billboard and goes sixty feet down a track to celebrate homeruns and victories. It looks like a Disney ride," Burke proudly stated. Others suggested that Burke should have used the money from the train to pave the parking lot. "However," Burke said, "no one has ever not come to one of our games because the parking lot is not paved, but I can tell you that people have come to see that train." He continued:

> In 1996, I had two live camels living in centerfield. I built a pen out there and leased two camels from a man in Indiana. On opening day, the newspaper had a huge picture of these two camels coming across the bridge from the zoo to our ballpark. They had little Lookouts helmets strapped on. They were Larry and Lumpy and I still get calls. In 1997, we had a cannon. A man in a military outfit named "General Admission" rode out in a miniature tank. After the national anthem and whenever the train came out he fired the tank's cannon.

The Results

In 1997, tickets started to become valuable. Burke's rescinding of many free tickets in 1995 and 1996 had caused attendance to suffer. (Attendance fell from over 290,000 in both 1994 and 1995 to under 230,000 for 1996.) In 1997, the per game figures were up from the prior season by 4.9%. Burke commented, "We focused on things people wanted to see. We were up even though we had several rainouts, including three weekend games. (Rainouts do not necessarily get made up at home because of the Southern League's split season.) In 1996, we only had two rainouts total." (See **Exhibit 4** for information on the Lookouts' Ticket Prices and Attendance.)

At each game, Burke tries to do something special for the fans. He remembered:

> Once a game I grab a baseball and find a child sitting with a grandparent. That's my favorite. It is unbelievable. I once took a little boy down to the dugout between innings. We went down on the field, walked right past the dugout and waved to all the players and went right back up to his seat. His father stopped me on the way out and said: "That was incredible. You have changed my son's life."

> I like to tell people that we are not only developing the players of tomorrow, we are developing the fans of tomorrow. It is incumbent on us to make sure they have a good time. I don't think that the major league owners necessarily recognize that. They recognize that we develop the players. Our success is because we do things that they ought to do (better).

The Lookouts were affiliated with the Cincinnati Reds of the National League. The Reds' farm system comprised Indianapolis (AAA), Chattanooga (AA), Burlington Iowa (A), Charleston W. Virginia (A), and Billings Montana (Rookie). Burke worked very hard at making Chattanooga a good place for players to come. He believes in treating his players well and that, in return, the parent Reds will send him better players. Lookouts alumni with the

EXHIBIT 4   LOOKOUTS TICKET PRICES AND ATTENDANCE

Section	1995, 1996, and 1997 Prices	1998 Prices	# of seats
Boxes	$7 ($5)*	$7 ($5)*	1,650
General Admission	$4 ($2)*	$4 ($2)*	4,300
LF Picnic Area	$6.50–$8	$7–$8.50	1,100
RF Picnic Area	$14	$14	150
Season Tickets	$175–$250**	$175–$250**	N/A

*Children's prices

**After November 1, the price of season tickets was $250

Year	Dates	Total Attendance	Per Game Attendance	# of Season Tickets
1994	67	292,920	4,372	N/A
1995	70	290,002	4,143	780
1996	69	227,885	3,303	785
1997	65	228,391	3,514	812

Reds in 1997 or 1998 included Aaron Boone (2 years with Chattanooga), Pokey Reese (2 years), Reggie Sanders (1 year), and five others, one of whom (Deion Sanders) had been with the Lookouts on a rehabilitation assignment. Others included Bobby Ayala (Seattle), Erik Hanson (Toronto), Trevor Hoffman (San Diego), Mark Langston (Anaheim), Keith Lockhart (Atlanta), Edgar Martinez (Seattle), Dan Wilson (Seattle), and ten others.

Burke told a few stories about some of the players:

> [Cincinnati General Manager] Jim Bowden told me that there were three players on my team whom he tried to promote [to AAA] at the half. They said "If I am not going to play every day and it's not going to get me to the big leagues any faster, I'd rather stay here with Frank."

> Pete Rose, Jr. went up to AAA and he called Cincinnati and said "if I am not going to play every day, I really would like to go back with Frank." He is the fourth one this year (1997) who has said that. Bowden told me, "You're killing me because these guys do not want to leave." The players know that if they are not going to play every day in AAA and if they hit .350 in AA, they can get to the big leagues.

He continued:

> I flew one player's wife to the AA All-Star game to see him play. It cost $125 to get her there. This guy will do anything for us now. That is not a big expense to get a guy to do something for you. Most of these guys do not make any money in AA.

> I groveled to have Terry Pendleton do his rehabilitation assignment in Chattanooga out of spring training.[81] Pendleton turned his nose up and said he wanted to play in Indianapolis (the Reds' AAA affiliate). Jim Bowden said, "I'm sorry, I really thought I could get him to play there." So, when Reggie Sanders was sent down on a similar short-term basis, he asked Reggie to come to Chattanooga. Reggie came in and he and I laughed for an hour about everything. He had such a good time here (Chattanooga), that when he left I asked Reggie if he wanted to keep his jersey. He said, "I'd love my jersey." I said he could have it if would go rub it in Pendleton's face, because I know the guy in Indianapolis didn't give him anything. I heard that Reggie went around the locker room showing Pendleton what he got. Sanders, a guy making $3.5 million-a-year, was thrilled he got that jersey from his rehabilitation assignment.

> The players and I have had a lot of laughs in the dugouts during rain delays and everything else. As a result, they go to spring training the next year telling guys that they should play in Chattanooga. The Reds are very happy with the care we take of them and the environment we provide for them.

> We also communicate with everyone who makes their debut in the big leagues. Every time a guy goes to the big leagues from Chattanooga, there is a fax waiting for him on his first day in Cincinnati. They never forget that. We have a kid who played for us last year who is 6–3 with the Reds right now. We saw him two weeks ago and he said, "I loved your fax."

They need to know that we give a damn and that the people here in town (Chattanooga) give a damn. It is just good business for me. The players do not turn their backs on a kid when he is asking for an autograph. They never say no. We got rained out one Saturday at 6:30, right before a game. There were 2000 people in the park who weren't going to get to see a baseball game; some of them had driven a long way. I went into the clubhouse and asked if any of the players could sign autographs for me. They all got up. You cannot pay for that.

The Offseason

During the offseason, from mid-September through March, Burke and his entire full-time staff of eleven sell advertising and tickets. (See **Exhibit 5** for the Lookouts full-time staff.) Burke stated, "Every single person needs to sell during the winter." From the groundskeeper through the president and general manager (Burke), the Lookouts staff tries to sell advertisements on every stationary object in the stadium. For example, Burke commented that "the groundskeeper sells to the company that sells John Deere tractors." Advertising billboards are sold all over the outfield fence and on signage at the concessions stands and even inside the bathroom facilities. Advertising is also sold for the souvenir program and yearbook. The Lookouts sell single-night and promotional sponsorships, for example Coca-Cola Fireworks Night on the Fourth of July.

The team also gears efforts toward group and season ticket sales. Group Sales people solicit churches, Little Leagues, social groups, and local businesses to purchase blocks of seats in Engel Stadium's picnic areas. The Lookouts have had a longtime practice to offer season tickets at a discount in the early portion of the offseason. Many season ticket holders take advantage of this period to renew their seats. It also provides the team with enough money to get through much of the offseason. After the cut-off point of the offer, November 1, the Lookouts staff works to attract new season ticket holders. (Refer again to **Exhibit 4** for Ticket and Attendance Information.)

EXHIBIT 5   CHATTANOOGA LOOKOUTS FULL-TIME STAFF

1. President and General Manager
2. Assistant General Manager
3. Public Relations and Administration Manager
4. Marketing, Promotions, and Merchandise Manager
5. Ticket Manager
6. Concessions Manager
7. Director of Stadium Operations
8. Groundskeeper
9. Radio Broadcaster and Traveling Secretary
10. Group Sales Person
11. Group Sales Person

During the Season

12. Stadium Maintenance Person

Overall Economics

Off the field of play, Burke says that the Lookouts do not compare favorably with other minor league teams. Engel Stadium continually reminds Burke and his staff of its age. The financial attention it requires draws on the team's resources which Burke would rather use for beneficial fan-building activities.

The Lookouts' $2.0 million of 1998 revenue consisted of Concessions (34%), Advertising and Sales (33%), Season Tickets and Gate Receipts (15%), Picnics (12%) and Souvenirs (6%). Expenses of $2.0 million comprised salaries and Wages (24%), Team Expenses (9%), Concession Food (9%), Advertising (8%) and Promotion (5%), Maintenance (7%), Depreciation (5%), Sales Tax (5%), Printing (3%), Insurance (3%), Payroll Taxes (2%), Souvenir Supplies (2%), Utilities (2%), and Miscellaneous (16%). The latter included tele-marketing, postage, grounds, broadcasting, and stadium lease expenses, as well as 2.5% (of total expenses) for League dues and National Association (Minor League Baseball) dues. Promotion and advertising (13% of overall expenses) includes the cost of all sponsored give-aways, and also trades for in-stadium advertising; the non-cash trades are recorded on both the revenue and expense side.

Burke described the Lookouts overall financial picture:

> The overall financial picture for the Lookouts has improved a lot since we bought it in March of 1995. It is still not where we need it to be in order to make this an attractive investment for us. From a pure investment standpoint, we can sell it for a nice return right now. From an operating standpoint we still have a way to go to make it a good operating investment. The bottom line is that we need to draw better and we have to keep a very close eye on the expenses because of the maintenance required with the facility. I don't want to raise ticket prices because it would threaten the progress the Lookouts have been making.

He continued:

> From an operating standpoint, success is driven by the facility and how people respond to the various attractions we have in place. By the time the first pitch is thrown this is a fixed cost business. We have variable costs in food and souvenirs. The rest are fixed, whether it's just me in the ballpark or people actually come. While we are in this facility, the key is to continue to try to draw more people to it and manage our expenses carefully. Right now there is barely a positive cash flow, but it is not significant enough to make this a really attractive operating investment.

The Future for Frank Burke

The stadium issue was the primary obstacle facing Frank Burke and his Chattanooga Lookouts in 1998. Historic Engel Stadium was 68 years old and looking every bit its age. Although they had a relatively inexpensive lease of $26,000 per year, the Lookouts repeatedly lost revenue opportunities by continuing to play at Engel Stadium. Burke stated:

> Right now, my only return on investment will come when I sell the team. The Lookouts are not making a significant profit and will not in this facility. It might look as if we have a good lease, but everywhere I turn the maintenance expenses are rising. I think we have one of the worst deals in the minor leagues. The Lookouts could easily turn a profit in another stadium. That would not only alleviate operations headaches but would drive up revenues in three key areas—ticket sales, concessions, and souvenirs.

Burke desperately wanted a new stadium for the Lookouts in Chattanooga. He thought that the public had taken the franchise for granted for years. Although he has promised not to move the Lookouts, he needed to consider selling the team. If that occurred, a new owner would likely seek another market with a new facility where the team prospectively could flourish. Since taking ownership of the team, Burke had become a staple of life in Chattanooga. He did not want to change that. However, he knew that the stadium issue would make or break his ownership.

Burke and his Lookouts staff worked hard to turn games into viable family entertainment. He promised that the 1998 season would be no exception. Burke brought in an expert from McDonald's to perform a time and motion study at Engel Stadium in order to serve concessions faster. In addition, he expected the camels to return to centerfield. As for his future beyond the coming years, Burke declared:

> In ten years I actually see myself coming to games and watching my team play. The minor leagues, as they are currently constituted, are a much more intrinsically interesting and rewarding place to be than the major league level because of the difference that you can see in the people that come to your park.
>
> I make less than what most HBS graduates will start out at. However, we make enough to live very nicely and I buy more equity from my partners each season. Although there is no guarantee, I do know that if I continue to improve profitability, the team's value will go up. We could sell the franchise tomorrow for more than we paid for it, perhaps 20–30% more. That's really where the value is in it for me.

Burke concluded:

> For me it is a labor of love for baseball and small business. I consider myself an entrepreneur. I have stayed awake at nights thinking about things and have felt the incredible highs and lows. I think it is an opportunity to have a small business where you can create value both financially and emotionally. You can have a lot of fun at it too. The vast majority of people absolutely hate what they do and I love what I do. My office is a ballpark. That grandparent sitting with his child, having a good time at a fair price while I still make a good living is, to me, very rewarding. Money cannot buy that.

Questions

1. What is different about minor league baseball compared to major league baseball? What are the implications of these differences for management and especially for marketing and for the skills and personality to be successful in the minors?

2. How does the team make money? Identify the Lookouts' revenue streams (existing or potential). How can Frank Burke grow them? Can Burke leverage the Chattanooga Lookouts name outside Engel Stadium? Will these ideas translate into ticket sales?

3. Has Frank Burke conquered the challenges he listed? Why does Burke want to avoid a price increase, even if it is only by $1 per ticket?

4. Explain the reasons behind all of the fanfare associated with minor league baseball (e.g., the camels in the outfield, mascots, etc.). Is this necessary for a team to thrive? or to survive?

5. Teams in both the major and minor leagues use stadium giveaways to draw fans to the games. What are the benefits and drawbacks of this?

6. How would a new stadium help the Lookouts? If the city of Chattanooga ultimately decides not to build a new stadium for the Lookouts, what other options should Burke consider before selling the franchise?

7. How does Burke's treatment of the Lookouts players help the franchise in the long run—considering that a player spends only a couple of seasons at most in Chattanooga?

8. Based on your reading and knowledge about other minor league sports, what additional observations do you have about opportunities and management in the minor leagues?

Footnotes

[1] This section was written by George Foster.

[2] In some leagues, such as soccer and rugby, clubs may be owned by nonprofit community organizations. Here members elect a Board of Directors, who in turn make decisions about the management team, coach, and so on.

[3] Dallas Cowboys is the only other NFL club with five Super Bowl wins (1972, 1978, 1993, 1994, and 1996).

[4] K. Lynch. "Homophobic Remarks Yield Muted Response." *San Francisco Chronicle* (November 22, 2002).

[5] Jessamy Tang and George Foster prepared this case as the basis for class discussion rather than to illustrate either effective or ineffective handling of a situation.

[6] "Inside the Huddle." *Forbes* (2 September 2003).

[7] *Arizona Cardinals Team History Franchise Page.* Arizona Cardinals website: http://www.azcardinals.com/history/franchise.php (5 May 2003).

[8] *Arizona Cardinals Franchise William Bidwill Bio Page.* Arizona Cardinals website: http://www.azcardinals.com/team/staffdetails.php?sid=16 (5 May 2003).

9   *Arizona Cardinals Meet The Team Front Office Page.* Arizona Cardinals website: http://www.azcardinals.com/team/frontoffice.php (6 June 2003).

10 Emmert, Erik. 2001. *Arizona—Big League Sports Mecca?* Erik Emmert personal website: http://www.users.qwest.net/~yarnspnr/opinions/azsports/azsports.htm (5 May 2003).

11 *Arizona Cardinals Team History Year by Year Results Page.* Arizona Cardinals website: http://www.azcardinals.com/history/franchise.php (5 May 2003).

12 *Summary of Stadium Features Page.* City of Glendale website: http://www.ci.glendale.az.us/stadium/facilityfeatures.cfm (5 May 2003).

13 *ESPN.com Page 2.* "Outside the Lines: Desert Showdown, Broadcast of Sunday, November 5, 2000." ESPN.com (5 May 2003): http://sports.espngo.com/page2/tvlistings/show32transcript.html

14 "Inside the Huddle," *Forbes,* (2 September, 2002).

15 NFLPA, "NFL 2002: Franchise History and Values Stadium Data," September, 2002.

16 Glendales' Game Plan, Presented by the City of Glendale. August 8, 2002.

17 *ESPN.com Page 2.* "Outside the Lines: Desert Showdown, Broadcast of Sunday, November 5, 2000." ESPN.com (5 May 2003): http://sports.espngo.com/page2/tvlistings/show32transcript.html

18 *ESPN.com Page 2.* "Outside the Lines: Desert Showdown, Broadcast of Sunday, November 5, 2000." ESPN.com (5 May 2003): http://sports.espngo.com/page2/tvlistings/show32transcript.html

19 Bickley, Dan. "Negative Valley Fans Have Ideal Target in Cards." The Arizona Republic, May 4, 2003.

20 *A Tune Up for April.* Tampa Bay Buccaneers website: http://www.buccaneers.com/newsroom/newspage.asp?newsid=2048&backpage=archive (3 June 2003).

21 Katz, Nancy. "Sports Teams as a Model for Workplace Teams: Lessons and Liabilities." *Academy of Management Executive* Vol. 15, No. 3 (2001) p. 56.

22 Morgan, Jon. "No Dynasties, No Problem for the NFL." *Baltimore Sun* (13 January 2002).

23 Sweeney, Ric. "The Future is Yao." *HoustonProFootball.com Quick Slant Page* (22 November 2002). HoustonProFootball.com (1 May 2003): http://www.houstonprofootball.com/slant/slant33.html

24 Lopez, John P. "McNair Deserves Much Credit for Job Well Done." *Houston Chronicle* (23 December 2002).

25 Duarte, Joseph. "Just Like Players, Tailgaters Take Preseason to Hone Skills." *Houston Chronicle* (2 August 2002).

26 *Houston Texans Staff Directory Page.* Houston Texans website: http://www.houstontexans.com/team/index.cfm?page_type=dept&cont_id=86228 (1 May 2003).

27 Duarte, Joseph. "What's in a Name?" *Houston Chronicle* (15 August 2002).

28 Calculations based on data from *Houston Texans History Top Attendance Page:* http://www.houstontexans.com/facility/index.cfm?page_type=dept&cont_id=26702 and *Houston Texans Reliant Stadium Facts and Figures Page:* http://www.houstontexans.com/history/index.cfm?page_type=sub&cont_id=172109. Houston Texans website (6 June 2003).

29 *Denise DeBartolo York Page.* The San Francisco 49ers website: http://www.sf49ers.com/team/officebio.asp?frontofficeid=2 (5 May 2003).

30 *ESPN.com NFL Page: 49ers Fire Mariucci After Six Seasons* (15 January 2003). Updated 31 March 2003. ESPN.com (7 May 2003): http://espn.go.com/nfl/news/2003/0115/1493146.html

31 *The DeBartolo Corporation Page.* The San Francisco 49ers website: http://www.sf49ers.com/team/officebio.asp?frontofficeid=82 (5 May 2003).

32 *Denise DeBartolo York Page.* The San Francisco 49ers website: http://www.sf49ers.com/team/officebio.asp?frontofficeid=2 (5 May 2003).

33 *John York Page.* The San Francisco 49ers website: http://www.sf49ers.com/team/officebio.asp?frontofficeid=99 (5 May 2003).

34 *Hall of Fame Page.* The San Francisco 49ers website: http://www.sf49ers.com/history/hall.asp (6 May 2003).

35 *History Page.* The San Francisco 49ers website: http://www.sf49ers.com/history/default2.asp (6 May 2003).

36 *NFL Super Bowl History Most Wins Record Page.* NFL Super Bowl History website: http://www.nflsuperbowlhistory.com/games.htm#3 (6 May 2003).

[37] Buchsbaum, Joel. *The End of the Eddie DeBartolo Era with the 49ers* (21 March 2000). Pro Football Weekly website: http://archive.profootballweekly.com/content/archives/features_1999/spin_032100.asp (6 May 2003).

[38] "Press Release: NFL Announces Settlement in 49ers Salary Cap Case: NFL, NFLPA Agree to Added Penalties for Future Violators" NFLmedia.com 2 (December 2000).

[39] Ibid.

[40] Peterson, Gary. "They Could Have Done Worse." *Contra Costa Times* (12 Feb 2003).

[41] Mayhew, Sydney. "49ers offense slow out of the gate." (27 September 2002). *49erswebzone* (6 May 2003): http://www.49erswebzone.com/cgi-bin/cgiwrap/49.../commentary.cgi?action=print&num=18

[42] New 49ers Stadium at Candlestick Park Page (6 May 2003). http://www.sfo.com/~csuppes/NFL/SanFrancisco49ers/newindex.htm. Original Source: Team Marketing Report and MediaVentures.

[43] NFLPA, "NFL 2002: Franchise History and Values Stadium Data," September, 2002.

[44] *Sports Business Daily* (8 February 2002). Original source: *San Jose Mercury News* (8 February 2002).

[45] Leuty, Ron. "Stuck with the 'Stick" *San Francisco Business Times* (30 August 2002).

[46] Major League Sports Stadium/Arena Referendums, Appendix 2 to Sports Facilty Reports, Volume 2, Number 2, National Sports Law Institute of Marquette University Law School.

[47] "Ownership of 49ers Goes to York, Pledge Made for New Stadium." (5 August 1999), MediaVentures.

[48] Hampton, Adriel. "Stick's Renaming Downed." *San Francisco Examiner* (6 August 2002).

[49] Leuty, Ron. "Stuck with the 'Stick'" *San Francisco Business Times* (30 August 2002).

[50] Epstein, Edward. "Fourth-Down Conversion for Stadium 49ers Not for Sale, Won't Leave S.F." *San Francisco Chronicle* (19 September 1998).

[51] Gigantino, Artie. "LA would love 49ers." *San Francisco Examiner* (21 May 2002).

[52] Hampton, Adriel. "Brown Surveys Political Scene." *San Francisco Examiner* (20 February 2003).

[53] *San Francisco 49ers History Page.* Official San Francisco 49ers website: http://www.sf49ers.com/history/default2.asp (7 May 2003).

[54] Bruton, Mike. "Owner Says He Will Keep Having Fun," *Philadelphia Inquirer,* (31 January 2003; and Georgatos, Dennis. "Hearst Offers Apology." *The San Jose Mercury News* (23 November 2002).

[55] This case was written by Alicia Seiger under the supervision of George Foster.

[56] The highest paid earned $200,000 and the lowest paid earned just $24,000 for the 5-month season.

[57] The cap was to rise to a minimum of 2% in the 2004 season and 3% in 2005.

[58] NFL team owners do not get preference on AFL players from their own teams.

[59] Numbers are approximate.

[60] Layden, Tim. "Through the Roof?" *Sports Illustrated* (March 10, 2003).

[61] Silver, Michael. "No Small Achievement." *Sports Illustrated* (June 2, 2003).

[62] Fatsis, Stefan. "NBC Sports Maps a Future Without the Big Leagues." *Wall Street Journal* (January 31, 2003).

[63] *Sports Business Journal* (December 1–7, 2003) reported "NBC would be due $200,000 from each of the recent $16 million deals to put teams in Philadelphia and Austin, Texas."

[64] The XFL was slotted for prime time, which increased its ratings expectations.

[65] *Chicago Sun-Times* (January 21, 2003).

[66] *TIME Magazine* (July 2003).

[67] Though not confirmed, the ratings goal was reported to be 2.7 and the advertising trigger to be $30 million. Source: Pastor, Frank, *St. Pete Times* (January 29, 2003).

68 "With TV Ratings Down, AFL Hires PR Firm to Boost Awareness." *Sports Business Daily* (April 17, 2003).

69 *TIME Magazine*, Special "Inside Business" section (July 2003).

70 "Lombardo, J. "AFL Banks on Regional Cable to Increase Reach." *Sports Business Journal* (December 15–21, 2003).

71 John Elway, a dual football-baseball college athlete at Stanford University, played quarterback for the Denver Broncos from 1983 to 1998 and led the Broncos to two Super Bowl championships. He is the all-time winningest starting quarterback in the NFL, guiding the Broncos to a 148–82–1 record (0.643 win %).

72 Michael Young, played football and baseball at UCLA. His NFL career as a wide receiver included the Los Angeles Rams, Kansas City Chiefs, Philadelphia Eagles, and Denver Broncos. He was the Broncos' leading wide receiver in 1991. Young joined the Broncos' management ranks starting in 1995.

73 Ron Sally captained the Duke University college football team as a quarterback. He has a law degree from UCLA and worked in private-sector law firms before joining the Kroenke Sports management team.

74 *Colorado Springs Gazette* (June 20, 2002). As it turned out, NBC was not able to execute on all of the promotions the network had planned and, according to Young, only succeeded in raising awareness to approximately 50%.

75 "With The AFL and NLL Now in Town, Denver Still Not Crowded." *Sports Business Daily* (January 28, 2003).

76 On a more positive note, the Crush took two teams into overtime and beat the Tampa Bay Storm, which ultimately hosted ArenaBowl XVII.

77 "Crush Announces Mike Dailey as New Head Coach." http://www.coloradocrush.com.

78 Research Associate Kirk A. Goldman and Professor Stephen A. Greyser prepared this case. HBS cases are developed solely as the basis for class discussion. Cases are not intended to serve as endorsements, sources of primary data, or illustrations of effective or ineffective management.

79 There are also the Independent Leagues whose teams are not affiliated with major league franchises. They operate in a manner similar to the traditional minor leagues.

80 Major League Baseball web site (http://www.majorleaguebaseball.com).

81 In his fourteenth major league season, Pendleton played in 50 games with the Reds prior to his July 1997 release.

SECTION 4... Players/Athletes and Agents[1]

Key Issues

- Team sporting leagues differ in their reliance on "free market" versus structured constraints (such as salary maximums or minimums) on clubs or individuals as regards player salary determinations.

- In team sporting leagues with no salary cap, there is a positive correlation between total club payroll and on-field club success.

- Strikes and lockouts are one observable aspect of the negotiation framework through which player salaries and player freedom to move to other clubs are determined.

- Elite players are important business assets as well as on-field assets. They have the capability of increasing club revenue as well as improving on-field success.

- Player income from off-field activities can be enhanced by developing and promoting a profile ("individual player brand") that is sponsor friendly.

Cases

A thlete salaries have increased dramatically in the last 20 years. Endorsement payments for a small set of select players and ex-players also have reached levels previously not achieved. This section outlines key features that affect both the total revenue pool available to athletes and how that pool is divided among individual athletes.

Exhibit 4-1 documents the 1994–2003 growth in average payroll per club across the NFL, MLB, NBA, NHL, and EPL. Clearly, players have been able to share in the growth in

EXHIBIT 4-1 GROWTH IN AVERAGE CLUB PAYROLL ACROSS LEAGUES: 1994–2003 ($ MILLIONS AND £ MILLIONS)

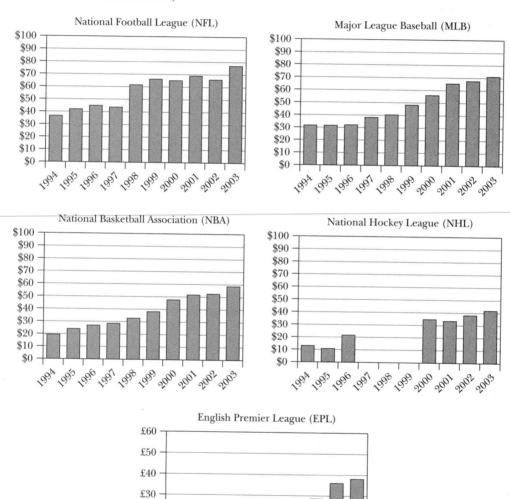

Source: Annual issues of *Forbes* and (up to 1997) *Financial World*, players' association data, and club documents; Deloitte, *Annual Review of Football Finance* (August 2004).

EXHIBIT 4-2   CLUB PAYROLL DIFFERENCES WITHIN EACH MAJOR LEAGUE: 2003 ($ MILLIONS AND £ MILLIONS)

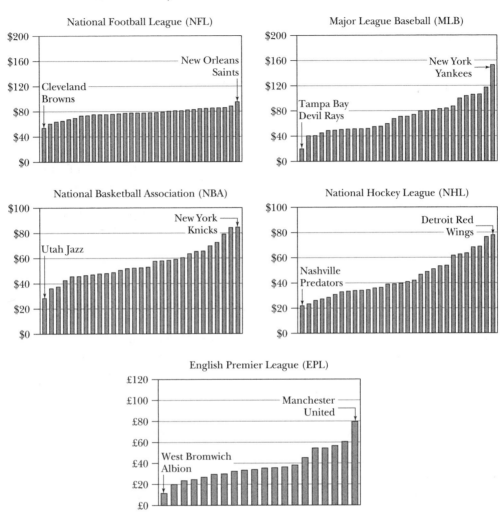

Source: Annual issues of *Forbes* and (up to 1997) *Financial World*, players' association data, and club documents; Deloitte, *Annual Review of Football Finance* (August 2004).

revenues that has occurred in these leagues. Exhibit 4-2 shows the distribution across clubs in each of the five leagues in 2003. The league with the tightest distribution across clubs in 2003 is the NFL (which has a hard salary cap).

Free Market Versus Agreed Salary Structure

There are fundamental differences across sporting leagues in how athlete compensation is determined. One approach is to allow the free market to operate on an individual player-by-player basis. In this case, there is no constraint on salaries at either the top or bottom end for each club or individual players. Soccer leagues in some countries come closest to this approach, for example, the English Premier League and the Spanish Primera Liga.

An alternative approach is to have an "agreed salary structure" that places constraints on salary payments. These constraints can operate at multiple levels:

League Level: This constraint is typically a formula that sets total player salary payments as a percentage of designated total league-related revenues. For example, total player salaries in the NBA are linked to a percentage of BRI (basketball-related income):

2001/2002	2002/2003	2003/2004	2004/2005
55%	55%	55%	57%

This revenue-sharing agreement is set out in the collective bargaining agreement (CBA) between the NBA and the NBA Player's Association.

The NFL and the NFL Player's Association have a revenue-sharing agreement that sets total player salaries at the following percentage of DGR (designated gross revenues):

2001	2002	2003	2004	2005	2006
63%	64%	64.25%	64.75%	65%	65%

In both the basketball and football agreements, there are agreed-upon definitions of what revenues fall into the BRI or DGR total revenue pools.

Club Level: Constraints on player salaries at the club level in some leagues are related to constraints agreed to at the league level. This is the case in both the NBA and the NFL. The NBA has what is called a soft salary cap—clubs can exceed the cap under certain conditions without penalties. The NFL has a hard salary cap—each club is given a set dollar salary cap for the coming season and cannot exceed it without severe penalties. In 2004, the cap was $80.6 million per club. There is also a minimum salary requirement for each club in the NFL ($67.3 million in 2004).

MLB has a salary tax model that sets constraints on individual club total salaries. MLB and the MLB Players' Association have agreed to a tax on clubs whose player payroll exceeds an agreed amount. For example, in 2003, MLB clubs had a $117 million salary threshold before they were taxed; clubs that exceeded $117 million were taxed at 15%. For 2003, the New York Yankees were the only club to be taxed—exceeding the $117 million by $67.540 million, they were taxed $11.82 million. Note that a salary tax penalizes but does not prevent a club from having a high player payroll. The MLB salary threshold for 2003 was $120.5 million, and is $128 million for 2005, and $136.5 million for 2006. A tax of up to 40% is levied on clubs exceeding the threshold in multiple years.[2]

Player Level: Minimum salaries for individual players are a frequent objective of player associations. For example, minimum salaries in the NBA are a function of years in the league:

Years in NBA	2001–2002	2002–2003	2003–2004	2004–2005
0	$ 332,817	$ 349,458	$ 366,931	$ 385,277
2	540,850	587,435	638,679	695,046
4	590,850	637,435	688,679	745,046
6	715,850	762,435	813,679	870,046
8	840,850	887,435	938,679	995,046
10+	1,000,000	1,030,000	1,070,000	1,100,000

Note that these minimums are unrelated to market forces for any specific player. A 10-year veteran player may be willing to play for much less than $1,100,000, but a club would be forced to pay the minimum. One consequence is that clubs have an incentive to replace veteran players with young players at an earlier stage vis-à-vis a system based on a free market.

Motivations for Player Salary Constraints/Caps

The motivations for departing from free market principles in the setting of player salaries include:

Promote Competitive Balance: Attempts to prevent one or several clubs from having payrolls multiple times those of other clubs in a league are often linked to competitive balance motivations. The evidence presented in the next section strongly supports the premise that in an unrestricted market, clubs with a higher payroll have a greater likelihood of on-field success.

Economic Viability of League: Having player salaries restricted to a level that ensures club profitability at the aggregate club level is one pillar on which league financial stability can be built. Whether this translates into individual club financial stability depends on other aspects of the league economic infrastructure. For example, the NFL combines the 64%–65% player salary/DGR revenue pillar with the largest league central revenue pool that is equally shared to create a league where there is widespread economic viability at the club level as well as the league level.

Promote a Broad Sharing by Players of the Total Revenues in a Sport: Having maximum and minimum salary levels for each team increases the likelihood that a broad set of players will receive sizable salaries vis-à-vis a free market system where one club can stockpile a small elite set of players by offering dramatically higher salaries than all other clubs.

On-Field Success and Club Player Payrolls

There is much support for the assumption that clubs with the highest payrolls have a higher likelihood of on-field success. This evidence is best collected from leagues where market forces are able to operate with minimal restrictions.

Exhibit 4-3 shows the correlation between the 5-year average club payroll and the 5-year average on-field season success (win/loss record in regular season for NFL, MLB, and NBA; season competition points in NHL and EPL). Correlations between club payroll and on-field success on a year-by-year basis as well as the 5-year averages are:

	1999	2000	2001	2002	2003	Average 1999–2003
NFL	−0.02	0.26	0.22	0.21	0.10	−0.05
MLB	0.74	0.43	0.32	0.47	0.43	0.48
NBA	0.59	0.37	0.13	0.42	0.24	0.47
NHL	0.54	0.68	0.69	0.56	0.30	0.66
EPL	0.67	0.86	0.70	0.88	0.73	0.93

The strongest positive correlations are for the EPL and NHL, whereas the NFL has no significant correlation.

EXHIBIT 4-3   CLUB PAYROLL AND ON-FIELD SUCCESS: AVERAGE 5-YEAR (1999–2003) PAYROLL
AND AVERAGE 5-YEAR WIN/LOSS % (OR POINTS) ($ MILLIONS AND £ MILLIONS)

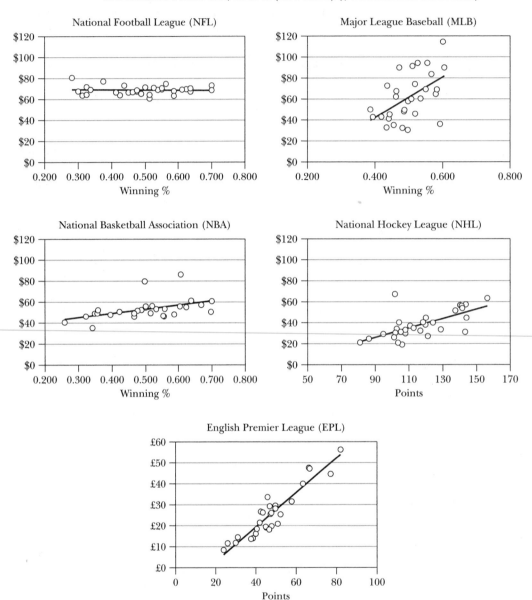

Source: Correlations run using data from Annual issues of *Forbes* and (up to 1997) *Financial World*, players' association data, and club documents.

The NFL's hard salary cap and other competitive balance parts of its infrastructure result in essentially zero correlation between 5-year average club payroll and 5-year average on-field success. Commentators widely credit the NFL as having the most "level competitive playing field" for its clubs. The other extreme is the EPL, which allows an open free market on salaries. Here, the correlation is 0.93. Many of the 20 clubs in the EPL at the start of their

38-game season have minimal chance of being the champion at season end. The NHL is the closest to the EPL in terms of players being able to contract without their being a salary cap on each club. It also has strong evidence of a positive association between the level of club payrolls and club success on the field.

Strikes and Lockouts

Players and owners in many sports have not always enjoyed harmonious relationships. Indeed, strikes and lockouts in professional sports are frequently cited examples in discussions of general labor negotiating history. A strike occurs when the players refuse to play under the conditions offered. A lockout occurs when the owners shut down operations on the pretext that the players will not agree to certain conditions the owners have offered them. Exhibit 4-4 shows a relatively comprehensive listing of strikes and lockouts in the NFL, MLB, NBA, and NHL since 1970. Major League Baseball is widely recognized as having a continued rocky (antagonistic) relationship between the player's union and club owners. The 1994–95 strike lasted more than 6 months and led to the cancellation of the World Series. Although there has been no subsequent strike in MLB, the two sides at the bargaining table continue to remain relatively militant and entrenched in their positions. At the other end of the spectrum is the NFL, where the league and the player's association have had an extended period of high cooperation over the last 15 years.

Player Contracting and Risk Sharing

Player contracts in different sports have different financial risk-sharing aspects. Several examples illustrate this aspect:

Guaranteed Contracts. Uncertainty exists about the future performance and future health of players. Who bears the risk of this uncertainty? The two main alternatives are:

(a) The club—in the MLB, contracts typically guarantee the base salary amounts for the length of the contract. Here the club rather than the player bears the risk for performance below expectation, or injury.

(b) The player—in the NFL, players receive their base salary amounts only as long as they remain on the active player list. Suppose a player signs a 5-year contract at $2 million a year. If, after year one, the club cuts the player from its playing squad, it is not obligated to make the $2 million-a-year payments for each of the remaining 4 years.

Up-Front Bonuses. Player contracts for highly demanded players often include an up-front bonus. This bonus is an especially important component when the player contracts are not guaranteed over the life of the contract. Consider Payton Manning's 7-year, $98 million contract with the Indianapolis Colts of the NFL. This 2004 contract had a $34.5 up-front bonus, which is not at risk to the player. Players' agents in the NFL attempt to increase the percentage of the player contract that is classified as a front-end bonus. The aim is to insulate the player as much as possible from the risk of performance below expectation, or injury.

EXHIBIT 4-4 STRIKES AND LOCKOUTS IN U.S. MAJOR SPORTING LEAGUES SINCE 1970

League	Year	Stoppage	Length	Games Lost	Main Issues
NFL	1970	Strike	2 Days	0	Minimum Salaries, Pensions, Health Benefits
	1974	Strike	40 Days	0	Free Agency, Minimum Salaries
	1982	Strike	57 Days	0	Percentage of Gross Proposal
	1987	Strike	24 Days	"Games Played with Substitutes"	Free Agency
MLB	1972	Strike	13 Days	86	Pensions
	1973	Lockout	17 Days	0	Salary Arbitration
	1976	Lockout	17 Days	0	Free Agency
	1980	Strike	8 Days	0	Free-Agent Compensation
	1981	Strike	50 Days	712	Free-Agent Compensation
	1985	Strike	2 Days	0	Salary Arbitration
	1990	Lockout	32 Days	0	Salary Arbitration and Salary Cap
	1994–95	Strike	232 Days	920	Salary Arbitration and Revenue Sharing
NBA	1998–99	Strike	191 Days	928	Salary Cap, Luxury Tax
NHL	1992	Strike	10 Days	Games Rescheduled	Free Agency, Arbitration, Pensions
	1994	Lockout	103 Days	468	Salary Cap, Luxury Tax, Free Agency

Sources: Compiled from multiple sources, including Staudohar, Paul D. "Baseball Negotiations: A New Agreement." *Monthly Labor Review* 125 (December, 2002): 15–22; NFLPA Playbook; http://www.bls.gov/opub/mlr/1999/04/art1full.pdf; http://www.cbc.ca/sports/indepth/cba/features/flashback.html; http://www.nflpa.org/aboutus/main.asp?subpage=history

Performance Bonuses. The Ricky Williams 1999 contract with the New Orleans Saints of the NFL illustrates the risk element of performance bonuses. The 7-year contract for the running back included an $8.84 million signing bonus and base salaries of between $175,000 and $400,000. If all the incentives had been met, Williams could have received $68.4 million. Some incentives related to on-field performance: "$1 million bonus for gaining 1,600 yards; $1.5 million bonus for 1,800 yards; $2 million for 2,000 yards; $2.5 million for 2,100; and $3 million for eclipsing the NFL single-season rushing record." Off-field incentives reflected a concern with Williams's possible behavior problems: "1.6 million in annual bonuses of $100,000 for doing such things as participating in off-season workouts and keeping his weight below 240 pounds."[3] This contract placed risk on Williams in the event he did not meet the milestones. Unfortunately, Williams did not meet as many of the milestones his agent believed to be within his reach. (As a follow-up, Ricky Williams subsequently transferred to the Miami dolphins. He walked out on the Dolphins just before the start of the 2004 season.)

Player contracting places a high premium on business acumen, whether from the player/player agent side or the club side. The escalating payments for elite athletes, the risks involved, and the increasing complexity of contracts makes this area of pivotal importance in the business of sports.

Player decisions are not just about financial issues. Exhibit 4-5 presents a list of 10 factors Bill Walsh recommends a player consider as regards possible retirement. Note the diverse mix of health, financial, and other factors included in this list.

EXHIBIT 4-5   THE PLAYER RETIREMENT DECISION: BILL WALSH'S PERSPECTIVE ON FACTORS FOR PLAYERS TO CONSIDER

1. Existing physical health. Ability to retain health if continuing to play.
2. Possible salary offer and potential ability and willingness of club to meet salary level desired by player.
3. Personal desire to continue playing. Is the thrill still there?
4. Ability to handle media pressure if continuing "old father time" comments.
5. Performance level. Is it declining? Is it competitive?
6. Desire of athlete. Go out on top? Stay on until cut?
7. Coaches'/Management's likely intentions to use athlete. Is a transition already being played out?
8. Future prospects for team. Player avoiding the "big regret" if team goes to top next year.
9. What postretirement career options are available to athlete. Personal fulfillment? Financial? Has athlete already been planning for next year?
10. Financial capacity of athlete to retire. Funds saved or invested (how secure)? Likely lifestyle demands for cash (himself, family, entourage)?
11. Agent and agent's ability to negotiate future deals.

Estimating the Value of Players

Estimating the financial value-add of a player is an important input in salary negotiations for new players. Consider the transfer of David Beckham from Manchester United to Real Madrid in June 2003. Beckham was near the end of his Manchester United contract. Under the Bosman rule, Beckham would be free to move to another club in 1 year without payment to Manchester United. By trading Beckham early, Manchester United would receive a transfer fee. That transfer fee was nominally listed at £24.25 million. It had three components:

- £5.25 million on completion of Beckham's transfer
- £12 million in installments over next 4 years
- £7 million based on Real Madrid's performance in Champions League (£875,000 every year they qualify; £875,000 every year they reach quarter finals)

The above transfer fee was from Real Madrid to Manchester United. In addition to these payments, Real Madrid would pay Beckham an annual player salary.

The revenue implications of Beckham playing at Real Madrid depend on factors such as the following:

1. Beckham's affect on on-field success. An increase in wins means a higher likelihood of winning the Spanish League and an increase in playing in the European Champions League. Winning The Champions league brings sizable additional television and trophy revenues.

2. Beckham's impact on attendance at home games. This will be affected by stadium capacity and the number of sellouts. The benefits of increased attendance include ticket revenue and concessions. If all games were sold out pre-Beckham, the upside here is limited. How Real Madrid gains from any attendance increases at away games is a function of the away game revenue-sharing formula.

3. Increased merchandising. Beckham's merchandising power was legendary, in part because of the media power of he and his wife Victoria Beckham ("Posh Spice"). More than 50% of Manchester United's 2002 sales worldwide were from his number 7 shirt.[4] Shirt number 7 was already taken at Real Madrid by Zinedine Zidane, the number one-rated skilled player in the world. Beckham took number 23 at Real Madrid. (It was no accident that this was Michael Jordan's number.) Real Madrid sold 8,000 Beckham replica shirts on Beckham's first day, beating the previous record of 2,000 when Ronaldo signed. By December 2003, sales had passed the million mark."[5] Even at a conservative £20 profit margin per shirt, 1 million shirt sales translates to a £20 million profit. This amount exceeds the £17.25 guaranteed part of the transfer fee!

4. Increased global brand power of Real Madrid. Beckham was one of the most globally recognized soccer players (despite not being ranked number one for his on-field performance). Real Madrid's current strategy is to further develop its global reach. The revenue implications here include game revenues from extra Asian and North American tours, extra merchandising, and more sponsors. Beckham was a superb additional asset in this strategy.

The above are some of the business considerations in Real Madrid's decision to bid for Beckham. The team aspect of soccer meant that relative salary levels vis-à-vis other soccer stars on the Real Madrid payroll also needed to be considered.

Player Agents

Most players/athletes are represented by agents in negotiations with clubs or tournaments and in endorsement-related dealings. The increasing acceptance of agents representing players is fueled by multiple factors. The financial stakes involved for players are large. Astute contracting can make an important contribution to a player's welfare. Contracts can involve complex options and clauses that have differing financial payoffs, risks, and taxation implications. Many players do not have the background to understand such complexity. For a small set of athletes, endorsement contracts provide the possibility of even greater payoffs. Agents can assist greatly in identifying and negotiating such contracts.

Players have multiple options regarding type of agent, including:

1. Large organizations, such as IMG, Assante, Octagon, and SFX. IMG, for example, has a broad set of athletes it represents and the capabilities to manage multiple aspects of a player's career, including on-field contracts, endorsements, personal appearances, financial planning, and media relations. IMG's beginnings were representing individual sports athletes (golf and tennis). It now includes athletes in multiple team sports as well as individual sports.

2. Small agent groups. An example is BDA Sports, which employs approximately 10 people in North America, and has a European office. BDA is led by Bill Duffy, and its clients include Yao Ming of the Houston Rockets.

3. Individual agent. One person represents a small set of athletes.

Player Endorsement Revenues

An important revenue source for a select set of athletes is player endorsements. Endorsement contracts with shoe and apparel companies and equipment companies are high-profile examples. By using athletes, such companies are seeking to achieve multiple purposes:

1. Drive higher revenues by attracting sales from people who positively identify with the chosen athlete.

2. Promote a distinctive brand image by selecting players with attributes that match or reinforce the desired image.

3. Use athletes to assist in new product development.

4. Use existing athlete endorsers to encourage other athletes to link up with the company.

Agents face the challenge of identifying the appropriate match between the athletes they represent and the potential companies that seek endorsement relationships. Consider Nike Inc. Exhibit 4-6 presents the magnitude of endorsement contracts of Nike each year of the 2002–04 period. As of May 2004, Nike had endorsement contracts of more than $1.7 billion! Exhibit 4-7 lists some factors that Nike finds attractive when identifying athletes of interest. Apart from the four generic purposes listed above, Nike seeks to achieve additional goals with its "athlete family," including helping serve the needs of serious athletes and assisting them to perform better, promoting athletes being change agents in their chosen sports, and promoting athletes becoming "heroes."

EXHIBIT 4-6 NIKE INC. ENDORSEMENT CONTRACTS ($ MILLIONS) AS DISCLOSED IN NIKE'S 10KS

	As of May 31, 2002	As of May 31, 2003	As of May 31, 2004
2003	$ 274.2		
2004	220.3	$ 338.6	
2005	166.1	292.1	$ 355.5
2006	135.5	247.2	322.7
2007	92.0	230.7	323.1
2008		129.1	208.6
2009			128.4
Thereafter	208.1	204.7	375.2
Total	$1,094.0	$1,442.4	$1,713.5

The amounts listed for endorsement contracts represent approximate amounts of base compensation and minimum guaranteed royalty fees we are obligated to pay athlete and sport team endorsers of our products. Actual payments under some contracts may be higher than the amounts listed as these contracts provide for bonuses to be paid to the endorsers based upon athletic achievements and/or royalties on product sales in future periods. Actual payments under some contracts may also be lower as a limited number of contracts include provision for reduced payments if athletic performance declines in future periods (2004, 10K, p. 23).

Source: Nike Inc., 10Ks.

EXHIBIT 4-7 WHAT ATTRACTS NIKE TO AN ATHLETE?

- Indications of greatness at early stage.
- Very highest tier performance over extended period.
- Successful on-field performance (and in team sports added provision of being on successful teams).
- Ability to transcend sports or attain celebrity status. Being on a broader radar screen.
- Ability to excite/enthuse viewers/fans by both on-field performance and off-field persona. Self-confidence? Pride? Guts? Attitude?
- Willingness to challenge existing tenets of sport or change agent.
- Athlete understands loyalty is a two-way street.
- Athlete is willing to take responsibility for own actions.

The *Sports Illustrated* list of the 2003 top American athletes with endorsement and appearance fees (and the percentage of total income from that source) were:

1. Tiger Woods $70.0 million (91.3%)
2. LeBron James $35.0 million (89.7%)
3. Andre Agassi $27.0 million (90.6%)
4. Lance Armstrong $16.5 million (97.3%)
5. Dale Earnhardt Jr. $15.0 million (67.9%)
6. Serena Williams $15.0 million (85.7%)
7. Phil Mickelson $14.0 million (88.5%)
8. Shaquille O'Neal $14.0 million (34.6%)

9. Venus Williams $14.0 million (92.6%)

10. Kobe Bryant $12.0 million (47.1%)

11. Jeff Gordon $12.0 million (64.4%)

The only two woman athletes on the top 50 list were Serena and Venus Williams. The top tier of the list was dominated by either individual-sport athletes (tennis, golf, cycling, and NASCAR drivers) or basketball players.

Athletes Behaving Badly: Athlete misbehavior stories are ever-present in all forms of the media. Exhibit 4-8 outlines a categorization relevant to decisions on who should respond to such stories and how best to do so. The categorization distinguishes between types of behavior issues, for example, legal violations (such as alleged rape or partner physical abuse); league-rule violations (such as use of performance supplements or gambling); club or coach rule violations (such as permitting women in hotel rooms the night before a game); and societal norm violations. Societal norms are a difficult area as they differ across segments of society. Moreover, athletes may have little respect for norms they do not believe in or those they feel restricted in adhering to. Responses from multiple parties to such misbehavior allegations may often be required. However, first and foremost, it is usually the role of the player to take responsibility for his or her own actions.

EXHIBIT 4-8   CATEGORIZING PLAYER BEHAVIOR ISSUES

Possible Responses		Possible Behavior Violations			
		Legal Violations	League Rule Violations	Club or Coach Rule/Edict Violations	Societal Norm Violations
	Player Involved Level				
	Agent of Player Involved Level				
	Other Player Level				
	Coach Level				
	Club/Team Level				
	Player's Association Level				
	League Level				
	Sponsor Company of Player Involved Level				

Case 4.1 A-Rod's Value Add: To the Rangers? To the Yankees?[6]

"I'm pretty excited. This is a big, big one . . . He'll be very big in New York"

— George Steinbrenner, owner of the New York Yankees

Introduction

On December 11, 2000, Alex Rodriguez (known to baseball fans as 'A-Rod'), the 25-year-old short stop for the Seattle Mariners, inked a deal that would send him to the Texas Rangers for a Major League record $252 million over 10 years. Although A-Rod was widely regarded as one of the best all-around player in the game—having already appeared in four All-Star games during his first seven seasons[7]—some commentators wondered whether his steep price tag was justified. Tom Hicks, owner of the last place Texas Rangers (the club finished 71–91 in the 2000 season) claimed that "Alex is the player we believe will allow this franchise to fulfill its dream of continuing on its path to becoming a World Series champion." Unfortunately for the Rangers, this prediction was not borne out. In 2004, eager to cut their losses, the Rangers traded A-Rod to the New York Yankees.

Although Rodriguez was unquestionably one of the best players in the game, some credited the blockbuster size of his contract to the savvy—and aggressive—negotiating style of his agent, Scott Boras. A former minor league baseball player himself, Boras represented much of the top talent in the game. Estimates of the total payroll of his clients for the 2004–05 season were in the neighborhood of $230 million.[8] Boras admittedly had no qualms about extracting as much as possible from baseball's owners for his clients. He defended this approach by claiming that "Big contracts are important . . . they create stars and bring people to the ballpark."[9] If this was the case, some felt that Boras outdid even himself with the Rodriguez deal.

EXHIBIT 1   ALEX RODRIGUEZ'S CAREER STATISTICS

Batting

Year	Team	Games Played	Batting Average	HR	RBI	Stolen Bases
1994	SEA	17	0.204	0	2	3
1995	SEA	48	0.232	5	19	4
1996	SEA	146	0.358	36	123	15
1997	SEA	141	0.300	23	84	29
1998	SEA	161	0.311	42	124	46
1999	SEA	129	0.285	42	111	21
2000	SEA	148	0.316	41	132	15
2001	TEX	162	0.318	52	135	18
2002	TEX	162	0.300	57	142	9
2003	TEX	161	0.298	47	118	17

Source: http://sports.yahoo.com/mlb/players/5275

The Early Years

In 1994, the Seattle Mariners choose Rodriguez as the number one overall pick in the amateur baseball draft. A-Rod made his major league debut in 1995 at the age of 18, making him one of the youngest players ever. He showed flashes of brilliance during his first season with Seattle, and was awarded the starting short stop position in the following season. The 1996 season established A-Rod as one of the best young players in the game and he finished second in the MVP voting. He compiled impressive statistics, including a .358 batting average, 36 home runs, and 123 RBI's. Rodriguez was a stand-out player on a team that included superstars such as Ken Griffey Jr. and pitching ace Randy Johnson. When those two players were traded, A-Rod became the sole superstar on the team going into the 2000 season. He led the Mariners to the American League Championship Series ('ALCS') where they lost to the eventual World Series Champion New York Yankees.

After the 2000 season, A-Rod became a free agent.[10] He was heavily courted by a number of teams and indicated that he wanted to play for a team that was a legitimate World Series contender. This fueled speculation that he was headed for the 2000 World Series runner-up New York Mets. However, on December 11, 2000, Rodriguez announced that he was becoming a Texas Ranger after singing a record 10-year $252 million contract (see Exhibit 2). He later confided that Texas narrowly beat out the Atlanta Braves offer of $128 million over 7-years because Atlanta refused to include a no-trade clause which the deal with Texas would include.[11]

The Texas Rangers

A-Rod's first year in Texas—the 2001 season—was difficult, as he was playing in the shadow of his large contract. It seemed as if nothing short of an immediate turn-around would justify his large salary in the eyes of fans and commentators alike. Indeed, many felt that the money spent on A-Rod could have been better spent on bolstering the club's pitching which was frequently cited as the reason for the Ranger's absence from postseason play. Despite the scrutiny, A-Rod was productive in 2001 hitting a career high 52 homers and 135 RBI's. However the Rangers failed to improve from their 2000 performance and again finished last in the AL West. Texas failed to make any major off-season improvements before the next two seasons and, consequently, finished last in the AL West for both the 2002 and 2003 seasons.[12] This is despite the fact that A-Rod finished second and first in the MVP voting in 2002 and 2003, respectively.[13]

After the 2003 season, the Rangers' front office apparently decided that young talent was the best way to rebuild their club. Rodriguez and his contract didn't fit well into this game plan. The Rangers started shopping A-Rod around and in early December 2003, it looked as if the Rangers were on the verge of striking a deal with the perennial American League Championship contender Boston Red Sox.[14] A deal that would have sent All-Star outfielder Manny Ramirez to Texas in exchange for Rodriguez fell through. The players' association—in a rare move—vetoed the deal which they claimed cut A-Rod's salary as part of the contract restructuring. Rodriguez said that he stood by the players' association even though he agreed in principle to the trade.

EXHIBIT 2   A-Rod's December 2000 Contract with the Texas Rangers

Base Salary: $242 million			Signing Bonus: $10 million	
Year	**Salary**	**Amount Deferred**	**Payday**	**Amount**
2001	$21 million	$5 mill. (3% interest)	March 1, 2001	$1 million
2002	$21 million	$4 mill. (3% interest)	Dec. 1, 2001	$1 million
2003	$21 million	$3 mill. (3% interest)	March 1, 2002	$1 million
2004	$21 million	$3 mill. (3% interest)	Dec. 1, 2002	$1 million
2005	$25 million	$4 mill. (3% interest)	March 1, 2003	$1 million
2006	$25 million	$4 mill. (3% interest)	Dec. 1, 2003	$1 million
2007	$27 million	$4 mill. (3% interest)	March 1, 2004	$1 million
2008	$27 million	$3 mill. (3% interest)	Dec. 1, 2004	$1 million
2009	$27 million	$3 mill. (3% interest)	March 1, 2005	$1 million
2010	$27 million	$3 mill. (3% interest)	Dec. 1, 2005	$1 million

Award Bonuses

- League MVP: First time, $500,000; Second time, $1 million; Third time and after, $1.5 million. Second- through fifth-place finish, $200,000; Sixth- through 10th-place finish, $50,000

- All-Star Game selection: $100,000

- Most All-Star Votes in League: $100,000

- Baseball America, The Sporting News, AP, UPI, USA Today All-Star: $100,000

- Baseball America, The Sporting News, AP, UPI, USA Today MVP or Player of the Year: $100,000

- World Series MVP: $200,000

- League Championship Series MVP: $150,000

- Gold Glove: $100,000

- Silver Slugger: $100,000

Base Salary Clauses

- During the years 2001–04 Rodriguez's base compensation of $23 million (which includes $2 million in prorated signing bonus) shall be increased $2 million above the highest average annual value of any other shortstop in major league baseball.

- After the 2007 season, Rodriguez has the right to void seasons 2008–10 of the contract and become an unrestricted free agent.

- After the 2008 season, Rodriguez has the right to void the 2009 and 2010 seasons and become an unrestricted free agent, unless the team increases his '09 and '10 salaries by the greater of $5 million or $1 million above the then largest salary of any position player.

- The deal also includes a no trade provision that allows Rodriguez to veto any potential trade.

Source: http://sportsillustrated.cnn.com/baseball/mlb/news/2000/12/11/arod_terms/

The New York Yankees

On February 15, 2004, the Texas Rangers again shocked the baseball world by announcing a deal that would trade A-Rod—along with a large part of what remained on his contract—to the American League champion New York Yankees. Under the terms of the deal, the Rangers would reportedly pay roughly $67 million of the $179 remaining on A-Rod's contract over a period that would stretch into 2025 (see Exhibit 4). In return, the Rangers got All-Star second baseman Alfonso Soriano along with a player to be named. MLB Commissioner Bud Selig grudgingly approved the arrangement but warned other teams that deals involving such large cash payouts wouldn't become the norm under his watch.

Although other teams expressed interest in dealing for Rodriguez, he found himself playing in the famed Yankee pinstripes at the start of the 2004 season. In addition to playing in a new uniform, A-Rod also found himself playing in a new position—third base. The Yankees already had a superstar short stop in 26 year old Derek Jeter who was also the team's captain. Despite their lack of need for a player in the short stop position, the Yankees apparently viewed the deal with Texas as "too good to pass up" given that A-Rod was the reigning league MVP.

Under the deal, the Rangers will have paid nearly $140 million to A-Rod for his three seasons with the team—and three last place finishes! The deal freed up funds for the Rangers to acquire players to fill other holes in their lineup. For the Yankees, they gained yet another power hitter in a batting lineup already replete with sluggers such as Jeter, Gary Sheffield, and Bernie Williams. In addition, Rodriguez adds fielding at the third base position.

The Economics of A-Rod's Deal

A-Rod's December 2000 contract with the Rangers eclipsed the previous Major League record set by Ken Griffey Jr.'s 9-year, $116.5 million contract signed in February of 2000 that sent him from Seattle to the Cincinnati Reds. In fact, the average annual payment of $25 million dwarfed those of the next three largest contracts in baseball: Carlos Delgado of the Toronto Blue Jays, Roger Clemens of the New York Yankees, and Mike Hampton of the Colorado Rockies who made average annual salaries of $17,000,000, $15,450,000 and $15,125,000 per year, respectively. Many commentators questioned whether it was worth spending so much to fill the void in a single position on a team with many glaring weaknesses—most notably pitching. Some thought the money could be better spent to bring on utility players at a number of positions which would, in turn, have a greater impact on the team's performance.

Ranger's owner Tom Hicks disagreed with the critics and believed that A-Rod would be the new face of the Rangers for years to come. Hicks believed that Rodriguez would be an instant fan favorite—especially in the Latino-heavy Dallas-Fort Worth metropolitan area where the Ranger's play. This, he thought, would translate into increased merchandise and ticket sales, not to mention the potential for an increased payoff associated with post-season play. Indeed, financial disclosures place the post-season 2000 revenue of the two World Series competitors—the runner-up New York Yankees and the victorious Arizona Diamondbacks—at $16 million and $13 million, respectively. Even the league champion runners-up Seattle Mariners and Atlanta Braves earned roughly $2.65 million each from their postseason

EXHIBIT 3   **SELECT STATISTICS FOR RODRIGUEZ'S TEAMS**

	Year	Regular Season Record	Ballpark	Capacity	Average Attendance	Season Attendance	League Avg. Attendance	Player Salaries	Revenues	Valuation
Seattle Mariners	1992	64/98	Kingdome	59,166	20,387	1,651,367	2,268,524	29.0	45.4	86
	1993	82/80	Kingdome	59,166	25,341	2,052,638	2,380,955	35.3	50.7	80
	1994	49/63	Kingdome	59,166	19,718	1,104,206	1,728,728	22.0	27.4	76
	1995	79/66	Kingdome	59,166	22,665	1,643,203	1,811,356	34.8	36.7	92
	1996	85/76	Kingdome	59,166	33,837	2,723,850	2,122,721	44.3	57.6	107
	1997	90/72	Kingdome	59,166	39,410	3,192,237	2,234,523	45.7	89.8	251
	1998	76/85	Kingdome	59,166	32,938	2,651,511	2,298,169	52.0	81.3	236
	1999	79/83	Kingdome/SAFECO	59,166	35,999	2,915,908	2,286,874	44.4	111.6	290
	2000	91/71	SAFECO Field	46,621	35,983	3,148,317	2,262,557	64.1	138.3	332
	2001	116/46	SAFECO Field	46,621	43,362	3,512,326	2,346,071	74.7	166.0	373
	2002	93/69	SAFECO Field	46,621	43,710	3,540,482	2,207,891	94.0	167.0	385
	2003	93/69	SAFECO Field	46,621	40,351	3,268,509	2,191,745	99.0	169.0	396
Texas Rangers	1992	77/85	Arlington Stadium	43,521	27,139	2,198,231	2,268,524	30.2	66.2	106
	1993	86/76	Arlington Stadium	43,521	27,711	2,244,616	2,380,955	41.6	60.3	132
	1994	52/62	The Ballpark at Arlington	49,178	43,916	2,503,198	1,728,728	25.5	50.1	157
	1995	74/70	The Ballpark at Arlington	49,178	27,582	1,985,910	1,811,356	32.9	61.9	138
	1996	90/72	The Ballpark at Arlington	49,178	35,448	2,889,020	2,122,721	42.8	87.7	174
	1997	77/85	The Ballpark at Arlington	49,178	36,361	2,945,228	2,234,523	42.9	97.6	254
	1998	88/74	The Ballpark at Arlington	49,178	36,142	2,927,399	2,298,169	54.7	108.1	281
	1999	95/67	The Ballpark at Arlington	49,178	34,253	2,774,501	2,286,874	81.3	117.5	294
	2000	71/91	The Ballpark at Arlington	49,178	31,956	2,800,075	2,262,557	71.7	126.5	342
	2001	73/89	The Ballpark at Arlington	49,178	34,952	2,831,111	2,346,071	88.6	134.0	356
	2002	72/90	The Ballpark at Arlington	49,178	29,043	2,352,447	2,207,891	108.0	131.0	332
	2003	71/91	The Ballpark at Arlington	49,178	25,856	2,094,394	2,191,745	106.0	127.0	306

New York Yankees									
1992	78/86	Yankee Stadium	57,545	21,589	1,748,737	2,268,524	43.5	94.6	160
1993	88/74	Yankee Stadium	57,545	29,839	2,416,942	2,380,955	54.2	107.6	166
1994	70/43	Yankee Stadium	57,545	29,656	1,675,556	1,728,728	37.1	71.5	185
1995	79/65	Yankee Stadium	57,545	23,521	1,705,263	1,811,356	50.5	93.9	209
1996	92/70	Yankee Stadium	57,545	27,789	2,250,877	2,122,721	63	133.3	241
1997	96/66	Yankee Stadium	57,545	31,856	2,580,325	2,234,523	65.0	144.7	362
1998	114/48	Yankee Stadium	57,545	36,484	2,955,193	2,298,169	63.2	175.5	491
1999	98/64	Yankee Stadium	57,545	40,662	3,293,659	2,286,874	88.1	195.6	548
2000	87/74	Yankee Stadium	57,545	37,956	3,227,657	2,262,557	104.7	192.4	635
2001	95/65	Yankee Stadium	57,545	40,807	3,264,552	2,346,071	112.3	215.0	730
2002	103/58	Yankee Stadium	57,545	42,736	3,461,644	2,207,891	141.0	223.0	849
2003	101/61	Yankee Stadium	57,545	42,785	3,465,600	2,191,745	187.0	238.0	832

Sources: http://baseballreference.com/teams,
http://www.ballparks.com/baseball/american
Financial information from *Forbes* Magazine

EXHIBIT 4   A-Rod's February 2004 Contract with the New York Yankees

Team	Original Contract Texas		New Contract Texas	New York	
Signing Bonus	$ 10		$ 10	0	
Assignment Bonus	0		36	0	
2001	21	(5)	16	0	
2002	21	(4)	17	0	
2003	21	(3)	18	0	
2004	21	(3)	3	15	(1)
2005	25	(4)	6	15	(1)
2006	25	(4)	6	15	(1)
2007	27	(4)	7	16	(1)
2008	27	(3)	8	16	
2009	27	(3)	7	17	
2010	27	(3)	6	18	
Total	$ 252	(36)	$ 140$	112	(4)

Numbers in parentheses indicate deferred payments.

Signing Bonus

Paid in $1 million installments each March 1 and December 1 from 2001–2005.

Assignment Bonus

The $36 million in deferred money from the original contract is converted to an assignment bonus, guaranteeing the money against work stoppages. The interest rate on the deferred money will be lowered from the original 3% to 1.75% starting with the date of the trade, and the money will be paid each June 15 from 2016–2025 instead of 2011–2020.

  2016—$5 million plus accrued interest
  2017—$4 million plus accrued interest
  2018—$3 million plus accrued interest
  2019—$3 million plus accrued interest
  2020—$4 million plus accrued interest
  2021—$4 million plus accrued interest
  2022—$4 million plus accrued interest
  2023—$3 million plus accrued interest
  2024—$3 million plus accrued interest
  2025—$3 million plus accrued interest

New Deferred Money

The Yankees will defer $1 million annually from 2004–2007 without interest January 15, 2011.

New Provisions

Rodriguez gets a hotel suite for road games and he gets the right to link his personal Web site to the Yankees Web site.

Opt Out Provisions

Rodriguez may terminate the contract after 2007, 2008 or 2009 seasons.

Escalator Provisions

Team must increase salaries for 2009 and 2010 by the higher of $5 million or $1 million greater than the average annual value of the highest-paid non-pitcher's contract.

No Trade Clause

Rodriguez may not be traded without his permission.

Award Bonuses

Same as prior contract.

Source: http://www.usatoday.com/sports/baseball/mlbfs41.htm

performance. Most of this added revenue comes from television contracts and ticket sales, which go predominantly to the home team.

Unfortunately for the Rangers, things did not work out as planned and they—some might say hastily—decided to ship Rodriguez off to the Yankees. For the Yankees, from an on-the-field perspective, the acquisition of A-Rod meant adding yet another superstar to a team already filled with All Star caliber players. Statistically, this might translate into a few extra wins each year—wins that have become increasingly important for the Yankees over the last few years as the Boston Red Sox have typically given close chase in the race for the AL Pennant. In addition, the Yankees would seem to be a better fit for A-Rod since he has always made it clear that he wants to play for a World Series caliber team. The New York Yankees unquestionably offer him that opportunity. From an off-the-field perspective, A-Rod's value to New York is less certain. Although he is one of the most personable players in the game, the Yankees already have such a player with A-Rod's long-time friend, Derek Jeter. Further, it is unclear how many more seats yet another All Star player could fill in Yankee Stadium. Nevertheless, no one—including New York Yankee's owner George Steinbrenner—doubts that Rodriguez will have an impact on the Yankees one way or another.

Questions

1. Consider the Texas Rangers 2000 contract for A-Rod:
   a. Estimate the expected financial benefits of having A-Rod be a Texas Ranger. Outline your assumptions.
   b. Estimate the incremental costs of the Rangers signing A-Rod.
   c. What factors would you recommend the Rangers consider in deciding whether to offer A-Rod the 2000 contract?

2. Consider the New York Yankees 2004 contract for A-Rod:
   a. Estimate the financial benefits of having A-Rod be a Yankee. Outline your assumptions.
   b. Estimate the incremental costs of the Yankees signing A-Rod.
   c. What factors would you recommend the Yankees consider in deciding whether to offer A-Rod the 2004 contract?

3. What inferences can you draw from your answers to requirements 1 and 2?

CASE 4.2   SPORTS AGENTS: IS THERE A FIRM ADVANTAGE?[15]

"Without an agent to pave her way, [professional tennis player] Debbie endured months of missed opportunities, punctuated by exhaustion and bouts of illness and self-doubt."

—Karen Stabiner, *New York Times Magazine*, February 2, 1986[16]

Eighteen year old Vince Holmcrist had an important decision to make. He had just won the world's most prestigious junior tennis tournament, and was ready to turn professional. Not wanting to miss out on any potential opportunities (like Debbie above), he was eager to sign with an agent. Choosing such a representative, however, was a real dilemma for Vince. He had narrowed his choices to Bob Guterton, a longtime family friend who had in the past represented baseball players and boxers, and John Andrews, a young tennis agent at the sports management and marketing firm ProServ. Vince knew that it was to his advantage to sign while he was still hot. The question was: with whom?

The Agent's Role

For a professional athlete, choosing the right agent was of the utmost importance. At various times during the athlete's career the agent might act as business manager, financial advisor, lawyer, confidante, friend, coach, and even pseudo-parent. So, it was essential that the relationship be based on a high level of trust. Unfortunately, the sports landscape was littered with stories of unethical and corrupt agents who had bilked their clients (including such stars as Kareem Abdul-Jabbar and Wayne Gretzky) of millions of dollars.

The role of tennis agent was even more complex and demanding than the similar role in a team sport like football or baseball. The simple reason for this was that a tennis player (similar to a golfer or other individual sport athlete) did not have a team to rely on for everything from scheduling to coaching to equipment to travel arrangements. Rather, it typically became the tennis agent's responsibility to deal with many of these often mundane, yet essential, details.

The standard duties of a tennis agent could be broken down into two categories: client management and revenue generation. Client management typically entailed tennis-related tasks such as developing an appropriate playing schedule, obtaining "wild card" entries into events, and finding the right coach and trainer, and administrative functions such as travel, hotel and visa assistance, contract invoicing, equipment stocking and distribution, appearance schedule coordination, and bill paying. Revenue generation consisted mainly of racquet, shoe, and clothing endorsements, non-tennis endorsements (ranging from patch sponsorships to international advertising campaigns), and appearance fees for participating in tournaments and exhibitions. An agent was typically paid a small management fee plus a 20% commission on the revenue he generated. (Tennis players usually kept 100% of their tournament prize money.)

The Sports Marketing Firm

ProServ was one of three generally recognized major international sports marketing and management firms, along with Mark McCormack's International Management Group and

Harvard Business School Case No 9-599-038. Copyright 1999 President and Fellows of Harvard College. All rights reserved. For information: permission@hbsp.harvard.edu. This case was prepared by Brian Harris under the supervision of Stephen A. Greyser. HBS cases are developed solely for class discussion and do not necessarily illustrate effective or ineffective management.

Advantage International. Similarly to its competitors, it had grown from a core athlete representation business to a full-service sports company providing such diverse services as corporate consulting, television production and rights sales, licensing, event management and marketing, sponsorship sales, and the marketing of stadium naming rights. (Attached as **Exhibit 1** are excerpts from a ProServ newsletter that provide details on some of these areas.)

ProServ's approach to athlete representation was hands-on and all-encompassing. In addition to the traditional services provided by an agent, ProServ had an in-house public relations department, a travel agency on the premises, and agreements with two large financial and investment planning firms to provide tax planning, estate planning, and investment counseling for an additional fee. The firm currently represented around forty professional tennis players ranging from up-and-comers (as Holmcrist would be) to stars like Stefan Edberg.

The Decision

As Vince contemplated his decision, he worried about several things. Would he be a big priority at ProServ, or just another name in their stable? Could ProServ match the personal attention Guterton would provide? Did the fact that ProServ represented many top players provide leverage to negotiate better deals for him? Or, should he be concerned about potential conflicts of interest? Would he really benefit from ProServ's scope of businesses, and if so, how? How important was it that his agent have a real "expertise" in tennis? And finally and most importantly, how could he know whom to trust?

Questions

1. What are your views on the questions raised in the last paragraph of the case, especially from the athlete's perspective?

2. What are the issues and challenges raised by the breadth, and particularly the integration, of a sports management firm's activities?

EXHIBIT 1   EXCERPTS FROM THE PROSERV NEWSLETTER

EDITORIAL

THE NEW PROSERV
There's a lot new at ProServ
By Bill Allard

This is to introduce you to all that is new at ProServ and how we are characterized today: energetic, creative, service-driven, enterprising and, above all, customer and client focused.

Today's ProServ offers our clients new lines of business and services, highlighted by an extremely successful consulting division. Recent initiatives in licensing, sponsorship of the arts, and alliances with stadium developers, as well as event opportunities ranging from grassroots to collegiate to professional, in a variety of sports, are compelling evidence that there is a lot new at ProServ.

Moreover, ProServ's approach to doing business is strategically-based, intent on targeting or creating properties that work for our corporate clients, ones that meet the client's objectives. These properties are results-oriented and devised with one overriding objective — to build our clients' business.

Our first task, and one that the company undertakes for each client, is to listen — simple, but key to any successful initiative. Throughout this important step our focus is firmly fixed on the client's objectives, targets and brand equities. For we believe that products are manufactured and services provided, but it is brands that are purchased. We take an objective approach to matching our client's goals with viable properties — be they events, athletes or promotions. These properties will be designed to, above all, drive results to the bottom line.

Why is ProServ uniquely qualified to do this? For two reasons. The first is our people. Embracing television expertise, client-side, brand and sponsorship marketers and agency-side advertising, public relations and promotional marketers, our people span the scope of the marketing industry, with vast experience in brand-building.

Second, in 25-plus years of doing business, ProServ boasts a distinct perspective, acquired from working across a breadth of properties, categories and industries. This hard-earned insight enables ProServ to lead the way in developing creative, effective solutions for our clients.

At ProServ, we are intent on establishing "the cult of the client." The value of each individual in our organization is measured by the value he or she can bring to our clients, for it is value that marketers are looking for today. Value to the client is often what distinguishes the truly successful property from its competitors. It's an adage as old as commerce itself: the companies that put the client first succeed. ProServ has succeeded and will continue to do so. But only if our clients succeed as well.

This energy and focus on our clients' business permeates ProServ, and is the principle thing we are about these days. Simply, we cannot build our business until we build that of our clients.

Bill Allard, COO of ProServ since 1993, was recently appointed President of the company.

CONSULTING TAKES FLIGHT

A segment of ProServ's business that has experienced exponential growth in the past year is consulting. The reasons lie in the single-mindedness of its mission: to identify and/or create strategically sound marketing opportunities, and deliver results-oriented and creative solutions that maximize the investment of its clients.

That approach is rooted in the experience of the consulting group, which is drawn from all facets of the business. The consulting team relies on the experience of agency professionals, with strong credentials in advertising, promotion and public relations, while also boasting an equal portion of marketing sophistication from the client and brand perspective. The approach of these professionals is strategically grounded and firmly focused on each client's objectives. ProServ Consulting uses sponsorship and events to build brands and businesses.

Boasting an impressive array of high profile Fortune 500 corporate clients, the consulting group has compiled a track record of developing and executing successful event marketing strategies and programs that make an impact in the marketplace, whether it be nationally, regionally and/or locally.

One of consulting's most recent clients is decidedly unique and demonstrates the division's marketing expertise as beyond the traditional sports marketing designation. Washington D.C.'s John F. Kennedy Center for the Performing Arts has retained ProServ consulting to assist them in bringing one of America's premier performing arts properties to market, seeking national corporate sponsorship for the first time in the Center's history.

Another departure for ProServ but one that has quickly produced remarkable success is its association with Magic: The Gathering. Called a phenomenon sweeping the nation by MTV, Magic is the fastest-growing, best-selling card game in the world. It incorporates competition and strategy with card-collecting, and has become an international sensation, especially among the 16-34 male demographic. ProServ consulting orchestrated a relationship bringing MCI into a multi-year agreement as an official sponsor of the six-city, $1 million Magic: The Gathering pro tour.

ProServ Consulting created a national NFL promotion for Hershey.

In addition to the Tour sponsorship, MCI's Prepaid Division will feature Magic: The Gathering images on calling cards and create an interactive platform where players around the world can receive ranking, scheduling and Pro Tour information. It is an integrated program never before seen in the trading card industry.

These are just the latest additions to the consulting division's client roster, which in addition to the Kennedy Center and Magic boasts an array of both product and service marketers, manufacturers and retailers and already includes Staples, Hershey's, SkyTel, Volvo, FootAction USA and Prudential Securities, among others.

Source: ProServ, Inc.

PROSERV EVENTS OFFER IMPACT IN MARKETPLACE

Event marketing is a big part of the sports business, and ProServ is big in events.

Among the jewels of ProServ's event marketing properties, and one that offers extraordinary opportunities for marketers, is the Franklin National Bank Classic. This college basketball tournament was created to fund programs benefiting children in Washington, DC, and boasts top teams and network television exposure via ABC.

This hugely successful tournament helps kick off the college hoop season and, with its line-up of national powers, attracts audiences nationwide. The 1997 Franklin National Bank Classic will undoubtedly set new standards, when powerhouses Kansas and LSU join DC favorites Maryland and George Washington at the new MCI Center in downtown Washington.

In a new endeavor for the fall of 1997, ProServ was instrumental in helping Kiawah Island, SC bring a major event to its resort. The leadership of Kiawah, one of America's premier golf resorts, laid out its objective: to bring a major event to the resort, one which would afford the site a great deal of national television exposure. ProServ then utilized its event, marketing and television expertise to pinpoint a tournament that would meet the resort's criteria, negotiating the agreement to

Capacity crowds in Washington

bring the World Cup Golf to South Carolina.

The event features the world's best golfers from 32 countries, and will be showcased by two days of national network television on NBC, as well as extensive international television. And Kiawah Island itself offers phenomenal corporate hospitality opportunities.

Tennis events are also a big part of the ProServ line-up, led by ATP Tour events in Washington, Los Angeles and Atlanta. This year will mark the 28th year of the D. C. tourney, with Andre Agassi confirmed to begin his summer there, challenged by the likes of defending champion Michael Chang and Wimbledon wonder MaliVai Washington.

Los Angeles and tennis go way back — 1927 to be exact — and all the greats have won in LA. More importantly, the Infiniti Open and Hollywood have a strong tie, as evidenced by the annual opening night festivities at the event. Top stars like Jay Leno, Jerry Seinfeld and Kelsey Grammer are among those who have helped meld tennis and Tinsel Town.

Atlanta's AT&T Challenge is among the most successful events on the ATP Tour, with Agassi going for his fifth title there in 1997. The host site, the Atlanta Athletic Club, will unveil a new permanent stadium for the event in 1997.

Whether it's being involved in some of our existing events or creating customized events for your marketing objectives, ProServ's event staff has demonstrated the ability to overdeliver.

Kiawah Island, SC

POP WARNER POPS WITH PROSERV MARKETING

ProServ has earned the selection as the marketing, licensing and television representative for Pop Warner football, the nation's only national organization for youth football and cheerleading.

Pop Warner is looking to expand its sponsorship base, with an eye toward a long-term agreement with major companies that will facilitate its efforts to get more kids involved in Pop Warner programs. To that end, ProServ has recently secured a major sponsor for Pop Warner in Reebok. The athletic shoe and apparel manufacturer is the official equipment supplier for Pop Warner, and plans to participate in a variety of promotions to highlight Pop Warner programs.

Pop Warner himself has been memorialized by the U.S. Postal Service

In 1997 ProServ is seeking to align the program with four corporate partners in long-term relationships. These partners will enjoy tremendous exposure among this desirable demographic, as well as enjoy the benefits of creative

cross-promotions.

In addition, ProServ and Pop Warner are looking to create a series of camps for boys and girls participating in Pop Warner leagues, as well as coaching clinics conducted by top professional and college coaches.

Founded in 1929, Pop Warner reaches some 250,000 boys and girls between the ages of 8 and 15. There are Pop Warner leagues in 40 states, with local and regional play culminating in the Pop Warner Super Bowl at Disney World in Orlando. An NBC television special on the Pop Warner Super Bowl airs nationally. Pop Warner is an ideal vehicle for reaching an age group that is highly desirable for marketers.

EXHIBIT 1 *(continued)*

ATHLETE REPRESENTATION

The business of managing the careers of the world's elite athletes is where ProServ began, and it remains a vital part of the ProServ portfolio. Team sports, in particular, are flourishing at ProServ, led by monumental signings of marquee athletes in football and basketball.

Kevin Hardy, the No. 2 pick in the 1996 NFL draft, and **Marcus Camby**, the Player of the Year in college basketball in 1996, are the latest elite athletes to join the ProServ team. But they represent just the cream of an outstanding crop of new clients for ProServ in team sports.

ProServ enjoyed its best year ever in football recruiting, signing a group of outstanding athletes, all of whom are forecast for bright futures in the pro ranks.

Kevin Hardy of the U. of Illinois was the winner of the Butkis Award in 1995, emblematic of the nation's top collegiate linebacker. The personable, engaging Hardy was the No. 2 selection overall, tapped by the Jacksonville Jaguars. His on the field ability is described as limitless, and he has already proven to have star quality on Madison Avenue.

Among the marketing successes ProServ has secured for Hardy is his being featured in a national TV advertising spot for **Degree** anti-perspirant. The thoughtful, articulate Hardy was selected to pen a rookie journal for the Internet, read by hundreds of thousands of fans during the 1996 season. In addition, Kevin boasts a local radio show in Jacksonville, as well as agreements with **Club Level** and **No Fear** for licensing and **Nike** and **Jaguar** automobiles.

Other NFL draft successes include defensive end **James Manley**, a second round pick by Minnesota after a stellar career at Vanderbilt. Quarterback **Bobby Hoying** of Ohio State was a third round selection by the Philadelphia Eagles. Hoying is to be groomed as the heir apparent to the Eagles quarterback job. And running back **Moe Williams** of Kentucky, a 1600-yard rusher his last season in Lexington, was another third round pick, by the Minnesota Vikings.

Among the factors that attracts these world-class athletes is ProServ's uniquely comprehensive approach to draft preparation. The company's Phoenix-based training and fitness facility allows athletes to prepare for league combines and training camps in an ideal setting, with the added bonus of the expertise of some of the best minds in psychology and fitness. Many a ProServ athlete has improved their draft position — and hence their immediate reward — by intense training at the Arizona site.

The ProServ draft class of 1996 joins such outstanding stars as All-Pro **Mark Chmura** (tight end, Packers) **Rob Fredrickson** (standout linebacker, Raiders) and super sensation **Joey Galloway** (wide receiver, Seahawks, third in Rookie of the Year balloting, who signed a major endorsement with Nike). Another long-time ProServ football client is offensive lineman **John Fina** of Buffalo, who signed an extension with the Bills that included a record signing bonus for the team.

Joey Galloway for Nike

Four NBA Picks Highlight Hoop Class

ProServ basketball can also claim a banner recruiting year, with the signing of **Marcus Camby**, the UMass star and consensus player of the year. Camby was the second player picked in the NBA draft, by the Toronto Raptors. Camby cited ProServ's full service capabilities and marketing expertise as important factors in his decision. And ProServ has already delivered for Camby, securing agreements with **Nike, Nissan, No Fear** and

Shawn Kemp for Reebok

American Express for the blue chip star.

Another ProServ first round selection was **Martin Muursepp**, a star in Europe whose talents caught the eye of the Miami Heat. In addition, Iowa star **Russ Millard** was a second round pick by the Phoenix Suns, and phenom **Moochie Norris** was a second round pick by Milwaukee.

These players join the ProServ roster headed by Seattle's **Shawn Kemp**, who had his finest NBA season in 1996. Other ProServ notables include **Sam Cassell** of Dallas, **Detlef Schrempf** of Seattle, sensational guard **Nick Van Exel** of the Lakers, Indiana's **Rik Smits** and **Gheorghe Muresan** of Washington, the tallest man in the NBA (7'7"), voted the league's most improved player in 1996.

These players have enjoyed substantial marketing success, with Kemp boasting a signature **Reebok** shoe, appearances in **McDonald's** advertising and promotions while continuing his relationship with **Logo 7** apparel. Muresan was a part of a series of promotional spots for **ESPN** and a national TV campaign for Snickers.

Tennis Loaded With Aces

For more than 25 years ProServ has managed the careers of the biggest stars in tennis, beginning with **Stan Smith** and the late **Arthur Ashe**. That truth still holds, with women's tennis leading the way.

Despite her retirement in October 1996, ProServ continues to record marketing success in representing **Gabriela Sabatini**. In fact, ProServ represented Sabatini throughout her 13 years as a professional, and helped make her the most marketable personality in women's tennis. Sabatini is poised to introduce her fourth line of perfume through Muelhens; past perfume lines have been the best-selling fragrances in many European countries.

Gabriela Sabatini for Milk

The Argentine star also continues to represent **Fila**, the international apparel company, for which she has made promotional tours in Asia since her retirement from the WTA Tour.

Natasha Zvereva stands as one-half of the No. 1 doubles team in women's tennis (with Gigi Fernandez), while also establishing herself as a top 10 player in singles. **Amanda Coetzer**, a favorite wherever she plays, began 1997 in impressive fashion, reaching the semifinals of the Australian Open.

An exciting new addition to the roster of female stars at ProServ is **Lindsay Lee**. A native Oklahoman who now lives in Atlanta, Lee was dubbed a "joy" and a refreshing new face by NBC commentator Dick Enberg during Wimbledon.

On the men's side, long-time ProServ client **MaliVai Washington** became the most talked about player in tennis this summer, reaching the Wimbledon final as an unseeded player and being named to the U.S. Olympic team. For more on Mal, see page 6.

Men's tennis at ProServ rocked to the exploits of the brothers **Jensen**. **Luke and Murphy** are the most popular pair to come into the men's game in years, with their enthusiasm for the game and rock and roll attitude. They added to their tennis resume in 1996 with a doubles victory at the Hamlet Cup on Long Island, and achieved genuine hero status with kids the world over.

The 1996 tennis year marked the farewell tour of long-time ProServ client **Stefan Edberg**. In his quiet, understated way, Edberg has won titles and fans for more than a decade, setting the standard for deportment and dignity in the sport. At every stop in 1996, audiences and tournaments demonstrated their appreciation to Edberg, and proved that although he may be leaving the game as an active player, his legacy will live on. The graceful champion will always be renowned for his ability - two Wimbledon and two U.S. Open titles - and his demeanor; in fact, his fellow players decided to name their annual sportsmanship award after him, evidence of his lasting influence on his sport.

On the other side of the career continuum, ProServ is celebrating the signing of two of tennis's most heralded young players: **Olga Barabanschikova** from Belarus and **Irakli Labadze** of Georgia. Both are regarded as "can't miss" prospects, and the two teenagers are likely to soon be atop the women's and men's rankings.

Johansson Leads Global Golf

ProServ's golf roster is headed by the exploits of Swedish star and Ryder Cup player **Per-Ulrik Johansson**. He will be making his debut in the Masters in 1997 — as a result of his stirring finish in the PGA Championship in the summer of 1996. He followed that up by winning the European Open in Dublin, Ireland, one of the European tour's biggest championships.

Johansson, one of Europe's top performers on the Tour, was an integral part of the 1995 Ryder Cup-winning team. The handsome Swede is leading a surge in golf talent — and interest — in his homeland.

Dawes Is On The Beam

An Olympic hero joined the ProServ ranks on the heels of her remarkable success in Atlanta. **Dominique Dawes**, a member of the gold-medal winning U.S. gymnastics team and one of the greatest gymnasts this country ever produced, is now being marketed by ProServ.

Olympian Dominique Dawes for Kodak

Dawes, a marquee star on the national tour of the gymnastics squad, won a team gold and the bronze medal in the floor exercise, to go with her bronze medal performance at Barcelona in 1992. A polished college student with an engaging demeanor, Dawes is bound to be a popular spokesperson.

Former Tour de France winner Greg LeMond for IBM

EXHIBIT 1 *(continued)*

PSTV BOASTS A GLOBAL PRESENCE

As a leader in sports television rights representation and production, ProServ Television is at the forefront of satisfying the world's insatiable appetite for sports. PSTV represents some of the most high profile properties in sports. Also a leader in production, PSTV produces the telecast for some 20 professional tennis events annually. All this adds up to PSTV being a leader in sports television opportunities for worldwide sponsors.

In 1996, PSTV was involved in the television marketing of the U.S. Open Tennis Championships for the sixth consecutive year. During its tenure with the Open, ProServ more than doubled the funds generated via domestic cable rights through its negotiations with USA cable. In addition, PSTV dramatically expanded the reach of the event, tripling the number of countries purchasing the telecast of the event.

ProServ Television is the exclusive international rights representative for all NCAA Championships, including basketball's Final Four. The NCAA's objective was to extend the reach of the tournament internationally, and PSTV has met that goal: in 1996 the Final Four was seen in 117 countries, nearly double the figure prior to PSTV's involvement.

For 1997 PSTV has the opportunity to incorporate an on-screen title sponsor into the international telecast of the tournament, a sponsorship not available in the U.S. market. This vehicle would enable a company to "present" the action from the Final Four to the millions of basketball fans around the world.

ProServ TV's tennis package of high-profile tournaments — including the International in New Haven, the St. Jude Classic in Memphis and the Infiniti Open in Los Angeles, among others — is an effective vehicle for reaching the sport's upscale demographic. Within each telecast, PSTV creates innovative promotional opportunities for sponsors to reinforce their message and solidify their link with the sport.

ProServ Television has a well-established relationship with the Boston Marathon, and was a major part of a milestone broadcast in the spring of 1996 with the 100th running of America's premier long distance race. The race was viewed in 90 countries, and was the largest clearance ever for a live event on Prime network. PSTV has

The Final Four is a top PSTV property and has experienced phenomenal international growth with PSTV.

produced and marketed the marathon telecast since 1989.

ProServ Television teamed with Ufa to bring the Golden Four, the foremost track and field events in Europe, to the U.S. via ESPN.

Another notable property of PSTV is the Canon Shoot-Out, a series of special golf events held at several European PGA tournaments. The Shoot-Out, with its unique offering of friendly competition, is seen throughout Europe courtesy of ProServ Television.

ProServ's television arm, with personnel boasting more than 50 years combined experience in the industry, enables our corporate clients to maximize the efficiency and impact of their television buys.

PROSERV JOINS FORCES WITH LICENSING LEADER CMG

ProServ has signed an agreement with CMG, the world's premier licensing and trademark representation firm. This new alliance will empower CMG to protect, enhance and license the names, likenesses and logos of ProServ clients, events and properties while both parties will seek new licensing clients.

CMG is the acknowledged leader in advertising, promotional and merchandise licensing, representing such notables as the Hollywood Chamber of Commerce, the city of Beverly Hills and the estates of Babe Ruth, Ty Cobb, Jim Thorpe and Marilyn Monroe.

The agreement with CMG is further indication of ProServ's comprehensive, full-service approach to doing business. This alliance gives ProServ a forceful tool in maximizing the benefits realized by ProServ corporate and athlete clients.

PROSERV AND CLARK SPORTS JOIN TO MARKET ARENA NAMING RIGHTS

As part of a strategy to provide owners with full service, turn-key development of sports facilities, ProServ has joined with Clark Sports to market the naming rights of stadiums or arenas developed or constructed by Clark.

This alliance melds ProServ's marketing expertise with Clark's turn-key develop/finance/construct capabilities within the sports facility marketplace.

Currently, Clark Sports is providing construction services to the new Redskins stadium in suburban Maryland, as well as the new Baltimore Ravens stadium, and consulting services for the forth-coming Cleveland NFL franchise. Clark is also building the MCI Center in Washington, D.C., the future home of the NBA Bullets and NHL Capitals. Other projects include the critically-acclaimed Oriole Park at Camden Yards in Baltimore. Clark Sports is a subsidiary of Clark Construction Group Inc., the nation's fourth largest general contractor.

Acquiring the naming rights for sports facilities has become a highly effective sales tool that is currently part of the marketing mix of companies like Delta Airlines, RCA, USAir, United Airlines and MCI.

PROSERV, INC. CORPORATE HEADQUARTERS: 1101 WILSON BOULEVARD, ARLINGTON, VA 22209 • TELEPHONE (703) 276-3030 • FAX (703) 276-3090
ATLANTA • LOS ANGELES • NEW YORK • OKLAHOMA CITY • PHOENIX • LONDON • TOKYO

CASE 4.3   MAGIC JOHNSON: ENDORSEMENTS "AFTER" . . . ?[17]

On Thursday, November 7, 1991, Los Angeles Lakers star Earvin "Magic" Johnson made an announcement that sent shock waves through the sporting world, and made front page news around the country. During a press conference in his team's home city, Johnson calmly disclosed that he had tested positive for HIV, the virus that causes AIDS. Johnson acknowledged that he would be retiring from basketball immediately, but added "I plan to go on for a long time. I will become a spokesman for the HIV virus because I want young people to understand they should practice safe sex."

Widely acknowledged as one of basketball's greatest players, Johnson was also one of the sport's most popular personalities. His popularity extended internationally. During his 12 years with the LA Lakers, Johnson was named Most Valuable Player three times (1987, 1989, 1990). He held the National Basketball Association record for career assists. He was a member of five world champion teams, and was named to the NBA All-Star team nine times. In the words of sports writer David DuPree, however, "[t]he statistics, the championships, and the individual awards barely scratch the surface of Johnson's value as a basketball player and his contribution to the game. He was an innovator, the consummate team player who had the rare gift of making all those who played with him better."[18]

For these reasons, beyond his skill as a player, Johnson was widely and consistently sought by marketers as a spokesperson for their products. Only Michael Jordan of the Chicago Bulls had a higher Q-rating, a measurement of the popularity and appeal of professional athletes conducted annually by Marketing Evaluations, Inc.[19] It was estimated that during 1991 alone, Johnson's endorsements for products such as Converse athletic shoes, Spalding basketballs, Pepsi-Cola, Kentucky Fried Chicken, Nestle's Crunch, and Nintendo video games could earn him as much as $12 million. In the aftermath of his announcement, individuals and corporations around the country voiced their admiration of, and support for, Johnson's courageous actions. At the same time, the marketing companies whom Johnson represented faced a potentially explosive dilemma: one of America's most well-loved sports heroes had contracted the virus that causes one of the most feared and stigmatized of diseases. No hope of a cure for AIDS currently existed. Each sponsor would have to make a decision, and soon, as to what would be done with Johnson's contracts.

In the hours that followed Johnson's announcement, some advertising and sports marketing executives suggested that Johnson would all but vanish from endorsements. Others voiced the opinion that companies which decided to end their relationship with Johnson could face a backlash from a sympathetic public.[20] Certainly, other athletes have been dropped from lucrative endorsement contracts when their health took a turn for the worse, or their private lives became too "messy." Yet both Johnson's stature as All-American sports hero, as well as the nature of his illness, could potentially change the rules of the game. Some thought that there was even a chance for good to come out of Johnson's personal tragedy. In the words of Al Cunningham, spokesperson for the National Taskforce on AIDS Prevention, "In many ways, [becoming a spokesman for the HIV virus] may be the greatest contribution Magic Johnson may be able to make beyond his contribution as a sports star. To make young people, to make the black community realize this is not something that just happens to somebody else . . . the wall of denial, especially in the Afro-American community, may begin to come down."[21] [Minority communities have long been disproportionately

Harvard Business School Case No 9-592-057. Copyright 1991 President and Fellows of Harvard College. All rights reserved. For information: *permission@hbsp.harvard.edu. This case was prepared by Wendy S. Schille under the supervision of Stephen A. Greyser. HBS cases are developed solely for class discussion and do not necessarily illustrate effective or ineffective management.*

affected by the AIDS epidemic—for example, blacks make up about 12 percent of the U.S. population, but almost 29% of all AIDS cases[22]—but this population also is considered to be one of the hardest to reach through education efforts.[23]]

Despite the contradictory opinions being expressed, marketing executives would have to make a decision: Was it worth the potential risk to their products to keep Johnson on as a spokesperson? If Johnson was kept on, how should the marketing campaigns proceed? A continuation of the light-hearted nature of Johnson's previous commercials might seem inappropriate to some, given the seriousness of Johnson's illness. If a decision were made to drop Johnson's contracts, how should that decision be implemented, and what should be its timing? Would the judgments be the same for sporting goods products as for other consumer products?

Questions

1. After the initial wave of sympathy, would you, as a sponsor, stay with Magic for an extended period or plan for separation? Why? Why not?

2. Would your responses to these questions be any different if you had been a long-term versus relatively recent sponsor? Would they be any different if you were a sporting goods sponsor versus a food company sponsor?

3. What effects, if any, on your company's or brand's use of Magic Johnson would there be from his several subsequent "returns to the game" and "retirements"?

4. In general, what criteria should be used by a marketer in considering or avoiding an athlete (or for that matter, another kind of celebrity figure) as an endorser?

CASE 4.4 NIKE CORPORATION AND ATHLETE ENDORSEMENTS[24]

You can't explain much in sixty seconds, but when you show Michael Jordan, you don't have to.

— Phil Knight, CEO, Nike Corporation[25]

On March 14, 2002, the *Herald Sun,* the largest circulation newspaper in Melbourne, Australia, announced that Wayne Carey had quit the North Melbourne "Kangaroos" Australian-rules football team. The story ran with a two inch, bold, banner headline "Carey Gone" and a large color picture of the superstar. The Carey story filled seven full pages of the issue, including the entire front and back pages. One columnist wrote: "On football's Richter scale, we are experiencing seismic activity measured in double figures."[26] The story received similar banner headlines, and extensive coverage, for the next four days. The March 17th front page of the *Herald Sun* showed Carey wearing Nike clothes in his hometown of Wagga Wagga.

At the time, Wayne Carey was captain of the Kangaroos and nicknamed "The King." He was considered "the best player of the past twenty years, and maybe the best to have played at [the Australian Football League (AFL)] level in more than 100 years."[27] He had brought strength and speed that had never been seen before to the AFL, changing the way the game was played.

Carey was brash and self-confident, with a presence that dominated his environment both on and off the field. He was "edgy," one of the guys, a very popular figure in Australia. The situation that led to his resignation had begun to become public two days before the resignation announcement. Carey, who had married his long-time sweetheart (Sally) just 14 months earlier in a well-publicized wedding, had been having an affair with the wife (Kelli) of his close friend and Kangaroo's vice captain, Anthony Stevens.

At the time of his resignation, Carey was earning nearly A\$1 million per year from his playing contract, and A\$500,000 through endorsements.[28] One of his major endorsement contracts was with Nike, who had contracts with four of the top AFL stars. Nike had portrayed him in an award-winning advertising campaign as the "Roo Boy"—raised in the wild by kangaroos, explaining his speed, strength, and jumping ability. Appendix A contains extracts from the *Herald Sun* of their coverage of the Carey story.

Tony Balfour, a Nike executive in Australia, described how the company learned of the situation. "We knew there'd been some team dispute, for want of a better word, and something had happened. There were rumors that it was involving partners, etc. But the fact that it was Stevens, and his wife, and it was at a team party, we didn't know any of that until we read about it in the paper."[29]

Carey's Nike contract had a standard clause that provided for cancellation if he behaved in a disreputable manner. Carey's manager Ricky Nixon reported that "Nike wants to know where he sits football-wise and whether he is going to play in 2003 and 2004. The possibility of me being able to give them an answer the next week is about five trillion to one. Things on the personal side have to be sorted out before we worry about other things."[30]

Journalists and television commentators engaged in a debate on how Nike should respond. For example, the *Herald Sun's* sports affairs reporter, in an article titled "Nike May Boot Carey," stated:

> *Nike is poised to use a contract morality clause to dump disgraced star Wayne Carey. The sporting goods giant has put Carey on notice after the revelation of his affair with teammate Anthony Steven's wife and split with the Kangaroos.*
>
> *Sources said there was no doubt the company would drop the fallen idol. It was a matter of when, and what spin the company would put on it. Industry experts said other sponsors would rush to invoke standard clauses that gave them an "out" if athletes behaved in a disreputable manner.*
>
> *. . . Sponsorship Solutions' Craig Richards said it was doubtful Carey could ever regain his commercial luster.*[31]

What should Nike do?

Nike Corporation

Nike Corporation had its roots in a partnership begun in 1962 between Bob Bowerman and Phil Knight.[32] Bowerman was a highly respected track and field coach at the University of Oregon, and Knight was a business student and middle-distance runner on Bowerman's team. Knight subsequently went on to an MBA at Stanford University. In a class on "small business," he wrote a paper describing a business idea for a high-performance track shoe made by a low-cost Japanese manufacturer.

After graduating from Stanford, Knight joined an accounting firm, but first took a trip around the world. While in Japan, he visited a company that made shoes which he thought met the needs of competitive runners. He bought a supply of the shoes, which Bowerman also liked, and the two started a shoe distribution company called "Blue Ribbon Sports." Knight went to high school track meets on the weekends, and on days off from his accounting job, selling shoes out of his car. In the first year, the revenues were $8,000, which was reinvested into an order for more shoes.

In 1966, Blue Ribbon Sports started having shoes made to Bowerman's design. Sales reached $1 million in 1969. In 1971, Knight decided that it was time to transition from a distribution company for the Japanese manufacturer, and to offer shoes under a new name and trademark. Nike was chosen as the brand name, after the winged Greek goddess of victory, and the "swoosh" symbol became the company's trademark. The first Nike shoes were used at the 1972 U.S. Olympic trials in Eugene, Oregon, and the company had revenues of $3.2 million that year.

By the end of the 1970's, Nike's sales were over $270 million. Nike went public in 1980, the same year it overtook Adidas as the leading selling athletic shoe in the U.S. However, in the mid 1980's Reebok, a company focused on shoes for the new aerobics fitness craze, surged into sales (especially with women's shoes). Reebok's sales went from $1.5 million in

EXHIBIT 1   NIKE INC 2003 REVENUE BREAKDOWN ($ MILLIONS)

	Footwear	Apparel	Equipment	Other	Total
USA	$3,019.5	$1,351.0	$287.9	-	$4,658.4
Other Americas	337.3	148.1	41.6	-	527.0
Europe/Middle East and Africa	1,896.0	1,133.1	212.6	-	3,241.7
Asia Pacific	732.4	499.3	127.1	-	1,358.8
Total	$5,985.2	$3,131.5	$669.2	$911.1	$10,697.0

Source: Nike Inc 2003 10K

1981 to $1.4 billion in 1987, when it passed Nike in shoe sales. The aerobics market, in part because it was not related to a specific professional sport or an identifiable elite athlete, did not hit Nike's radar screen as early as they would have liked. Since the late 1980's Nike has broadened its focus to embrace all athletic activity. Its mission statement in 2002 reflected that orientation: "To bring inspiration and innovation to every athlete in the world." The statement defined "athlete" with a quote from Bill Bowerman, "if you have a body, you are an athlete."[33]

By fiscal year 2003 (ended May 31) revenues were over $10 billion—see Exhibit 1. The company had over 23,000 employees in 2003, half in the United States.

NIKE AND ATHLETE ENDORSERS

Well orchestrated marketing campaigns designed around highly visible elite athletes included Michael Jordan (basketball), John McEnroe (tennis), Andre Agassi (tennis), Jim Courier (tennis), Pete Sampras (tennis), Bo Jackson (baseball and football), Deion Sanders (baseball and football), and Nolan Ryan (baseball), Tiger Woods (golf), and the U.S. Women's World Cup championship soccer team. The company also maintained close relationships with leading coaches and teams, at both the professional and college levels.

Nike was so tightly connected to leading athletes and teams that in 1993 Phil Knight was named "the most powerful man in sports" by The Sporting News. He was also the first sports executive to be featured on the cover of Sports Illustrated.[34] Donald Katz, in his book about Nike, described Knight's philosophy:

> [Knight felt] that if a company could somehow manage to project everywhere his own incorrigible sports-fan's urge to ascribe glory to gifted athletes, the results could be magical. If the general public could be helped to imagine great athletes as he imagined them—as having implications of the very best that the human spirit had to offer—then those athletes would become heroes like the heroes of old . . . like the heroes in books. And the people would come to these heroes and listen to what they had to say, Knight believed, because superior athletic ability speaks to everyone's belief in some primordial capacity for a kind of true greatness that has been obscured over time by expediency and disappointment and the general clutter of contemporary life.

People don't concentrate their emotional energy on products in the way fans abandon themselves to the heroes of their games. But great products that were necessary to great athletic figures, Knight reasoned, could create customers who were like fans. "Nobody roots for a product," Knight would say; the products needed to be tethered to something more compelling and profound.[35]

This philosophy had important implications for Nike: Nike should strive to help star athletes transcend their sports and become true heroes in the public mind. The association between Nike and these heroes would turn customers into dedicated fans of its products.

The first Nike athletes were track and field stars. In the early 1970s, leading shoe companies commonly paid top "amateur" runners money under-the-table to use their products. This practice was known, but ignored, by the sports' governing boards. Nike openly offered Steve Prefontaine, the great Oregon middle-distance runner, five thousand dollars to wear its shoes and a shirt bearing the Nike name in competition. The American Athletics Union (AAU) officials opposed this, and were unhappy that the sports' hypocrisy (sometime derisively referred to as "shamateurism") was being exposed. Prefontaine, the antiestablishment free spirit, ignored the officials.

Prefontaine was killed in an auto accident in 1975, but his spirit made a lasting impact on Knight and Nike. In 1992, Knight said in an in-house film on the company's first twenty years: "To many he was the greatest U.S. middle-distance runner ever, but to me he was more than that. Pre was a rebel from a working-class background, a guy full of cockiness and pride and guts. Pre's spirit is the cornerstone of this company's soul."[36]

Nike's priority was clear from the beginning. The company was focused on the athlete, not the sports establishment. From the beginning, the company had also provided exceptional service to its athletes, ensuring that they had the products they needed, when they needed them, and that their suggestions for improvements were acted upon. It promoted its athletes, and stood by them. In response, athletes were fiercely loyal to Nike.

In 1985, Nike took its relationship with athletes a step further, actively working to turn star athletes into figures that transcended sport. This was most dramatically, and successfully, seen in the case of Michael Jordan, a rookie basketball player from North Carolina. Jordan was not widely known at the time, but was catapulted into the public's imagination by a Nike ad, "Jordan Flight," in which he seemingly flew. The advertisement was produced with such creativity that it captivated viewers. Jordan and Nike assumed the mythical proportions Knight had imagined when pondering sports-fans relationships with their heroes. The new Air Jordan basketball shoes were an instant success. There was a buying frenzy, complete with long lines in stores to buy them, hoarding, shortages, and marked-up prices. Jordan's on-court performance was so spectacular that it reinforced the image Nike created, and his grace off the court gave him a broad appeal to the general public. Jordan exemplified Nike's approach to its athletes, and illustrated the way that turning athlete endorsers into heroes could have a powerful affect in the marketplace. Shortly before retiring (for the first time) from basketball in 1993 to pursue a baseball career, Jordan reflected on the impact that Nike had made on his public image, saying "what Phil and Nike have done is turn me into a dream."[37] Jordan was fiercely loyal to Nike.

Howard White, Nike's professional basketball manager, described the types of people that Nike wanted as endorsers:

> If I was pulling together a competitive basketball team . . . I might need a great center . . . Someone who'll get everybody involved and help you win. . . . But when we go after somebody for Nike, that player has to represent something more. There are elements of style to consider. Does he excite anyone? Does he get up real high on his dunks? Cause if he can't move people and offer an attitude we can work with, then he just won't do much for us as an endorser.[38]

Nike executive Mike Wilskey described the company's athlete endorsers in this way:

> Very few people change the sport. The ones who do have a tendency to have an approach that is what I would describe as multidimensional. They love the sport for a lot of reasons. At the same time that they love it, and have a certain respect and reverence for that sport, they also challenge it. And what is controversial, usually, is the individual that challenges the heritage of the game, or maybe the way the game should be played. People who challenge a sport have a tendency not to be very popular early in their careers.

Nike made its athletes into stars beyond the limits of their sports. Donald Katz compared two exceptional basketball players, Charles Barkley and Karl Malone. On the basis of pure talent, Malone was superior. However, Malone was virtually unknown outside the basketball world. Barkley was a celebrity. The difference was in the shoes. Malone had signed with another shoe company. Nike had developed the image of Barkley, elevating his celebrity beyond the basketball court.[39]

The Nike/Athlete "Family"

Nike preferred to begin their formal relationship with athletes early in the athlete's career, before they became prominent. In order to identify the athletes Nike wanted as endorsers, the company generally began to establish relationships long before entering into any formal agreement. Nike executive Scott MacEachern described the development of their relationship with athletes as follows:

> We are in the locker rooms, we are on the buses, we are on the trains. We are with these guys in minor leagues, in junior leagues and coming up through the ranks. And if we aren't personally, we have people that are. So, we . . . have a very good understanding as to who this individual is on a personal [level]—not just how great they are at athletics or in sports . . . That's what separates us from everyone else. . . . Before I would sign individuals, even before I went up and shook the individual's hand, I would take a few weeks just observing them. How do they handle the media? How do they handle other athletes around them? How do they handle themselves in the locker room? It's an observation before I even went up and introduced myself.

It viewed its sponsored athletes as "family," a characterization commonly used by Nike employees to describe the relationship between the company and its athletes. When asked about dealing with its athletes during difficult times, the Nike representatives consistently discussed the issues in a familial manner, rather than as business issues.

A classic example of the strong family bond between Nike and its athletes is the case of bicyclist Lance Armstrong. In his autobiography, Armstrong described his relationship with Nike and Scott MacEachern, his Nike Representative. Shortly after joining the Nike family, Armstrong was diagnosed with testicular cancer, which had spread throughout his body. The prognosis for survival was poor, and the prospects for continuing a world-class cycling career seemed out of the question. Armstrong continued:

> . . . It was no accident that [Scott] was one of the first people I told about my cancer. In my conversation with Scott that night after returning home from [the doctor's] office, all the horrible emotions I had suppressed broke loose. I started crying as I told Scott the whole story . . . After awhile, I stopped crying. There was a moment of silence on the other end of the line, and then Scott spoke calmly, almost casually: "Well, don't worry about us," he said. "We're with you." . . . Scott was true to his word; Nike didn't desert me. As I got sicker, it meant everything.[40]

Asked about this, MacEachern elaborated:

> At Nike, we have these relationships and beliefs about how we treat individuals, and athletes, and just people in general. After talking with Lance, I just knew the company was behind me when I said that we were not going anywhere. We were going to stick by Lance. That's just part of our core values.

The loyalty Nike showed to its athletes resulted in strong loyalty from the athletes to Nike.

Changes in On-Field Performance

An athlete's performance from year to year couldn't be predicted in advance. An endorsement contract was entered into with certain expectations, which might be met, not met, or exceeded. If an athlete greatly exceeded expectations, becoming a superstar, the company would want to ensure that he/she remained an endorser and didn't leave to join a better-paying competitor.

Holding the athlete to the compensation negotiated before he/she became a superstar might alienate the athlete and make him/her consider endorsing competitive products when the current contract expired. On the other hand, if an athlete's performance declined dramatically, or did not meet the expectations of the company, the company would be paying far in excess of the value that the athlete brings to endorsements. Including a performance clause in Nike's contracts was intended to address these issues until the contract expired and could be renegotiated upon renewal.

In some cases, an athlete might suffer a career-ending injury that forced retirement.[41] This happened to Nike when Bo Jackson, a star in both football and baseball, and around whom the company had built a major marketing campaign for cross-training shoes (the "Bo Knows" series of advertisements), suffered a career-ending football injury. It was thought that he might never walk again, but through hard work he made a baseball comeback. Nike supported Jackson through his comeback, even to the point of creating an advertising campaign focused on his return to baseball.

The performance of an athlete in an individual sport (such as tennis, golf, running, cycling, or swimming) was easy to measure—there was a clear, unambiguous ranking that could be used to determine one athlete's performance compared to others in the sport. In addition, the athlete received public notice based on this performance—with more successful athletes generally getting more attention. The winner of the Wimbledon tennis championship, or the Masters golf tournament immediately became a high-profile individual who attracted attention to a sponsor's products, and could be used in promotional campaigns.

The situation in team sports was somewhat different. There were high-profile athletes in team sports, but their overall success depended on team performance, and their commercial impact was decreased if the team was unsuccessful. Statistics could be used to demonstrate an individual's excellence, but they couldn't be a "winner" by themselves—and the perception that an athlete is a winner was an essential element of their marketing value.

ADDITIONAL SITUATIONS

The Wayne Carey situation described earlier and in Appendix A is one example of athlete issues that arise when a company like Nike uses athletes to endorse its products. Exhibit 4-8 of the Section 4 text presents four general categories of possible situations—legal violations; league-rule violations; club or coach rule/edict violations; and, societal norm violations. Examples of other specific instances are now given:

Randy Moss

Randy Moss was the Minnesota Vikings highest paid player, in the second year of a $75 million, eight-year contract. He had set a National Football League record for receiving yards for his first four years in the league, and had scored more touchdowns since joining the league than all but one other player.

However, Moss had a troubled history. He had begun his college career at Notre Dame, but had lost his scholarship after pleading guilty to battery after beating up a high school classmate. He then went to Florida State, but was kicked off the team for violating his parole. He then went to Marshall, becoming a star. Moss joined the NFL in 1998, but was fined in 1999 for squirting water at a referee, and fined again in 2001 for verbally abusing corporate sponsors on the team bus.

In September 2002 Moss was arrested after he allegedly made an illegal turn, then used his car to push a traffic officer along the street. The officer was slightly hurt when she fell off Moss's car after he finally stopped. Moss was initially charged with felony assault, but the charge was reduced to two misdemeanors when prosecutors decided they couldn't prove he had tried to hurt the officer. Moss was later charged with possession of a small amount of marijuana that was found in his car.[42]

Moss was fined by the Vikings, and faced disciplinary action from the NFL due to the marijuana charge. He was a Nike athlete. Should Nike take any action against him?

Gold Club

In November 1999, federal racketeering charges were filed against Steve Kaplan, the owner of the Gold Club, Atlanta's most popular "adult/striptease" club. Kaplan had long been suspected by the FBI of having connections to organized crime, beginning in 1988 when he had been investigated after the murder of a mob figure.

The Gold Club catered to star athletes, who were provided free service when they frequented the establishment. Elite clientele helped give the club a status symbol, attracting large numbers of patrons, who paid high prices. Among the allegations against Kaplan and the Gold Club was the charge that they provided the athletes with female companions, who provided free sexual services at the club. Multiple star athletes were named. Some denied the charges. Others, such as NBA star Patrick Ewing (a Nike endorser), and baseball player Andruw Jones, admitted the charges and testified against Kaplan in court. Jones admitted visiting the club about 30 times. In August 2002, the trial was stopped when Kaplan pled guilty to racketeering. He was later sentenced to 16 months in prison. Eight other defendants also made plea agreements. The club was confiscated by the federal government.

Should Nike take any action regarding Ewing? What about contracts with players who were implicated but did not admit their involvement?

Tiger Woods and Augusta National Golf Club

On June 12, 2002, Martha Burk, chair of the National Council of Women's Organizations (NCWO) wrote to the chairman of the Augusta National Golf Club requesting that the club admit women members. Augusta National was an exclusive club, with just 300 members, that hosted the Masters Golf Tournament, one of golf's "majors," and arguably the sports' most prestigious event. The club chairman responded that women might be invited to be members in the future, but "not at the point of a bayonet." Burk then wrote to the CEOs of the companies planning to advertise at the tournament, asking them to withdraw their sponsorship. NCWO also requested that the PGA Tour not recognize the Masters, that CBS not televise the tournament. To continue pressure on the club, NCWO posted a web page of the "Hall of Hypocrisy" listing companies whose executives were Augusta members, under the title "corporations that sanction sex discrimination at Augusta."[43]

Augusta National refused to change its rules in response to the NCWO demand. CBS did not cancel plans to televise the event, which would be played in April 2003.

The story gained increased attention in November 2002, when the *New York Times* published an editorial calling for Augusta National to admit a woman member, and for Tiger Woods to boycott the event. Woods had won the tournament three times, and was the two-time defending champion. He would be trying to become the first person to win the tournament in three consecutive years. The *Times* editorial said:

> *Tiger Woods . . . could simply choose to stay home in April. The absence of golf's best player would put a dreaded asterisk by the name of next year's*

winner. And a tournament without Mr. Woods would send a powerful
message that discrimination isn't good for the golfing business. Of course,
if Mr. Woods took that view, the club might suddenly find room for a few
female members. Justice Sandra Day O'Connor, for example, is said to be a
very good golfer.[44]

Jesse Jackson, threatening to organize boycotts against the tournament, also called for Woods to boycott, saying, "He's much too intelligent and too much a beneficiary of our struggles to be neutral. His point of view does matter."[45]

Woods, who had repeatedly said that he thinks women should be allowed to join Augusta National, expressed frustration that he was the only player that was being asked to boycott, and that he was tiring of having to continually comment on the issue. He noted that it wasn't his decision, as he was not a voting member of the club. The press, particularly the *New York Times* continued to pursue the story, focusing on Woods.

Woods thus found himself being used to promote a political agenda and news story. What should he do? Should Nike ask Woods to take a stand?

Shane Warne

Cricket was a major sport in most British Commonwealth countries such as Australia, India, New Zealand, Pakistan, South Africa and the West Indies. It was a very British sport, gentlemanly and proper, with tradition, culture, and unwritten rules of behavior establishing expectations for athletes. Cricket was one of the few truly national sports in Australia, and thus cricket stars were important sports personalities. In the early 1990s, Australian cricket was at a low point, searching for stars.

Shane Warne was a young spin (slow) bowler, a traditionally unglamorous role, compared to the more high-profile batsmen and fast bowlers. However, Warne reintroduced the idea of using spin bowling as an attacking role to take wickets, rather than its usual defensive focus. Furthermore, in the conservative world of cricket, he was an iconoclast — he had bleach-blond hair, drove a Ferrari, was a party animal, and wore an earring. Nike's Balfour observed, "He stood out unbelievably. The sport was desperately looking for heroes at that time."

In addition to his cricket prowess and the fact that he stood out in the conservative world of cricket, Warne was well suited to appeal to Australians. Balfour described his appeal, saying, "Shane is the archetypal lovable rogue. He has this really endearing smile. He doesn't care what people think about him. There's a little bit of Shane in every Australian. For us, Shane was a big part of Australianizing the Nike brand." With few established world-class Australian cricket stars at the time, Warne captured the fans' imagination. Nike spotted him early, signing him to a A$1.1 million, five year contract in 1994.[46]

On August 5, 2000, a *Herald Sun* article titled "Bad Boys" reported on the most recent of Warne's indiscretions, which led to his termination as vice-captain of the Australian national team:

Superstar bad boy Shane Warne crashed to a new low. Warne yesterday
was sacked as Australia's cricket vice-captain after a series of humiliating

scandals. Warne was stripped of the cricket honor because of off-field indiscretions, most recently a phone sex-talk scandal involving a young British nurse while he was in England playing with county side Hampshire. Warne, 30, had pleaded with Australian authorities, asking he be allowed to keep the job. But the controversies proved too much for the Australian Cricket Board (ACB).

ACB chairman Denis Rogers said Warne's off-field behavior cost him the job. "We have counseled him over the years and he's been very honest with us, but it's got to the point where we think it's time for a change," Mr. Rogers said.

It was revealed Warne left obscene messages on the mobile phone of a woman he met in a nightclub last month. [The woman then shared the messages with a national tabloid newspaper.] That episode seemed to be the last straw for the board after he and [another player] admitted taking money from an Indian bookmaker in 1994. In [New Zealand] last year, he allegedly tried to take a camera away from a young man who snapped him with a cigarette while he was being sponsored to give up smoking.[47]

The article also included a chronicle of other indiscretions by Warne, which included a fine for criticizing another player, unacceptable public behavior while drunk, attacking the media, associating with illegal bookmakers, and being photographed smoking despite being paid $200,000 by a pharmaceutical company to quit smoking. The article pointed out that, "critics argue Warne's antics are a bad influence on youngsters who model their behavior on sporting heroes."

In 2001, Warne's Nike contract was up for renewal. He appeared to be at the twilight of his career. He smoked and had gained weight. The public was tiring of his off-field antics. His on-field performance, however, was still good. Nike had a limited budget for athletes in Australia, and Warne was one of the three highest paid Nike athletes.

Should Nike renew Warne's contract, and if so, what considerations would be important in a new contract?

SUMMARY

Athlete endorsements were an essential part of the Nike marketing strategy. Working closely with star athletes, and creating a public image based on its relationship with athletes, had helped Nike become a major corporate power, and the leaders in their business. Yet depending on the public perception of a relatively small number of high-profile sports stars, who had a wide variety of interests, backgrounds, and maturity levels, contained an element of risk. Nike's ongoing challenge was to manage these relationships for the company's long-term benefit.

APPENDIX A
Extracts from *Herald Sun* Detailing the Wayne Carey Saga

A. "Carey's Rise and Fall" (Thursday, March 14, 2002 Issue)

June 10, 1989. Wayne Carey makes his debut for North Melbourne Kangaroos

March 11, 1993. Becomes the youngest captain in the AFL competition when he is named skipper of the Kangaroos at 21.

June 1994. Reported four times (for on-the-field infractions) during the season and eventually suspended for three matches.

September 24, 1995. Carey is charged with indecent assault after grabbing a young women's breast outside the Sports Bar in King St. He had been drinking with teammates after a finals defeat the previous night. The Kangaroos skipper lunged at the woman's breast, squeezed hard and allegedly said: "Why don't you go and get a bigger set of tits?" Carey subsequently pleads guilty in the Melbourne Magistrates Court to indecent assault over the breast-grabbing incident. He is released without conviction and placed on a 12-month good behavior bond.

September 28, 1996. Leads the Kangaroos to a Grand Final ("Super Bowl") victory over Sydney Swans.

September 25, 1999. Leads Kangaroos to second Grand Final ("Super Bowl") win over Carton Blues.

August 30, 2001. Carey's star-studded career is capped when he is named captain on the Kangaroos' Team of the Century.

B. "How The Drama Unfolded" (Friday, March 15, 2002 Issue)

Sunday (March 10) night, Party at Glenn Archer's Warrandyte house for his wife Lisa's 30th birthday. (Archer is a ten-year veteran player with the Kangaroos and named to their Team of the Century).

11PM Kangaroos captain Wayne Carey and Kelli Stevens (wife of vice-captain) caught in the bathroom together. Scuffle follows.

Tuesday (March 12) AM. Sally Carey is admitted to an exclusive Melbourne psychiatric clinic after a breakdown.

Wednesday (March 13) AM. Kelli Stevens tells Anthony that she has been having an affair with Carey. The club is contacted. The club is told neither Stevens, Archer nor any of the senior players would play with Carey in the team. Carey speaks with the club and his manager, and the Kangaroos superstar decides to quit.

6PM Carey tearfully announces he has quit the Kangaroos with the following statement:

> *The matters leading to the statement I am about to make are of a
> personal nature and I will not discuss them. For the wellbeing of all
> concerned I have taken the decision to cease my playing career with the*

Kangaroos. I regret the circumstances of my actions, which have led to this decision and the pain it has caused to my wife and my family. I apologize to all my teammates and all the Kangaroos supporters; I believe this is the only proper and responsible course of action.

Questions

1. From an athlete's viewpoint, what factors should be considered in choosing a shoe/apparel company to endorse?

2. What is Nike seeking to accomplish with athlete endorsements?

3. What factors should Nike consider in responding to "problem situations"? Develop your set of factors at a general level and then apply them to recommending what Nike should do regarding:

   a. Wayne Carey

   b. Randy Moss

   c. Gold Club

   d. Tiger Woods

   e. Shane Warne

4. What steps can athletes take to increase the likelihood that their endorsement relationships are win-win for the endorser and the endorsee?

CASE 4.5   CAN KOBE'S ENDORSEMENT DEALS MAKE A REBOUND?[48]

On September 2, 2004, Kobe Bryant issued the following statement:

First, I want to apologize directly to the young woman involved in this incident. I want to apologize to her for my behavior that night and for the consequences she has suffered in the past year. Although this year has been incredibly difficult for me personally, I can only imagine the pain she has had to endure. I also want to apologize to her parents and family members, and to my family and friends and supporters, and to the citizens of Eagle, Colorado.

I also want to make it clear that I do not question the motives of this young woman. No money has been paid to this woman. She has agreed that this statement will not be used against me in the civil case. Although I truly believe this encounter between us was consensual, I recognize now that she did not and does not view this incident the same way I did. After months of reviewing discovery, listening to her attorney, and even her testimony in person, I now understand how she feels that she did not consent to this encounter.

I issue this statement today fully aware that while one part of this case ends today, another remains. I understand that the civil case against me will go forward. That part of this case will be decided by and between the parties directly involved in the incident and will no longer be a financial or emotional drain on the citizens of the state of Colorado.

The incident to which 26-year-old L.A. Lakers superstar Kobe Bryant was referring was the allegation of criminal sexual assault brought by a 19-year-old worker at a Colorado health spa where Bryant was staying while undergoing knee surgery. This statement was released after the prosecution dropped felony charges against Bryant, ending a 14-month ordeal that was one of the most followed news stories during 2003 and 2004.[49] Although this meant Bryant would not serve time in prison, in no way did it exonerate his reputation.

The Makings of a Superstar

Kobe Bryant had all the makings of a basketball superstar prior to his joining the NBA. The son of long-time NBA player Joe ("Jellybean") Bryant, Kobe grew up surrounded by the game. Although he moved around early in his life, Kobe finally ended up in Philadelphia in time to enroll in Lower Marion High School. There, he showcased his talent as a basketball prodigy. He capped his career by leading the school to a Pennsylvania State Championship—and, incidentally, breaking a Pennsylvania high school scoring record set by NBA hall-of-famer Wilt Chamberlain!

On June 26, 1996, after passing up scholarship offers to play at college powerhouses such as Duke, Michigan, and North Carolina, Kobe was selected by the Charlotte Hornets as the 13th pick in the NBA draft.[50] Within weeks, he was traded to the Los Angeles Lakers and signed a 3-year deal worth a reported $3.5 million. Kobe made his NBA debut on November 3, 1996 at the age 18 years and 2 months, making him the second youngest NBA player ever. He immediately made an impact with his new team. In a game against the Chicago Bulls during his second season, Kobe scored 33 points while being guarded by one of the greatest players the game has ever seen—Michael Jordan. That prompted some sportswriters to compare—albeit prematurely—the young star to His Airness (i.e., Michael Jordan). Later that season, Kobe became the youngest player ever to appear in an All-Star game where he turned in an 18 point performance.

Early in his career, Kobe acquired the nickname "Showboat" from his teammates for his flamboyant—and, according to some, borderline arrogant—style of play. But he also developed a reputation for his competitiveness, his work ethic and, most important, his desire to win. On the road, Kobe would reportedly stay in his hotel room and study videotape of games while his teammates ventured out for a night on the town. This contributed to what would eventually become his public persona as a "wholesome" and "squeaky-clean" player.

During his third season, Kobe began to blossom and was awarded a starting spot on the lineup. Eager not to loose the young star to free-agency, the Lakers re-signed him to a 6-year, $71 million contract during his third year. In 1999, the Lakers hired ex-Chicago Bulls Coach Phil Jackson after the team experienced yet another early elimination from the playoffs.[51] During Jackson's first year with the team, Kobe—along with superstar teammate Shaquille O'Neal—helped lead the Lakers to their first NBA title in over a decade. They followed their 2000 performance by winning two more consecutive titles during the 2001 and 2002 seasons.[52] By that time, at only 24 years of age, Kobe had established himself as one of the most dominant—and highest paid—players in the game.

Kobe's Endorsements

Before he ever appeared in an NBA game, Kobe had already signed a six-year endorsement deal with shoe-maker Adidas that was worth an estimated $10 million to the young phenom. His performance on the court soon drew the attention of other potential sponsors. By the end of his second season, Bryant had added Sprite, Spalding, and McDonalds to his endorsement portfolio. This was followed by other, smaller deals with companies such as Mattel, Upper Deck, Nintendo, Nutella, and Mercedes, making Kobe one of professional sports most widely-recognized and highly visible pitchmen.

In July of 2002, Kobe and Adidas broke off their six-year relationship after the shoe-maker decided not to exercise a two-year extension in the contract.[53] This paved the way for Kobe to sign one of the most lucrative endorsement deals in all of sports—a coveted Nike shoe contract. Although terms of the June, 2003 agreement weren't disclosed, it was worth an estimated $40–45 million over five years to Bryant and easily eclipsed the payoff from any of his other deals.

Sports Illustrated, in May of 2004, reported Bryant to be the 3rd highest paid athlete in the NBA in terms of 2003 endorsement income (see Exhibit 1). Bryant's playing statistics and on-court accolades are summarized in Exhibit 2.

EXHIBIT 1 TOP 10 NBA ENDORSEMENT EARNERS IN 2003 ($ MILLIONS)

Player (Club)	Endorsement Income	Salary	Total Income
1.) LeBron James (Cleveland Cavaliers)	$ 35.000	$ 4.018	$ 39.018
2.) Shaquille O'Neal (Los Angeles Lakers)	14.000	26.518	40.518
3.) Kobe Bryant (Los Angeles Lakers)	12.000	13.498	25.498
4.) Grant Hill (Orlando Magic)	11.000	13.279	24.279
5.) Vince Carter (Toronto Raptors)	8.000	16.000	24.000
6.) Tracy McGrady (Houston Rockets)	8.000	13.279	21.279
7.) Kevin Garnett (Minnesota Timberwolves)	7.000	29.000	36.000
8.) Allen Iverson (Philadelphia 76ers)	7.000	13.500	20.500
9.) Anfernee Hardaway (New York Knicks)	4.250	13.500	17.750
10.) Tim Duncan (San Antonio Spurs)	3.500	12.676	16.176

Source: "SI's Fortunate 50," *Sports Illustrated* (May 14, 2004)

The Allegations and Fallout

Just days after signing his Nike deal, the nation was stunned to learn of Kobe Bryant's arrest in connection with a sexual encounter while he was in Colorado for knee surgery after the 2002–03 season. On July 18, 2003 more details surfaced when Bryant was formally charged with felony sexual assault against a 19-year-old woman that allegedly occurred at an up-scale Eagle County spa where Kobe had stayed. If convicted, the charge carried a sentence of four years to life in prison or 20 years to life on probation, and a fine of up to $750,000. What was once one of the cleanest, most likable images in all of professional sports was instantly sullied by the ensuing media fallout. Through his agent, Bryant released the following statement:

> *I am innocent of the charges filed today. I did not assault the woman who is accusing me. I made the mistake of adultery. I have to answer to my wife and my God for my actions that night and I pray that both will forgive me. Nothing that happened June 30th was against the will of the woman who now falsely accuses me.*

Eager to stem the damage to his reputation, a contrite Bryant appeared at a news conference holding hands with wife Vanessa to proclaim his innocence. He tearfully admitted that he was "furious at myself, disgusted at myself for making the mistake of adultery," but went on to repeatedly deny the other allegations.

The media pundits immediately began to speculate about the repercussions to Bryant both on and off-the-court. Kobe continued to practice and play with the Lakers in late 2003, making periodic trips to Colorado to appear in court during the preliminary phases of his trial. Although he was noticeably distracted during some games, he turned out All-Star caliber performances in others, which helped propel his team to the NBA finals. The Lakers were ultimately upset in the 2004 Championship Series by the Detroit Pistons in only five games. In July of 2004, the Lakers re-signed Bryant—despite the looming criminal trial—to a new, seven-year, $136 million contract in July of 2004. The contract was structured so that Bryant would receive $9.7 million of his first-year salary of $14.1 million as a lump sum, upfront

EXHIBIT 2

Panel A: Kobe Bryant's Playing Statistics

Year	Team	Games	Average Minutes	Field Goal pctg.	3-point pctg.	Free-throw pctg.	Rebounds per Game	Assists per Game	Steals per Game	Points per Game
1996	LA Lakers	71	15.5	41.7	37.5	81.9	1.9	1.3	0.7	7.6
1997	LA Lakers	79	26.0	42.8	34.1	79.4	3.1	2.5	0.9	15.4
1998	LA Lakers	50	37.9	46.5	26.7	83.9	5.3	3.8	1.4	19.9
1999	LA Lakers	66	38.2	46.8	31.9	82.1	6.3	4.9	1.6	22.5
2000	LA Lakers	68	40.9	46.4	30.5	85.3	5.9	5.0	1.7	28.5
2001	LA Lakers	80	38.3	46.9	25.0	82.9	5.5	5.5	1.5	25.2
2002	LA Lakers	82	41.5	45.1	38.3	84.3	6.9	5.9	2.2	30.0
2003	LA Lakers	65	37.7	43.8	32.7	85.2	5.5	5.1	1.7	24.0
Career		561	34.4	45.4	33.1	83.4	5.0	4.3	1.5	21.8

Panel B: Kobe Bryant's Accolades

- In 1995, Kobe was named Most Valuable Player of the Adidas ABCD Summer Camp, one of the top high school camps in the U.S.

- In 1996, Kobe leads his high school (Lower Merion High) to the Class AAAA Pennsylvania state championship in his senior year. On the way, Kobe averages 30.8 points, 12.0 rebounds, 6.5 assists, 4.0 steals and 3.8 blocked shots and surpasses all-time great Wilt Chamberlain to become Southern Pennsylvania's all-time leading scorer with 2,883 points. He is also named Naismith Player of the Year.

- On June 26, 1996, Kobe is selected as the 13th pick in the NBA draft by the Charlotte Hornets.

- On November 3, 1996, Kobe makes his NBA debut and becomes the second youngest player ever to appear in an NBA game.

- In February of 1997, during All-Star Weekend, Kobe wins the Gatorade Slam Dunk Championship and sets a new Rookie Game record by pouring in 31 points.

- On February 8, 1998, Kobe becomes the youngest player ever to appear in an All-Star game. He finishes with 18 points for the game.

- Kobe appears in the 50th annual NBA All-Star Game after garnering the most fan votes (1,433,747). Bryant leads the Western Conference in scoring with 19 points for the game, including three jumpers in the final 90 seconds. The Western Conference ends up loosing one of the most exciting All-Star games in NBA history 111–110.

- On February 10, 2002, Kobe scores 31 points and earns MVP honors in the All-Star game.

Sources: http://www.allstarz.org/kobe/time.htm
http://sports.yahoo.com/nba/players/3118/career

payment. This signaled his team's willingness to stand by their star during his trial since, if convicted, Kobe's contract would likely be declared null and void.[54]

Despite the negligible impact of the allegations and trial on Kobe's basketball career, the effect on his endorsements was another matter. Two of Kobe's deals—with McDonalds and Ferraro, the maker of the chocolate spread Nutella—expired shortly after the charges were brought. Neither sponsor renewed and both companies limited their comments about the allegations to denying that they had any bearing on their decision. Although none of Kobe's other endorsement deals had expired since the allegations were brought against him, it appeared as if some of his sponsors were hesitant to use his image. Around the same time the allegations against Kobe surfaced, Coca-Cola reduced running Sprite ads that featured Kobe. This contract runs through 2005 and it is unclear whether the star will be re-signed. Even if Kobe's image is never used, most sponsors are obligated to pay him unless there is a breach of his contract—and the dismissal of felony charges would appear to preclude such an outcome.

Exhibit 3 includes examples of comments made by observers on Bryant's endorsement future. These comments were all made before the September 2, 2004 announcement that the prosecution was dropping the felony charge against Bryant.

EXHIBIT 3   **COMMENTARY ON BRYANT'S ENDORSEMENT FUTURE PRE-SEPTEMBER 2004**

"If it's like O.J., he'll never have another endorsement contract again."

—Bob Williams, Burns Sports and Celebrities Inc.

"I think consumer product companies, the McDonald's and Sprites of the world, have really washed their hands of him at this point. I believe that by the time he's able to restore his reputation, if he's ever able to do that, he'll be old enough to be pitching denture cream and prune juice."

—David M. Carter, Los Angeles-area sports business consultant

"I think right now, the watch word is hesitation. This is an eye opener, making many advertisers step back and say, 'If it can happen to Kobe Bryant, it can happen to anyone.'"

"Advertisers would still want to make sure the whole situation is played out before they would want to associate themselves with Bryant again."

—Bob Williams, president of Burns Sports & Celebrities

"Convicted of a felony is not a high enough standard. They (advertisers) are buying reputation. If the reputation gets sullied, they're not getting what they paid for."

—Marc Ganis, sports marketing expert

"It's going to take time, if he can recover at all. He's going to have to do a lot for the public to respond because he has publicly admitted to adultery and that offends a great number of people."

—Jeff Chown, managing director of The Marketing Arm

"I think it would take three years and almost flawless behavior for him to get back on top. Even then I don't think it ever will be quite the same for Kobe. Certainly over time things will get a lot better for him."

—Andy Appleby, CEO of General Sports and Entertainment, LLC

"Someone's reputation is priceless and there are hundreds of other celebrities and athletes companies can use to pitch products. If I was on the marketing side, I would say, 'Why Kobe?' And I don't really have a great answer."

—Peter Land, general manager of sports and entertainment for the Edelman public relations company

"Chances are that companies will come calling on Bryant again, particularly if he plays at a high level and continues to lead his team far in the playoffs."

—Kurt Badenhausen, Forbes Magazine

Sources: http://sportsillustrated.cnn.com/2004/basketball/nba/wires/08/29/2030
ap.bkn.bryant.future.bjt. 0819
http://news4colorado.com/localnews/kobe_story_247131604.html
http://money.cnn.com/2003/07/21/news/companies/kobe_impact
http://www.forbes.com/2004/09/03/cz_kb_0903kobe.html
http://www.washingtonpost.com/wp-dyn/articles/A54506-2004Sep1.html
http://www.usatoday.com/sports/basketball/nba/2004-09-02-kobe-image_x.html

Questions

1. Why was Kobe Bryant so attractive to companies as an endorser of their products?

2. Categorize the difficulties an elite athlete like Bryant faces in his off-the-court life.

3. What factors should potential endorsers consider in deciding, post September 2004, whether to sign Bryant to endorse their products? Consider the comments made in Exhibit 3 of the case in your analysis.

4. Post September 2004, what can Bryant do to maximize his future endorsement income?

Footnotes

[1] This section was written by George Foster.

[2] "CBA: The MLB Model," http://www.andrewsstarspage.com (December 28, 2003).

[3] Mark's Sportslaw News. "Thought of the Week—The Incentive-Based Contract." www.sportslawnews.com (May 25, 1999).

[4] M. Klein. "Beckham Inc." *Sunday Times* (16 September 2004).

[5] Paul Siddall. "The David Beckham Pages." (15 September 2004) website page.

[6] This case was written by Chris Armstrong under the supervision of George Foster.

[7] A-Rod was named to the American League All-Star team in 1996, 1997, 1998, and 2000. In addition, A-Rod has appeared in every All-Star game since 2000.

[8] Benjamin, Matthew. "Agent Scott Boras is changing the business of baseball." *U.S. News and World Report* (10 May 2004).

[9] Ibid.

[10] A player with free-agent status is allowed to sign a contract with any team. This typically happens when a player's old contract expires. After the 2000 season, free agency in Major League Baseball was celebrating its twenty-fifth anniversary.

[11] Re-signing with Seattle was reportedly third on A-Rod's list; however, the Mariners were apparently unwilling to negotiate in the salary range offered by Atlanta and Texas.

[12] Meanwhile, A-Rod's old team, the Seattle Mariners, finished first, third, and second in the AL West in 2001, 2002, and 2003, respectively.

[13] Many felt that Rodriguez should have won the 2002 AL MVP instead of the Oakland Athletics' Miguel Tejada. Rodriguez put up better numbers that season, but Tejada played for a club with a better record and postseason prospects.

[14] Convinced of this imminent trade, one story even ran with the opening line "Alex Rodriguez will soon join the Boston Red Sox because major league baseball wants it to happen as much as Red Sox management does." For details, see "Stroke of Genius by Red Sox, Epstein: Get Best Player, Dump Manny, and Annoy Steinbrenner" at http://msnbc.msn.com/id/3668340.

[15] Brian Harris, MBA '97 prepared this case under the supervision of Professor Stephen A. Greyser as the basis for class discussion rather than to illustrate either effective or ineffective handling of an administrative situation.

[16] *An Athlete's Guide to Agents,* Robert Ruxin. (Boston: Jones and Bartlett, 1993) p. 115.

[17] This case was prepared from public sources by Research Associate Wendy S. Schille, under the supervision of Professor Stephen A. Greyser, as the basis for class discussion rather than to illustrate either effective or ineffective handling of an administrative situation.

[18] *USA Today,* "His was the name of the game," by David DuPree, November 8, 1991, p. 1C.

[19] *NBA News,* October 28, 1991.

[20] *The New York Times,* "Athletes' Endorsements May Now Be in Doubt," by Stuart Elliot, November 8, 1991, p. B13.

[21] *USA Today,* "Reactions mix emotion with sense of purpose," November 8, 1991, p. 1C.

[22] *The Boston Sunday Globe,* "Magic Johnson gave AIDS prevention a needed jolt," by Richard A. Knox, November 10, 1991, p. 28.

[23] *The New York Times,* "Magic's Loud Message For Young Black Men," by Michael Specter, November 8, 1991, p. B12.

[24] Research Associate David Hoyt prepared this case under the supervision of Professor George Foster as the basis for class discussion rather than to illustrate either effective or ineffective handling of an administrative situation.

[25] Donald Katz. *Just Do It* (Random House, New York, 1994), p. 25.

[26] Mike Sheahan. "Blow-Up to Beat Them All." *Herald Sun* (March 14, 2002), p. 5.

[27] Mike Sheahan. "Roos on the Edge." *Herald Sun* (March 14, 2002), p. 96. The AFL is the premier league of Australian rules football.

[28] Shaun Phillips. "Nike May Boot Carey." *Herald Sun* (March 15, 2002), p. 7.

[29] Quotations in this case that are not otherwise attributed were from personal conversations with the author.

[30] Daryl Timms. "Fans Rally Behind Kangaroos, for Now." *Herald Sun* (March 15, 2002).

[31] Phillips, loc. cit.

[32] The early Nike history in this section is from Katz, pp. 58–69.

[33] Nike website: http://www.nike.com/nikebiz.jhtml?page=4 (July 15, 2002).

[34] Ibid., p. 10.

[35] Katz, op. cit. p. 6

[36] Ibid., pp. 63–64.

[37] Ibid., p. 8. Jordan later returned to basketball (1994–95 to 1997–98 with the Chicago Bulls). He returned again in 2001–02 and 2002–03 with the Washington Wizards.

[38] Ibid., p. 221.

[39] Ibid., p. 44.

[40] Ibid.

[41] In high-risk sports such as auto racing, the worst case might be death.

[42] "Vikings' Moss Now Facing Two Misdemeanor Charges." CNN/SI.com (26 September 2002): http://sportsillustrated.cnn.com/football/news/2002/09/25/moss_arrest_ap/index.html (23 October 2002).

[43] http://www.augustadiscriminates.org (April 4, 2003). For a chronology of the controversy, see Associated Press, "Masters Controversy Chronology." http://sports.espn.go.com/golf/masters/story?id=1533550 (April 6, 2002).

[44] "America's All-Male Golfing Society," *New York Times* (November 18, 2002), p. A2.

[45] King Kaufman. "Tiger's Burden." Salon.com (November 27, 2002). http://www.salon.com/news/sports/col/kaufman/2002/11/27/woods/print.html (April 4, 2003).

[46] Malcolm Conn and Michael McGuire. "Warne Just Won't Do It Any More." *The Australian* (6 July 2001), Sport page 18.

[47] Tim Jamieson and Mark Dunn. "Bad Boys." *Herald Sun* (August 5, 2000).

[48] This case was written by Chris Armstrong under the supervision of George Foster.

[49] Despite the dismissal of criminal charges against Bryant, he still faced a civil trial with the potential for either a large settlement or judgment against him.

[50] One of the main reasons Kobe cited for skipping college and going straight to the pros was so that he could play against Michael Jordan before he retired.

[51] Playing for the legendary Coach Jackson had been one of Kobe's childhood dreams.

[52] The 2000, 2001, and 2002 championships were Coach Jackson's third "three-peat." He had two other strings of three consecutive championships (1991–93 and 1996–98) while coaching Michael Jordan and the Chicago Bulls.

[53] Some sources reported that Kobe made a sizable payment to Adidas to break off their relationship.

[54] NBA contracts typically contain a "morals" clause which gives the player's team the right to terminate the contract if the player "at any time fails, refuses or neglects to conform his personal conduct to standards of good citizenship, good moral character (defined here to mean not engaging in acts of moral turpitude, whether or not such acts would constitute a crime), and good sportsmanship, to keep himself in first-class physical condition, or to obey the team's training rules." A felony conviction would undoubtedly constitute a breach of this clause.

SECTION 5... College Sports[1]

Key Issues

- College sports management faces the ever-present struggle to balance academic program integrity, sporting program demands and success, and the business opportunities sports programs provide for a college and its athletic department.

- College sports decision making is heavily constrained by regulatory bodies (such as the NCAA) as well as legislative bodies (such as the U.S. Congress with Title IX).

- Title IX has profoundly changed resource allocation in college sports and has greatly expanded the opportunities for women's participation in sports.

- College sports under the NCAA regime strongly adheres to athletes maintaining their amateur status in their chosen college sports. This constrains the ability of elite student athletes to capture a meaningful part of the revenues they are pivotal in creating for their college.

- Revenue pools and revenue allocation rules are a central part of college sports management. In many colleges, men's football revenues and men's and women's basketball revenues cross-subsidize costs in many other sports on campus.

Cases

College sports programs are an essential part of the life of many students while in college and as alumni after leaving college. Athletic departments are an important part of the budget of many colleges. This section outlines a selection of topics that highlight some of the complexity of the issues on the business side of college sports. The relationship between student academic and personal development issues and college sport business issues has long been debated and likely will continue to be so without any common agreement.

The National Collegiate Athletics Association

The National College Athletics Association (NCAA) plays a pivotal role in the administration of college sports. It is "a voluntary association of over 1000 colleges and universities, athletic conferences and sports organizations devoted to the sound administration of intercollegiate athletics." The NCAA's origins date back to 1905, when representatives of 13 colleges met to propose football rule changes to make the game safer for students. On December 28, representatives of 62 schools met in New York City to found the Intercollegiate Athletic Association of the United States (IAAUS). The group changed its name to the National Collegiate Athletics Association in 1910.

For the first several years, the NCAA was a forum for discussion and rule making. It held its first national championship in 1921, for track and field. Over time, the NCAA became active in more sports, and added more championships. By the end of the twentieth century, the NCAA defined its mission as to "strive to maintain intercollegiate athletics as an integral part of the educational program and the athlete as an integral part of the student body." Its goals were to promote intercollegiate sports, protect student-athletes, prepare student-athletes for lifetime leadership, and provide funding to help meet the goals.[2]

In 1973, the NCAA's members divided into three divisions for legislative and competitive purposes, and in 1978, the Division I members further subdivided.[3] Division I-A schools are required to meet spectator attendance minimums for football, whereas Division I-AA have football programs with no attendance minimum requirements. Division I-AAA institutions do not have football programs.[4]

Division II and III colleges have fewer sports than Division I. Division II colleges provide partial academic scholarships for their student-athletes, whereas Division III colleges provide no such financial support. Active members in each division, as of July 2004, are:

I-A	I-AA	I-AAA	II	III	Total
117	121	88	279	419	1,024

As intercollegiate athletics grew, there was concern that it would interfere with the academic mission of universities. The NCAA philosophy was that student-athletes were students first, yet the pressures on athletes to perform, and teams to win, created an environment in which athletics could easily overwhelm the academic mission. In 1989, after several years of highly public scandals in intercollegiate sports, *TIME Magazine* characterized the problem as "an obsession with winning and moneymaking that is pervading the noblest ideals of both sports and education in America." *TIME* then noted that the victims included the athletes who were not receiving a quality education, as well as "the colleges and universities that participate in an educational travesty—a farce that devalues every degree and denigrates the mission of higher education."[5]

In October 1989, the trustees of the Knight Foundation created a commission (the Knight Commission) to propose reforms. The first Knight Commission report was issued in 1991, and most of its recommendations were implemented by the NCAA, which embraced the Commission's efforts. Ten years later, the Commission revisited the issue, finding that "it is clear that good intentions and reform measures of recent years have not been enough—The Commission is forced to reiterate its earlier conclusion that 'at worst, big-time college athletics appear to have lost their bearings.' Athletics continue to 'threaten to overwhelm the universities in whose name they were established.'"[6]

College Athletics Department Financials

Exhibit 5-1 presents the University of Michigan Department of Athletics' financial budget for 2004–05. Also included are the actual financials for 2002–03, and an estimate from July 2004 of what the 2003–04 actuals would be. Several aspects are worth highlighting. First, the total 2004–05 budget of $61.390 million signals the high financial amounts involved in a major college sports program. Second, the two dominant revenue contributors are spectator admissions (49% of 2004–05 total revenues) and conference distributions (17% of total revenues). Football (men only) and basketball (men's and women's) are the leading components of both admission revenue and conference revenue. Third, salaries, wages, and benefits of $21.299 million (including $8.564 to coaches and team staff) and financial aid to students are the two largest cost items. Fourth, the importance of football attendance is highlighted by the 2004–05 football admissions revenue of $25.769 million being below the $29.067 million for 2003–04. In 2004–05, the Michigan Wolverines have a six home-game schedule ($4.295 million per game) compared to a seven home-game schedule in 2003–04 ($4.152 million per game)!

The University of Michigan's athletic department budget showed a surplus for 2002–03 and 2003–04, and is budgeted to be in surplus for 2004–05. It is one of a small number of athletic programs in the country that are both well-resourced and self-supporting from an economic perspective. The University of Michigan is widely acknowledged to have broad-based excellence in its academic programs as well as across many of its college sports.

College Sports Decision Making

Decision making for college sports operates within a complex set of guidelines and constraints. The NCAA rules provide explicit guidelines (such as Title IX adherence) as well as constraints and prohibitions (such as gambling and drugs). The academic faculty at many universities are heterogeneous in their appreciation of the role of athletics and of the importance of dollars spent by an athletic department. Some academic faculty are highly supportive of many aspects of college sports; others find little rationale for anything beyond student participation in intermural sports and student workouts in gymnasiums. University presidents and administrators must juggle the academic mission of a university, the financial demands of athletic programs, and the potential benefits from alumni support associated with successful athletic programs. Presidents and administrators also juggle the tension of compensation levels for leading academics vis-à-vis leading football and basketball coaches.

This section highlights some key factors that influence the business aspects of college sports.

EXHIBIT 5-1

UNIVERSITY OF MICHIGAN DEPARTMENT OF ATHLETICS FINANCIALS ACTUAL 2002–2003/ESTIMATE 2003–2004/BUDGET 2004–2005

	2002–2003 Actual	2003–2004 Estimate	2004–2005 Budget	2004–2005 Budget %
Revenues				
Spectator admissions*	$31.649	$33.357	$29.897	48.7%
Conference distributions**	10.084	10.617	10.530	17.2
Corporate sponsorships	4.340	5.000	4.525	7.4
Licensing royalties	3.206	3.800	2.200	3.6
Athletic scholarship fund	3.744	4.750	2.027	3.3
Proceeds from priority seating	—	—	3.600	5.9
Radio	1.090	1.710	1.485	2.4
Facilities	2.033	1.900	1.900	3.1
Concessions and parking	1.591	1.904	1.448	2.3
Other income	0.871	1.380	1.628	2.6
Investment income	2.168	2.100	2.150	3.5
Current Fund Revenues	60.776	66.608	61.390	100.0%
Expenses				
Salaries, wages and benefits	18.986	20.581	21.299	34.7%
Financial aid to students	10.617	10.900	12.125	19.8
Team and game expenses	9.531	10.528	10.787	17.6
Facilities	4.618	4.632	4.712	7.7
Other	10.551	11.878	10.110	16.4
Current Fund Expenses	54.303	58.519	59.033	96.2
NET OPERATING SURPLUSES	$ 6.473	$ 8.089	$ 2.357	3.8
				100.0%
*Spectator Admissions				
Football	$27.599	$29.067	25.769	86.2%
Basketball	2.243	2.365	2.200	7.4
Ice Hockey	1.564	1.775	1.765	5.9
Other	0.243	0.150	0.163	0.5
Total	$31.649	$33.357	$29.897	100.0%
**Conference distributions				
Television (football and basketball)	$ 5.745	$ 6.101	$ 6.210	59.0%
Football bowl games	1.848	1.993	1.801	17.1
NCAA basketball-based distributions	2.085	2.232	2.169	20.6
Other	0.406	0.291	0.350	3.3
Total	$10.084	$10.617	$10.530	100.0%

Source: University of Michigan (July 2004).

Title IX: Throughout much of U.S. history, men have had more economic opportunities than women. In 1972, the U.S. Congress enacted Title IX of the Educational Amendments of 1972:

> *No person in the United States shall, on the basis of sex, be excluded from participation in, be denied the benefits of, or be subject to discrimination under any education program or activity receiving Federal financial assistance.*

Although Title IX did not refer specifically to athletic programs, lawsuits and guidelines have made such coverage explicit. In 1979, the U.S. Department of Health, Education, and Welfare outlined three criteria that could be used to assess whether a college complied with Title IX:

- The male/female ratio of athletes at an institution is "substantially proportionate" to the male/female ratio of undergraduate enrollment.

- The institution has a "history and continuing practice of program expression" for women.

- The institution is "fully and effectively" accommodating the interests and abilities of women.

Most colleges find the first criterion the most clear-cut one to adopt. College athletic directors have implemented multiple strategies to increase the ratio of female to male athletes, such as:

- Increase the number of funded women's sports. Funded here includes both scholarships and funds for coaching staff and equipment.

- Reduce the number of funded men's sports.

In 2001, the Government Accounting Office (GAO) issued a report evaluating the addition and elimination of teams in intercollegiate athletics. The GAO reported that between 1981–82 and 1998–99, the number of women's teams had increased by 3,784, or 55% (from 5,695 to 9,479). The number of men's teams had remained nearly unchanged, at 9,149 in 1998–99, just 36 more than in 1981–82.[7] Between 1981–82 and 1998–99, the sport that added the most teams was women's soccer, going from 80 to 926 teams and adding 18,132 participants. Of the 25 women's sports surveyed, all but 6 had increased both teams and participants.[8] Of the 26 men's sports included in the report, 15 had remained unchanged or had suffered decreases in teams over the 17-year period. The sport with the most teams eliminated was wrestling, losing 171 teams of the 426 that had been in existence in 1981–82.[9]

Exhibit 5-2 shows the average number of undergraduate participants for men and women over the 1991–92 to 2001–02 period. Football dominates men's participation in Division I, with often more than 100 student-athletes playing on a college team. Examples of other high-participant college sports for men include rowing, lacrosse, track and field, baseball,

EXHIBIT 5-2   AVERAGE NUMBER OF MEN AND WOMEN STUDENT-ATHLETES IN COLLEGE ATHLETIC PROGRAMS: 1991/1992 TO 2001/2002

	1991–1992	1995–1996	1999–2000	2001–2002
Division I				
Men's	250	226	233	262
Women's	112	130	163	204
Division II				
Men's	167	149	155	166
Women's	79	80	96	108
Division III				
Men's	216	190	184	213
Women's	116	116	123	143

Source: NCAA, 2001–02 NCAA Gender Equity Report.

ice hockey, soccer, and swimming. High-participant sports for women in Division I include soccer, rowing, track and field, lacrosse, swimming, field hockey, and ice hockey.

Although debate over the justification for Title IX continues, it is one of the single most important factors affecting the business of college sports.

NCAA Rules on Compensation for Student-Athletes: The NCAA requires colleges to take a hard line on payments that students can receive for athletic-related activities. The NCAA Bylaws define the organization's intent with respect to amateurism and intercollegiate athletics:

> *12.01.2 Clear Line of Demarcation. Member institution's athletics programs are designed to be an integral part of the educational program. The student-athlete is considered as an integral part of the student body, thus maintaining a clear line of demarcation between college athletics and professional sports.*[10]

The NCAA views athletes as students pursuing an education, whereas professional sports sees athletes as business resources. The NCAA Bylaws (12.02.3) define a professional athlete as "one who receives any kind of payment, directly or indirectly, for athletics participation except as permitted by the governing legislation of the [NCAA]."[11] Athletic administrators are not able to use financial rewards beyond scholarships to attract student-athletes or to retain such students in their college programs.

The NCAA rules on "amateur status" mean that individual star athletes who are major contributors to college revenue creation are not able to capture any meaningful amount of that revenue. This "non-pay for play" aspect of college sports creates economic incentives for star athletes, especially in basketball and football, to go to the professional ranks before graduation. In basketball, the NBA permits high school graduates to directly enter its professional ranks. Superstar high school players often bypass the college ranks—examples include Kobe Bryant to the Los Angeles Lakers and Lebron James to the Cleveland Cavaliers. The NFL has a 3-year post–high school graduation hurdle before an athlete is eligible to enter the NFL. This NFL rule, coupled with the NCAA "amateur" rule, enables colleges to capture rents from star footballers for at least the athlete's first 3 post–high school playing years.

Revenue Implications

Exhibit 5-3 reports average revenue and profit breakdown for the Division I-A U.S. college conferences. The composition of these conferences is shown in Exhibit 5-4. Several features are apparent from Exhibit 5-3 and other related data:

(a) Many college athletic programs are, at best, marginally profitable. Three of the six largest college conferences have average revenues less than their average costs. The University of Michigan budget surplus reported in Exhibit 5-1 is the exception rather than the norm. The University of Michigan athletic program is underpinned by one of the best revenue-generating football programs in the country. With a 100,000+ capacity football stadium sold out each game, and an intensely loyal and large alumni base, Michigan has sizeable built-in revenue predictability in its budgeting. Most other programs have much lower revenue potential and

EXHIBIT 5-3   AVERAGE 2002–2003 REVENUES AND NET PROFITS OF ATHLETIC DEPARTMENTS OF DIVISION I-A COLLEGE CONFERENCES ($ MILLIONS)

Conference	Total Programs*		Men's Programs		Women's Programs		Men's Football Programs		Men's Basketball Programs		Women's Basketball Programs	
	Total Revenues	Net Profit	Total Revenues	Net Profit	Total Revenues	Net Profit	Total Revenues	Net Profit	Total Revenues	Net Profit	Total Revenues	Net Profit
Big Ten	$44.507	$4.193	$33.236	$16.419	$1.354	($6.028)	$21.533	$12.730	$8.170	$5.208	$0.383	($1.132)
SEC	41.192	5.889	34.465	17.490	1.863	(5.376)	26.901	18.134	5.687	2.923	0.618	(0.948)
Big 12	34.397	2.500	22.472	9.024	1.138	(4.631)	16.187	8.249	4.146	1.610	0.501	(1.096)
Pac 10	33.014	(0.883)	21.719	5.633	1.214	(5.622)	15.904	6.210	4.986	2.314	0.457	(0.944)
ACC	31.332	(0.350)	21.187	6.677	1.696	(4.529)	11.755	4.083	8.148	5.104	0.192	(1.266)
Big East	27.184	(3.787)	17.416	2.068	1.540	(4.527)	12.992	3.735	3.615	0.750	0.599	(0.986)
Mountain West	18.428	0.472	9.059	0.301	1.420	(2.353)	4.991	(0.059)	2.857	1.095	0.312	(0.564)
C-USA	14.421	(3.287)	8.021	(0.686)	0.564	(2.602)	4.529	(0.452)	2.865	1.060	0.161	(0.774)
WAC	11.704	(2.941)	5.208	(1.382)	0.492	(3.048)	3.112	(0.825)	1.701	0.500	0.111	(0.772)
MAC	10.102	(1.965)	2.277	(2.931)	0.531	(2.526)	1.440	(1.469)	0.504	(0.355)	0.141	(0.549)
Independent	8.670	(2.512)	3.798	(1.137)	0.990	(0.882)	3.017	0.148	0.344	(0.382)	0.060	(0.291)
Sun Belt	6.783	(2.510)	3.084	(1.483)	0.523	(1.533)	2.258	(0.791)	0.594	(0.279)	0.202	(0.395)
Average	25.358	(0.090)	16.634	4.971	1.128	(3.934)	11.483	4.897	3.900	1.781	0.336	(0.859)

*Total program revenues and net profits include men's programs, women's programs, and non-gender designated revenues (such as interest on athletic department general endowment funds).

Source: D. H. Fulks and NCAA Research Staff, *Revenues and Expenses, Profits and Losses of Division I-A Intercollegiate Athletic Programs Aggregated By Conference—2003 Fiscal Year.*

EXHIBIT 5-4   COMPOSITION OF MAJOR DIVISION I-A COLLEGE CONFERENCES IN 2004

Big Ten	Southeastern Conference (SEC)	Big 12	Pacific 10	Atlantic Coast Conference (ACC)
Illinois	Alabama	Baylor	Arizona	Clemson
Indiana	Arkansas	Colorado	Arizona State	Duke
Iowa	Auburn	Iowa State	California	Florida State
Michigan	Florida	Kansas	Oregon	Georgia Tech
Michigan State	Georgia	Kansas State	Oregon State	Maryland
Minnesota	Kentucky	Missouri	Southern California	Miami (FL)
Northwestern	Louisiana State	Nebraska	Stanford	North Carolina
Ohio State	Mississippi	Oklahoma	UCLA	North Carolina State
Penn State	Mississippi State	Oklahoma State	Washington	Virginia
Purdue	South Carolina	Texas	Washington State	Virginia Tech
Wisconsin	Tennessee	Texas A&M		Wake Forest
	Vanderbilt	Texas Tech		

Boston College (join in 2005)

Big East

Boston College (leave in 2005)
Connecticut
Georgetown*
Notre Dame*
Pittsburgh
Providence*
Rutgers
St. John's*
Seton Hall*
Syracuse
Temple
Villanova*
West Virginia

Cincinnati (join in 2005)
DePaul (join in 2005)
Louisville (join in 2005)
Marquette (join in 2005)
South Florida (join in 2005)

Sun Belt

Arkansas-Little Rock*
Arkansas State
Denver*
Idaho (football only; leave in 2005)
Louisiana-Lafayette
Louisiana-Monroe (football only)
Middle Tennessee State
New Mexico State (leave in 2005)
New Orleans*
North Texas
South Alabama*
Troy (football only)
Utah State (football only; leave in 2005)
Western Kentucky*

Florida Atlantic (join football in 2005 and all sports in 2006)
Florida International (join football only in 2005)

Conference USA

Alabama-Birmingham
Army
Charlotte
Cincinnati (leave in 2005)
DePaul (leave in 2005)
East Carolina
Houston
Louisville (leave in 2005)
Marquette (leave in 2005)
Memphis
Saint Louis
South Florida (leave in 2005)
Southern Mississippi
Texas Christian (leave in 2005)
Tulane

Central Florida (join in 2005)
Marshall (join in 2005)
Rice (join in 2005)
Southern Methodist (join in 2005)
Texas-El Paso (join in 2005)
Tulsa (join in 2005)

Western Athletic Conference (WAC)

Boise State
Fresno State
Hawaii
Louisiana Tech
Nevada
Rice (leave in 2005)
San Jose State
Southern Methodist (leave in 2005)
Texas-El Paso (leave in 2005)
Tulsa (leave in 2005)

Idaho (join in 2005)
New Mexico State (join in 2005)
Utah State (join in 2005)

Mountain West

Air Force
Brigham Young
Colorado State
Nevada-Las Vegas
New Mexico
San Diego State
Utah
Wyoming

Texas Christian (join in 2005)

Mid-American Conference (MAC)

Akron
Ball State
Bowling Green
Buffalo
Central Florida (leave in 2005)
Central Michigan
Eastern Michigan
Kent State
Marshall (leave in 2005)
Miami (OH)
Northern Illinois
Ohio
Toledo
Western Michigan

Independent

Navy
Notre Dame (football only)
Troy State*

*Indicates that the football team does not compete in the respective conference.

Source: Compiled from conference websites.

198

EXHIBIT 5-5   Conference Revenue Pools for Distribution to Member Colleges: 2001–2002

Conference (1)	Total Revenue Pool for Distribution (2)	Regular Season Football Conference Pool for Distribution (3)	Regular Season Basketball Pool for Distribution (4)	Football Bowl Games Pool for Distribution (5)	NCAA Basketball Tournament Pool for Distribution (6)
Big 10	$97.8	$62.4	$3.9	$24.7	$8.9
SEC	95.7	51.0	3.5	30.7	7.9
Big 12	84.0	43.0	4.0	26.6	6.4
Pac 10	64.0	37.8	4.0	19.3	6.9
ACC	87.6	49.1	5.3	20.5	7.6
Big East	55.4	28.0	N/A	18.7	7.3

Source: Street & Smith's *Sports Business Journal,* "By the Numbers" 2004.

greater revenue uncertainty. These uncertainties create the potential for operating losses to occur with some frequency. Many of the cost items in a college budget are committed at the start of the academic year and cannot be easily downsized if revenues fall short of budgeted amounts.

(b) Men's football and basketball programs are the major contributors (in both revenue and profit) to the finances of most Division 1-A and II-A athletic programs. These two men's programs effectively cross-subsidize many other college sports programs (men's and women's).

(c) Women's college athletic programs struggle to attract revenues in an absolute sense. Women's programs have total costs well above total revenues. Women's basketball is invariably the dominant revenue generator, followed by sports such as volleyball, softball, soccer, and gymnastics.

(d) College budgets benefit greatly from television contracts, many of which are negotiated at the NCAA or conference level. Exhibit 5-5 reports the size of the 2001–02 conference revenue pools that are distributed to member colleges. Column (2) reports the total amounts. Columns (3) to (6) report key individual components. There are two main conference revenue sources for football (men's) and basketball (men's and women's): regular season television contracts and postseason television contracts (for bowls in football and for tournaments in basketball). Exhibit 5-5 highlights the high drawing power of college football.

One issue in college budgeting and reporting is the diverse buckets where revenues are assigned. Alumni who feel intensely loyal to a college, in part because of its football team's success, may still make their alumni donations 100% at the university level, rather than assigning a part to athletics. Athletic departments often do not always receive credits for that part of donations (or increased donations) that alumni give due to the prowess and accomplishments of the current student athletes.

The tension between the academic side of a university and the revenue side of college sports plays out in the debate over "Who is the number one college football team?" At present, the Bowl Championship System (BCS) is structured without a sequence of elimination games that end up with a single "final college super game." The revenue attraction of adding extra bowl(s) to have the equivalent of "Playoffs and a Super Bowl" of college football is both self-evident and alluring. However, adding more bowls (and extending college football well into January) means disrupting the academic balance of college student-athlete life even more than does the current system. University presidents, to date, have not supported the development of a College Super Bowl elimination playoff-system. Some commentators on college sports, however, argue that if you "follow the money," it is just a matter of time before college football has its own annual "playoffs and mega-bowl event." The power of money in college athletic decisions is evident in some recent conference realignment decisions. The 2003 blockbuster announcement that the Atlantic Coast Conference (ACC) would include Miami and Virginia Tech starting in 2004 and Boston College in 2005 had a strong conference revenue growth motivation.

CASE 5.1 JEREMY BLOOM: "SHOW US THE MONEY"[12]

*When I was a kid, I remember my parents telling me that going to college
would broaden my horizons and give me all the opportunities in the world.
What I've found out, though, is that the benefits of being a student become
clouded when you add the word "athlete."*

— Jeremy Bloom[13]

Jeremy Bloom was an Olympic skier at age 19 when he made the U.S. skiing team for the 2002 Salt Lake City Winter Olympics and placed 9th in the mogul event. Later in 2002 he became the #1 ranked mogul skier in the World, and won first place in the 2002 U.S. Nationals. Bloom had attracted media attention long before reaching this status. Most Beautiful Man made him their "Most Beautiful Man of October 2002," citing his athletic prowess and his "toned and extremely physically fit body."

Professional skiing was populated with many athletes receiving money from endorsement and sponsorship contracts. Bloom was a natural to receive such contracts. However, accepting money from such contracts would potentially create problems with his eligibility to play college football for the University of Colorado Buffaloes. At Loveland High School in Colorado, Bloom was "member of the state championship football team, a two time state champion in track and field, a black belt in karate, and a student with a 3.4 grade point average."[14] He received a football scholarship to the University of Colorado (CU) in 2001, but delayed entry to train and compete in the 2002 Winter Olympics.

Prior to enrolling at CU, Bloom "earned income from wearing ski goggles and ski thermal underwear" bearing the manufacturers' logo while competing in World Cup Events. He also obtained paid on-camera acting opportunities with Nickelodeon and Music Television (MTV)."[15] In addition, Bloom was contracted to model clothing for Tommy Hilfiger. This income put Bloom in conflict with the NCAA and jeopardized his eligibility to play intercollegiate football.

Bloom's difficulties arose from NCAA rules, which had been developed using the single-sport assumption for a student-athlete. The NCAA required a student to be an amateur in their chosen college sport, which meant receiving no money from either participation or from endorsement/sponsorship contracts. Bloom was a two-sport athlete—football as well as skiing. NCAA rules permitted a student to be simultaneously an amateur in the college sport and a professional in the non-college sport. Being a professional enabled the athlete to accept payments to play and receive prize money. However, the NCAA prohibited two-sport student-athletes from receiving money from endorsement or sponsorship contracts in any sport, including those in which the student was a professional athlete. NCAA Bylaw 12.5.2.1 stated:

> *Subsequent to becoming a student-athlete, an individual shall not be
> eligible for participation in intercollegiate athletics if the individual:
> (a) Accepts any remuneration for or permits the use of his or her name or
> picture to advertise, recommend or promote directly the sale or use of a
> commercial product or service of any kind, or (b) Receives remuneration
> for endorsing a commercial product or service through the individual's use
> of such product or service.*[16]

For Bloom, this was a severe prohibition. Professional mogul skiers competed for minimal prize money—their income came from endorsement contracts, which could be very lucrative. This money was needed for them to practice and travel to remain among the elite skiers of the world.

Bloom discussed with CU officials the potential problems his commercial endorsements and other paid activities might have on his college football eligibility. The university requested a waiver for Bloom from the NCAA, meaning (if approved) that he could both continue such commercial arrangements for his skiing activities while playing college football for CU.

In August 2003, Bloom moved into a dormitory at CU. The previous week, a judge ruled in favor of the NCAA, denying an injunction that Bloom had sought in order to allow him to play football while receiving skiing endorsement money. Bloom announced that he was giving up his corporate endorsements in order to live in the university dorm and play football. He explained, "Everyone is here because they had a big dream when they were young, and pursuing that dream is worth more than any amount of money."[17] While he appealed the ruling, he focused on being a "typical freshman," temporarily foregoing his skiing career, which he could not maintain without corporate sponsorship.

In his freshman year, Bloom was both a wide receiver and special teams player for the University of Colorado Buffaloes. The first punt return of his college football career was a 75-yard touchdown against Colorado State. During his freshman year, he set records for the longest pass reception in CU history and longest punt return in Big IV Championship history.

Following his freshman football season, he returned to the slopes, winning multiple gold medals as well as a silver medal at the 2003 World Championships.

As he prepared to enter his sophomore year, Bloom again challenged the NCAA rules. In addition to challenging the rule that prohibited earning endorsement income in one sport while maintaining amateur status in another sport, Bloom's attorneys also fought the NCAA's prohibition against Bloom's television employment. They argued that this restriction diminished his education and his chance for a career after graduation.[18]

Bloom's opening brief for the appeal, dated July 2, 2003, stressed that his endorsements and sponsorship contracts arose "strictly by virtue of his skiing skills; they have 'absolutely' nothing to do with football." The brief also noted that "television opportunities had nothing to do with sports." Gary Barnett, the University's head football coach, stated that "Jeremy's 'once in a lifetime' television offers constitute 'educational opportunities.'"[19]

In August 2003 Bloom wrote an opinion piece titled "Show Us The Money" that outlined his position. He began by describing how he had looked forward to college since childhood, anticipating that it would "broaden my horizons" and provide lots of opportunities. However, he found that the NCAA limited those opportunities. He observed that the NCAA had changed from its initial focus on establishing rules for competition, and that it had become a big business, "a multibillion dollar organization that holds a monopoly on college athletics." As it had made this change, bringing in huge amounts of revenue from television and other sources, it had prevented the student-athletes from benefiting.

Bloom noted in his column that student-athletes received none of the $6 billion that CBS paid to the NCAA for television rights to the national basketball championship, while at the same time enforcing regulations that prevented the student-athletes from earning their own money. He found the response that student-athletes' scholarships should be sufficient to be inadequate, noting that with the heavy time commitments, if scholarships were considered payment, "we are recompensed at far less than the minimum wage." He observed that by the time any changes would be made, he would be long gone from intercollegiate athletics. Bloom then proposed a "Student-Athletes' Bill of Rights" that he had sent to state legislators nationwide, and that he felt would help the next generation of student-athletes.

> *Among other things, my proposal would allow student-athletes to "secure bona fide employment not associated with his/her amateur sport" and collect money generated by the sale of apparel that bears their names and jersey numbers. At the very least this would help student-athletes cover school-related costs, like travel and books, over and above what their scholarships pay for. Also, because the NCAA doesn't allow universities to cover a student-athlete's health insurance during the summer, the bill would assure student-athletes a full-time policy. It would also help financially burdened family members travel to post-season tournaments.[20]*

In his sophomore year, Bloom continued on the starting football squad of the University of Colorado. He also continued with his legal challenge to the NCAA's position regarding his non-eligibility to play college football if he accepted skiing related endorsements and sponsorships.

The Colorado Court of Appeals denied Bloom's request for an injunction against the NCAA in May 2004. It agreed with the lower court that Bloom had not shown that he would probably win his case, or that the NCAA was inconsistent in applying its rules. The court also stated that, "although student-athletes have the right to be professional athletes, they do not have the right to simultaneously engage in endorsement or paid media activity and maintain their eligibility to participate in amateur competition."[21]

Bloom responded in a statement saying:

> *While I certainly respect the court's decision to not overturn the lower court, it is still my intention to play college football, it is the NCAA's responsibility to determine if I will be eligible for collegiate competition next fall. I believe I should have the right to be a professional in the sport of freestyle skiing, as well as an amateur in the sport of football, the NCAA needs to evaluate the growing number of athletes competing in alternative sports such as the Summer X Games and the Olympics. It is my hope that the NCAA will realize it is unfair to exclude all of us from collegiate competition."[22]

BACKGROUND ON NCAA RULES ON COMPENSATION FOR STUDENT-ATHLETES

Athletes were required by the NCAA to be amateurs, with strict limitations on payments they could receive. The NCAA Bylaws clearly defined the organization's intent with respect to amateurism and intercollegiate athletics:

> *12.01.2 Clear Line of Demarcation. Member institution's athletics programs are designed to be an integral part of the educational program. The student-athlete is considered as an integral part of the student body, thus maintaining a clear line of demarcation between college athletics and professional sports.[23]*

The NCAA viewed athletes as students pursuing an education. The NCAA Bylaws (12.02.3) defined a professional athlete as: "one who receives any kind of payment, directly or indirectly, for athletics participation except as permitted by the governing legislation of the [NCAA]."[24] They then provided detailed rules on payments that were and were not permitted to student-athletes.

Student-athletes could not be paid for participating in a sport, or as a result of their public recognition as an athlete. They could receive financial aid from their schools (tuition, room, and board), as well as reimbursement for actual costs incurred (e.g. travel) when participating in their sport. They could work, but could only be paid for work actually performed, at a market rate. (This was intended to prevent inappropriate payments to student-athletes in the form of high-paying jobs that required little actual work.) They were not allowed to receive payments as a result of their athletic reputation.[25]

CHALLENGES FOR STUDENT-ATHLETES

The primary financial compensation for student-athletes was in the form of scholarships. At one time, scholarships were awarded for the student-athlete's entire four-year college experience, regardless of on-field performance. Over time, single-year scholarships, renewable annually, became the norm. This changed the perception of the scholarship, so that it was viewed as dependent on athletic performance rather than as a vehicle to provide an education to a student who participated in sports. This also threatened to change the relative priority of academics and athletics as perceived by student-athletes.

Scholarships typically did not cover a student-athlete's entire college cost. For instance, the room payment was based on the school's "official on-campus room allowance as listed in its catalog, or the average of the room costs of all of its students living on campus."[26] However, in many schools there was insufficient on-campus housing, so student-athletes needed to live elsewhere, often at higher cost than they received as a room allowance. Scholarships did not cover other costs, such as travel to school or trips home for breaks. They did not cover the cost of the student-athlete's family traveling to watch their child or sibling perform. Nor did they cover the cost for a student-athlete to return home for a family emergency. (The NCAA did, however, have a fund that student-athletes could apply to help with specific emergencies.)

Student-athletes could work, provided that the job fell within the NCAA's rules. However, student-athletes were at a disadvantage compared to other students. Participation in their sport took a substantial amount of time. The NCAA placed limits on the time requirements for student-athletes, but the time commitment was still high. During a sport's season, the NCAA Division I limitation was 4 hours of practice or competition per day, with a maximum of 20 hours per week.[27] During the off-season, the limit was 8 hours per week. Time spent in school-sponsored workouts was also limited during school holidays. The NCAA restricted the type of workouts that athletes could be required to attend in the off-season, primarily related to conditioning. Off-season workouts were supposed to be voluntary, but were often viewed by the student-athletes as required in order to maintain their standing on the team. As a result of these commitments and expectations, student-athletes had little time available for paying jobs, and had to find jobs with enough flexibility to enable them to continue their athletic training. And, if they didn't there was the possibility that their scholarships would not be renewed.

Student-athletes could not be provided medical insurance unless it was part of the required coverage for the general student body, and thus generally did not receive school-paid insurance for the summers. Injuries suffered in "voluntary" summer workouts, therefore, were not covered by insurance. Finally, student-athletes were not allowed to accept gifts from people other than family and "established family friends."

BLOOM DROPS LEGAL ACTION, CU PETITIONS NCAA ON BLOOM ELIGIBILITY

After the end of his second football season at the University of Colorado (December 2003), Bloom made several decisions. First, he began accepting ski-related endorsements and sponsorship money. Second, he decided not to pursue his legal challenge to the validity of the NCAA rules on college eligibility and receipt of endorsement/sponsorship money. The University of Colorado made a related decision to petition the NCAA to enable Bloom to continue playing college football on the grounds that the endorsements and sponsorships were skiing-specific and had no link to his amateur college sport of football—a petition that was denied in August 2004.

Bloom's attorney, Jim Smittkamp, commented: "Frankly, Jeremy said, 'I don't want to go this [legal appeal] route anymore' . . . We have dismissed the lawsuit and stopped."[28] University of Colorado football coach Gary Barnett doubted that Bloom would return to play his junior season. Bloom's father speculated that his son would not return to school for the following year, opting to fulfill his recently signed sponsorship commitments.

Questions

1. Why does the NCAA impose a requirement that student-athletes in their college years have an amateur as opposed to a professional status?

2. Outline the issues in the Jeremy Bloom case from:

   a. Jeremy Bloom's perspective

   b. The University of Colorado's perspective

   c. NCAA's perspective

3. Assume you are an elite student-athlete. You have just finished your third year at an NCAA-accredited college. What factors would you consider in deciding whether to (1) continue being a student-athlete or (2) enter the professional ranks of your chosen sport?

4. Who would benefit financially if the NCAA allowed student-athletes to receive payments for on-field performance and from sponsors/endorsements? Who might be disadvantaged?

CASE 5.2 MARQUETTE AND BUCKNELL WRESTLING PROGRAMS: WERE THEY PINNED BY TITLE IX?[29]

> *No person in the United States shall, on the basis of sex, be excluded from participation in, be denied the benefits of, or be subjected to discrimination under any education program or activity receiving Federal financial assistance.*
>
> — Title IX of the Education Amendments of 1972.[30]

Jim Schmitz, head coach of Marquette University's (MU) men's wrestling program will never forget June 15, 2001. That day the MU Athletic Director announced, effective immediately, that the men's wrestling program was being eliminated. The WrestlingMall.com commented in November 2002, "The elimination of a self-supporting program to merely comply with a quota law that has developed because of Title IX could not have been the original intent of this law. Could it?"[31]

At the time of the announcement, Schmitz had been at Marquette for 16 years, as a wrestler and coach. He stated, "I am all for athletics for everybody. It's a tremendous learning tool and I think athletics are for both men and women. I am all for women being in athletics, but I don't think dropping wrestling at Marquette is going to help any women anywhere."[32]

The problem, as seen by the Marquette wresting program, was that the school had not been able to grow its women's athletic program sufficiently to achieve a ratio of women to men athletes that was the same as the gender ratio in the student population (the "proportionality test")—one of the evaluation criteria used to evaluate compliance with Title IX of the Education Amendments of 1972 ("Title IX"). It was a law intended to provide equal educational opportunities for women.

The MU female student population was growing, to about 55 percent in 2001. Despite offering many scholarships, and adding women's soccer in 1992, the school was unable to sufficiently increase sports participation by women. Marquette had even limited the size of its men's track, soccer, tennis, and golf teams, but was unable to achieve the desired proportionality. Adding additional women's sports would be expensive. Coaches would have to be hired, facilities built, athletes recruited, and scholarships provided.

When the university had cut funding for the wrestling program in 1992, in response to a financial shortfall, the team built a network of donors, so that the program could continue independent from university financial support. Achieving independence from university support took a toll on the athletes and coaching staff. Athletes felt isolated from the university. Coaches added fundraising to their normal recruiting and coaching responsibilities. In spite of these obstacles, and despite the scheduling problems that resulted from Marquette having the only wresting program in their conference, the program continued, although with limited success. The team had posted a winning record in just two of the 11 years prior to the 2001 termination.

However, the university could not meet the proportionality requirements of Title IX, which were also required by the NCAA, and was faced with losing its standing in the NCAA.[33] Thus, the wrestling program was terminated, reducing the number of male athletes, and increasing the proportion of female athletes. Schmitz said of the June 15 announcement, "They announced the dropping on a Friday night, so it got buried in the news for the most part." [34]

The Marquette decision drew immediate criticism, with condemnation of the unintended consequences of Title IX. The Milwaukee Journal Sentinel commented:

> *This was not what women fought so hard for, this was never the intention of Title IX. What has happened in colleges across the country, and at Marquette University, is disturbing to a lot of supporters of men's non-revenue sports.*
>
> *Another team, Marquette wrestling, has been eliminated because of budget cuts and equity laws. How could this happen? Women just wanted the same chances men have to compete. They didn't want to take away men's opportunities, thus setting men's athletics back 30 years to where women's athletics were. Title IX was supposed to make things fair for women in the classroom and on the field. Instead, men's programs die out by the dozens in an ugly side effect to the federal law. NCAA wrestling alone has lost 56 teams in the last 20 years. . . .*
>
> *It was an agonizing choice for the MU staff, but the only practical one. So even though the wrestling team was privately funded, even though those wrestlers brought in money to the school by paying their own way, even though the team was also an academic success, the sport was dropped because it skewed the male-to-female proportionality requirement of Title IX.*[35]

Seven months after the Marquette wrestling program was terminated, on January 16, 2002, the Marquette Wrestling Club joined the National Wrestling Coaches Association (NWCA) and three other co-plaintiffs in suing the United States Department of Education. Their complaint stated:

> *Plaintiffs bring this action on behalf of their members to protect intercollegiate and scholastic athletic opportunities and teams from further elimination caused directly and indirectly by the unlawful rules that Defendant United States Department of Education (USDE) has issued under the color of implementing Title IX of the General Education Amendments Act of 1972.*[36]

Committee to Save Bucknell Wrestling

One of the NWCA co-plaintiffs was the "Committee to Save Bucknell Wrestling." Bucknell University, located in the central Pennsylvania town of Lewisburg, had discontinued men's wrestling as a varsity sport in 2001. During the school's initial Title IX NCAA Certification Review in 1995, the school was found to be out of compliance. In 1998, it initiated a 42-point Gender Equity Plan that was intended to bring the athletic program into compliance with Title IX requirements within five years. A particular focus of the plan was to achieve a ratio of male-to-female proportionality in varsity sports participation that reflected the ratio within the overall student body. Two women's sports were added in the 1998–99 academic

EXHIBIT 1

EXHIBIT 1 HIGH SCHOOL AND 4-YEAR COLLEGE WRESTLING PARTICIPATION

Year	State High Schools		NCAA 4-Year Colleges		
	Number of School Teams	Number of Participants	Number of College Teams	Number of Participants	Average Squad Size
1981–1982	8,512	245,029	363	7,914	21.8
1984–1985	8,273	248,300	325	8,572	26.4
1987–1988	8,426	251,281	289	7,031	24.3
1990–1991	8,416	233,856	280	7,092	25.3
1993–1994	8,438	222,025	264	6,468	24.5
1996–1997	8,738	227,596	248	6,510	26.3
1999–2000	9,046	239,105	234	6,279	26.8
2000–2001	9,404	244,984	225	5,966	26.5

Sources: High school data from National Federation of State High School Associations Participation Study 1971–2001.

NCAA data from "NCAA Year-By-Year Sports Participation 1982–2001," NCAA Research, http://www.ncaa.org/library/research/participation_rates/1982-2001/009-056.pdf (August 17, 2004).

year to increase women's participation. Team rosters were also managed to increase the proportion of women participating in varsity sports.

Discontinuing men's sports was also considered as part of the plan. In 2001, Bucknell terminated wresting and men's crew programs. The school later described the basis for the decision, saying, "To achieve 'substantial proportionality' under Title IX guidelines, Bucknell chose to discontinue wrestling and men's crew as varsity sports, later reclassifying them as club-varsity, so that they would not draw any university funds."[37]

The experiences of Marquette and Bucknell were not unique. Over the 20-year period from 1981 to 2001, there was a 38 percent decrease in 4-year college men's wrestling teams, and a 25 percent decrease in the number of participants. The NWCA listed 378 programs in 2-year and 4-year colleges that had been discontinued since Title IX was enacted in 1972.[38] This was in contrast to what was happening in high schools. Over the 1981–2001 period, there was a 10 percent increase in high school men's wrestling teams (although the total number of participants remained relatively constant). (Exhibit 1 provides details on high school and college teams and participation.)

TITLE IX BACKGROUND

Congress enacted Title IX of the Education Amendments of 1972 ("Title IX") in order to address the problem of discrimination against female students, and the lack of opportunities provided for girls and women by educational institutions.[39] Title IX provided that, "No person in the United States shall, on the basis of sex, be excluded from participation in, be denied the benefits of, or be subjected to discrimination under any education program or activity receiving Federal financial assistance."[40]

Over the years after Title IX was enacted, women made tremendous inroads into academic fields that had previously been dominated by men. For instance, in the 1971–72 academic year, just 9 percent of medical school graduates were women. Twenty years later, women received 41 percent of the medical degrees awarded. During the same period, women increased from 1 to 17 percent of engineering graduates, from 12 to 49 percent of business graduates, and from 7 to 44 percent of law school graduates.[41]

While it was clear that Title IX applied to academic programs, there was not a clear consensus that the statute applied to athletics. However, this was confirmed over the next several years by a number of lawsuits, which ruled that athletic programs were covered by Title IX, and validated the rules that USDE had established to implement the law. While Title IX did not specifically refer to athletic opportunity, and sports programs did not receive federal funding, these programs were covered because the colleges and universities received federal funding.

Title IX Evaluation Criteria

In 1979, the Department of Health, Education and Welfare adopted a policy interpretation of Title IX that included three criteria to evaluate compliance. An institution would be held to be in compliance if they could demonstrate that:

1) The male/female ratio of athletes at an institution is 'substantially proportionate' to the male/female ratio of undergraduate enrollment, or

2) It has a 'history and continuing practice of program expansion' for women, or

3) It is 'fully and effectively' accommodating the interests and abilities of women.[42]

The first criterion compared the gender percentage among student-athletes with that among the overall student body. In practice, most schools used this metric, as it was easily calculated, and was viewed as a "safe harbor" test by the government. Some claimed that this resulted in a quota system. To meet the requirements of Title IX, as measured by the proportionality yardstick, schools had to increase women's sports participation and/or decrease men's participation.

The second and third criteria (steadily increasing opportunities for women, and demonstration that the athletic program was meeting women's needs) were seldom used due to their subjectivity. By 2004, the "steadily increasing opportunities" criterion was considered by some to be obsolete. The Title IX law was over thirty years old, and one would be hard pressed to demonstrate that a school had been providing steadily increasing opportunities for that period of time without achieving some objective measure of equal opportunity.

In the thirty years following the enactment of Title IX, women athletes made impressive advancements. For 2001–02, the NCAA reported that women accounted for 44 percent of student-athletes. In Division I-AAA, which did not have football, women and men had equal participation.[43]

CONTROVERSIAL ISSUES IN MEETING TITLE IX OBJECTIVES

The statistical gains made by women athletes indicated that progress was being made in meeting the objectives of Title IX. However, this success had not come without controversy. The controversy centered on several issues which represented a conflict, in the minds of some, between the objectives of increasing opportunities for women, and steps taken to meet numerical participation ratio requirements. Problem areas included: treatment of football (a sport that produced significant revenue and involved a high number of athletes, all of whom were male), elimination of male non-revenue sports programs to reallocate funding to women's teams, and the treatment of "walk-on" and other non-recruited student athletes.

The Impact of Football on Title IX Compliance

Most intercollegiate sports programs made little, if any, net profit. For the vast majority of schools, the only sports that generated significant revenue were football and men's basketball. By far the largest sport, in terms of numbers of participants per institution, was football—solely a men's sport.

In the 2001–02 school year, Division I football teams averaged 106 student-athletes, by far the most of any sport.[44] For Division I, II, and III, nearly a quarter of male student-athletes were on football teams.[45] The average number of participants per Division I institution was 262 men and 260 women.[46] Thus, if an institution had equal numbers of men and women in its student body, had a football program, and wanted to have sports participation that was proportional, there would have to be many more women's teams than men's teams. Since most sports had 15–30 student-athletes per team, to counter the large football team an athletic department would need to have about 5 more non-revenue teams for women than it had for men.

Elimination of Men's Non-Revenue Sports Programs

In order to meet proportionality objectives, women athletes needed to be added at a higher rate then men. If not enough women could be added to an athletic program, a numerical proportionality target could be achieved by reducing the number of male athletes. In order to evaluate this, the GAO issued a report in 2001 on the addition and elimination of teams in intercollegiate athletics. The GAO reported that between 1981–82 and 1998–99, the number of women's teams had increased by over 65 percent (from 5,695 to 9,479). The number of men's teams had remained nearly unchanged, at 9,149 in 1998–99, just 36 more than in 1981–82.[47]

Between 1981–82 and 1998–99, the sport that had added the most teams was women's soccer, increasing from 80 teams to 926 and adding 18,132 participants. Of the 25 women's sports surveyed, all but six had increased both teams and participants.[48] Of the 26 men's sports included in the report, 15 had remained unchanged or suffered decreases in teams over the 17 year period. The sport with the most teams eliminated was wrestling.

The GAO surveyed the reasons for discontinuing teams. For men's teams, the reason cited most often as "greatly or very greatly" affecting the decision was "insufficient student interest" (33 percent), followed closely by "gender equity goals/regulations" (31 percent), and "resources needed for other sports" (30 percent).[49]

The Walk-On Issue

An additional consideration was the question of walk-on athletes. Many of the student-athletes participating in intercollegiate sports were recruited and offered some form of scholarship. However, students that were not recruited ("walk-ons") could attempt to qualify for teams. In evaluating a school's progress toward Title IX goals, walk-ons counted equally with recruited players. If a school planned its athletic program to meet Title IX objectives, it had control over the number of athletes it recruited, and could focus its recruiting efforts towards attracting women. However, if a significant number of men walked-on, the gender equity metrics would be skewed, even if the additional male participants created only minimal additional expense or resource demand on the institution. In this situation, the school might feel pressure to limit the number of men allowed to participate, denying opportunities to those who had not been recruited.

NWCA LOSES TITLE IX CASE

On June 11, 2003, Emmet G. Sullivan, United States District Court Judge for the District of Columbia dismissed the NWCA v. USDE lawsuit. Sullivan stated in his ruling opinion:

> *Before entertaining claims which contemplate taking the dramatic step of striking down a landmark civil rights statute's regulatory enforcement scheme, the Court must take pains to ensure that the parties and allegations before it are such that the issue will be fully and fairly litigated. This is particularly true where the challenged enforcement scheme is one which has benefited from more than twenty years of study, critical examination, and judicial review, and for which a demonstrated need continues to be recognized by the nation's legislators. In the Court's view, plaintiffs have failed to meet their burden of persuasion on the question of whether they are the proper parties to be asserting the claims they raise against the defendant.*[50]

The Women's Sports Foundation lauded the decision, stating in a press release:

> *The court's decision made it clear that Title IX cannot be blamed for cuts to men's teams because educational institutions make decisions based on multiple unrelated factors. The court also recognized the importance of Title IX, characterizing it as a "landmark" civil rights statute with implementing policies and a significant flexibility built into the Department of Education's enforcement considerations, thus negating the allegation of "quotas". The court specifically stated that every federal appellate court that has considered the issue has upheld the Title IX policies.*
>
> *Dawn Riley, President of the Women's Sports Foundation stated, "This is absolutely the right decision. It reflects the intent of the law, the fact that the public wants our sons and daughters to be treated fairly and equitably and it allows everyone to focus on moving forward to achieve the promise of Title IX. The Women's Sports Foundation applauds the court's decision."*[51]

In May 2004, The U.S. Court of Appeals for the District of Columbia Circuit upheld Sullivan's decision to dismiss the NWCA lawsuit.

Bucknell Wrestling to be Reinstated

By 2003, Bucknell had reached full compliance with the NCAA's requirements under Title IX. Men's participation was 51 percent, while 49 percent of the school's varsity athletes were women.[52]

On May 7, 2004, Bucknell announced that it had received a $5.6 million donation from William Graham, chairman and chief executive officer of Philadelphia-based The Graham Company. Graham had been co-captain of the Bucknell wresting team in 1962, and a long-time supporter of the school's athletic program.

Graham's grant was structured as two equal distributions—half to support men's wrestling, and half to support a variety of women's sports, with an emphasis on women's crew. Thus, it was expected to provide an equal number of new varsity opportunities for both men and women, enabling the university to maintain its Title IX compliance.

The men's wresting program would be reinstated as a varsity sport in the 2005–2006 academic year, underwritten entirely by endowments from the Graham gift. The women's crew program would be enhanced beginning in 2006, with additional coaches and increased funding. A new women's lacrosse and field hockey field was also built with money from the grant, and an endowment established to support women's athletics.

The press release announcing the gift stated:

> "We are extremely pleased to accept Mr. Graham's generous donation," said Judge Susan Crawford, chairwomen of Bucknell's Board of Trustees. "This is the latest step in a long line of efforts to work within the mandates of Title IX for the betterment of the institution and student-athletes alike."

> "Bucknell's decision to reclassify the men's wrestling team in 2001 was extremely difficult to make. This donation gives us the opportunity to reinstate the varsity program to provide our students the quality opportunities they deserve while complying with Title IX requirements," said John Hardt, Bucknell's director of athletics and recreation. "We hope that Bill Graham's leadership and financial support can serve as a model for other institutions seeking to improve their programs for both male and female students."[53]

Mike Moyer, the Executive Director of the National Wrestling Coaches Association (NWCA), called the restoration unprecedented:

> "All I can say is 'wow!' This is a great day for athletics. To our knowledge, there's never been a Division I program that's been either reclassified or discontinued and has been resurrected several years later. We can only hope this inspires other universities to develop innovative strategies for reinstating discontinued programs while bolstering their women's programs at the same time."[54]

Questions

1. Why was the Title IX legislation passed? Why has it had an important effect on the business side of college sports?

2. Assume you are the athletic director at Marquette University:

   a. What was the sequence of events that led to the men's wrestling program being eliminated?

   b. What options do you have other than eliminating the men's wrestling program? Discuss the viability of each.

   c. How should you "manage" the anticipated negative reaction to your decision to eliminate the men's wrestling program?

3. Repeat Question 2 for Bucknell University.

4. One proposal to make Title IX compliance have less impact on men's sports is to exempt the number of athletes in men's football when computing the ratio of male to female athletes vis-à-vis the ratio for the undergraduate enrollment. What are the pros and cons of this proposal?

Case 5.3 Notre Dame: What Price Independence?[55]

In June 2003 three Division I-A institutions announced they were leaving the Big East Conference in order to join the Athletic Coast Conference (ACC), bringing the conference to 12 schools, including several traditional football powerhouses such as Miami and Florida State. The new ACC members would be Miami and Virginia Tech in 2004, and Boston College in 2005. The ACC also included perennial basketball powerhouses Duke and North Carolina. The announcement took three premier schools from the Big East, which was losing one additional football school (Temple) in 2004 to independence. The Big East acted quickly to fill the vacancies, resulting in a wave of realignments as conferences scrambled to adjust.

Officials at the University of Notre Dame watched these conference realignments with interest. The school was the premier Catholic university, with a rich football tradition. It was private, and had fostered a national following in part due to the independence of its football program. Notre Dame had previously considered conference membership, most recently in the late 1990s, ultimately deciding to forego Big Ten membership to remain independent. With the changing conference landscape, the issue resurfaced. Should it join the ACC, with its roster of strong football and basketball programs? Should it take another look at the Big Ten, which included some long-time football rivals as well as a prestigious academic collaboration? Or should it remain independent?

The College Conference System

The conference system grouped institutions into leagues sharing similar characteristics, such as geographical location. Conferences fostered inter-school rivalries, which increased fan interest. Participation in conferences enabled schools to join together to negotiate financial arrangements, such as television or post-season bowl contracts.

In 2004 there were six major Division I-A athletic conferences that participated in the football Bowl Championship Series (BCS) program (the Big Ten, ACC, Big East, Southeastern Conference, Big 12, and Pacific Ten). Other conferences were made up of schools with smaller athletic programs or in different NCAA divisions. Some conferences also had non-football schools, and some schools were members of multiple conferences—one for football and one for other sports. Football, and its large revenue generating capacity, was a key driving force for most of the changes in conference structure. Exhibit 5-4 of the Section 5 text outlines the composition of the Major Division I-A conferences in 2004.

The importance of the conference structure could also be seen in NCAA Division I governance. In 1997, the division changed from a legislative system based on member schools to one based on conferences. An 18-member Division I Board of Directors, consisting of conference representatives, voted on proposed legislation, replacing the previous system of voting by all schools at an annual convention.[56]

Conference Championships, Bowls, and the Bowl Championship Series

Conferences were originally formed to standardize rules and develop competitive leagues for intercollegiate sports. As football bowl games and television became substantial revenue generators, conferences took a leading role in negotiating deals, and distributing revenues to each school in the conference. In this way, a conference could package a series of games to sell to a television network, wielding far greater leverage than the individual schools negotiating alone. For instance, the Southeastern Conference (SEC) had television contracts that were expected to generate $101 million in 2003 for its 12 schools. The SEC had long-term contracts with CBS, ESPN, and a local television station for broadcasting football and basketball.[57] Notre Dame was a notable exception to the conference system. It kept its football program independent and negotiated a national television contract with NBC worth about $9 million per year, while joining the Big East for other sports.

For conferences, football was by far the largest revenue generator.[58] Revenue could be increased by adding more games—particularly championship games, but the NCAA limited the number of football games per season to 11. A conference could add an additional game if it had 12 teams. In that case, the NCAA bylaws allowed the conference to divide into two divisions, and to add a 12th game as a championship game between the winners of each division.[59] This offered the potential for substantial increased revenue, from both ticket sales and television. Thus, there was a financial incentive for conferences to have 12 football schools.

Bowl games were another important conference revenue source. Many of the major bowls, such as the Rose Bowl, were played between the winners of two conferences—in the case of the Rose Bowl, between the winners of the Pacific Ten and the Big Ten conferences. The conferences negotiated with the bowls, and distributed funds to the conference schools.

In 1998, four major bowls joined with six major conferences (plus Notre Dame) to form the Bowl Championship Series (BCS).[60] The purpose was to establish a system by which the top two teams in the country would play for the national championship. Previous attempts had been made to increase the likelihood that the top two teams would play against each other in a post-season bowl game by eliminating some conference tie-ins to bowls, increasing the potential number of at-large invitations, and allowing the bowls to invite the best teams. The BCS was the first system devised specifically to determine a national champion.

The BCS agreement ran through the 2005 season (and 2006 bowl games). The four bowls rotated as hosts of the national championship game, played between the top two teams as determined by a rating system devised by BCS. When not hosting the national championship, bowl participants would include regional conference considerations—the FedEx Orange Bowl would include either the ACC or Big East champion, the Rose Bowl would be played between the champions of the Pac-10 and Big Ten, the Nokia Sugar Bowl would have the SEC champion, and the Tostitos Fiesta Bowl would include the Big 12 champion. If one of these champions was one of the top two ranked teams, that team would play in the national championship game, and the bowl could select a replacement as long as it met certain BCS criteria.

The BCS received money from ABC Sports for television rights, plus money from each of the bowls (not including the Rose Bowl, which paid the Pac-10 and Big Ten conferences directly). In 2004, this was estimated at nearly $90 million. $6 million was distributed to Division I-A and I-AA conferences that did not have automatic births in the BCS bowls for the general support of college football, with another $600,000 used to support other college football-related activities. The balance, over $83 million, was distributed among the BCS conferences. (The total amount going to the BCS conferences was actually closer to $115 million, including the $14-17 million paid to each of the Pac-10 and Big Ten directly by the Rose Bowl.)[61] Conferences generally split bowl revenue evenly among member institutions, after reimbursing the team playing in the bowl game for its budgeted expenses.

Thus, the BCS was a mechanism for both determining a national champion in football as well as coordinating post-season revenue generation for conferences, both those with automatic participation in BCS games, as well as those that did not participate in BCS games. There were many other bowl games, whose organizers could contract directly with conferences for their games. However, the most lucrative games were those in the BCS system.

Historical Conference Changes

Changes in the composition of conferences were not a new phenomenon. For instance, in the early 1990s one of the important conferences was the Southwest Conference, founded in 1914 and including such institutions as the University of Texas, Texas A&M, Texas Tech, Baylor, and University of Arkansas (the only non-Texas school in the conference). The conference began to suffer in the 1960s when professional football came to Texas and began to compete with the intercollegiate game for spectators and television money. By the 1980s, attendance at conference games was significantly lower than historical levels, and the large schools became unhappy with their share the conference's revenue sharing plan, complaining that too much was going to support smaller schools. In 1990, Arkansas left to join the SEC.

In 1977, more than 60 major football colleges (not including those in the Pac-10 and Big Ten), formed the College Football Association (CFA), which provided leverage in negotiating television contracts. Notre Dame left the CFA in 1990 to negotiate its own national television deal. In 1994, a television contract between ABC and the CFA fell apart when the SEC left to sign a separate agreement with CBS. Conferences then scrambled to negotiate the best deals they could make on their own. With the weakness of the Southwest Conference, Texas, Texas A&M, Texas Tech, and Baylor left for the Big Eight, forming the Big 12. The four remaining schools in the Southwest Conference were forced to look for new conference homes, and the Southwest Conference died.[62]

Notre Dame and Conference Affiliation

The University of Notre Dame, founded in 1842, was located in South Bend, Indiana, about 90 miles southeast of Chicago. It was a private, independent, Catholic university with a national scope. The school's enrollment was just over 11,000 students.

The Notre Dame "Fighting Irish" had a rich football tradition, coming to national attention in 1913 when the team beat Army by using the then-revolutionary forward pass. Notre Dame achieved national prominence under famed coach Knute Rockne (a receiver in the victory over Army), who led the team to a 101-12-5 record from 1918 to 1930. Rockne's exhortation to "win one for the Gipper" in a victory over heavily favored Army in 1928 became the stuff of legends, and was later immortalized in film. From 1887 to 1999, Notre Dame had the best overall winning percentage of any school, winning 75.7 percent of its games, including eight national championships. While a football powerhouse, Notre Dame also had a strong undergraduate academic program, graduating 98 percent of scholarship players who stayed four years.[63]

Notre Dame's nationwide popularity could be seen in the results of a poll conducted by ESPN in 2004 (Exhibit 1). The "Favorite College Football Teams" poll surveyed 6,949 respondents, who ranked Notre Dame number one nationwide. In addition to a nationwide ranking, the poll surveyed popularity in each of four regions. Notre Dame was the only school in the top nine in each of the four regions, confirming both its nationwide and regional popularity.[64]

Notre Dame football could also be seen by its attendance figures. It filled its stadium, which had been renovated to hold 80,000 in 1997, in 209 out of 210 games prior to the 2004 season. It also had an impressive record of selling out nearly 60 percent of its road games. Over the school's history, it had played to capacity crowds in 66.8 percent of its games, both home and away.[65]

While Notre Dame's football program had always been independent, the school had periodically considered conference membership, particularly in the Big Ten, which was well suited geographically and included some of the school's traditional rivals. In 1999, the Big

EXHIBIT 1   NOTRE DAME FOOTBALL: AN ELITE PROGRAM AT AN ELITE SCHOOL

Panel A: Favorite College Football Teams, 2004 (ESPN Sports Poll Results)

	Overall	Northeast	North Central	South	West
1	**Notre Dame**	Penn State	Ohio State	Texas	UCLA
2	Ohio State	**Notre Dame**	Wisconsin	Tennessee	USC
3	Penn State	Syracuse	Michigan	Georgia	**Notre Dame**
4	Michigan	Boston Col.	**Notre Dame**	Florida	Washington
5	Miami (FL)	Miami (FL)	Nebraska	Florida State	Oregon
6	Texas	Pittsburgh	Minnesota	Miami (FL)	Colorado
7	Nebraska	Michigan	Michigan St.	Oklahoma	Oregon State
8	Wisconsin	Ohio State	Iowa	**Notre Dame**	Nebraska
9	Florida State	North Carolina	Missouri	Alabama	Michigan

Source: "ESPN Sports Poll: Notre Dame Reigns as Top Football Program," *Sports Business Daily*, August 27, 2004.

Panel B: Top Ten Schools with Most NFL Players: 1998–2002

Rank	School	Number of Players	Starters	% Starters	With Degrees	% Degrees
1	Notre Dame	218	96	44%	136	62%
2	Florida State	211	117	55	83	39
3	Miami	186	82	44	68	37
4	Texas A&M	182	73	40	36	20
5	Tennessee	181	76	42	60	33
6	Penn State	173	80	46	77	45
7	Michigan	172	78	45	61	35
8	Florida	169	73	43	51	30
9	Ohio State	168	74	44	40	24
10	North Carolina	161	67	42	81	50

Source: M.J. Duberstein, "Schools Producing the Most NFL Players: 1998–2002," NFLPA.org (document dated November 2003)

Ten courted Notre Dame, but the school decided to remain independent. In announcing the decision, Father Malloy, the university president, noted that, "Notre Dame has a core identity, and at that core are these characteristics—Catholic, private, and independent." He contrasted Notre Dame with other members of the Big Ten, "Notre Dame would be one of only two private universities . . . and the only one with a religious affiliation." It would also be much smaller than any of the other Big Ten schools.[66]

Others speculated that economics might have played an important role in the decision. After all, the school did have a conference affiliation with the Big East for 21 sports. The Notre Dame basketball program had moved to the Big East in 1995 in order to improve the quality of its competitive schedule.[67] Independence was reserved for its football program.

Economic Benefits of Independence

Football was the economic engine of the Notre Dame athletics program, with $39 million of the school's $44 million in allocated revenue coming from football (the school generated an additional $10 million in unallocated revenue. Football generated a surplus of $28 million (Exhibit 2).

Independence enabled Notre Dame to schedule games with top schools throughout the country, without having to reserve schedule dates for conference obligations. Playing a nation-wide schedule enhanced its national reputation and fan following. The school was able to capitalize on its independence and national following economically by directly negotiating a television contact. It initially signed a contract with NBC in 1990, covering every Notre Dame home game. The contract was renewed at the end of 2003, covering the period from 2005 to 2010. Although terms were not disclosed, the extension was estimated to be worth about $9 million per year.[68] In addition to being able to keep all its television revenue, Notre Dame did not need to share post-season bowl revenue with other institutions, as was the case with conference members.

EXHIBIT 2   NOTRE DAME ATHLETIC DEPARTMENT FINANCIAL INFORMATION (FOR 2002–2003, VALUES IN $)

Revenues	Men's	Women's	Total
Basketball	3,163,537	334,285	3,496,822
Football	39,103,268		39,103,268
All other sports	936,266	492,949	1,429,215
Total Revenues	43,202,071	827,234	44,029,305
Not allocated by sport			10,162,257
Grand Total Revenue			54,191,562
Expenses			
Basketball	2,735,627	1,790,882	4,526,519
Football	11,212,130		11,212,130
All other sports	5,552,017	6,406,750	11,958,767
Total Expenses	19,499,784	8,197,632	27,697,416
Not allocated by sport			11,916,935
Grand Total Expenses			39,614,351
Total Surplus			14,577,211

Source: Equity in Athletics Disclosure Act filing for academic year 2002–2003, http://ope.ed.gov/athletics/InstDetail.asp?CRITERIA=3 (September 7, 2004).

Benefits of Conference Affiliation

As the intercollegiate sports landscape evolved, conferences had become the primary power brokers. Notre Dame was an exception, but there was no assurance that it could retain its position in the face of powerful conferences.

While the NBC television contract was an incentive to remain independent, there were other factors that favored a conference affiliation. For instance, participation in a conference could ensure year-to-year consistency in scheduling. It could cushion the impact of a series of years with poor on-field performance, which had historically resulted in decreased television viewership and might jeopardize future contracts. It could also enhance the school's opportunities for participating in post-season bowl games.

As a member of a major conference, Notre Dame would automatically receive access to the BCS, as well as secondary bowl games. It would have an eight game conference schedule (with three additional games open for non-conference teams), and would receive a television package negotiated by the conference. As an independent, each of these had to be directly negotiated by the school. Schedules, for instance, were directly negotiated with other schools, most of which had conference commitments that impacted their availability. This made it difficult to schedule top-flight opponents, potentially reducing fan interest as well as making it more difficult to qualify for the BCS pool and major bowl games.

Conference participation also increased access to post-season bowl games. Members of the major conferences were automatically included in the BCS pool. Notre Dame negotiated separately for BCS access, but the criteria for inclusion had become increasingly restrictive. Most of the non-BCS bowls chose teams based on conference affiliations, limiting opportunities for independents.

As a member of a conference, Notre Dame would still receive bowl money. In 2004, each BCS conference was expected to receive more than $17 million, which would be distributed among its members.[69] In the seven seasons before 2004, Notre Dame had qualified for the BCS pool three times, but went to only one top-tier bowl game (the Fiesta Bowl following the 2000 season). Despite records of 9–2 in 1998 and 10–2 in 2002, the team was invited only to the second-tier Gator Bowl,[70] which paid less than $4 million.[71]

For a conference, adding Notre Dame and its national following would provide additional clout in negotiating television and other agreements. Even before the NBC deal expired, the presence of Notre Dame in a conference would increase the value of television rights for the team's games that were hosted by other conference members. (See Exhibit 3 for members of the Big Ten, ACC, and Big East conferences, together with football revenues for each of these institutions.)

The Big Ten

Notre Dame had a long history of discussions with the Big Ten, dating back to the days of Knute Rockne, when the conference decided not to admit Notre Dame, continuing to the 1999 decision by the university not to join the conference.

Then Big Ten (which consisted of eleven teams in 2004), was based in the Midwest, and included such traditional football powerhouses as Ohio State and Michigan. It was a natural

EXHIBIT 3 CONFERENCE CONFIGURATION AND FOOTBALL REVENUES OF POTENTIAL NOTRE DAME AFFILIATIONS (FOOTBALL REVENUE IN $ MILLIONS)

Atlantic Coast Conference	Rev.	Big East	Rev.	Big Ten	Rev.
Boston College (starting 2005)	13.0	Boston College (leaving 2005)	13.0	Illinois	16.0
Clemson	22.8	Connecticut	3.2	Indiana	13.3
Duke	7.0	Pittsburgh	16.1	Iowa	23.7
Florida State	18.7	West Virginia	13.8	Michigan	36.7
Georgia Tech	12.2	Syracuse	17.2	Michigan State	21.1
Maryland	9.2	Temple (leaving 2005)	7.1	Minnesota	14.7
Miami	21.9	Rutgers	5.9	Northwestern	13.9
North Carolina	15.2	Cincinnati (starting 2005)	7.2	Ohio State	52.7
North Carolina State	9.8	Louisville (starting 2005)	11.3	Penn State	46.2
Virginia	13.2	South Florida (starting 2005)	5.0	Purdue	19.8
Virginia Tech	20.2			Wisconsin	24.6
Wake Forest	7.1				

Football revenues from disclosures made under the Equity in Athletics Disclosure Act, for the 2002–2003 academic year. Revenues do not include revenues that are not allocated by sport.

Sources: Conference web sites for conference membership. US Department of Education, Office of Postsecondary Education website for revenues: http://ope.ed.gov/athletics/Search.asp (September 7, 2004)

fit geographically with Indiana-based Notre Dame, which would be a particular benefit to non-revenue sports teams, whose schedules would be relatively close to home. Most of the Big Ten schools were large land-grant colleges. Northwestern, the only private institution in the Big Ten in 2004, was considerably smaller than the other schools, with an enrollment only slightly larger than Notre Dame. None of the Big Ten schools had a religious affiliation.

With eleven schools, the Big Ten was one short of the 12 needed to qualify for a conference championship game. Notre Dame would provide the 12th team, enabling the conference to divide into two divisions and conduct a championship game, increasing revenues for conference members.

There were also broader academic considerations. The Big Ten schools and the University of Chicago combined to form the "Committee on Institutional Cooperation (CIC)" a highly prestigious consortium. CIC shared ideas, resources, and facilities, with a graduate school focus. Advocates argued that participation in the CIC would help develop the school (particularly its graduate school program) to world-class status. In the late 1990s, Notre Dame faculty representatives had voted 25–4 to join the CIC, which would have also resulted in Notre Dame joining the Big Ten.[72]

The Atlantic Coast Conference

In 2004 the ACC was on the rise, having added three schools in 2003, including the extremely successful football program of the University of Miami. Another top football school, Florida State, was also part of the ACC. Two of the finest basketball programs were in the ACC—Duke and North Carolina.

Geographically, Notre Dame was somewhat far afield from the rest of the ACC institutions, which were located along the Atlantic Coast. Attracting Notre Dame would increase the conference's geographic reach and national exposure. From Notre Dame's perspective, it would align the school with some of the most prominent athletic programs in the country, ensuring high quality schedules.

The ACC member institutions were more diversified than those in the Big Ten, however, with several institutions of similar size to Notre Dame. Duke, for instance, was a private institution of about 11,000 students—about the same as Notre Dame. While not a religious school, Duke had religious roots. Wake Forest was a private institution even smaller than Notre Dame, with an enrollment of about 6,400. Clemson was a public university, but also relatively close to Notre Dame's size, at 16,000 students.

The Decision for Notre Dame

Notre Dame had been independent throughout its illustrious football history. In 2004, the school had a national following and was able to command a lucrative television contract as well as access to BCS and other bowl games. However, the intercollegiate football landscape was changing. Powerful conferences negotiated for television and post-season bowl rights. Ensuring a high-quality schedule without a conference affiliation was increasingly difficult. Many bowl games were restricted to conference members, and thus inaccessible to the school.

Would Notre Dame's prestige and national fan base be sufficient to enable it to maintain its position over the long term in the face of these pressures—particularly if it had a few poor seasons (as it had experienced in the recent past)? Or did it need to make plans to eventually become a conference member?

Questions

1. Describe Notre Dame's (ND) affiliation status as regards NCAA sports as described in the case.

2. What are the benefits and costs of ND's football team retaining its independent status?

3. Assume ND's president and his advisors decide to pursue affiliation with a conference for its football program (such as the ACC or the Big Ten). What factors should guide the choice of a specific conference?

4. In November 2004, ND made a dramatic announcement: it was firing its football coach (Tyrone Willingham) at the end of year 3 of a 5-year contract. His 2004 (3-year) record was 6 wins 5 losses (21 wins 15 losses). Willingham was one of only three remaining black head coaches among the 117 Division I-A football programs. It was the first time ND had fired a coach before the original contract length had expired. What factors might have led to this decision?

5. Do you agree with the following comment: "The firing of Willingham highlights what we already knew. College sports are about money, even at schools like Notre Dame that profess otherwise. College sports and professional sports are now the same as regards why key decisions are made."? Explain.

CASE 5.4 SAN JOSE STATE'S FOOTBALL PROGRAM: IS IT THE FINAL PLAY FOR THE SPARTANS?[73]

"You take football out . . . and it affects everything."
— John Twining, former Athletic Department CFO,
San Jose State University.

As the 2004 college football season kicked off, the San Jose State Spartans[74] were at a crossroads. If the critics of the program had their way, it would be the Spartans' last season. In the face of continuing budget cuts from the state legislature, some students and faculty questioned the need for a sub-par football team that continued to lose money year after year. They argued that the "resources could be better spent on education—which was, after all, the mission of the university." The supporters of the football program countered that despite the team's poor performance in recent years, the team fostered school spirit among the student body and provided the university with name recognition that it would not otherwise have. They also noted that part of student education occurred while participating in sports programs. Education and sports were not "either/ors" as critics of SJSU's football program often implied. Despite their differences, both sides agreed on one thing—a swift decision about the fate of the football team was necessary. Nobody wanted the program to have the slow "death of a thousand cuts."

The debate over the financial consequences of SJSU dropping the football program was literally put on the "front page" when Jon Wilner of The San Jose Mercury News wrote a three-part series a week before the Spartans opened their 2004 season against the Stanford Cardinals. Exhibit 1 shows summary data on SJSU's football on-field success and attendance for 1998 to 2003. Exhibits 2 and 3 are reproduced from The San Jose Mercury series—they are based on a combination of "official school documents" and "estimates/analysis" by Wilner.

San Jose State University

San Jose State University (SJSU) is a large, urban, commuter school. It is located in the heart of California's Silicon Valley in downtown San Jose. Founded in 1857, SJSU was the first in what would later become the California State University system—a system which now

EXHIBIT 1

Season	Win/Loss	Number of Home Games	Average Home Game Attendance	Total Number of Division I-A Programs	SJSU Attendance Rank in Division I-A Programs
1998	4/8	5	12,532	112	105
1999	3/7	4	7,973	114	113
2000	7/5	5	12,103	114	106
2001	3/9	4	10,207	115	112
2002	6/7	4	10,360	117	115
2003	3/8	5	15,080	117	106

EXHIBIT 2   **ATHLETIC DEPARTMENT BUDGET**

	2003–04 Budget (1)	Internal Projection: 2003–04 Budget Without Football (2)	Mercury Projection: 2003–04 Budget Without Football (3)	Notes
Revenues				
General fund support	5,864,536	4,188,137	4,188,137	Decline proportional to reduction in state funding because of fewer student athletes
General fund support - benefits	987,966	791,735	716,735	Decline because of staffing reduction
Student IRA	798,000	798,000	798,000	
Spartan Foundation	1,235,906	125,000	588,977	Decreased alumni giving to athletics department
Ticket sales	481,098	75,000	75,000	Football ticket sales eliminated
Athletic revenue-guarantees	1,125,000	—	—	
WAC	635,000	—	10,000	Big West conference revenue estimate in Scenario II
NCAA	300,000	140,000	185,000	Big West per team revenue from NCAA in Scenario II
Sponsorships	295,000	75,000	75,000	75% reduction if football is eliminated
Champs/life skills program	3,000	3,000	3,000	
Camps	50,000	50,000	50,000	
	11,775,506	6,245,872	6,689,849	
Expenses				
Salaries	3,984,440	3,166,940	2,866,940	
Benefits	987,966	791,735	716,735	Reduction proportional to staffing reduction
Grant-in-aid	2,624,000	1,700,000	1,700,000	Elimination of football scholarships
Event related	1,060,100	740,100	740,100	Elimination of football game expenses
Travel	1,418,500	838,500	400,000	Column (3) based on estimates from Big West Travel
Phones/postage	170,550	120,550	120,550	
Supplies/equipment	434,950	300,000	252,950	
WAC dues/bowl	429,000	125,000	30,000	WAC dues replaced by Big West dues
Debt service/other	616,000	425,000	425,000	
Misc./camps	50,000	50,000	50,000	
Marketing factor	—	—	(100,000)	Column (3) assumes other savings from marketing
	11,775,506	8,257,825	7,202,275	
Net Operating Income	—	(2,011,953)	(512,426)	

Source: SJSU numbers come from official school documents. San Jose Mercury News estimates based on reporting and analysis by Jon Wilner.

223

EXHIBIT 3   FOOTBALL PROGRAM'S BUDGET

Revenues	San Jose State Internal Figures	Alternative Figures	Notes
University support/benefits	161,708	279,385	Offset by increased benefits expense below
Ticket sales	350,000	350,000	
Guarantees	1,125,000	1,125,000	
WAC/BCS	96,000	96,000	
Sponsorships	221,250	221,250	Assumes that 75% is football related
Spartan Foundation	927,000	927,000	Assumes that 75% is football related
	2,880,958	2,998,635	
Expenses			
Salaries	817,540	1,117,540	Internal figures exclude certain support personnel
Benefits	161,708	279,385	
Travel (team)	505,000	505,000	
Travel (recruiting)	75,000	75,000	
Grants	960,000	960,000	Football scholarship costs
Operations	580,000	580,000	
Supplies/equipment	182,000	182,000	
Marketing	0	100,000	Cost of football marketing.
WAC/BCS	0	120,000	All WAC schools must pay bowl expenses which are excluded in the internal figures
	3,281,248	3,918,925	
Net Operating Income (loss)	**(400,290)**	**(920,290)**	

Source: SJSU numbers come from official school documents. San Jose Mercury News estimates based on reporting and analysis by Jon Wilner.

consists of 23 teaching-oriented schools. Enrollment at SJSU for the 2003 academic year was nearly 30,000 students, of which roughly 75% were undergraduates. Since the school caters to nontraditional and part-time students, 43% of the student body was older than 25 in the most recent academic year.

As a public institution, SJSU is highly dependent on California state funding which, in turn, affects the budget of every department of the university—including the athletic department. The state's funding of SJSU was heavily influenced by the state government's revenues as well as the legislature's commitment to funding higher education. As budgets had become increasingly tight, some students and faculty questioned the need for a football team that reportedly lost money and appeared to have limited support from the students and local fans.

The Spartan Tradition

The SJSU Spartan football program was almost as old as the university, fielding its first team in 1893. It had a historical winning percentage of .515. Since the team's inception more than 100 players had been selected in the NFL draft, including six in the first round. Although the football team had experienced success in the past, it had struggled in recent years, having produced only one winning season since 1993 (in 2000). The team was coached by Fitzgerald

("Fitz") Hill who took over in 2001 and had compiled a 12 and 24 record in his first three seasons. Despite his less than stellar record, Coach Hill was convinced that the team was poised for a turnaround. Bolstered by additional scholarships in the current season as well as the next as a result of a new NCAA requirement for Division I-A programs,[75] the team had added depth which Coach Hill believed would turn some of the Spartan's close losses of recent years—such as last year's season-ending 34–32 home loss to Tulsa—into victories.

The athletic department was headed by Athletic Director Chuck Bell who came to San Jose State from Utah State University in February of 1998. Bell has had a relatively successful tenure as Athletic Director and is credited with bringing the Silicon Valley Football Classic to San Jose State's Spartan Stadium as a postseason bowl. Bell was extremely committed to the Spartan's football program and maintaining its status as a Division I-A competitor.

The Western Athletic Conference

In addition to Spartan football, San Jose State athletics consisted of five other men's and nine women's sports[76] that also competed at the Division I-A level in the Western Athletic Conference (WAC). Exhibit 5-4 of the Section 5 text shows the composition of the Major Division I-A conferences in 2004. San Jose State had been a member of the WAC since 1996. The ten members of the WAC in 2004 came from seven different states:

- Fresno State (California)
- San Jose State (California)
- University of Hawaii (Hawaii)
- Boise State (Idaho)
- Louisiana Tech (Louisiana)
- University of Nevada (Nevada)
- University of Tulsa (Oklahoma)
- Rice University (Texas)
- Southern Methodist (Texas)
- Univ. of Texas—El Paso (Texas)

A realignment of the WAC was scheduled for July, 2005. New colleges joining the WAC would be The University of Idaho, New Mexico State University, and Utah State University. Some commentators suggested that The University of Idaho—the last school to be added—was a hedge against the possible loss of San Jose State from the conference. The colleges scheduled to exit the WAC were The University of Tulsa, Rice, Southern Methodist, and The University of Texas at El Paso.[77] The WAC was founded in 1962 as a conference of six teams and had seen a number of programs enter and leave its ranks since that time. The current commissioner of the WAC was Karl Benson who was appointed in April of 1994. During his tenure, Commissioner Benson had enhanced the name recognition of the WAC through expansion of the conference and through a series of television deals for its football as well as men's and women's basketball teams. In addition, Commissioner Benson entered into contracts with a number of bowls for postseason football play for members of his conference.

Prior to joining the WAC, San Jose State was a member of the Big West Conference from 1969 – 1995. The ten college composition of the Big West (a Division I-AAA conference) in 2004 was as follows:

- Cal Poly—San Luis Obispo (Cal.)
- Cal State Fullerton (Cal.)
- Cal State Northridge (Cal.)
- Long Beach State (Cal.)
- Univ. of Cal—Irvine (Cal.)
- Univ. of Cal—Riverside (Cal.)
- Univ. of Cal—Santa Barbara (Cal.)
- Univ. of Pacific (Cal.)
- Univ. of Idaho (Idaho)
- Utah State Univ. (Utah)

The Big West Conference was also scheduled for realignment in 2005. The University of California at Davis was slated to join while The University of Idaho and Utah State University planned to switch to the WAC. Starting in 2005, the Big West would consist only of colleges located in California.

The Debate

Although there had been talk of eliminating the SJSU football program for years, those in favor of its elimination had become increasingly vocal in recent months. Members of the faculty senate were among the most ardent supporters of eliminating the football team. Last year they recommended, by a margin of 3–to–1, reducing the amount spent on the various sports programs in general and withdrawing from Division I-A competition—which would effectively result in the discontinuance of the football program.

The main arguments cited by those in favor of discontinuing San Jose State's football program included the following:

- Poor attendance was a manifestation of student apathy towards the team. Attendance at the Spartans' home games was consistently at the bottom of the rankings of all Division I-A schools (see Exhibit 1). Further, student attendance was only a very small fraction of the overall student population—it ranged from 310 to 1,433 (out of a total student population of nearly 30,000) last season. This poor attendance was despite the fact that tickets and even parking to football games were free to all students with a valid SJSU ID.

- In the face of continuing budget cuts, the resources that were spent on the football program could be better used to spare cuts in other areas of the university. In addition, cutting the football program would free up resources in the athletic department budget to fund other men's and women's sports teams. The overall performance of the athletic department (exclusive of football) had been ailing in recent years in the annual Sears Director's Cup rankings.[78]

- Long Beach State and Cal State Fullerton dropped their football programs after the 1991 and 1992 seasons, respectively. There was little evidence that dropping these programs damaged either school's other athletic programs. In particular, both schools maintained the success of their other intercollegiate sports after dropping their football programs and had even placed higher than San Jose State in recent years in the annual Sears Director's Cup rankings.

Those in favor of keeping the football team included Athletic Director Chuck Bell (who was on the record as saying that he would resign his post if the football team was eliminated), Coach Hill, the president of the student body, acting university president Don Kassing, as well as a number of other school administrators. They countered the charges of the critics with the following arguments:

- Despite low student turnout in recent years, the football team fostered a sense of school spirit which is typically lacking in commuter schools with an older student body. They claimed that one cure for this lack of school spirit was to build a sense of community by increasing student attendance at football games. Although this had proven to be a difficult task, they felt that an improvement in team performance would directly result in increased attendance at home games.

- New student housing that was scheduled to open in the next year would increase the number of students who lived on campus from 2,000 to 3,200 (and then possibly 6,000) in future years if all of the residence halls were completed. An increase in the number of students living on campus, they said, would result in increased attendance at football games.

• Eliminating the football team would undoubtedly result in lower alumni giving—particularly to the Spartan Foundation which was the athletic department's fundraising organization. Even the opponents of football conceded that alumni giving would suffer if the football team were dropped; however they claimed that the decrease would be more in the 50–75% range as opposed to 90% as claimed by the supporters of the team.

• The football team allowed San Jose State to compete at the Division I-A level in an athletic conference with a national reputation. This provided the university with name recognition that it wouldn't otherwise have which benefited its academic as well as its athletic programs.

• An improvement in the team's performance could result in a change of fortune for the program. In particular, a winning season could send the team to postseason play in a bowl game with an accompanying payout that could turn the team profitable. In addition, postseason play would further enhance the name recognition of the school.

Several consequences follow from eliminating the football program. First, without a football team, San Jose State would be required to withdraw from the WAC. This would entail upfront exit fees of roughly $3,000,000, the majority of which would be paid to already scheduled opponents for canceled games. Second, the university would need to find a new athletic conference in which to compete. The most likely candidate would be the revamped Big West Conference. Although this conference is less prestigious than and lacks the name recognition of the WAC, it would save the athletic department travel expenses associated with away games for all of its sports. Third, dropping the football team would result in the cancellation of roughly 80 scholarships to male athletes. Due to Title IX requirements and the Cal NOW decree that collectively require gender equality in collegiate athletics, San Jose State would be required to eliminate two women's sports and add one men's sport in order to comply with their rules.[79] These programs would require an upfront investment and would probably need to be subsidized for at least a few years.

Perhaps the biggest point of contention between the two sides was the profitability of the football program. The supporters of the team believed that the team's current budget deficit was manageable and could even be eliminated with more success on the field and better marketing—Exhibit 3 reports a $400,290 deficit. This deficit was below the average Men's Football Program deficit for all ten WAC colleges. A study of college athletic department budgets reported an average deficit of $825,000 across all ten members of the WAC for 2002–2003:

	Total Programs in Athletic Department	Men's Football Program
Revenues	$11,704,000	$3,112,000
Expenses	14,645,000	3,937,000
Net Profit	(2,941,000)	(825,000)

The opponents countered that the SJSU budget for the football team failed to include certain expenses directly attributable to the football team in the income statement.[80] As an example, all WAC schools are required to pay the bowl expenses of the conference's football teams that are involved in postseason play. In return, all members of the conference share in the bowl payouts. San Jose State included its share as revenue of the football team but failed to include its share of the expenses. The opponents argued that inclusion of these expenses painted a more accurate picture of the team's financial difficulties and served to support to their position that the team should disband after the current season.

The Future of Spartan Football

Even if the football team was allowed to continue, its future (at least at the Division I-A level) still remained uncertain. The NCAA recently imposed an attendance requirement of all Division I-A football programs. The rule was subsequently modified and its current form required all Division I-A programs to average 15,000 fans at their home football games for the season. Failure to meet this requirement once in a ten year period would result in a notification from the NCAA. A second violation in a ten year period would result in NCAA sanctions. Last year, the Spartans barely met the requirement with an average of 15,080 fans at their five home games. However, one of their games—the Literacy Classic against Grambling—drew a Spartan Stadium record 34,345 fans that purportedly came more to see the opposing team's marching band (the legendary Tiger Band) than to root for the Spartans. Without this game, the average attendance would have been 10,264 which is well short of the NCAA requirement.

The requirement that all Division I-A schools play at least five home games per season limited the Spartan's ability to schedule so-called "money games" where the school travels to a tough opponent for a large payout (which can reach upwards of half-a-million dollars). The host school typically draws a large number of fans who come to witness their home team defeat the visitor as in the University of Florida Gator's 65–3 defeat of the Spartans' last season.

Despite their differences, both sides agreed on one thing—a swift resolution of the outcome was necessary. Those in favor of discontinuing the program were eager to stop the losses they claimed the team generated which—if their accounting was correct—would free up resources that could be used elsewhere in the university. Although Coach Hill downplayed its significance, the uncertainty of the program undoubtedly affected his recruiting ability. Some of the older players were less muted in their opinion and suggested that the uncertain fate of the program limited their ability to recruit the talent necessary to be competitive at the Division I-A level. In addition to these players, the Athletic Director Chuck Bell agreed that the uncertainty added to the school's recruiting challenges.

Questions

1. What are the benefits of SJSU having a "respectable" Division 1-A football program?

2. What are the financial consequences of discontinuing the SJSU football program? What areas have the most uncertainty and how would you seek to gain further information on those areas?

3. What factors should SJSU take into account in deciding whether to discontinue the football program?

4. The case highlights much movement in conference membership. Why might such movement occur? Is it a good thing?

Footnotes

1 This section was written by George Foster with assistance of Dave Hoyt.

2 http://www.ncaa.org/about/purposes.html (April 20, 2004).

3 NCAA history from http://www.ncaa.org/about/history.html (April 20, 2004).

4 Report to Congressional Requestors GAO-01-297, "Intercollegiate Athletics: Four-Year Colleges' Experiences Adding and Discontinuing Teams," General Accounting Office, March 2001, p. 6. Available online at http://www.aahperd.org/nagws/title9/pdf/GAOReport.pdf (May 4, 2004).

5 Knight Commission Report, op. cit., p. 8.

6 "A Call to Action: Reconnecting College Sports and Higher Education," Report of the Knight Foundation Commission on Intercollegiate Athletics, June 2001, p. 11. Available online at: http://www.ncaa.org/databases/knight_commisssion/2001_report/2001_knight_report.pdf (April 13, 2004). The quotation refers to the Knight Commission's first report in March 1991.

7 "Intercollegiate Athletics: Four-Year Colleges' Experiences Adding and Discontinuing Teams," GAO 01-297, March 2001, p. 4.

8 Ibid. pp. 9, 12.

9 Ibid. p. 13.

10 NCAA Division I Manual, p. 60. Online at http://www.ncaa.org/library/membership/division_i_manual/2003-04/2003-04_d1_manual.pdf (April 28, 2004).

11 Ibid.

12 David Hoyt prepared this case under the supervision of George Foster.

   Copyright © 2004 by the Board of Trustees of the Leland Stanford Junior University. All rights reserved. To order copies or request permission to reproduce materials, e-mail the Case Writing Office at: cwo@gsb.stanford.edu or write: Case Writing Office, Stanford Graduate School of Business, 518 Memorial Way, Stanford University, Stanford, CA 94305-5015. No part of this publication may be reproduced, stored in a retrieval system, used in a spreadsheet, or transmitted in any form or by any means—electronic, mechanical, photocopying, recording, or otherwise—without the permission of the Stanford Graduate School of Business.

13 Jeremy Bloom, "Opinion: Show Us The Money," *New York Times*, August 1, 2003.

14 Plaintiff's Opening Brief, Jeremy Bloom vs. NCAA and the Regents of The University of Colorado, Court of Appeals, State of Colorado (July 2,2003) p. 7.

15 Ibid, pp. 8–9.

16 NCAA Division I Manual, p. 81. Online at http://www.ncaa.org/library/membership/division_I_manual/2003-4/2003-4_d1_manual.pdf (April 28, 2004).

17 "Bloom Chooses Football over Endorsements," www.thedenverchannel.com (August 19, 2002).

18 Legal Battle: CU's Bloom makes appeal to earn skiing endorsements," Sports Illustrated.com (July 3, 2003).

19 Plaintiff's Opening Brief, op. cit., p. 9.

20 J. Bloom, "Opinion: Show Us The Money," loc. cit.

21 "Court Tells Bloom He Can't Accept Endorsements for Skiing," www.thedenverchannel.com (May 6, 2004).

22 Ibid.

23 NCAA Division I Manual, op. cit. p. 60.

24 Ibid.

25 There were some exceptions to these general principles. See Division I Manual, op. cit. pp. 60–83 for details.

26 NCAA Division I Manual, op. cit. pg. 186.

27 Division I Manual, Section 17.1.5, op. cit. p. 238. There was an exemption to the daily maximum for golf rounds, although the weekly maximum remained 20 hours.

28 C. Dempsey, "Bloom makes last challenge to play," Denver Post.com (July 18, 2004).

29 David Hoyt prepared this case under the supervision of George Foster.

[30] "'Open To All': Title IX at 30," The Secretary of Education's Commission on Opportunity in Athletics, February 28, 2003, p. 12. Online at http://www.ed.gov/about/bdscomm/list/athletics/title9report.pdf (April 13, 2004).

[31] Andy Berglund, "Death of a Dream: The Demise of Wrestling at Marquette University," TheWrestlingMall.com, November 18, 2002. http://www.thewrestlingmall.com/htmls/news.asp?Cat=3&View=4561 (August 16, 2004).

[32] Ibid.

[33] Lori Nickel, "Title IX Proving to be More Fatal," *Milwaukee Journal Sentinel*, November 30, 2001.

[34] Burglund, op. cit.

[35] Nickel, op.cit.

[36] National Wrestling Coaches Association, Committee to Save Bucknell Wrestling, Marquette Wrestling Club, Yale Wrestling Association and the National Coalition for Athletics Equity v. United States Department of Education, "Complaint for Declarative and Injunctive Relief," filed in the United States District Court for the District of Columbia, January 16, 2002, p. 2. Online at http://www.nwcaonline.com/title9/nucafinalcomplaint.doc (April 13, 2004).

[37] Bucknell Media Release, "Bucknell University Receives Major Donation By Alumnus, William Graham, To Bolster Sports Programs," May 7, 2004.

[38] List can be found at: http://www.nwcaonline.com/title9/discontinued.xls (August 17, 2004).

[39] "Open To All," op. cit., p 12.

[40] Ibid., p. 14.

[41] "Gender Equity: Men's and Women's Participation in Higher Education," General Accounting Office GAO-01-128, December 2000, pp. 37, 38. Online at: http://www.aahperd.org/nagws/title9/pdf/GAO-01-128report.pdf (May 7, 2004).

[42] "'Open To All' Title IX at 30," op. cit., p. 15.

[43] "2001–02 Gender Equity Report," NCAA, p. 1. Online at: http://www.ncaa.org/library/research/gender_equity_study/2001-02/2001-02GenderEquityReport.pdf (May 7, 2004).

[44] Men's rowing had second largest teams among men's sports, averaging 42 student-athletes per team, but there were just 19 institutions contributing to the NCAA report that had men's rowing teams, compared to 232 that reported football teams.

[45] NCAA Gender Equity Report, op.cit, pp. 20, 78, 94. Note that not all schools had football programs.

[46] Ibid., p. 14.

[47] "Intercollegiate Athletics: Four-Year Colleges' Experiences Adding and Discontinuing Teams," GAO 01-297, March 2001, p. 4. Online at: http://www.aahperd.org/nagws/title9/pdf/GAOReport.pdf (May 4, 2004).

[48] Ibid. pp. 9, 12.

[49] Ibid. p. 19.

[50] United States District Court for the District of Columbia, National Wrestling Coaches Association et al., v. United States Department of Education, Memorandum Opinion of Emmet G. Sullivan, June 11, 2003, pp. 116–117.

[51] Press Release, "National Wrestling Coaches Association Law Suit," Women's Sports Foundation, June 11, 2003.

[52] "Bucknell University Receives Major Donation," op. cit.

[53] Ibid.

[54] R. Todt, "Bucknell Reinstates Wrestling Program," *The Daily Item* (May 8, 2004).

[55] David Hoyt prepared this case under the supervision of George Foster.

[56] NCAA website: http://www1.ncaa.org/membership/governance/division_I/index.html (April 26, 2004).

[57] Tony Barnhart, "SEC to Divvy Up Record $101 Million," *Atlanta Journal-Constitution*, May 19, 2003.

[58] The NCAA men's basketball championship (and other national championships) was controlled by the NCAA, which negotiated its own television agreement.

[59] Bylaw 17.11.5.2 (c), NCAA Division I Manual, op. cit. p. 270.

[60] The bowls were the FedEx Orange, Nokia Sugar, Rose, and Tostitos Fiesta Bowls. The conferences were the ACC, Big East, Big 12, Big Ten, Pacific Ten, and SEC.

[61] BCS Media Guide, pp. 2–3, 7–8, 16. Online at http://www.bcsfootball.org/mediaguide.pdf (May 17, 2004).

[62] Jennifer Lee, "Who Pays, Who Profits in Realignment," *Street & Smith's SportsBusiness Journal*, December 8–14, 2003, pp. 25, 32.

[63] Dick Heller, "Irish Independence is a Tradition Worth Cheer, Cheering For," *The Washington Times*, February 11, 1999, p. B. 3.

[64] "ESPN Sports Poll: Notre Dame Reigns as Top Football Program," *Sports Business Daily*, August 27, 2004.

[65] University of Notre Dame, http://und.collegesports.com/facilities/nd-stadium-history.html (September 7, 2004).

[66] "Notre Dame Decides Not to Join the Big Ten," *Notre Dame Report*, February 19, 1999, p. 301.

[67] John Heilsler, "Athletic Conference Affiliation: Is Notre Dame Still in a League of Its Own?" *Notre Dame Magazine*, Winter 2003–2004.

[68] Andrew Soukup, "NBC Extends Football Contract Through 2010," *The Observer*, January 14, 2004.

[69] BCS, online at http://www.bcsfootball.org/revenue.shtml (May 17, 2004).

[70] Heisler, loc. cit.

[71] http://www.gatorbowl.com/tgb/history/yby.asp (September 1, 2004).

[72] Tom Oates, "Big Ten Better Off Without Golden Torch," *Wisconsin State Journal*, February 7, 1999, p. 1D.

[73] This case was written by Chris Armstrong under the supervision of George Foster. It was prompted by a series of articles by Jon Wilner in The San Jose Mercury, August 29–31, 2004. The assistance of Jon Wilner is gratefully acknowledged.

[74] The San Jose State mascot is the Spartan, which was the name given to warriors from the ancient Greek city of Sparta.

[75] This is part of a broader set of new requirements that Division I-A schools must (i) sponsor a minimum of 16 varsity sports, (ii) provide a minimum of 200 scholarships, (iii) have a football program with a minimum of five home games, (iv) provide 76.5 football scholarships (over a rolling two-year period), and (v) average 15,000 fans per home game.

[76] The five other men's sports were baseball, basketball, cross country, golf, and soccer. The nine women's sports were basketball, cross country, gymnastics, soccer, softball, swimming, tennis, volleyball, and water polo.

[77] All four schools were scheduled to join Conference-USA upon their departure from the WAC.

[78] The Sears Director's Cup is awarded annually by the National Association of Collegiate Directors of Athletics (NACDA), United States Sports Academy, and USA TODAY to the school with the "best overall collegiate athletics programs in the country." San Jose State's close neighbor, Stanford University, won its 10th

consecutive Sears Director's Cup in the 2003–04 season. Stanford was followed by The University of Michigan, The University of California at Los Angeles, and Ohio State University. San Jose State finished 193 out of the 274 programs that competed. The scoring system is based on the "on-field" performance of a college's men's and women's teams across a broad number of sports.

[79] If San Jose State ultimately joins the Big West Conference, the additional men's sport will have to be track and field, which is a requirement for Big West membership.

[80] Column (2) of Exhibit 2 is San Jose State Athletic Department's projected budget without a football team. Column (3) is The San Jose Mercury's projected budget. Together, columns (2) and (3) highlight the main differences between the two sides of the debate.

SECTION 6... Sports Marketing (1): Advertising, Sponsorship, and Endorsements[1]

Key Issues

- Companies have multiple options in how they structure their links to sports when seeking to promote their products and further build links to targeted customer bases. Sporting bodies need to recognize these options in any of their decisions that may impact the economic interests of their marketing/sponsorship/advertising partners.

- Major advertisers are continually evaluating their total advertising spend and how that is allocated between sports-related properties and other properties.

- Company sponsorship programs should articulate the objectives of their sporting sponsorships to facilitate both before-the-decision informed choice and after-the-event informed evaluation of success.

- The deliverables from sporting sponsorship include association related (such as "official sponsor"), visual image use, event day activities, player-related appearances, and ambush marketing protection.

- Methods used to evaluate sponsorship effectiveness include sales tracking analysis, targeted objectives analysis, brand awareness/recall measures, and media exposure analysis.

Cases

$\mathbf{M}$arketing partners such as advertisers, sponsors, and endorsers are a key pillar of most successful sporting leagues, events, and clubs. Unsuccessful efforts to build sporting properties fail in part because of lack of marketing support. Sections 6 and 7 of this book present text and cases related to the marketing pillar of sports. Section 6 concentrates on advertising, sponsorship, and endorsements. Section 7 focuses on club marketing with its emphasis on ticketing, fan avidity, and club branding.

Marketing Financial Outlays Are High! and Pivotal!

Sporting events, leagues, and clubs receive payments from broadcast (e.g., television, radio) partners that collectively exceed many billions each year (see Section 8). Advertising expenditures are crucial to enabling these broadcast partners to pay the rights fees to the relevant sporting bodies. Exhibit 6-1 reports the top 12 U.S. companies based on advertising expenditures during sporting events.[2] Also included are the total advertising outlays by these companies. For six of these companies, sports-related advertising is more than 50% of their total advertising outlays. Street & Smith reports that the total sports advertising by the top 50 companies exceeded $3.4 billion in 2002.

Sponsorship outlays also occur at the multibillion-dollar level. Exhibit 6-2 reports IEG's[3] listing of the top 12 U.S. companies by sponsorship outlays in 2003. The total outlays by the top 50 companies exceed $3 billion. IEG, a leading authority in this area, estimates that 69% of all sponsorship outlays in 2004 are sports related.[4] The 12 companies in Exhibit 6-2 include 5 that are TOP Olympic Games sponsors—Coca Cola, Nike, McDonald's, Eastman Kodak, and Visa. (TOP stands for "The Olympic Partner" program.) Each of these companies pays the International Olympic Commitee (IOC) at least $50 million every 4-year cycle to be an official TOP Olympic sponsor. This $50+ million payment does not include the additional outlays (e.g., advertising, hospitality) Olympic sponsors incur to "activate" (extract value

EXHIBIT 6-1 TOP 50 SPORTS ADVERTISERS IN 2002—STREET & SMITH'S RANKING (RANKED BY TOTAL SPORTS ADVERTISING SPENDING IN 2002)

Rank		Total 2002 Sports Advertising Spending ($ Millions)	Total 2002 Advertising Spending ($ Millions)	% of Total Advertising Spending Devoted to Sports
1	Anheuser-Busch Cos.	$264	$322	82%
2	Chevrolet Motor Division	201	370	54
3	AT&T	134	340	39
4	Visa International	129	255	51
5	Ford Motor Company	120	430	28
6	Miller Brewing Company	110	181	61
7	Coors Brewing Company	105	135	78
8	American Honda Motor	86	217	40
9	Nike, Inc.	86	142	61
10	McDonald's Corp.	84	383	22
11	Pepsi-Cola Company	79	204	39
12	Coca-Cola USA	79	173	46

Source: Street & Smith's *Sports Business Journal, By the Numbers 2004.*

EXHIBIT 6-2 Top U.S. Sponsors in 2003—IEG Ranking ($ Millions)

Rank	Company	Amount ($ Millions)
1	PepsiCo, Inc.	$250–$255
2	Anheuser-Busch Cos.	240–245
3	General Motors Corp.	185–190
4	Coca-Cola Company	180–185
5	Nike, Inc.	160–165
6	Miller Brewing Company	155–160
7	Daimler-Chrysler Corporation	125–130
8	Ford Motor Company	100–105
9	McDonald's Corporation	95–100
10	Eastman Kodak	95–100
11	Visa International	90–95
12	Master Card International	85–90

Source: IEG, Inc.: *IEG Sponsorship Report* (December 22, 2003).

from) their sponsor fee. IEG reports survey results that the ratio of activation outlays to sponsor fees averages above 1 each year of the 2001 to 2003 period:

2001	2002	2003
1.2	1.7	1.3

An activation ratio of 1.3 means that a sponsor paying a $50 million Top-Tier Olympic sponsor fee outlays an additional $65 million (1.3 × $50 million) to extract value from the Olympic official sponsor status.

Sponsorship dollars can mean the difference between success and failure for some sporting leagues. Consider the WUSA, the women's professional soccer league. The WUSA commenced in 2001 and shut down in 2003.[5] In late 2003, proposals were made to restart the league. Exhibit 6-3 shows estimated financials for the last year of the league and a budget for the first year of the restart. The restart has budgeted expenses similar to the 2003 financial year. However, the budgeted revenues for the restart show sponsorship revenue of $21 million vis-à-vis $8.6 for 2003. Clearly, the restart of the WUSA under this budget rests on its ability to substantially expand the sponsorship base of professional women's soccer.

Multiple Decision Points

Companies investing in sports marketing programs have multiple decisions to make, such as:

1. Total marketing spend decisions. Marketing is but one of several business areas where corporations make investments. Other areas include manufacturing, distribution, and new product development. Eastman Kodak is an Olympic Games Top-Tier Sponsor. This cost Kodak more than $100 million for a 4-year cycle of a summer and a winter Olympics (including activation costs). Kodak's investment in Olympic Games sponsorship ideally should continue to provide competitive returns vis-à-vis further investments in, say, new

EXHIBIT 6-3   SPONSORSHIP AS A KEY PART OF PROPOSALS TO RESTART THE WUSA ($ MILLIONS)

	Estimated WUSA Financials 2003 ($ Millions)	Budget of Proposed Restart in 2005 ($ Millions)	Variation ($ Millions)
Revenue			
Sponsorship Revenue	$ 8.6	$ 21	$12.4
Ticket Sales Revenue	4.7	8	3.3
Merchandise Sales Revenue	0.6	2	1.4
Other Revenue	1.8	1	(0.8)
	15.7	32	16.3
Expenses			
Player Salaries/Costs	9.6	10	0.4
Staff Salaries/Costs Team	11.0	7	(4.0)
Operations/Venue Costs	8.5	6	(2.5)
TV Expenses	2.5	4	1.5
Marketing	3.5	8	4.5
Other	0.5	1	0.5
	35.6	36	0.4
Profit	$(19.9)	$(4)	

Source: "Details and Analysis of WUSA's Comeback Plan," *IEG Sponsorship Report* (December 8, 2003).

photographic technology. A company may decide to cut back its investments in sports marketing because new opportunities in other parts of its business increase in attractiveness.

2. Marketing mix decisions. Decisions here include the different types of marketing outlays and the different areas for each type. Consider the following options:

	Advertising	Sponsorship	Player Endorsement	Other (e.g., hospitality)
Sports Related	I	II	III	IV
Non-Sports Related	V	IV	VII	VIII

Companies have multiple alternatives when allocating their marketing outlays, both within and outside the sports arena. Many companies allocate their outlays across the multiple I to VIII categories. Exhibit 6-1 highlights the sizable differences across 12 companies in terms of the percentage of their total advertising spending they devote to sports advertising—from a low of 22% (McDonald's Corp.) to a high of 82% (Anheuser-Busch).

3. Focus of sports marketing outlays. Companies can invest their marketing outlays at multiple levels, including the league, event, club, and player/athlete levels.

Companies investing in marketing outlays have many options. Sports properties can build stronger relationships with their corporate marketing partners by better understanding the objectives of such outlays and providing information on their results.

Marketing Contracts, Risk Sharing, and Incentives

Many marketing contracts present substantial risks to one or both parties. An advertiser may commit to several 30-second slots for a prime-time event, such as the Super Bowl, months in advance of the event date. However, the actual ratings may be below expectations. The Super Bowl could have involved two teams from small markets with little national following, or it could have been already a one-sided game by halftime. Uncertainty also exists with other areas. A sponsor or endorser may commit to sizable support for an athlete who subsequently becomes injured for an extended period or who suffers major loss of form. Mechanisms exist in sports business to incorporate these risks into contracts.

- Television advertising for major sporting events have high 30-second advertising rates. These rates are premised on high television ratings. Advertising contracts can include "make-good" clauses: in the event that the sporting broadcast does not achieve the expected high ratings, the broadcast network provides additional advertising slots that "make up" for the lower-than-expected minimum ratings. Advertisers with these clauses bear less risk of lower-than-expected ratings vis-à-vis a contract with no such clauses.

- Shoe and apparel endorsement contracts with athletes can include upside and downside protection clauses. Consider an endorsement contract for a tennis player currently ranked number 2 in the world. Assume it pays $2 million per year for 3 years, with a $1 million bonus each year if the athlete is ranked number 1 in a particular year, and a penalty each year of $500,000 if the athlete falls out of the top 5 ranking and $1 million if the athlete falls out of the top 10 ranking. This contract has both incentive and risk-sharing components. The athlete has the financial incentive to improve his or her world ranking, but has the risk of lower endorsement payments if he or she is injured or performs much below the expectations at the time the contract is written. The endorsing company carries less downside risk than if the contract were a guaranteed $2 million a year for 3 years.

Sponsorship Alternatives in Sports

The IEG definition of sponsorship highlights several key elements: "A cash and/or in-kind fee paid to a property in return for access to the exploitable commercial potential associated with that property." [6] Exhibit 6-4 illustrates some key categories of deliverables a sponsor may receive in consideration for the rights fee.

The deliverables in Exhibit 6-4 are relatively generic. Each sport has its own textual richness. Motor sports represents a fascinating arena for sponsorship. Exhibit 6-5 is based on Octagon's analysis of sponsorship alternatives for NASCAR, the premier stock car racing

EXHIBIT 6-4 **DELIVERABLES TO OFFICIAL SPORTING-RELATED SPONSORSHIP**

Association Type Deliverables

- Name association recognition—"official sponsor"
- Sport association recognition
- Athlete association recognition

Visual Image Deliverables

- At event site
- At event surroundings
- On direct transmission of event
- On replays of events
- Use in advertisements/promotions

Event Day and Related Deliverables

- Tickets/tickets in preferred zones
- Hospitality suites/facilities
- Access to off-limit areas—e.g., pits in F1/NASCAR events

Athlete/Team/Facility Deliverables

- Athlete appearance deliverables
- Athlete endorsement deliverables
- Athlete image deliverables
- Use of facilities for corporate events

Ambush Marketing Protection

- Aggressive stance against "ambushers"

EXHIBIT 6-5   Sponsorship Options in NASCAR

Panel A: Estimated NASCAR Sponsorship Avenues

Point of Entry	Annual Cost	Benefits
Series Title Sponsor	>$60MM	Category Exclusivity (Teams, Tracks, Drivers, and Media) Use of all marks and likenesses
Event Title Sponsor	$1–2MM	Naming rights to a Winston Cup Series Race Television exposure Opportunity for promotion using race as a platform
Official NASCAR Sponsor	$2–10MM	Use of NASCAR mark Use of NASCAR in promotions Participation in special NASCAR programs
Team Sponsor	$6–20MM	Exposure on vehicle Opportunity to use driver likeness Use of vehicle in promotion
Driver Sponsor	$150–500k	Opportunity to use driver likeness Opportunity to use driver in employee programs Direct link to NASCAR's most prized asset

Panel B: Sponsor Activation Avenues

Activity	Drivers Level Sponsorship	Team Level Sponsorship	Event Level Sponsorship	Title Sponsor
Driver Uniform Logo				
Placement on Race Car				
At-Track Fixed Media				
Themed Marketing				
In-Store Appearances				
Driver Appearances				
Licensed Merchandise				
Hospitality Suites at Events				
Access to Pit Lane During Event				
Branding				
Wireless Content				
Access to NASCAR Fan Database				
At-Track Product Displays				
Ability to Showcase Technology				
Level of Exposure	*	*		
Based on Performance				

Key	
No Exposure	
Minimal Exposure	
Moderate Exposure	
Event-Specific Exposure	
Maximal Exposure	

Source: Octagon (internal documents)

organization. Octagon is a leading sports marketing company, with many offices around the globe. Exhibit 6-5 Panel A illustrates how sponsorship can exist at different levels and with different costs for the sponsorship alone (i.e., before activation costs). Panel B highlights the various types of activation avenues with a driver level, team level, event level, and title level sponsorship. In 2003, NEXTEL and NASCAR announced a 10-year, approximately $700 million sponsorship—NEXTEL became the Series Title Sponsor of NASCAR's premier racing series (replacing Winston, the tobacco brand of R.J. Reynolds).

Sponsorship Objectives and Evaluation

There are multiple objectives for companies investing in sponsorship relationships. These include:

Stimulate Sales—generate increased purchases from existing customers or attract new customers.

Brand Awareness—increase a consumer's favorable recognition of a product by exposure to the name.

Brand Personality/Image—promote a product having distinctive and memorable attributes by association with a sporting league, event, club, or player.

Customer Reach—access a desired customer base in a targeted way.

Exclusivity—provide a platform where the products of potential competitors are precluded from obtaining customer mind share.

Employee Motivation—promote greater loyalty and commitment from employees.

Community Citizenship—promote company as supporting events and clubs to which many members of the community are emotionally attached.

IEG's survey of sponsorship objectives ranked the following in order of importance: (1) create awareness/visibility, (2) increase brand loyalty, (3) change/reinforce image, (4) drive retail/dealer traffic, (5) stimulate sales/trial usage, (6) showcase community responsibility, and (7) showcase products.[7]

Evaluating Sponsorship Effectiveness

The objectives sought with a sponsorship will guide the types of measures that can provide insight into effectiveness. Investing resources in collecting and analyzing data assists in making informed decisions on effectiveness. Some examples are:

Sales Tracking Analysis: The most elementary approach is a simple comparison of sales before and after the start of the sponsorship (pre- and postsales analysis). More sophisticated analysis attempts to take into account nonsponsorship factors that help explain pre- and postsales changes. It is important to specify the targeted sales area expected to be affected; for example, a single club sponsorship may be expected to have a more narrow area of sales improvement than sponsorship of a nationwide league.

Targeted Objectives Analysis: Some companies set quantifiable objectives as justifications for sports sponsorship. For example, one objective is to increase sales coupon use of a product in the belief that exposure to use of that product increases the likelihood of future sales. Sophisticated tracking information now exists to assess coupon use in regions that have different exposures to a sponsorship.

Brand Awareness/Recall Measures and Purchase Likelihood Measures: Survey methods can be used to probe whether a sponsorship has increased potential customers' awareness of a product or sponsor, the likelihood of trialing a product, or the likelihood of purchasing a product. Existing customers can be surveyed to examine whether their likelihood to continue purchasing or even increase the amount they purchase has increased because of the sponsorship.

Media Exposure Analysis: Sponsorship for some sporting properties results in brand-name exposure to the viewer. The "viewer" can be on-site at the game or event, or can be at home viewing a broadcast of the event. Many sponsors of NASCAR events and teams see television media exposure as a key benefit of their sponsorship investment. NASCAR fans have a high passion for their sport and sponsors hope this translates to an increased fan interest in the products of NASCAR sponsors. A frequently used evaluation methodology in this area is media exposure analysis. Joyce Julius and Associates is a leading consulting firm in this area. Its *2003 NASCAR Winston Cup Series Year-End Report* included the following:

> [This] Report contains exposure information accumulated during telecasts of the season's 36 events, starting with the Daytona 500 and ending with the Ford 400. In all, a total of 37 telecasts—airing on Fox, FX, NBC, and TNT—chronicled the series when taking replays into consideration.
>
> During each broadcast, all clear, in-focus exposure was recorded and tabulated by the Sponsors Report. In addition, mentions of a sponsor's name or products) were counted and valued at :10 each.
>
> To determine a dollar value for each sponsor's exposure, on-screen time and mentions were compared to the network's estimated or non-discounted cost per :30 commercial rate for each particular telecast.
>
> Throughout the 2003 broadcast season, 1,087 sponsors joined forces to secure 263 hours, 13 minutes, 19 seconds (263:13:19) of clear, in-focus exposure time, 7,295 mentions, and $3,692,281,465 of comparable earnings.

This analysis tracks the time each sponsor's name was clearly exposed and then converts it to a dollar value using the 30-second commercial advertising rate for that telecast. Exhibit 6-6 reports the total media value and the five largest exposure points contributing to that value. Note that such information can be used to predict which parts of the car or driver are most likely to be exposed to the viewer.

EXHIBIT 6-6 MEDIA EXPOSURE ANALYSIS FOR 2003 NASCAR WINSTON CUP SERIES: JOYCE JULIUS AND ASSOCIATES ANALYSIS FOR TOP FOUR SPONSORS

	Chevrolet	Winston	Ford	Dodge
Exposure Time	15.06:34	9.17:00	9.08:26	7.12:09
Sponsor Mention	447	1,209	367	325
Media Value ($ millions)	$209.695	$164.306	$133.241	$110.001
Top Five Sources				44.124
Front Bumper Identity	$ 68.751		15.855	
Graphics Accompanying				3.813
Running Order	32.074		25.547	24.555
Running Order Graphics	27.071		44.405	7.849
Rear Bumper Identity	21.487			12.466
Verbal References	16.940	42.996	13.661	
Driver Uniforms		30.401	9.286	
Event Title Graphics		19.230		
Retaining Walls		15.053		
Series Title Graphics		14.513		

Source: Joyce Julius and Associates, *2003 NASCAR Winston Cup Series Year-End Report.*

Joyce Julius is a leading provider of sponsorship evaluation services. Other firms include: Bonham Group, Front Row Marketing, and Opinion Research Center. These firms offer a broad set of quantitative and qualitative approaches to assist sponsors in planning and evaluating the effectiveness of sponsorship outlays.[8]

CASE 6.1 NEXTEL's NASCAR Sponsorship Decision[9]

INTRODUCTION

In May 2003, Mark Schweitzer, Senior VP of Marketing for NEXTEL Communications, had a recommendation to make. For the first time in over 30 years the title sponsorship position for NASCAR, the most successful auto racing organization in the United States, was available. The current sponsor, RJR Reynolds and its Winston brand, was stepping back from its position as title sponsor. This was due to increasing pressure from anti-smoking activists and the worldwide voluntary elimination of tobacco related motorsports sponsorships enacted by the tobacco industry by 2006. Estimates for the cost of the current RJR Reynolds sponsorship agreement ranged from $40 to $50 million annually in direct sponsorship and at track events, and with NASCAR's popularity reaching all-time highs this number would more than likely increase. The numbers being thrown around were enormous, with proposals that topped $700M for a 10 year sponsorship—which would make this the largest sports related sponsorship deal ever. While the past few years had seen explosive growth for NASCAR, with TV ratings second only to the NFL, could this momentum be maintained into the future? And was the expected return enough to justify the price? Mark's instructions from Tim Donahue, CEO of NEXTEL, were to "go do a deal—but don't do a bad deal." What should Mark do?

NEXTEL COMPANY BACKGROUND

Former FCC member Morgan O'Brien founded Fleet Call in 1987 as an alternative technology to the burgeoning cellular industry that was forming. It was based on a specialized mobile radio platform that was used extensively by transportation and mobile service operators. The technology utilized radio frequencies as opposed to the traditional cellular networks being developed by the other major carriers at the time. The key differentiating feature of their product was the unique direct connect option that allowed the phone to be utilized like a walkie talkie. This provided the users with a quick, efficient way to connect with other NEXTEL subscribers. With a virtual lockup of the frequencies it operated on, due to its quiet acquisition of radio dispatch companies in the late 1980s, NEXTEL had guaranteed itself a sustainable advantage.

At the time, most wireless carriers relied upon analog signals to carry the signals between the handsets and the receiving towers. While this technology allowed cellular systems to cover large amounts of area with relatively few towers, the analog signals were more expensive and power consuming than the newer digital systems that were being developed. The benefits to the digital format were extensive, allowing for improved clarity, extended battery life, and most importantly—cheap connections. The drawback to digital service was that the towers used to service the network were required to be much closer together, which required the provider to spend several times more on infrastructure than a traditional analog system. In the beginning, service was spotty and customers complained about the poor service NEXTEL offered. In 1995 however, Motorola entered into a partnership with NEXTEL and brought along its 800-MHz SMR licenses. This allowed NEXTEL to offer a higher degree of service to its customers across the country. After a cash infusion by cell phone pioneer Craig

McCaw in 1996, NEXTEL was able to roll out its national Motorola integrated digital enhanced network (iDEN), which combined their trademark two-way radio transmission option along with a digital cellular phone service in one handset.

Based on its trendsetting history, NEXTEL was able to begin developing cutting edge services for its users. These included web based applications and offering services to its users that other companies didn't, such as one-second rounding for billing purposes and eliminating out-of-area roaming fees. The combination of these innovations and the unique direct connect option lead to a user base that was primarily business oriented, from Fortune 500 companies to local construction companies. These customers tended to spend more on average than non-business users and also tended to be more loyal to one particular carrier over time. The key customer bases for NEXTEL included computer services, construction, education, field sales and service, financial services, government sector, healthcare, hospitality, manufacturing, professional services, real estate, retail and transportation.

Appendix A reports summary annual financials for NEXTEL over the 1996 to 2002 period. The 2002 revenues were $8,721 million while sales, general and administrative (SG & A) expenses in 2002 were $3,039 million. Included in this SG & A line item were direct sales and marketing payroll; commissions and residuals earned by indirect dealers and distributors; facilities costs of opening new NEXTEL stores; and advertising expenses. The advertising expenses included sports-related sponsorships and television commercials. Up to 2002, sports-related sponsorship had been minor—less than $10 million total in 2002.

NASCAR Background

NASCAR was initially conceived in the economic boom that followed the completion of the Second World War. As the nation settled down from the war, the attention to heroes shifted from the battlefield to the ball field and from the front line to the track. All over the country, local race tracks were recording increased attendance. As the attendance increased, so did the number of drivers and teams. However, not all of the local tracks had a common rules system to allow teams to compete on a weekly basis at neighboring facilities. Also, while some tracks were well suited for both racing and viewing, there were lots of tracks that were not good for spectators. Some were good for spectators but proved difficult to race on. All of these issues lead to a meeting in 1947 at the Streamline Hotel in Daytona Beach, Florida, hosted by Bill France Sr., to discuss the future of stock car racing in America. From this initial meeting, the foundations for NASCAR were born.

The first NASCAR sanctioned event was held on February 15, 1948 on Daytona's beach course, just two months after the initial organizational meeting was held. It was the next year, however, when the first race in the NASCAR Grand National was held in Charlotte, North Carolina. The fan reaction to the event was tremendous, and NASCAR began its long climb to motorsports supremacy in North America. Immediately following the success in Charlotte, plans were drawn up to develop bigger tracks and races for the growing fan base. Darlington Raceway in South Carolina was completed one year later and became the first asphalt superspeedway in the country.

Over the next decade, the popularity of NASCAR continued to spiral upwards. In 1959 the Daytona International Speedway in Florida, the crown jewel of NASCAR, was built by Bill France Sr. The first race at DIS proved that the formula envisioned by NASCAR produced high quality, intense competition to the fans. The first race at DIS was so close that it took 72 hours to determine the winner, Lee Petty, as the margin of victory was so small. These dramatic finishes and intense competition lead to ABC televising the 1961 Firecracker 250 from Daytona, the first national broadcast for NASCAR.

1971 ushered in the modern era of NASCAR. R.J. Reynolds Tobacco Company provided corporate sponsorship to the sanctioning body, and the NASCAR Grand National Series was transformed into the NASCAR Winston Cup Series. The new sponsorship allowed NASCAR to associate itself with a highly visible consumer brand and gain further nationwide exposure. Within 5 years of the deal, NASCAR captured the worldwide lead in motorsports attendance with more than 1.4 million spectators attending events annually—this lead has never been relinquished.

Throughout the 1980s, NASCAR's presence on the nationwide stage continued to grow. The 1979 Daytona 500 was the first 500 mile race in history to be broadcast live in its entirety. By 1989 every race in the NASCAR Winston Cup Series was televised, nearly all of them live. Throughout the 1990s attendance figures once again surged ahead. There was also a 57% growth from 1993 to 1998 to a total of 6.3 million broadcast viewers. The major television networks saw this explosive growth in available viewers and aggressively bid for the rights to broadcast NASCAR races. In 1999 a consolidated television package between Fox Sports/FX and NBC Sports/TNT was announced. The package was valued at over $2.4B for 6 years of event coverage. It was made possible by the ability of NASCAR to convince the individual track owners to allow them to negotiate the television rights package as a whole, where traditionally the individual tracks negotiated separately with the broadcasters. This deal allowed NASCAR to design a viewer experience that would remain consistent from week to week.

NASCAR has enjoyed a run of unparalled growth, and seems poised to continue growing into the future. There are some questions that remain to be answered: Can NASCAR continue to grow in an increasingly fractured marketplace? With long time series Title Sponsor Winston departing, who will they choose as the successor? Has NASCAR reached its peak?

MOTORSPORTS SPONSORSHIP

The ways that corporate sponsors can become involved in motorsports has grown drastically over the past 20 years. In the early days, most sponsorship was limited to the cars entered in the race and signage at the track. However, following the growing popularity and visibility of professional racing leagues, there has been an increase in the ways that a sponsor can be associated with motorsports. See Exhibit 6-5 of the Section 6 text.

League Level

Within NASCAR there are various levels of sponsorship available to a potential client that allows them to tailor an exposure package that suits their desired visibility objectives.

The highest level of league sponsorship is the Title Sponsor role. This is the position that RJR Reynolds and their Winston brand had held with NASCAR for over 30 years. A sponsorship at this level guaranteed a sponsor exposure at every venue, including media placement at every track, on every uniform and mentions by the on air broadcasters. In addition, the Title Sponsor gains access to the series drivers, or their likenesses, for use in promotional activities and events. The cost for this sponsorship would likely exceed $60 million annually.

Another option for potential sponsors is the Event Title Sponsorship. In this case, a company is paying to have the official name of the race include their name as well. An example of this is the Coca Cola 600 (held in Charlotte each year), where Coke is the official Event Sponsor for the race and all media relating to that specific race is branded with the Coke label. This type of sponsorship generally provides a large amount of publicity over a short time frame (around the race) and generally receives the largest advertising return over the race period (measured in terms of on air mentions and visible logo placement). Generally the cost for this type of sponsorship runs between $1–2 million. One risk associated with this type of sponsorship is that the race may be delayed due to weather conditions, which would significantly lower the value of the sponsorship as weekday TV ratings would be significantly lower than the expected weekend ratings. Also, depending on the Driver's Championship race, the individual race ratings will tend to vary significantly. If a driver has locked up the championship, this tends to greatly depress ratings and lower the value to the individual event sponsor.

There is also the opportunity to become an Official Sponsor of NASCAR. This option allows a company to gain category exclusivity with regards to using the NASCAR name and logo in advertising and promotions. This also gains the sponsor full exclusivity across all NASCAR properties with regard to promotional and sponsorship activities. This type of sponsorship typically does not include any exposure for the company and costs between $2–10 million.

Team Level

The most common form of sponsorship is in the form of team sponsorship. This deal typically involves the exchange of either funds, products, or both from the sponsor company to the team. In return, the team promises to attend a certain number of races and prominently display the corporate logo of their sponsors. The value of the sponsorship is directly related to the company's logo placement on the vehicle, with the more visible areas costing more. For example, a typical lead sponsor on a vehicle would get logo placement on the hood, the sides of the car and the rear quarter panels—while associate sponsors would get logo placement on the rear wing and front fenders. Depending on the placement of the decals, and the prestige of the team, the dollar amount associated with individual sponsorships can vary greatly. Team sponsorship levels are one of the more closely guarded secrets of the individual racing teams, but generally, a primary team sponsorship can run between $6–20 million for the premier series and $2–4 million for the second tier Busch Grand National Series. The risks associated with this type of sponsorship include the possibility of the team not qualifying for a race, or finishing poorly and not receiving media attention.

Driver Level

Finally, a sponsor could elect to sponsor a driver personally. This contract would allow the sponsor to use the driver for promotional activities and personal appearances. The driver agrees to also wear branding reflecting their personal sponsorship and include their names in any interviews held during the race weekend. This type of sponsorship generally costs

$150,000–$500,000 per season. Once again, there is a risk that a driver will not perform well and therefore receive little media attention during an event. Several companies have mitigated against this risk by signing up stables of drivers in the hopes that at least one of them will be successful in a given week. These include the Gillette NASCAR Young Guns and the Coca Cola Racing Family.

VALUING THE SERIES TITLE SPONSOR OPPORTUNITY

Based on the risks and costs associated with each sponsorship opportunity, NEXTEL decided that it made the most sense to pursue the Title Sponsor opportunity. This position would allow NEXTEL to capitalize on several dominant facts about NASCAR:

- Fans tended to be loyal to the league's most prominent sponsor
- Prevent the fan alienation that naturally comes from sponsoring an individual team
- Win every Sunday as opposed to not being shown on TV or not making the race
- NEXTEL brand attributes more easily conveyed to fans when involved with every team/driver
- Series-wide exclusivity removes competition from using this media outlet
- Sponsorship integration is easier with a series wide commitment

The Title Sponsor opportunity also provided many additional sources of value for NEXTEL over a traditional Team or Event level sponsorship. Exhibit 6-5 of the Section 6 text shows a breakdown of the activation elements associated with each of the sponsorships available to NEXTEL. With the Title Sponsor role, NEXTEL would be able to impact fans at every NASCAR event, as opposed to an Event Sponsor, and provide an outlet at each event for Product Demonstrations. By showcasing NEXTEL's technological abilities, as all NASCAR officials and teams will be using NEXTEL equipment, they will be able to demonstrate the advantages of their product over traditional cellular operators.

CURRENT SITUATION

Replacing a long time sponsor like RJR Reynolds was not going to be easy, and with NASCAR popularity reaching all time highs—current ratings put the Winston Cup series second only to the NFL in TV ratings (see Exhibit 8-3 of the Section 8 text)—the bidding was going to be fierce. Not only would NEXTEL need to field a highly competitive bid, but they would also need to convince NASCAR that they were the right fit for the role. One of the unique aspects for this sponsorship is the ability of NASCAR to be highly selective about which company it would want to align with. In this regard, NEXTEL has an advantage in that the tech-savvy image it portrays was one that NASCAR desperately wanted to bring to the sport. In addition, the telecommunications industry does not carry with it the negative connotations associated with the tobacco or alcohol industries—another plus for NEXTEL. With NASCAR approving NEXTEL as a potential replacement for Winston, it came down to NEXTEL determining the return it could expect for the sponsorship.

Direct Media Valuation

Motorsports sponsorship is tracked and valued based upon several key metrics. Most importantly is the amount of clear, in-focus exposure time that the vehicle receives during the event. This amount of time is then multiplied by the average advertising slot sold during the event to determine the total advertising value generated for the sponsor during the event. This system takes into account the network airing the program and the viewership of the event. This provides companies with a valuation for what their sponsorship dollars are returning to them in the form of direct advertising. It does not, however, include the additional return from the at-track audience that is being impacted by the sponsor's placement. An example of the 2002 Winston Title Sponsorship valuation is given in Exhibit 1, computed using the traditional valuation technique, an adapted advertising agency valuation and a valuation from a market research firm. Exhibit 2 shows selected media valuations for the 2002 NASCAR Winston Cup Series.

Examining data from the 2002 NASCAR season shows that Title Sponsor Winston received annual advertising value equivalent to $160,158,235. Compared to this are the leading team sponsorship, which generated $166,404,630 in media value for Budweiser, and the leading Official Sponsor, which generated $53,820,930 in valuation for Pepsi (excluding the auto manufacturers).[10]

EXHIBIT 1   MEDIA VALUATION EXAMPLE—WINSTON 2002 NASCAR SPONSORSHIP

Valuation Techniques	Element	Value
Based on NASCAR/Joyce Julius reporting (15 hours and 1877 mentions), evaluating one :30 spot at $87,337 advertising agency's assigned value), and one verbal mention as :10		
Traditional	Logo Exposure	$157,206,600
(second of exposure/30) × (average spot rate)	Verbal Mentions	$ 54,643,850
	Total	**$211,850,450**
Advertising Agency View	Logo Exposure	
	100%	$157,206,600
Value = 10% to 100% of a :30 TV spot for the event	10%	$ 15,720,660
	Verbal Mentions	
	100%	$ 54,643,850
	10%	$ 5,464,385
	Total Range	
	100%	**$211,850,450**
	10%	**$ 21,185,045**
Market Research View	Logo Exposure	$225,720,000
Sponsorship Media Value = (Seconds of Exposure/30) × (Audience/1000) × CPM × Weighting	Verbal Mentions	$ 78,458,600
CPM = $22	**Total**	**$304,178,600**
Audience = 19,000,000		
Weighting = 0.3 (Average for recall between on screen graphics (0.5) and shirt (0.2))		

Source: Joyce Julius and Associates *2002 NASCAR Winston Cup Year-End Report*

EXHIBIT 2 **SELECTED MEDIA VALUATIONS FOR 2002 NASCAR WINSTON CUP SERIES**

League Level Sponsor	In-Focus Exposure Time	Sponsor Mentions	$ Value Based on Cost Per :30
Winston	15:00:46	1,877	$160,158,235
Pepsi	5:56:48	249	$ 53,820,930
MBNA America	5:01:52	29	$ 39,772,980
Coca-Cola	4:29:32	102	$ 39,619,360
3M	4:44:15	1	$ 34,471,770
Stacker2	3:07:36	83	$ 26,833,380
Subway	1:47:54	135	$ 24,218,695
Team Level Sponsor			
Budweiser	19:40:52	350	$166,404,630
Lowe's	10:06:48	242	$ 90,958,200
Alltel	5:21:12	39	$ 42,710,605
Cingular Wireless	5:59:05	102	$ 54,650,935
Sprint	2:48:20	54	$ 21,141,025
Sharpie	3:43:14	117	$ 26,850,020
Rubbermaid	3:06:47	47	$ 24,225,750

Source: Joyce Julius and Associates *2002 NASCAR Winston Cup Year-End Report*

EXHIBIT 3 **CONSUMER BRAND LOYALTY BY SPORT**[11]

Percentage of fans within each sport/event that claim to "Almost always" or "Frequently" purchase a sponsor's product over a non-sponsor's product.

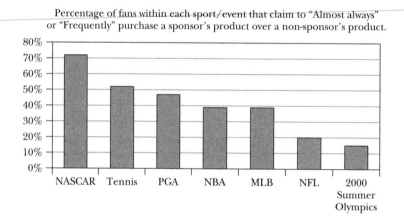

New Subscriber Valuation

The largest potential area for value to NEXTEL lies in the conversion of NASCAR fans from other wireless carriers to their wireless service. NASCAR's fan base is estimated at 72 million, and only 5% of them currently are NEXTEL customers. There is tremendous potential for NEXTEL to grow its user base by converting NASCAR's highly brand loyal customers (Exhibit 3 shows a comparison of the brand loyalty characteristics of fans across sports) to their service. Aiding this is the fact that NASCAR's demographics and NEXTEL's desired customer base align well. With the average NEXTEL customer's yearly bill at $720, the value to NEXTEL of a 1% conversion of NASCAR fans to their service generates $514 million in additional revenue.

TIME TO CHOOSE

With the numbers worked out and the blessing of NASCAR, it was time for Mark to recommend whether to accept or decline this opportunity. There could be a tremendous upside to the deal if the growth of NASCAR continued, and if the fan base could be converted over to NEXTEL service. However, the large scale of the agreement, almost 5% of net income in 2002, was inherently risky. NEXTEL had never been associated with NASCAR, and NASCAR had never been partnered with a technologically focused sponsor before. Would the partnership work out? Do the benefits outweigh the risks? Is NASCAR the right vehicle to hitch their wagon to?

APPENDIX A
NEXTEL Communications: Summary Financials

Panel A: Financial Statement Information ($ Millions: As Reported Each Year)

	1996	1997	1998	1999	2000	2001	2002
Revenue	$ 333	$ 739	$ 1,847	$ 3,326	$ 5,714	$ 7,689	$ 8,721
Cost of Revenues	248	289	516	697	2,172	2,869	2,516
Selling, General and Admin. Expenses	330	862	1,550	2,094	2,278	3,020	3,039
Restructuring and Impairment Charge	—	—	—	—	—	1,769	35
Depreciation and Amortization	401	527	832	1,004	1,265	1,746	1,595
Operating Income	(646)	(938)	(1,052)	(469)	(1)	(1,715)	1,536
Net Income Attrib. To Common Stockholders	(556)	(1,643)	(1,801)	(1,530)	(1,024)	(2,858)	1,660
Total Assets		9,228	11,573	18,410	22,686	22,064	21,484
Long Term Debt		5,038	7,710	10,925	14,731	14,865	12,550
Stockholders' Equity		230	1,912	2,574	2,028	(582)	2,846

Source: Nextel SEC Form 10K filings.

Panel B: Capital Market Information (as at December 31)

	1996	1997	1998	1999	2000	2001	2002
NEXTEL							
• Shares Outstanding ($ millions)	455	540	578	738	763	799	1,004
• Closing Price	6.53	13.00	11.81	51.56	24.75	10.96	11.55
• Market Capitalization ($ millions)	2,878	6,801	6,693	75,514	18,917	8,757	11,864
Industry/Stock Market Indexes							
• NASDAQ Telecom Index	216	307	501	1,015	463	237	108
• S and P 500	741	970	1,229	1,469	1,320	1,148	880

Source: Bloomberg.

Questions

1. Why should NEXTEL consider NASCAR sponsorship? Should it be considered a substitute for or a complement to other forms of NEXTEL marketing (such as advertising or in-store promotions)?

2. How should NEXTEL decide between the major different types (levels) of NASCAR sponsorship—league level as series title sponsor, league level as event title sponsorship, league official sponsor, team level, and driver level?

3. Exhibits 1 and 2 of the case show "valuation techniques" often used in sports sponsorship presentations. Discuss the usefulness of these valuation techniques.

4. Focus on NEXTEL's series title sponsorship decision. Evaluate whether NEXTEL should bid in the range being discussed ($700 million for a 10-year sponsorship).

CASE 6.2 "I LOST MY VOLVO IN NEW HAVEN": TENNIS EVENT SPONSORSHIP[12]

As the 1995 Volvo International Tennis Tournament (VITT) in New Haven, Connecticut began, tournament owner Jim Westhall walked his dog Aztec (a gift from Ivan Lendl) around the site. He was met with a flurry of questions from inquisitive spectators: "Jim, who's going to be the title sponsor in 1996? . . . Is Volvo really out? . . . Is it true you're selling the tournament?"

Volvo Cars of North America was in its 23rd and final year as title sponsor. Volvo was the longest running title sponsor in professional tennis. However, in Westhall's view, Volvo was not paying enough in sponsorship fees to enable the tournament to keep up with the financial changes in the sport. Prize money had more than doubled since the tournament had moved from Stratton Mountain, Vermont, six years earlier, yet Volvo's annual financial participation had remained about the same. Westhall was looking for a title sponsor at approximately $1.4 million annually for a minimum three-year period.

Westhall was now in the final round of negotiations with The Pilot Pen Corporation of America and Diners Club International to take over the title sponsorship in 1996 and beyond. He wondered whether he should accept one of these offers now, or keep searching.

Event History

Westhall had founded the tournament in 1970. His company, JEWEL Productions, organized and promoted two tennis tournaments. This constituted his principal activity year-round.

The 1970 inaugural tournament offered $5,000 in prize money and featured the star Australian players Rod Laver, Roy Emerson, Ken Rosewall and Fred Stolle. Spectators sat along a grassy hillside above a red clay court at the world-famous Mount Washington Hotel in Bretton Woods, New Hampshire (year-round population of two). In 1973, Volvo Cars of North America became the title sponsor. In 1974, the tournament relocated to the Mt. Cranmore ski area in North Conway, New Hampshire. It remained at North Conway for ten years, before moving to a bigger site at Stratton Mountain in Vermont in 1985. At these classic destination resorts, the event was among the most successful and respected on the tour. (**Exhibit 1** lists past champions of the VITT.)

In 1989, the Association of Tennis Professionals (ATP) and the tournament directors joined forces to organize a new men's professional tennis tour (The ATP Tour). The Tour regulations specified that beginning in 1990 all Championship Series events would have to be played in a permanent facility. Stratton Mountain was able to raise $10 million of the $14 million needed for a new stadium. Tournament owner Westhall was unable to raise the rest. Approval of a state tax proposal and/or state bond issuance to fund this gap was considered highly unlikely.[13]

In September of 1989, Westhall announced that he had selected New Haven, Connecticut as the site for the 1990 VITT. The State of Connecticut had financed a 15,000 seat ultra-modern stadium located on the Yale University campus, adjacent to the 70,000 seat Yale Bowl and

Harvard Business School Case No 9-599-037. Copyright 1999 President and Fellows of Harvard College. All rights reserved. For information: permission@hbsp.harvard.edu. This case was prepared by Stephen A. Greyser, Brian Harris, and Mitchell Truwit. HBS cases are developed solely for class discussion and do not necessarily illustrate effective or ineffective management.

EXHIBIT 1   VITT Past Champions

Year	Champion	Location
1994	Boris Becker	New Haven
1993	Andrei Medvedev	New Haven
1992	Stefan Edberg	New Haven
1991	Petr Korda	New Haven
1990	Derick Rostagno	New Haven
1989	Brad Gilbert	Stratton
1988	Andre Agassi	Stratton
1987	John McEnroe/Ivan Lendl[a]	Stratton
1986	Ivan Lendl	Stratton
1985	John McEnroe	Stratton
1984	Joakim Nystrom	North Conway
1983	Jose-Luis Clerc	North Conway
1982	Ivan Lendl	North Conway
1981	Jose-Luis Clerc	North Conway
1980	Jimmy Connors	North Conway
1980	Harold Solomon	North Conway
1978	Eddie Dibbs	North Conway
1977	John Alexander	North Conway
1976	Jimmy Connors	North Conway
1975	Jimmy Connors	North Conway
1974	Vijay Armitraj	Bretton Woods
1973	Cliff Richey	Bretton Woods

Source: *1995 Volvo International Tournament Magazine.*

[a] Final not played due to rain.

6,000 seat Yale Field (baseball). In return for use of the stadium, Westhall was to pay 8% of all ticket, merchandise, and food and beverage revenues and 15% of all in-state sponsorships to the Tennis Foundation of Connecticut, Inc. (TFC). Further, Westhall was to remit a 10% tax on all tickets to the State of Connecticut (to repay construction bonds) and a 3% ticket tax to the city of New Haven. Additionally, Westhall volunteered to donate $100,000 or more per year for a tennis program for inner-city children.[14] In negotiating the arrangements with Yale for the use of the university's land for the stadium, Westhall committed to including the phrase "from Yale University" on promotional material on tickets, etc. Yale also could buy a number of boxes for its own hospitality purposes.

Westhall believed New Haven would be a terrific venue in which to grow his event. New Haven County bordered on Fairfield County, one of the wealthiest counties in America. Connecticut was domicile to a multitude of corporate headquarters. By leveraging his working relationship with Yale University to gain access to alumni executives and by marketing his event throughout Connecticut, Westhall planned to sell more corporate sponsorships and tickets than for any other all-male tennis event in North America.

By the summer of 1995, Westhall's plans had not yet come to fruition. On the positive side, the VITT sold more box seats and event tickets than any other one-week male tennis event in the world.[15] Additionally, Westhall had developed the SNET Classic, a successful professional women's tennis exhibition played on the heels of the VITT, sponsored by the local telephone company, Southern New England Telephone. Connecticut, however, had gone through its worst recession in years. Corporations had been reluctant to spend sponsorship money in this economic climate. Furthermore, many fans and corporations were turned off by New Haven's crime-related problems. New Haven also lacked the beautiful natural resources and accommodations of Stratton Mountain. The press continued to focus on the weather and the ever-present threat of rain. Westhall had invested heavily in trying to enhance the player and fan experience, e.g., via offering hot air balloon rides, street hockey clinics, picnics, raffles, etc. Yet in his opinion the tournament needed the lift of a new image. (**Exhibit 2** provides details on some tournament-related special events.)

Men's Professional Tennis and New Haven's Sanction

The men's professional tennis tour was governed by the ATP (the players' union), and the tournament directors. By 1995, the Tour had grown to over 80 international events featuring more than $60 million in prize money.[16] These tournaments were organized according to location, prize money, and calendar date. The ATP Tour controlled each of these elements to varying degrees, thus limiting a tournament's ability to change.

New Haven's sanction (i.e., event eligibility) was for a Championship Series Double-Up event in August, two weeks prior to the U.S. Open. This meant that the tournament would compete directly with the RCA Championships being held during the same week in Indianapolis.[17] In exchange for accepting this date on the calendar and maintaining certain levels of prize money, the ATP Tour guaranteed both the RCA and the VITT three of the top ten players in the world. Unfortunately, Westhall considered this guarantee of three top players as potentially insufficient for New Haven. The reason, as Westhall saw it, was the difference between having marquee American stars (i.e., truly well-known names) and lesser-known foreign players. The top 10 players for August were: Andre Agassi, Pete Sampras, Thomas Muster, Boris Becker, Michael Chang, Goran Ivanisevic, Yevgeny Kafelnikov, Thomas Enquist, Marc Rosset, and Wayne Ferreira. There were a number of factors that influenced the tournaments in which a player chose to play. Among these were location, date, climate, tournament amenities, and event sponsors.

There were also rumors that certain tournaments paid illegal appearance fees to induce top stars to play in their events. While New Haven's climate and scheduled week made it an excellent preparation for the U.S. Open, some top players were tired from the long, hot summer and chose to rest that week. Other players were reluctant to play in New Haven due to its lack of a first class hotel. Additionally, corporate sponsors were beginning to play a more active role in determining where players played. Westhall was concerned that Nike, a major sponsor of the Indianapolis event, might flex its muscle and induce its contracted players such as New Haven's top seed, Andre Agassi, to alter their schedules. Because the player field was directly related to the VITT's ability to attract sponsor revenue and sell tickets, it was essential that star players decide to come to New Haven.

At Stratton Mountain, Westhall's event had been chosen consistently as the players' favorite stop on the tour. Players brought their entire families to the tournament. They were provided with ski lodges and treated to golf, fishing, softball games, fireworks displays, and Westhall's famous lobster cookout. The tennis was just part of the total experience. Many fans also took the week off from work to enjoy the attractions of the resort destination, and

EXHIBIT 2   TOURNAMENT RELATED SPECIAL EVENTS

Volvo International
August 12–20

The ABCs of tennis: **Agassi. Becker. Chang** begin the alphabet of top tennis players in the 1995 Volvo International. **Michael Stich, Luke and Murphy Jensen, Sergi Bruguera,**

Richard Krajicek

and over 50 more players make it letter perfect. Your ticket to great tennis starts here but the best prices end July 21. Boxes, day & night series, session and group tickets are still available. Call 1-800-548-6586 or 203-772-3838.

players/times subject to change

Volvo International Best Buys

Kids 14 and under - They get in for half-price.
Families - With half-price kids and low-priced tickets it's no contest when it comes to a great family outing.
Early buyers - Ticket prices are inexplicably inexpensive for anyone who buys on or before July 21.
Big shots - Our corporate package includes a 4-seat box, 100 session tickets and a spot in the Legends Tennis Clinic.
Cheap shots - Get a group of 20 together and get tickets for $5. That's not just cheap, that's smart!

A Whole Bunch of Special Events

All kinds of exciting activities will be served on and off court during the Volvo International and the SNET Classic. ReMax hot air **balloon rides** will keep you on top of things. The **Peter Burwash International Tennis Show** is a sophisticated production combining music, humor and slick racquet and ball control skills. **Libor Karas** will show why he is a stunt bike champion. The **Hartford Whalers** will put on street hockey clinics and exhibitions. Incredible **Rollerbladers** will be spinning their wheels throughout both events. The **Tennis Legends** return to display their skills. **JEWEL Grassroots Excellence Team** will "court" your attention. And overhead, after some of the evening sessions, you can look up to a colorful display of **fireworks.**

Softball, Aug. 12
Basketball, Aug. 13

Tom Brokaw's team will play softball against **Doc Rivers'** team in the CT Special Olympics Celebrity Softball Game, Sat. Aug. 12, 7pm, Yale Field. For softball tickets call (203) 782-1666. Sunday, Aug. 13, 3:00pm, on the Grandstand Court, Doc Rivers and players from the knicks, Celtics and San Antonio Spurs will play basketball alongside the tennis pros in the **FootAction Shootout.** For basketball info call 1-800-548-6586.

Source: *1995 Volvo International Tournament Magazine.*

bought courtside boxes to the entire week of play. Thus far, New Haven had been unable to replicate the appeal of Stratton Mountain.

Tournament Economics[18]

Professional tennis tournaments generated revenue from a variety of sources. Among these were sponsorships, ticket sales, and food and beverage and merchandise concessions. An event like New Haven might generate 55% of its revenue from tickets, 40% from sponsorships, and 5% from concessions.

Box seat tickets were the largest single revenue source, accounting for 40% of sales. (**Exhibit 3** lists the range of box seat prices for 1995.) This money was particularly significant from a cash flow perspective, in that 80% of box seat holders renewed their seats for the following year during the week of the tournament and in the month immediately following. These advance sales provided essential working capital for much of the year.

General admission tickets represented 15% of revenue. These, however, were very unpredictable and could drop dramatically due to inclement weather, player injury, or early round upsets. These sales were usually made either several weeks prior to the event or, more often, on the day of the match.

The title sponsorship generally made up 20% of revenues. Additionally, the title sponsor was typically responsible for purchasing television time to air the event. Due to tennis' poor ratings, networks were unwilling to pay for the rights to broadcast events such as New Haven. However, such television coverage was necessary in order to maximize sponsor value. From Westhall's perspective an ideal sponsor would add prestige to the event through its affiliation, dedicate meaningful resources beyond its sponsorship fee, be a consistent and visible supporter of tennis, and encourage its corporate business partners (e.g., major vendors) to be involved with the event.

Lower-level sponsorships generated another 20% of revenues. The majority of this money came from a "Presenting Sponsor" and a limited number of "Supporting Sponsors." New Haven's current sponsors included a combination of global, national, regional, and local organizations in addition to Volvo: TIME (Magazine), Shawmut Bank, Footaction USA, Unisource, RADO Swiss Watches, IBM, the ATP Tour, Toshiba, Polo Sport (Ralph Lauren), US Air, SNET, New England Brewing Co., the Connecticut Lottery, local business-to-business and specialty retail firms, and a local network TV channel. Additionally, many local sponsors provided trade benefits. These consisted of essential goods and services including airfare, advertising, automobiles, office equipment, catering, etc.

Sponsor Search

In the fall of 1994, Volvo Cars of North America gave private notice to Westhall that it would not renew its title sponsorship after 1995 at the new increased rate of $1.2 million annually. Westhall immediately began his search for a replacement. Due to the investment necessary to change all tournament signage and collateral material and to promote the new title sponsor, a one-year or two-year deal was deemed infeasible.

Westhall aimed to target companies with products or services that matched the upscale demographics of tennis fans. Based on research conducted at earlier Volvo events, the average

EXHIBIT 3   1995 Box Seat Price Information

Box seats are the premier seats in the stadium and you get to select the one that's right for you. The accompanying stadium diagram shows the availability.

Your box includes:

- One to ten seats for 15 sessions of tennis (9 days and 6 nights)
- Personalized identification plaque
- Access to boxholder restaurant
- Option to purchase preferred parking (limited availability)
- Renewable option on seats
- First right-of-refusal on other JEWEL Productions events in the Connecticut Tennis Center

Call (203) 776-7331 and ask for a sales representative. We'll be happy to answer any of your questions.

Volvo International dates:
August 12-20, 1995

Source: 1995 Volvo International Ticket Brochure.

1995 BOX SEAT PRICES

ROWS	1995 PRICE
Baseline North & South Boxes	
1	$3632
2-4	$2946
5-8	$2740
9-12	$2604
13-16	$2398
17-19	$2262
Courtside West & East Boxes	
1	$3496
2-4	$2740
5-8	$2604
9-12	$2466
13-16	$2330
17-20	$2056
Courtside West Boxes	
21-24	$1918
25	$1782
Courtside East Boxes	
21-24	$1748
25-26	$1624
Baseline Concourse Luxury Boxes	
Luxury	$6029

Prices based on 4-seat boxes and 8-seat Lux Boxes. 2-seat boxes available at 1/2 the listed prices.

VITT customer was 39.5 years of age and had a household income of $89,500. About 70% were college graduates and 66% held professional degrees; 40% reported that they were involved in investing. Further, some 82% said they would return to the next year's tournament. The average customer attended 3.6 of the 15 sessions of play.[19] At first glance, financial service companies, luxury automobile manufacturers, and insurance companies (an industry with strong Connecticut presence) seemed the most logical fits.

Westhall's sales team also searched for companies with previous involvement in professional tennis, as well as companies looking to make a major move into the Connecticut market. Other recent title sponsors of major U.S. tennis events included AT&T, Comcast, Diet Pepsi, Legg Mason, Lipton, Miller Lite, Newsweek, Nuveen, Purex, RCA, and several major supermarket chains. Due to tennis' declining television ratings and level of participation, it was difficult for tournament owners to find interested major sponsors. Some U.S. tournaments did not have title sponsors.

Sponsor Benefits

The event had much to offer a title sponsor. Specifically, the title sponsor would benefit from international, national, and regional media coverage, promotional rights, hospitality opportunities, and community visibility. Title sponsorship also guaranteed category exclusivity. This made it both an "offensive" opportunity (strategically) to promote goods and services, and a "defensive" one to block competitors from this high-profile event.

The title sponsor's name would appear on television through end-court identity, title graphics, on-air mentions, and promotional advertising. **Exhibit 4** is a summary of exposure Volvo was estimated to have received from its title sponsorship of the VITT in 1992. The value of the exposure was estimated at $7,713,809.[20] (It should be noted that many sponsors did not accept such exposure valuations at their full estimated value and instead chose to discount them.) In 1994, the tournament received over 20 hours of national cable television coverage on ESPN and ESPN2. Volvo received 25% of the advertising inventory on these telecasts.[21]

EXHIBIT 4   **1992 VITT EXPOSURE SUMMARY**

Volvo International

Exposure Section	Exposure Time	# of Articles Mentioned	Impressions	CP:30/NTIV
1) National television	6:35:42	205	162,226,420	$4,515,785.26
2) International television	NTIV	NTIV	8,144,850	48,787.65
3) Local television	NTIV	NTIV	46,951,586	281,239.99
4) National radio	NTIV	NTIV	2,332,800	13,973.47
5) Local radio	NTIV	NTIV	10,039,074	60,133.97
6) Event site & local market	NTIV	NTIV	108,884,520	652,218.27
7) Cross-corporate advertising	NTIV	NTIV	17,647,250	105,707.03
8) Print	NTIV	224	356,505,530	2,096,097.75
Total	6:35:42	429	712,732,030	$7,713,809.42

Source: VITT.

Note: Values may vary ± 5.00 due to rounding.

EXHIBIT 5   1992 VITT EVENT SITE AND LOCAL MARKET EXPOSURE

	Impressions	NTIV
Total	108,884,520	$652,218.27

Event site and local market impressions are calculated by a formula that compares the level of involvement at the event site in terms of exposure vehicles the sponsor utilizes (signage, handouts, fliers, marquees, etc.), the number of people attending, and impressions created from the "life" of the exposure vehicles.

Contributing to Volvo's impressions at the Volvo International and in the marketplace were the following:

Item Distributed	Number	Impressions	NTIV
Attendance	165,000	19,800,00	$118,602.00
Food court	10,000/day	2,240,000	13,417.60
Ticket brochures	180,000	1,440,000	8,625.60
Mailers	35,000	280,000	1,677.20
Postcards/mailers	5,000	40,000	239.60
Posters	5,000	22,610,000	135,433.90
Programs/magazines	13,500	162,000	970.38
Drawsheets	40,000	480,000	2,875.20
Tickets	152,000	608,00	3,641.92
Credentials	13,500	54,000	323.46
Champion club brochures	3,500	28,00	167.72
Stationary	25,000	150,000	898.50
Media release letterhead	10,500	63,000	377.37
Mailing labels	1,200	14,400	86.26
Christmas cards	17,500	420,00	2,515.80
Postcards yearly	15,000	90,000	539.10
Sponsor brochures	1,250	10,000	59.90
Press releases	18	43,200	258.77
Phone calls to ticket office	50,000	50,000	299.50
Billboard/95-New Haven	1	6,951,300	41,638.29
Billboard/95-Bridgeport	1	5,610,000	33,603.90
Billboard-Hartford	1	2,320,500	13,899.80
Bus tails	60	5,348,200	32,035.72
Bus signs	12	393,550	2,357.36
Mugs	233	111,840	669.92
Water bottles	186	122,760	735.33
Aprons	48	720	4.31
Cloth hats	1,443	1,082,250	6,482.68
Visors	300	144,000	862.56
Straw hats	50	110,000	658.90
T-shirts	9,731	11,677,200	69,946.43
Sweatshirts	4,191	23,469,600	140,582.90
Volunteer shirts	800	2,960,000	17,730.40
Total	**750,025**	**108,884,520**	**$652,218.27**

Source: VITT.

EXHIBIT 6   1992 VITT Cross-Corporate Advertising Exposure

	Impressions	NTIV
Total	17,647,250	$105,707.03

Included in this section is exposure derived from cross-promotional activity performed by other sponsors or organizations involved with the Volvo International.

Cross-Corporate Advertising

Item	Number Distributed	Impressions	NTIV
Chase Manhattan/mailers	300,000	1,200,000	$7,188.00
Chase Manhattan/display	100	357,000	2,138.43
Finast shopping bags	17,000	102,000	610.98
Coca-Cola cut-outs	50,000	300,000	1,797.00
Mobil coupons	1,000,000	8,000,000	47,920.00
Mobil display	250	7,675,000	45,823.50
Volvo test drives	10	38,250	229.12
Total	**1,367,360**	**17,647,250**	**$105,707.03**

Source: VITT.

Event site and local market exposure was valued at over $650,000. (**Exhibit 5** breaks down total impressions from this visibility in 1992.) The title sponsor was recognized on over 150,000 tickets, 180,000 ticket brochures, three highway billboards on Connecticut's busiest highway, and at a myriad of other areas. Innovative programs included printing tournament name and information as the background on the ticket stock for the Connecticut lottery for over one month. (Other cross-corporate promotional opportunities from 1992 are summarized and valued at $105,707 in **Exhibit 6.**)

Print advertising and articles were valued at over $2 million. The tournament reached over 400 newspaper markets and received several thousand press clippings. Coverage in major newspapers in the previous year had extended for a full week or longer in many instances; in *USA Today*, it was 12 days.

Beyond media value, the tournament offered an opportunity to entertain current and prospective corporate clients, reward employees, and network with other corporate sponsors. Air-conditioned hospitality tents were located adjacent to the stadium court. The hospitality tents featured international cuisine, open bars, and closed circuit television coverage of the matches. The title sponsor received forty invitations per session and a party for 250 at the "Sponsor Promenade." Westhall paid tennis legends such as Rod Laver, Vijay Armitraj, Ken Rosewall, Fred Stolle, Cliff Drysdale, Roy Emerson, and Ilie Nastase to put on clinics for sponsors and their guests and to mingle in the Promenade. Other title sponsor perks included several spots in the sponsor golf tournament with past and current players, recognition as a sponsor of a celebrity fund-raiser softball event for the Connecticut Special Olympics, and participation in the tournament awards ceremony live on television on center court. The title sponsor also received ten baseline four-seat boxes in the first and second row, two eight-seat Concourse Luxury Boxes, and Gold Club parking passes.

The title sponsor could donate up to 15,000 tickets to charitable organizations. (The organizations encompassed a wide range of civic, charitable, school, church/synagogue, community, arts, and youth groups.) The title sponsor was also recognized prominently in the Grassroots Tennis program Westhall ran for inner-city youths. This program was formed to expand and initiate year-round activities that introduced tennis to Connecticut's inner-city youth while fostering self-discipline, pride, and good health and fitness habits. There were activities throughout the year in each of the nine Grassroots cities. In the past, these had included appearances by MaliVai Washington, Luke and Murphy Jensen, and the late Arthur Ashe. There was also an opportunity for title sponsor employee participation in the year-round volunteer program.

In spite of all these benefits, nearly a year of effort yielded only a limited number of interested companies.

AT&T

AT&T was making a move for in-state long-distance market share in the newly deregulated Connecticut market. Southern New England Telephone (SNET) had maintained a monopoly on this service until 1994. Title sponsorship would provide AT&T with tremendous exposure and allow it to entertain big accounts. AT&T was already involved in men's professional tennis as the title sponsor of the AT&T Challenge in Atlanta every spring. SNET, however, was the title sponsor of Westhall's women's tennis exhibition and a supporting sponsor of the men's event. SNET was headquartered in New Haven and had been a sponsor since 1990. If Westhall actively pursued AT&T, SNET indicated that he risked losing them for both events. Furthermore, he worried that this move might agitate local politicians and other New Haven-based companies. He decided not to pursue AT&T.

Pilot Pen

Westhall had a longstanding friendship with Ron Shaw, CEO and President of The Pilot Pen Corporation of America. Pilot had previous title sponsorship experience through a men's tennis event in California (1985–1987) and a minor $50,000 event with Westhall in New Haven. Ron Shaw was a major figure in New Haven. He was the Chairman of the Shubert Theater's Board of Directors and was involved with the Jewish Community Center. Westhall was hopeful that Shaw could open doors to corporations in Connecticut that had previously been shut to him. Shaw started his career as a stand-up comic and Westhall was confident Shaw would be willing to take some chances to stir up tennis. Shaw thought the demographics of his product's consumers and the audience of the tournament overlapped, and that ESPN's reach was a perfect complement. It was unclear, however, whether Shaw would be willing to spend large sums of money above and beyond his sponsorship fee to highlight Pilot's participation. In contrast, Volvo for example, had supplemented its involvement by sponsoring amateur leagues, a collegiate tennis series, and seven other professional tennis events. Westhall was also concerned that Pilot's name might not have the same awareness and image value as Volvo's and wondered how this might affect the image of the tournament.

Diners Club

Diners Club International (DCI) was working with sports marketing consultants Harlan Stone and Ron Erskine of Advantage International to find an event which would serve as a "bookend" on the east coast for their Diners Club Matches golf event in California. DCI wanted the exposure of title sponsorship and an opportunity to entertain major accounts in and around New York City. DCI was committed to a world class image and was willing to purchase time on ABC or CBS for the finals weekend. (NBC was already under contract to broadcast the semi-finals and finals of Indianapolis.)

DCI recognized that network coverage would be far more valuable than ESPN cable coverage, but it would also be more expensive. Therefore, DCI wanted Westhall to purchase some of the advertising time on the telecast to help offset the cost. ESPN coverage had typically cost Volvo around $200,000 per year, while network time would likely be around $800,000. Westhall considered this plan viable, although far from ideal. While he would assume great risk in purchasing the advertising time, he hoped to package it with lower-level event sponsorships in order to increase their value.[22] Additionally, sponsorships which included courtside signage would be elevated in value due to the higher ratings for tennis on ABC and CBS. In 1994, comparable men's tennis broadcasts on ESPN ranged from ratings of 0.3 to 0.9, while those on ABC, CBS, and NBC ranged from 1.5 to 2.0.[23] Ratings aside, the tournament would experience an image boost simply by being on one of the national networks.

Westhall believed that Diners Club could be just the lift the tournament needed. He was sure that they would partake in additional spending to extend the reach of their sponsorship and thus the event.

The Diners Club deal, however, presented many potential negative financial consequences for Westhall. The 15% commission Advantage would charge on the deal made it less lucrative than the Pilot deal. Moreover, Westhall feared that his internal sales force would be adversely affected if the deal and commission went to an outside firm. Furthermore, he risked losing Fleet Bank as a major supporting sponsor. Fleet maintained that its exclusivity in financial services extended to credit cards as well as to banks. Because Fleet was the largest bank in New England, Westhall would be hard pressed to find another bank with the ability to match Fleet's sponsorship dollars.

Westhall also worried that his lack of financial latitude with the DCI deal might hamstring his relations with the ATP Tour. The Tour had just announced Mercedes-Benz as its official car. While it was not mandatory, ATP officials were encouraging tournaments to strike separate deals with Mercedes. Mercedes knew that their relationship with the Tour provided them with some leverage in dealing with the individual tournaments. Therefore, their sponsorship offers to Westhall and other tournament directors were not nearly as lucrative as deals the tournaments could obtain on the open market. ATP officials were instrumental, behind the scenes, at balancing the player field between New Haven and Indianapolis. It behooved Westhall to find a way to accommodate the ATP's request. He feared the Diners Club deal would limit his financial flexibility to do so. His company's resources had been impaired in 1992, when a court surface de-lamination on center court canceled several sessions of the 1992 VITT.

The Decision

By August 1995, news of Volvo's pending departure had reached the *New Haven Register*. Westhall needed to make a decision and an announcement right away. Without a new title sponsor, he feared that box holders would delay their purchases until they were sure there would be an event in 1996. This was an untenable thought from a cash flow perspective, since Westhall needed these sales to fund any potential shortfall from this year's event, as well as to cover his operating expenses for the next eleven months (until next year's revenues came in.) He also worried that once lost, these box holders would be much harder to regain.

Westhall evaluated his options. Should he accept Pilot Pen and risk being seen as a regional event with less reach? Should he go with Diners Club and assume the financial risk of purchasing expensive network inventory? If he expected to be in the business of selling advertising inventory, would he be better off trying to get Presenting Sponsor *TIME* to step up to the role of the title sponsor in exchange for a substantial number of ad pages? Or, should he delay the decision and search for a better deal?

Questions

1. Which title sponsor opportunity do you think is best for Westhall? Why?

2. What has been distinctive about this tournament? Is it still as distinctive as it used to be?

3. What are the problems raised by the tournament scheduling "double-up" with Indianapolis?

4. What are the advantages and disadvantages of having a major sports management firm be the source of a tournament title sponsor?

CASE 6.3 VISA OLYMPIC SPONSORSHIP MARKETING[24]

Visa was the world's leading payment brand and its vision was to be "The World's Best Way to Pay." In 2003, Visa-branded cards[25] had sales volume exceeding $2.7 trillion in annual volume; totaled more than 1.2 billion cards worldwide, and were accepted in over 150 countries. Visa was among the most globally recognized brands. Its advertising tagline, "It's everywhere you want to be," had become part of the lexicon in many countries. Visa attributed an important part of its success to high profile sponsorships such as its Olympic Games sponsorship which began in 1986—see Exhibit 1. In the fall of 2002, Visa announced its decision to extend its Olympic Games sponsorship through 2012.

Visa International was comprised of six regional operating organizations: Asia-Pacific; Canada; Central & Eastern Europe, Middle East & Africa (CEMEA); European Union; Latin America & Caribbean; the United States. Despite its global reach, Visa remained very much a local organization. Its regional offices had a high degree of operating and marketing autonomy. Thomas Shepard, Visa's executive vice president of international marketing, partnerships, and sponsorship, played a key role in convincing Visa's six regional boards and its international board to allow Visa to extend its Olympics and Paralympic sponsorship. The sponsorship gave and would continue to give Visa and its member financial institutions (i.e., banks and credit unions) exclusive marketing rights, including advertising and promotional use of the Olympic rings and other graphics. Visa also would be entitled to exclusivity with transactions under Olympic control, including online transactions, ticket sales, and Olympic-themed events.

VISA SPONSORSHIP MARKETING STRATEGY AND PROCESS

Visa sponsored events such as the Olympic games, the Paralympics, the Best of Broadway, NASCAR, NFL, the Visa Triple Crown, and the Walt Disney Company. Shepard discussed

EXHIBIT 1   WORLDWIDE OLYMPIC (TOP) 2004 SPONSORS

Company/Brand	Category	First Olympic Association
Kodak	Film/photography & imaging	1896
Coca-Cola	Nonalcoholic beverages	1928
Swatch	Timing, Scoring Systems	1932
Xerox	Document publishing & supplies	1964
Sports Illustrated—Time	Periodicals/newspapers/magazines	1980
Panasonic	Audio/TV/video equipment	1984
Visa	Consumer payment systems	1986
John Hancock	Life insurance/annuities	1994
McDonald's	Retail food service	1996
Samsung	Wireless communications equipment	1997
Altos Origin	Information technology	2001

Source: http://www.athens2004.com/en/OlympicPartners

how sponsorship could help Visa improve upon and alter its brand image:

> *Within the payment service industry, we're doing research that shows how consumers view the brand. We've learned that we are very relevant in the minds of consumers and have a significant impact on consumer lifestyle. Visa gives people piece of mind and people use their cards everyday. They believe we're a quality organization, but we're not perceived as unique. That's what we have worked on and that's what sponsorship can help us achieve. Visa's sponsorship portfolio was also skewed [toward] male and low-end [markets] in some cases and we are balancing our portfolio as a result of this research.*

Periodically, Visa embarked on a "sponsorship refresh" where the sponsorship team made sure that its objectives paralleled Visa's corporate objectives. "Our sponsorship marketing objectives are grounded in corporate objectives and executed through the brand value proposition," explained Shepard. In the Spring of 2004, Shepard and his team assembled to work on the next "sponsorship refresh." They planned to discuss the current corporate strategy and through this process refine the existing Olympic sponsorship strategy. The current corporate strategy emphasized greater involvement in the field of entertainment. An outgrowth was selecting and working with new partners such as The Walt Disney Company.

Sponsorship Development Cycle and Selection Criteria

Visa divided its sponsorship opportunities into three development cycles: 1) emerging markets (name recognition, branding, and product sampling), 2) maturing markets (name building, signage, advertising, public relations, and promotions), and 3) mature markets (presence, products, partnerships, and alternative media). In this final mature market category, Visa sought to differentiate its product from competitors.

Visa's sponsorship selection criteria included the following: 1) brand fit, 2) usage stimulation on behalf of Visa's members, 3) event history/credibility, 4) broad reach, 5) governing body control, 6) advocacy creation, 7) low risk, 8) event's marketing plan, 9) ease of implementation, and 10) strong member interest. Shepard commented on the challenges of evaluating long-term sponsorship opportunities: "There are a lot of new payment schemes out there in the payments industry and looking out into the future to try to figure out what the landscape is going to look like is probably the hardest part of evaluating any sponsorship opportunity."

Sponsorship Marketing Platforms and Marketing Mix

Shepard used the "virtuous cycle" shown in Exhibit 2 to illustrate Visa's sponsorship marketing platforms and marketing mix:

> *The property Visa is associated with is all about creating platforms. From an advertising platform standpoint, we seek to build awareness and imagery and support member acquisition/usage. From a promotional*

EXHIBIT 2   VISA SPONSORSHIP MARKETING PLATFORMS AND MARKETING MIX

Advertising
Build Awareness and Imagery
Support Member Acquisition/ Usage

Promotions
Increase Usage
Partner with Strong Brands

Corporate Relations
Enhance Impact/Reach of Other Marketing Efforts
Strengthen Corporate Reputation/Image
Employee Programs

Product Platform
Showcase New Technologies
Launch New Products
Infrastructure

Source: Visa.

> *platform standpoint, we seek to increase usage and partner with strong brands. From a corporate relations platform, we seek to enhance impact/reach of other marketing efforts, strengthen our corporate reputation and image, and improve employee relations through employee programs (e.g. an event with Disney, Visa's sponsor, to show employees why Visa decided to partner with Disney). From a product platform standpoint, we seek to showcase new technologies; launch new products; and develop infrastructure on site.*

To implement sponsorship marketing platforms, Visa first conducted core/primary consumer research and then held an initial task force meeting and promotional briefing. It believed in developing a multi-agency "promotional platform" where various advertising agencies and internal constituents developed and tested the marketing and promotional concepts as a team.

THE OLYMPIC GAMES

Overview

The Olympic Games transcended political and geographical boundaries to deliver international exposure, broad-based audience appeal, and a wide range of cultural and sporting events appealing to virtually every demographic group. During the 2002 Winter Olympics in Salt Lake City, 2.1 billion global viewers in 160 countries amassed 13.1 billion viewer hours. (Exhibit 3 shows U.S. television coverage and ratings for each Games since 1984.) Despite recent Olympic scandals, many corporations still continued to sponsor the event. Indeed, many of the current worldwide sponsors had very long associations with the International Olympic Committee.

Although exact sponsorship figures were not disclosed, in 2002, TOP (The Olympic Partners) sponsors paid the IOC over $50 million for a four-year sponsorship cycle. In

EXHIBIT 3   OLYMPIC GAMES SINCE 1984 AND U.S. TELEVISION COVERAGE

Year	Games	Location	USA Television Network	Average Prime Time Rating	Total Network Hours	Number of Nations Competing	Number of Olympic Events
1984	Winter	Sarajevo, Yugoslavia	ABC	18.4	41.5	49	40
1984	Summer	Los Angeles, USA	ABC	23.2	180	140	221
1988	Winter	Calgary, Canada	ABC	19.3	95	57	46
1988	Summer	Seoul, South Korea	NBC	17.9	176	160	237
1992	Winter	Albertville, France	CBS	18.7	107	64	57
1992	Summer	Barcelona, Spain	NBC	17.5	148	171	257
1994	Winter	Lillehammer, Norway	CBS	27.8	110	67	61
1996	Summer	Atlanta, USA	NBC	21.6	164	196	271
1998	Winter	Nagano, Japan	CBS	16.3	124	80	68
2000	Summer	Sydney, Australia	NBC	13.8	162.5	199	300
2002	Winter	Salt Lake City, USA	NBC	16.9	168.5	80	78

Source: Street and Smith's *Sports Business Journal, By the Numbers 2003* (December 30, 2002).

addition, Visa incurred additional costs to "activate" its sponsorship, e.g., advertising costs and other marketing program costs. Visa's members received hospitality benefits due to Visa's sponsor status, as well as a guaranteed number of rooms and tickets for member and client entertainment (e.g., Visa had invited approximately 800 guests to Salt Lake City). Visa's members could also sponsor an individual athlete or team, use the Olympic theme in marketing promotions (from TV advertising to product literature), or issue Olympic cards with the Olympic rings or a picture of the specific athlete or team they were sponsoring without paying extra fees. Since Visa began its Olympic sponsorship, its members had issued more than 21 million Visa cards bearing the exclusive Olympic rings.

Shepard explained Visa's rationale for sponsoring the Olympics:

> We look at the equities that a property brings to us to develop our business. We seek out sponsorships that generate advocacy at the highest end of the consumer spending pyramid. If you look at the Olympics, it's a perfect fit for us. Olympic brand equities include being at the pinnacle of its category; having universal appeal; standing for excellence; having broad-based consumer awareness and acceptance; having global reach with local impact and participation; and standing for leadership. Visa's brand equities of industry leadership; global yet local; accepted everywhere; innovative and modern; and service excellence parallel Olympic brand equities. Visa probably could work on innovativeness, though, because we're not known as the most innovative brand.

In November 2002, Visa announced that it would be renewing its Olympic sponsorship through 2012. As a result of the renewed agreement, Visa would be the exclusive payment card and official payment service for the four Olympic Games following the 2004 Summer Olympics in Athens. This included the Winter Games in Torino, Italy in 2006, the Summer Games in Beijing, China in 2008, the Winter Games in Vancouver, Canada in 2010, and the

2012 Games (locations yet to be determined). Shepard discussed Visa's continuation of its Olympic sponsorship through 2012:

> *I presented to Visa's six regional boards to get the international board to allow us to sponsor the Olympics through 2012. They asked us, "Aren't you subject to exorbitant fees to make sure that Visa owns the category in TV in the U.S.?" and that's something that we and other sponsors must evaluate. It is a costly opportunity. We cannot just look at the cost of the property. We have to look at the cost of the property plus the television rights that we have to acquire, the manufacturing of all the commercials that we have to do, etc. Millions of dollars were rolled up into this decision. The question is, how can we best leverage the property and how can we make a business case for sponsoring the property?*

Evolution of Olympic Sponsorship

Shepard discussed the progression of Visa's involvement with the Olympics: "We've raised the bar with the Olympics. When we first started with the Olympics, we were just trying to get our name out and use it as an advertising platform. Our sponsorship strategy has evolved to one with a global platform with local relevance; an integrated marketing approach; and an expanded window of opportunity beyond just the Olympic Games." Shepard continued:

> *In [the 1992 Winter Games in] Albertville, we started to engage and build marketing programs for all of our member financial institutions. We expanded member and merchant participation globally. In [the 1992 Summer Games in] Barcelona, we expanded Visa's presence in the host city for the first time by engaging the merchant community and having onsite visibility with our own service centers. In [the 1994 Winter Games in] Lillehammer, it was the first time we rolled out a global corporate relations platform and really started to get visibility throughout the city and we began sponsoring teams. In [the 1996 Summer Games in] Atlanta, it was the first time we did anything comprehensive on site with our products. We issued a stored value product [pre-paid cards] that was marginally successful. Our hospitality program, ATM infrastructure, and Customer Service Center hosting were all significantly larger than those at previous games. In [the 1998 Winter Games in] Nagano, we had overkill in terms of our visibility and we learned that we needed to have a comprehensive effort because at Nagano we had five different Visa logos.*

OLYMPICS INTEGRATED MARKETING PROGRAM

For the Olympic Games, Visa focused on creating an integrated marketing program which included creating a central marketing theme, a look of the Games, member and merchant programs, advertising, promotions, public relations, athlete relationships, host city partner/presence programs, onsite activation capabilities, and hospitality.

Central Marketing Theme and Look of the Games

For the 2002 Olympic Winter Games in Salt Lake City, Visa created an integrated marketing platform centered on a marketing theme, "You've got what it takes." Shepard said this central marketing theme "spoke to the core brand position of superior acceptance, to the athletes who were the core of the Olympics, to Visa cardholders, and to Visa employees. Visa's look also complemented the Salt Lake Olympic Committee's look and feel."

Member and Merchant Programs and Promotions

For the 2002 Salt Lake City Games, Visa created member and merchant programs in which 500 members around the world utilized Visa's rights in the form of statement inserts, templates, and other promotional campaigns. Members were its banks, credit unions, and other financial institutions issuing Visa products. More than 50 million statement inserts highlighting Visa's Olympic marketing programs were distributed to consumers. Visa received an unprecedented 100 percent participation in its member programs from its top 12 U.S. members during the Salt Lake City Games. Of the top members, 75 percent conducted multiple programs that covered multiple lines of business (credit, debit, commercial, employee incentives, etc.).

Merchants received indirect association with the Olympics through Visa. For the Salt Lake Games, statement inserts included offers such as Olympics-related sweepstakes. Fifty-four member sweepstakes programs were also developed during the Salt Lake City Games. For example, each time cardholders used their Visa cards, they were automatically entered to win a trip to the Olympics. Linda Cullinan, a vice president of Intrust Bank of Wichita, Kansas, said it had chosen to ally with Visa over MasterCard in part because of the prestige associated with the Olympic Games. Intrust used some of the Visa Olympic promotional inserts in statements sent to its 100,000 card account holders. Though Visa offered Intrust a better deal financially, "Visa's standing in the market was the single most important factor in the branding decision, "followed by the promotions they run and the acceptability of those promotions," she said.[26]

In 1994 Visa also launched another worldwide public relations program effort—a children's art contest called the "Visa Olympics of the Imagination." Children ages 9 to 13 from various countries were invited to submit art around a designated theme. For the Atlanta Summer games, Visa asked children to invent and then illustrate an Olympic sport of the future, and write about how that sport would promote global peace and unity. For the contest in Nagano, children were asked to create artwork featuring a person they admired, engaged in a Winter Olympic sport. Winners received free trips to the Olympic Games. For the Atlanta Games, the contest garnered positive coverage in more than 1,000 newspapers, print, TV, and radio outlets in more than 50 countries and Visa received approximately 600 million media impressions. Mike Sherman, vice president of corporate relations at Visa in San Francisco said: "That's like getting a story in *The Wall Street Journal* every day for a year."[27]

Merchant programs included online and offline efforts. During the Salt Lake City Games, merchants such as Federated, Nordstrom, CompUSA, and Gap.com participated in merchant programs by promoting trips to the Olympics if consumers used their Visa cards. Prior to Salt Lake, merchants ordered over 1 million point-of-sale signs and over 15,000 merchants participated in merchant programs.

Advertising

Advertising was a significant part of Visa's integrated marketing program. During the Sydney Games, Visa launched two television spots highlighting its Olympic ties during the Super Bowl (nine months early). Visa typically tailored its advertising to reflect the unique aspects of each Olympic setting. "As you go from Olympics to Olympics, each one has a different feel and tone. We try to develop a concept that suits each one," said Matt Beispiel, former Vice-President of Visa. "What we wanted to exploit this year [Sydney 2000] are the unique aspects of the Australia Olympics. The 'dream with no boundaries' theme is a way to capitalize on the magnitude and boundless nature of that continent."[28]

Television dominated the advertising mix for the Sydney campaign. Visa purchased exclusive rights on the NBC Olympic broadcast and was the only advertiser in its category during the Games coverage on that network as well as MSNBC and CNBC. Visa also bought exclusive rights on the local NBC stations in the top dozen markets. Other advertising included radio, print, and online advertising. Early Visa television advertisements highlighted places that accepted Visa but not American Express. This campaign was developed in 1985 by BBDO. "It was intended to separate the Visa brand from MasterCard," said Beispiel. "We have both brands that functionally do the same thing and we needed to somehow separate the brands in the mind of the consumers to move our business ahead."[29]

Athlete Relationships

Visa developed relationships with athletes around the world. In the U.S., Visa had sponsored the ski team since 1986 and for Salt Lake, extended its athlete sponsorship into other sports such as snowboarding, bobsledding (e.g., Jean Racine and Jen Davidson), freestyle, figure skating (e.g., Sasha Cohen) and other athletes in the Paralympics. Visa also sponsored the Canadian bobsleigh team, the Russian hockey team, and the Japanese ski jumping team.

Destination Marketing—Host City Partner/Presence Programs

Visa was the first worldwide Olympic partner to launch "destination marketing" programs linked to the Olympic Games' host cities. Visa's strategy was to extend the benefit of its Olympics sponsorship beyond the actual Olympic Games: "We have been able to stretch the marketing window from the duration of the Olympics to a four to five year period," said Shepard. "We have a worldwide sponsorship of tourism, merchants, and advertising, which never stops." Visa assisted its partners and members in creating local and regional incremental value and benefits around the Olympic Games. Sydney proved to be the "gold standard" of Visa's destination marketing efforts, according to Shepard. In Sydney, Visa generated more than $40 million in marketing value for Australia for the Sydney Olympic Games over the four-year period leading up to the Olympic Games in 2000.[30] Shepard stated:

> Sydney was our most robust case of generating volume for our Visa
> network of members. We still have partnerships from that time period that
> are around today such as the Australian Tourism Commission, the Sydney
> Convention and Visitors Bureau, etc. We've really penetrated the merchant
> community in Sydney. Sydney became our gold standard. And we
> continued this effort in Salt Lake City. In [the 2004 Summer Games in]

*Athens, we're looking to use Athens as a pan-European footprint,
extending our reach beyond Greece.*

In the Salt Lake Games, Visa created national television commercials that highlighted Olympic athletes and Utah as a destination during the Games. One spot titled "Surfing," featured the Wasatch Powderbird Guides, a Utah-based helicopter ski and snowboard company. "We have changed our methodology in the 16 years since we first started sponsoring the Olympic games," said Sherman.

> *Our campaign for the 1988 Calgary Olympics was all about branding
> and we focused on the 17 days surrounding the games. Then in 1994, we
> saw that Visa was going to have to adapt its marketing to make it closer to
> tourism and spread its efforts over a much longer period. We realized that
> we had to work with the Olympic city before, during, and after the Games
> in order to derive the best benefits for our members. We asked ourselves why
> host cities bid for the games and we realized the answer came down to
> showcasing the city to the world. Not only do the games bring tourists to
> the Olympic city, but also they create a large halo effect that lasts beyond
> the games. Prior to the 1992 Olympics, Barcelona was the 16th most
> popular tourist destination in Europe. In 1993, it was the third. There
> was a similar kind of lift in Australia after the 2000 games.*[31]

During the Salt Lake Games, surrounding areas saw sales on Visa payment cards increase 30 percent over the same period in 2001, and 23 percent over the prior month. The Salt Lake Convention and Visitor's Bureau reported that overall, 55 percent of reservations were made on Visa cards, up from 46 percent in 2001 and 41 percent in 2000.[32]

Onsite Activation and Marketing

Onsite marketing activities were also an important component of Visa's integrated marketing program. At Salt Lake City, Visa had its ATM networks at or near all competition and non-competition venues, including two mobile ATMs, 650 new point-of-sale acceptance terminals at Olympic venues, and a customer information center to help visitors with lost or stolen cards and Games-related questions. Visa believed these efforts helped build consumers' awareness and reinforced Visa as the payment brand of choice. Visa pointed to its improvements by showing that Visa's volume throughout the Olympic venues at Salt Lake City exceeded the 2000 Sydney Games by more than $2 million, even though the Sydney Games were four times larger.[33]

ATHENS SUMMER GAMES 2004

For the Athens Olympics, there would be 11 worldwide or TOP sponsors, each in a different product category. As one of the worldwide sponsors, Visa was the exclusive payment card and official payment service of the Athens Games and would be the only card accepted at all Olympic Games venues for all official Olympic-related transactions. Visa planned to install a special Olympic ATM network and hundreds of point-of-sale acceptance devices at the International Press Centre, the International Broadcast Centre, and the Olympic Athletes

Village. The Visa Service Centre (VSC) would provide multilingual emergency services and general assistance to cardholders. Visa also sponsored the Visa Olympians Reunion Center where Olympians could congregate and relax. It had also planned to support teams such as the U.S. gymnastics, track and field, ski and snowboard, hockey, and figure skating teams.

For its members, Visa planned to utilize the Games as a sponsorship platform by offering marketing tie-ins and opportunities for international exposure and image enhancement. Similar to Sydney and Salt Lake City, Visa planned to conduct destination marketing campaigns with the host city during future Games. In November 2002, Visa and the Greek National Tourism Organization (GNTO) formed a global alliance to promote Greece worldwide as a key travel destination and showcase Visa's sponsorship of the Athens Games. Visa planned to use advertising, direct mail, cardholder communications, and Olympic promotions in more than 50 countries to promote Greece as a travel destination. One program would feature the joint development and creation of an information booth to service visitors, providing information concerning tourist issues. Visa also planned to feature Greece on its "Visa Destinations" online travel site and planned to promote Greece with its hotel and airline travel partners. "We are packaging trips to Greece and to the Greek islands which can be offered as prizes to Visa card users," said Shepard.

As an extension of its Olympic sponsorship, Visa was sponsoring the Paralympic Games in Athens in 2004 for the first time (Visa had supported the Paralympic Games in other ways at various other Olympics). Visa's sponsorship resulted in the first Visa Paralympic Website, accessible to people with vision, hearing, and mobility challenges. Visa's members would help deliver the messages of the Paralympic Games (Pursuit, Strength, Inspiration, and Celebration). Visa hoped that its sponsorship of the Paralympic Games would create an affinity between its brand and the disabled community and their families worldwide. Shepard noted: "There are 750 million people worldwide with disabilities. If we can create something relevant for them and their families, we will be creating a partnership with them for mutual benefit."

SPONSORSHIP PERFORMANCE MEASUREMENT

As sponsorships grew in popularity and became more expensive, sponsors began looking for ways to quantify event marketing value. One of the first techniques used was tracking televised logo time, i.e., the amount of time a sponsor's logo is visible to a television viewer. However, over time, marketing professionals began to question the value of this analysis, as flashing a company's logo during an event may have been cheaper than running advertising during the event, but the two may not have been interchangeable in terms of effectiveness. Companies began to use a variety of research techniques to measure pre- and post-event results ranging from focus groups to onsite surveys.

Visa often used external consultants to quantify the value generated by the Olympic sponsorship to "persuade us first as a management team and the board second" that there was a business case for a sponsorship. The results showed that a sponsorship translated directly into tangible benefits such as brand recognition and market share and "has a significant value."[34] Since 1986, the number of Visa cards in issue grew from 137 million to just over one billion, while global volume grew from $111 billion to $2.3 trillion. Since it started sponsoring the

Olympics in 1986, Visa's market share had risen by 33 percent, to 53 percent, the company said. "And when you gain the leverage from the member banks," said Malcolm Williamson, CEO and President of Visa International, "[the Olympics is] an amazing property."[35] Moreover, during the span of Visa's Olympic involvement, it had seen brand preference in the U.S. go up—with its rating as "best overall card" rising to 50 percent.[36] Visa cited research showing that more than 66 percent of Americans thought Olympics sponsors deserved their business. "Obviously, not all of that is from the Olympics," said Michael Lynch, senior vice president of event and sponsorship marketing. "But we're finding that those who are aware of our Olympic sponsorship are more likely to use the Visa card than those who are unaware."[37]

According to Becky Saeger, executive vice president of brand marketing:

> At Visa, we frequently review our efforts to ensure a return on investment for our members. Since 1986, no single property has allowed us to build our brand and drive use better than the Olympic Games. . . . Since 1986, Visa volume has grown at a compounded annual rate of 16 percent. Unaided consumer awareness of Visa's sponsorship after Sydney was an unprecedented 72 percent, and research shows sponsorship awareness drives Visa brand preference. Finally, the 2002 Games scored record ratings on NBC, enabling Visa to reach a larger, more diverse audience than ever before.[38]

Visa measured specific campaigns as well. For example, in 1992, it advertised that it would donate a percentage of each card transaction to the U.S. Olympic team. Transactions increased by 17 percent. Up until that point, Visa had never received more than a 3 percent increase from any advertising or promotional campaign that it had run.[39]

THE FUTURE

Visa had "raised the bar" during each of the Olympics it had sponsored since 1986. It had created an integrated marketing program that ranged from advertising to host city partner/presence programs. In the spring of 2004, Shepard and his team gathered at Visa's international headquarters located in Foster City, California. The plans for the 2004 Olympics were in place. Shepard and her team wanted to continue the "sponsorship refresh" of its Olympic and Paralympic activities. With rights to the 2006, 2008, 2010, and 2012 Olympics now in place, there was much to gain from continuing to innovate and seek new ways to extract maximum value from its association with the Olympic five rings.

APPENDIX A
Overview of Visa

Visa was jointly owned by 21,000 financial institutions (members) such as banks and credit unions worldwide. It was a private, for-profit association whose members offered credit cards and other payment solutions for both consumers and businesses. Cards were issued by Visa's member financial institutions, not by the Visa association. Its members also signed up (acquired) retailers, recruited cardholders, set fees and determined spending limits and interest rates on outstanding balances.

Visa products and services were offered directly by members to their customers. Visa did not issue cards, set annual fees on cards, determine annual percentage rates (APRs)[40], solicit merchants to accept cards, or set discount rates.[41] Members managed the relationships with consumers and merchants. Visa's goal had been to create a brand that was a trusted seal of approval so that members could use Visa as a platform to meet their objectives. Shepard elaborated on Visa's relationship with its members:

> Our 21,000 member financial institutions own us. Visa's international role is to coordinate the six regions and try to provide innovative solutions for the properties that we have. Our primary job is to help members grow their business by offering them payment solutions; new payment technologies; dynamic, efficient, and secure processing services; and the global Visa brand.

Revenue Model

Visa's revenue model included a series of fees from merchants who accepted Visa cards. Typical fees included 1) discount rate (a percentage of sales which could range from 1.99 to 2.54 percent on Internet accounts and 1.35 to 1.79 percent on retail accounts),[42] 2) per item fee or transaction fee (this fee occurred whenever merchants processed and charged a customer's credit card, usually between 20 to 50 cents per transaction), 3) monthly minimums (fee imposed if merchants' credit card charges did not add up to a monthly minimum—usually $25 or $50), 4) statement fees (merchants received a monthly statement detailing all transactions and deposits—usually approximately $15 per month for this service), 5) chargeback processing fees (a chargeback occurred when a customer refused to pay a charge that had been placed on their credit card statement—ranging from $5 to $25 per chargeback), and 6) terminal lease or rental fee (merchants needed to purchase or lease out a terminal machine in order to be able to process credit cards using a terminal—generally starting around $200 or $15 to $50 per month).

Visa operated on a break-even basis, collecting membership dues from its members based on their respective sizes. Credit card associations such as Visa did not generally earn profits. In instances where profits did occur, Visa reinvested these back into the association for development. To become a member of the Visa association, an institution needed to pay an initial service fee that depended on the type of membership applied for, the type of cards to be issued, and the number of accounts projected after three years.

Questions

1. Describe the Visa brand. What attributes make for it being either a good fit or bad fit for:

   a. Sponsorship?

   b. Sponsorship of sports?

   c. Sponsorship of Olympic sports?

2. The Olympics sponsorship is a central part of Visa's strategy. Outline and evaluate ways that Visa has leveraged being a Tier-One (TOP—The Olympic Partners) Olympic sponsor.

3. "Activating" a sporting sponsorship is a central issue to Visa. Assume that Visa "spent an additional two times that of the sponsorship fees . . . to maximize the value of the sponsorship." Evaluate the nature and rationale for these additional outlays.

4. What are the major challenges Visa faces in extracting maximum value from its sporting-related sponsorships? How is it addressing these challenges?

CASE 6.4 JOHN HANCOCK SPORTS SPONSORSHIP: 1993–2000 AND BEYOND[43]

By early 1998, after over a decade of Boston Marathon involvement, sports sponsorship had become a major part of John Hancock's marketing strategy. Under the leadership of David D'Alessandro, now president, the financial services company had continued its key sponsorship role with the Boston Marathon and the sport (also sponsoring the New York City Marathon). Also, with the Nagano, Japan Winter Olympic Games in February 1998, John Hancock was sponsoring its third, consecutive Olympiad. The company had already extended its substantial Olympics sponsorship, initiated in 1993, through the 2000 Summer Olympic Games in Sydney, Australia.

John Hancock was also deeply involved with the sport of gymnastics at various levels, including sponsorship of the popular "John Hancock Tour of World Gymnastics Champions," and a four-year sponsorship of the sport's governing body, U.S.A. Gymnastics. In searching for a winter Olympics property equivalent to the gymnastics tour, John Hancock had just reached agreement to sponsor the soon-to-be-renamed, "John Hancock Champions on Ice" Tour, the premier skating tour in the world.

After some dozen years of sponsorship experience, D'Alessandro thought that he had developed some principles regarding effective sports sponsorship. He and Tod Rosensweig, the company's general director of Olympic and event marketing, were planning to apply these principles in deciding what directions to take John Hancock's sports involvement in the new millennium. Should they continue Olympics sponsorship—for Salt Lake City in 2002 and Athens in 2004? Should they maintain the momentum of "Olympic umbrella" sponsorships, in particular, gymnastics and ice skating? How else could John Hancock broaden or deepen its sports sponsorship efforts, within and/or outside the Olympics? And, of course, there was the Boston Marathon: should John Hancock extend its primary sponsorship until 2008?

Marathon Sponsorships

John Hancock was generally credited as having been responsible for elevating the Boston Marathon to its current status as the best in the world. After losing ground during the prior decade to other marathons in New York, Chicago, London, and Tokyo, in 1986, John Hancock, led by David D'Alessandro, began the successful rescue operation with sponsorship money and managerial skills. As Will McDonough, sports columnist of *The Boston Globe*, wrote after the running of the race in 1993, "There is no greater success story in Boston sports than that of the Boston Marathon's revival at the hands of John Hancock Financial Services and senior vice president David D'Alessandro over the last 10 years."

The Boston Marathon sponsorship accounted for a large share of Hancock's total sports marketing budget—it was second only to Olympics sponsorship. Yet, Hancock executives considered it a "subtle sponsorship," an event that belonged to the people of Boston, and with no Hancock title sponsorship to the race. John Hancock's contract with the Boston Athletic Association extended through the 2003 Marathon, with an option of extending the agreement for five more years.

Harvard Business School Case No 9-599-027. Copyright 1998 President and Fellows of Harvard College. All rights reserved. For information: permission@hbsp.harvard.edu. This case was prepared by John Teopaco and Stephen A. Greyser. HBS cases are developed solely for class discussion and do not necessarily illustrate effective or ineffective management.

With its Boston Marathon success, Hancock expanded its involvement in running with the sponsorship of the New York City Marathon beginning in the late 1980s. Hancock wanted a greater presence in an important geographic market for the company. The race itself had three to four times the number of runners than did Boston, and it was also a bigger street event. The sponsorship provided Hancock with a first-class hospitality opportunity, for at least 700 guests, with the booking of the Tavern on the Green restaurant near the finish line in Central Park.

Whereas the 10-year Boston Marathon contract called for more than $1 million a year, the New York Marathon sponsorship started at $800,000. As with its hometown race, Hancock refrained from demanding title sponsorship to the New York City race. Recently, Hancock's involvement had dropped considerably, and the company was now just a second-tier sponsor. Hancock's 1997 agreement with the New York Road Runners' Club was a one-year deal, viewed as a stop-gap measure between the previous three-year deal and any future contracts.

The John Hancock Bowl

Separate from its Boston Marathon sponsorship, in 1986, John Hancock sponsored and placed its name on the John Hancock Sun Bowl, a college football bowl game held in El Paso, Texas. Although not one of the major bowls in terms of visibility or television viewership, the Sun Bowl was the first bowl to provide a title "naming" opportunity. However, the media continued to refer to it as the Sun Bowl, so D'Alessandro paid the organizers $150,000, or as he put it, "$50,000 a letter"—to remove Sun from the name a few years later.

The main appeal of the Sun Bowl sponsorship was the immense visibility that it offered at very low cost, initially $500,000 per year for three years. Over the years, however, several factors contributed to Hancock's decision to terminate sponsorship after the 1993 game. The media buy became inefficient—between 1989 and 1993, TV ratings dropped 14% while cost per thousand viewers increased 62%. Too many shifting sponsorships in other bowls were confusing football fans, diminishing the value of Hancock's title sponsorship—once unique in college football. Finally, the agreements of the NCAA Bowl Alliance determined that the John Hancock Bowl would never become a championship game, relegating it to third-class status. D'Alessandro put it in perspective: "Continuity can be important in a sponsorship because it can take time to figure out how to make the most of your investment; but there is also the possibility of diminishing returns."

A major business reason for entering the 10-year deal with the Boston Marathon had been to reshape John Hancock's image from an old-fashioned, conservative insurance company to an innovative financial services supplier. The company worked to reposition the brand from an insurance provider, to that of a provider of insurance and investments. In the 1990s, the brand image challenge became more focused—to gain credibility as an investment provider and to break through the competitive clutter. To D'Alessandro, the Olympic Games presented just such a vehicle for image-building.

Olympics Sponsorship

In 1993, John Hancock became a sponsor of the U.S. Olympic Committee. The following year, the company expanded its relationship with the Olympics by becoming a "Top

Sponsor," joining an elite group of only ten companies in the world. (By 1998, the number had increased to eleven. The other 10 were Panasonic, Kodak, Xerox, Sports Illustrated, Visa, UPS, Motorola, McDonald's, IBM, and Coca-Cola.)

Hancock maintained a strong advertising and hospitality presence at the Lillehammer Winter Games of 1994 and the Atlanta Summer Games of 1996. Subsequently, the sponsorship was extended for another Olympic quadrennium, encompassing the Nagano Winter Games of 1998 and the Sydney Summer Games of 2000.

Tod Rosensweig had joined John Hancock in 1995 to help direct its Olympic marketing efforts. Prior to that, he had spent 21 years in marketing for the Boston Celtics (professional basketball team), of which he headed the team's marketing activities for the last fifteen years. Referring to the benefits of being an Olympic Top Sponsor, Rosensweig explained: "Those companies have exclusive rights in their specific categories to associate themselves internationally with the Olympics and the Olympic rings—the most recognized logo and most marketable sports property in the world. The rings are more familiar than the next most recognizable logo, McDonald's arches, or the third and fourth finishers—the Shell Oil logo, and amazingly, the Christian cross."

Why the Olympics?

A four-year sponsorship of the Olympics cost John Hancock $30 million, and with advertising media cost added in, the total was closer to $40 million. It clearly was a high-cost sponsorship, but was it also high-value? David D'Alessandro explained:

> *Success is not about having the marketing dollars to buy in. Instead, it's about being smart enough to make the investment pay off. And, when you're considering an Olympic sponsorship, only one thing matters: Will it help or hurt your bottom line?*
>
> *At Hancock, we make a point of not being blinded by the glamour. There are six basic questions that we ask ourselves before we sign on to anything, and they're the same six questions whether the event in question is the Olympics or a marshmallow roast.*
>
> *First: Will it enhance our brand in ways that matter to consumers? At Hancock, we aggressively co-brand our name with the rings on letterhead, business cards, brochures, sales materials, and TV tag line.*
>
> *Second: Will this event generate leads and sales?*
>
> *Third: Will the sponsorship provide us with a unified, cost-effective marketing platform? Is it something we can use for many different kinds of promotions? It is impossible to justify the price tag of the Olympics if you don't use it to create a unified and co-branded marketing platform that covers everything from high-end advertising to grass roots promotions around the globe.*
>
> *Fourth: Can we use it at home? In other words, to motivate our sales people and employees? John Hancock uses trips to the Games as a sales*

> *incentive, as a reward for key employees, and as an opportunity to entertain major clients.*

> Fifth: *Can we sustain the association long enough to get the most out of it and benefit from economies of scale?*

> And sixth: *Can we quantify the results? Because if you can't prove that it's working for you in concrete and measurable ways, you probably shouldn't be investing in it in the first place.*

For Hancock, the Olympics just happen to be a ringing "yes" on all counts.

Hancock's president continued to elaborate on specific benefits that the Olympic sponsorship provided John Hancock:

> *The Games allow us to reach a public that is no longer easily persuaded by traditional advertising. Let's face it, consumers are getting too sophisticated for jingles and self-serving pitches. Try to show people a commercial, and they're off the couch and on their way to the refrigerator. However, allow them to rub elbows with an Olympic athlete—or invite them to bring their kids to a clinic run by gymnastics legend Bela Karolyi—and you have their rapt attention. You might even have their loyalty for life.*

> *This is the essence of event marketing, if you do it right—winning the goodwill and consideration of consumers by bringing them something of value.*

In 1996, when Hancock decided to extend its Olympic sponsorship for another quadrennium, they continued to hold to the same objectives which had served as the foundation of the company's association with the Olympics since 1993. These were to:

- Enhance the image of the John Hancock brand by co-branding with the Olympics both nationally and locally
- Assist the field force in growing sales through Olympic-sponsored events that enhance relationship marketing efforts
- Generate new college recruits into the agency system with Olympic-sponsored college events
- Build incentive programs for agents and home office associates that leverage the sponsorship
- Boost employee morale by being part of something special

Olympic Sponsorship Results

Hancock surveyed 5,000 consumers before and after the 1994 Winter Games about their willingness to buy Hancock products. After the Games, positive response went up from 58% to 70%. After the Atlanta Games of 1996, the percentage of consumers who thought of Hancock as a large investment company, and as a leader in the investment industry, increased by 40% and 42%, respectively.

The Olympics provided Hancock with free publicity estimated to be worth $7 million, and they generated thousands of business leads.

By using trips to Lillehammer and Atlanta as incentives for field sales representatives, Hancock generated over $50 million in new sales.

Most importantly, according to Hancock executives, the Olympics strengthened the Hancock brand for the long-term, and cemented the loyalty of many of their biggest and most profitable clients.

The Olympics apparently also boosted employee morale. Some 95% of Hancock's employees attended some Olympic-connected event. In a survey, 85% said they were proud of Hancock's Olympic sponsorship. Sales to employees of such Hancock merchandise as jackets and gym bags jumped almost five-fold when the five-ring Olympic logo was added.

"When you add in the excitement of our agents and employees and being seen as a good corporate citizen, we're getting an awful lot for our dollars," Stephen Brown, Hancock's chairman, said.

One of John Hancock's tenets regarding effective Olympic sponsorship was leveraging and amortizing the Olympic investment, particularly over the off-years. According to D'Alessandro, "the key to a successful Olympic sponsorship is not [just] making a big splash once, but instead, finding a direct and emotional way to bring the Olympics home to consumers year after year."

For instance, before the Lillehammer Winter Games of 1994, the company spent $300,000 and sponsored the John Hancock USA Hockey Tour, a 24-city, pre-Olympic series that included games between the U.S. Olympic hockey team and the Russian team. Team members conducted hockey clinics for young players in each city, which allowed local Hancock agents to meet the kids' parents.

Leveraging the Olympics: Gymnastics Sponsorship

A principal component of Hancock's Olympics association had been its gymnastics sponsorship—considered an effective way to help Hancock's field agents leverage the Olympic rings. Gymnastics was the most popular of the Summer Olympics Games, and it attracted an audience with an income and education profile that matched Hancock's target demographics.

Hancock created the first-ever sponsorship of the sport at the grass roots level (the clubs). It supported nine of the top gymnastics clubs in the U.S., including those owned and operated by all the top coaches—Bela Karolyi, Tim Daggett, Mary Lee Tracy, and Steve Nunno. The company also sponsored several college-level men's programs, and helped to save the UCLA's gymnastics program which produced 1984 Olympic Gold medalists Peter Vidmar, Tim Daggett and Mitch Gaylord. (The program would have been abandoned due to Title IX gender equity issues.)

In 1995, in coordination with U.S.A. Gymnastics (the sport's governing body), Hancock sponsored a 20-city Mall Tour. This gave Hancock the first opportunity to use the sport for grass roots marketing on a personal level, using the Olympics as a "hook." John Hancock agencies used the tour as an opportunity to provide consumers with information on the company's college funding product, "College Plus."

The John Hancock Tour of World Gymnastics Champions

Also in 1995, well before the U.S. women's gymnastics team surprised the world by winning its first gold medal ever in Atlanta, Rosensweig's Olympic and Event Marketing group bought the title sponsorship of a nationwide tour by the women's and men's teams. This gave birth to the "John Hancock Tour of World Gymnastics Champions." Compared to the Mall Tour, the Champions Tour was more highly-produced and theatrical.

After the Atlanta Games, the Tour covered 34 cities in the fall of 1996. In early 1997, the second phase of the Tour came to 23 "secondary" markets, while the third phase (late 1997) visited another 31 primary markets. Hancock also elected to buy the title sponsorship of NBC's telecast of the 1997 Tour.

At the local level, the Olympic and Event Marketing group contacted agency management, arranged the tickets, hospitality and marketing booth opportunities, and worked to help the Hancock agencies develop relationships with their local gymnastics clubs. The thousands of gymnastics club owners across the U.S. were themselves small-business owners to whom Hancock wanted to market. The Tour offered the agencies a major opportunity to build relationships, recruit, host clients, and gain recognition in their communities.

Prior to each show, a selected agent addressed the crowd and welcomed them on behalf of John Hancock. During the show, Hancock gained good exposure with well-lit signs on the floor, and the company name on the arena marquee, promotional materials, event program, and all merchandise. Hancock hosted post-event hospitality attended by all of the performing gymnasts.

The Fall 1996 Tour saw arenas filled to 90% of capacity. Half a million people attended in the 34 cities. It generated 460 news articles and $2.9 million in P.R.-advertising equivalency, and 10,000 sales leads. However, attendance began to lag after the first phase (which was carried by its post-Atlanta flush of success), hovering at the 50%–60% capacity range for the latter two phases.

The Tour's three phases involved a total sponsorship cost of $1.5 million. The deal with the production company had ended, and Hancock was presented the opportunity to continue sponsorship through 2000.

U.S.A. Gymnastics (USAG) Sponsorship

Based on its experience with the Mall and Champions Tours, in 1997, John Hancock enhanced its sponsorship of the sport of gymnastics by entering into a four-year sponsorship of USAG, the national governing body. The agreement, costing the company $1 million annually, gave Hancock exclusivity in the entire financial services category (except credit cards) and title sponsorship of USAG's major championship, the John Hancock U.S. Gymnastics Championships. This event selected the national team which represented the U.S.A. at all world competitions. The championships were held in Denver in August 1997, and were to be held in Indianapolis in 1998, Sacramento in 1999, and St. Louis in 2000.

In other USAG promotional programs, Hancock gave $1,000 grants to each of eighty gymnastics clubs in the U.S., travel grants to send parents of gymnasts to the World

Championships, $1,000 to each of eight Regional Congresses for guest clinicians or other speakers, and developmental grants for promising gymnasts.

The title sponsorship of the national championships provided Hancock with advertising and other exposure via tickets, signage, and awards presentations; local agency marketing opportunities (marketing booth, tickets, hosting recruitment and/or financial seminar); tickets and hospitality; and public relations/media coverage. The sponsorship also provided Hancock access to USAG's extensive membership list for marketing purposes.

In 1996, John Hancock and the Massachusetts Sports Partnership (a private, not-for-profit corporation established to attract significant sporting events to the state) hosted the U.S. Gymnastics Trials, the event that determined who would represent the country at the Summer Games. By capitalizing on its USAG sponsorship, and by providing half of the site bid fee, in 1997 Hancock once again joined with the Partnership to bring the 2000 Trials to Boston.

The sponsorship provided Hancock with significant promotional opportunities. These included public relations—Hancock handled the media relations for the Trials; a photo and autograph session with team members; 1,000 complimentary tickets and the opportunity for agents and employees to purchase a similar amount (Hancock donated 1,000 tickets to the Boys & Girls Clubs of Boston); hospitality; advertising; and other corporate visibility—street banners, venue signage, athlete clothing; marketing booths; and award presentations.

"Living with Balance" Program

In looking for a way to leverage the USAG sponsorship, and to reach gymnastics families, John Hancock had begun to design a grass roots program that addressed life-issues facing young athletes. Called "Living with Balance," the program would deal with the issues facing gymnasts and their parents, such as nutrition, stress management, and social integration.

Hancock was planning to launch the program in mid-1998 with workshops across the country. Approximately twenty gymnastics clubs would be targeted, and they would be matched with an equal number of Hancock agencies. For the future, the goal would be to expand the gymnastics club/agency relationship into other markets each year. Hancock's commitment to "Living with Balance" would run concurrently with the USAG sponsorship—through 2000.

Hancock executives were confident that gymnastics was a meaningful and beneficial way to leverage the Olympic sponsorship. They recognized a need, however, to balance this effort with a similar one that leveraged the Winter Games, and with the same level of impact.

"John Hancock Champions on Ice" Tour

In search of a winter Olympic property to complement the gymnastics tour, Hancock found the "Champions on Ice" skating tour. This was the premier tour in the world, featuring every Olympic and World Champion still skating. Campbell's Soup had been sponsoring the tour since the mid-1980s, but they decided not to renew their sponsorship after the '98 tour. Hancock signed a four-year agreement—for $2 million annually—as the tour's title sponsor, extending through the 2002 Olympic Games in Salt Lake City.

Contractually, Hancock was guaranteed a minimum of 45 tour stops each year, with an average of 50. The tour would run April through July each year. As the title sponsor, Hancock would gain exposure in all promotional materials, tickets, merchandise, and event programs; two rink board signs at each performance; tickets; marketing booth; and right of first refusal on TV sponsorship.

The company was also entitled to hospitality opportunities and athlete appearances. Prior to each of four shows, the entire ensemble of athletes would make an appearance at Hancock's hospitality areas; prior to the remainder of the shows, two athletes would make an appearance.

Several advertising/promotional opportunities would also come with the sponsorship—an $80,000 media package for each tour stop; a full-page, four-color ad on the back of the show program; the Hancock logo projected on the ice; public address announcements promoting the title sponsorship and the marketing booth; and an on-ice presentation by a Hancock agent.

Beyond the Olympics: The Ryder Cup

The Olympics and Olympics-related events clearly were central components of Hancock's sports sponsorship program. The company was presented with the opportunity, however, to sponsor The Ryder Cup in 1999, the most prestigious golf event in the world.

The Cup was a competition held every two years between the best golfers of the U.S. and those of Europe. Players competed as a team, with no money and only international prestige at stake. The players were chosen based on their competitive performances prior to the Ryder Cup. Only the best players in the world competed.

The location alternated between the two continents. For the 1999 Ryder Cup, the competition was going to be held at The Country Club in Brookline (a community near Boston). The event was scheduled to be held over three days in September. There would be extensive television coverage on the NBC and USA networks.

The sponsorship fee for John Hancock would be $350,000 paid over three years. In the classic sense, The Ryder Cup was not a real sponsorship in that it provided no advertising or public relations benefits. It offered, instead, 150 complimentary tickets to each day of competition, and to each of three practice days. It also would give Hancock the opportunity to purchase a hospitality tent.

In planning for John Hancock's future sports marketing program, D'Alessandro and Rosensweig were faced with the immediate decision of whether to seize the opportunity to sponsor the prestigious Ryder Cup right in the company's hometown. Rosensweig's position was clear:

> *The Ryder Cup will be the biggest thing to hit Boston in years. The eyes of the nation will be on Boston during the competition.*
>
> *Many of our agents love golf. I contend that, to a lover of golf, the opportunity to go to the Ryder Cup is every bit as inviting an incentive as a trip to the Olympics. A week of golf and hospitality around this event would make the elements of a strong sales incentive program. For instance, we could have a golf celebrity not playing in the competition—like a Jack Nicklaus or Jay Sigel—host our guests on the course and in the tent.*

1998 and Beyond: Some Key Decisions

Aside from The Ryder Cup decision, D'Alessandro and Rosensweig were also facing decisions on the renewal of several of the existing sponsorships. (**Exhibit 1** lays out Hancock's committed and proposed sponsorship events through 2002.)

Hancock's Olympics contracts with the U.S. Olympic Committee, International Olympic Committee, and organizing committees of the Nagano and Sydney Games ran through the 2000 Summer Games. The two executives had to decide on whether to extend sponsorship through the Salt Lake City Winter Games of 2002 and the Athens Summer Games of 2004.

D'Alessandro and Rosensweig saw the Olympics as a strong brand-building association, and among all of Hancock's sponsorships, they believed the Olympics set the company apart from competitors. Rosensweig saw it this way: "When you have a great property with which to sell, gather all your resources to leverage it. Great opportunities require creative and immediate action." D'Alessandro summed up the situation: "In the end, the Olympic brand is absolutely unique. It remains consistently inspiring to consumers and to the sponsors themselves." The Olympics also provided the "umbrella" for two other major Hancock sponsorships—gymnastics and ice skating.

The U.S.A. Gymnastics sponsorship, and the "Living with Balance" program, were also going to end by 2000. The sponsorships provided Hancock with excellent grass roots marketing opportunities (at the field agency and club level). Did they meet the other Hancock sponsorship criteria?

The gymnastics Champions Tour sponsorship had ended in 1997. Should Hancock extend sponsorship for another three years? Could the interest and excitement surrounding the Atlanta Games performance be revived? Could attendance be boosted beyond the 60% capacity mark? What would be the impact of a non-renewal on Hancock's field agencies and their grass roots marketing programs?

And, in the marathon field, should Hancock consider itself a de facto, "perpetual" sponsor of the Boston Marathon? For a local event, the sponsorship did require a high level of financial commitment. Were business results commensurate with the investment? Did the Boston Marathon provide relationship-building opportunities for Hancock agents? D'Alessandro provided perspective on the subject: "We invest in the people of Boston because it's the right thing to do, and it's crucial to build a reservoir of goodwill in our hometown."

Hancock's other marathon sponsorship, in New York City, had decreased to almost one-fourth of its original level. Should Hancock accept the offer to continue sponsorship for another five years—through 2002? If so, at what level?

In reflecting on these options, D'Alessandro reminded himself and Rosensweig of some of the key sponsorship principles that he had learned over the past decade:

> *Success in event marketing doesn't really depend as much on flashing the cash as on knowing where to spend it. Spend on properties that are well-run, and that are run like businesses. Spend on events that you can own, manage and measure. Spend also on opportunities that enhance your brand, involve your customers, and extend your marketing reach.*

EXHIBIT 1 JOHN HANCOCK OLYMPIC AND EVENT MARKETING SCHEDULE OF EVENTS, 1998–2002

YEAR	JAN	FEB	MAR	APR	MAY	JUN	JUL	AUG	SEP	OCT	NOV	DEC
1998		Nagano Olympics Olympic Recruitment Events	Olympic Recruitment Events	Boston Marathon Living w/Balance				Gym Nationals	Elite Club Grants Gym Tour (proposed)	Gym Tour (proposed)	NYC Marathon (proposed) Gym Tour (proposed)	
1999				Boston Marathon Living w/Balance	Champions on Ice	Champions on Ice	Champions on Ice	Gym Nationals	Ryder Cup (proposed) Elite Club Grants		NYC Marathon (proposed)	
2000				Boston Marathon Living w/Balance Champions on Ice	Champions on Ice	Champions on Ice	Champions on Ice	Gym Nationals Gym Trials	Sydney Olympics Elite Club Grants		NYC Marathon (proposed) Gym Tour (proposed)	Gym Tour (proposed)
2001	Gym Tour (proposed)			Boston Marathon Champions on Ice	Champions on Ice	Champions on Ice	Champions on Ice				NYC Marathon (proposed)	
2002		Salt Lake Olympics (proposed)		Boston Marathon Champions on Ice	Champions on Ice	Champions on Ice	Champions on Ice				NYC Marathon (proposed)	

Questions

1. On reflection, what do you think about Hancock's decisions both to sponsor and to abandon sponsorship of the Sun Bowl?

2. What is your assessment of each major component of Hancock's sponsorship—the Boston Marathon, Olympics "Top Sponsor," USA Gymnastics, and Champions on Ice?

3. What are your views of D'Alessandro's "six basic questions" as principles of sports sponsorship?

4. Overall, where is Hancock at the end of the case in terms of sponsorship?

5. What are your recommendations on the several new and renewal sponsorships?

6. How, if it all, do you think the importance of sports sponsorship to Hancock will change after the company was bought by Manulife, a Canadian firm? (Assume the Hancock brand continues.)

Case 6.5 Tarnished Rings? Olympic Games Sponsorship Issues[44]

During a January 22, 1999 speech in New York, U.S. Olympic Committee Marketing Director John Krimsky acknowledged that "we have been bruised" by the scandal [Salt Lake Olympic Committee]. These comments came after the troubled International Olympic Committee had already hired public relations giant Hill & Knowlton Inc. to try to restore its image.

"Make no mistake about it, the scandal and the flap surrounding it are not helping the Olympic brand," said Lance Helgeson, senior editor of Chicago-based IEG Sponsorship Report, which tracks corporate sponsorships. In 1996, Olympic sponsorship dollars totaled $290 million, according to IEG, compared with $433 million this year.[45]

Emerging Scandal

Early 1999 was awash with international discussion of an emerging scandal within the powerful Olympic movement. "The IOC's [International Olympic Committee] sponsorships have become radioactive," said David D'Alessandro, the president of John Hancock Mutual Life Insurance, one of a dozen worldwide sponsors of the Olympics. "All corporate Geiger counters are going off the chart. They've got to find a way to make sponsorships safe again." D'Alessandro said that he had begun to wonder whether Juan Antonio Samaranch, the 78-year-old president of the IOC, would or could remain in his job if the scandal escalated and corporate sponsorship was seriously imperiled. (See **Exhibit 1** for a brief chronology of the scandal.)

Hancock and other sponsors were eagerly awaiting the IOC meeting to be held in Lausanne on the weekend of January 24, 1999. "The question is whether they can achieve reform with credibility under the current leadership," D'Alessandro said. "Only the IOC can answer that question. Can Samaranch go into a boardroom and credibly sell a sponsorship? I don't know the answer to that. I think he survives if his changes are extraordinary, sweeping, and he shows enormous courage as a leader . . . and recognizes that all he has built is in jeopardy." Samaranch, a Spanish marquis who became IOC president in 1980, stated emphatically during the first week of January 1999 that he would maintain his position until his current term ends in 2001. He seemed to be qualifying his remarks somewhat later in the month,[46] when he said he would rely on the judgment of IOC members acting as a body.

Organization of the Modern Olympics[47]

At the Congress of Paris in 1894, the control and development of the modern Olympic Games was entrusted to the International Olympic Committee (IOC; Comité International Olympique), with headquarters to be established in Switzerland. It is responsible for maintaining the regular celebration of the Olympic Games, seeing that the Games are carried out in the spirit that inspired their revival, and promoting the development of amateur sport throughout the world. The original committee in 1894 consisted of 14 members and Baron

Harvard Business School Case No 9-599-107. Copyright 1999 President and Fellows of Harvard College. All rights reserved. For information: permission@hbsp.harvard.edu. This case was prepared by John A. Clendenin and Stephen A. Greyser. HBS cases are developed solely for class discussion and do not necessarily illustrate effective or ineffective management.

EXHIBIT 1   SCANDAL TIME LINE

SALT LAKE CITY 2002

DEC. 12—Charges of bribery and vote-buying in the Olympic bid process are made by Marc Hodler of Switzerland, a senior member of the IOC executive board.

DEC. 13—IOC President Juan Antonio Samaranch vows to crack down on corruption.

DEC. 14—Billy Payne, head of the Atlanta Games, says he was aware of influence peddlers in the Olympic movement, but denies Atlanta "bought" the '96 Games.

DEC. 17—The Justice Department says it will review allegations that the Salt Lake Olympic Committee bribed IOC members.

DEC. 20—Samaranch says the IOC will establish a new process for determining future Olympic sites.

DEC. 23—The Justice Department and FBI announce an investigation of the Salt Lake scandal.

JAN. 3—Utah Gov. Mike Leavitt asks that SLOC members involved in the bid process be put on leave.

JAN. 7—The New York Times reports that Salt Lake made payments of $5,000 to $70,000 to IOC members from Africa and Latin America.

JAN. 8—SLOC President Frank Joklik and Vice President Dave Johnson resign.

JAN. 11—IOC Vice President Anita DeFrantz predicts that as many as 12 IOC members may be forced to resign. Hodler says the Salt Lake Games could be in jeopardy.

Source: Compiled from media reports.

Pierre de Coubertin, the first President. Membership since then has been self-perpetuating. Convinced that the downfall of the ancient Olympic Games had been caused by outside influences that undermined the spirit of the Games, Coubertin believed that the revived Games would go the same way unless they were in the hands of people whose concern was to keep the spirit of amateur sport alive and who were responsible in no way to any outside influences.

International Olympic Committee[48]

IOC members are regarded as ambassadors from the IOC to their national sports organizations. They are in no sense delegates to the committee and may not accept from the government of their country, or from any organization or individual, any instructions that in any way affect their independence. The IOC is a permanent organization that elects its own members. Each member—the present membership is about 118 (prior to recent departures)—must speak French or English and be a citizen of or reside in a country that has a National Olympic Committee. With very few exceptions, there is only one member from any one country. Members were originally elected for life, but anyone elected after 1965 must retire at 75. The IOC elects its president for a period of eight years, at the end of which he is eligible for reelection for further periods of four years each. Juan Antònio Samaranch (Spain) was elected in 1980. Previous presidents were Dimitrios Vikélas (1894–96, Greece), Baron Pierre de Coubertin (1896–1925, France), Count Henri de Baillet-Latour (1925–42, Belgium), J. Sigfrid Edström (1946–52, Sweden), Avery Brundage (1952–72, United States), and Michael Morris, Lord Killanin (1972–80, Ireland). The executive board of 11 members holds periodic meetings with the international federations and National Olympic Committees. The IOC as a whole meets annually, and a meeting can be convened at any time that one-third of the members so request. Known as the "Lords of the Rings" the committee had an elite membership that included several members of royalty and aristocrats from the member nations.

Site Selection

Since the success of the 1984 Olympic games in Los Angeles, the selection of Olympic sites had grown increasingly competitive. Los Angeles had been the only site to bid for the 1984 games. Under the leadership of Peter Ueberroth, the Los Angeles Organizing Committee's Chief Operating Officer, the City of Los Angeles was able to run the games successfully, survive a Soviet bloc boycott, and actually make a profit. (The net for the city was $222.7 million; this earned Ueberroth a $475,000 bonus.[49]) Since 1984 cities around the world have formed organizing groups in order to present bids for consideration of the IOC.

The Olympic Brand

In recent years, the Olympics has been generally considered to be one of the world's premier brands. The value of the Olympic brand and the "selling" of the Olympic Five Rings logo has become a major factor in attracting quality companies worldwide in the effort to associate their names with the prestige of the Olympic Games. Although not without the influence of politics,[50] the Games were positioned as representing the world's best efforts in excellence of ideals. The Olympic motto of "Citius, Altius, Fortius" (Swifter, Higher, Stronger) was widely recognized worldwide along with the interlocking five rings. Also recognized was the Olympic ideal of participation in the games being paramount rather than winning.

Sponsorship

With the success of the brand came the increasing value of sponsorship. Companies competed vigorously for rights to official Olympic sponsorship and paid substantial dollars for the right to license Olympic Merchandise. For example, the dozen major (TOP) sponsor companies paid $40 million per quadrennium for worldwide sponsorship. IOC global sponsors for the 2002 Winter games were: Coca Cola, IBM, John Hancock, Kodak, McDonald's, Panasonic, Samsung, Sports Illustrated, UPS, VISA, and Xerox. USOC National Sponsors, according to Olympic Properties, included: General Motors, US WEST, Texaco, Budweiser, AT&T, The Home Depot, Blue Cross and Blue Shield, Delta Air Lines, United Airlines, Seiko, Lucent Technologies, General Mills, York, NationsBank, and Merrill Lynch.

The revenue stream associated with these sponsor arrangements became the lifeblood of success for a city hosting the Olympics. Television rights and the high ratings value of the Olympics created additional pressure on cities and the IOC concerning the process used for awarding the games to a host city. Ethical norms and procedures were known to vary widely in the international arena. The behavior of the members of the IOC was under increasing scrutiny in determining the appropriateness of tactics used by the competing cities in soliciting votes.

Sydney, Australia—2000 Summer Olympics

In January 1999, organizers of the 2000 Summer Olympics were also concerned about the spreading international bribery scandal. They were still $130 million shy of the $455 million they hoped to raise from corporate sponsors. The Games' marketers have enlisted some 60 companies who already have signed contracts to help convince about 40 potential sponsors that a multimillion-dollar investment would not leave them tainted by association.

"Brand association is what the Olympics is all about," said John Moore, head of marketing and image for the Sydney Organizing Committee for the Olympic Games (SOCOG). "Nobody's called and said they want to stall until they see what happens. But they're asking us to reassure them as we build the case for an Olympic investment."[51]

Further complicating matters was the bombshell dropped during the last week of January 1999. Australian Olympic Committee President John Coates had released written agreements to provide $1.2 million in sports funding for 11 African countries in the weeks before Sydney won its bid in 1993, fending off its main rival Beijing by just two votes. Much of it was conditional on Sydney winning. And some of it, totaling $70,000, was offered at a dinner with the Kenyan and Ugandan delegates on the eve of the vote in Monte Carlo.

Television Broadcast Rights

Television rights fees provide the majority of revenue for the IOC. NBC, which holds broadcast rights to upcoming Olympic Games, maintained that advertising, which is sold in multi-year packages, was not being hurt by the influence-peddling scandal. The NBC network has agreed to pay $3.5 billion for the television rights to all five Winter and Summer Games to be held between 2000 and 2008.[52]

"We've seen absolutely no impact on Olympic advertising, and we don't expect any," said NBC spokesman Ed Markey. NBC continues to superimpose the familiar Olympic rings on sports programs, but it has pulled the rings from news shows that are covering the scandal.

Historically, television rights fees have provided the majority of revenues for the IOC. The majority of all revenues (95%) came from television in 1980, with more than 85% of these revenues coming from the US Network. Today, although U.S. television rights fees are worth eight times more than in 1980, they account for less than 25% of total revenues. Total television rights fees now account for just under 50% of all marketing revenues.

Additionally, the IOC is paving the way to using TV revenue to finance the Olympic Movement as a whole, in addition to the Games themselves. From 2004, Olympic Host Cities will receive only 49% of revenue instead of 60%. This shift in the distribution of television income is to serve the progress of sports in the Olympic Movement worldwide rather than financing the long-term capital/structural investments of host cities. Although there is a reduction in the percentage to the OCOGs, the real value to the cities will increase due to the increasing amounts of the TV rights fees.[53]

Salt Lake City Potential Sponsors

Any growing reluctance on the part of sponsors to get involved with the 2002 Games could have serious consequences for American efforts to stage a full Winter Olympics. United States Olympic officials as of January 1999 still have to raise $250 million in sponsorship money in a joint-marketing agreement with Salt Lake City to reach the proposed budget of $1.45 billion. Olympic officials had said that the Games may have to be reduced in size if the full budget figure cannot be reached.

"Some potential sponsors reportedly had decided not to sign final marketing agreements with the troubled Salt Lake City Organizing Committee until investigators determine the breadth of that city's problems. But other companies were moving ahead with Olympic sponsorships. Visa International, a major IOC sponsor of the 2000 Summer Games in Sydney, Australia, was "still in discussions" about a possible corporate sponsorship of the Salt Lake City Games. And, as allegations of vote-buying spread to Australia, the Visa spokesman said the credit card company "continues to work toward a successful marketing and hospitality effort in Sydney."

Denver-based US West Communications reversed a decision to withhold a $5 million sponsorship payment from the Salt Lake City Games. The telecommunications company said it sent the payment after Utah Governor Mike Leavitt pledged to reform the organizing committee. "The governor has made major progress in pushing forward an open investigation," said US West spokesman Davie Beigie. "He's cleaning things up, bringing the spirit of Utah and the West into making the Games the focus again instead of the selection process. We're encouraged that it's moving in the right direction."

For better or worse, sports marketers say, scandal-weary Americans seem to be taking the sports world's latest woes in stride. A Denver-based market research firm reported January 22 that 43% of Olympics fans who know about the scandal have a "less favorable" view of the Games. But the slew of investigations by federal, state and Olympics officials "has triggered a positive response among some fans and a mending of the Olympics' image is underway," said Tim Taylor, chief operating officer of the Bonham Group Market Research Co."[54]

> *"It's premature to revise any estimates, but obviously we will be watching for any developments that may require us to look at things again," says Utah State Olympic Coordinator John Fowler. In July, he had issued a report predicting state tax revenues from the Games would be $19 million more than the direct cost to the state for hosting the events. "Our hope is there will be no reason to revise those estimates."*

Key IOC members have maintained that despite a slew of investigations into alleged bid-rigging by Utah Games boosters, the 2002 events will not be moved. At the same time, an outspoken IOC member and leaders of some cities that lost out to Salt Lake City in the bid competition have suggested relocating the Games. Quebec officials even broached the possibility of suing to get the Games.

New Olympic Sponsors

John Krimsky, who had responsibility for signing corporate sponsors for the Winter Games and for the U.S. Olympic Committee (USOC), made the following assessment in late January 1999: "Don't look for any new Olympic sponsors to be announced until the bumper-to-bumper investigations into the escalating scandal are complete."

He went on to say: "Two companies that plan to sponsor the 2002 Winter Olympics are holding off on announcing their agreements." One of the two companies was rumored to be BMW, which had been a sponsor of the 1996 Summer Olympics in Atlanta. The prospective sponsors' wariness made clear the potential problem facing Krimsky as he tried to recruit new sponsors during an unfolding scandal. "We will know Monday after the IOC's initial report as to how fast we can really begin the healing process," said Krimsky.

The Future

For big companies that will pour an estimated $443 million into Olympic Games sponsorships and advertisements during 1999, the looming question is how badly the Salt Lake City bribery investigation will tarnish the Olympic rings that already have endured terrorism, Cold War boycotts, and the dulling impact of performance-enhancing drugs.

But, so far, many corporations with rights to use Olympic logos and athletes in advertising say they are not ready to abandon the highly effective international marketing tool. "We can either look at the Games themselves and the spirit behind them, or look only at the scandal and begin wringing our hands," said Burke Stinson, spokesman for AT&T, whose sponsorship of the U.S. Olympics Team runs through the 2004 Games in Greece. "We've chosen to take the long view. It's an awkward time for the Games, and by inference the sponsors, but it's a time for sponsors to close ranks, not kick someone when they're down."

Similarly, Coca-Cola Co., an Olympic sponsor since 1928, "isn't going to discard that relationship," said spokesman Ben Deutsch. "This is a serious issue and a cause of great concern for us. But we've expressed our concerns to the organizing committees and the IOC, and we've been assured that they will take swift steps to bring the situation to a positive closure." But while some big corporations say they are unlikely to abandon the Games, some corporate executives frustrated by the skyrocketing costs of sponsorship fees took the position that they will try to use the scandal as leverage when contracts are renegotiated. "Make no mistake about it, the scandal and the flap surrounding it are not helping the Olympic brand," said Lance Helgeson, senior editor of Chicago-based IEG Sponsorship Report, which tracks corporate sponsorships. In 1996, Olympic sponsorship dollars totaled $290 million, according to IEG, compared with $433 million this year.

The president and chief operating officer of John Hancock Mutual Life Insurance Company was reported by *The New York Times* to have "sternly admonished the IOC to extend its investigation of irregular bidding practices beyond Salt Lake City and the 2002 Winter Games. "If they fail to do that and something else comes up, the rings won't be tarnished, they'll be broken," said David D'Alessandro. He urged the IOC to expand its examination of cash payments, tuition aid, and lavish gifts acknowledged by Salt Lake City officials to include the bidding procedures of the 1996 Summer Games in Atlanta, the 1998 Winter Games in Nagano, Japan, as well as the coming 2000 Summer Games in Sydney, Australia, and the 2004 Summer Games in Athens.

The IOC commission investigating Salt Lake City's Winter Olympics bid was scheduled to present its initial report to the IOC's 11-person executive board on January 24, 1999. Whether the report could provide the closure the IOC hoped for was now threatened by new bribery allegations out of Sydney. "Can the boat take any more hits?" asked Rick Burton, director of the Warsaw Sports Marketing Center at the University of Oregon."[55]

In the future, D'Alessandro also said, he expected that sponsorship deals with the IOC would contain the equivalent of morals clauses, which would presumably allow corporations to escape their contracts. "You only get one bite of this apple," he said, referring to the IOC.

"They can't come back a year from now and say, "Oops, here's another one, there was a leak and we happened to hear about it." "Boardrooms will shake if this is mishandled," D'Alessandro said. "That includes NBC's boardroom."

Questions

1. In light of what is known about the Olympic bribery scandals and the related news and publicity about them *at the time of case* (February 1999), how concerned would you be as a major Olympic sponsor? On a scale of seriousness from 1 (low) to 10 (high), how would you rate this as of early February (1999)?

2. As of early February, what would be your principal specific worries? Are they short term, long term, or both?

3. As of early February, what actions do you believe the IOC should undertake to shore up its reputation?

4. What research, if any, would you undertake as a major sponsor? As NBC? As the IOC?

5. As a major Olympic sponsor, what actions would you take if the scandals continued to be in the news through summer (a year before the Sydney Olympics)? Why?

6. What reflections do you have on this in light of 2002–03 events involving the United States Olympic Committee (USOC)?

Footnotes

[1]   This section was written by George Foster.

[2]   Street and Smith's SportsBusiness Journal, *By the Numbers 2004*, p. 32.

[3]   IEG's website is http://www.sponsorship.com; its bimonthly *IEG Sponsorship Report* is a rich source of information on many aspects of the sponsorship arena.

[4]   The other 31% of sponsorship outlays were entertainment, tours and attractions (10%); cause marketing (9%); festivals, fairs, and annual events (7%), and arts (5%).

[5]   www.soccerhall.org. See "Soccer Research Library" section.

[6]   IEG Inc., *Measuring Sponsorship's Return on Investment* (Chicago: 2003), p. 145.

[7]   IEG's Guide to Sponsorship (Chicago: 2004).

[8]   "The Price of Pricing: Breakdown of Sponsorship Analysis Companies and Why or Why Not to Hire One." *Team Marketing Report* vol. 16, issue 09 (June 2004).

[9]   Ron Johnson prepared this case under the supervision of George Foster.

[10]   Valuations taken from Joyce Julius and Associates 2003 NASCAR Winston Cup Year-End Report. The advertising agency in Exhibit 1 is Mullen. The market research firm is TNS.

[11]   Information taken from NASCAR Marketing Publication.

[12]   Professor Stephen A. Greyser and Brian Harris and Mitchell Truwit (MBAs '97) prepared this case. Some financial information in the case has been disguised. HBS cases are developed solely as the basis for class

discussion. Cases are not intended to serve as endorsements, sources of primary data, or illustrations of effective or ineffective management.

[13] Allen Sack and Arthur Johnson. "Politics, Economic Development, and the Volvo International Tennis Tournament." *Journal of Sport Management* (1996).

[14] Tennis Foundation of Connecticut Agreement with JEWEL Productions, Inc., 1990.

[15] JEWEL Productions internal sales data.

[16] *1995 ATP Tour Player Guide.*

[17] The July–August North American tour schedule (between Wimbledon and the U.S. Open) consisted of events in Newport, RI, Washington, DC, Montreal, Los Angeles, Cincinnati, New Haven/Indianapolis (2 events, same week), and Long Island. The European tour was also active in July and early August.

[18] Some financial information in this case has been disguised.

[19] JEWEL Productions Title Sponsor Presentation, 1995.

[20] Joyce Julius and Associates, "The 1992 Volvo International," October 19, 1992.

[21] JEWEL Productions Title Sponsor Presentation, 1995.

[22] Many events packaged advertising pages in *TIME* or *Newsweek* in their sponsorship proposals. Events could charge more for these packages and found them easier to sell because companies sometimes could nearly justify the sponsorship buy on media value alone. Westhall had in fact, in the past, capitalized on his relationship with *TIME*, accepting ad pages in addition to cash.

[23] Joyce Julius and Associates, 1994.

[24] Victoria Chang prepared this case under the supervision of George Foster.

[25] Visa-branded cards included credit, debit and prepaid, corporate, purchasing, and business products. Debit products allowed consumers to access their checking or bank deposit accounts directly. Debit products gave consumers the choice to "pay now," whereas credit products allowed consumers to "pay later," and prepaid products to "pay before."

[26] Lavonne KuyKendall. "Gauging Value Has High Degree of Difficulty." *American Banker* (February 27, 2002), p. 1.

[27] Visa Press Release, September 8, 1997, volume 53, issue 25.

[28] "Visa Kicks Off Olympic-Themed Campaign." *Bank Advertising News* vol. 24, issue 4 (February 21, 2000), p. 1.

[29] Ibid.

[30] Visa website: http://www.visa.com/globalgateway/gg_selectcountry.html?retcountry=1.

[31] "Visa Launches Marketing for 2004 Olympics." *Bank Marketing International* (December 31, 2002), p. 4.

[32] Visa website: http://www.visa.com/globalgateway/gg_selectcountry.html?retcountry=1.

[33] Becky Saeger. "Visa Has What It Takes at the Olympics." *Marketer's Forum* vol. 6, no. 3 (April 2002), p. 30.

[34] "Visa Breaks Olympic Record for Sponsorship." *Bank Marketing International* (January 22, 2003), p. 8.

[35] Ibid.

[36] "Visa Extends Olympic Games Sponsorship for Eight More Years; Most Successful Sponsorship to Deliver Support Through the Games of the XXX Olympiad in 2012." *Business Wire* (November 11, 2002).

[37] Miriam Kreinin Souccar. "Visa's Sponsorship Gives It Inside Lane for Olympic Games." *American Banker* vol. 264, issue 216 (November 9, 1999), p. 1.

[38] Becky Saeger. "Visa Has What It Takes at the Olympics." *Marketer's Forum* vol. 6, no. 3 (April 2002), p. 30.

[39] http://www.onlinesports.com/sportstrust/sports13.html.

[40] The APR was the yearly interest charge on outstanding credit card balances.

[41] The discount rate was the fee a merchant paid a member financial institution to process a purchase charged to a Visa card.

[42] The national average for the discount rate was 2.35%. MasterCard's fees were comparable to Visa's fees, whereas American Express and Discover typically charged 3%.

[43] Dr. John Teopaco and Professor Stephen A. Greyser prepared this case as the basis for class discussion rather than to illustrate either effective or ineffective handling of an administrative situation.

Copyright © 1998 by the President and Fellows of Harvard College. To order copies or request permission to reproduce materials, call 1-800-545-7685, write Harvard Business School Publishing, Boston, MA 02163, or go to http://www.hbsp.harvard.edu. No part of this publication may be reproduced, stored in a retrieval system, used in a spreadsheet, or transmitted in any form or by any means–electronic, mechanical, photocopying, recording, or otherwise–without the permission of Harvard Business School.

[44] John A. Clendenin, Senior Lecturer, and Professor Stephen A. Greyser prepared this case. This case was developed from published sources. HBS cases are developed solely as the basis for class discussion. Cases are not intended to serve as endorsements, sources of primary data, or illustrations of effective or ineffective management.

Copyright © 1999 President and Fellows of Harvard College. To order copies or request permission to reproduce materials, call 1-800-545-7685, write Harvard Business School Publishing, Boston, MA 02163, or go to http://www.hbsp.harvard.edu. No part of this publication may be reproduced, stored in a retrieval system, used in a spreadsheet, or transmitted in any form or by any means–electronic, mechanical, photocopying, recording, or otherwise–without the permission of Harvard Business School.

[45] Johnson, Greg. *Los Angeles Times* (January 23, 1999), Part A, p. 20.

[46] Longman, Jere. *New York Times* (January 21, 1999), Section D, p. 1.

[47] Source: *Encyclopedia Britannica* Globe.

[48] http://www.olympic.org.

[49] Melvin Helitzer. *The Dream Job: Sports Publicity, Promotion and Marketing*, p. 44.

[50] Notable past political actions have included the United States Boycott of the 1980 games in Moscow, the Soviet Bloc Countries Boycott of the 1984 games in Los Angeles, and the killing of Israeli athletes by Arab extremists in the Olympic Village in Munich during the 1972 games. Adolf Hitler had attempted to restrict facilities during the 1936 games in Berlin but backed down after being told that "when the Olympic Flag is raised, commencing the Olympic Games, the location becomes international and no longer Germany."

[51] Morello, Carol. *USA TODAY* (January 28, 1999), Sports, p. 7C, Sydney, Australia.

[52] Longman, Jere. *New York Times* (January 13, 1999).

[53] Adapted from Olympic website and media sources.

[54] Johnson, Greg. *Los Angeles Times* (January 23, 1999), Part A, p. 20.

[55] Boulton, Guy. *Salt Lake Tribune* (January 23, 1999), Nation/World, p. A1.

SECTION 7... Sports Marketing (2): Club Marketing, Branding, and Fan Avidity[1]

Key Issues

- Revenue enhancement at the local level occurs within a framework set by past and current decisions, including decisions about stadium capacity, season ticket packaging, ticket price tiering, and variable pricing strategies.

- Clubs are exploring ways (such as secondary ticket options) to capture additional rents from high demand events that currently go to "black market" ticket operators.

- Increasing attention is being given to the varying dimensions of fan satisfaction. These include a winning team on-the-field, competitive ticket pricing, access to players, in-stadium experience, and quality of game promotions.

- Key sporting club brand drivers include management initiatives to build and exploit the brand, long-run winning record, home market strength, and stadium/arena strength.

- Athlete branding is of growing importance. Factors influencing its value include popularity of the sport, on-field ability, winning tradition, charisma, public recognition, and media face/talk time.

Cases

Club marketing covers the related challenges of local revenue enhancement and club brand management. There are dramatic differences across clubs in both the magnitude of their local revenues and in the strength of their brand. A major source of these disparities is differences in the size of a club's fan base and its avidity.

This section covers several related topics:

1. Local revenue enhancement and ticket pricing
2. Promoting fan satisfaction
3. Branding challenges at the club and player levels

Local Revenue Enhancement and Ticket Pricing

Ticket revenues are the single largest local revenue source for many clubs. Decisions regarding ticket pricing can have an important effect on club profitability and on the number of fans in attendance. The 2001 MLB disclosures included individual club-by-club ticket revenues. The average across the 30 clubs was $45.700 million. The top three and bottom three in ticket revenues and their ratio relative to the average is:

Top 3			Bottom 3		
1. New York Yankees	$98.000	(2.14)	28. Minnesota Twins	$17.605	(0.39)
2. Boston Red Sox	$89.743	(1.96)	29. Florida Marlins	$16.756	(0.37)
3. Seattle Mariners	$76.570	(1.68)	30. Montreal Expos	$ 6.405	(0.14)

Underpinning such vast ticket revenue differences are multiple decisions:

Capacity of the Stadium: Stadium construction time is clearly when there is most flexibility in determining capacity. However, clubs frequently reconfigure seating in an attempt to add more seats, or create higher-premium ticket areas. Section 9 provides further discussion of stadium issues.

Season Ticket Packaging: The decisions to be made here include whether to require season ticket-holders to purchase all games or to allow a subset of games to be packaged. Much depends on the level of demand and the number of games. Each NFL club has only eight home games, all typically on a Sunday. NFL clubs that invariably sell out offer only full-season packages. In contrast, MLB clubs have 81 home games, which occur on all days or nights of the week. Many clubs sell both full 81-game season packages and smaller packages.

Ticket Price Tiering: Tiering relates to both the number of different price points in a stadium and the slope of the price points from highest to lowest and points in between. High and low single-game ticket prices for many North American sporting leagues are

EXHIBIT 7-1   TICKET PRICE TIERING: EVIDENCE USING SINGLE GAME TICKET PRICES.
2004 REVENUES FROM SPORTS VENUES SURVEY

League (1)	Average Highest Single Ticket Price (2)	Average Lowest Single Ticket Price (3)	Tiering: Ratio of Highest/ Lowest (4)=(2)/(3)	Stadium/ Arena Average Capacity (4)	Stadium/ Arena Average Attendance (5)
Football—NFL	$111.37	$36.52	3.05	69,828	66,662
Baseball—MLB	59.12	7.11	8.32	46,278	28,025
Basketball—NBA	222.28	10.87	20.45	19,353	16,833
Hockey—NHL	166.75	19.10	8.73	18,490	16,589
Arena Football	81.72	10.03	8.15	16,196	11,397
Soccer—MLS	35.20	14.10	2.50	21,174	14,898
Basketball—WNBA	90.35	8.38	10.78	18,705	8,933
Baseball—Minors					
International League	9.07	5.82	1.56	12,333	6,706
Pacific Coast League	11.07	5.33	2.08	12,582	6,283
Texas League	9.56	5.88	1.63	7,571	5,017
Hockey—Minors					
American HL	25.69	12.98	1.98	11,748	5,741
Central HL	22.910	10.74	2.13	8,445	4,520
ECHL	20.58	10.29	2	9,744	4,109

Source: Based on source data in *2004 Revenues From Sports Venues.*

reported in 2004 *Revenues From Sports Venues.* Exhibit 7-1 draws from this publication. The ratio of the highest single price to the lowest indicates the extent of price tiering across leagues. In basketball, both the NBA and the WNBA have the highest degree of price tiering—ratios of 20.45 to 1 and 8.73 to 1, respectively. Front-row seats in the NBA and WNBA are in premium positions. They offer a level of involvement close to the game not found in many other leagues. Within each individual sporting league, there are sizable differences across clubs in their price tiering.

Related to price tiering is the number of different price points in a stadium. Again, clubs differ greatly here, for reasons not always related to revenue maximization. The San Francisco Giants in MLB have 13 different price categories at SBC Park. The Giants sell out many but not all games. In contrast, the San Francisco 49ers of the NFL play to sellouts for all their regular season games. The 49ers charge the same amount ($64 in 2004) for every seat in Candlestick Park! Seats are allocated based on when the season package was purchased. Longtime season ticket-holders have lower deck, 50-yard line tickets, whereas most recent ticket purchases sit in the top ends of the upper deck ("binocular land"). This single-ticket price is relatively rare, but has its roots in Candlestick Park being 100% publicly financed.

Variable Pricing: A growing trend in ticket pricing is to charge different prices for the same seat depending on one or more of the following:

- By opponent—higher prices for higher demanded visitors
- By day of week—higher price for weekend games
- By season—higher prices for summer games

Variable ticket pricing is appealing from an economic perspective, provided reliable information exists on differences in demand across the chosen pricing parameter. This can be challenging in some sporting settings. An opponent assumed to be a strong draw at the start of the season when prices are set might dramatically underperform during the season and draw lower crowds (even at nonpremium prices). There also can be a fan backlash to variable pricing, as it has been portrayed as owners opportunistically seeking to extract as much "rent" from fans as possible.

Secondary-Market Ticket Pricing: Ticket scalping has long been a part of sports. Fans not able to obtain tickets from the club for sold-out games can and do venture to the black market, which can be illegal. Some clubs now are seeking to capture rents from this secondary ticket market. The San Francisco Giants provide their season ticket-holders with the "Double Play Ticket Window." This enables season ticket-holders to place on a website (Tickets.com) tickets for games they wish to sell. There is no ceiling on the upside, but there is a floor equal to the face value of the ticket. Currently, the average ticket sold in the "Double Play Ticket Window" has commanded a 40% premium over face value. There is a total commission on the transaction of 21%, which is collectively paid by both the buyer and seller. This commission is split between "the Giants, the on-line provider, and Tickets.com that does all the record keeping." The Giants see multiple benefits from participating in this secondary market. First, season ticket-holders have fewer unused tickets, which helps increase season ticket-holder renewal rates. Second, fans have access to premium location seats, which can increase their interest in subsequent stadium visits. Third, the Giants also receive part of the 21% total commission on the transaction. The black market can cause much pain to fans when the ticket they purchase is a fake. Fans purchasing tickets on the Double Play Ticket Window are guaranteed their ticket is a genuine one.

Promoting Fan Satisfaction

Fans, directly or indirectly, are a central part of the money-generating machine that underlies much of the business of sports. Fans pay for tickets and concessions on game day. They help create the game atmosphere and pageantry that make moments in sports "live forever." They pay for the merchandise they wear as a symbol to the world of their passion and support. They also provide "eyes and ears" for all different forms of media that in turn attract advertisements, sponsors, endorsements, and the like.

Studies of fans report multiple factors that drive their behavior. An extensive study by *ESPN The Magazine* and the Warsaw Sports Marketing Center at the University of Oregon highlights eight variables:

1. BNG (Bang for the Buck)—Revenues directly from fans divided by wins in the last 3 years.

2. FRL (Fan Relations)—Ease of access to players, coaches, and management.

3. OWN (Ownership)—Honesty; loyalty to players and city.

4. AFF (Affordability)—Price of tickets, parking, and concessions.

5. STD (Stadium Experience)—Friendliness of environment; quality of game-day promotions.

6. PLA (Players)—Effort on the field; likeability.

7. CCH (Coach/Manager)—Strong on-field leadership.

8. CHA (Championships)—Titles already won or expected soon.

These eight variables came from a national poll to determine "what sports fans most care about 'getting back'" from their clubs. Fans then rated on ESPN.com their responses to 21 questions that were used to compute the eight variables. Fans of every club in the NFL, MLB, NBA, and NHL provided input. For each of the eight variables, all clubs were ranked from top (1 = "giving back" the most to their fans) to bottom. The eight variables were also weighted to develop a single ranking of the "ultimate standing" of clubs to their fans—the weights were based on fans' perception of their "relative importance" of the eight variables.

Exhibit 7-2 presents 2004 results for 24 of the 120 clubs—the top 3 and bottom 3 in each of the MLB, NBA, NFL, and NHL. The top-ranked and bottom-ranked clubs overall were:

2003	2004
1. Green Bay Packers	1. San Antonio Spurs
2. Arizona Diamondbacks	2. Dallas Mavericks
117. New York Knicks	119. Arizona Cardinals
118. Cincinnati Bengals	120. Chicago Blackhawks

The variables underlying this research highlight how efforts to enhance fan experience have to work at multiple levels. On-the-field success, while important, is far from being the only area important to fans. For example, the stadium experience and the affordability of tickets, parking, and concessions also are important to fans.

The affordability of a family attending a sports event is important to fans and attracts a lot of media attention. *Team Marketing Report* conducts a "Fan Cost Index" (FCI) survey on a regular basis. This index tracks the "cost of attendance for a family of four. The FCI includes: two adult average price tickets; two child average price tickets; four small soft drinks; two small beers; four hot dogs; two programs; parking; and two adult-size caps." Exhibit 7-3 shows large difference across leagues and across clubs in affordability. Summary results are:

League	Average FCI	Highest FCI	Lowest FCI
MLB	$156	$263 (Boston)	$108 (Montreal)
NBA	261	387 (LA Lakers)	185 (Golden State)
NFL	302	405 (New England)	230 (Arizona)
NHL	254	318 (Detroit)	193 (Carolina)
Minor Baseball	81	98 (Charlotte)	56 (Burlington)

Media frequently use such data in reports on different clubs. Fans who are required to pay top-tier prices likely will be well informed when the press writes "fan-gouging" stories about clubs at the high-price end for stadium-related tickets, parking, or concessions. A challenge for such high-pricing clubs is to provide an exceptional within-stadium experience so that their fans believe they are getting value for their money.

EXHIBIT 7-2 FAN SATISFACTION RANKINGS: 2004 *ESPN THE MAGAZINE*'s ANNUAL SURVEY
(120 CLUBS RANKED IN 2004; 118 CLUBS RANKED IN 2003)

	BNG	FRL	OWN	AFF	STD	PLA	CCH	CHA	2004 Overall Rank	2003 Overall Rank
NFL: 1. Green Bay Packers	24	3	1	6	4	19	51	8	3	1
2. Kansas City Chiefs	44	4	4	19	10	5	2	33	5	28
3. Tennessee Titans	48	9	19	13	11	2	7	21	7	25
29. Cleveland Browns	84	118	95	94	79	108	97	97	110	64
30. San Diego Chargers	94	116	118	111	117	114	114	110	118	80
31. Arizona Cardinals	64	119	117	95	121	117	104	120	119	112
MLB: 1. Anaheim Angels	19	11	18	21	19	15	5	11	6	10
2. Arizona Diamondbacks	5	18	20	34	17	38	61	14	9	2
3. St. Louis Cardinals	49	15	15	18	37	26	57	24	18	17
28. New York Mets	107	112	69	114	114	111	100	38	111	88
29. Milwaukee Brewers	75	106	119	58	66	84	66	119	112	107
30. Detroit Tigers	114	117	108	96	68	118	65	65	113	116
NBA: 1. San Antonio Spurs	4	1	2	4	7	1	18	2	1	3
2. Dallas Mavericks	12	2	5	20	3	7	17	34	2	5
3. Detroit Pistons	18	7	17	9	18	3	24	23	4	13
27. Portland Trail Blazers	55	121	100	103	92	121	56	81	115	110
28. New York Knicks	116	114	102	119	82	115	117	104	116	117
29. Atlanta Hawks	98	115	113	110	99	113	113	118	117	111
NHL: 1. Edmonton Oilers	1	16	57	8	44	41	44	41	8	9
2. Ottawa Senators	6	17	26	27	41	51	38	42	10	26
3. Minnesota Wild	79	6	14	14	2	9	4	36	11	N/A
28. Washington Capitals	54	88	75	112	71	116	119	112	109	68
29. New York Rangers	119	107	86	116	74	120	111	43	114	109
30. Chicago Blackhawks	101	120	120	121	120	119	106	121	120	108

*BNG = Bang for the Buck; FRL = Fan Relations; OWN = Ownership; AFF = Affordability; STD = Stadium Experience;
PLA = Players; CCH = Coach/Manager; CHA = Championships.

Source: © 2005 ESPN Magazine, LLC. Reprinted courtesy of *ESPN The MAGAZINE*.

Clubs are continually seeking many ways of providing extra fan experiences as well as new game-day revenues. For example, the Chicago White Sox of MLB offer on game day an "array of pricey on field activities, including raking the infield between innings ($1,500 to $2,000), delivering the lineup card to the umpire ($1,500 to $2,000) and swapping the bases mid-game ($1,000 to $1,500)." The challenge here is to balance the extra fan options provided without creating a negative, overly mercenary image that "everything and anything has a price." The White Sox donate "ten percent of the 'White Sox Experience,' which also includes game tickets for friends and family, good and souvenirs, to charity."[2]

EXHIBIT 7-3   FAN COST INDEX: COMPARISON ACROSS LEAGUES

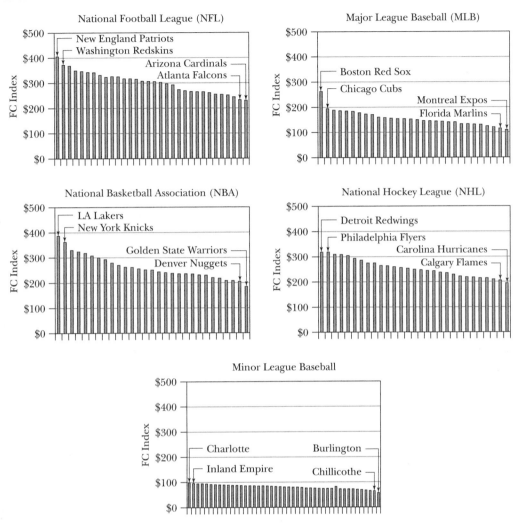

Source: Based on Information on Team Marketing Report website (Sept. 2004).

Club Branding

Branding occurs at many levels in sports including leagues, events, clubs, and players. Branding of clubs and players is an essential element of club marketing.

Branding of Clubs: Clubs with strong brand names have many commercial advantages, such as more leverage to negotiate better sponsorship deals, and higher likelihood of game-day sellouts. Clubs that understand the drivers of brand value develop a road map of ways to enhance that value.

FutureBrand, a global marketing firm, has conducted extensive research on sporting brands. It uses the following definition of brand:

A brand can be defined by identity *and* reputation.

- Identity *is the visual, verbal, audible, and environmental expression of a brand positioning—how a brand is communicated to a customer and how a customer ultimately identifies with a brand.*[3]

- Reputation *can be broken down to the promise and performance associated with product or item.*

The key brand value drivers for a sporting club were identified to be:

1. Strength of fan base
2. Management exploitation of brand
3. Long-run winning record
4. Home market strength
5. Stadium/Arena strength[4]

FutureBrand "based the value of sporting brand on its ability to generate current earnings and future earnings." Current earnings was related to leveraging the brand financially through a range of activities from team logo, merchandise sales or television rights. Future earnings was related to how strong the brand was able to continuously capture such revenue streams. Its survey evidence found that the four most important factors driving fans to support a team in the first place are:

- My parents/friends/children/others support the team (31.7%).
- My favorite player(s) play(ed) there (21.7%).
- It is my hometown team (21.7%).
- They have won trophies and titles (6.8%).

Note that on-the-field performance was fourth rather than the leading reason for fan support (or at least the fourth "admitted" reason).

Exhibit 7-4 lists two FutureBrand rankings of the brand values of sporting clubs in Europe and North America. The elite brand names in Exhibit 7-4 are underpinned by the large fan bases and management creatively exploiting multiple revenue sources from their fan base and other assets of the sporting club.

Branding of Players: Branding of players is one of the least explored areas of sports marketing. It applies to both individual athletes in team sports and athletes in individual sports such as golf and tennis. Factors relevant to building and enhancing an athlete brand include:

- Popularity of the sport
- On-field ability and consistency of performance
- Winning tradition (either of team or individual)
- Charisma/Persona

EXHIBIT 7-4   FUTUREBRAND'S RANKINGS OF MOST VALUABLE SPORTING BRANDS

Panel A: Most Valuable Brands in NFL, MLB, NBA & NHL (2002)

League	Rank/Club	Brand Value $ Millions	Overall Rank (1 = Most Valued)
NFL	1. Dallas Cowboys	$300	2
	2. Washington Redskins	192	5
	3. New York Giants	167	6
MLB	1. New York Yankees	$334	1
	2. New York Mets	135	12
	3. Boston Red Sox	111	15
NBA	1. Los Angeles Lakers	$272	3
	2. New York Knicks	238	4
	3. Chicago Bulls	156	7
NHL	1. New York Rangers	$155	8
	2. Detroit Red Wings	152	10
	3. Chicago Blackhawks	64	30

Panel B: Most Valuable Football (Soccer) Brands in Europe (2004)

Rank/Club	League	Brand Value (Euros Millions)
1. Manchester United	England	288
2. Real Madrid	Spain	278
3. AC Milan	Italy	197
4. Bayern Munich	Germany	149
5. Barcelona	Spain	141

Source: FutureBrand, *The Most Valuable Football Brands in Europe: The 2004 Report,* and *The Most Valuable Brands in Sports: The 2002 Report.*

- Public image
- Media face/talk time

Branding of individual athletes in team sports can be a juggling act. Conflicts between the individual athlete brand and the club brand can dilute the marketing power of both. An athlete with a "bad boy" image may have difficulty projecting this image in a club that promotes itself as "family friendly." Sports vary in the extent that individual athletes' facial images are exposed during broadcast time. Soccer and basketball are on one end of the spectrum while football and hockey are on the other end of the spectrum.

Section 4 introduced the topic of "players behaving badly." This behavior may in some cases reinforce a consciously developed player brand. However, in other cases, it can reduce the value of endorsement opportunities. Short of criminal or extremely offensive behavior, players' brands can rise above past behavior problems, especially if the athlete continues to be highly successful on-the-field. Winning in sports can be a deodorant for many past "smells"/problems!

CASE 7.1 VARIABLE TICKET PRICING: SHOULD THE MINNESOTA TWINS CATCH THE WAVE?[5]

Scott O'Connell, director of ticket sales for the Minnesota Twins, reviewed the pre-game ticket sales for the upcoming Tuesday-Wednesday-Thursday series to be played August 17 to 19, 2004 against the visiting New York Yankees. The Twins sat at the top of the American League Central Division. The Yankees likewise led the American League East Division. Pre-game sales were very strong, and since the advent of on-line secondary ticket companies, it was easier to get insight into the demand for premium tickets than it had been when there had been only a poorly organized scalping market. ShowMeTickets.com listed three different lots of four premium seats for the Twins-Yankees games at $260 each, well over the $35 face value. HotShotTickets.com listed two different lots of five premium tickets for $275 each $35 face-value seat. While these high markups were great for the sellers, O'Connell wondered whether something could be done by the Twins to capture more value from the high-demand games, rather than have the benefit go to ticket resellers. At present, the Twins did not charge different prices for different opponents. A ticket to a highly demanded New York Yankees game cost the same as a game for less-in-demand Tampa Bay Devil Rays.

Twins History

In 1960, Calvin Griffith, owner of the Washington Senators, decided to move his club to the Minneapolis/St. Paul ("Twin-City") area, with "Twin City" inspiring the club's new name: the Minnesota Twins. The Twins had some success early in their history. They made it to the 1965 World Series where they lost to the Dodgers, and won American League West Division pennants in 1969 and 1970. In 1987, the Twins won the World Series, and in 1988 became the first American League team to have attendance exceed 3 million. The Twins again won the World Series in 1991, accomplishing a "Worst to First" turnaround. The club struggled for the rest of the 1990s, but saw improvement at the start of the millennium. In 2001, they finished 2nd in their division. The following year they lost to the eventual 2002 World Series Champions, the Anaheim Angels, in the American League Championship Series. In 2003, the Twins won their Division but lost to the New York Yankees in the first playoff series.

Revenue Generation

The Twins consistently ranked in the bottom quarter of MLB teams in annual total revenue. Two factors were the main contributors: (a) their stadium, and (b) the size of the local market. The Twins played in the Metrodome, owned by a public entity—Metropolitan Sports Facilities Commission. It was built in 1982 at a cost of $75 million, with $55 million coming from revenue bonds. The two main tenants were the Minnesota Twins of MLB and the Minnesota Vikings of the NFL. In 2004 it was one of the few remaining stadiums housing both MLB and NFL teams—other remaining examples were the Oakland Coliseum (home to the Oakland Athletics and Oakland Raiders) and Pro Player Stadium (home to the Florida Marlins and Miami Dolphins).

The Metrodome was a multipurpose, non-retractable domed stadium, built for football and retrofitted for baseball. The capacity for baseball was approximately 50,000, but average attendance figures for the Twins in the previous three years had ranged from 22,287 to 24,025. Seating was primarily designed for the rectangular shape of a football field with the focal point on the 50-yard line. Despite this, when the stadium was filled, the indoor facility created an electric, loud atmosphere. The Twins typically sold out for their home opener. However, for the rest of the season, they averaged approximately half capacity or less.

Exhibit 1 is a seating plan of the baseball configuration for the Metrodome with details of the seven 2004 individual game and group ticket price zones. The left field seats faced the football 50-yard line instead of home plate, forcing baseball fans to rotate to the right to watch the batter. The stadium had approximately 6,600 prime seats that were sold at a premium price of $35. Many new stadiums had 13,000 to 15,000 premium priced seats. The Twins had less than 9,000 season ticket holders in 2004, one of the lowest numbers in MLB.

2004 Revenues in Sports reported that the Twins receive 100 percent of the parking revenue on game days, 100 percent of concession revenues, 50 percent of signage, and nothing from suite revenues. It noted, "At the Metrodome, the Vikings get the suite revenue, but the Twins get more than $1 million in signage revenue. Half of the signage money goes to the Metropolitan Sports Facilities Commission."[6]

MLB club revenue information was not normally disclosed to the public. However, in 2001 the Commissioner of Major League Baseball released this information in a Congressional hearing. The Minnesota Twins were reported to have the second lowest 2001 operating revenues ($56.3 million):

Local	
Ticket revenue	$17.6 million
Local media revenue	7.3
Other local revenue	7.0
National	31.9 million
National MLB Revenue	24.4
Total	$56.3 million

The New York Yankees had the highest 2001 ticket revenues ($98.0 million) while the Montreal Expos had the lowest ($6.4 million).

Likely Continuing Stadium Woes For Twins

It was well recognized that the Metrodome was "economically outmoded" for both baseball and football. However, financing new stadiums in the Twin Cities proved difficult to achieve. In the 1990s several unsuccessful attempts were made to put together a mixture of public and private financing for separate new baseball and football stadiums. Debate continued without any agreement on how to move forward. For example, in 2002 an 18-member "Stadium Task Force" made recommendations to the Minnesota State Legislature. In 2004 Minnesota Governor Pawlenty supported a new stadium bill, but it failed to pass the State Ways and Means Committee. Much as O'Connell believed in the economic benefits of a new baseball stadium, realism told him that moving to a new stadium was probably at least 5 years out.

EXHIBIT 1   MINNESOTA TWINS 2004 TICKET PRICES

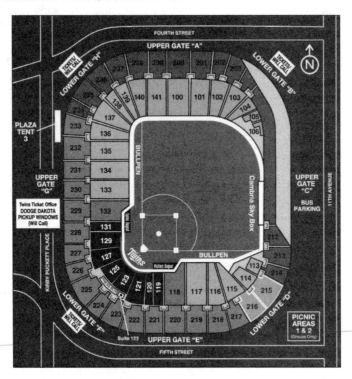

2004 Ticket Prices		
	Individual Price	**Group Price***
Lower Club:	$35	$35
Diamond View:	$33	$33
Lower Reserved:	$23	$20
Upper Club:	$15	$13
Lower Pavilion:	$15	$13
Family Section (ticket, pop):	$15	$15
Upper GA:	$6	$5

* Discounts apply to groups of 25 or more.

Source: Minnesota Twins; website is updated for each season or when prices change.

Twin Cities Professional Sports Market

The Twin Cities had teams in multiple major professional sporting leagues—MLB (Twins), NBA (Timberwolves), NFL (Vikings), NHL (Wild), and WNBA (Lynx). There was also much interest in college sports. The University of Minnesota Gophers played their college football games at the Metrodome, with an average 2003 attendance of approximately 45,000 for the

EXHIBIT 2   TWIN-CITY 2004 TICKET PRICING FOR PROFESSIONAL SPORTS

Club Arena/ When Built	League	Number of Games	Season Ticket Prices	Single Ticket Prices	Average 2003 Attendance/ (Approx Capacity)
Twins Metrodome/1982	MLB	81	$2,430 (H) 200 (L)	$ 35 (H) 6 (L)	24,025 (50,000)
Timberwolves Target Center/1990	NBA	41	$7,525 (H) 430 (L)	$375 (H) 10 (L)	15,700 (19,000)
Vikings Metrodome/1982	NFL	8 (+2 preseason)	$ 860 (H) 270 (L)	$ 94 (H) 15 (L)	64,180 (65,000)
Wild Xcel Center/2000	NHL	41	$2,924 (H) 440 (L)	$ 76 (H) 15 (L)	18,500 (18,500)
Lynx Target Center/1990	WNBA	17	$1,512 (H) 144 (L)	$ 86 (H) 8 (L)	7,074 (19,000)

Source: *2004 Revenues From Sports Revenues* (Milwaukee, Wisconsin: MediaVentures, 2004).

four conference games and 30,000 for the two non-conference games. Minneapolis-St. Paul was the 17th ranked television sized market using Nielsen Media Research estimates for the 2003–2004 television season.

While the Twins were the only men's professional sport game in town from June–August, from April–May and September–October there was significant overlap. The beginning of the baseball season corresponded with the end of the NBA and NHL seasons. When the Wild and Timberwolves were playing well enough to participate in the playoffs, many fans would have a choice between attending an important playoff game or an early season baseball game in the Metrodome. This happened in the 2003 season when on one night the Timberwolves were facing the Los Angeles Lakers in a playoff game and the Wild were in an exciting game seven of their playoff series with the St. Louis Blues. That same night the Twins faced the Devil Rays in an early season game.

Minnesota is known as the land of 10,000 lakes, and during the summer the Twins had to compete with the state's abundant outdoor activities. For example, fishing season started in early May and ran through the entire baseball season. In many cities good weather helped attendance, but in Minnesota, some Twins' fans stayed away in the summer, preferring to remain outdoors rather than be in a domed stadium.

The Twins competed with these other sports and leisure activities for a share of their fans' entertainment budget. Exhibit 2 presents summary information on 2004 ticket prices for each of the five professional sporting teams playing in the Twin City market. Season ticket prices in 2004 for non-college students for the six University of Minnesota Gophers football games at the Metrodome ranged from a high of $198 to a low of $99. Single tickets for the conference games ranged from a high of $40 per game to a low of $20 per game.

Demand Based Pricing

Given the importance of ticket sales to the Twins revenue, and their large swings in attendance, O'Connell was interested in a more flexible, demand based pricing system. Demand based pricing was a simple type of variable ticket pricing where tickets for games that generate more demand were sold at a higher price. Variable ticket pricing was most prevalent in the airline industry. Airlines called their strategy "revenue yield management," and it was based mostly on the timing of the ticket purchase and the demand for a certain route. For most airlines, proper yield management was critical to their success.

The Twins had many options on how to implement a demand based pricing scheme:

By Opponent. Ticket prices could be based on the level of fan interest in the opposing team. Exhibit 3 outlines 2003 data on the 81 home games of the Twins, showing average attendance varying from a high of 34,529 against the Toronto Blue Jays to a low of

EXHIBIT 3   MINNESOTA TWINS 2003 HOME GAMES ATTENDANCE

Opponent	Average Attendance	Games
Toronto Blue Jays	34,529	3
Arizona Diamondbacks	28,965	3
New York Yankees	28,411	4
Chicago White Sox	27,857	9
Kansas City Royals	25,067	10
Milwaukee Brewers	25,014	3
Cleveland Indians	24,734	10
Boston Red Sox	23,474	3
Detroit Tigers	23,095	9
Oakland Athletics	22,391	6
Texas Rangers	22,220	3
Baltimore Orioles	21,813	3
Seattle Mariners	21,812	6
Colorado Rockies	18,277	3
Anaheim Angels	15,583	3
Tampa Bay Devil Rays	13,585	3
Grand Total	24,022	81

Day of Week	Average Attendance	Games
Monday	19,770	5
Tuesday	20,318	12
Wednesday	22,499	12
Thursday	21,823	13
Friday	28,341	13
Saturday	28,017	13
Sunday	24,370	13
Grand Total	24,022	81

Month	Average Attendance	Games
April	23,771	12
May	20,151	16
June	23,274	13
July	22,217	15
August	28,983	11
September	27,395	14
Grand Total	24,022	81

EXHIBIT 3 (continued)

2003 DETAILED ATTENDANCE

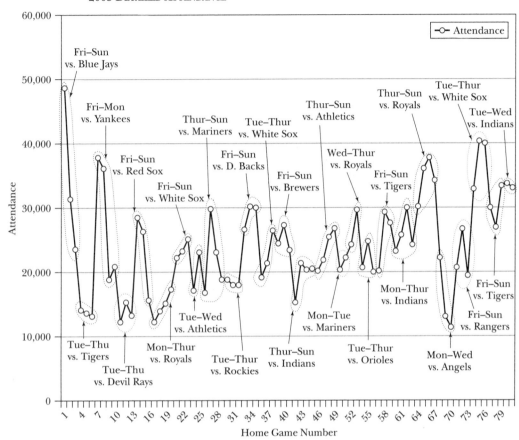

13,585 against the Tampa Bay Devil Rays. The Blue Jays played the Twins in the season opener, Friday April 4, Saturday April 5th and Sunday April 6th. The New York Yankees consistently drew above-average attendance. The Twins intra-divisional rivals (Chicago White Sox, Cleveland Indians, Detroit Tigers and Kansas City Royals) also traditionally draw well.

In 2004, the Twins charged the same price for each opponent. O'Connell was aware other teams were experimenting with higher prices for games with stronger drawing visitors. The New York Mets classified games into Gold, Silver, Bronze or Value categories. These categories are based on the opposing team as well as the time of year and day of week. 2004 Gold dates included "weekend dates with cross-town rival Yankees, World Champion Marlins, and Division Champion Braves and Chicago Cubs, along with Opening Day and Fireworks night on July 16th." Examples of 2004 price differences across the four categories for the same seat were:

Seating Zone	Game Category			
	Gold	Silver	Bronze	Value
Inner Field Box	$53	$48	$43	$38
Outer Field Box	39	36	33	30
Upper Box	27	25	23	19
Upper Reserved	16	14	12	5

The New York Mets used the value-based ticket prices for games with the Montreal Expos, Milwaukee Brewers, Cleveland Indians, and San Diego Padres. Such variable pricing was not without its critics. Phil Mushnick of the New York Post argued strongly against it, saying, "The notion that all Braves-Mets games will provide more satisfaction than all Brewers-Mets games thus Braves-Mets tickets should cost more is a ridiculous one. . . . Where is the media on this? Where is its outrage? Where's its sense of consumerism, its sense of sport and plain, old-fashioned fair play?[7]

By Day-of-the-Week. This version of variable pricing has many variants. One approach was to systematically price weekend games higher than mid-week games. The San Francisco Giants priced Friday, Saturday, and Sunday games higher than Monday thru Thursday games. The 2004 Giants single price tickets for the same seat in selected seating zones were:

Seating Zone	Friday to Sunday	Monday to Thursday
AAA Club Infield	$65	$60
AAA Club Outfield	50	47
AAA Club Left Field	45	40
Lower Box	34	32
Bleachers	21	16
Standing Room	12	10

By Month of Year. Some times of the year were more attractive for fans, which could be built into a variable pricing program. The Colorado Rockies classified home games into one of four categories for pricing purposes—Marquee, Classic, Premium, and Value. Marquee games were the highest price and include the July 4th fireworks game and the Boston Red Sox games in 2004 (as Boston was visiting the Rockies for the first time). Opening day was in the Classic category. Games in July, and August games were classified in the Premium category, while games in April, May and September were classified in the value category. Examples of pricing differences for the same seat in August and September games in 2004 are:

Seating Zone	August (Premium)	September (Value)
Infield Club	$41	$41
Lower Reserved Infield	24	18
Rightfield Box	20	14
Upper Reserved Corner	15	9

Regular Promotions

While the Twins in 2004 did not adopt variable pricing by opponent, day-of-the-week, or month-of-the-year, it did have a rich array of promotions/special packages regularly available for its fans. The "Continuity Programs" available to fans in 2004 included:

Monday. Star Tribune "Every Fan Counts" ticket offer featured a five-dollar off coupon printed in that Monday's newspaper good towards all price level seats.

Tuesday. McDonald's "Half Price Night" offered half-price on $15 lower pavilion seats. Included was a "buy one get one free" coupon for a McDonald's McGriddle.

Wednesday. Davanni's (pizza) Student Night half-price upper deck general admission tickets to students with an active school ID. Plus bounce back coupon to Davanni's.

Thursday. WCCO TV Bargain Night featured one Lower Pavilion seat and a $5 food voucher for $15 (compared with a normal value of $20).

Friday. Cub Foods Value Pack featured Lower Pavilion ticket, Hormel hot dog, soft drink for $16.

Saturday. Dairy Queen Family Pack featured a Lower Pavilion Seat, Papa John's personal pan pizza, soft drink, and a bounce back coupon from Dairy Queen for $16.

Sunday. SuperAmerica Kids Day in the Lower Pavilion features kid's tickets at $4 and adult's full price.

Resale of Tickets By Season Ticket Holders

As O'Connell struggled with the problem of filling the Metrodome, he also saw another potential application of demand based pricing. Despite the fact that the Twins rarely sold out, there was an active secondary market for some of the better seats in the stadium. Many of these seats commanded significant premiums to face value, but the Twins did not capture any of the revenue from the resale of tickets. There were multiple on-line options available to Twins ticket holders to resell their tickets, such as ShowMeTickets.com and HotShotTickets.com. Transactions on these on-line services highlighted how much money potentially was being left on the table by the Twins policy of not playing a role in ticket reselling.

A number of baseball teams, including the Giants, Red Sox, Cardinals, Mariners, Cubs and Diamondbacks, had implemented season ticket exchanges to allow fans to buy and sell season tickets. These exchanges had realized varying degrees of success. The Giants "Double Play Ticket Window" had been highly successful. It facilitated the resale of seats previously paid for by their season ticket holders. The Giants allowed the seller to set the price greater than face value. The Giants charged the buyer and the seller a commission on the sale. The benefits of this program potentially included higher renewal rates from season ticket holders (who had fewer "unused tickets in the drawer") as well as additional commission-based revenues.

Original Sale of Tickets By Teams at Market-Determined Prices

Attempts by the teams themselves to move to market-based variable pricing for initial ticket sales had met with resistance. In the 2003 season, both the Chicago Cubs and the Seattle Mariners began testing programs to let the market determine the price of some of their tickets. The Mariners implemented their program by offering some of their unsold charter tickets (premium seats located directly behind the dugouts) for sale on a per game basis. The tickets were previously only sold as part of season ticket packages. The Mariners planned to put as many as 111 charter seats up for sale for whatever price the market would bear. The program realized some early success with the club selling 1,800 club seats on a per game basis through the first 3 months of the 2003 season.[8] However, the Mariners were criticized for pushing the envelope on scalping laws. One fan was quoted as saying: "It's kind of hypocritical. I don't see how they can sit back and say that it's not scalping whether it's on the Web site or the corner of Royal Brougham . . . They (the M's) can sell it for more than $32 and I can't. I'll get arrested."[9]

The Mariners experiment may have opened up a new set of competition from previously illegal scalping. In January 2004 a Seattle judge overturned convictions of two ticket scalpers saying that the Mariners were engaging in the same conduct online.[10]

The Chicago Cubs faced an even more severe backlash when they started their own legal ticket broker, Wrigley Field Premium Ticket Services, and began selling tickets at above face value. These tickets were from the Cubs' own inventory and not from season ticket holders reselling their previously purchased tickets. When the New York Yankees visited the Chicago Cubs in 2003 (the first such visit since the 1938 World Series), individual tickets were listed from $200 to $745 on Wrigley Field Premium Ticket Services.[11] Legal ticket brokers in Chicago went so far as to file suit against the Cubs. The lawsuit was eventually dismissed in November 2003, but the lawsuit raised questions about how accepting fans would be of teams trying to sell their own tickets at above face value.

Decision Time

While demand-based pricing seemed like a good idea on paper, O'Connell had questions about how to apply it for the Twins. Given that the Twins were usually only at half capacity, he wondered if he should be using demand-based pricing to reduce prices in low demand sections throughout the stadium. Seats that were facing centerfield and seats that are high in the upper deck were always a tough sell. He was skeptical of assuming what worked well in other parks would have similar success at the Metrodome. For example, The San Francisco Giants had a relatively new stadium (SBC Park, with a capacity of 41,584) in a relatively large market (5th ranked television market using Nielsen data). The Giants had a high number of season ticket holders, and there was a scarcity factor associated with good tickets to Giants home games. The Twins faced a different situation. Most games had large numbers of unsold tickets, even at prices 40 percent and more below those charged by the Giants.

O'Connell wondered if building more flexibility into the pricing system could help him increase game-day revenue. He already offered a variety of season ticket and multi-game packages at different prices as well as seven tiers of pricing for any individual game. The Twins also sold about 1,300 upper deck season ticket packages for just $200 for all 81 home games. How would reducing ticket prices for sections that never sold out affect attendance and game-day concession and merchandise revenue? How would any dramatic discounting affect the perceived value of other seats in the stadium or the sale of tickets for games when the seats weren't discounted?

Questions

1. What are the different forms of variable ticket pricing?
2. Evaluate the main arguments used to oppose variable pricing. Distinguish between arguments based on opposing it on principle and arguments based on difficulties in its implementation.
3. Evaluate the main arguments used to justify variable pricing.
4. Assume the Minnesota Twins decide to adopt variable pricing. Recommend the approach they should use. Include in your analysis how the Twins should justify the chosen approach.

CASE 7.2 THE "FRIENDLY FENWAY" PROGRAM: THE VALUE OF EXPERIENCE ENHANCEMENT[12]

*Of course team performance in the field is the key driver of revenues. But the calibre of the fan experience **beyond** team performance adds to revenues and asset value.*

—Larry Cancro, Vice President Sales-Marketing, Boston Red Sox

In 1997, Boston Red Sox marketing head Larry Cancro was reviewing the "Friendly Fenway" fan satisfaction program that had been instituted several years before.

The Boston Red Sox

The Boston Red Sox are one of the most well-known franchises in professional sports, and also one of New England's most familiar institutions. The team's Fenway Park home, first opened in 1912, is one of the most recognizable venues in sports, particularly its 37-foot left-field wall (the "Green Monster") topped by a large screen. According to consumer research, many baseball fans consider Fenway Park to be "a shrine." It is a major tourist attraction for many summer visitors to Boston, and the team conducts group tours of the ballpark. Some marketing experts characterize Fenway Park as another "brand" in addition to the team itself.

Through the years, the Boston Red Sox team has had peaks and valleys in terms of winning. After being one of the American League's dominant teams in the league's first two decades through 1918, the sale of star pitcher-outfielder Babe Ruth to the New York Yankees ushered in a long period of second-division performance; this included nine last place finishes in eleven years ending in 1932.

The purchase of the team by Thomas Yawkey in 1933 soon signaled a new era for the team, particularly through acquiring many high quality future Hall of Fame players, such as pitcher Lefty Grove, slugger Jimmy Foxx, and shortstop and player-manager Joe Cronin. In addition, there was a reconstruction and modernization for Fenway Park. Often contenders in the 1930s and 1940s, the Red Sox's first pennant since 1918 came in 1946 (the first year of post-war baseball) when the legendary Ted Williams (baseball's last .400 hitter) led the team to 104 wins, never achieved since (although 8 more games are played now). In that year, and in 1967 ("the Impossible Dream" team), 1975 (Carlton Fisk's oft-viewed World Series Game Six homerun), and 1986 (Bill Buckner's notorious error), American League pennant-winning Red Sox teams lost the World Series to National League teams 4 games to 3. In 1988, 1990, and 1995 the Red Sox won division championships but were defeated in American League post-season play. Thus the team has had long periods of performance drought (notably the 1920s and 1960s), recent regularly very competitive teams, a few division and league champions, but no World Championship since 1918.

Fenway Park

Fenway Park is the smallest park in the major leagues, with a seating capacity of less than 34,000. It remains basically a single-deck park, with a modest number of rooftop seats and

Harvard Business School Case No 9-599-035. Copyright 1999 President and Fellows of Harvard College. All rights reserved. For information: permission@hbsp.harvard.edu. This case was prepared by Stephen A. Greyser. HBS cases are developed solely for class discussion and do not necessarily illustrate effective or ineffective management.

private suites built in 1982–3, but not a full upper deck. Some 610 club seats were constructed above the grandstand behind home plate in 1988–9. Although the small size prevents large crowds for very desirable games (e.g., vs. the New York Yankees), it helps sell season tickets and early-season purchase of seats for later games, because of the threat of scarcity. In fact, Red Sox home attendance has been strong since 1967 when it reached 1.7 million. Starting in the mid-1980s, attendance topped 2,000,000 per year except for the 1994 season shortened by the work stoppage caused by management/player conflict. Three times, attendance exceeded 2.5 million, well over 90% of capacity. Nonetheless in 1996, about one quarter of the 81 individual home dates drew less than 25,000; four of these drew under 20,000. Fans came from throughout New England (and beyond). The nearest major league franchises were in New York City; the latter drew many fans from Connecticut.

Although very high as a percentage of capacity, Red Sox total home attendance trailed that of franchises with very new stadiums, such as Toronto (which sold out its 50,000 per game capacity for several years); Baltimore; Texas; and Cleveland (which sold out all its seats before the season's start in 1996 and 1997). These franchises thus had an economic advantage of size over the Red Sox, in addition to more potential revenue from luxury boxes and premium-priced seats. The Red Sox ownership had recently expressed a strong interest in building a new facility in Boston with 40%–50% more seats than in Fenway Park, including substantial additional luxury box and club (premium-priced) seating. Management cited an area adjacent to Fenway Park as the preferred location.

The price of Red Sox tickets had been increasing steadily in the wake of rapid growth in player payrolls. For 1997, the price of field box seats was $26, upper boxes (i.e., further back from the field) $21, reserved grandstand $16, and bleachers $9. Red Sox season ticket plans included full season (all 81 home games), nights (approximately 52 games), and weekends/holidays (about 28 games).

All Red Sox games were broadcast on radio on a network covering New England. All non-national network games were televised, some on local broadcast TV and many on the NESN cable network (80% owned by the Red Sox). Most of the latter games were rebroadcast late that night and/or early the next morning.

Information about Fenway Park and Red Sox attendance appears as **Exhibits 1** through **4.**

Cancro's Views

Larry Cancro had joined the Red Sox in 1985 after six years with the Atlanta Braves, where he had managed group sales and merchandise operations. He was responsible for creating MLB's first mail order catalog of team merchandise. His Red Sox responsibilities over the years had grown to encompass food services and concessions, promotions, advertising, ticket sales (including premium sales) and operations, and fan research. He is a graduate of Boston University with a degree in psychology.

As marketing head of the Red Sox, Larry Cancro knew that revenues from game attendance, season ticket purchases, food and beverage sales, and souvenir sales were important to the team's ability to compete in the increasingly expensive player re-signing and free agent market. He also wanted to attract some season ticket-holders as well as Red Sox business partners and others to buy seats in the special 600 Club (above the stands, behind home plate); these

EXHIBIT 1   A VIEW OF FENWAY PARK FROM ABOVE THE HISTORIC LEFT-FIELD WALL

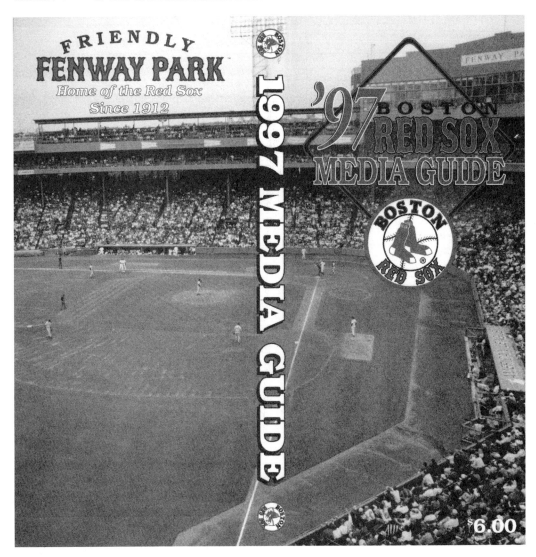

600+ seats (with dining and bar privileges) cost about three times as much as field box seats and had to be purchased for a full 81-game season.

[Sponsorships, several Red Sox retail outlets, and licensed merchandise are beyond the specific scope of this case.]

Cancro believed in consumer and customer service, and he thought that more active marketing and improved customer service initiatives would result in more revenue through increased fan satisfaction. He thus developed the "Friendly Fenway" [registered] program.

EXHIBIT 2   RED SOX YEAR-BY-YEAR AND HOME ATTENDANCE TOTAL 1960–1996

RED SOX YEAR-BY-YEAR

Year	Pos.	W - L	Pct.	GA GB	Manager	Attendance
1996	3E	85 - 77	.525	7	Kevin C. Kennedy	2,315,231
1995	1E	86 - 58	.597	7	Kevin C. Kennedy	2,164,410
1994	4E	54 - 61	.470	17	Clell L. Hobson	1,775,818
1993	5E	80 - 82	.494	15	Clell L. Hobson	2,422,021
1992	7E	73 - 89	.451	23	Clell L. Hobson	2,468,574
1991	2TE	84 - 78	.519	7	Joseph M. Morgan	2,562,435
1990	1E	88 - 74	.543	2	Joseph M. Morgan	2,528,986
1989	3E	83 - 79	.512	6	Joseph M. Morgan	2,510,012
1988	1E	89 - 73	.549	1	McNamara, Joseph M. Morgan	2,464,851
1987	5E	78 - 84	.481	20	John F. McNamara	2,231,551
1986	1E§	95 - 66	.590	5½	John F. McNamara	2,147,641
1985	5E	81 - 81	.500	18½	John F. McNamara	1,786,633
1984	4E	86 - 76	.531	18	Ralph G. Houk	1,661,618
1983	6E	78 - 84	.481	20	Ralph G. Houk	1,782,285
1982	3E	89 - 73	.549	6	Ralph G. Houk	1,950,124
1981	5E†	59 - 49	.546	2½†	Ralph G. Houk	1,060,379
	2TE	29 - 23	.558	1½	second half	
	5E	30 - 26	.536	4	first half	
1980	4E	83 - 77	.519	19	Zimmer, John M. Pesky	1,956,092
1979	3E	91 - 69	.569	11½	Donald W. Zimmer	2,353,114
1978	2E	99 - 64	.607	1	Donald W. Zimmer	2,320,643
1977	2TE	97 - 64	.602	2½	Donald W. Zimmer	2,074,549
1976	3E	83 - 79	.512	15½	Johnson, Donald W. Zimmer	1,895,846
1975	1E§	95 - 65	.594	4½	Darrell D. Johnson	*1,748,587
1974	3E	84 - 78	.519	7	Darrell D. Johnson	*1,566,411
1973	2E	89 - 73	.549	8	Edward M. Kasko	1,481,002
1972	2E	85 - 70	.548	½	Edward M. Kasko	1,441,718
1971	3E	85 - 77	.525	18	Edward M. Kasko	*1,678,732
1970	3E	87- 75	.537	21	Edward M. Kasko	*1,595,278
1969	3E	87- 75	.537	22	Williams, Edward J. Popowski	*1,833,246
1968	4	86 - 76	.531	17	Richard H. Williams	1,940,788
1967	1	92 - 70	.568	1	Richard H. Williams	*1,727,832
1966	9	72 - 90	.444	26	Herman, James E. (Pete) Runnels	811,172
1965	9	62 - 100	.383	40	William J. Herman	652,201
1964	8	72 - 90	.444	27	Pesky, William J. Herman	883,276
1963	7	76 - 85	.472	28	John M. Pesky	942,642
1962	8	76 - 84	.475	19	Michael F. Higgins	733,080
1961	6	76 - 86	.469	33	Michael F. Higgins	850,589
1960	7	65 - 89	.422	32	Jurges, Higgins, Del Baker	1,129,866

§Won A.L.C.S.

†Overall record

*Led league

Source: '97 Boston Red Sox Media Guide

EXHIBIT 3 ᴀᴍᴇʀɪᴄᴀɴ Lᴇᴀɢᴜᴇ Aᴛᴛᴇɴᴅᴀɴᴄᴇ (ʙʏ ᴛᴇᴀᴍ) 1991–1996

AMERICAN LEAGUE 6-YEAR ATTENDANCE

	AVG.	1996	1995	1994	1993	1992	1991
Toronto	3.40M	2,559,573	2,826,483	2,907,933	4,057,947	4,028,318	4,001,527
Baltimore	3.17M	3,646,950	3,098,475	2,535,359	3,644,965	3,567,819	2,552,753
Texas	2.35M	2,889,020	1,985,910	2,503,198	2,244,616	2,198,231	2,297,720
Boston	2.28M	2,315,231	2,164,378	1,775,818	2,422,021	2,468,574	2,562,435
Chicago	2.20M	1,676,403	1,609,773	1,697,398	2,581,091	2,681,156	2,934,154
Cleveland	2.10M	3,318,174	2,842,725	1,995,174	2,177,908	1,224,274	1,051,863
California	1.94M	1,820,521	1,748,680	1,512,622	2,057,460	2,065,444	2,416,236
New York	1.94M	2,250,877	1,705,257	1,675,556	2,416,965	1,748,733	1,863,733
Seattle	1.89M	2,723,850	1,640,992	1,104,206	2,051,853	1,651,398	2,147,905
Oakland	1.80M	1,148,380	1,174,310	1,242,692	2,035,025	2,494,160	2,713,493
Minnesota	1.79M	1,437,352	1,057,667	1,398,565	2,048,673	2,482,428	2,293,842
Kansas City	1.67M	1,435,997	1,232,969	1,400,494	1,934,578	1,867,689	2,161,537
Milwaukee	1.45M	1,327,155	1,087,560	1,268,399	1,688,080	1,857,314	1,478,729
Detroit	1.43M	1,168,610	1,180,979	1,184,783	1,971,421	1,423,963	1,641,661
Lg. Totals	29.4M	29,718,093	25,356,158	24,202,197	33,332,603	31,759,501	32,117,588

Source: *'97 Boston Red Sox Media Guide*

With top management support, the activity encompassed task forces of staff members focused on suggesting improvements in different areas of the fan experience (e.g., security, concessions, look of the park); an extensive research program; and a search for ideas from other parks and teams.

In focusing on improving the fan experience, Cancro recognized that there was a somewhat fragile foundation for the active delivery of many components of consumer service at the ballpark. For example, during the season, there were hundreds of day-of-game staff, including ticket-takers, ushers, some security people, and vendors at concession stations and in the stands. Beyond the day-of-game people, some staff were seasonal, e.g., some ticket-selling employees. The vending staff, including its management personnel, worked for Aramark (a national venue food operations firm), not the Red Sox. However, to the fan, everyone working at the park was seen as working for the Red Sox, whether or not they were personally paid by the Red Sox.

A few initiatives in the program were undertaken in 1994, more in 1995 and 1996. This included a website and "fan chats" with General Manager Dan Duquette. Typical questions addressed the status of injured players, where new players would play (or share playing time), minor league player progress, Duquette's philosophy of player development and free agent signings, players' contract negotiations, and coaches.

In-season changes were made in the program, as well as between-season ones. As described in the two-page summary of the presentation made about the "Friendly Fenway" program at the December 1996 baseball meetings, the goal was to enhance the total fan experience. (See **Exhibit 5.**)

EXHIBIT 4   1996 Red Sox Home Attendance (day by day)

1996 RED SOX HOME ATTENDANCE

Date No.	Date	Day	D-N	Opp.	Game No.	Attendance	Series	Season
1	4/09	Tue.	D	Minn.	1	30,812		30,812
2	4/11	Thur.	D	Minn.	2	15,594	46,406	46,406
3	4/12	Fri.	N	Clev.	3	26,703		73,109
4	4/13	Sat.	D	Clev.	4	31,827		104,936
5	4/14	Sun.	D	Clev.	5	31,796		136,732
6	4/15	Mon.	D	Clev.	6	32,861	123,187	169,593
7	4/24	Wed.	N	Tex.	7	19,217		188,810
8	4/25	Thur.	N	Tex.	8	20,350	39,567	209,160
9	4/26	Fri.	N	KC	9	22,385		231,545
10	4/27	Sat.	D	KC	10	29,455		261,000
11	4/28	Sun.	D	KC	11	32,485	84,325	293,485
12	4/30	Tue.	N	Det.	12	18,504		311,989
13	5/01	Wed.	N	Det.	13	20,828		332,817
14	5/03	Fri.	N	Tor.	14	25,507		358,324
15	5/04	Sat.	D	Tor.	15	29,785		388,109
16	5/05	Sun.	D	Tor.	16	29,866	85,158	417,975
17	5/14	Tue.	N	Cal.	17	22,450		440,425
18	5/15	Wed.	N	Cal.	18	23,455	45,905	463,880
19	5/17	Fri.	N	Oak.	19	28,690		492,570
20	5/18	Sat.	D	Oak.	20	31,663		524,233
21	5/19	Sun.	D	Oak.	21	32,601		556,834
22	5/20	Mon.	N	Oak.	22	20,890	113,844	577,724
23	5/21	Tue.	N	Sea.	23	24,528		602,252
24	5/22	Wed.	N	Sea.	24	26,753		629,005
25	5/23	Thur.	N	Sea.	25	31,551	82,832	660,556
26	6/04	Tue.	N	Chi.	26	23,715		684,271
27	6/05	Wed.	N	Chi.	27	24,248		708,519
28	6/06	Thur.	N	Chi.	28	24,382	72,345	732,901
29	6/07	Fri.	N	Milw.	29	26,861		759,762
30	6/08	Sat.	D	Milw.	30	30,399		790,161
31	6/09	Sun.	D	Milw.	31	28,120	85,380	818,281
32	6/13	Thur.	N	Tex.	32	32,645		850,926
33	6/14	Fri.	N	Tex.	33	29,689		880,615
34	6/15	Sat.	N	Tex.	34	33,186		913,801
35	6/16	Sun.	D	Tex.	35	30,461	125,981	944,262
36	6/25	Tue.	N	Clev.	36	33,576		977,838
37	6/26	Wed.	N	Clev.	37	33,727	67,303	1,011,565
38	6/27	Thur.	N	Det.	38	29,582		1,041,147
39	6/28	Fri.	N	Det.	39	27,578		1,068,725
40	6/29	Sat.	N	Det.	40	33,509		1,102,234
41	6/30	Sun.	D	Det.	41	31,217	121,886	1,133,451

1996 RED SOX HOME ATTENDANCE

Date No.	Date	Day	D-N	Opp.	Game No.	Attendance	Series	Season
42	7/15	Mon.	N	NY	42	33,263		1,166,714
43	7/16	Tue.	N	NY	43	34,676		1,201,390
44	7/17	Wed.	N	NY	44	34,082	102,021	1,235,472
45	7/18	Thur.	N	Balt.	45	33,014		1,268,486
46	7/19	Fri.	N	Balt.	46	32,262		1,300,748
47	7/20	Sat.	D	Balt.	47	33,590		1,334,338
48	7/21	Sun.	D	Balt.	48	34,423	133,289	1,368,761
49	7/22	Mon.	N	KC	49	28,109		1,396,870
50	7/23	Tue.	N	KC	50	23,711		1,420,581
51	7/24	Wed.	N	KC	51	33,381	85,201	1,453,962
52	8/02	Fri.	N	Minn.	52	28,041		1,482,003
53	8/03	Sat.	D	Minn.	53	19,860		1,501,863
	8/03	Sat.	N	Minn.	54	29,135		1,530,998
54	8/04	Sun.	D	Minn.	55	29,939	106,975	1,560,937
55	8/05	Mon.	N	Tor.	56	23,884		1,584,821
56	8/06	Tue.	N	Tor.	57	25,264		1,610,085
57	8/07	Wed.	N	Tor.	58	30,442		1,640,527
58	8/08	Thur.	D	Tor.	59	32,696	112,286	1,673,223
59	8/16	Fri.	N	Cal.	60	30,689		1,703,912
60	8/17	Sat.	D	Cal.	61	32,497		1,736,409
61	8/18	Sun.	N	Cal.	62	25,224		1,761,633
62	8/19	Mon.	N	Cal.	63	25,779	114,189	1,787,412
63	8/20	Tue.	N	Oak.	64	25,094		1,812,506
64	8/21	Wed.	N	Oak.	65	26,362		1,838,868
65	8/22	Thur.	N	Oak.	66	30,503	81,959	1,869,371
66	8/23	Fri.	N	Sea.	67	33,079		1,902,450
67	8/24	Sat.	D	Sea.	68	32,928		1,935,378
68	8/25	Sun.	D	Sea.	69	34,370	100,377	1,969,748
69	9/09	Mon.	N	Milw.	70	22,386		1,992,134
70	9/10	Tue.	N	Milw.	71	20,487		2,012,621
71	9/11	Wed.	N	Milw.	72	21,308	64,181	2,033,929
72	9/13	Fri.	N	Chi.	73	28,907		2,062,836
73	9/14	Sat.	D	Chi.	74	31,841		2,094,677
74	9/15	Sun.	D	Chi.	75	32,452	93,200	2,127,129
75	9/24	Tue.	N	Balt.	76	28,557		2,155,686
76	9/25	Wed.	N	Balt.	77	28,432	56,989	2,184,118
77	9/26	Thur.	N	NY	78	32,367		2,216,485
78	9/27	Fri.	N	NY	79	32,573		2,249,058
79	9/28	Sat.	D	NY	80	33,610		2,282,668
80	9/29	Sun.	D	NY	81	32,563	131,113	2,315,231

Source: '97 Boston Red Sox Media Guide.

EXHIBIT 5 THE MARKETING PROGRAM THAT MADE FENWAY PARK "FRIENDLY FENWAY" (TWO-PAGE SUMMARY OF PRESENTATION AT DECEMBER 1996 BASEBALL MEETINGS, BY STEPHEN A. GREYSER AND LARRY CANCRO.)

Summary of Presentation

THE MARKETING PROGRAM THAT MADE
FENWAY PARK "FRIENDLY FENWAY"

Professor Stephen A. Greyser, Harvard Business School
Larry Cancro, Boston Red Sox
Baseball Meetings, Boston, December 1996

The "Friendly Fenway" program is first and foremost a *fan experience-enhancement program* undertaken by the Boston Red Sox for fans at Fenway Park. Beyond that, it is a "way of doing business" intended to extend the Friendly Fenway concept through broadcasts, community relations, and business relationships with Red Sox marketing partners.

The essence of the Friendly Fenway program is "customer service and satisfaction for a services customer." By "customer," we mean both individual game consumers, season ticket-holders, and luxury box customers—i.e., consumers and business-to-business customers of the Red Sox. We recognize that the dominant driver of fan satisfaction comes from a winning team on the field. However, we believe that the experience at the park also is a significant source of fan satisfaction. Further, that fan satisfaction can manifest itself in added revenues—from more fans, more money spent per visit (e.g., concessions, souvenirs), more games per fan, better word-of-mouth, and to some extent increased probability of buying season tickets.

The "Friendly Fenway" program is driven by marketing and fan/customer orientation. It has support from the very top of the organization (particularly Executive Vice President John Buckley and CEO John Harrington) and involves many staff members in proposing and considering new initiatives to improve the fan experience. It is rooted in extensive fan research with individual game consumers and season ticket-holders. It is reflected in efforts at continuous improvement, so in-season changes are made as well as between-season ones.

What do we mean by "the total experience" mentioned above? The total experience encompasses ticket buying, signage to ease the task of finding one's seat, ushers, security, scorecards and souvenirs, and concessions (both at stands and at one's seat). (Note that parking is *not* on this list; it is basically not controlled by the Red Sox unlike the case for many clubs.) Not all of those who deliver these services are full-time staff or in some instances even employees of the Red Sox. But to the fans, *everyone* who works at Fenway Park works for the Red Sox; management's recognition of this is a central element in developing and implementing the "Friendly Fenway" program.

To try to understand the Fenway fan experience, we undertook comprehensive fan research. This encompassed both specific assessment of different facets of the experience via in-park questionnaires (mostly using four-point scales) as well as open-end exploration of suggestions for change. We also did some limited comparison with analogous information from other teams. Thousands of completed questionnaires were returned in our 1994, 1995, and 1996 (largest of all) studies.

From the research, we can track fans' ratings of individual attributes (e.g., courtesy of ushers, and price/value relationship of concessions) of entire zones (e.g., food and beverage stands, the ticket office); and also the "overall experience" (other than game results). We can also analyze the data by light/medium/and frequent attendees, etc. We can also examine mid-summer vs. late-season ratings, and year vs. year assessments. We know there is always room for improvement—e.g., increases in the excellent + good percentage, increases in the excellent percentage, reduction in the poor percentage, etc. We often focus on specific problem areas, including inputs from both fans and staff groups dedicated to those areas.

What are some of the initiatives that have become part of the "Friendly Fenway" program? In 1994, organized tours were begun, on the field and behind the scenes. Also a spruced-up "look" was given to the interior and exterior of the park, including banners along the adjacent streets. Significant changes in concessions came in 1995, especially branded foods and more efficient service. A "Fanfest" was also mounted. Changes in 1996 included smoke-free stands and further improved concessions, and a Red Sox Website (including an interactive session for computer-using fans with GM Dan Duquette).

By way of reminder, we know that team performance on the field is the main element driving revenues and increased asset value. But we also know that the fan experience *beyond* team performance can add to revenues and enhance the franchise's asset value. We believe that the "Friendly Fenway" program truly helps make going to Fenway Park a very special experience.

* * * * *

Larry Cancro is Vice President, Marketing and Sales of the Boston Red Sox. A graduate of Boston University, he worked with the Atlanta Braves for 6 years during which time he created baseball's first mail order catalog of team merchandise. In 1985, he joined the Red Sox, where he oversees all ticket sales functions, promotions, advertising, and food services. He chairs MLB's Research Committee. He has the primary responsibility for the "Friendly Fenway" program.

Stephen A. Greyser is Richard P. Chapman Professor at Harvard Business School, specializing in consumer marketing and corporate communications. He is responsible for 12 books, numerous articles, and some 250 published case studies. He has been active as a corporate board member; non-profit trustee; and consultant in the advertising, marketing, and sports management fields, including work with the Boston Red Sox. At HBS, he teaches MBA courses on Corporate Communications and the Business of Sports and executive seminars in non-profit management. A former three-sport sports broadcaster, for seven years he also wrote and produced a Red Sox pre-game radio fan participation quiz program at Fenway Park.

In the winter of 1997, Cancro was reviewing the program. He knew there was more still to do to increase fan satisfaction at Fenway Park—from the ticket-buying process to directions to the park to finding one's seat, etc. He also knew there were constraints on what could be done in a facility built in 1912 with limited space to implement what in new parks was standard (e.g., more backroom space for concessions, team-controlled parking, team-managed outdoor vendors).

His experience and philosophy supported the concept that it was valuable to enhance the fan experience. The "brands" of Fenway Park and the Red Sox were valuable, leverageable assets in doing so. But major questions remained: Was the model of basic revenue (**Exhibit 6**) incorporated in the presentation really valid? Could he determine the contribution the Friendly Fenway program was making?

As he considered these questions, he recognized the special enthusiasm New England fans had for the Red Sox, particularly when the team played well. The coming season marked the 30th anniversary of one of the team's most memorable performances, by the "Impossible Dream Team" in 1967. (The eventual six-page souvenir pamphlet for the anniversary, prepared by Harvard Business School Professor Stephen A. Greyser, was entitled "And All New England Cheered." It chronicled the emotional and competitive highlights of the season and its key players, the team's second-half surge, and the dramatic last-game victory that won the pennant in the closest multi-team pennant race since 1908. The Red Sox had finished the previous season 18 games under .500, in ninth place in the then one-division ten-team league. The 1967 team's nickname, "The Impossible Dream Team," and its anthem, were from the Broadway hit of that name based on Cervantes' fictional hero Don Quixote.) Cancro also had to take into account an additional question: How important to fan satisfaction—even in a special place like Fenway Park—is team performance?

EXHIBIT 6   **BASIC REVENUE MODEL**

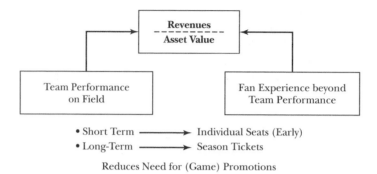

• Short Term ⟶ Individual Seats (Early)
• Long-Term ⟶ Season Tickets

Reduces Need for (Game) Promotions

Going to Park as "An Experience"

Impacts on Ancillary Revenues:
  - Concessions
  - At-Park Merchandise
  - Out-of-Park Merchandise
  - Broadcast

Questions

1. What is your opinion of the concept of the "Friendly Fenway" program as a fan experience enhancement program?

2. How, if at all, does the program impact on revenues? In your view, is the model and the effect shown in Exhibit 6 accurate? How important do you think team performance is? What level of team performance do you think Red Sox fans expect? (Across MLB, consider four basic levels: top tier, competitive/upper middle, might become competitive, bottom tier.)

3. How does one measure and evaluate this kind of program? What criteria and measures would you use?

4. How would you go about determining the financial value of this kind of program?

5. Would this program be as effective (however effective you consider it to be) if the Red Sox home park did not have the heritage it does? If the home park were a 45,000-seat modern ballpark?

6. Is the Friendly Fenway concept applicable to other aspects of how the Red Sox interact with their fans, the community, and marketing partners? (If yes, how? If no, why not?)

CASE 7.3 RED SOX 2004: TIMES OF CHANGE[13]

By 2004, major changes had taken place with the Red Sox and Fenway Park. In the winter of 2001–02, the 6-plus decades of the Yawkey era had ended, as the Yawkey Trust sold the team, ballpark, and the club's 80% share of the cable New England Sports Network. The new ownership group was led by John Henry (former principal owner of the Florida Marlins), entertainment executive Tom Werner (former owner of the San Diego Padres), and incoming CEO Larry Lucchino (former CEO of the Baltimore Orioles and San Diego Padres). The price was a MLB record high, estimated at approximately $700 million.

In less than 3 seasons (through summer 2004), the Red Sox had made significant changes both on and off the field. The former led to the exciting 2003 team, which lost its League Championship series to the New York Yankees in an emotional (and to Red Sox fans, tragic) seventh game. General Manager Theo Epstein (youngest in the majors) was leading the effort to build a team that could rise to the long-sought plateau of winning the World Series, a goal last achieved by the Red Sox in 1918.

Off the field, numerous improvements had been made to Fenway Park in ways that substantially increased revenue. The new ownership had expressed its desire to improve Fenway Park rather than to pursue a new ballpark, although the latter was not ruled out for the future. (State and city economic conditions had rendered unlikely any public funding, even for infrastructure; some $150 million in funds had been voted for the latter in conjunction with previous management's plans.)

Among the initiatives undertaken were:

- "Capturing" Yawkey Way (the street adjacent to the main entrances) for pregame and during-game fan activity, particularly a variety of food, beverage, and souvenir sales.

- The addition of several hundred "Monster seats" via construction of a special section atop the left-field wall. Although initially considered by some to be inappropriate invasion of a hallowed area, fan research indicated support for the idea. The seats, first available in 2003, became highly sought.

- The addition of a family-oriented picnic and relaxation area beneath the right-field stands.

- For 2004, the construction of a special section on the top of the right-field roof, with tables and several hundred seats. A large Budweiser sign provides sponsor identification of the area.

- Two additional rows of very highly priced field box seats in front of the existing lower boxes from dugout to dugout.

- Enhanced additional club dining facilities with naming sponsors.

At the heart of the strategy for increased revenue generation were two premises, according to experienced observers. One was to "leverage space," that is, to convert either previously unused space or low-revenue space for much higher-revenue uses. (Other revenue-generating activities, for example, increased ballpark signage and expanded pregame and postgame cable TV coverage on NESN, are not the focus here.) Many of the physical changes at

Fenway Park were developed by Red Sox architect Janet Marie Smith, whose work at Baltimore's Camden Yards had been widely praised as creating a "retro ballpark with modern amenities."

The second strategic premise was an emphasis on fan satisfaction. This element was led by Executive Vice President Dr. Charles Steinberg, Lucchino's longtime colleague. Steinberg's responsibilities extended across a wide range of public affairs and external relations areas, including "game presentation." Steinberg's philosophy was reflected through a very large pegboard that dominated his office walls. A wide variety of aspects of the "total fan experience" were reflected in the main sections, from ease of finding one's way to the ballpark and then to one's seats, to ticketing, concessions, restrooms, ushers, security, and so forth. The vast majority of these were the same attributes that Larry Cancro had incorporated into the Friendly Fenway program and its associated research. (Cancro had assumed other duties.) Steinberg posted a 1–10 rating for each element, based on his own and others' detailed evaluations and fan input.

Even though a formal Friendly Fenway program no longer existed, the idea of fan orientation across the spectrum of the fan experience was deeply imbedded in the operating approach of the Red Sox. Via media reports, talk show comments, and general fan reaction, it was clear that a sense of closer "connection" between the fans and the team had been built.

By incorporating Yawkey Way into the ballpark on game days, more space was provided for fans. A physically expanded interior (because inside ticket gates could be removed) did the same. New seating areas, as noted, provided additional opportunities for fans seeking very-high-price and medium-to-high-price seats. (Ticket prices had increased considerably overall; field box seats cost $75 in 2004.)

During the first 3 years of new ownership, the consequences of these initiatives and the underlying strongly fan-oriented attitude were significantly increased revenues and continued growth in home attendance. Attendance in 2004 was almost 2.74 million, the seventh consecutive year of increases. (Capacity by 2004 had increased to 35,000.) By the end of the 2004 season, a string of 145 consecutive sellouts had been recorded, including every home date in 2004; a seasonlong home sellout had been achieved by only three other teams.

Improbably, and amazingly, the Red Sox won the 2004 World Series, after trailing the New York Yankees three games to none in the American League Championship Series. An unprecedented four consecutive victories captured the pennant, followed by four more wins over the St. Louis Cardinals. The eight straight wins were a "first" in postseason play.

Amid great joy in all of "Red Sox Nation," management would soon confront questions of raising ticket prices (already the highest in baseball) and other revenue-increasing initiatives while fans were in euphoria.

Questions

1. What ways are best for Red Sox management to extract financial value from the 2004 Championship? How much higher should ticket prices be raised, particularly the field boxes ($75 now)?

2. More generally, when teams are at or near capacity in ticket sales, what are the pros and cons of meaningful price increases in tickets?

CASE 7.4   ATLANTA FALCONS (A): BRANDING/MARKETING CHALLENGES FOR NEW OWNERSHIP[14]

The Atlanta Falcons were created on June 30, 1965, when the National Football League (NFL) awarded an expansion franchise to Atlanta businessman Rankin Smith for $8.5 million. At the time, the nearest location of another professional football franchise was St. Louis, about 570 miles away. Smith hoped that the Falcons would capitalize on the growth of Atlanta as a major city in the southern United States.

Despite Smith's intentions, the Falcons struggled through the years. The team made its first NFL playoff appearance in 1978, after 13 seasons of play. Over the next 19 years, the team made the playoffs just four times. In 1998, the team finally had a breakthrough year, finishing with a 14–2 record in the regular season and advancing to the NFL Super Bowl championship game.[15] However, the success was short-lived, as the Falcons dropped to 5–11 the following season. Overall, from 1966 through 2001, the Falcons were 202–327–6 in regular season games (a dismal .393 winning percentage), had four playoff game wins in 36 years, had never had back-to-back winning seasons, and were without a league championship. The team was synonymous with losing, and had struggled to develop a fan base.

Atlanta Demographics

Atlanta is a large, geographically dispersed city in the heart of the "deep south" region of the United States. According to the 2000 US Census, the population in the Atlanta metropolitan area is over 4.1 million, making it the 11th most populous area in the US. In addition, Atlanta's population grew 40% from 1990–2000, representing the 11th largest growth rate among US cities during that period.[16] Among the 30 most populous metropolitan areas in the US, the closest to Atlanta is Cincinnati, Ohio, about 500 miles away.[17]

Atlanta's demographics are similar to that of other large US cities, with one distinction being that Atlanta has a high percentage of African-Americans among its residents. African-Americans represent 28.9% of the population in the Atlanta metropolitan area, versus 12.3% for the US as a whole.[18]

The Atlanta Sports Market

Given the size and growth of the Atlanta metropolitan area, and its geographic separation from other large cities, Atlanta was seemingly an attractive sports market. Unfortunately for Smith, he was not the only person to notice, and franchise owners in other professional sports leagues also attempted to capitalize on Atlanta as an emerging opportunity. The Braves of Major League Baseball (MLB) moved to Atlanta from Milwaukee in 1966. The Hawks of the National Basketball Association (NBA) moved to Atlanta from St. Louis in 1968. The Atlanta Flames were created as an expansion National Hockey League (NHL) franchise in 1971. The Flames relocated to Calgary in 1980, but the NHL returned to Atlanta in 1999 with another expansion franchise, the Atlanta Thrashers. Although the seasons in each major professional sport did not fully overlap, the Atlanta teams did compete with each other for local brand stature and for share of Atlanta fans' yearly sports expenditures. The Braves play at Turner Field (opened in 1997). Both the Hawks and the Thrashers play at Phillips Arena (opened in 1999).

February 2002: Arthur Blank Purchases the Falcons

In December 2001, Arthur Blank, the retired co-founder and former CEO of The Home Depot, agreed to purchase the Atlanta Falcons from the Rankin Smith family for $545 million.[19] The NFL approved the deal in February 2002.

Blank had been a successful executive for many years at The Home Depot, and his decision to purchase the Falcons surprised some outsiders who questioned his purchase price. For $545 million, Blank inherited an ailing franchise with weak brand stature and a history of poor performance. However, Blank made it clear that his motivation went beyond pure financial returns, and that he primarily viewed the Falcons as a community and cultural asset.[20] Blank had been an Atlanta resident since 1978, and he sought to energize the Atlanta community by turning around what had been a troubled franchise. Blank said of his purchase:

> Purchasing the Falcons was a way for me to be more strongly connected to sports and give back to the community. Although I own the team, I really see myself as a custodian of the team for the fans in Atlanta.[21]

In his efforts to turn the Falcons franchise around, Blank vowed to apply management philosophies that had proven to be successful at The Home Depot. Specifically, Blank emphasized the principles of active listening, diligent responsiveness, and continuous learning, all of which were instrumental in building The Home Depot into a $50 billion corporation. At the NFL press conference in February 2002 announcing the approval of his purchase, Blank reiterated his philosophy:

> The last two months for me have been filled with learning in every sense of the word. I will continue to listen. I will continue to learn. Our obligation is to produce the best product both on and off the field. We understand that fans are our customers. I am reading all of the fan mail. I have responded to every single one. We built a great company at The Home Depot on a very simple philosophy.[22]

Blank promised to listen to fans, players, coaches, and the entire Atlanta community in order to build an organization that was not only successful on the field, but that also generated tremendous goodwill for each group that it served. His style was active, visible, and hands-on, quite different from the more aloof nature of the Smith family.[23] Blank also made a commitment to winning, saying, "I will not rest until I have the opportunity to wear a Super Bowl ring on behalf of everybody in Atlanta and everybody in the state of Georgia."[24]

Blank hires Dick Sullivan. Following his purchase, Blank immediately began transforming the Falcons organization to meet his objectives and management style. On the marketing side, Blank turned to Dick Sullivan, a long-time colleague from The Home Depot. Sullivan had spent nine years at The Home Depot, culminating as Senior Vice President of Marketing responsible for the company's marketing campaigns and global brand strategy.[25] He was well-versed in Blank's management philosophy. After joining the Falcons in April 2002, Sullivan was charged with a key strategic initiative: developing and executing a plan to put new life into the Falcons brand.

April 2002: Sullivan Contemplates Falcons' Brand Strategy

Sullivan had significant brand building experience at The Home Depot, and although he knew that some traditional brand strategies would apply to the Falcons, he also knew that sports brands have unique characteristics. For example, sports brands have a much stronger emotional component than do traditional corporate brands, with consumers identifying with sports brands more deeply than via purely functional benefits. This leads to a potentially stronger opportunity to market sports brands to emotionally charged consumers, but it also means that negative consumer perceptions of sports brands can be more difficult to overcome.

In addition, sports team organizations are governed by league rules around territorial rights and revenue sharing, and they therefore have less competitive freedom in which to operate than traditional corporate entities. As such, home market success is particularly important to sports team brands.

Sullivan realized the challenge he faced with the Falcons. Some NFL teams had done a tremendous job of brand positioning, such as the Dallas Cowboys as "America's Team" and the Green Bay Packers as a community-based organization with deep local roots.[26] He wondered how to create a valuable brand identity for the Falcons, given their dismal past. In addition, the NFL had fewer games than other professional sports, and hence fewer direct branding opportunities. What was the right brand strategy to get there?

April 2002: Sullivan Evaluates Falcons Situation

Sullivan acknowledged the unique characteristics of sports brands when considering his plan for the Falcons, but he first evaluated the Falcons' current situation in critical areas that could provide input into his brand strategy.

Fan perception. Given the Falcons' history of losing, local and national fan perception of the team was awful. Home attendance ranked near the bottom of the league, and research indicated that for some Falcons home games, opposing fans outnumbered Falcons fans.[27]

In addition, Falcons home games were often "blacked out" in the Atlanta television market, meaning that local residents could not watch Falcons home games on television. The NFL's blackout policy began in the 1970s, and requires that a game be "blacked out" in its home television market if tickets to the game are *not* sold out 72 hours before the game begins.[28] Because of poor ticket sales, 18 of the previous 20 Falcons home games had been blacked out in the Atlanta area, and therefore local fans who did not attend games in person had inconsistent connections with the team.[29]

Stadium. The Falcons played their home games in the Georgia Dome, a stadium in the heart of downtown Atlanta. The Georgia Dome opened in 1992 with a development cost of $214 million, and was built adjacent to the Georgia World Congress Center and Centennial Olympic Park, creating one of the largest convention center and entertainment complexes in the world.[30] The area also included the Philips Center arena, which opened in 1999 as the home of both the Atlanta Hawks and the Atlanta Thrashers. The complex was served by two lines of MARTA, Atlanta's public transportation rail system.[31]

The Georgia Dome was owned by the State of Georgia and leased to the Falcons and other tenants.[32] Although the Falcons were the Georgia Dome's primary tenant, the team used the stadium for less than 15 days a year.[33] The Georgia Dome was also used for events such as concerts, professional wrestling, college basketball, college football, gymnastics, rodeos, tractor pulls, and track and field.[34]

The Georgia Dome was considered a prime venue when it opened, but a stadium development "blitz" in the United States and Canada meant that the Georgia Dome had been surpassed by newer, more elaborate venues with development costs in the $400 million and $500 million range. Specifically, from the time the Georgia Dome was opened in 1992 to the time Blank agreed to purchase the Falcons in December 2001, 10 new NFL stadiums had opened, and 43 new venues had opened in the NBA, NHL, and MLB combined.[35]

Players and On-Field Performance. The Falcons were coming off a 7–9 record in 2001—an improvement from their 4–12 record in 2000, but still well below a championship contending team.

Despite the team's losing record in 2001, the most exciting aspect of the season was the encouraging play of quarterback Michael Vick. Vick was an extremely athletic player, possessing tremendous speed, agility, and arm strength. The Falcons selected Vick with the #1 overall pick in the 2001 NFL draft, after Vick had decided to forego his remaining two years of college in order to enter the NFL. Vick signed a 6-year contract with the Falcons worth a guaranteed $15.3 million over three years, with incentives that could pay him up to $62 million over the 6-year contract duration. It was the richest rookie contract in NFL history.[36] Many analysts questioned the risk the Falcons took on an unproven professional player, but the Falcons felt that Vick was an exceptional talent that could not be ignored.[37]

Although Vick started just two games for the Falcons in his rookie season of 2001, he displayed flashes of greatness, and the Falcons felt justified in their investment. Before the 2002 season, the Falcons named Vick, at the tender age of 21, their 2002 starting quarterback. Incumbent quarterback Chris Chandler, the third leading passer in Falcons history and a veteran of 14 seasons, was released.[38] Falcons Head Coach Dan Reeves said at the time about Vick, "I think he's as ready as you can have a second-year quarterback in this league."[39]

After naming Vick the starting quarterback, the Falcons made a number of additional football changes, eventually re-tooling the roster with 21 new players for the 2002 season.[40]

Ticket Sales and Attendance. The Falcons consistently struggled to sell tickets for home games, which was both frustrating for management and de-motivating for players. Ticket sales fluctuated higher around more successful seasons and immediately after the Georgia Dome opened, but average yearly sales were dismal by NFL standards. See **Exhibit 1** for data on Falcons ticket sales from 1992–2001.

EXHIBIT 1 FALCONS TICKET SALES, 1992–2001

Year	Regular Season Win/Loss Record	Win %*	Average Ticket Price	Average Tickets Sold Per Home Game**	% Available Tickets Sold†
1992‡	6–10	.375	$28.28	68,246	95.4%
1993	6–10	.375	$28.41	60,894	85.2%
1994	7–9	.438	$28.37	58,160	81.3%
1995	9–7	.563	$31.75	52,283	73.1%
1996	3–13	.188	$31.31	46,311	64.8%
1997	7–9	.438	$31.09	44,387	62.1%
1998	14–2	.875	$30.51	51,786	72.4%
1999	5–11	.313	$38.02	54,708	76.5%
2000	4–12	.250	$38.52	49,585	69.3%
2001	7–9	.438	$36.58	53,855	75.3%

*Win % = Wins/(Wins + Losses).

**Includes preseason games.

†Calculated based on Georgia Dome capacity of 71,500.

‡Year Georgia Dome opened.

Source: Internal Falcon Records.

Exhibit 2 shows how for the 2001 season there were two pricing tiers sold by the Falcons—a $370 per season ticket zone and a $330 per season ticket zone. Exhibit 2 also shows a "Club Level Section" that was sold by the Georgia Dome Authority. When the Georgia Dome opened in 1992 it sold club seats on a 7-year multi-year license. This license ($1,500 per seat per year) gave access to all events in Dome (including the SEC Championship and the Peach Bowl). After the initial seven year period expired, ticket holders were offered by the Georgia Dome Authority another multi-year flat price deal for either three or five years.

Comparison with other NFL Franchises. Despite the seemingly attractive sports market in Atlanta, the Falcons ranked second lowest of the NFL in both average attendance and venue utilization in 2001. The Arizona Cardinals with average 2001 attendance of 38,414 and utilization of 52.2 % was the lowest in both areas. NFL team averages were 65,791 for attendance and 93.0% for utilization.

Comparison with other Atlanta Professional Sports Franchises. Like the Falcons, the Atlanta Hawks of the NBA and the Atlanta Thrashers of the NHL ranked near the bottom of their respective leagues in both winning percentage and attendance. Conversely, the Atlanta Braves had won more games than any other MLB team since 1992, but despite their unprecedented success on the field, the Braves ranked just 12th in total attendance and 15th in venue utilization among MLB teams in 2001. See **Exhibit 3** for a comparative list of Atlanta professional sports franchises prior to the 2002 NFL season.

Falcons within NFL Revenue Sharing Structure. The Falcons are governed by significant NFL revenue sharing policies that give the NFL more financial parity than other professional sports leagues. For example, all NFL television rights are negotiated at the league level, and the resulting revenues are distributed equally to each team.[41] Revenue from the current NFL television deal amounts to about $75 million per team per year, and for many

EXHIBIT 2   GEORGIA DOME STADIUM MAP, 2001 FALCONS TICKET PRICING TIERS

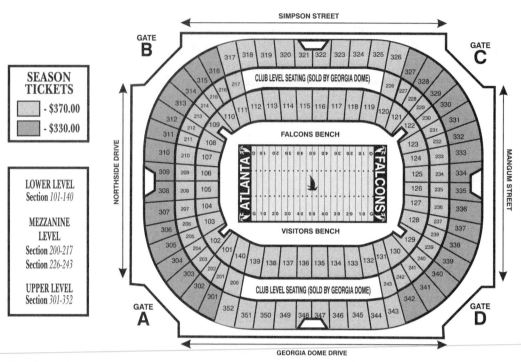

Note: Season tickets covered 10 total games (2 pre-season and 8 regular season). Individual game tickets were sold at approximately the same per-game rate.

Source: Falcons internal records.

EXHIBIT 3   ATLANTA PROFESSIONAL SPORTS FRANCHISES (START OF 2002 NFL SEASON)

Atlanta Team Name	Win %[*]	Team Average Ticket Price (Rank Within League)	League Average Ticket Price	Venue Capacity	Average Home Game Attendance (Rank Within League)	Venue Utilization (Rank Within League)[**]	2002 Forbes Estimated Franchise Value (Millions)
Falcons (NFL)	0.438	$36.58 (30)	$47.41	71,500	54,251 (30)	75.9% (30)	$407M
Braves (MLB)	0.543	$20.78 (9)	$17.69	49,831	34,858 (12)	70.0% (15)	$424M
Hawks (NBA)	0.402	$39.02 (17)	$42.02	20,000	12,344 (27)	61.7% (27)	$199M
Thrashers (NHL)	0.268	$40.26 (17)	$41.02	18,750[†]	13,668 (28)	72.9% (29)	$134M

[*]Win % = Wins/(Wins + Losses).

[**]Venue Utilization = Average Home Game Attendance/Venue Capacity.

[†]The capacity of Philips Arena is slightly less for hockey than for basketball, because of reconfiguration of the stadium.

Source: *2004 Revenues From Sports Venues; Forbes 2003* issues.

teams, this is their largest revenue source.[42] In addition, the NFL has a policy of sharing gate and merchandise revenues. Gate revenues are split 60/40, with the home team keeping 60% of the gate, and the remaining 40% going into a pool that is distributed equally across teams.[43] Finally, merchandise revenues come primarily from NFL deals with national retailers, and these revenues are shared equally. However, the league allows teams to distribute some merchandise in their own local "stores" and markets, for which no revenue sharing is required.[44] In summary, over 60% of the NFL's revenue is divided evenly among the league's teams.

Although the NFL's broad revenue sharing policies have facilitated desired competitive balance, the downside is that each individual team has less control over their ability to reap the value of their own individual initiatives. As such, team brand building is potentially more difficult in the NFL than in sports such as MLB with fewer revenue sharing requirements. From a pure revenue perspective, the biggest competitive levers that each NFL team controls are home ticket sales and ancillary stadium revenues,[45] with smaller impacts possible via local merchandising, pre-season television, and radio.

April–May 2002: Sullivan Makes Final Assessments

Sullivan did not have much time. The NFL pre-season was set to begin in August, and the Falcons needed to make a strong branding statement that exemplified its new management and ownership. In addition to his personal assessment of the Falcons' situation, Sullivan quickly conducted a series of fan focus groups, in line with Blank's philosophy of active listening. Sullivan targeted three main fan segments: season ticket holders, single-game attendees, and people who had not attended a Falcons game in the past two years. The main takeaways from those sessions were that professional sports in general were overpriced, that the Falcons' overall game day experience could be improved, and that it was important for the Falcons to integrate themselves into the community.[46] Sullivan evaluated this feedback and wondered how to address it given his primary focus of growing the value of the Falcons brand. With a healthy budget in hand, there were many alternatives for Sullivan to consider as he prepared for his strategy announcement in June.

Questions

1. What are the major reasons for the Atlanta Falcons brand being in the bottom tier of the NFL club brands at the time of the change of ownership?

2. What are the strengths the new Falcons management can draw on in drafting a new branding/marketing strategy?

3. What are the broad areas Sullivan and the Falcons management should consider in developing a new branding/marketing strategy?

4. Recommend a Falcons branding/marketing strategy and a series of implementation steps starting in April/May 2002.

Case 7.5 Atlanta Falcons (B): Ongoing Branding/ Marketing Challenges[47]

In June 2002, Arthur Blank and Dick Sullivan announced their strategy for the 2002 Atlanta Falcons season. Two key components of their strategy were to 1. lower ticket prices, and 2. improve the overall game-day experience for fans. Blank and Sullivan felt that investing in these initiatives would significantly increase fan participation, excitement, and loyalty. They thought that this in turn would invigorate the team's performance on the field, leading to further fan appreciation. Together, the strategy components were expected to significantly strengthen the Falcons' brand value.

Lower ticket prices. The Falcons were already near the bottom of the league in average ticket price, and lowering prices further was counter to some classic brand building strategies that consider price a driver of brand value. However, Sullivan felt that increased fan attendance would strengthen the Falcons brand far more than lowered prices would weaken it. Specifically, increased attendance would create added player motivation, greater in-game excitement and emotion critical to sports brands, and opportunities for higher ancillary stadium revenues. Perhaps most importantly, if lowered prices led to "sold out" games, the Falcons would eliminate television blackouts to 4+ million Atlanta area residents. Sullivan elaborated on the impact of televised games:

> We were only at 50,000 tickets sold per game. If we could get to 70,000, then four million people would get to try our product [on television]. We thought that would give us a much better chance of creating brand affinity, strength, and ultimately stature.[48]

Sullivan also recognized the Falcons' suboptimal pricing structure, in that tickets for some upper level and end zone seats had the same prices as tickets for the best seats in the building. Invariably, the good tickets were sold, and the bad seats were left empty. Sullivan explained:

> The front row 50-yard line seat and the top row corner [seat] were priced exactly the same. We had to scale the building. One price in an airplane may work but it also may be a disadvantage if you have $800 first class seats and $200 coach seats, and try to price everything at $500. What happens is you sell the first class and the coach doesn't sell.[49]

The Falcons lowered prices on more than 23,000 Georgia Dome seats for the 2002 season, reducing their average ticket price by nearly 20% to $29.78.[50] Most notably, the Falcons offered a large block of season tickets (9,996 seats[51]) for just $100, an amount unheard of by NFL standards, and a figure that matched the lowest-priced tickets to Atlanta Hawks and Atlanta Thrashers games on a per-game basis.[52] The Falcons also price-tiered the Georgia Dome in a fashion that better aligned seat value with price—see **Exhibit 1.** For the Club Seats, the Falcons negotiated with the Georgia Dome to restructure the sale of any new seats

EXHIBIT 1   Georgia Dome Stadium Map, 2002 Falcons Ticket Pricing Tiers

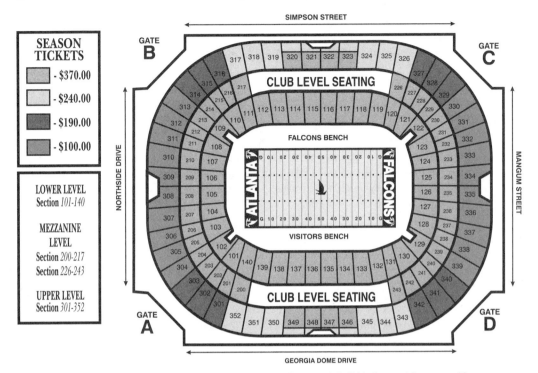

Note: Season tickets covered 10 total games (2 pre-season and 8 regular season). Individual game tickets were sold at approximately the same per-game rate.

Source: Falcons internal records

and to share some of the revenue. They raised the price per club seat and built in an annual escalator—a 3 year contract has a 9% annual escalator while a 5 year contract has a 6% annual escalator.

Sullivan noted how the low-priced $100 season tickets addressed recent focus group feedback that asked the Falcons to be more integrated into the community:

> *The commissioner of the NFL would say that the best-sized building is between 62,000 and 65,000 [seating capacity] . . . we have 72,000. So what if we took those 10,000 seats and in a sense gave them back to the community? If we gave back 10,000 seats then we're really working with a 62,000 seat building . . . the other 10,000 [seats] are our goodwill back to those fans that couldn't normally afford to come to a game.*[53]

Improve the overall game-day experience for fans. As a further strategy to increase fan participation and appreciation, Blank and Sullivan announced a plan to improve the overall "driveway to driveway" game-day experience for fans. This included making improvements to parking and traffic control, investing in the Georgia Dome venue, and adding entertainment attractions to the entire day.

First, the Falcons improved parking around the Georgia Dome. The team contracted with nearby parking lot owners and assumed game-day management of nine new parking lots for the 2002 season, increasing managed parking spaces for season ticket holders from 2,000 to 20,000. Prices for most of the new parking spaces were set at $8 per game, down from the $12 per game many fans had paid in 2001.[54] In addition, the Falcons branded their primary parking area as "The Gulch," intended to be a tailgating paradise. To encourage tailgating and fan enthusiasm before games, the Falcons hung team banners in The Gulch, and ensured physical security of the space. Regarding The Gulch, one season ticket holder said, "You know you're at a Falcons game before you're even at the game."[55]

Second, the Falcons improved traffic flow around the Georgia Dome on game days. The team worked with the City of Atlanta and the Department of Transportation to provide more traffic lanes going in and out of the area, ultimately controlling traffic at 53 nearby intersections (a 70% increase over 2001). The Falcons also partnered with MARTA to offer special discounts for Falcons game attendees, a move that increased MARTA ridership to/from games by 150%.[56]

Third, the Falcons invested heavily in the Georgia Dome venue. They spent $1.5 million to resurface the playing field with new, high quality turf[57], and they invested $5 million to upgrade the technology and video systems to a state-of-the-art level.[58] In addition, the Falcons removed revenue-generating commercials from the stadium scoreboard after fans had indicated that the commercials were an annoying distraction. The Falcons also improved their attention to detail for things such as maintaining adequate bathroom and concession supplies.[59] Matt Winkeljohn, a writer for the *Atlanta Constitution*, noted that the Falcons' enhancements to the Georgia Dome made it seem "less like an antiseptic barn with a plastic lid, and more like a true NFL venue."[60]

Finally, the Falcons invested in new entertainment events before, during, and after Falcons games, in order to make the overall game-day experience a "larger than life" attraction. They booked locally popular entertainment acts—including James Brown, the Atlanta Symphony, the Pointer Sisters, and the Temptations—to perform for fans both inside and outside the Georgia Dome. The team also created Falcons Landing, a new entertainment complex outside the stadium for pre-game and post-game festivities. Falcons Landing opened three hours before Falcons games and provided attractions such as live music acts, face painting booths, autograph sessions with cheerleaders and former players, and interactive football-oriented contests. It was an alternative for fans that preferred active pre-game entertainment over leisurely tailgating. Regarding Falcons Landing, one Atlanta fan said: "It gives you something to do other than sitting around . . . it gets you pumped up and excited."[61]

June 2002–January 2003: Falcons Implement Strategy for 2002 Season, Observe Results

The Falcons strategy was radical and expensive, but the message was clear. At a news conference announcing the decisions, Blank summed up the focus:

> *Our goal is to fill the Georgia Dome with the energy, noise and excitement our fans and players have told us they want.*[62]

Sullivan said of the Falcons' approach:

> *We invested a lot of money, but we did what the fans told us to do. At The Home Depot, we used to say that 99 percent of the answers are on the floor of our store. The customers . . . they'll give you the answer. We went through the same steps with the Falcons. I could give you thousands of examples of times we were about to make a decision, and message boards lit up that said, we don't think that's the right decision. But we thought it over and we said, the fans are probably right, so let's go in that direction . . .*[63]

The results of the strategy were phenomenal. Once the Falcons began implementing their plan, they sold 10,000 season tickets in 11 days.[64] By September 2002, before the Falcons played their first regular season game under Blank's ownership, the team had doubled its season-ticket base. They had also "sold out" three regular season games, compared to just one sell-out the entire previous year.[65] By the end of the 2002 season, the Falcons had sold 21,000 new season tickets in total, and had broken an 83-year NFL record for the largest ticket sales increase year over year.[66] Average regular-season home game tickets sold jumped to 64,506, up from 53,855 in 2001.

During the 2002 season, the Falcons continued their policy of active listening by installing 20 polling stations at the Georgia Dome that surveyed fans during games. Blank and Sullivan compared the polling stations to The Home Depot strategy of store "intercepts," people paid to ask shoppers about their experience.[67] The input from these polling stations helped the Falcons refine their decision-making throughout the season.

On-field results. On the field, the Falcons' 2002 results were also dramatic. The Falcons went 4–0 in the preseason, creating considerable excitement about what the team could accomplish. They finished the regular season with a 9–6–1 record, earning a spot in the NFL playoffs for just the seventh time in 37 years. Furthermore, under watchful eyes, phenom quarterback Michael Vick had a breakthrough season, exciting fans with his tremendous athleticism and leadership. Vick finished fourth in the NFL's 2002 Most Valuable Player voting, and according to many football writers, turned every play into "something you had to watch."[68]

In January 2003, the Falcons traveled to Green Bay to face the Packers in their first game. The Packers were 8–0 at home during the regular season (12–4 overall), and 13–0 in home playoff games since 1933. Despite a game-time temperature of 31 degrees and snowy weather, the Falcons pulled off an incredible upset, defeating the Packers 27–7. Although the Falcons lost their next playoff game to a strong Philadelphia Eagles team, the victory over the Packers was indicative of the Falcons' physical and psychological emergence.

January 2003: Falcons Evaluate Brand Impacts

Despite the fact that total ticket revenues in 2002 were essentially flat compared to 2001, Sullivan was confident that the Falcons' brand value had increased dramatically. One thing was certain: the Falcons were listening to their fans, and responding. In a January survey of season-ticket holders, 53.2 percent said that the best way to describe the Falcons organization was that it "cares about its fans."[69]

In addition, every 2002 Falcons home game eventually sold out,[70] creating two dramatic brand impacts. First, the increase in attendance created a "full stadium" excitement experience that touched on the emotional factor so critical to sports brands. Second, the Falcons avoided the NFL television blackout policy, giving the team access to 4+ million television viewers for every home game, compared to just one locally-televised home game in 2001. This expanded local television coverage strengthened the team's identification with the local community.

Finally, surveys showed that the number of Falcons fans nationwide had increased. One fan study published in *Sports Business Journal* rated the 2002 Falcons an astonishing #1 among all NFL fans aged 18–49, representing a significant turnaround in fan perception.[71] Blank and Sullivan were greatly encouraged by these developments, and looked to continue the upward trend in 2003.

Impact of players and on-field performance. Although the Falcons' brand development results in 2002 were significant, observers noted that the upturn in results coincided with both a substantial improvement in the team's on-field performance and the emergence of Michael Vick, the league's newest superstar player. Some wondered how effective the new brand strategy would have been without such dramatic on-field improvements, and whether the team could sustain its brand momentum if it were unable to sustain its on-field success. Joe Cooper, president of the Falcons official fan club, surmised: "The honeymoon will come to an end if the Falcons don't win."[72]

Sullivan clearly recognized the positive impact that Vick and the rest of the Falcons players had on ticket sales and the overall Falcons brand. Vick was a superstar player and a fan favorite, and Sullivan was grateful for the opportunity to include Vick in future team branding efforts. However, Sullivan was also confident that the new ownership's brand strategy would not be dependent on one player. In addition, although Blank planned increasing investments in football talent, Sullivan was confident that a strong brand strategy could withstand periodic down years on the field:

> I think there's an expectation in our city that we will win . . . but because the philosophy and culture of this organization is to really listen to and respond to fans, I'd like to think that if we don't have a playoff run or a Super Bowl run every season, it won't matter as much . . .
>
> . . . I think it goes to brand equity. If you have a lot of deposits in your account, you can have one or two withdrawals; you just can't have many of them. You have to continue to add to the deposit side of the ledger. This team had one good deposit in 1998 when it went to the Super Bowl, and it's had a lot of withdrawals because of no back-to-back winning seasons, but by the changes we've made this past year, we've put a lot of deposits in that account.[73]

Several Falcons players had the opportunity to market themselves independently of the team, creating a potential conflict of interest with the team brand. In response, Blank and Sullivan developed a culture of providing assistance to players who were seeking and/or evaluating their own independent endorsement deals. The Falcons also helped players connect with the Atlanta business community during and after their playing careers.[74] This culture influenced Falcons players to consider the impacts of their own individual business affairs on the Falcons as a whole. The Falcons' support policies also improved the organization's reputation among players throughout the NFL, strengthening the team's brand image further.

January 2003–September 2003: Falcons Look to Continue Brand Momentum

The Falcons hoped that their new brand strategy had established a fan base that would be loyal year after year. After such a dramatic improvement in 2002, the Falcons went to work on the challenge of continuing the brand's momentum in 2003.

Logo. One major initiative in 2003 was the design of a new Falcons logo to represent the new personality of the team and organization. Sullivan surveyed key fan segments on key attributes of various logo designs. The existing logo uniformly received negative responses. When the new logo and new uniforms were launched in March 2003, *The Sporting News* commented: "the old Falcons logo, in which the poor, beaten bird appeared to be gasping for air, has been updated with a meaner, more aggressive look."[75] See **Exhibit 2** for a comparison of the old logo and new logo.

Broadcasting and the Internet. In addition, the Falcons undertook initiatives in broadcasting and the Internet in 2003. Realizing the ethnic diversity of their fan base, the Falcons announced new television and radio broadcast partners that addressed both the Hispanic and the African-American markets. The team also updated its Internet presence, redesigning its website based on feedback from a fan advisory board.[76]

Merchandising. Furthermore, the team boosted its merchandising efforts in an effort to grow the brand. Sullivan noted how growth strategies for the Falcons compared to growth at The Home Depot:

> At The Home Depot, we could always order more circular saws or lumber, but with the Falcons, we couldn't order more seats. So we had to build brand extensions quickly to create inventory. With the Falcons, building market share meant increasing the share of wallet from the consumer from all the brand extensions we could create . . . it could be merchandise, special trips, or other things that are different.[77]

EXHIBIT 2 FALCONS OLD LOGO AND NEW LOGO

Old   New

Source: Falcons internal records

The Falcons created a new merchandising concept, known as the "Atlanta Falcons Mobile Museum and Mobile Store," that consisted of two trailer rigs outfitted with Falcons memorabilia, interactive audio/video displays, and merchandise. The trailers served as a "mobile brand presence" for the Falcons, and traveled to locations in Atlanta and surrounding areas throughout the year.[78]

Meanwhile, Michael Vick had become a cultural icon. In the period from April 1, 2003 to July 31, 2003, Vick's jersey became the top selling jersey among NFL players up from the third best selling jersey in the 2002 fiscal year. The first half of 2003 saw the Falcons' total jersey sales increase 600% over the same period in 2002,[79] bolstered not only by Vick, but also by the newly designed logo and uniform style launched in March. Sullivan said of the results: "what it means is that our team is not just a local team, [but] a national product."[80]

Pricing. For 2003, the Falcons retained their lowest-priced season-ticket seat blocks at $100 and $190 respectively, which was a core part of the 2002 strategy. However, the team raised prices on tickets for higher quality seats, and created several additional pricing tiers in those seating areas—see **Exhibit 3.** Sullivan explained: "We held firm on the cheapest seats in the building, but we tried to get our first class seats to be the right price." Overall, the Falcons' average ticket price in 2003 rose 16% to $34.63, with the increase coming exclusively from prices for the better seats in the building. Even with the price increase, the Falcons still had the lowest average ticket price in the NFL.[81]

Despite the price increase for some tickets, the Falcons still faced considerable new ticket demand for the 2003 season. By June, the team had sold out all of its season tickets, had limited single-game tickets available, and had 2000+ people on its ticket waiting list.[82] Sullivan was encouraged by the continued demand, and attributed it largely to growth in the Falcons' brand value over the previous 12 months.

August 2003–September 2003: Falcons Prepare for 2003 Season

The Falcons approached the 2003 season with significant momentum, and some writers labeled them legitimate Super Bowl contenders. However, on August 16, during the second game of the preseason, Michael Vick fell awkwardly while being tackled, and suffered a broken right fibula. The club subsequently finished 0–4 in the pre-season, and although pre-season games had no bearing on end-of-season results, the discouraging record and the injury to Vick raised many questions. Fans wondered whether the team had enough talent and resolve to overcome the loss of its franchise player. Sullivan wondered whether the Falcons brand had enough inherent value to sustain a potentially down year on the field. As the Falcons prepared for their opening game against the Dallas Cowboys on September 8, the prognosis was for Vick to miss 4–6 regular season games. Sullivan reflected on a statement he had made in July:

> *Whether it's brand personality or brand attributes, you need to ask*
> *everyone, "When you think of your team, what do you think of?" Is it*

EXHIBIT 3   GEORGIA DOME STADIUM MAP, 2003 FALCONS TICKET PRICING TIERS

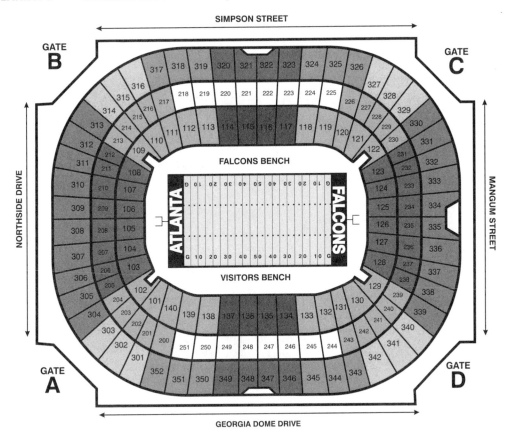

Note: Season tickets covered 10 total games (2 pre-season and 8 regular season). Individual game tickets were sold at approximately the same per-game rate.

Source: Falcons internal records.

toughness, is it offense, is it defense, is it speed, is it the owner, what is it? There needs to be a focus around the brand or otherwise there won't be [a brand]. When I think of Volvo, I think of safety. When I think of Disney, I think of the magic of childhood.

Our brand is focused around the fans.[83]

With the recent turn in events, Sullivan pondered how to best manage the Falcons' brand for the 2003 season and beyond.

Questions

1. What information can be gathered to evaluate the branding/marketing decisions made in June 2002?
2. Evaluate the brand positioning decisions announced by Blank & Sullivan in June 2002.
3. What changes would you recommend for the 2003/2004 season in its branding/marketing?
4. How should the Falcons handle the Michael Vick August 16, 2003 accident from a branding/marketing viewpoint?

Footnotes

[1] This section was written by George Foster.

[2] A. Herrmann. "Reporter Learns the Base-ics of Sox Park." *Chicago Sun Times* (May 19, 2004).

[3] S. Shapiro, The Most Valuable Brands in Sports, FutureBrand, 2002, p. 2.

[4] Ibid, p. 5.

[5] Todd Bello (Stanford MBA, 2004) and Steven Sibley (Stanford MBA, 2004) prepared this case under the supervision of George Foster.

[6] *2004 Revenues in Sports* (Milwaukee, WI: MediaVentures, 2004), p. 11.

[7] *New York Post* (December 1, 2002).

[8] "M's Put Prime Seats Up for Online Bids." *Seattle Times* (June 28, 2003).

[9] Ibid.

[10] "Judge Tosses Ticket-Scalping Cases, Cites M's Internet Sales." *Seattle Times* (January 31, 2004).

[11] D. Rovel. "Bankable Product: Yanks in Town, Rocket Pitching," ESPN.com (June 3, 2003).

[12] Professor Stephen A. Greyser prepared this case. HBS cases are developed solely as the basis for class discussion. Cases are not intended to serve as endorsements, sources of primary data, or illustrations of effective or ineffective management.

[13] This case was written by Stephen A. Greyser.

[14] Chris Boni prepared this case under the supervision of George Foster.

[15] The Falcons lost Super Bowl XXXIII to the Denver Broncos by the score of 34–19.

[16] By comparison, the San Francisco/San Jose/Oakland metropolitan area ranked 7th in overall population (7.0 million) and 138th in population growth (12.6%).

[17] Source: 2000 U.S. Census.

[18] Ibid.

[19] Smith family average annual return (1965–2001).

[20] Interview with Dick Sullivan, September 2, 2003.

[21] *NFL Insider,* Postseason Issue 2002.

[22] NFL Arthur Blank press conference, February 2, 2002.

23 NFL.com wire report, July 25, 2002.

24 NFL Arthur Blank press conference, February 2, 2002.

25 http://www.atlantafalcons.com, Dick Sullivan bio.

26 The Green Bay Packers have one of the most unique ownership structures in sports, with each resident of Green Bay owning shares in the team.

27 Dick Sullivan presentation, *Stanford Program for NFL Managers*, June 2003.

28 "NFL Blackouts Tackle Weakest Teams." *CNN SportsBiz* (October 14, 2002). The idea behind the NFL blackout policy is to encourage home market fans to attend games in person, as opposed to "allowing" fans to watch games on television when stadium tickets are still available. The NFL felt that the blackout policy would both increase ticket revenues and provide more "full-stadium" entertainment experiences for fans in the stadium and people watching on television, hence increasing the overall value of the product. Satellite and cable television networks also follow the blackout policy.

29 Interview with Dick Sullivan, September 2, 2003.

30 http://www.gadome.com.

31 Unlike rail systems in other large cities, MARTA has limited city coverage.

32 The specifics of the Falcons' lease arrangement for the Georgia Dome are not published, but a recent study by *MediaVentures* rating the favorability of sports teams' venue arrangements gave the Falcons a score of 85, below the NFL average of 100. Lease arrangements typically cover areas such as financing, ticket sales, luxury boxes, parking, concessions, and signage, with the team and venue owner often sharing both costs and revenues. Source: "2003 Revenues From Sports Venues." *Mediaventures* (February 24, 2003).

33 The typical NFL schedule runs from August to December, including 4 preseason games (2 home, 2 away) and 16 regular season games (8 home, 8 away). Games are played once a week. If a team makes the playoffs, it can play up to 4 additional games in January, with home/away locations based on team performance.

34 The stadium also hosted Olympic events during the 1996 Atlanta Summer Olympic Games, and was the NFL Super Bowl venue in both 1994 and 2000.

35 Specifically, the NBA had 18 new arenas (some of which had NHL teams as cotenants), the NHL had 11 new arenas (without NBA teams as cotenants), and MLB had 14 new ballparks. Sources: http://www.nfl.com, http://www.ballparksofbaseball.com, http://www.hoopscorner.com, http://www.hockeyzoneplus.com.

36 "Vick Signs Richest Rookie Contract in NFL History." *Sporting News* (May 9, 2001).

37 Just before the 2001 NFL draft, the Falcons—still owned by the Smith family at the time—traded their first round pick (#5 overall), their third-round pick, their second-round pick in 2002, and wide receiver Tim Dwight to the San Diego Chargers for the right to select Vick #1. Vick's agents had previously negotiated with the Chargers and determined that the Chargers were unwilling to pay what Vick's agents were seeking.

38 "Five Questions Facing the Falcons." *Gainesville Times* (July 25, 2002).

39 "Packers Fortunate to Face Vick Early." http://www.packers.com (September 5, 2002).

40 http://www.atlantafalcons.com.

41 This is in stark contrast to MLB, in which teams independently sell broadcast rights for most games to local television stations, keeping 100% of the resulting revenues.

42 The NFL has the highest television ratings among U.S. sports, and the NFL television deal is the largest in sports, generating $17.6 billion for the league from 1998–2005. The deal includes ABC, CBS, FOX, and ESPN.

43 Rodney Fort. *Sports Economics*, p. 160.

44 "Oakland Raiders to Fans: Just Buy, Baby." *San Francisco Business Times* (December 10, 2001). Local merchandise sales are subject to NFL royalties, but the team still keeps a much higher percentage of revenues than in the national retail case.

45 Ancillary stadium revenues include parking, concessions, signage, naming rights, and so on. In some cases, ancillary revenues can be substantial; for example, Federal Express paid $205 million for naming rights of the Washington Redskins' venue through the year 2026. However, the competitive value of ancillary stadium revenues to an NFL team is dependent upon the arrangement the team has with its stadium owner.

46 Interview with Dick Sullivan, September 2, 2003.

47 Chris Boni prepared this case under the supervision of George Foster.

48 Interview with Dick Sullivan, September 2, 2003.

49 Interview with Dick Sullivan, September 2, 2003.

50 Independent of the Falcons, the average NFL ticket price between the 2001 and 2002 seasons increased from $47.77 to $50.68 (+6.1%). Only two other NFL teams lowered average ticket prices between the 2001 and 2002 seasons: the New Orleans Saints dropped from $47.07 to $46.32 (-1.6%), and the Seattle Seahawks dropped from $44.99 to $43.28 (-3.8%). Source: *Team Marketing Report,* Fan Cost Index, 2002.

51 Falcons internal records.

52 "Blank Aims to Grow Crowds as Falcons Cut Ticket Prices." *Sports Business Daily* (June 21, 2002).

53 Interview with Dick Sullivan, September 2, 2003.

54 "Falcons' Innovative Owner Giving Football Back to Masses." *Pro Football Weekly* (July 1, 2002).

55 "Fans like revelry at Dome." *Atlanta Journal-Constitution* (August 9, 2002).

56 Dick Sullivan presentation, *Stanford Program for NFL Managers,* June 2003.

57 The new turf was both softer and faster, leading to less stress on players' bodies, and also allowing players to run and pivot more quickly, increasing fan excitement. Furthermore, the Falcons' team emphasized quickness, so the new turf provided an advantage for the Falcons versus bigger, slower teams.

58 Interview with Dick Sullivan, September 2, 2003.

59 "Falcons Discover the Value of Surveying Fans." *Sports Business Journal* (August 11–17, 2003).

60 "Georgia Dome on Blank's Mind: Falcons Get 'Cozier' Home." *Sports Business Daily* (August 9, 2002).

61 "Fans Like Revelry at Dome." *Atlanta Journal-Constitution* (August 9, 2002).

62 "Falcons announce price cut on tickets." *NFL.com wire reports* (June 20, 2002).

63 Interview with Dick Sullivan, September 2, 2003.

64 Dick Sullivan presentation, *Stanford Program for NFL Managers,* June 2003.

65 *NFL Insider,* Postseason Issue 2002.

66 Dick Sullivan presentation, *Stanford Program for NFL Managers,* June 2003.

67 "Falcons Discover the Value of Surveying Fans." *Sports Business Journal* (August 11–17, 2003).

68 "Falcons Season in Review." *Pro Football Weekly* (February 4, 2003).

69 "NFL Taps into Falcons Expertise." *Athens Banner-Herald* (July 5, 2003).

70 A "sold out" game does not necessarily mean that every seat is physically attended on game day, as evidenced by the Falcons' average home game attendance of 68,872 versus a Georgia Dome capacity of 71,500.

71 Dick Sullivan presentation, *Stanford Program for NFL Managers,* June 2003. The *Sports Business Journal* study was based on the number of fans who attended, watched, or listened to one or more games of a team in the fan's market in 2002.

72 "From One Company to Another: Blank's Plans with Falcons." *Sports Business Daily* (August 23, 2002).

73 Interview with Dick Sullivan, September 2, 2003.

74 Interview with Dick Sullivan, September 2, 2003.

75 *Pro Football* (a publication of the *Sporting News*), 2003 Edition.

76 Dick Sullivan presentation, *Stanford Program for NFL Managers,* June 2003.

77 Interview with Dick Sullivan, September 2, 2003.

78 "Falcons Unveil New Mobile Museum." http://www.atlantafalcons.com (July 10, 2003).

79 "NFL Taps into Falcons Expertise." *Athens Banner-Herald* (July 5, 2003).

80 Interview with Dick Sullivan, September 2, 2003.

81 Independent of the Falcons, the average NFL ticket price between the 2002 and 2003 seasons increased from $50.68 to $53.54 (+5.7%). The New Orleans Saints were the only team with a significant decrease in average ticket price for 2003, dropping from $46.32 to $43.87 (−5.3%). Source: *Team Marketing Report,* Fan Cost Index, 2003.

82 Dick Sullivan presentation, *Stanford Program for NFL Managers,* June 2003.

83 "NFL Taps into Falcons Expertise." *Athens Banner-Herald* (July 5, 2003).

SECTION 8... Broadcasting, Media, and Sports[1]

Key Issues

- Sports content is increasingly on cable rather than broadcast (free-to-air) television for many sports. Cable operates with a two revenue stream model (cable subscription fees and advertising) as opposed to the single revenue stream model (advertising) for broadcast.

- Cable content channels and cable distribution platform companies are two important parts of the cable industry. Only a small subset of sports cable content companies (such as ESPN and FOX Sports) have sizable leverage with the distribution platform companies.

- Sporting bodies are negotiating more diverse contracts with their television partners. The upfront fixed fee model is still common, but other alternatives (such as revenue sharing and buying time) are increasingly on the negotiation table.

- Cable sports has been an area of high innovation. Diverse types of regional sports networks (RSNs) as well as league owned cable content channels are being rolled out.

Cases

B roadcast, cable, radio, Internet, and print media play many roles in sports. A subset can bring sports events and games live to fans and other viewers who are not in attendance. Such live coverage enables fans to remain emotionally connected and to experience the uncertainty of outcome that is a hallmark of sports competition. Media is also part of the publicity machine promoting sports. Before-game and after-game analysis heightens fan interest in individual events, games, and clubs and their leagues. Media also shapes sports. Leagues have switched the time of their playing season to better accommodate broadcast network schedules.[2] Media coverage can lead to changes in game-day events—such as the length and timing of breaks in a game. Coverage and replay can shape the enforcement of game rules and even the rules themselves. Analysis of the business side of the media/sports interface is essential to an understanding of the business of sports.

This section covers several interrelated topics:

- Alternative delivery mechanisms for sports content on television
- Alternative contracting models for sports rights negotiations
- Trends in sports broadcasting, including the growth of RSNs (regional sports networks)

Television Coverage of Sports

The television industry distinguishes two different formats by which sports programming is delivered to viewers: free-to-air broadcasting and cable television. Exhibit 8-1 provides an overview of these two sides of the television market.

Free-to-Air Broadcast: The genesis of television and of its sports coverage is the free-to-air broadcast side. For many years, this was the only way to receive television content. Houses or apartments carried outside aerials that picked up broadcast signals. Broadcast networks developed to bring nationwide coverage to viewers in many parts of the country. The initial Big 3 networks (ABC, CBS, and NBC) became the Big 4 when FOX emerged as a major force in the 1990s. FOX's rapid growth was in part fueled by its acquisition of NFL sports rights for the (at the time) record fee of $395 million per year. Each television area typically has access to both free-to-air network television stations and stations of local independents. Sports coverage is included on both the network stations and the independents.

The revenue model underlying free-to-air broadcasting is the 30-second advertising commercial. Advertisers are charged based on the expected ratings and the expected demographics of that rating. Sports historically have been among the highest rated programs shown on free-to-air broadcast television.

Cable: The cable side of television has two pillars—cable content channels and distribution platforms:

- **Cable Content Channels.** These channels deliver content to different target audiences. Sports channels are among the highest rated cable channels. Exhibit 8-2 illustrates the

EXHIBIT 8-1   U.S. TELEVISION—BROADCAST (FREE-TO-AIR) AND CABLE SIDES

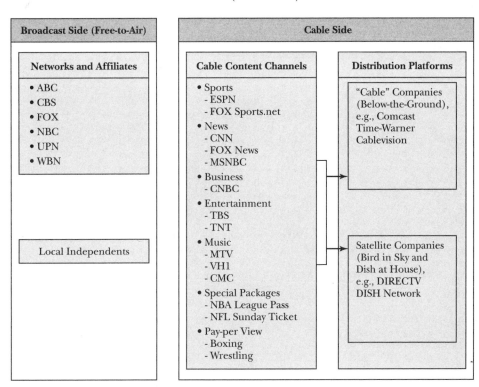

sports channels on two packages available to DIRECTV subscribers. The "Basic Package" costs $39.99 per month. It includes at least nine channels carrying sizable sports content, including four channels from ESPN. The "Total Choice Premier Package" includes more than 210 channels for $90.99 per month. It includes all channels on the Basic Package plus another 80 channels, including an additional 24 carrying sizable sports content. These include 18 FOX Sports Net regional channels.

A recent trend in cable sports is "Special Sports Packages" that provide seasonlong access to out-of-town games that local broadcast or local cable channels may not include. Exhibit 8-2 includes five such packages for DIRECTV. For example, the NBA League Pass provides "up to 40 regular season games a week from outside the viewer's local area." It costs $169 for the season.

Most cable content channels have two major revenue sources: (1) carriage payments from cable distribution platform companies like Comcast and DIRECTV and (2) advertising revenues. Carriage fees differ dramatically. Most contracts between cable content channels and their distribution platform partners are on a monthly per subscriber basis. Being on a high-volume subscriber package (such as Comcast's Standard Cable or DIRECTV's Basic Package) typically is the preferred position for a cable content channel. This results in higher revenues to the cable content channel—for a given monthly carriage fee, the more subscribers, the higher the revenues of the cable content channels. In some cases, cable content channels are willing to reduce the carriage fee they would charge to be positioned on a higher-volume subscriber package.

EXHIBIT 8-2   SPORTS CABLE CHANNELS ON **DIRECTV (2004)**

BASIC PACKAGE – More than 130 channels: $39.99 per month. Channels carrying sports include:

- ESPN
- ESPN2
- ESPN News
- ESPN Classic
- Speed Channel
- Superstation WGN
- TBS
- TNT
- Turner South

TOTAL CHOICE PREMIER PACKAGE – More than 210 channels: $90.99 per month. Channels carrying sports include those in Basic Package plus 18:

- FOX Sports Net Channels (Arizona, Bay Area, Chicago, Cincinnati, Detroit, Florida, Midwest, New England, New York, North, Northwest, Ohio, Pittsburgh, Rocky Mountain, South, Southwest, West, West2)
- FOX Sports World
- Golf Channel
- MSG
- NESN
- Sunshine Network
- YES Network

SPECIAL SPORTS PACKAGES

NFL Sunday Ticket	$219	(2004–05 Season)
MLB Extra Innings	$169	(2004 Season)
NBA League Pass	$169	(2004–05 Season)
Mega March Madness	$59	(2005 Season)
English Premier League	$299	(2004–2005 Season)

A major cost category for sports cable content companies is the rights fees they pay to sports leagues or sports clubs. For example, ESPN pays the NFL, under its 1998–2005 contract, $600 million annually for the rights to carry NFL night games on a Sunday night.

- **Distribution Platform Companies.** These companies package multiple individual "cable" channels and deliver them to viewers using one of two technologies:

1. Below-the-ground cable. Examples of leading companies and their 2003 U.S. subscribers are Comcast (22 million in 2003), AOL Time Warner (13 million), and Charter Communications (7 million).[3]

2. Satellites that convey signals to dishes attached to houses or apartment complexes. The two major companies and their 2003 U.S. subscribers are DIRECTV (11 million) and DISH Network (7 million).[4]

The revenue model underlying cable distribution platforms is a monthly fee from subscribers. For example, Comcast offered subscribers several packages in September 2004 for its below-the-ground cable service:

- Standard Cable $43.99 per month
- Digital Classic $53.94 per month
- Digital Silver $71.94 per month
- Digital Gold $83.94 per month
- Digital Platinum $94.94 per month

Exhibit 8-2 shows the DIRECTV packages available on its "bird in the sky" satellite services. Sports channels are included in each package. Additional sports channels can be purchased in any of the digital packages for an extra $4.99 per month. Comcast aims to grow revenues by both increasing its number of subscribers and having existing customers upgrade to more expensive subscriptions (e.g., Standard Cable to Digital Platinum).

The major cost category for distribution platform companies like Comcast are "carriage payments" to cable content channels for the rights to carry each channel on its platform. Sports channels are among the most expensive to carry. Kagan Research[5] reports the following average 2003 license fees per subscriber per month: ESPN ($1.93), FOX Sports ($1.21), TNT ($0.77), Disney Channel ($0.75), USA ($0.42), and CNN ($0.38).

Television Sports Ratings and Alternative Contracting Models

Television ratings are central to determining what broadcasters and cable companies are willing to bid for sports media rights and the contracts they are willing to sign. Exhibit 8-3 summarizes recent television ratings for selected leagues and events. Broadcast ratings reported in Exhibit 8-3 are averaged across multiple stations on the broadcast side while reported for the highest rated channel on the cable side.

There are many different contracting models that media companies and sporting rights holders can adopt. We now consider three examples:

Media Company Pays Fixed Up-Front Fee Model: This is the most commonly used model for major sporting properties. Exhibit 8-4 shows the magnitude of the rights fees paid over multiple contracts and multiple leagues. This data relates to national television contracts on broadcast or cable coverage. Exhibit 8-4 does not include local television contracts that individual MLB, NBA, and NHL clubs have for local area television or the special outside-local-area packages (such as the "NBA League Pass" and "NFL Sunday Ticket").

The guaranteed fixed fee aspect of this model provides "revenue certainty" to the sporting league. It puts the risk of any downturn in ratings or advertising rates on the media company. For the year ended June 30, 2002, News Corp. wrote off approximately $900 million (U.S.)

EXHIBIT 8-3 SPORTS TELEVISION (TV) NIELSEN RATINGS[a]—2000 TO 2003: BROADCAST NETWORK TV (FREE TO AIR) AND CABLE TV[b]

LEAGUE/SPORT	BROADCAST (FREE-TO-AIR) TV				CABLE TV[b]			
	2000	2001	2002	2003	2000	2001	2002	2003
NFL—MEN								
Regular Season	10.7	10.1	10.3	10.3	7.0	6.3	7.4	7.7
Playoffs	17.2	17.8	18.9	19.0	—	—	—	—
Super Bowl	40.4	40.4	40.7	41.4	—	—	—	—
MLB—MEN								
Regular Season	2.6	2.6	2.5	2.7	1.3	1.2	1.1	1.0
Division Playoffs	4.9	5.2	6.2	7.5	2.9	—	—	3.9
League Championships	6.9	7.0	6.5	10.7	—	—	—	—
World Series	12.4	15.7	11.9	12.8	—	—	—	—
NBA—MEN								
Regular Season	3.3	2.9	2.9	2.6	1.3	1.3	1.3	1.2
Playoffs	5.7	4.9	5.6	4.8	2.9	2.3	2.5	3.2
NBA Finals	11.6	12.1	10.2	6.5	—	—	—	—
WNBA—WOMEN								
Regular Season	1.4	1.1	0.9	0.8	0.5	0.4	0.3	0.2
Playoffs	1.4	1.1	1.0	0.9	0.4	0.4	0.3	0.4
NHL—MEN								
Regular Season	1.3	1.1	1.4	1.1	0.6	0.6	0.5	0.5
Playoffs	1.5	1.5	1.5	1.3	1.1	1.0	1.0	0.7
Stanley Cup Finals	3.7	3.3	3.6	2.9	—	—	—	—
MLS—MEN								
Regular Season	0.8	0.8	0.7	0.9	0.3	0.3	0.3	0.2
Playoffs	0.7	1.0	0.8	0.6	0.3	0.3	0.4	0.2
WUSA—WOMEN								
Regular Season	N/A	—	0.1	0.1	—	0.4	—	0.2
Playoffs	N/A	—	0.1	—	—	0.1	—	—
ARENA FOOTBALL—MEN								
Regular Season	1.2	0.9	0.8	0.8	0.6	0.4	0.4	—
Playoffs					0.8	0.7	0.9	—
COLLEGE FOOTBALL—MEN								
Regular Season	3.8	3.3	3.6	3.5	1.9	1.6	1.9	1.8
Post Season/Bowl Games	8.3	7.0	7.6	8.1	2.6	2.8	2.8	2.7
COLLEGE BASKETBALL—MEN								
Regular Season	1.8	1.9	1.8	1.9	0.9	0.9	0.8	0.9
Post Season Tournament	6.4	6.5	6.5	5.5	0.8	0.7	0.9	1.6
Championship Game	14.1	15.6	15.0	12.6	—	—	—	—
COLLEGE BASKETBALL—WOMEN								
Regular Season	—	—	—	—	0.6	0.4	0.3	0.3
Post Season	—	—	—	—	1.1	1.1	1.2	1.1
MOTOR SPORTS—MEN								
NASCAR	5.1	5.5	5.5	5.3	4.0	3.8	4.6	4.3
IRL (With Indy 500)	2.3	2.0	1.6	1.5	0.6	0.5	0.5	0.5
CART	—	—	—	—	0.8	0.5	0.4	0.2

LEAGUE/SPORT	BROADCAST (FREE-TO-AIR) TV			
	2000	2001	2002	2003
GOLF—MEN AND WOMEN				
PGA—Men	3.4	3.6	3.4	2.9
LPGA—Women	1.3	1.2	1.2	1.
TENNIS—MEN AND WOMEN				
GRAND SLAM—Men	—	2.94	2.77	
GRAND SLAM—Women	—	3.72	3.42	.
OLYMPICS—MEN AND WOMEN				
Prime Time (M and W Combined)	13.8	—	19.2	—

[a]A single Nielsen ratings point represents 1% of the total number of television households in the U.S. The estimate .
of television households for the 2000, 2001, 2002, and 2003 seasons was 100.8 million, 102.2 million, 105.5 million, and
108.4 million, respectively. Therefore, 1 ratings point in 2002 represents 1% or approximately 1,055,000 households.

[b]Cable Television ratings are for national cable stations such as ESPN, FX, Lifetime, Oxygen, TBS, and TNT. Ratings on Regional
Sports Networks are not included.

Source: Nielsen Television Index Sports Decks, Nielsen Galaxy Explore/Tennis from *By The Numbers 2004*.

against its sports properties, which had failed to attract the levels of advertising the company had hoped for. Its *Annual Report for 2002* stated:

> As a result of the downturn in sports-related advertising during the year,
> together with the reduction in long-term forecast advertising growth rates,
> in accordance with the company's accounting policies, the directors
> reevaluated the recoverability of the costs of certain sports contracts,
> principally in the United States. Accordingly, the company recorded a
> one-time other expense of [$900] million relating to the National Football
> League [$367 million], NASCAR [$280 million], Major League
> Baseball [$210 million] and non-U.S. cricket programming rights
> [$43 million].[6]

This write-down highlights the risks inherent in the fixed up-front fee model.

Revenue-Sharing Model: Under this model, a component of the sports rights fee (or even all of the fee) is a function of revenues associated with broadcast of the event. This model works cleanest with a broadcast free-to-air partner where the advertising revenues stream can be identified with the sports broadcast. The XFL, a joint venture between NBC and World Wrestling Entertainment (WWE), operated a 50/50 sharing of revenues for its two joint venture partners after production costs were covered. This was joint risk sharing of the uncertainty over future revenues.

Sports Rights Holder Buys Time on the Media Outlet and Keeps All Advertising Revenue It Sells: Here there is revenue certainty to the media outlet. The risk of a downturn in ratings or advertising revenues falls on the sports rights holder. An extreme version is where the sporting rights holder sets up its own cable content channel and carries its own games on that network.

U.S. NATIONAL TELEVISION RIGHTS DEALS ($ MILLIONS)

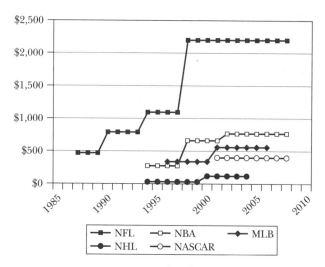

League	Contract Period	Broadcast (Free-to-Air) Partner	Cable Partner	Average Annual Rights Fee
NFL	1987–1989	CBS, NBC, ABC	ESPN	$ 468
	1990–1993	CBS, NBC, ABC	ESPN	789
	1994–1997	FOX, NBC, ABC	ESPN, TNT	1,097
	1998–2005	FOX, CBS, ABC	ESPN	2,200
MLB	1996–2000	FOX, NBC	ESPN	$ 340
	2001–2006	FOX	ESPN	559
NBA	1994–1998	NBC	TNT	$ 275
	1998–2002	NBC	TNT, TBS	660
	2002–2008	ABC	ESPN, TNT	767
NHL	1994–1999	FOX		$ 31
	1999–2004	ABC	ESPN	120
NASCAR	2001–2008	FOX, NBC	FX, TNT	$ 400
OLYMPIC GAMES (Winter/Summer)	1980(W), 1980(S)			$ 122
	1984(W), 1984(S)			390
	1988(W), 1988(S)			728
	1992(W), 1992(S)			928
	1994(W), 1996(S)			1,251
	1998(W), 2000(S)			1,845
	2002(W), 2004(S)			2,215

Source: Street & Smith's *Sports Business Journal, By the Numbers 2004,* individual leagues.

These three alternatives have many variants in practice. In some leagues, a media partner may look beyond the advertising revenues or increased cable subscribers as the value drivers in a sports rights fee contract. Consider the current contract between the Arena Football League (AFL) and NBC. NBC in 2003 became the AFL's broadcast partner in an advertising revenue-sharing model with no up-front fee. Previously, the AFL was shown on cable with limited ratings. NBC believed it was providing the AFL with a broader and higher-profile promotional opportunity. This likely would increase the market value of individual AFL clubs. The 2003 AFL/NBC contract provides that NBC will share in any club appreciation (beyond the 2003 benchmark) when they are sold. NBC believed its broadcast muscle increased the AFL's value and contracted to capture part of that appreciation for itself!

Sports Rights Fees—A Perspective From the Rights Holder

Negotiation experts recommend each party look at what the other side expects and will consider in the negotiations. A sports rights holder has several factors to consider when choosing a media partner, including:

- Size of rights fees bid. Other things being equal, the highest bidder is typically the most attractive.

- Financial solvency of the potential high bidder. Several leagues have awarded sports rights to the highest bidder and subsequently been straddled with the bidder not paying the committed fees because of bankruptcy.

- Broadness of coverage. Ability to provide coverage to as broad a base of viewers as possible (typically higher on the broadcast side than the cable side).

- Capability of bidders to broadcast the event. This includes technical capacity and ability to innovate in coverage.

- Capability of bidders to market and cross-promote the sporting league.

- Long-term relationships. It takes time to develop trust and confidence in a broadcasting partner. An incumbent partner delivering innovative and highly rated broadcasts is a positive to a league.

Creating a negotiating dynamic of more bidders than slots is important to a sports rights holder. More bidders than slots can cause media companies to increase their bids because of the risk of being left out of the final winning bids. Consider the "NFL Sunday Ticket," which is a seasonlong pass that enables the purchaser to view all nonlocal NFL games every Sunday of the season. The NFL in its negotiations had the option of making it available on all cable platforms to all subscribers in the same way that ESPN is available. However, it restricted the bidding to pit the cable platform players against each other. In 2004, DIRECTV renewed its exclusive rights to the "NFL Sunday Ticket" for a five-year period through the 2010 season for $3.5 billion. This was a 75% increase over the then existing five-year contract of $2.0 billion. DIRECTV is the sole provider of the NFL Sunday Ticket. A passionate NFL fan currently using a "cable-in-the-ground" cable company now has to switch to DIRECTV to access the NFL Sunday Ticket. One factor that led DIRECTV to bid high to the NFL for the right to carry this package was the expectation that it could attract and retain households away from cable-in-the-ground companies or from DISH Network. The potential revenues from such new customers include premium cable packages and any telephony (DSL) associated packages. The NFL Sunday Ticket would enable DIRECTV to "asset build" its year-round subscriber base. The NFL structured the bidding in a way that enabled it to capture some of the rents DIRECTV likely would gain from this asset build.

Cable Sports Networks and Regional Sports Networks

ESPN launched as a cable content channel in September 1979. It was a bellwether event in sports broadcasting. It has since become the most financially valued cable channel, capable of bidding against national broadcast networks for sporting rights. The ESPN model is a nationwide 24-hour sports network. There are multiple developments in cable sports broadcasting that attempt to compete for ESPN's focal market or create new areas that ESPN and other sports broadcasters are not addressing.

Local Sports Networks: Fan interest in club sports is typically strongly regionally focused. Sufficient sports products are available in many areas to support local cable sports content channels. For example, the Sunshine Network in Florida was launched in March 1988 and had more than 3 million subscribers in 2004. Its website notes that "each year over 600 live telecasts are showcased on Sunshine Network." Coverage includes Florida State Seminoles (College), Florida Gators (College), Miami Heat (NBA), Orlando Magic (NBA), and Tampa Bay Lightning (NHL).

National/Regional Hybrid Sports Networks: Although individual region-focused cable content channels have the benefit of a local focus, viewers also are interested in what is happening at the national level. In 1997, FOX Sports launched FOX Sports Networks. This was a new national sports channel with a local emphasis. By 2002, FOX had acquired equity interests in more than 20 local regional sports networks (RSNs). The aim was to create an umbrella brand (FOX Sports Net) that provided consistent national content to each RSN that would be supplemented by local programming—such as MLB, NBA, NHL, or college games featuring local clubs and colleges.

Sporting Club "Controlled" RSNs: The traditional RSN has an arms-length relationship with individual sporting clubs. There is growing interest in the creation of RSNs where a sporting club is an equity investor. For example, the New England Sports Network (NESN) is 80% owned by the owner of the Boston Red Sox. Not surprisingly, the Red Sox are the lead programming content on NESN. There are multiple reasons for clubs exploring such an encroachment into the television part of the sports value chain. If a club's games are key content for an RSN, owning the RSN creates the opportunity to capture rents on the television component as well as the club and stadium components of the value chain. Owning the RSN as well as a club or stadium gives the owner group more control over its brand management.

Existing RSNs without club equity ownership argue that the benefits of a sporting club "controlled" RSN are overstated. The core competency of most sporting clubs currently does not include television production and coverage. It is costly and uncertain as to whether clubs can develop this competency. Clubs that own a related RSN add an extra financial risk to their strategy. The guaranteed long-term fixed rights fees from an independent RSN enables the club to contract with players with more revenue certainty vis-à-vis the club facing uncertainty over cable subscription rates or advertising with a club-owned RSN.

High-profile RSNs with club equity interests include the New York Yankees (YES Network), in addition to the Red Sox (NESN) link. Clubs in Chicago, Denver, and Houston are also exploring this area. It is widely acknowledged that combining an MLB club with either (or both) an NBA or NHL club provides potential minimum content to explore a 24-hour, year-round, club-owned RSN. The very threat of such RSNs being set up has prompted existing RSNs to either increase their bids for sports rights with local clubs, to restructure contracts so that multiple club contracts in a city do not simultaneously expire, or even to offer clubs equity (but not control or operating rights) in the existing RSN.

Single-Sport-Related Networks: Avid fans of particular sports can find a dedicated channel a compelling proposition. They are guaranteed regular and detailed coverage of their sporting passion. The launch and growth of the Speed Channel illustrates this business opportunity. It covers motor sports, including open-wheel (such as Formula 1 and IRL), NASCAR, and bike racing, as well as replays of classic motor sports events. The Speed Channel provides advertisers with a very targeted audience, and one that has high loyalty to advertisers sponsoring their sport. One challenge here is, how many sports can both provide enough content and attract enough viewers to replicate the success of the Speed Channel?

League-Owned-and-Operated Cable Content Channels: Major league bodies are moving to own and operate cable content channels that are dedicated to their respective sports. NBA TV is a cable station available on DIRECTV, DISH Network, and multiple cable operators (such as Comcast, Cox Communications, Time Warner, and Cablevision). It describes itself on its website as "your all-access channel for everything basketball, featuring live games, behind-the-scenes access, live high-definition (HDTV) game broadcasts, new original programming and more."

Many of the benefits for single-sport-related networks also apply here. For a league, there are additional benefits. Brand management at the league level can be better promoted via a league-owned cable content channel. In addition, the league builds up expertise in television. This may be beneficial when negotiating for higher sports rights fees with independent networks and cable companies. Not surprisingly, existing sports rights holders for NBA games have very mixed reactions to the NBA starting its own NBA TV cable channel. They like its role in increasing fan interest but are leery that it is a "stalking horse" to create an extra bidder at the table to drive up NBA sports rights fees.

CASE 8.1 THE NATIONAL HOCKEY LEAGUE'S NEW TELEVISION CONTRACT FOR 2004 AND BEYOND[7]

It's much more exciting in person, even than on television—no offense to ESPN.

— United States President Bill Clinton to ESPN's Brian Hayward[8]

In May 2004, NBC and the National Hockey League announced a two-year television agreement for the 2004–2006 period. The contract was renewable by NBC for an additional two years.[9] NBC will televise seven regular season games and six Stanley Cup playoff games in regular Saturday afternoon time periods, plus games 3 through 7 of the Stanley Cup finals in primetime. (The finals are best four of seven.)

Separate from the NBC broadcast agreement, NHL extended its ESPN cable contract for three years for 40 games (instead of 70) and annual rights fees of $60, $70, and $70 million over the three years. All regular season cable games will be on ESPN2, rather than on a mix of ESPN and ESPN2 as in recent years. However, ESPN will televise some playoff games as in the prior contract, and games 1 and 2 of the Stanley Cup finals. Some 70 games a year were televised under the prior cable contract, for an average of $120 million annually. ESPN2 has 87 million subscribers, slightly fewer than ESPN.[10]

The NBC financial arrangement for the league was unusual in that no upfront money was involved. (This was analogous to NBC's arrangement with the Arena Football League.) NBC and the NHL will share revenues, according to the press release. NBC will retain enough advertising to pay its production and related costs (including pre-empting evening programs during the Finals). The revenue-sharing arrangement favors the NHL after NBC recaptures its expenses, but after an (unannounced) point, equal shares will go to each partner.

Overhanging the new television agreement was the question of whether there would be any NHL games at all in 2004–05. A serious dispute between the league and the NHL Players Association threatened the season. The two sides seemed far apart, with the NHL reportedly seeking some form of salary cap (aggregate team payroll), and the NHLPA strongly opposed. (The league had commissioned a widely-reported study led by former SEC chairman Arthur Levitt which concluded that combined team losses were $273 million during the 2002–3 season.) The possibility of a strike or lockout loomed over the coming season, since the current NHL-NHLPA agreement was to expire in September (2004).

NHL television ratings had traditionally been low. During the 1999–2004 period, regular season broadcast ratings ranged between 1.6 and 1.2, and regular season cable ratings from 0.6 to 0.5 (under 1 million households), according to sports media reports. For the playoffs, broadcast ratings were between 2.5 and 2.0 (about ten games) and cable ratings from 1.1 to 0.7 (typically 30–36 games). Ratings for the 2004 playoffs were reported at the lower end of these ranges, although slightly higher than for the 2003 playoffs.

As was true for major broadcast networks, NBC would be able to promote its NHL games to broad audiences during its regular evening schedule; it was expected that on-air promotion would be in the late week period. Separately, however, NBC was considered to have several advantages over other broadcast networks, including ABC, which had been the NHL's

Harvard Business School Case No 9-599-108. Copyright 1999 President and Fellows of Harvard College. All rights reserved. For information: permission@hbsp.harvard.edu. This case was prepared by Stephen A. Greyser and Elizabeth E. Smyth. HBS cases are developed solely for class discussion and do not necessarily illustrate effective or ineffective management.

broadcast television partner under the prior joint ABC-ESPN (Walt Disney Company) contract. NBC was first in reaching 18–49 age viewers. Also, it had a "heritage" with the NHL, having been its first broadcast network partner (1966), airing playoff games. "Peter Puck," a TV vehicle for educating viewers about hockey, appeared on NBC for three seasons starting in 1972–73.

The new contract, obviously reflecting the league's strained economic situation, represented much lower revenues for the NHL compared to the existing (and concluding) five-year deal for 1999–2004 with Disney, announced almost six years earlier.

The 1999–2004 NHL Television Contract

In August 1998, the Walt Disney Company (owner of both the ABC broadcast network and sports cable channel ESPN) had startled the sports and broadcast worlds by purchasing the rights for the national schedule of National Hockey League games for the five-year period 1999–2004. The rights were then held by both FOX Sports Net and ESPN. FOX had been televising the NHL since the 1994–95 season, and would continue to do so through 1998–99. ESPN and ESPN2 were in the last year of a seven-year cable deal.[11] The FOX schedule called for up to 19 dates; ESPN had over 100 regular season dates on a combination of ESPN and ESPN2.

Disney's contract called for paying a record (for hockey) $600 million during the five-year period. This would yield approximately $4.5 million per year for each NHL team.[12] The offer was nearly four times the five-year $155 million total package negotiated between the NHL and FOX in 1994. ESPN had paid $100 million for the seven-year cable contract in 1992. The reason many were surprised at the amount was that it was widely considered that the ratings for the NHL on FOX were not only low, but were not showing signs of improvement. More specifically, FOX's ratings had plunged 30% from a 2.0 to a 1.4 rating between the 1996–97 and 1997–98 seasons. The drop translated to a revenue loss to the network of nearly $1 million per game as a result of lower rates paid by advertisers for smaller audiences. During the same period, ESPN had shown a decline in viewership, dropping 13% from a 0.8 to a 0.7 rating; ratings for NHL games on ESPN2 remained flat at a 0.4 rating.[13]

FOX executives had linked the previous season's ratings drop to a two-week break in the regular 1997–98 NHL season. The NHL schedule break occurred in February 1998. This permitted many of the league's players to represent their countries in the Winter Olympic Games at Nagano, Japan. The break in turn delayed the NHL Stanley Cup playoffs so that they overlapped more than usual with the very popular National Basketball Association postseason.[14] Another break took place for the 2002 Salt Lake City games.

The principal intent of the NHL's participation in the Olympics was to generate interest on the part of current or prospective fans. (See "NHL 1998: 'The Coolest Game in Nagano,'" HBS Case 599-024 for a detailed description.) However, many observers questioned whether a meaningful degree of fan interest had resulted. Most of the US team's games were on TV at late night or early morning times in North America. The team's performance at the Games was sub-par; it won only one of three games and did not earn a medal. Further, the team's off-ice conduct (e.g., "trashing" some of their Olympic Village dorm rooms) cast a shadow on its image.

More on the 1999 NHL TV Contract

The 1999 NHL TV contract permitted ABC to air up to seven regular season games annually, plus six early round playoff games, up to five Stanley Cup Finals games, and the NHL All-Star game. ESPN and ESPN2 would air close to 200 games per year. ESPN would air up to 27 regular-season games, All-Star Weekend activities, and parts of the Stanley Cup Playoffs; ESPN2 would air three or four games per week for a total of 104 games.[15]

According to media sources, Disney did not enter into negotiations with the NHL, but simply placed its bid.[16] FOX had one year left on its NHL contract, and could extend that agreement by matching ABC's $250 million offer (i.e., the network portion of the $600 million). In essence, games currently televised by FOX were those that would revert to ABC if FOX did not renew its contract. The NHL gave FOX until August 14, 1998 to meet or beat the Disney offer. The deadline passed. On August 25, 1998, the NHL accepted Disney's record-breaking bid. "This is good for the sport, great for ABC and ESPN," said Steve Bornstein, president of ESPN and ABC Sports.[17] League Commissioner Gary Bettman announced:

> *This is a landmark occasion for the NHL. These agreements are the culmination of a long-standing and successful partnership with ESPN. . . . ABC, a leader in sports broadcasting for more than 30 years, and its formidable network of stations, is uniquely positioned to showcase our great game.*[18]

Although FOX would be withdrawing from the NHL's national TV schedule, it would continue to televise local games of many NHL teams. Through its various local broadcast and cable outlets, FOX was a television partner of 20 of the 27 NHL teams in 1998–99.[19]

Questions

1. What does the case tell you about the attractiveness of the NHL as a television sport? Be specific regarding the pros and cons for the NHL of the 2004 NBC contract, the 1999 ABC/ESPN contract, and the 1994 FOX contract.

2. In your view what role, if any, does television play for hockey in grass-roots fan attraction, in fan building for those interested in the game, and in fan retention?

CASE 8.2 FOX SPORTS AND FREE-TO-AIR BROADCAST TELEVISION[20]

We have the long-term rights in most countries to major sporting events and we [intend to] use sports as a battering ram and a lead offering in all our pay TV operations.

—Rupert Murdoch's speech to shareholders in 1996

The key phrase that describes what happened at FOX Sports is "asset build." Everyone traditionally talked about P&L as a key driver in television versus asset building. What Rupert Murdoch and Chase Carey did by signing on the NFL was centered on an asset building strategy.

—David Hill, CEO FOX Sports Television

In late April 2004, David Hill, the head of FOX's worldwide sports media activities at the News Corporation Limited (News Corp.), waited in his Los Angeles office for the arrival of Rupert Murdoch, the head of News Corp. News Corp. was one of the world's largest media companies, with total annual revenues of $US17.474 billion in 2003—see Appendix A. Murdoch was flying in from London to Los Angeles after checking up on his media and entertainment properties there. Hill and Murdoch planned a conference with Chase Carey, chief negotiator behind News Corp.'s sports deals, and now a key player in News' DIRECTV subsidiary, which it acquired in May 2003. Murdoch wanted to discuss with Carey and Hill a number of strategic questions relating to News Corp.'s sports future, with the focus on free-to-air broadcast television.

By 2004, Murdoch and his team had built an impressive global sports regime within News Corp., while transforming the industry with innovative strategies, implementation, and technologies. Appendix B summarizes some key events in the development of FOX Sports in the U.S. Murdoch had used FOX's acquisition of the National Football League (NFL) rights in 1993 to launch an attack on the entrenched Big Three broadcasters—CBS, ABC, and NBC. On the cable side of the business, FOX had identified a gap in the market where unbranded and ungrouped regional sports networks (RSNs) aired local team games. FOX believed in the increasing regional emphasis of America and set out to join the regional networks together. Despite these successful moves, Murdoch knew all too well that the sports industry never remained static and many key decisions remained in the future.

FOX ENTERTAINMENT GROUP

FOX Entertainment Group, Inc. (FEG), 82% owned by News Corp., developed, produced, and distributed feature films and television programs, television broadcasting, and cable network programming worldwide. FEG had total annual revenues of approximately US$11.78 billion in 2003.

FEG's studios, production facilities, and film and television library provided high-quality creative content, and FEG's broadcasting and cable networks provided extensive distribution platforms for its programs. FEG's major assets included the Twentieth Century FOX studio, The FOX Television Network, 33 full-power television stations, 20 Regional Sports

Networks (RSNs), and various cable networks, including FOX News, FX, Speed Channel, and FOX Sports Net. The genesis of FEG began in 1985 when News Corp. acquired a 50 percent stake in Twentieth Century FOX. News Corp. improved the financial performance of the then ailing film and television studio and also transformed the entity into a complete and highly integrated media and entertainment company. This process began when in 1985 News Corp. defied conventional wisdom by building FOX Broadcasting Company, a fourth broadcast network to compete with NBC, CBS, and ABC, with its $1.9 billion acquisition of six major metropolitan TV stations from Metromedia. FEG took major programming risks with the development of unconventional and creative programming such as "Married with Children," "The Simpsons," and "Ally McBeal."

SPORTS AT FOX ENTERTAINMENT GROUP

In the U.S., two different sports programming businesses existed within FEG:

- Free-to-Air broadcast television—called FOX Sports. Programs get "carried" on either FOX-owned stations or FOX-affiliated stations.[21] FOX's major competitors were ABC-, CBS-, and NBC-owned or affiliated stations.

- Cable (Pay) television—called FOX Sports Networks. Individual FOX Sports channels get "carried" by operators on both the cable ("hardware" below the ground—such as Comcast or Cablevision) and the satellite ("bird in the sky"—such as DIRECTV and DISH Network) distribution platforms.

FOX Sports generally aired NFL and MLB games and related sports newscasts. David Hill headed up FOX Sports as the chairman and CEO of FOX Sports Television Group. The group reported into the FOX Broadcasting Company (FBC). "As far as FOX Sports and FOX Sports Networks, everything reports to me with regards to what appears on air [development of programming]," said Hill. "On business issues, they report to Tony Vinciquerra, the president of FOX Television Network."

FOX Sports Networks was different from the broadcast side in that it was a 24-hour national cable sports programming service. FOX Sports Networks was located within the operating unit, FOX Cable Networks Group. Bob Thompson, president of FOX Sports Networks, led the sports cable arena and reported to the CEO of FOX Cable Networks Group as well as to David Hill in terms of programming. Thompson discussed business issues with Vinciquerra. Beyond the two U.S.-related sports properties located within FEG, a series of other sports properties existed globally. For example, FOX Sports International also reported into FOX Cable Networks Group. Other properties included ESPN STAR sports and Sky Sports.

Sports Rights Contracts: Bidding and Evaluation Process

When FOX bid for sports rights contracts, it modeled both the cost and the revenue sides in order to determine what to bid for the contracts. On the cost side, FOX included the production costs (cameras, equipment, operators, tape machines, graphics machines, etc.) and the labor costs (skilled labor, cameramen, graphic operators, sideline people, etc.). In addition, the model included studio costs if pre-game shows were involved, such as costs for opening the studio and operating the control room. FOX then had to factor in the "above-the-line" costs or the "talent," such as the announcers, producers, directors, and associate directors ("below-the-line" people included technical people that operated cameras and tape machines and did not generally make creative decisions). Finally, FOX budgeted in operations costs, such as the cost related to the satellite connection, uplinks, integration of commercials, and getting signals out to all of its television stations.

On the revenue side, in the world of Free-to-Air television, this only included advertising revenue. In order to estimate ad revenue, FOX first determined the amount of commercial units it would receive contractually from the sports league. This figure varied from sport to sport, but typically included 30-second commercial units or 15-second units. FOX's research department then projected ratings for the sport such as the NFL or NASCAR. The sales department used these ratings figures to determine the associated CPM (cost per thousand) rates for the particular ratings. This figure multiplied by the number of units gave FOX a revenue estimate for the contract. FOX also included revenue from ad units given to local stations it owned. "In theory, your revenue should exceed your cost," explained Larry Jones, chief operating officer, FOX Sports Television Group. "The difference would tell you where your break even is, so if you can generate a hundred million dollars worth of revenue in year one, and you have fifty million dollars worth of costs in year one, you can spend fifty million dollars for rights to break even, assuming you want to be in the break even business."[22] When estimating revenue for its cable channels, FOX included advertising revenues and the effect of the sports property on retaining and growing subscribers. FOX receives from cable and satellite distribution platforms a per-subscriber fee when those platforms carry a FOX cable channel.

U.S. TELEVISION BROADCAST BUSINESS: FOX SPORTS

The NFL Deal

In December 1993, Murdoch, Carey, and Hill, then head of Sky Sports in the U.K., approached the NFL in an attempt to acquire broadcast rights to NFL football games. "Chase was the primary negotiator on the deal," said Hill. "My job was simply putting pictures in a box. Chase and I complemented each other because Chase had the business side covered and I made everything happen." Murdoch and Carey had decided that football would be a crucial part of the audience-building drive at the new FOX Free-to-Air network. Carey explained: "We always looked at the television business as being one where the core was really entertainment, sports, and news. We also recognized that as we moved into a more and more fragmented world, events (sporting, entertainment, etc.) would become more and more important and would be the things that would distinguish us and give us strength. We knew that strategically, we needed these events to be able to have an identity, build an audience, and deal with advertisers. At that point, in 1993, we had launched the FOX Network and led the industry in terms of vertical integration, production, programming networks, and distribution. We had done a good job of establishing the FOX brand, but it was probably still a bit niche. At the end of the day, network has to be your big broad flagpole, so we were always looking for new opportunities and in the world of events, there was no second event to the NFL."[23] Hill provided his perspective: "This was all about an affiliate play. A lot of the FOX affiliates in those days were UHF,[24] compared to VHF stations. The brilliance of what Murdoch and Carey did, was to realize that if we had football, every cable channel in the country would carry us. Murdoch and Carey were trying to increase the penetration of the FOX network. What was the single product that would make every cable system carry it? Football."

That year, FOX outbid CBS for television rights to the NFL (FOX ultimately paid $1.58 billion for a four-year deal), while NBC had acquired the rights to the NFL's AFC games and ABC had Monday night games. FOX spent 49 percent more than CBS had paid for the previous four years. When the rights charges of $395 million per year were added to the operating costs for football programming at $100 to $150 million annually, no one expected FOX to make a profit on its deal. Murdoch did not disagree: "Did we overpay? Of course we did."[25] "It was an asset play for FOX," said Hill. "FOX in those days wasn't even secondary or tertiary. We just tried to make the network work." At the time of the NFL deal, several analysts expressed concern over Murdoch's high-paying decision: "For a company like FOX to try to create a brand, using clearly definable programming like the NFL makes great strategic sense," said Christopher Dixon, an analyst at Paine Webber. "The question is at what cost. The jury will be out on the question until the end of the season."[26] Many more analysts and top studio executives in Hollywood called FOX's move "foolish." Tracy Dolgin, former president of FOX Sports Networks, defended FOX's price paid to the NFL: "When Murdoch looked at the NFL, he didn't look at it as 'how much am I going to make in ad sales revenue versus how much am I going to pay for the rights fees and production costs.' He wanted to get stations to defect to FOX. The genius of Murdoch was to look at the decision to get the NFL based on the big picture, as opposed to looking at it based on how it would perform economically on a stand-alone basis so he was able to make a substantially higher bid than competitors. We never thought we were going to get NFL rights because we only had the low quality UHF stations, but we did and that changed media and sports history."[27]

When FOX landed the deal, David Hill moved over from London to launch the business. "Ed Goren had been a senior producer at CBS working on football and we brought him over," said Hill. "It was Ed and I who did the whole thing. We had nobody. No announcers, nothing." Hill's team worked long hours such as hundred hour weeks with high stakes at risk. "It was like any startup," said Hill. "We worked our asses off and had a lot of guts." Hill was a no-nonsense Australian who joined the core FOX Sports launch team from News Corp.'s Sky Sports, where he had led the sports programming entity since 1991. Sky Sports was the U.K.'s only dedicated sports service and was often referred to as the fastest growing subscription channel in television history. Hill brought to FOX Sports his philosophy of sports as entertainment: "Too many people treat sport like a requiem mass," asserted Hill. "They make it seem like World War III. Television sport is entertainment. We want people to sit down and laugh. The philosophy has gone through to all of our sports shows."[28] One newspaper dubbed Hill as a "TV sports' gimmick gamesman." He had earned much of this reputation at Nine Network, an Australian broadcasting company where he was an executive producer and vice president of sports.

After he joined FOX Sports, Hill began working with his launch team to "FOXize" the NFL: "We felt enormous pressure to do something big when we actually won the NFL deal," recalled Dolgin. The FOX Sports team created a promotional campaign nine months prior to the first game, which was more typical of movie than television marketing. "Traditionally, television didn't start marketing until two months out because it was general consensus that viewers had short attention spans," said Dolgin. "But we had this sports property and we were betting the whole future of FOX on this property so we came up with this in-your-face marketing campaign to do a few things—to try to change the way sports was viewed on television, to build a FOX brand, and to turn FOX into a real network." The team used the tagline, "Same Game—New Attitude" and created a series of outrageous promotions that included famous football players who wanted to try new things. "We were extremely nervous about this approach, though," recalled Dolgin. "We were paranoid that our idea was going to be rejected by the traditional sports fan. The media was predicting that Bart Simpson would be in our announcer booth." Murdoch hired John Madden, paying him $30 million for four years, making him the highest paid man in the sport, including players. Madden was one of football's most well known NFL figures as head coach of the Oakland Raiders and as an expert NFL analyst for 22 years. Hill also hired Pat Summerall, Madden's longtime partner at CBS for $1.5 million per year, Terry Bradshaw, a former Pittsburgh Steelers quarterback for $1.75 million per year, and Jimmy Johnson, former Dallas Cowboys coach for $600,000 per year.

In terms of production changes, Hill came up with the FOX BOX, or the now standard constant score and clock graphic used by every sports network. This, among other technical innovations, led the industry to label him the "P.T. Barnum of sports coverage." "It's very common sensical what I do," said Hill. "You have to put yourself in the role of the viewer." Carey recalled the FOX BOX discussion with Hill: "David [Hill] told me he wanted to do the FOX BOX and as someone who has been watching football for decades, I didn't want to do it and thought I'd hate it. But I had more confidence in David's judgment than my own and so I told him to try it and now you can't turn on a football game without seeing it." Later on, the "FOX NFL Sunday" pre-game show became the most watched program of its genre and has since won two Emmys for "Outstanding Studio Show." Following FOX's broadcast of Super Bowl XXXVI in 2002, the most-watched program of the year on any network, "Malcolm in the Middle," the Emmy Award-winning FOX Television Studios comedy, drew an extraordinary 31 million viewers. Carey commented on FOX's production: "We knew that we needed to be able to present and broadcast NFL games with the quality that stood up to certain standards and expectations. I give tremendous credit to David Hill and the people he put into place to get the job done. My side is really the business side only. I'm not a creative executive or a production executive. I think there's a dimension that exceeded our expectations and it's probably what David and his team have done in terms of presenting those games. That was a dimension that none of us really dreamed of—that we'd actually do it better than everyone else did."

Just four years after signing its watershed 1993 NFL deal, FOX Sports stood as the leader in TV sports. Football propelled FOX into mainstream America: "FOX became, with the NFL, a place," said Hill. "FOX moved into people's consciousness and forced cable operators to put it on the air. It established itself in 100 percent of the market and that could never have happened without football."[29]

NHL, MLB, and NASCAR Deals

Following the success of the NFL, the struggling NHL pursued FOX. FOX paid $155 million for the four-year deal from 1994 to 1998, almost double what ESPN had paid for the previous four years. "Our bet on the NHL was that you could really grow that sport," said Carey. "It was a sport that hadn't been on television a lot and we thought we could take the sport ahead." "Hockey saw what FOX did with the NFL and they wanted us to market their sport to the mainstream," said Dolgin. "We did the same thing for hockey that we did for the NFL. We conducted this huge marketing campaign, tried to make stars out of their players, did crazy promotions, made the puck glow, etc. Everyone thought we were crazy." The glowing puck Dolgin referred to was the "FOXTrax" system or "Glow Puck" that had begun appearing on FOX televised hockey games in 1996. The technology was developed in response to one of the most common complaints television viewers had about watching hockey; namely, that it was sometimes difficult to follow the puck. With the FOXTrax system, the puck on TV glowed blue during most of the play, and when the puck traveled over 70 mph, a red comet tale appeared on the screen. The Glow Puck eventually disappeared when FOX lost the NHL. "We had a little bit of bad luck with the NHL," noted Hill. "Until we took the NHL over, there hadn't been a sweep in the Stanley Cup since 1916 or something. We had three straight. If I had to do it again, I don't think I would have done anything differently. We thought we might be able to replicate the stadium experience with television, but we couldn't—maybe 20 or 30 years from now. We didn't bid for the NHL deal after our contract ended in 1998." Carey reflected on the NHL: "I'm not sure we could ever really put our hand on why the NHL was never that successful. I think at its core, there was a longer-term issue of whether the sport translates well to television. It turned out to be a bigger challenge than we had originally expected."

In 1996 FOX began its broadcast relationship with MLB. NBC shared postseason (playoffs and World Series) with FOX from 1996 to 2000. In 2000, FOX Sports signed a six-year deal locking up nearly all of MLB's national TV and cable rights, including the All-Star Game, American League Division Series, National League Division Series, American League Championship Series, National League Championship Series, and the World Series. The flagship FOX network would carry every All-Star and postseason game through 2006. The FX cable network would air Saturday night games and the FOX Family Channel would air Thursday night games. During this period, the only non-FOX national baseball broadcasts would be ESPN's Wednesday and Sunday night cablecasts. FOX paid $2.5 billion for this package, an increase of 44 percent over the previous contracts signed five years before. The contract protected MLB in the event of a labor dispute—if some of the games were canceled by a strike or a lockout, MLB would still get all its money, but needed to compensate FOX with additional telecasts. "Baseball was the most traditionalist sport in the world and they wanted to change the way it was covered," said Hill. "Chase Carey assessed the situation and saw an opportunity in baseball. So he started talking to baseball and they listened to him. Eventually, we ended up with the contract." FOX introduced the "Catcher Cam" which gave viewers a view from the catcher's mask, in-base microphones, and microphones on the outfield walls. Before 2001, MLB's national television rights had been divided between two networks for 21 of the past 25 seasons. NBC shared the package with ABC from 1976 to 1989 and again as part of "The Baseball Network" in 1994 to 1995.

The televising of auto racing had changed dramatically in the first years of the 21st century. There was a new NASCAR television contract in place beginning in 2001, an extension of the Indy Racing League (IRL) contract with ABC and ESPN, and a new CART (Champion Auto Racing Teams—a company that put on major races throughout the year) television agreement with CBS and FOX replacing an earlier deal with long-time TV partners ABC and ESPN. NASCAR racers used racing versions of cars purchased by consumers. IRL and CART racers used cars similar to that in Formula 1 (F1) racing. While the networks had rotated frequently in terms of televising auto racing, many events in the sport had held and even improved their ratings as other sports events had lagged. In 1999 FOX reached an agreement with NASCAR, giving FOX broadcast and cable rights for Winston Cup and Busch Grand National Series racing over eight years. FOX, along with sister cable network FX, had broadcast and cable rights for the first half of the season, while NBC and Turner Sports had broadcast and cable rights for the second half of the season. FOX Sports and NBC Sports alternated coverage of the Daytona 500.

The 2001 inaugural season of NASCAR on FOX received critical accolades and attracted record-high ratings. Hill called the inaugural NASCAR telecasts "probably the most enjoyable start-up in sports I've ever been involved in. I liked the people involved with NASCAR." NASCAR realized that they had one race one week on one network and the next race on another week on another network. They realized that for them to become a major player in sports, they had to consolidate. They went through a three-year period where they brought the rights back from all the tracks, which had previously owned them. They then went to the broadcasters and offered different options such as multiple races to a single network and half season packages to networks. This way networks could create promotions week after week and maximize promotional opportunities. As a result, NASCAR ratings went up more than any other sport has ever gone up in a single year. Hill and his team also "lowered the cameras and cranked up the audio," said Hill. They used FOX's hockey puck technology (with the assistance of Sportvision) to help viewers identify cars.

A CHANGING LANDSCAPE

Fragmentation of Entertainment Choices

Over the decade of the 1990s, the free-to-air broadcast networks were increasingly affected by fragmentation of entertainment choices. Consumers faced increased programming choices besides free-to-air networks that carried major sports, placing the burden to lure viewers onto the major networks. While the number of programming options had increased dramatically, the amount of people sitting in front of televisions had not. These trends led to lower television ratings across the board, including sports ratings (although sports ratings remained the least affected by fragmentation).

Despite the ratings decline of nationally televised sports events, according to Gould Media, regionally delivered sports were thriving. "While this is good in local markets, it is a negative in the overall picture of television sports [as regional sports viewership often took away from national sports programs]."[30] Hill gave his perspective on sports viewership: "Sports will always be the most bullet proof in terms of entertainment. The bottom line is, sports is probably one of the very few things that isn't going to live on a video-on-demand situation—that is, it has to be watched live. It will still create an audience that will never be created in any other form of broadcast television."

Sports Rights Contracts

For the year ended June 30, 2002, News Corp. wrote off AU$1,861 million (US$906 million) against its sports contracts, which had failed to attract the levels of advertising the company had hoped for, according to its annual report—"The company recorded a one-time other expense of AU$1,861 million relating to the National Football League (AU$753 million), NASCAR (AU$578 million), Major League Baseball (AU$437 million) and non-U.S. cricket programming rights (AU$93 million)."[31]

The FOX write-down underscored the difficulties experienced by all networks that paid high prices for rights fees. The FOX write-downs were announced after NBC reported losses on its NBA deal, estimated at US$300 million over the prior two seasons. NBC cited those losses as the reason it dropped out of the bidding on NBA rights beginning in the 2002 to

2003 season. Thompson reflected on FOX Sports' rights contracts historically: "In a narrow sense, we probably overpaid for the first NFL, but it increased the asset value of the FOX network and our local television stations. NASCAR has also been successful. The NHL, on the other hand, was not as successful, even though we made money on the deal. We had the right idea, but it just didn't work. The MLB contract was challenging as well. All you have to do is to look where we took write-downs to see where we had challenges." "The prices being paid to sport and sporting bodies have got beyond an economic level," said Murdoch. "And that's not just in the U.S. but everywhere else as well."[32]

Jones discussed the challenges of bidding for rights in 2002: "It is very different today than it was in 1993 when we were willing to truly stretch the bidding model much more because the value of the NFL to us was significant, in the sense that at that time, the FOX Network was still relatively new. It didn't have full coverage in the country. FOX's acquisition of the NFL rights gave the network the ability to get more stations to take its programming. FOX factored in potential station acquisition when trying to decide how much to overspend for the NFL. This is not a factor today, because we already have the 98 percent so we would not receive any extra value by overspending." In addition, the first NFL contract allowed FOX to switch from its weaker stations around the country to stronger stations more valuable to the company as a whole.

In 2002, FOX applied its more conservative bidding strategy to other sports: "We are not going to stretch the numbers anymore for the PGA or MLB," said Jones. "If our model does not show us at least breaking even or making money, then we're simply not going to bid any higher than that. We used to do that, but not anymore." Hill agreed to some extent, but emphasized bidding on a case-by-case basis: "Anyone who thinks they know what's going to happen in the sports rights business is either a fool or a liar. Things will change dramatically and there's no way you can make a blanket statement in terms of what you will do during a bidding process. You have to analyze what's going on in the current environment at a given time."

The End of Free Television?

Fragmentation and sky-high sports rights contracts led many to question the economic viability of the broadcast television model. "The biggest problem right now is that free over-the-air television is becoming a dying breed," said Jones. "We're limited to only one source of revenue and on top of that, the sports leagues are selling sponsorships to people who traditionally buy advertisements from us. For example, Nike will buy a sign in the stadiums instead of buying a TV ad with us. To make money, the NFL could move over to cable or a pay package. However, the government will never allow that to happen and the NFL is quite aware of that. Baseball could migrate to cable, except for the World Series." Hill agreed: "Television must change. Economic forces will dictate this. To me, it's similar to book production in the Middle Ages when books were produced one by one by monks until moveable type was invented. Television is going to go exactly the same way. The sporting rights economic model worked fine when there were only three networks. It's simple supply and demand. The average American will have 600 channels by 2006. The great thing about FOX is that we're a content company. Whatever technological changes occur, we will be ready for it. We've been working on various technological things for three to four years. It all depends on whether set-top boxes will be rolled out. The bottom line is that viewers don't care how they get their programming—if it's brought in by over-the-air, through cable, by satellite, or brought in by a pack rat. The programming is key—content is key."

Other sports such as basketball had already begun to partially shift to cable. The NBA entered the 2002 to 2003 season with new television partners ABC, ESPN, and AOL Time Warner, replacing NBC and TNT/TBS. On January 22, 2002, ESPN announced that, along with ABC, a sister unit of Walt Disney, it had outbid NBC for six years of NBA games for $2.4 billion, or just over a year's worth of ESPN revenues. Basketball was a sport that had seen its TV ratings plummet 40 percent since 1996 and ESPN's NBA foray was the first time a cable player had grabbed a major sports contract from the broadcast networks. NBC, which had held the contract for the past 12 years, refused to shell out more than $1.3 billion, after losing money in two of the four years on its last contract.

An important watershed in the trend to "non-free sports television" was the "NFL Sunday Ticket" package first introduced in 1995. DIRECTV was awarded the exclusive rights to this package. It was not available on free-to-air, cable, or on DISH Network (DIRECTV's satellite competitor). Subscribers to this service could view all NFL games each weekend through the 17-week regular season. In December 2002, DIRECTV renewed its "NFL Sunday Ticket" agreement with the NFL. It was reported that: "The five-year deal is said to be worth close to $2 billion. It calls for about three times the annual fee of the current pact. About 1.5 million of DIRECTV's 11 million subscribers pay the additional $180 a year for the service, and it's a key marketing draw in signing up new customers."[33]

THE FUTURE

During Murdoch's late April 2004 meeting with Hill and Carey, they planned to discuss the need for continuous innovation in order to remain ahead of the competition. As they had in the past, numerous industry changes complicated their task. In the U.S., industry fragmentation made competing for viewership increasingly difficult, thus making the hunt for advertising revenues and subscriber fees on the cable and satellite side all the more challenging. Meanwhile, costs were at all time highs with record-high sports rights contracts on the free-to-air network and the networks/channels on the cable and satellite distribution platforms. All of this led to a big question mark in terms of the future of sports on free-to-air broadcast television.

APPENDIX A
News Corp. Timeline

1952: Rupert Murdoch inherits the Adelaide News from his father, Sir Keith Murdoch.

1953: Takes over News Ltd in Australia.

1964: Launches the Australian, his first national newspaper.

1969: Takes over the News of the World and The Sun in the U.K.

1973: Buys San Antonio Express News in the U.S.

1976: Buys the New York Post from Dorothy Schiff.

1980: Establishes News Corporation.

1981: Takes over the Times and Sunday Times in the U.K. with a controversial deal that passes the U.K. monopolies commission.

1983: Launches the first ever satellite TV channel, Sky. Sky uses a European telecommunications satellite, Eutelsat, owned by European state post and telecoms operations, including British Telecom.

1985:	Takes control of 20th Century FOX in the U.S. Acquires Metromedia's independent television stations from John Kluge for £1.5 billion, giving News Corp. a presence in six major U.S. cities.
1988:	Forced to sell the New York Post to the real estate developer, Peter Kalikow, when media ownership rules are tightened. Pays Walter Annenberg £2 billion for Triangle Publications, owner of TV Guide. News Corp. announces plans for the Sky satellite channel across Europe. Revenues of News Corp. are $5,976 million in Australian dollars.
1990:	British Satellite Broadcasting merges with Sky to form British Sky Broadcasting (BSKYB). Revenues of News Corp. are $8,736 million in Australian dollars.
1992:	BSKYB buys the broadcasting rights to the Premier League for £300 million in a joint bid with the BBC. Four years later, it pays £670m to renew the contract and in 2001 it paid £1.1 billion. Revenues of News Corp. are $10,189 million in Australian dollars.
1993:	Buys back the New York Post after a financial crisis plunges the publication into turmoil. News Corp. pays £325 million to take control of Hong Kong-based STAR TV.
1998:	Floats 18 percent of FOX Entertainment Group. News Corp. retains 82 percent.
2000:	Buys Chris Craft Industries and United Television in the U.S. (10 TV stations in total) for £3.6 billion.
2003:	Reaches agreement with General Motors to acquire a controlling interest in Hughes Electronics, whose DIRECTV subsidiary is the leading satellite company in the U.S. Revenues of News Corp. in 2003 are $US 17,474 million whilst net income is $US 947 million.
2004:	News Corp. shifts primary sharemarket listing from Australian Stock Exchange to New York Stock Exchange.

Source: Adapted from Dan Milmo, "How Murdoch Built His Empire," *Guardian*, November 20, 2001.

APPENDIX B
FOX SPORTS TIMELINE

December 1993:	NFL announces that the FOX Broadcasting Company was awarded the rights to broadcast the NFC package for the next four seasons.
April 1994:	FOX begins marketing the NFL with the groundbreaking "Same Game, New Attitude" slogan.
September 1994:	Regular season NFL action premiers on FOX Sports with double-header coverage of six games.
April 1995:	After almost half of the NHL season lost due to a lockout, the "NHL on FOX" premiers with regional coverage of six games. Regular season NHL games are seen on broadcast television for the first time in 20 years.
January 1996:	FOX Sports unveils FOXTrax, a computer tracking and graphics system that creates a glow around the puck, at Boston's FleetCenter prior to the 1996 NHL All Star Game.
June 1996:	FOX Sports premiers its MLB coverage with a four-game regionalized schedule of the FOX Saturday Baseball Game of the Week.
July 1996:	FOX enters into a 50/50 joint venture with Liberty Media to start a national regional sports networks.
November 1996:	FOX Sports debuts with 21 million subscriptions formed from original Prime Ticket regions.

July 1997:	FOXsports.com launches under the direction of News Digital Media.
January 1998:	FOX/Liberty and Rainbow (owned by Cablevision) form the first national sports network made up of the best regional sports networks. Rainbow's regions are rebranded FOX Sports Net and distribution grows to 60 million.
March 1998:	The FOX Group is given a positive vote and approval by MLB team owners for the purchase of the Los Angeles Dodgers.
April 1998:	FOX enters into joint venture with Phil Anschutz under which FOX takes a 40 percent ownership in the new Staples Center arena to be built in downtown Los Angeles.
July 1999:	Host Marriott opens its first FOX Sports SkyBox at the Chicago Airport, under a license deal with FOX Sports.
August 2000:	FOX Sports Radio Network debuts under a license deal with Premier Radio, a division of Clear Channel.
January 2001:	FOXSports.com is folded under FOX Sports and re-launched.
February 2001:	FOX Sports launches NASCAR coverage with Daytona 500.
October 2002:	FOX Sports Interactive TV launched Insight cable systems. FOX Sports partners with Verizon and ActiveSky to create premium mobile phone sports service.
November 2002:	The first FOX Sports Grill Restaurant is opened under a license agreement with B&B Restaurant Ventures.
May 2003:	News Corp.'s acquisition of DIRECTV includes rights to "NFL Sunday Ticket" package.

Source: FOX Sports.

Questions

1. Assume you are a senior executive of News Corp. in 1993. On the table is a proposal for a 4-year NFL bid for $395 million annual rights fees plus $100–$150 million additional annual operating costs.

   a. Make the case against the proposal.

   b. Make the case for the proposal.

   Why might the NFL be willing to risk using FOX given it was not (then) a "full-fledged network"?

2. What were the key dates/points in the evolution of FOX Sports (the free-to-air broadcasting side)? Of the dates/points you identify, choose two where you believe the chosen course of action was far from obvious. Give your reasoning.

3. For the year ended June 30, 2002, News Corp. wrote off $AU 1,861 million ($U.S. 906 million) on its sports rights, including NFL ($AU 753 million), NASCAR ($AU 578 million), and MLB ($AU 437 million). What strategy would you use on bidding on the next round of NFL, NASCAR, or MLB contracts? Give your reasoning.

4. Comment on News Corp.'s acquisition of a controlling interest in DIRECTV in May 2003. What extra strengths does this acquisition bring to News Corp.'s portfolio of sporting assets? How best can it "exploit" these extra strengths?

CASE 8.3   YES NETWORK AND CABLEVISION: WILL THE YANKEES FANS CONTINUE TO STRIKE OUT?[34]

Cable industry veteran Leo Hindery hung up the telephone in disgust. It was June 2002, and he had just received a call from his one of his lawyers, telling him that Cablevision had requested 660 days to prepare to defend the lawsuit filed against them by the YES (Yankees Entertainment and Sports) Network. This stall tactic was not good news for Hindery, the CEO of YES. Each day that Cablevision did not carry YES was a financial dagger, since Cablevision's nearly 3 million customers represented a major chunk of the region's cable subscribers. Without Cablevision on board, YES was destined to lose out on approximately $65 million annually in subscriber fees and advertising revenue, nearly a third of their projected $200 million in revenue.[35] Furthermore, 2.7 million New Yorkers were up in arms that they could not watch their beloved New York Yankees in 130 televised games on YES. As their first baseball broadcast season came to a close, Hindery, the Yankees, and YES were faced with one major obstacle blocking the path to success: Cablevision.

Hindery was a Stanford MBA (1971) who had an extensive background in media and cable television. In 1988 he founded InterMedia Partners. In 1997, Hindery was elected President of Tele-Communications, Inc. (TCI), then the world's largest cable distribution entity. In March 1999, AT&T bought TCI for $52 billion, and Hindery became the CEO of AT&T Broadband. He was one of Business Week's "Top 25 Executives of the Year" for 1999.

MAJOR LEAGUE BASEBALL

In 2002, Major League Baseball (MLB) was struggling with multiple issues—major revenue imbalances across teams, potential contraction to eliminate weaker teams, and television ratings. Team revenues related to television consisted of (1) a shared component from the national TV contract, and (2) local revenues. In 1999, MLB signed a seven-year $2.5 billion national TV contract with FOX Sports for a select number of regular season games and all post season games.[36] This contract averaged out to $11.9 million annually for each of the league's 30 teams.

The major factor explaining revenue differences across MLB teams was the size of the local TV revenues—see Exhibit 1. In most cases, each MLB team negotiated their local TV contract with an independent third party. For example, the Florida Marlins (owned by John Henry) had local contracts with free-to-air (WAM-TV) and cable (Sports Channel Florida), both of which were unrelated to John Henry. Where commercial ownership overlapped between an already strong MLB team and a television network, the potential for enlarging the revenue imbalance in MLB was increased. The 2002 sale of the Boston Red Sox for $660 million highlighted the value of owning both a MLB team and a RSN (regional sports network).[37] The $660 million included an estimated $320 million for 80 percent of NESN (The New England Sports Network). The Boston Red Sox could use profits from its ownership of NESN to further strengthen its on-field team.

EXHIBIT 1   Major League Baseball 2001 Local TV Revenues, Summary Financial Estimated by Forbes, and Free-to-Air TV/Cable Breakdown

Team	Number of Free-to-Air TV Cable Games	Local TV Revenue ($ Millions)	Forbes Estimates		
			Total Revenues ($ Millions)	Operating Income ($ Millions)	Team Valuation ($ Millions)
1. New York Yankees	50/100	$56.750	$215	$18.7	$730
2. New York Mets	50/100	$46.251	169	14.3	482
3. Seattle Mariners	34/106	$37.860	166	14.1	373
4. Boston Red Sox	67/85	$33.353	152	−11.4	426
5. Chicago White Sox	53/99	$30.092	101	−3.8	223
6. Los Angeles Dodgers	50/80	$27.342	143	−29.6	435
7. Texas Rangers	75/80	$25.284	134	−6.5	356
8. Chicago Cubs	78/72	$23.559	131	7.9	287
9. Cleveland Indians	75/75	$21.076	150	−3.6	360
10. Baltimore Orioles	65/85	$20.994	133	3.2	319
11. Atlanta Braves	90/59	$19.988	160	9.5	424
12. Detroit Tigers	40/100	$19.073	114	12.3	262
13. Philadelphia Phillies	45/113	$18.940	94	2.6	231
14. Colorado Rockies	75/50	$18.200	129	6.7	347
15. San Francisco Giants	62/60	$17.197	142	16.8	355
16. Tampa Bay Devil Rays	65/64	$15.511	92	−6.1	142
17. Florida Marlins	55/95	$15.353	81	1.4	137
18. Toronto Blue Jays	40/110	$14.460	91	−20.6	182
19. Arizona Diamondbacks	75/60	$14.174	127	−3.9	280
20. Houston Astros	62/75	$13.722	125	4.1	337
21. San Diego Padres	25/115	$12.436	92	5.7	207
22. St. Louis Cardinals	45/59	$11.905	123	−5.1	271
23. Anaheim Angels	40/50	$10.927	103	5.7	195
24. Oakland Athletics	50/60	$ 9.458	90	6.8	157
25. Pittsburgh Pirates	15/105	$ 9.097	108	9.5	242
26. Cincinnati Reds	0/85	$ 7.861	87	4.3	204
27. Minnesota Twins	25/105	$ 7.273	75	3.6	127
28. Kansas City Royals	51/30	$ 6.505	85	2.2	152
29. Milwaukee Brewers	50/80	$ 5.918	108	18.8	238
30. Montreal Expos	0/48 (French)	$ 0.536	63	−3.4	108

Sources: *USA Today,* December 7, 2001.

Baseball Prospectus, Doug Pappas, December 12, 2001 (http://www.baseballprospectus.com/news/20011212pappas.html).

Broadcasting and Cable, April 2, 2001.

Regional Sports Network Economics

The major free-to-air networks (ABC, CBS, FOX and NBC) and their affiliates had a single revenue model—from the sale of advertising spots. In contrast, cable stations had a dual revenue model—1. Sale of advertising spots, and 2. Cable subscriptions fees. Cable content channels typically received a per subscriber fee from their cable distributors (such as

Comcast, Time Warner, Cablevision, DIRECTV, and DISH). Examples of payments made by cable distributors to cable content stations are ESPN, ($1.84 per month per subscriber), Disney ($0.73), TNT ($0.72), USA ($0.39), and CNN ($0.37).[38]

The Boston Red Sox-owned NESN was carried by AT&T Broadband in its Boston market at a monthly fee to NESN of $1.40 per subscriber.[39] With 3.1 million subscribers, NESN received $52.080 million in annual subscriber revenues (3.1 million × $1.40 per subscriber × 12 months). This subscriber revenue, combined with advertising revenue, enabled NESN to cover its own production costs and then contribute a healthy profit to the Boston Red Sox.

THE YES NETWORK

In 1999, New York Yankees owner George Steinbrenner merged his team with the NBA's New Jersey Nets, creating a holding company called YankeeNets. Under the structure of YankeeNets, the teams were to be run by their principal owners: George Steinbrenner of the Yankees, and Lewis Katz and Ray Chambers of the Nets. In 2000, YankeeNets purchased a majority interest in the National Hockey League's (NHL) New Jersey Devils for $175 million. This MLB-NBA-NHL partnership enabled the creation of the YES Network, a viable alternative to the Cablevision stronghold over local television broadcast rights.

For several years, Steinbrenner and YankeeNets envisioned a golden opportunity to capitalize on the popularity of the Yankees and their other sports properties. Rather than merely collect a fee for Yankees television rights, they could create additional sources of revenue by creating their own cable television network. This new network would have the dual revenue opportunity: per-subscriber cable fees as well as advertising. First, however, the Yankees had to carry out the remainder of their multi-year contract with the Madison Square Garden (MSG) Network. Steinbrenner also needed a leader who could quickly convince the cable operators to carry this network at the right price. Steinbrenner hired media and cable veteran Leo Hindery.

In June 2001, Hindery met with Steinbrenner and Goldman Sachs executives at the Regency Hotel in New York, and began carving out a deal to raise equity for the new venture. Hindery committed several million dollars of his own money to the venture. In the end, the YES Network was valued at approximately $850 million,[40] with the YankeeNets owning a 60 percent stake, and four private investors comprising the other 40 percent. Included in this group was Goldman Sachs at 30 percent, Providence Equity Partners 8 percent, Hindery 1.5 percent, and cable veteran Bill Bresnan 0.5 percent. Hindery signed a three-year agreement to be CEO of the Yankees Entertainment and Sports Network LLC (YES). The majority of YES's content was to be Yankee and Nets-related, including 130 Yankee games and 75 Nets games.

YES Network Business Model

The success of the YES network hinged on four key factors: predictable broadcast rights contracts with local professional sports teams, attractive long-term carriage agreements with cable distribution operators, a constant stream of quality advertisers, and premium-quality 24-hour programming. Exhibit 2 is a summary of key players in the YES sports broadcasting landscape.

EXHIBIT 2   Sᴘᴏʀᴛs Bʀᴏᴀᴅᴄᴀsᴛɪɴɢ Lᴀɴᴅsᴄᴀᴘᴇ ғᴏʀ **YES**

Arenas/Venues	Leagues/Teams	Content	Distribution
Yankee Stadium	**Governing - Bodies** MLB NBA NHL **Teams** New York Yankees (MLB) New York Knicks (NBA) New York Rangers (NHL) New York Liberty (WNBA) New York Mets (MLB) New Jersey Nets (NBA) New Jersey Devils (NHL)	1. Free-to-Air Broadcasting (Advertising Revenue) Networks & Affiliates • ABC • CBS • FOX • NBC • UPN • WBN Local Independents 2. Cable Content Channels (Subscription Revenue and Advertising Revenue) YES Network MSG Network FOX Sports New York ESPN 3. Pay per View (PPV Event Review)	1. Free to Air Distribution 2. Cable Distribution • Time Warner Cable • Comcast • AT&T Broadband • Cablevision 3. Satellite Distribution • DIRECTV • DISH
Madison Square Garden			
Continental Airlines Arena			
Shea Stadium			

Team Broadcast Rights

Since YankeeNets was a significant stakeholder in YES, YES had a built-in advantage to secure quality sports programming content at a competitive price. According to Hindery, baseball was the key to a 24-hour regional sports network. "Baseball and its 162 games are necessary to provide enough content for a local sports network like YES," said Hindery.

The Yankees were also a popular programming component because of their longtime success on the field as well as their storied tradition. By 2002, they had won 26 World Series, 17 more than any other team. Yankee Stadium, "The House That Ruth Built," was a historic landmark in the Bronx. The Yankees had the second-highest home attendance in 2002 (second only to the Seattle Mariners), drawing nearly 3.5 million fans.[41] As YES was launching, the Yankees had won four of the last six World Series championships.

For years, the MSG Network and FOX Sports New York (both joint-ventures between Cablevision and FOX Sports and operated by Cablevision) held all of the local broadcast rights to all professional baseball, basketball, and hockey teams in the greater New York area. The NFL television rights were locked up in national contracts, with only pre-season games and supplementary programming available to local networks. For the past 12 years, Cablevision's MSG held the local broadcast rights for the Yankees. The Yankees' 12-year, $486 million cable deal with MSG expired in 2000, but the original contract contained a clause that gave MSG the first right of refusal for a new deal. MSG refused to let the Yankees slip away without compensation. In 2001, exercising one of the options available pursuant to a lawsuit settlement with MSG, the Yankees paid MSG $30 million to buy back its local broadcast rights for the 2002 season (making 2001 effectively the last year for the MSG/Yankees contract).

For approximately $54 million per year (commencing in 2002), YES purchased all television broadcast rights for the New York Yankees, who played a 162 game schedule.[42] YES did not televise the entire season, however. FOX and ESPN owned the national rights to up to 12 Yankee games over the course of the season. YES also signed a three-year, $36 million contract with WCBS/Channel 2 in New York, guaranteeing the local network 20 games per season.[43] Thus, YES was left with 130 regular season games to televise. YES also acquired Yankee radio rights and re-licensed them to Infinity Broadcasting/WCBS-AM, agreeing to a five-year deal worth $48.75 million. Infinity paid more for Yankee radio rights in 2002 than Cincinnati, Minnesota, Kansas City, Milwaukee, and Montreal received for television and radio rights combined in 2001.[44]

In August 2002, YES signed a 10-year agreement to carry New Jersey Nets games. The Nets made it to the 2002 NBA Finals. In exchange for paying the Nets $8 million per season, YES acquired the rights to televise around 75 Nets games. The Nets were previously on the MSG network for just over $7 million per season. The New Jersey Devils were under contract to FOX Sports NY (FSNY) until 2007.

Other sports featured on the YES network included: NY Giants and Jets pre- and post-game shows, Canadian Football League (CFL), minor league baseball, and Ivy League and other college events. After discussions with FOX, which held the broadcast rights for the English Premier League, YES was also planning to carry Manchester United soccer games from the UK, beginning in 2003.

Carriage Agreements with Cable Operators

There are over 8 million cable subscribers in the greater New York area. There are 5.745 million cable subscribers in the advertising industry's designated market area (DMA) for New York. The DMA is what local advertising rates are based on. The top six DMA markets and their cable penetration are New York (7.282 million/78.9% = 5.745 million), Los Angeles (5.318 million/62.4%), Philadelphia (2.830 million/82.0%), San Francisco-Oakland-San Jose (2.436 million/76.4%) and Boston (2.353 million/82.5%). New York, unlike most cities, is a very fragmented cable environment, with over 30 cable operators in the area. According to Nielsen, 78.9% of New Yorkers subscribe to cable.[45] There are over 8 million cable subscribers in the greater New York area.

YES sought agreements with cable operators to be broadcast on their expanded basic cable tier, the most popular tier of subscription television service. In 2001–2002, YES signed 3 to 10 year carriage agreements with over 30 regional cable operators, including for outer market areas such as Connecticut and Eastern Pennsylvania. Every cable operator in the region, except one, agreed to pay YES an average of $1.85 per subscriber per month. Cablevision, with 2.7 million subscribers (comprising nearly half of the area's DMA[46]), refused to carry YES at that price.

Satellite TV offered YES an opportunity for expanded regional and some national coverage, and it signed a three-year agreement with market leader DIRECTV. MLB restrictions, however, required that live Yankee games be televised only in the designated New York region. For example, DIRECTV customers in California could receive the YES Network, but live Yankee games were blacked out unless the subscriber also paid for an MLB-approved regional sports package called "Extra Innings." These restrictions were designed to protect the interests of local teams, who did not want other televised MLB games to damage their own attendance and broadcast value.

EchoStar's DISH Network was the second biggest satellite network in the region. DISH refused to carry YES, claiming that it would have to raise national rates by one dollar to do so. EchoStar CEO Charlie Ergen said that he offered to carry YES on an a la carte basis, allowing the network to charge viewers what it wanted. YES declined the option, however, since to do so would contravene YES's basic carriage agreements with cable operators and DIRECTV.[47]

Advertisers

Advertising rates for sporting events vary, depending on the number of households reached and the expected Nielsen rating for the event. In 2002, according to one New-York based ad buyer, New York regional rates ranged from $3,500 for a 30-second ad on ESPN to $35,000 for a similar ad during a New York Giants game on FOX's free-to-air channel.[48] Initially, advertisers clamored for Yankee game spots on the new YES network. YES intended to charge them $7,500 per 30-second ad, even more than the $6,500 MSG had charged for Yankee games the previous year.[49] YES believed that part of this additional cost was justified by each game being rerun at least one time. Ads during pre-game and post-game shows cost about half of a 30-second in-game ad.[50] In total, YES forecast nearly $55 million in ad revenue for 2002.[51] However, without Cablevision on board, YES took an advertising hit. Without nearly half of the DMA's cable subscribers, YES could only charge advertisers about $5,000 per 30-second spot.[52] "We also disproportionately lost upscale advertisers," said Hindery. "Chrysler Jeep, Toyota, and GM, for example, pulled out. Cablevision owns Long Island, and that is where a high concentration of these car dealerships are."

YES sold ad packages that often included non-game programming. "These rates vary and range from a time-buy concept to a revenue share depending on the program," said YES Executive Vice President of Development Derek Chang. "Rates are considerably less than during a Yankee game." YES sometimes carried programming content under a revenue sharing agreement. For example, the Canadian Football League (CFL) did not collect a rights fee from YES, instead opting to share advertising revenues during game broadcasts.

Exhibit 3 presents some summary YES Financials, including advertising information. Variable cost items per game included leases of trucks, cameras, and crews. There were also subcontractors who provided satellite uplinks and backhaul (sending the signal to other locations). An estimate of production costs, based on comparable sporting events, was approximately $40,000 per Yankees or Nets game.[53]

Premium Programming Content

To please viewers as well as to make the network more attractive to cable operators and advertisers, Hindery wanted to build high-quality programming content. "We use 12 cameras for every Yankees game; something no other network does except for the playoffs and World Series," said Hindery. "We also have top notch announcers and production teams." Besides Yankee games, which were shown two to three times daily, YES programming featured other professional and collegiate sports teams as well as classic sports footage. The YES schedule also included original biography, interview, and magazine programs, as well as live simulcasts of the very popular top-rated sports radio show in NY, "Mike and the Mad Dog."

EXHIBIT 3   YES FINANCIALS

Number of Yankee Games: 130
Number of Nets Games: 73

Per-Game Production Costs

Fixed Costs:

Director/Producer/Broadcaster Salaries

Variable Costs (Outsourced):

Lease of trucks, cameras, crews

Satellite uplink

Backhaul (sending signal to other locations)

Total Per-Game Production Costs	**$40,000**

(*Note: Assume home and away games have same costs and that costs for each Yankee game and each Nets game are the same.*)

Advertising Revenue

NYC Advertising Households (Designated Market Area): 5,500,000

Game & rerun revenue:

Cost of 30 sec ad during Yankee game	$5000
Total ads per game	40
Cost of pre-game and post-game ad	$2500
Total pre-game and post-game ads per game	8
Cost of 30 sec ad during Nets game	$1500
Total ads per game	40
Cost of pre-game and post-game ad	$ 750
Total pre-game and post-game ads per game	8

Non-game revenue:

All other advertising and infomercials	$500,000 per month

Source: Estimated figures based on comparable sporting events, interview with Dave Ianucci, Zimmerman & Partners (advertising industry buyer), November 18, 2002.

YES primarily outsourced the production of Yankee games. YES's main studio was housed in Stamford, Connecticut, and was a 24x7 operation, leased to YES by a subcontractor, Liberty Livewire. Producers and directors were salaried, but nearly everything else was outsourced.

THE BATTLE WITH CABLEVISION

For the first few months of the 2002 baseball season, almost every New York sports radio, television, and print item was dominated by the YES-Cablevision battle. It was obvious that the millions of fans who could not watch their Yankees were not going to be shut out quietly.

Cablevision owned and operated cable television systems in various areas of New York, New Jersey, and Connecticut. They also had a vertically integrated sports business. As of 2002, Cablevision had amassed a regional sports empire of $2.7 billion in sports commitments, ranging from athlete contracts to regional television rights deals.[54] Cablevision had a controlling interest in Regional Sports Programming Partners, which owned Madison Square Garden LP, which in turn owned Madison Square Garden, the New York Knicks and the New York Rangers, as well as MSG Network and FOX Sports New York (FSNY). News Corp. (FOX) also had ownership in these entities. Besides the previous history between

Cablevision's MSG Network and the Yankees, there was also a personal aspect to the stalemate with YES. The Dolan family, who operated Cablevision, was close to a deal to buy the Yankees in 1998. It fell through at the last minute, however, when Steinbrenner demanded that he retain operational control of the team.

When YES and Cablevision attempted to negotiate the carriage agreement in the spring of 2002, they could not reach a deal. YES wanted carriage on extended-basic at $1.85 per basic subscriber per month, a price that Hindery argued was purposely and comfortably in the middle of the range of what other RSNs charged for a single channel. YES's asking price was also based upon the large number of live sporting events offered (nearly 200 Yankees and Nets games annually), and the high television ratings that the Yankees commanded. Cablevision offered YES two options:

> OPTION 1: Carriage on extended basic at $0.50 per basic subscriber (later raised to $0.55 after litigation was underway, or
>
> OPTION 2: Carriage on an a-la-carte/premium tier (like HBO or Showtime).

To Hindery and YES, there was no general precedent for sports programming to be a premium tier channel. Premium channel penetration rates were typically very low, usually around 10 percent.[55] "There is also an ethical issue here—people in the Bronx need YES on basic cable to be affordable" said Hindery.

If YES were to accept a $0.55 per subscriber fee or any other discount to their asking price, a "most-favored-nations" clause in their other major contracts would be triggered. This would force YES to lower the fees for most, if not all other cable operators, eliminating any possibility of profitability and likely putting YES out of business. YES turned down both options as unfair, and encouraged Cablevision subscribers to speak up to their cable provider in support of YES. "The reason we're not on is not our economics," said Hindery. "It's because we compete against programming that Cablevision has." Exhibit 4 is an open letter from YES Network to Cablevision subscribers sent on April 5, 2002.

On April 29, 2002, YES filed a lawsuit against Cablevision, citing anti-trust and anti-competitive behavior in an effort to put YES out of business, as well as to protect its own less attractive RSNs from competition from YES. YES hired high-profile lawyer David Boies, the lead attorney for the Justice Dept. in its anti-trust suit against Microsoft. With the lawsuit, YES was hoping to put enough pressure on Cablevision to get a deal done. The 2002 baseball season came and went, however, without an agreement between the two companies.

YES Arguments

YES cited several issues in their anti-trust suit against Cablevision, including:

- Cablevision attempted to monopolize the regional sports programming market, in violation of Section 2 of the Sherman Act.
- Cablevision held exclusive access to the homes in its geographic regions, giving it a lawful monopoly. What was unlawful was that Cablevision used this monopoly over access in order to give it an unlawful competitive advantage in the RSN market. Moreover, while DIRECTV was an alternative for some Cablevision subscribers, YES claimed that there were financial, logistical, and environmental barriers for subscribers to switch.

YES LETTER TO CABLEVISION SUBSCRIBERS

A Message to Cablevision Subscribers from YES

April 5, 2002

Dear Yankee fans:

For months we have asked Cablevision to simply treat the YES Network in the same way as Time Warner Cable, Comcast, RCN, Cox, Charter, AT&T Broadband and DIRECTV. All these area cable and satellite operators have agreed to carry the YES Network on the basic tier.

For years, Cablevision has insisted that other area cable operators carry MSG and FOX Sports NY, which Cablevision owns, in the basic tier. All we are asking for is the same treatment. And, the price we are asking for is the same as MSG. Why is Cablevision discriminating against Yankee fans?

YES Network will not negotiate in public, and we are available at any time to talk with Cablevision about fair carriage of the YES Network.

We hope that a satisfactory conclusion can be reached that will best serve Cablevision subscribers, who right now are being very ill-served by Cablevision management.

Please contact Cablevision at 516-803-2300 to let them know you want the YES Network and Yankees baseball included in your basic cable package.

Alternatively, you can call DIRECTV at 1-800-DIRECTV if you would like to watch the Yankees immediately.

Sincerely,

YES Network

Source: YES.

- Cablevision, in violation of FCC regulations, stated that it would carry YES only if there was cable exclusivity (which meant that YES could not reach a deal with DIRECTV or other satellite distributors).

- Cablevision did not grant YES what it was legally entitled to: "reasonable, non-discriminatory access." The offer to carry YES on a premium tier was "atypical of the cable industry and without precedent in regional sports programming."[56]

YES sought an immediate trial, in an effort to resolve the dispute quickly. However, Cablevision requested a 660-day discovery period. "Cablevision asked to trim down the case, but we don't want to give up our rights in exchange for speed," said Alan Vickery, lead YES lawyer and partner at Voies, Schiller & Flexner, LLP. "We do, however, want the trial to begin as soon as possible." Vickery estimated that an end of 2003 start date for the trial was the most likely scenario.

Cablevision Arguments

Cablevision CEO James Dolan summarized the company's position on its disagreement with YES: "Customers who don't want to see the Yankees shouldn't have to pay for the network. The proper place for the YES Network, given its expensive asking price, is on a premium tier."[57] Cablevision had several reasons not to accept YES's demand of $1.85 per subscriber on an expanded basic tier. First, the company believed that YES's asking price was exorbitant.

Another expensive sports network would have significantly increased its programming costs, forcing Cablevision to raise customer rates even further. Cablevision was already charging customers $3.50 to $3.70 per month for the MSG/FOX Sports NY package. Cablevision felt that YES's demands were based on a bloated value of the network. "I can't accept that valuation without the marketplace telling us that it is correct," said Dolan. "We do think right now that the Yankees are overinflated in their importance."[58] Another possible reason to refuse YES was that Cablevision wanted to protect its regional sports network (MSG and FOX Sports NY) properties from a competing RSN, particularly given their loss of the Yankees and Nets to YES.

Since the spring of 2002, Cablevision faced significant pressure from its communities, with nearly three million subscribers unable to watch Yankees games. Fans were in an uproar over the situation. Some defected to DIRECTV, but most were left out in the cold with no access to 130 Yankees games. While some fans were angry at YES or the Yankees for not dropping their asking price, most of the fan backlash was directed at Cablevision. The $0.55 rebate Cablevision gave MSG subscribers was not enough. They wanted their Yankees.

The YES dispute could hurt Cablevision's bottom line. Although Cablevision potentially saved approximately $54 million in sports rights fees by not carrying Yankees in 2002, subscriber losses mounted. With cable subscribers then valued by Wall Street at over $3,300 each, losing thousands of subscribers would cost Cablevision dearly.[59] From April–November 2002, Cablevision attributed subscriber losses of approximately 30,000 to the YES dispute.[60] Cablevision said that it "expected to lose up to 45,000 subscribers by the end of the year—a sharp reversal from last year, when the company gained almost 47,000 customers."[61] Hindery, however, estimated Cablevision's subscriber loss to be approximately 100,000; a number based on the latest tally of new DIRECTV subscribers in Cablevision areas. Others also believed that Cablevision lost more subscribers than it admitted. Some customers downgraded from pricier expanded basic and pay services (keeping Cablevision only for basic tier/low-end broadcast service) and added DIRECTV.

DIRECTV, which had no incentive to end the YES-Cablevision dispute and thus jeopardize its customer windfall, declined to discuss its new subscriber figures in Cablevision areas. It was estimated, however, that new DIRECTV subscriptions increased as much as 25 percent in the New York area.[62]

Cablevision stock, reflecting in part the YES uncertainty as well as capital structure concerns, declined from $34 in pre-season March 2002 to a 10-year low of just over $9 in September 2002.[63]

Outlook

In May 2002, Cablevision gave a rebate to its subscribers of $0.55 per month, since MSG no longer carried Yankees games. Management asserted that the worst of the company's subscriber losses was over. Yet Cablevision remained in financial trouble. It remained unclear whether an agreement with YES was achievable. The longer Cablevision held out, the more difficult it would be for YES to become financially viable. The Dolans and Cablevision avoided media contact as much as possible. "The more we keep talking about YES with the press, the more we keep telling potential customers that there is a product we don't have," said James Dolan.[64]

THE CURRENT SITUATION FOR HINDERY AND YES

With the Cablevision dispute still unresolved, fans losing patience, and YES barely breaking even, Hindery and his staff were weighing at least the following options in October 2002:

1. Let the legal and/or legislative process carry out, but otherwise maintain status quo.

This option would be very time consuming, but according to Hindery, YES had an excellent chance of eventually coming out on top. Cablevision remained under heavy political pressure from millions of Yankee and Nets fans. The lawsuit was expected to go to trial near the end of 2003, with a jury trial lasting several weeks, thus prolonging the standoff into the following baseball season. Legislative action or regulatory intervention was possible yet unlikely, since government traditionally had proved reluctant to interfere with contracts between two private corporations. By maintaining the status quo for an extended period, however, there was a chance that YES could not survive. "It's possible that YES could struggle along, laboring under anti-competitive conditions, doing the best it can under the circumstances," said Vickery. "But our belief is that that would eventually lead to YES going out of business." According to Hindery, they were barely breaking even without Cablevision's 2.7 million subscribers.[65]

2. Find middle ground with Cablevision and reach a carriage agreement.

Was there a point between a premium-only offering and $0.55–$1.85 per basic subscriber that would satisfy both YES and Cablevision? "Cablevision has backed away from every proposal," said Hindery. "But we will keep on trying." A summer 2002 offer by Hindery to discount the first two years of a proposed long-term agreement was also declined by Cablevision.

3. Buy MSG and/or FOX Sports NY from Cablevision.

Putting a valuation on these properties would be difficult, and it was questionable whether Cablevision would sell or YES would have the financial capability to acquire these properties. However, Cablevision was facing severe financial difficulties, and had already committed to unload other assets. YES also raised a $120 million war chest in spring 2002 (a credit line from GE Capital and Lehman Brothers) to either provide seasonal working capital or to support a possible acquisition, although not one of this magnitude. If the regional sports network entities were under one umbrella, however, it would be challenging to devise a per-subscriber fee that would be acceptable to cable operators.

4. Merge FOX/MSG/YES, creating a joint venture with Cablevision.

If the networks merged, it would be unclear what positions YES and Cablevision would hold in the new entity (due to various valuation issues), but realistically it would seem that the two companies would hold relatively equal positions. However, the merger option became more unlikely after the lawsuit was filed, since Cablevision would still retain ownership interest in the new entity. This option would eliminate Cablevision's motivation to exercise its monopoly power in cable distribution to hurt YES, but it does not solve some of the antitrust allegations leveled by YES in its lawsuit (since Cablevision would still influence the programming and distribution). Also, Cablevision would still need to approve any carriage agreement with itself or other cable operators, creating a potentially unstable situation.

With the future of the YES network hinged on Cablevision's next move, Hindery had several options to consider. YES investors, professional sports team owners and, of course, George Steinbrenner waited anxiously to see what he would do.

Questions

1. The dominant pattern for many years has been that ownership of a RSN is separate from ownership of the sporting club whose games are shown on the RSN. From the club's perspective, what are the strengths and weaknesses of this separation of ownership?

2. What were the major motivations for setting up YES? What were the major challenges in setting up YES? How were these challenges handled? (Assume that if YES is on extended basic, 90% of cable subscribers get the extended basic package as part of their subscription. Assume that if YES is on à la carte premier tier, 10% of cable subscribers will subscribe to YES. You can do sensitivity analysis on these assumptions.)

3. What are the key areas of dispute between YES and Cablevision? Present three different ways that YES and Cablevision could resolve their dispute. Outline why you think each way helps resolve the dispute and its attraction to each of the disputing parties.

4. Assume it is February 2004. You are the arbitrator. Outline your decision with key reasons supporting it.

5. Outline the factors that will influence whether club-owned RSNs will become a widely adopted approach in media broadcasting.

CASE 8.4 THE NFL-NETWORK TELEVISION CONTRACTS, 1998–2005[66]

In the summer of 1997, National Football League executives were preparing for the upcoming reopening of the national television contracts with their major broadcast and cable TV partners. Television was a central component of the economics of the NFL and its 30 individual teams. (The latter shared national TV rights revenue equally. This currently yielded about $39 million per team annually, over half a typical team's revenue.)

Television was also widely considered to have been the principal driver of the growth in the NFL's popularity that had led to its leadership position on the American sports landscape. **Appendix A,** "NFL Television History," is a September 1997 NFL document that describes the development of NFL TV policy, current home and road televising practices, and the sequence of growth in NFL television rights revenues. (In addition, a 90-minute video was being produced, for April 1998 showing, that focused on the history of the NFL on television.) **Exhibit 1** shows the NFL's national television rights income since 1970, by season and by contract.

Current Packages

As of 1997, there were four current NFL national TV packages:

Sunday afternoon (AFC)	NBC
Sunday afternoon (NFC)	FOX
Sunday evening (cable)	TNT (first half of season); ESPN (second half)
Monday Night Football	ABC

EXHIBIT 1 NFL NATIONAL TELEVISION RIGHTS INCOME ($000 OMITTED) 1970–1997 SEASONS

Year	Regular Season						Total	Post-Season	Total	Average Per Club
	ABC*	CBS	NBC	FOX	ESPN	TNT				
1970–1973	$ 34,632	$ 73,000	$ 49,000				$ 156,632	$ 29,000	$ 185,632	$ 7,140
1974–1977	72,000	88,000	74,000				234,000	35,000	269,000	9,970
1978–1981	232,000	192,000	168,000				592,000	54,000	646,000	23,071
1982–1986[a]	650,000	665,000	590,000				1,905,000	171,000	2,076,000	74,143
1987–1989[b]	360,000	450,000	360,000		$ 153,000		1,323,000	105,000	1,428,000	51,000
1990–1993[c]	888,000	1,052,000	744,000		445,500	445,000	3,575,000	41,000	3,616,000	129,143
1994–1997	920,000		868,000	1,580,000	525,500	496,000	4,389,500	0	4,389,500	152,612
1970–1997	3,156,632	2,520,000	2,853,000	1,580,000	1,124,000	941,500	12,175,132	435,000	12,610,132	447,078

*ABC figures include mini-package in 1979–1985 seasons and assume 5 game mini-package per season from 1984–85.

[a]Strike impact (not reflected): Due to 1982 regular season strike, total reduced from $300 million to $216,416,664 (Post season reduced by $380,000). Also due to 1982 strike, 1983 total reduced from $345 million to $318,419,048. Total cost of strike was $110,554,288.

[b]Strike impact (not reflected): Due to 1987 regular season strike, total reduced from $475 million to $417,669,00.

[c]Schedule adjustment: Reducing 1992 season from 18 to 17 weeks resulted in $28 million giveback of 1993 rights fees ($ million per club).

Source: National Football League.

Harvard Business School Case No 9-599-039. Copyright 1999 President and Fellows of Harvard College. All rights reserved. For information: permission@hbsp.harvard.edu. This case was prepared by Stephen A. Greyser. HBS cases are developed solely for class discussion and do not necessarily illustrate effective or ineffective management.

EXHIBIT 2   CURRENT SPORTS TV RIGHTS TIMELINE ($ IN MILLIONS)

	1994	1995	1996	1997	1998	1999	2000
NFL							
ABC	195.0	230.0	247.5	247.5			
FOX	340.0	385.0	436.0	419.0			
NBC	237.0	217.0	197.0	217.0			
TNT	115.0	120.0	128.0	133.0			
ESPN	127.8	127.8	135.0	135.0			
Total	**1,014.8**	**1,079.8**	**1,143.5**	**1,151.5**			
NBA							
NBC		187.5	187.5	187.5	187.5		
TNT		88.0	88.0	88.0	88.0		
Total		**275.5**	**275.5**	**275.5**	**275.5**		
MLB							
FOX			115.0	115.0	115.0	115.0	115.0
NBC			95.0	95.0	95.0	95.0	95.0
ESPN			91.0	91.0	91.0	91.0	91.0
Liberty/FOX			—	43.0	43.0	43.0	43.0
Total			**301.0**	**344.0**	**344.0**	**344.0**	**344.0**
NHL							
FOX		31.0	31.0	31.0	31.0	31.0	
ESPN	12.5	12.5	12.5	12.5	12.5	12.5	
Total	**12.5**	**43.5**	**43.5**	**43.5**	**43.5**	**43.5**	
OLYMPICS							
CBS-Winter	295.0		—		375.0		—
NBC-Summer	—		456.0		—		715.0
Total	**295.0**		**456.0**		**375.0**		**715.0**

Source: National Football League.

In combination, the four packages with five partners represented over $1.1 billion in annual rights fees, the largest for any league or sport. The four-year total under the current contracts, negotiated in late 1993, was approximately $4.4 billion. This was far larger than the rights fees for the other principal leagues and for the Olympics, as shown in **Exhibit 2.**

According to the contractual process, each incumbent partner had an exclusive negotiating period with the NFL for its existing package until mid-to-late-fall. The NFL was obligated to give each incumbent a dollar amount for the renewal of its package. Only if the incumbent did not accept the NFL amount would that package become open to other bidders.

A similar process four years before had led to the blockbuster bid by FOX for the NFC portion of the Sunday afternoon games. FOX had paid the record-breaking amount of $1.58 billion for the NFC Sunday games in the 1994–1997 four-season period, well above the $1.05 billion CBS had paid for them in the previous contract for the four seasons of 1990–1993.

For 1994–97, CBS was out of the NFL TV lineup. Executives in many CBS affiliate stations had expressed displeasure over the network's loss of NFL football. Now, in 1997, CBS executives had spoken in public of the network's interest in returning to the NFL TV lineup. Obviously this prospectively provided the NFL with an added bidder as well as a signal for further upward prices for the TV rights.

NFL Preparation

As the 1997 negotiation period neared, NFL senior executives prepared for what they hoped would be another significant increase in the League's television rights revenues. Among their actions was the organizing of a task force of broadcasting, finance, and marketing people to help determine the "maximum reasonable amount" the networks would be capable of paying. Meaningful time from NFL Commissioner Paul Tagliabue and President Neil Austrian was also contributed to the project.

Hundreds of pages of projections were incorporated into models of network/cable channel revenues and the profitability derived from NFL football telecasts. Illustratively, for "Monday Night Football," the first component of revenue potential was estimated based on each season's number of regular season games (17), the number of 30-second commercials per game (56), and the approximate price to advertisers per commercial (estimated from advertising cost trends). To this was added analogous estimates of advertising revenue potential for two pre-season primetime games (lower price per commercial), two wildcard post-season Saturday afternoon games, and each SuperBowl during the contract (much higher price per commercial). To the SuperBowl were added estimated revenues from pre- and post-game programs. For the networks, estimates of additional revenue potential were made for the local portion of revenues earned from the NFL telecasts by a network's owned-and-operated stations (typically in major markets). Analogous detailed estimates were made for each NFL TV package.

From these amounts were subtracted estimated production costs, talent costs, and relevant operating overhead.

Inputs to these estimates came from a wide variety of sources. These included trends in TV network primetime ratings, which had declined from a four-network total of 46.9 (76% share) in 1987–88 to 43.1 (72% share) for six networks in 1996–97; in TV sports ratings, including ratings for the highly desirable (to advertisers) males 18–49 and 25–54 **(Exhibit 3)**; in TV sports ratings for the regular season and post-season for the different sports leagues **(Exhibit 4)**; in TV ratings by package; in total network and cable households; and in several other relevant aspects of television, such as broadcast vs. cable share of primetime viewing and fourth calendar quarter viewing. In the fourth quarter, the three months dominated by the NFL, the primetime viewing share for broadcast stations declined from 76% to 64% between 1990 and 1996. The share for cable network viewing increased from 22% to 34%.

From 1981 to 1996, U.S. TV households had grown from 81.5 million to 97.0, cable homes from 31.5 million to 68.5 (all of which had ESPN and 37.8 million had ESPN2), and satellite TV homes from less than a million in 1991 to 6.8 million; also DIRECTV homes numbered 2.1 million in 1996. The growth of cable and satellite viewing was reflected in the decline of the broadcast network share of the primetime viewing audience from 92% in 1981 to 88% in 1986, 77% in 1991, and 64% in 1997.

The percentage of regular season blackout lifts had been relatively stable in recent years. (NFL television policy called for all games to be televised. However, if a game did not sell out in advance, it would not be televised in the home team's city. Each "blackout" reduced the league's overall TV ratings.)

The senior staff task force also determined the timing and sequencing of discussions with network/cable channel sports heads. A key role was played by members of the owners television

EXHIBIT 3   **TV SPORTS NETWORK RATINGS 1988–1996**

SPORTS NETWORK RATINGS (Full Season)

	1988	1989	1990	1991	1992	1993	1994	1995	1996
NFL									
Total US Households	14.2	14.2	13.9	13.9	13.9	14.1	14.4	13.7	12.9
Men 18–49	11.9	12.0	11.8	11.8	11.9	12.0	12.2	11.2	10.4
Men 25–54	12.8	12.7	12.7	12.7	12.6	12.9	13.1	12.0	11.4
NBA									
Total US Households	8.1	7.5	7.3	6.8	6.8	7.9	6.8	7.2	7.7
Men 18–49	7.1	6.4	6.2	5.9	5.9	6.8	6.0	6.1	6.6
Men 25–54	7.1	6.6	6.3	5.9	5.8	6.6	5.9	6.0	6.6
MLB									
Total US Households	9.5	7.7	9.3	11.0	9.0	9.3	8.9	11.0	7.1
Men 18–49	6.0	4.7	5.8	7.3	5.9	6.1	5.9	7.4	4.6
Men 25–54	6.6	5.1	6.3	8.0	6.4	6.7	6.1	8.2	5.3
NHL									
Total US Households				2.4	2.2	1.8	1.8	2.2	2.6
Men 18–49	NO SIGNIFICANT			1.9	2.0	1.7	1.6	2.0	2.3
Men 25–54	NETWORK COVERAGE			1.8	2.1	1.7	1.7	1.9	2.3

Source: National Football League.

EXHIBIT 4   **TELEVISION RATINGS FOR SPORTS LEAGUES 1990–1997**

	1990	1991	1992	1993	1994	1995	1996	1997
NFL								
ABC Monday Night Football	17.2	16.8	16.8	16.8	17.8	17.0	16.2	15.0
NBC NFL Regular Season	11.0	10.9	11.2	11.3	12.5	11.1	10.9	10.4
FOX NFL Regular Season[a]	13.5	13.1	13.0	12.9	12.1	12.5	11.3	10.7
TNT NFL Regular Season	7.0	6.4	6.9	7.6	8.8	8.1	7.3	7.3
ESPN NFL Regular Season	9.8	8.4	8.4	8.2	10.5	9.0	8.1	7.6
NBC AFC Championship Game	23.6	27.4	25.5	28.6	28.3	27.1	28.5	25.0
FOX NFC Championship Game[a]	30.2	29.5	33.3	31.6	34.2	33.3	30.1	26.2
SuperBowl	**41.8**	**40.3**	**45.1**	**45.5**	**41.3**	**46.0**	**43.3**	**44.5**
NBA								
NBC NBA Regular Season	5.0	4.5	4.8	5.0	4.6	5.2	5.3	4.9
NBC NBA Playoffs	7.3	6.7	7.2	8.2	7.2	8.1	8.0	7.4
NBC NBA Finals	**12.3**	**15.8**	**14.2**	**17.9**	**12.4**	**13.9**	**16.7**	**16.8**
MLB								
League Championships								
Primetime Games	13.5	13.7	12.7	13.2	—	13.1	9.5	9.6
Weekday Games	8.5	8.3	7.3	8.8	—	—	8.0	7.1
World Series	**20.8**	**24.0**	**20.2**	**17.3**	**—**	**19.5**	**17.4**	**16.8**
NHL								
FOX Regular Season (ABC 93–94)				2.2	1.7	2.0	2.1	1.9
FOX NHL All Star Game (NBC 89–94)	3.6	2.7	2.3	2.4	2.5	—	4.1	2.7
FOX Stanley Cup Playoffs (ABC 93–94)				1.7	1.6	2.3	2.7	2.4

[a]CBS from 1990–1993.

Source: National Football League.

committee. This small group of owners assisted both other owners and the network executives whom they saw in negotiating meetings with an understanding of where reality was in the discussions. Since ultimately the TV contract packages require a three-quarters approval (23 of 30) by the owners, the committee members provide input regarding both the current negotiation and the caliber of the management of the rights negotiations process by NFL executives.

The Negotiations

The big news from the 1993 negotiations had been the emergence of FOX as a serious bidder. At that time, according to NFL executives, long discussions with CBS and NBC led the NFL executives to conclude that neither considered FOX to be a serious bidder. Initial 1993 offers from both CBS and NBC were below the then current rate (from the preceding contract). The NFL was seeking 10%–15% increases. After CBS declined to accept the NFL's price of $295 million per year, FOX eventually bid $395 million to assure its NFC package. (Because of the size of NFC markets compared to AFC ones, the price for the former is typically higher.)

As noted above, by late 1997 it was clear that CBS wanted to return to the NFL TV lineup. Its affiliates were urging the network's new CEO to do so. Also, it seemed that the NFL TV audience fitted CBS' needs regarding programming and audiences desired by advertisers.

Another pertinent event in late 1997 was the signing of new four-year contracts by the NBA with NBC and Turner. Initial reports were that the value of the new contracts was substantially greater than the 1995–1998 $1.1 billion aggregate deal. (Details, as discerned by the NFL, are in **Exhibit 5**).

* * * * *

A separate but strategically-related strand of the TV negotiation was taking place on the player relations front. The intent was to reach an accord with the NFL Players Association such that the NFL could seek an **eight**-year television arrangement, rather than the typical four-year one. Indeed, the eventual packages all were for eight years (through the 2005 season), and provided that the NFL could **unilaterally** re-open all the contracts (not selective ones) after five years.

* * * * *

Among the numerous specific ideas suggested by one or another rights-seeker during the series of discussions with the NFL were that:

- the NFL institute a new 14-game **Thursday** series
- the now separate two Sunday evening cable series (first half of the season, and second half) be combined on a single cable network
- NBC seek Monday Night Football rather than stay with the Sunday AFC package
- ABC consider how to leverage its control of both ABC and ESPN

* * * * *

The NFL decided that the price for the Sunday AFC package to be offered to NBC as the incumbent would be $500 million per year. This would make the offering price for the NFC package for FOX approximately $550 million, and for Monday Night Football at least $500 million. The Sunday evening cable packages would be offered for at least $280 million each.

EXHIBIT 5   Known Specifics of NBA TV Deal

Overall Deal Points:

- Deal is for four years covering 1998/99 through 2001/02 seasons.

- Networks are protected against labor work stoppage by paying its annual rights as scheduled and League reimbursing Networks at a later date, if necessary .

- Revenue sharing is again part of both the over-the-air and cable deals.

Over-the-air Deal:

- NBC retains rights for $1.75 billion or $437.5 million per year.

- NBC will add seven (7) regular season games, all in the 5:30–8pm or 6:30–9pm time slot, increasing game inventory to 33 (includes All-Star game).

- NBC will also add eight (8) playoff games (mostly early round games that were regionalized on Turner) increasing minimum number of playoff games from 23 to 31.

- NBC will add two (2) commercial units per game, increasing average national units to 58.

- Current deal of $750 million over four years included revenue sharing. NBC netted $1.10 billion in revenue over current deal which means, after taking out approximately $50 million in production costs and overhead, profit on the deal was $300 million.

- With revenue sharing, $300 million profit means $150 million is currently going to NBC and $150 million going to NBA.

- Although rights fees will be reported as more than doubled (133%), actual increase for NBA is 94% ($1.75 billion versus $900 million—$750 million in rights plus $150 million in revenue sharing).

- NBC has reported that, due to increased game and commercial inventory, Network will only be asking for 10% increases from current League sponsors. In actuality, Network will most likely ask for 30% increases from current big-ticket sponsors (autos, beers, etc.) and will fill in the gaps with new and smaller categories.

Cable Deal:

- Turner retains rights for $890 million or $222.5 million per year.

- Turner will add nine (9) regular season games for a total of 80 games.

- Current TBS package of Wednesday night games moves to Monday night following the NFL season.

- Turner loses the seven playoff games that NBC picked up (seven games that were previously broadcast on TBS in the same time slot as TNT), leaving a total of 40 playoff telecasts.

- Current deal of $352 million over four years included revenue sharing. Turner netted approximately $492 million in revenue over current deal which means, after taking out approximately $50 million in production costs and overhead, profit on the deal was $90 million.

- With revenue sharing, $90 million profit means $45 million is currently going to Turner and $45 million going to NBA.

- Although rights fees will be reported as two and one-half times the current amount (153%), actual increase for NBA is 124% ($890 million versus $397 million—$352 million in rights plus $45 million in revenue sharing).

Source: National Football League.

September 1997

NFL TELEVISION HISTORY

The NFL's television history is a story of stability, innovation and timely strategic decisions. It is a tale of thoughtfully maximizing the NFL television product, while continuing to be sensitive to the issues of overexposure and marketplace saturation.

When looking at the $39 million teams receive per year under the current contracts, it is easy to forget that clubs averaged less than $2 million per season 20 years ago and less than $6 million per year as recently as 1981.

A chronological view of the League's TV history follows:

Our television beginnings were rather humble . . . from the initial telecast of a Brooklyn Dodgers-Philadelphia Eagles game on what is now New York station WNBC back in 1939 through the 1940s and early 1950s . . . when college football remained in an extremely prominent position.

In 1949, as an example, League television rights totaled $75,000.

By 1950 several NFL clubs were contracting for selected road games to be televised back to their home cities. However, the policies to be adopted for NFL telecasts grew from an unusual contract entered into by the Los Angeles Rams as that decade opened.

In 1950, the Rams contracted with a maker of television sets, Admiral Television, to televise all of the team's away games back to Los Angeles. The Rams also made an agreement for the sponsor to televise their home games live in the local L.A. market, but with the stipulation that Admiral would have to make up the financial difference in lost stadium attendance compared with the previous season's crowds for those six contests.

Although the Rams had an outstanding team and played in the Championship Game, home attendance for the locally televised games dropped appreciably. Admiral Television by contract had to pay the Rams $307,000, a staggering amount at that time, particularly in light of the number of television sets in the area as compared with today. In 1950, there were sets in only 690,000 homes in the L.A. area, some 42 percent of the 1,643,000 households. Today there are sets in some 5.0 million L.A. area homes, or over 98 percent of the total households.

On the basis of this experiment 45 years ago, NFL teams became convinced they could not routinely televise their home games locally and expect to also attract significant crowds to the stadium. (Several Admiral executives also learned a lesson when they were asked to seek new employment.)

All NFL teams then began televising their away games back to the home city during the 1950s and this was gradually broadened to include outlying regional networks.

However, League rules precluded not only a local telecast of the game being played, but also prevented *any other* NFL game being televised into a city on the day a game was being played there. This latter rule was challenged by the Department of Justice in 1953, but the League was able to establish the detrimental effect on attendance that such telecasts would cause and Judge Allan K. Grim's decision upheld the NFL policy in a Federal Court in Philadelphia.

So the then twelve NFL teams continued their practice of negotiating the best individual contracts they could, normally for about $100,000 each for the season, throughout the

1950s. In each case, the contracts covered only the six "away" games that were televised back to their home areas.

By 1960, the medium of television had become much more national in scope and changes took place. The Cleveland Browns' rights were owned by a brewery and this sponsor began maximizing utilization of the rights of the popular and successful team by televising its games on the independent Sports Network throughout the country except in cities where NFL games were being played the same day.

NBC-TV took a cue from this pattern and signed contracts with two NFL teams, the Johnny Unitas-led Baltimore Colts and the Pittsburgh Steelers. Each Sunday NBC would telecast either a Colts or Steelers game throughout most of the country in the same manner in which Cleveland games were being carried.

CBS-TV was left with the other nine teams and carried their games on regional networks throughout the nation.

This created a situation wherein three NFL telecasts were seen each Sunday in most parts of the country with subsequent sharing of the football audience. The situation became intolerable for CBS, because it found it was paying rights directly or indirectly to nine teams to reach a nationwide audience, while Sports Network and NBC were reaching the same audience by paying rights to only one and two clubs, respectively.

There were strong indications that CBS would drop some of the clubs it was carrying and simply maximize the coverage of select big city teams throughout the country. This would have meant that some teams would lose all television income as well as the promotional benefit of having all road games televised back home.

The result was a decision by the League to sell the rights for all NFL teams in a package to a single network, something that was already being done by both the NCAA on the collegiate level and the new American Football League. At this time, the big city teams, such as the New York Giants, Chicago Bears and Los Angeles Rams, agreed to relinquish the value of their large population home television market and accept an equal share of the income from a League package sale with their partners.

This was to be done for the 1961 season. However, the Department of Justice blocked the plan in court, contending the teams should individually compete in the sale of their television rights.

On September 18, 1961, Rep. Emanual Cellar introduced a bill in the House of Representatives legalizing single network television package sales by professional sports leagues. The bill was passed by the Congress and signed into law by President John F. Kennedy on September 30.

It was too late to implement the plan for the 1961 season, but on January 10, 1962, the NFL entered into a League television rights agreement with CBS-TV for 1962 and 1963 for $4,650,000 annually. The contract was negotiated with CBS because that network was the only one that held valid contracts with individual teams that were effective through 1963. Our 14 teams received almost $400,000 per club per year.

After the 1963 season the League was free from any contractual or legal obstacles and was able to put its TV rights up for bid to all three networks, ABC, CBS and NBC.

In a highly publicized bidding contest, sealed envelopes were opened revealing the amounts offered by these growing and highly competitive television entities. The first envelope opened by Commissioner Pete Rozelle in front of the network representatives was NBC's. It contained an offer of $10.75 million for each of the 1964 and 1965 seasons. This was followed by the ABC proposal, which was for $13.2 million a year. The final offer read was the winning bid of $14.1 million a year by CBS—a total of $28.2 million. The 14 NFL clubs received just over $1 million per year.

One significant change in NFL television policy was implemented in 1964, the first year of that agreement. CBS was permitted to televise a second, usually late-starting, game into any city that did not have a game being played that day. Thus, the so-called "doubleheader" game was launched. However, if an NFL team was playing at home, there was still *no NFL game* on television in that city that day.

When NFL rights next became available, for the 1966 season, the NFL did not have the luxury of three bidders. By this time NBC had contracted with the American Football League and ABC was privately committed to the NCAA college package.

Dissatisfied with the progress of negotiations with CBS, the League seriously studied the feasibility of placing its games on an independent network of stations. The clubs made the decision to take this gamble. However, last minute negotiations with CBS were successfully concluded and that network retained the rights under a two-year escalating contract that began in 1966 at $18.8 million and included an option for the 1968 season. NFL clubs now reached the level of roughly $1.6 million per club.

A significant feature of this agreement was a major change in NFL policy. The clubs felt they had reached the stage where they could sustain their home attendance and still permit the telecast of another NFL game to be seen in their cities when they were playing at home. Thus, there was a lift of what had been a total "blackout." As a result, an NFL game was shown for the first time in cities where the local NFL teams were playing at home that day.

During this period the NFL cracked the prime time barrier when CBS agreed to nationally televise a limited number of night time games as "specials." Five such games were televised from 1966 to 1969 and when all but one attained in the range of 40% shares of the viewing audience, the groundwork was laid for the regular Monday night football programming of the 1970s.

The merger of the AFL into the NFL to form a single League was announced in June of 1966. NFL games continued on CBS and AFL games on NBC for the next four years until the merger was fully implemented with the 1970 season. A World Championship Game, or Super Bowl, was inaugurated after the 1966 season . . . and ultimately became this country's No. 1 event (television and otherwise) each year. Through the 1996 season, nine of the top ten highest-rated sports events of all time are Super Bowls, topped by SB XVI's 49.1 rating, the highest rated television sports event ever.

It was in 1970 that the League began its contractual arrangements with all three television networks. Contracts were signed with CBS to televise the newly structured National Football Conference Sunday afternoon games and with NBC to carry similar games of the AFC. For interconference games, the conference affiliation of the visiting team determined which network carried the telecast.

Inasmuch as CBS and NBC had been the most recent televisers of professional football, they were approached regarding their interest in a regular series of Monday night NFL games.

Although CBS' prime time night experiments in the 1960s had been successful, first CBS . . . and later NBC . . . declined, because they felt they could not afford to gamble on dropping their general interest prime time programming for a steady diet of Monday night football.

Negotiations then began with ABC and later the independent Hughes Sports Network for the Monday night rights. Roone Arledge, head of ABC Sports, shared Pete Rozelle's confidence that the series could be successful. ABC also feared losing affiliates to the prospective Hughes network . . . and opted to gamble on prime time football. It was a courageous decision at the time to commit to such programming for four years, 1970–73, but ABC did it and it paid off for both the network and the NFL. Since those beginings, Monday Night Football has become an ABC prime time institution and has enjoyed a string of six consecutive years among the top 10 prime time television shows from 1991–1996.

The 1970s began with the following pattern, a pattern that remains the cornerstone of NFL television 25 years later:

1. Contracts with all three networks assure that the hometown fans receive the telecast of every road game of their team.

2. Three NFL telecasts are seen each Sunday afternoon throughout the country, except in cities where NFL games are played the same day.

3. When a NFL team is playing at home on a Sunday afternoon, two telecasts, one by CBS (and later FOX) and one by NBC, are seen in that city. If a team is playing at home in the Sunday night game, two afternoon telecasts are still shown in the home market.

4. A weekly Monday night game is televised nationwide by ABC.

5. Late season Thanksgiving and Saturday games are televised by both CBS (and later FOX) and NBC.

The new agreements with CBS, NBC and ABC for the four years from 1970 through 1973 . . . based upon the popularity of our sport and the expanded NFL . . . totaled over $185 million for four years, an average of roughly $1.7 million per club per year for the 26 member clubs.

In 1973 the excitement created by the sold-out games played in Washington, D.C., by the Redskins triggered action by Congress. As the 1973 season opened, a law was passed that had the effect of forcing the NFL to make available for local television any home game sold out 72 hours prior to kickoff. The League feared this law, because it was felt that many people holding tickets would not attend games, if they could enjoy them in the comfort of their living rooms. In time, it was reasoned that such "no shows" would become no buyers. To a degree, that occurred.

While the law was passed for only a three-year duration, concern that it would be adopted again on a permanent and perhaps even more restrictive basis prompted the NFL to inform Congressional leaders that it would voluntarily continue to follow the spirit of the law after its 1975 expiration.

While we had been able to show a drop in season ticket sales after enactment of the law, as well as a financial impact on our clubs from what became known as "no shows," there has been no climate in Congress . . . then or now . . . for the NFL to win a battle on the issue of not telecasting home sellouts. Moreover, a return to the old policy would trigger negative economic reactions from the television networks.

Shortly after the enactment of the 1973 law, the League entered into new contracts with the three networks for games to be played from 1974 through 1977. The packages remained the same, with one basic exception. ABC added a 14th game . . . to the then 13 Monday nights . . . and telecast a Saturday night game on the 14th and final week of our season.

Financially, the new four-year contract jumped from a total of $185 million for the 1970–1973 period to $269 million for the period from 1974 through 1977. The member teams received roughly $2.5 million per year from television per year . . . with Seattle and Tampa Bay joining the fold for the 1976 season.

The 1978 through 1981 agreements with CBS, NBC and ABC added a new element, a so-called package of "special" prime time games . . . games played on a night other than Monday, generally Sunday or Thursday. The contract with ABC called for from four to six special games each year . . . at $3 million per game . . . and with the decision on the number of games to be made by the NFL . . . our concern for over-exposure was such that we decided to limit the specials package to four games each season. Thus, the League concern for too much football was not philosophical . . . it was practical. We left $24 million on the table over the four years . . . 1978 through 1981.

The increasing popularity of NFL football during this period was evidenced by the substantial increase in rights fees that we were able to negotiate . . . from $269 million in 1974 to $646 million in 1978, an increase of 42 percent. Per club income now jumped to more than $5.5 million per year.

Coming off a banner 1981 season . . . a year in which we set an all-time high in television ratings, the Broadcasting Committee negotiated a new five-year agreement . . . from 1982 through 1986 . . . for just under $2.1 billion. It was the largest rights deal in the history of the television industry, and remained so until the NFL's next deal of $3.6 billion.

Under the five-year contracts with CBS, ABC and NBC, per club income escalated to almost $15 million per year . . . with a high of over $17 million in the final season. ABC contracted for the first time to televise a Super Bowl Game.

In just five years . . . from 1977 to 1982 . . . NFL per club revenue jumped from $2.5 million per year to $15 million per year!

Interestingly, the 1982 arrangements added just one additional regular season telecast. When some were suggesting that the NFL should go to a full Thursday night package, or enter cable TV, it was our view that more football on television could have an overall negative effect at that point. Thus, we added just *one game* . . . going from four to five on the number of ABC specials.

Our reluctance did not stop others. In 1982, the NCAA went from one network (ABC) to two networks (ABC and CBS) and also put together a cable package with Ted Turner.

In 1983, the United States Football League came into being and gave us year round football.

In 1984, the Supreme Court decision against the NCAA opened the door to anyone interested in televising college football . . . and viewers in many markets could suddenly select from as many as 10, 12, or more college games on Saturdays.

The major increase in the amount of football could not have happened at a worse time . . . from our standpoint.

In 1982, our player strike not only cost the League revenue in the range of $200 million . . . the public perception of the greedy players battling with rich owners took its toll . . . adding another negative element.

That same 1982 through 1984 period saw the three major networks continue to watch their audience shares erode. What had been more than a 90 share for ABC, CBS and NBC combined began to tumble. With independent stations and cable entities increasing their percentage, the networks fell to the high 60s.

At the same time, the video cassette craze set in . . . with a cross section of the nation seeking out home movies as major entertainment fare.

The net result of the glut of football, triggered by the colleges and the USFL . . . the 1982 NFL player strike and its aftermath . . . network sales problems that ranged from prime time to sports . . . a decline in rating levels . . . the added strength of independent cable programs against the networks . . . and the increased interest in video cassettes and other new forms of entertainment . . . impacted on the NFL in a very negative way as the NFL negotiated its next television contracts.

Yet, in 1987 the League was still able to use entrance into the cable television market as a means of maintaining its premier place in the sports marketplace. Three-year agreements with ABC, CBS, NBC and ESPN for the 1987, 1988 and 1989 seasons total $1.42 billion. Each NFL team realized $17 million each year of contracts.

The new ESPN contract called for Sunday night cablecasts on the all-sports network the final eight weeks of the season, and also gave ESPN post-season rights to the AFC-NFC Pro Bowl game. ESPN averaged a 10.0 rating for those regular season telecasts for 1987–89, making NFL football the highest-rated programming series in cable history, an achievement which ESPN has maintained through the 1996 season. A unique aspect of the regular season package called for each game to also be telecast back to the home city of the visiting team (and in the site city as well, if sold out 72 hours in advance) on over-the-air broadcast television.

It was the view of the Broadcasting Committee (and ultimately the membership) that the modest escalation in rights from the 1982–86 package to the 1987–89 agreements would allow the networks, who fared badly from a financial standpoint on the previous five-year deals, to regain a measure of health . . . and allow the NFL to make a major step forward in rights levels following the 1989 season.

The networks did get healthy and the NFL, in a robust economy and a positive television environment, negotiated a five-network, four-year 1990–93 arrangement that dwarfed the five-year $2.1 billion deal of 1982. The new $3.6 billion deal saw club rights levels soar from the $17 million level to $32.5 million, an increase of almost 48 percent.

To reach the new rights level, the NFL extended its Sunday cable package to a full season of games by contracting with Turner Broadcasting for a first half of the season package on TNT, added ABC to the pre-Super Bowl post-season mix with two new Saturday Wild Card games, extended the season to 16 games over 17 weeks and later 16 games over 18 weeks, added additional weeks of late-season Saturday afternoon games on CBS and NBC, and increased the number of per-game television advertising units.

In March of 1990, in a seller's market and a strong economy, more looked like better to the NFL and to its television partners. But, a few short months later an about-face rapidly began.

Ultimately, the early 1990s recession struck the networks across the board . . . primetime and other dayparts as well as sports. Unit pricing increases were minimal or non-existent.

While NFL rating levels remained strong, compared to the decreases suffered by baseball and other sports, the marketplace had been unable to sustain the new NFL rights levels. With ramped up rights fees, particularly in 1992 and 1993, our broadcast partners found themselves in a loss situation.

Thus, the climate was not good for negotiations in the fall of 1993. However, the environment changed dramatically when FOX entered the picture as a serious contender for a Sunday afternoon package. Commissioner Tagliabue and the Broadcasting Committee spent considerable time weighing the effects of awarding one of the packages to a young network, one without a sports division.

In December of 1993, the League announced new four-year agreements with incumbents ABC, NBC, ESPN and Turner and with newcomer FOX replacing CBS as the rightsholder of the NFC package. The value of the agreements totaled a staggering $4.4 billion. FOX brought full-year promotion of the NFL through its "Under The Helmet" public service announcements; a one-hour pregame show; the innovative FOX Clock and an expanded network that reached 98% of the nation, compared to 92% before obtaining NFL rights. While industry projections foresaw a 10–15% potential decline for NFC ratings with the move from CBS to FOX, FOX's first two years of coverage averaged an impressive 12.3 rating, a mere 4% off CBS's 1993 ratings level.

The current contracts with NBC and FOX added a new feature called NFL SUNDAY TICKET, a joint venture between the League, FOX and NBC in satellite transmission via C-Band and DSS dishes that is an outgrowth of a presentation made to the then Commissioner Pete Rozelle by current League President Neil Austrian way back in 1985.

NFL SUNDAY TICKET provides dish owners with the opportunity to view out-of-market games on sunday afternoons (as well as the local market game if it is sold out 72 hours in advance), and has been saluted by many relocated NFL fans anxious to follow the team from their former locale. While the initial revenue stream from NFL SUNDAY TICKET is conservative, the long range prospects are quite positive, and the promotional values are significant.

At this juncture, the broadcasting environment continues to evolve with the establishment of new sports cable entities as well as CBS's publicly-stated desire to return to the NFL family. Promotionally, the NFL benefits from expanded pre-game shows and other shoulder programming.

Whatever the road ahead, the NFL can look back on successful negotiations that have taken its clubs from $1 million for each of the 14 teams in 1964 and 1965 to an average of over $39 million a team in our present contracts–rights levels that place the League far ahead of any other team sport and make it the premier attraction in sports programming.

Questions

Consider the following questions as a network/cable channel participant in the NFL-Network Television negotiations.

First, take into account the other major sports television properties your network/cable channel already has in the fall of 1997:

NBC	**CBS**	**ABC**
Olympics '00–'08	NCAA Football	NCAA Football
NBA	NCAA Basketball Final Four	NCAA Basketball
Golf	'98 Olympics	NFL-Mon. Night Football
MLB	Golf-The Masters	Golf
NFL-AFC		Wide World of Sports
Notre Dame Football		

FOX	**ESPN**	**TNT**
NHL	NCAA Basketball	NBA
MLB	NCAA Football	NFL-1/2 Sunday Nights
NFL-NFC	NFL-1/2 Sunday Nights	
	MLB (including Sunday night)	
	NHL	

1. Why are the NFL TV rights so important for networks and cable channels?

2. How important is its NFL package to each incumbent?

3. As a network or cable channel, how does one assess the present or prospective value of having an NFL TV package? What elements enter into the consideration?

4. In light of the decline in overall network ratings for sports, why is the price for the new NFL packages up so much?

5. How does a network/cable channel try to recover big increases in its NFL costs?

6. As CBS, why is it important to return to the NFL TV lineup? Is it worth more than the likely advertising revenue from NFL telecasts and pregame/half-time programs?

7. As NBC, how important is it to retain the Sunday afternoon AFC package—even if *not* at a profit? (NBC claimed each winning network would lose $150m–$200m a year on the new contract.)

8. As FOX, was it worth the huge additional fee you paid in 1993 for the 1994–97 NFL NFC Sunday afternoon package? Why? Why not? Is it worth another big increase for the next contract?

9. As ABC, how important is it to retain Monday Night Football? How far would you go financially to do so?

10. As ESPN, are you willing to pay about double for your new NFL package (second half, Sunday night)? Is it worth paying even more to take over the current TNT package as well?

11. Does it make sense for the NFL to institute a Thursday night package at rates proportional to those for Monday Night Football?

12. What is the NFL's rationale for seeking an 8-year, rather than a 4-year, TV contract? Why should the networks agree? What about the NFL's unilateral option to reopen in the fifth year?

CASE 8.5   NBC's Olympics Broadcast Strategy[67]

The 2004 Athens Summer Olympics were the most extensively televised Olympics in U.S. television history. NBC and its several associated cable channels—CNBC, MSNBC, Bravo, USA, and Telemundo—provided more than 1,200 hours of Olympic coverage (compared to 441 from Sydney in 2000), supported by some $1 billion in advertising.

The coverage on NBC (broadcast network) itself was the most extensive. It also was the coverage most directed to sports in which women would have an interest. The presentation continued to be based on an explicit philosophy and strategy that had been developed after the 1988 Seoul games, which had not been a ratings (viewership) success. The telecasts had emphasized a large number of events and did not attract what NBC considered a substantial enough women's audience.

The focus for NBC's coverage of subsequent Olympics, according to former NBC research director Nicholas P. Schiavone, was on "story-telling rather than solely on competition." The approach was explicitly intended to attract both men and women viewers, in short "to bring everyone into the tent."

As described in a lengthy article in *The New Yorker,*[68] the strategy adopted by NBC Sports president Dick Ebersol was based on extensive research involving thousands of interviews over the years. Ebersol himself, widely considered one of the most powerful people in sports, had worked with the legendary Roone Arledge, the late head of ABC Sports (and News), when ABC telecast the Olympics in the 1960s. Arledge had coined the phrase "up close and personal" to characterize the approach to presenting background information on Olympic athletes.

Five core components were identified in the research. Schiavone considered them "the foundation of the NBC Olympic television philosophy." They are:

- Story—"narrative momentum, a story that builds"
- Reality—unscripted drama (inherent in sports)
- Possibilities—victory and defeat, especially the path to achievement by athletes, symbolizing one's own possibilities to achieve
- Idealism—"purity and honor" are still seen as significant Olympic values
- Patriotism—pride and pageantry, incorporating athletes' love of their own nations, echoed by viewers

Schiavone added that balancing "thought" and "feeling" was an important element. Women, he said, were found to see a story "from the inside out," that is, more focused on the people. Men see sports "from the outside in," with the event dominant. Keeping score is a part of the story, but not the whole story.

Hence, the coverage, particularly in more recent Olympics, is based on *story*. This emphasis also fits with another element affecting NBC's coverage for the United States, namely the reality of Olympics in cities many time zones away from the United States, for example, Sydney 2000, Athens 2004, and in 2008 Beijing. With few telecasts actually live, the intent is to make them seem so, which NBC calls "plausibly live."

To help "train the viewers," human interest features were run before the Games, in the Olympic Trials and in pre-Olympics specials. These features took viewers to the athletes' roots.

In the 2004 telecasts, "story" had become a well-recognized key element of NBC's coverage. Illustratively, a column in *The Boston Globe* emphasized the importance of storytelling in NBC's coverage, especially in light of the ready prior availability of results because of the 7-hour time difference from the East Coast to Athens (longer in other parts of the country). "That's where NBC's test for storytelling comes in."[69] *The New York Times* flagged the Jimmy Roberts's feature on ancient Olympia, praising him as "a skilled interviewer and storyteller."[70]

Implications for Advertisers

Schiavone also described how major Olympic advertisers were shown how NBC thought the advertisers could link their messages to the program (editorial) coverage. In a presentation[71] before the 1992 Barcelona summer games, Schiavone reported on research conducted to help advertisers "signal" their association with Olympic values, and thus (in his view) help create value for the advertiser's brand.

Effective Olympic advertising, according to study respondents, was distinguished by one or more of five characteristics—high production values, future promise (the joys of children and hope for the future), flag-waving (capturing pageantry and patriotism for Americans), goose bumps and tears (high emotion), and inspiration and reward (appreciation for the story behind the victory or effort). From Schiavone's perspective, "there is a strong link between how viewers respond to the Olympics and the way they respond to good Olympic advertising."

He went on to cite five principles of Olympic advertising and their implications for message/content.

- Linkage—Advertising connected to the Olympic story helps "maintain . . . the narrative momentum" by providing "an understandable connection to the Olympics" for viewers.

- Credibility—Advertising that is seen as involving real people in real situations generates "greater impact" compared to advertising that does not.

- Identification—Advertising that expresses a feeling of hope "has the potential to hold the attention of viewers."

- Reverence—"Advertising that respects the athletes and the Olympic spirit" is appropriate, although in non-Olympic program settings the same commercials "may be out of place."

- Celebration—The Olympics "offer a rare opportunity for expression of patriotic feelings."

The heart of Schiavone's own message is that viewers "welcome advertising [done] in the context of the Olympic coverage," a melding of commercial content with the program content. In the communications field, this is known as "fitting" one's message (presentation style and/or content) to the editorial climate in which it will appear.

* * *

Ratings data on the Athens Olympics showed that more than 70% of the U.S. population had watched some portion of Olympics coverage on NBC or one of its family of cable channels.[72]

Questions

1. What were NBC's objectives regarding the Olympics telecasts?

2. What are your reactions to each of the five elements of the NBC Olympics television philosophy? To its totality?

3. To the extent you recall watching the 1996 Atlanta, 2000 Sydney, and 2004 Athens games on TV, what were your reactions then? How did the ideas in the case affect them? What about NBC's "plausibly live" approach to time-delayed competition?

4. If you watched any of the recent summer games on TV outside the United States, what differences were there compared to what you read (or saw) in terms of coverage in the United States?

5. In light of the brevity and the intensity of the Olympics, how does a network try to "train the fan" for Olympics TV viewing?

6. What are your views of Schiavone's suggestions to advertisers about linking their Olympics advertising to the NBC programming approach?

CASE 8.6 THE WOMEN'S SPORTING MAGAZINE MARKET: IS THERE A VIABLE POSITION FOR A NEW STARTUP?[73]

Sarah Driver was in two minds as she walked off the field with her college team winning the 2004 NCAA women's soccer final. It was her final college game. Winning the game was an accomplishment she would treasure for life. However, she loved soccer and doubted if she was likely to be selected this year for the U.S. national team. Two years ago, being selected for a team in the WUSA, the women's professional soccer league, was a viable option after her senior year. However, that league folded in late 2003. Driver was sad that her future now as a player was uncertain.

Driver was a communications major and was contemplating an "off-field" career in the magazine industry. Her parents had successfully launched three magazines that were all subsequently sold to major publishing houses. *Forbes* recently estimated the family wealth at $250 million. The Driver family was intensely committed to women's sports. They were a sponsor of two of the WUSA teams. During a family retreat, Sarah discussed her desire to do something positive for lifting the profile of women's sports. Her parents response took her by surprise. "Bring us a viable business plan." Sarah had observed enough business conversations of her parents that she knew they were serious. "Bring us a viable business plan" was code for "we are very interested and willing to commit sizable resources if the proposal is a commercially viable one."

The 1996 to 2004 period in Sarah's life was one in which women's sports achieved much publicity in the U.S. For example, the U.S. women's basketball team won the gold in the 1996, 2000, and 2004 Summer Olympics. The U.S. women's soccer team won the 1999 Soccer World Cup and won the gold medal in the 2004 Summer Olympics. Women's professional tennis attracted comparable ratings to the men, and included high profile U.S. stars such as Lindsay Davenport, Monica Seles, Serena Williams, and Venus Williams.

Potential Market Analysis

Sarah was about to start her senior year thesis. She decided to examine the viability of a new women's sporting magazine. As a first pass, she interviewed many of her fellow students and numerous people at local coffee shops on what the target audience for such a magazine might be. There were a diversity of responses. The possible target audiences included:

1. Women and men who watch professional women's or college women's sports.
2. Women who participate in sports. These include:
   a. Girls up to the end of high school
   b. College women's sports
   c. Professional women's sports
   d. Amateur women's sports (including recreational sports)
3. "Family and friends" of women who participate in sports. This includes parents and siblings of women playing sports at any level.

4. Women who are interested in an active lifestyle. This could include outdoor recreation (such as hiking) as well as sports-related activities (golf, tennis, skiing, etc.)

5. Women interested in fitness and wellness/health.

6. "Physical appearance" interested readers. Sports Illustrated's Swimsuit Issue is a major commercial success.[74] Several of Sarah's friends expressed interest in a magazine showcasing male or female athletic bodies.

Sarah was aware that magazines differed greatly in their readership/subscribers and in their content. Two obvious issues to her were (a) the sex of the possible readership, and (b) the sex focus of the magazine's photos and stories. Exhibit 1 summarizes nine possible combinations she sketched out. She knew that part of her research would be to examine the potential viability of the combinations in Exhibit 1. The only combination in Exhibit 1 she was not interested in was a readership that was predominantly male with content (photos and stories) that was predominantly male.

Statistics published in Street and Smith's *Sports Business Journal: By The Numbers 2004* (the premier magazine in sports business) indicated women constituted an important component of the fan base in major U.S. men's sports—NFL (43.4%); MLB (46.6%); NBA (45.7%); NHL (41.0%); MLS (48.5%); and NASCAR (41.2%). A stereotype is that it is mostly women who watch women's sports. However, one survey (Harris Poll #16, March 10, 1999) reported that "men are more likely than women to watch not just all sports but also women's sports. Fully 81 percent of men watch some sports and 46 percent of men watch some women's sports, compared to 60 percent of women who watch any sports and 33 percent who watch any women's sports." Sarah was not sure how generalizable this result was to specific sports.

Magazine Publishers of America publishes an annual list of the Top 100 Consumer Magazines in the U.S. The 2003 list included 18 magazines that had a sports or fitness or health focus in its title—see Exhibit 2. Sarah Driver was disappointed but not surprised that women's sports was not a central element of any of the magazines on the Top 100 list in 2003.

Sarah knew that in identifying her target market, the issue of lesbianism would arise. There was a belief of some that women's sports had an above-average lesbianism component, both on-the-field and in its supporter base. The *New York Post* had run stories on the "Lesbians for [the WNBA's New York] Liberty," a group seeking more recognition for its strong support of the WNBA team. One *New York Post* article (8/3/2002) noted that "WNBA teams, such as Seattle, Sacramento, Los Angeles, Minnesota and Miami, have acknowledged the large lesbian fan base with special promotions such as discounts for gay groups." How should a new magazine address this issue, if at all? What impact does it have on possible advertisers? On possible subscribers?

EXHIBIT 1   MATRIX OF POSSIBLE READERSHIP/CONTENT COMBINATIONS FOR MAGAZINES

	FOCUS OF MAGAZINE PHOTOS/STORIES		
SEX OF READERSHIP/SUBSCRIBER	Predominantly Male	Mix of Male and Female	Predominantly Female
Predominantly Male	I	II	III
Mix of Male and Female	IV	V	IV
Predominantly Female	VII	VIII	IX

EXHIBIT 2

SPORTS/FITNESS/HEALTH MAGAZINES IN TOP 100 CONSUMER MAGAZINES 2003

Rank In Top 100/Title	Paid Circulation (Millions)	Rank In Top 100/Title	Paid Circulation (Millions)
15. Prevention	3.275	57. Golf Magazine	1.413
16. Sports Illustrated	3.238	58. Fitness	1.408
25. Maxim	2.510	59. American Rifleman	1.404
40. ESPN: The Magazine	1.726	60. Health	1.389
41. Men's Health	1.686	67. Motor Trend	1.270
45. Shape	1.638	78. FHM	1.106
51. Golf Digest	1.570	81. American Hunter	1.070
52. Field and Stream	1.520	96. Outdoor Life	0.936

Source: Audit Bureau of Circulations. Tabulated by Magazine Publishers of America.

The Rocky Road of Past "Women's Sports" Magazines

Sarah's research uncovered a *Folio* (December 1, 1999) article on "Women's Sports Titles Gain Momentum." The article cited "rate bases" (the circulation figures used to set advertising rates) for several "women's sports titles" with circulation above 50,000 per issue:

	1999	2000
Women's Sports and Fitness	475,000	650,000
Sports Illustrated for Women	250,000	300,000
Golf for Women	370,000	380,000
Amy Love's Real Sports	75,000	100,000

By 2004, only *Golf for Women* had survived as a regular magazine. *Real Sports* had moved to a annual "Collector's Edition" cycle with much lower circulation. Both the *Women's Sports and Fitness* and *Sports Illustrated for Women* titles had been discontinued.

CONDE NAST'S SPORTS FOR WOMEN/WOMEN'S SPORTS AND FITNESS. October 1997 saw the launch of its monthly *Conde Nast's Sports For Women*. Conde Nast was a magazine publishing powerhouse. Its magazines included *Vogue, Vanity Fair, Glamour, Self,* and *Bride's.* Its strengths were in women's magazines rather than in sports. In January 1998, Conde Nast purchased Women's *Sports and Fitness* (circulation approximately 200,000) from Sports and Fitness Publishing for a reported price of $5 to $7 million. Conde Nast then announced it was retitling its own magazine to *Women's Sports and Fitness* and moving it from a monthly to a bi-monthly schedule. *Folio* (January 13, 1998) noted:

> Conde Nast Sports for Women *publisher Susan Grimes insists that the switch to a bi-monthly schedule isn't a setback. She admits that* CNSFW *was obscured by being placed too often with newstands's sports magazines rather than where Conde Nast would prefer it with women's titles.*

Lisa Granatstein (Media Week, 4/27/1998) noted that "Conde Nast says that the name change reflects the [magazine's] focus on healthy, active lifestyle through both sports and fitness."

On February 27, 1998, Sports Business Daily reported that:

> Conde Nast Sports For Women *"is now headed for a major relaunch at mid-year" according to Keith Kelly of the* New York Daily News. *After conducting recent focus groups, the title hired Mary Murray as its new Executive Editor in charge of "stepping up fitness and nutrition coverage." Conde Nast Editor James Truman "insisted the company has not hit the panic button." But Kelly notes "one sign of potential circulation weakness" is that after "slicing back" to six issues a year and "buying"* Women's Sports and Fitness *it "has no plans to boost" circulation beyond 350,000. . . . The magazine also plans to hire another senior editor to "focus entirely on fitness" and will come up with a new logo that could debut in June.*

In June 2000 Conde Nast Publications announced that the September issue of *Women's Sports and Fitness* would be its last. Factors cited by commentators and in a *Sports Business Daily* (June 28, 2000) review of the press reaction to the decision included:

1. Slower than expected growth in circulation and advertising.—"Insiders say that circulation growth 'proved tough, and without a big readership, the company could not charge high enough prices to advertisers.' Its advertising pages last year [1999] as a bimonthly publication dropped 25.6 percent to 408.7, while advertising revenues dropped 10.6 percent to $11.3 million. This year [2000], publishing monthly, it was 'rebounding through May, with advertising pages up' 30.3 percent to 234 pages, but circulation was still growing too slowly."

2. Changing publication cycle. A *Wall Street Journal* article (6/28/2000) by Matthew Rose noted that "the four year old title flip-flopped between being a monthly and a bi-monthly, confusing some readers."

3. Struggle to define identity. One observer noted that "from the first issue in 1997, the magazine ambled from one editorial identity to another." A Conde Nast Executive observed: "What else could they have done to that magazine? Could they have possibly made any more switches to it?"

4. Failure to yet achieve profitability. The Founding Editor in Chief of WSF (Lucy Danzinger) was quoted as saying "[The closure] not a huge surprise to me. Our successes were steady, but profitability was in the distant future." Internal sources were said to estimate 1999 losses at $14 million with Conde Nast spending at least $45 million since its launch in October 1997.

SPORTS ILLUSTRATED FOR WOMEN. Time Inc is a leading magazine publisher, with tiles across multiple areas including *People*, *Sports Illustrated* (SI), and *Time*. SI was the leading sporting magazine, both in terms of circulation and advertising revenues. On January 7, 1997 *Sports Business Daily* noted that *SI* will test a sports magazine for women in April 1997:

> *The yet-to-be-titled magazine, with a working title of* Sports Illustrated Woman, *will be published twice in 1997, with frequency to be determined. Targeted to the "Title IX generation" women, ages 18–34, the magazine will cover personalities and issues of sports and the April issue will consist*

> *of more than 100 editorial pages. Initial distribution will include SI's*
> *450,000 female subscribers and a newsstand shipping of 150,000 at a*
> *cover price of $2.50. The magazine will launch with a rate base of*
> *600,000 and a page rate of $25,000.*

The second issue of *Sports Illustrated Women* hit the newsstands in September 1997. The cover story was on Mia Hamm, the U.S. soccer star.

On October 7, 1998, *Sports Business Daily* reported a *New York Post* article that Time Inc was "'laying plans to revive' a women's title from *Sports Illustrated,* an idea many assumed—was dead." *SI* President Michael Klingensmith "confirmed that the magazine was planning another run in 1999, after two test issues were published in 1997, but he stopped short of calling it a full scale launch." He said that *SI* could "publish one to four shots with 300,000 to 500,000 copies available on newsstands only, and the first expected to roll out around the women's World Cup in June 1999." In 1999, four special issues were published under the *Sports Illustrated for Women* title.

Time Inc. officially set the launch of its bimonthly *Sports Illustrated for Women* (SIFW) for March 2000. *Sports Business Daily* (October 6, 1999) noted:

> *The magazine will launch with a circulation base of 300,000 and a cover*
> *price of $3.50.* SIFW *Editor Sandy Bailey said the magazine will be*
> *aimed at women 18–34, and "will cover the current landscape of women's*
> *sports," and it will "also offer our readers insights on issues of health,*
> *nutrition, and fitness, news about products, gear and clothing that fit*
> *their lifestyles." A six-issue subscription will cost $11.94.*

Media Week (quoted in *Sports Business Daily,* February 1, 2000) noted that the March 2000 issue differed from its earlier trial issues in 1997 and 1999:

> *Time's* SIFW *"still got game" thanks to "major editorial repositioning"*
> *and "considerable buzz" in women's sports.* SIFW *"has evolved from an*
> *avid fan book to more of a lifestyle magazine for active women."*
> *Beginning with its March/April 2000 issue,* SIFW *will increase to a*
> *bimonthly frequency, while boasting its rate base from 250,000 to*
> *300,000.* SIFW *Group Publisher Cleary Simpson says that* SIFW*'s "own*
> *sales force" will "drive sales this year." Last year SI handled the ad sales*
> *and it will continue to call on a number of advertisers," but Simpson now*
> *has "her own team in place."*

The Boston Globe reported (March 15, 2000):

> SIFW *Editor Sandy Bailey said the magazine conducted market research*
> *over the past two years to determine its target readership. Bailey quoted as:*
> *"The common denominator for the women who read us was that they*
> *played sports, they weren't just spectators. Our target is the 18 to 34 year*
> *old women—even younger, say a 16 or 17-year older preparing for*
> *college—who is interested in sports as a participant."*

Bailey noted that one reason for Time Inc.'s delay in launching SIFW was ESPN's launch in 1998 of ESPN: The Magazine. *This magazine competed with Time Inc.'s* SI *and the top priority in 1998 and 1999 was maintaining SI's market position. Bailey noted that in 1997 they "were not nearly as focused on what [SIFW] was and how we are different from the men's magazine, as we are now." SIFW had 5 issues in 2000, 8 issues in 2001 and 10 issues in 2002.*

In October 2002, Time Inc. announced that it would cease publication of SIFW after its December 2002 issue. Reasons cited for this decision included:

1. Economic factors. The Communications Director for *SIFW* (Allison Keane) state that "A lot of magazines are really feeling it right now because it's such an unforgiving time. Obviously, there's a market out there (for women's sports coverage). In a better (economic) time, maybe this would have had more of an opportunity to grow" (Chicago Daily Tribune, 9/9/2002).

2. Struggle to define identity—Matthew Rose in *The Wall Street Journal* (10/17/2002) stated that SIFW "flip-flopped from concentrating on spectator sports to focusing on personal fitness and athletics." *SIFW* editor Susan Casey observed that its "name was a problem, giving the misleading impression that the magazine was for viewers of sports events. We defined sports as anything outside of sitting in a La-Z-Boy recliner which is different than Sports Illustrated." One observable switch near its demise was the *SIFW* July/August 2002 "Swimsuit Issue." It featured the "Sexiest Men in Sports 2002" and included 30 pages of men in swimsuits or board shorts.

3. Competition from other magazines. After Conde Nast's *Women's Sports and Fitness* closed in June 2000, *SIFW* had *Real Sports* as its only focused competitor covering women athletes. However, when *SIFW* broadened to include fitness/health, its range of competitors expanded. One commentator quoted in Sports Business Daily (10/23/2002) noted: "Lets face it. There are more than enough magazines out there already covering [fitness] topics."

4. Lack of profitability at parent and at magazine level. AOL Time-Warner (the parent) was suffering major shortfalls. This increased the reluctance of Time Inc. to carry magazines not year making money. MediaWeek.com (10/16/2002) noted that "While *SIFW*'s circulation 'improved recently' executives felt that Time Inc. 'couldn't afford to wait for the loss-making title to turn around financially.'"

REAL SPORTS: Amy Love founded *Real Sports* magazine in July 1997. Love was a Harvard Business School graduate with a strong consumer marketing background. In her youth, she successfully challenged a youth soccer association rule prohibiting girls playing on "All-Star" teams. Love's vision for *Real Sports* was to "seize an opportunity to change the way women's sports are covered and treated in this country." She wanted to use the *Real Sports* magazine as a way to present female athletes playing on the field and on the court, as opposed to using "glamour shots" done in the studio. Love felt that the growing world of female athletes and fans wanted top rate photography and editorials that focused on women playing their sport.

The magazine began as quarterly, with the first edition running in November 1998 at a cover price of $3.95. Initial circulation was 55,000. The next few editions continued *Real Sports'* positive momentum. Circulation increased dramatically to a peak level of 150,000 in late 1999. The magazine moved to bi-monthly frequency. While readers were rating the new magazine a rousing success, the response from advertisers was less promising. "We couldn't get any of the big names to make long-term commitments," commented Love. One issue here was Love's decision to have athletes in "playing mode" rather than pose or have "re-worked" photos. This policy did not appeal to potential advertisers from the cosmetics industry.

Even at a circulation level of 150,000 *Real Sports* was still not yet breaking even financially. Love hoped that a continuation of the recent positive momentum in women's sports would bring on bigger advertisers and put the magazine in the black. In 2000, the "dot com" bubble burst. The resulting economic crisis, especially in Real Sports' backyard of Silicon Valley, had serious impact on the magazine business. Advertising revenues plummeted, and four companies who owed money to Real Sports filed for bankruptcy. In the midst of revenue shortfalls, Love had to make some tough decisions. She dropped the page count of the magazine from 84 to 40, and moved back to quarterly frequency.

At the end of 2001, while still facing a difficult financial situation and a diminishing circulation, Love decided to consolidate and focus on her core market. She made the first editorial change for the magazine, moving to a Collector's Edition annual format, increasing the page count to 100 and raising the price from $3.95 to $9.95 per issue. The first such edition recapped the year in sports for 2001, and the second in Spring 2002 focused on a preview of the upcoming WUSA season. Since the move, Real Sports began to stabilize. Circulation was down dramatically, to around 15,000 for the Spring 2002 edition. However, the magazine had broken even in three of its last five issues.

"Playing the Skin" Card

The increasing interest in nude or "cheesecake" photos of women athletes was something Sarah Driver had been observing. Lauren Jackson, the WNBA's Most Valuable Player in 2003, posed nude in *Black and White* magazine for its 2004 Olympic Tribute issue. In the week of June 14, 2000 Jackson "shattered the WNBA.com record for player-page views, registering more than 90,000 visits . . . Seattle Storm Sue Bird had held the weekly record with more than 20,000 during the week of July 21, 2003" (Sports Business Daily, 6/29/2004). Women athletes from the 2004 Olympics posed for *MAXIM*, *FMH* and *Playboy* magazines. The August 2004 issue of *MAXIM* featured pictures of six female Olympian athletes under the caption "Action Figures—These sexy athletes have spent a lifetime honing their bodies to absolute perfection. The least you can do is gawk." These magazines had high sales. *FMH's* Olympic Issue had its highest sales for a single issue. *Sports Business Daily* (8/16/2004) noted: "Former U.S. swimmer Diana Nyad said [in the New York Times that] she was disheartened by *FMH's* "Sexy Olympic Special." However, she wrote that September issue of *Playboy* features "12 elegant full-page photographs of female Olympians who are decidedly more athletic than they are sexy. Or, rather, they are both athletic and sexy-the new sexy." An alternative view was expressed by a *New York Daily News* writer (Stanley Crouch—8/16/2004). He called the *Playboy* photographs "whorish" in an article titled "Porn A Leap Backwards for Olympic Women."

Sepp Batter, the President of FIFA (the world soccer federation) broke rank with "political correctness" when he suggested a way for female soccer players to increase the popularity of their sport: "Let women play in more feminine clothes like they do in volleyball. They could, for example, have tighter shorts" (*London Guardian*, 1/16/2004). While Batter was widely criticized for his comments, Sarah pondered if what he said was "commercial reality." Anna Kournikova had graced the cover of many magazines, albeit more for her "looks" than for her on-court tennis accomplishments. Sarah wondered whether one explanation for women's tennis attracting more viewers than men's tennis was viewers wanting a combination of sports and voyeurism. Even if this was true, was this in the best interest of promoting women's sports?

Where To From Here

Sarah Driver's challenge was to "bring a viable business plan" to her parents. She knew that family money potentially would be at stake. Her agenda included doing something positive to lift the profile of women's sports. Her initial focus was to be in the sports magazine area. However, part of her research aimed to explore additional areas if it was deemed the women's sporting magazine market was "too tough a nut to crack."

APPENDIX
U.S. Women's Professional Sports Landscape

Exhibit 3 shows broadcast television ratings for selected sports. Sports with female and male tracks include individual sports (tennis and golf) and team sports (basketball and soccer). Women's tennis has comparable or better ratings to men's tennis in recent years. Women's professional golf television ratings typically average less than half that of men's golf.

Professional women's team sports have struggled. The WUSA (soccer) shut down operations in its third season (2003). One of the two most recent women's basketball leagues (ABL), also shut down in its third year (1998). Only the WNBA has survived and continued to be shown on leading cable stations. The regular season ratings of the WNBA averaged 30–40 percent of those of the NBA in recent years. Exhibit 4 shows average regular season attendance for the ABL, WNBA and WUSA. In 2003 the WNBA averaged 52 percent of the NBA per game attendance. For 2003, the WUSA averaged 45 percent of the MLS per game attendance.

EXHIBIT 3   BROADCAST TELEVISION RATINGS (2003) FOR SELECTED PROFESSIONAL SPORTS[a]:

Sport (1)	Mens/Women's (2)	Ratings: Men's Professional (3)	Ratings: Women's Professional (4)	Ratings: Women's/ Men's (5) = (4)/(3)
Football:	NFL/-	10.3	—	—
Baseball:	MLB/-	2.7	—	—
Basketball:	NBA/WNBA	2.6	0.8	0.31
Hockey:	NHL/-	1.1	—	—
Soccer:	MLS/WUSA	0.9	0.1	0.11
Golf:	PGA/LPGA	2.9	1.2	0.41
Tennis:	Grand Slam Finals: Men's/Women's	2.2	2.3	1.05

[a]A single Nielsen ratings point represents 1% of the total number of television households in the U.S. Regular season ratings are shown for team sports.

Source: Nielsen Television Index Sports Decks, Nielsen Galaxy Explore.

EXHIBIT 4   **AVERAGE REGULAR SEASON GAME ATTENDANCE FOR WOMEN'S PROFESSIONAL TEAM SPORTS**

	Year	Number of Teams	Average Attendance	% Change Prior Year
A. Basketball/ABL	1996/97	8	3,536	—
	1997/98	9	≈4,400	24.4%
	1998/99	10	≈4,000	−9.1
B. Basketball/WNBA[a]	1997	8	9,669	—
	1998	10	10,869	12.4%
	1999	12	10,207	−6.1
	2000	16	9,074	−11.1
	2001	16	9,075	0.0
	2002	16	9,228	1.7
	2003	14	8,830	−4.3
C. Soccer/WUSA[b]	2001	8	8,104	—
	2002	8	6,957	−14.2%
	2003	8	6,667	−4.2

[a]Average NBA (men's) regular season basketball attendance per game in 2002/2003 season was 16,883

[b]Average MLS (men's) regular season soccer attendance per game in 2003 season was 14,898

Source: Street and Smith's *Sports Business Journal, By The Numbers 2004.*

American Basketball League (ABL): 1996–1998. This women's professional basketball league operated for the 1996/97 and 1997/98 seasons and part of the 1998/99 season. The 8 teams in 1996 were Atlanta; Colorado; Columbus; New England; Portland; Richmond; San Jose; Seattle. The ABL announced on December 22, 1998 it was suspending operations and was seeking protection under Chapter 11 of U.S. Bankruptcy Law. It had unpaid net liabilities of approximately $24 million in December 1998. The ABL struggled to attract broad-based sponsors and high-profile broadcast/cable television contracts.

Women's National Basketball Association (WNBA): 1997–Present. In April 1996, the NBA announced the formation of the WNBA with summer 1997 as the first season. Eight teams played in the first season, each of which was affiliated with an NBA team (Charlotte; Cleveland; Houston; Los Angeles; New York; Phoenix; Sacramento; Utah). The WNBA has been financially supported by the NBA since its start. In a 2004 press conference, WNBA President Val Ackerman predicted the league "will be profitable by the 2007 season" (Sports Business Daily, 10/12/2004).

WUSA: 2001–2003. This women's professional soccer league played games for the 2001, 2002 and 2003 seasons. There were 8 teams in the league (Atlanta; Boston; Carolina; New York; Philadelphia; San Diego; San Jose; Washington). On September 16, 2003, the WUSA announced plans to discontinue operations. WUSA Chairman John Hendricks stated, "An independent women's professional league can survive, if it has corporate support. Quite frankly, we didn't get that support." *Sports Business Journal By The Numbers: 2004* reported the following financials ($ millions):

Year	Revenues	Expenses	Loss
2000		$ 6.0	$ 6.0
2001	$12.2	64.5	50.2
2002	15.6	41.1	25.5
2003	15.7	35.6	19.9

Questions

1. Outline the highs and lows associated with U.S. women's professional sports in the decade up to 2004. First, focus separately on the "on-the-field" arena and, second, on the "business side."

2. What are the key reasons for the demise of major women's sporting magazine titles such as *Women's Sports and Fitness* and *Sports Illustrated for Women*?

3. Sarah Driver seeks your help in developing a proposal for an economically viable (3 to 5 years out) new women's sporting magazine. What would you recommend?

4. What other business areas might Sarah Driver pursue to positively lift the profile of women's sports?

Footnotes

[1] This section was written by George Foster.

[2] The Arena Football League in 2003 moved from a May to August season to a February–June season to better fit in with NBC programming schedule.

[3] "Clash of the Titans." *Daily Variety* (25 March 2003).

[4] Ibid.

[5] 2004 Kagan Research LLC, Private research e-mail to author.

[6] News Corporation *Annual Report,* June 30, 2002, p. 65.

[7] Professor Stephen A. Greyser and Research Associate Elizabeth E. Smyth prepared this case. HBS cases are developed solely as the basis for class discussion. Cases are not intended to serve as endorsements, sources of primary data, or illustrations of effective or ineffective management.

[8] Howard Manly. "Dollars Make No Sense; Ratings Don't Justify $600 Million for the NHL.." *The Boston Globe* (August 23, 1998).

[9] NBC Press Release (May 19, 2004).

[10] Richard Sandomir. "NBC and N.H.L. Announce a Deal to Skate as a Pair." *The New York Times* (May 20, 2004).

[11] Joe Schlosser. "FOX Divided over Chasing Puck." *Broadcasting & Cable* (August 10, 1998).

[12] Howard Manly. *The Boston Globe* (August 23, 1998).

[13] Schlosser. *Broadcasting & Cable* (August 10, 1998).

[14] Marianne Bhonslay. "NHL Sales Slip into Summer." *Sporting Goods Business* (June 10, 1998).

[15] NHL website: http://www.nhl.com.

[16] Joe Schlosser. "Disney Grabs the Puck." *Broadcasting & Cable* (August 24, 1998).

[17] Rudy Martzke. "NHL OKs TV Deal, Which Could Get an Early Start." *USA TODAY* (August 21, 1998).

[18] NHL website: http://www.nhl.com.

[19] Howard Manly. *The Boston Globe* (August 23, 1998).

[20] Victoria Chang prepared this case under the supervision of George Foster.

21 Examples of FOX-owned stations are WNYW (New York), KTTV (Los Angeles), and WFLD (Chicago). A FOX-affiliated station is a station owned by a third party (such as Sinclair, Belo Corp., or Cox) but that carries FOX programming. An example is KTVU (Oakland-San Francisco), which is owned by Cox.

22 Interview with Larry Jones. Subsequent quotes are from this interview unless otherwise noted.

23 Interview with Chase Carey. Subsequent quotes are from this interview unless otherwise noted.

24 The Federal Communications Commission originally allocated 12 channels for television broadcasting. These channels, numbers 2 through 13, were in the "very high frequency" or VHF band. (Originally Channel 1 was also included, but was soon reassigned to other purposes.) The tremendous growth in television broadcasting following World War II made it obvious that 12 channels were not enough. So in 1952, the FCC allocated 70 additional channels above the VHF television band and called them "ultra high frequency" or UHF band. The channels were 14 through 83.

25 Richard Sandomir. "The Man Carrying the Ball for Murdoch." *The New York Times* (September 4, 1994), Section 3, p. 1.

26 Ibid.

27 Interview with Tracy Dolgin. Subsequent quotes are from this interview unless otherwise noted.

28 Barry Layne. "Aussie Hill Gets FBC Start." *Hollywood Reporter* (December 23, 1993), p. 9.

29 Anand, op. cit., p. 11.

30 *Television Sports Rights, 2003 Edition*, Gould Media, 2003, overview.

31 News Corporation Annual Report, June 30, 2002, p. 65.

32 David Teather. "News Corporation Loses $606m." the *Guardian* (February 13, 2002).

33 D. Lieberman, "DIRECTV keeps NFL games in $2B deal," *USA TODAY* (December 12, 2002).

34 Amy Wustefeld prepared this case under the supervision of George Foster.

35 Peter Kafka. "Brushback." *Forbes* (May 27, 2002).

36 Staff. *Sports Business Daily* (June 15, 2001).

37 Frank Deford. "Suicide Squeeze." *Sports Illustrated* (July 8, 2002), p. 70.

38 *The Wall Street Journal* (October 14, 2002).

39 Berkowitz and Joshi, loc.cit.

40 Diane Mermigas. "Hindery Returns." *Electronic Media* (September 17, 2001).

41 Staff. "Major League Attendance." ESPN.com (October 3, 2002).

42 Chris Isidore. "Cable Clout Going, Going . . . Gone?" *CNN/Money* (April 12, 2002).

43 Katie Sheehy. "Boss Yanks More Games Off Free TV." *New York Post* (November 6, 2001).

44 Ronald Blum. "Yankees Move to WCBS." *Yahoo Sports* (December 27, 2001).

45 World Business Report. "Cable Penetration Analysis by DMA." Nielsen Media Research, 2002 (http://www.wbrtv.com/distribution/cnbc.html).

46 DMA: Designated Market Area, or inner market of a television region. DMA, a registered trademark of Nielsen Media Research, Inc., is what advertising CPM (cost per thousand impressions) is based upon.

47 Staff, *Sky Report* (April 9, 2002).

48 Interview with Dave Ianucci, Zimmerman & Partners, November 18, 2002.

49 Harry Berkowitz. "Many Advertisers Say No to YES." Newsday.com (April 2, 2002), and interview with Dave Ianucci, Zimmerman & Partners.

50 Interview with Dave Ianucci, Zimmerman & Partners, November 18, 2002.

51 Berkowitz, loc. cit.

52 Interview with Dave Ianucci, Zimmerman & Partners, November 18, 2002.

53 Brian Davis, "Kyle Field Only Place to See Texas A&M", *Dallas Morning News*, October 3, 2002.

[54] Kaplan and Bernstein. "Cablevision $2.66B into Sports." *Street & Smith's SportsBusiness Journal* (April 8–14, 2002).

[55] YES vs. Cablevision Complaint, *YES Network v. Cablevision*, U.S. District Court, Southern District of New York (April 29, 2002), p. 26.

[56] YES Memorandum in Opposition to Defendants' Motion to Dismiss, *YES Network v. Cablevision*, U.S. District Court, Southern District of New York (July 1, 2002), p. 19.

[57] "Sub Losses, MSG Revenue Hurt Cablevision's Financial Picture." *Sports Business Daily* (August 9, 2002).

[58] Richard Sandomir and Mike Wise. "James Dolan in Center of Storm." *The New York Times* (April 3, 2002).

[59] Andy Bernstein. "Saying No to YES Bolsters Carriers." *Street & Smith's SportsBusiness Journal* (July 1–7, 2002).

[60] "Cablevision Says It Has Lost Less Than 1% Due to YES Dispute." *Sports Business Daily* (December 6, 2002).

[61] "Sub Losses, MSG Revenue Hurt Cablevision's Financial Picture." *Sports Business Daily* (August 9, 2002).

[62] Joe Concha. "CBS, DIRECTV, Mets are Big Winners in Battle Between Cablevision, YES." *New York Sun* (May 6, 2002).

[63] Summary Capital Market information is:

Date	Cablevision Stock Price	Cablevision Market Capitalization ($millions)	S&P 500 Stock Index	Bloomberg Cable Stock Index
12/29/2000	$72.15	$11,257	1,321	334
12/31/2001	47.45	6,318	1,148	249
3/29/2002	34.00	4,532	1,147	202
6/28/2002	9.46	1,261	990	103
9/30/2002	9.06	1,208	916	96

[64] Harry Berkowitz. "Dolans Downplay Stock, YES." Newsday.com (June 5, 2002).

[65] Staff. "YES Sues Cablevision Over Yankee Games." *CNN/Money Magazine* (April 29, 2002).

[66] Professor Stephen A. Greyser prepared this case. HBS cases are developed solely as the basis for class discussion. Cases are not intended to serve as endorsements, sources of primary data, or illustrations of effective or ineffective management.

[67] This text material was prepared by Stephen A. Greyser from presentations by former NBC research director Nicholas P. Schiavone at several class sessions of "The Business of Sports," and in interviews, and approved by Mr. Schiavone.

[68] David Remnick. "Inside-Out Olympics." *The New Yorker.* (August 3, 1996), p. 26.

[69] Bill Griffith. "NBC Relies on Storytelling for Continuity." *The Boston Globe.* (August 20, 2004).

[70] Richard Sandomir. "NBC's Gymnastics Team Masters Difficult Routine." *The New York Times.* (August 19, 2004).

[71] "The Five Rings of Advertising Opportunity." TOP Sponsor Workshop, October 1991.

[72] *USA TODAY* (August 30, 2004).

[73] This case was written by George Foster. It draws on Stanford MBA assignments written by Sonia Axter, Catherine Beam, Kevin Bryant, Martin Plettner, Daniel Schlafman, Jeff Siemon, and Amy Wustefeld.

[74] *SI's* Swimsuit Issue was a major financial contributor. CNNMoney.com (2/20/2003) reported that SI expects the issue to "sell an extra 1.4 million copies over its normal weekly circulation of 3.15 million, which at $5.99 a copy, would mean about $8 million more in revenue. Also, advertisements in the issue are sold at an 18 percent premium over normal ad rates."

SECTION 9... Stadiums and Arenas[1]

Key Issues

- Stadium decision making is affected by who owns the stadium , who has stadium operating rights, the number of anchor tenants in the stadium, and the number and diversity of other events being run in the stadium.

- New stadiums (or old stadium revamps) are an essential component of the relentless search for new revenues in the business of sports. Key revenue sources include naming rights, personal seat licenses, suites, in-stadium advertising, and innovative ticketing strategies.

- Planning stadium capacity is a pivotal front-ended decision that has dramatic effects on both subsequent revenues and fan experience for many years out.

- Public financing has played an important role in many recent stadium construction projects. Debate over the size of the benefits and who captures those benefits is an ongoing part of the political process that accompanies new stadium proposals.

- Where new stadiums are privately financed, the owners can have a broader set of decision rights. However, the additional costs of extra debt with private financing adds to the financial challenges for groups that own both a club and its stadium.

Cases

Stadiums and arenas are a pivotal component of the business of sports. They are a major revenue source for many clubs. The difference between the highest and lowest revenue-earning clubs in many leagues is often associated with either (1) differences in their stadium revenue-generating capabilities or (2) differences in contracts with which those stadium revenues are shared. Stadiums and arenas also play an important role in the economic revival of cities and in attracting major events to those cities. For example, Houston attracted Super Bowl XXVIII in 2004 as part of public financing assistance for Reliant Stadium, the home of the Houston Texans. The added attraction of bringing a Super Bowl to Houston was a factor in how much the Houston syndicate bid for this NFL expansion franchise in 1997.

This section outlines three key business issues related to the construction or operation of stadiums and arenas (hereafter referred to as stadiums):

1. Key decision makers in business-related stadium activities
2. Stadiums as multiple revenue-generating assets
3. Seeking public funding assistance for stadium construction and operation

Ownership, Operator, and Anchor Tenant Influences on Stadium Decision Making

Three factors influencing decisions related to the business side of stadium management are:

- Who owns the stadium?
- Who operates and manages the stadium?
- How many sporting clubs are tenants of the stadium?

Exhibit 9-1 illustrates combinations of these three factors. The simplest case is Case I in Exhibit 9-1 where a club owns, operates, and is the sole major tenant in the stadium. Examples include FedEx Field/Washington Redskins in the NFL, SBC Park/San Francisco Giants in the MLB, and Old Traford/ Manchester United in the English Premier League. Here the sporting club has great flexibility in decision making in multiple areas, for example, naming right sponsors, ticket pricing, and other possible renters of the stadium.

For stadiums with a single anchor tenant, complexities arise when the stadium is either owned or operated by a third party. Here contracts over decision rights, revenue sharing, and cost responsibilities have to be negotiated between the sporting club, the stadium owner, and the stadium operator. An example is the Louisiana Super Dome. The New Orleans Saints of the NFL is the anchor tenant. The Super Dome is owned by the State of Louisiana and

EXHIBIT 9-1 STADIUM/ARENA OWNERSHIP, OPERATOR, AND NUMBER OF ANCHOR TENANT RELATIONSHIPS

	Owner: Sporting Club Operator: Sporting Club	Owner: Third Party Operator: Sporting Club	Owner: Third Party Operator: Third Party
Single Anchor Tenant	I	II	III
Multiple Anchor Tenants	IV	V	VI

managed by SMG Facility Management (a public-sector body). Decisions relating to the stadium can involve all three different parties—the club, the owner, and the operator.

A further layer of complexity is added when we recognize multiple anchor tenants. Multiple tenants occur most frequently in indoor arenas. The simplest case is Case IV where the owner of the multiple anchor tenants also owns and operates the arena. The Pepsi Center in Denver is an example. Stan Kroenke owns and operates the arena as well as owns the two main anchor tenants—the Colorado Avalanche of the NHL and the Denver Nuggets of the NBA. Both the NBA and the NHL require financials on an individual sporting club basis. This will necessitate a rule to allocate the Pepsi Center shared revenues (such as arena naming rights and suite revenues) between the Avalanche and the Nuggets and possibly the other events. Suite holders buy a package that covers all events in the Pepsi Center.

The most complex case is where there are multiple tenants and a different entity owns and operates the arena. Staples Center in Los Angeles is a classic example. Staples is jointly owned by Phil Anschutz and Edward Roski, Jr. It is operated by AEG (Anschutz Entertainment Group) and has five anchor tenants (Los Angeles Lakers and Los Angeles Clippers of the NBA, Los Angeles Kings of the NHL, Los Angeles Sharks of the WNBA, and Los Angeles Invaders of the AFL). These anchor tenants do not all have the same ownership groups. Even where the same individuals overlap in ownership, equity percentages in individual clubs or the arena differ. The result is a negotiated set of sharing rules at the Staples Center.

Stadiums as a Multiple-Revenue-Generating Asset

Managers in all areas of sports face the seemingly endless need to expand their revenue base. The multiple revenue sources associated with a state-of-the-art stadium can be illustrated with Reliant Stadium, home of the Houston Texans. The stadium has a retractable roof and a natural grass field. The Texans, an expansion franchise in the NFL, played their opening season game against the Dallas Cowboys in September 2002 (Houston won 19–10!). The Texans paid a record $700 million new franchise fee to the NFL, payable over a 5-year period. The total project cost for Reliant Stadium was $310 million. The owner of the stadium is the Harris County—Houston Sports Authority. This public-sector authority put up $195 million toward the construction cost, based on a hotel and motel tax public financing. The remaining $115 million came from the two major tenants—the Houston Texans (led by Bob McNair) and the Houston Livestock Show and Rodeo.

Capacity Decisions: Reliant has capacity for approximately 69,500. In the planning stage, a balance was struck between the costs of adding extra capacity versus the likely demand for seats (including demand at peak events). The costs of having too much capacity include the construction and operating costs of an "oversized" stadium as well as the diminution in fan value when games are played with many empty seats. In addition, leagues can impose additional costs. The NFL has a "blackout policy"—only games sold out 72 hours before kick-off time can be televised in the home city. The loss of a televised market at home is a negative for sponsors and fans. This blackout policy creates an incentive for new NFL stadiums to have lower capacities than might otherwise be the case.

Exhibit 9-2 presents summary data on the stadium sizes in selected professional leagues. MLS, NFL, and EPL generally play in outdoor stadiums, whereas the NBA, NHL, and WNBA

EXHIBIT 9-2

STADIUM CAPACITIES FOR SELECTED PROFESSIONAL SPORTING LEAGUES

League	Highest	Lowest	Average Capacity	Average Attendance	Average # of Suites (Range)	Average # of Club Seats (Range)	# of Home Games
NFL (National Football League)	85,407 Washington Redskins FedEx Field	60,272 Indianapolis Colts RCA Dome	69,828	66,662	141	7,636	8 + 2 preseason
MLB (Major League Baseball)	57,545 New York Yankees Yankee Stadium	33,950 Fenway Park Boston Red Sox	46,278	28,025	75	3,983	81
NBA (National Basketball League)	22,076 Detroit Pistons Palace Auburn Hills	17,100 Seattle Supersonics Key Arena	19,353	16,883	89	2,024	41
NHL (National Hockey League)	21,631 Montreal Canadians Bell Centre	11,000 Nashville Predators Gaylord Center	18,490	16,589	94	2,094	41
MLS (Major League Soccer)	25,576 Metro Stars Giants Stadium (NJ)	8,500 Dallas Burn Dragon Stadium	21,174	14,898	82	4,463	15
WNBA (Women's National Basketball League)	24,042 Charlotte Sting Charlotte Coliseum	10,000 Connecticut Sun Mohegan Sun Arena	18,705	8,933	84	1,780	17
EPL (English Premiere League)	67,630 Old Trafford Manchester United	19,148 Fullham Craven Cottage	37,784	35,445	N/A	N/A	19

Sources: Prepared from information in *2004 Revenues From Sports Venues* (Media Ventures, 2004) and Deloitte, *Annual Review of Football Finance* (2004).

play in indoor arenas (although the distinction between outdoor and indoor now is less clear-cut with some outdoor stadiums having retractable roofs).

Personal Seat Licenses: A personal seat license (PSL) is a one-time purchase of the underlying rights to a particular seat (typically in a premium location) in the stadium. PSLs offer fans control over their tickets and seat location as well as future ownership of the seat. The stadium owner receives a front-end payment from the sale of the PSL as well as the annual season-ticket revenue for the seat. The PSL owner, in most cases, has the right to resell the PSL and personally capture any increase in its market value.

The Houston Texans sold approximately 41,000 PSLs at prices ranging from $600 to $4,200. Assuming a mid-range price of $2,400, this translates to $98.400 million up-front cash. This early cash infusion was pivotal to the investor group being able to manage its share of the $310 million construction cost as well as make payments on the $700 million expansion fee.

Naming Rights: An attractive naming rights deal offers a stadium a long-term sequence of cash inflows. The Harris County—Houston Sports Authority signed a $300 million, 30-year deal with Reliant Resources. This is one of the most lucrative naming rights deals in all sports. Exhibit 9-3 reports the five highest naming rights deals as of 2003. The Houston Texans receive 75% of the annual naming rights payment.

Suites: Suites offer occupants viewing of a game in an upscale setting—more space, ready access to catered food and beverages, and privacy. Suites typically are sold on a multiyear basis. There were 165 suites at Reliant the first season. Given the high demand, it was decided to add another 19 new luxury suites. Most suites average 17 to 21 people. For 2004–05, the price range is $55,000 to $225,000. At an average price of $154,000, the 184 suites yield more than $28 million in annual revenue each year.

Season Ticket-Holders: This source of revenue is highly attractive in the annual financial planning for a sporting club. It is paid in full at the start of the season. In the extreme case, if the stadium is completely sold out with season ticket-holders, no subsequent marketing of

EXHIBIT 9-3   NAMING RIGHTS DEALS AT MAJOR LEAGUE FACILITIES

Facility Total Amount	City League	Expiration Year/Length	Average Annual Value (Millions)	Major Tenants
1. **Reliant Stadium** $300 million	Houston Texas/NFL	2033/30 years	$10.00	Houston Texans
2. **FedEx Field** $205 million	Landover, Maryland/NFL	2025/27 years	$7.59	Washington Redskins
3. **American Airlines Center $195 million**	Dallas, Texas NBA/NHL	2030/30 years	$6.50	Dallas Mavericks Dallas Stars
4. **Philips Arena** $185 million	Atlanta Georgia, NBA/NHL	2019/20 years	$9.25	Atlanta Hawks Atlanta Thrashers
5. **Minute Maid Park** $170 million	Houston, Texas/MLB	2029/28 years	$6.07	Houston Astros

Source: Street & Smith's *Sports Business Journal, By the Numbers 2004.*

tickets is required. There are approximately 38,000 season ticket-holders with PSLs at Reliant Stadium. The annual season ticket costs range from $500 to $2,680. At a mid-range price of $1,590, the estimated revenues are $60.420 million. An additional 16,700 non-PSL holders have season tickets in the $300 to $430 range. The additional estimated annual revenue here at a mid-range price of $365 is $6.095 million.

Other revenue sources at Reliant include in-stadium sponsorship and signage, and parking. In addition, the Texans earned $1.5 million from a hospitality village. This area is adjacent to the stadium and includes tents and other facilities for parties and tailgating.

In summary, the Houston Texans have bolted out of the gate as regards building an impressive "revenue-generating machine" at Reliant Stadium. The club has won business awards for these "off-field" efforts.

Seeking Public Funding Assistance for Stadium/Arena Construction or Operation

The costs of new sports stadiums continue to escalate. Exhibit 9-4 summarizes new stadium construction for MLB teams over the 1990 to 2004 period. The three new stadiums in the 1990–92 period averaged a cost of $148 million, 99% of which was publicly financed. The three new stadiums in the 2003–04 period averaged $362 million, 67% of which was publicly financed. Public funding can take multiple forms. These include hotel-motel tax; car-rental

EXHIBIT 9-4   MAJOR LEAGUE BASEBALL (MLB) NEW STADIUM OPENINGS: 1990–2004

Year Opened	Team	Name	Approx. Cost	% of Public Funding
1990	Tampa Bay Devil Rays	Tropicana Field	$ 85	100%
1991	Chicago White Sox	U.S. Cellular Field	150	100
1992	Baltimore Orioles	Camden Yards	210	96
1994	Texas Rangers	Ballpark at Arlington	191	71
1994	Cleveland Indians	Jacobs Field	180	82
1995	Colorado Rockies	Coors Field	215	75
1996	Atlanta Braves	Turner Field	232	100
1998	Arizona Diamondbacks	Bank One Ballpark	354	75
1999	Seattle Mariners	Safeco Field	517	76
2000	Detroit Tigers	Comerica Park	295	45
2000	Houston Astros	Minute Maid Park	248	68
2000	San Francisco Giants	SBC Park	350	0
2001	Milwaukee Brewers	Miller Park	312	71
2001	Pittsburgh Pirates	PNC Park	320	85
2003	Cincinnati Reds	Great America Ballpark	289	90
2004	Philadelphia Phillies	Citizen Bank Park	349	50
2004	San Diego Padres	Petco Park	450	66

Source: *2004 Revenues From Sports Venues* (Milwaukee, WI: Media Ventures, 2004).

tax; parking tax; airport travelers tax; "sin-taxes," which are levied on alcohol and cigarettes; city, county, or state sales tax; or city, county, or state general borrowings.

Proponents and opponents of the use of public financing for new sporting stadiums have sparred multiple times over the last 20 years. The arguments that each side will put forward are relatively predictable, although their applicability in any specific stadium situation can vary somewhat. Proponents for the use of public funding typically will cite any or all of the following arguments:

- Additional revenues from the new stadium accrue to the city because of visiting supporters of teams—for example, within-stadium revenue (such as parking and concessions) and outside-of-stadium revenue (such as hotel/lodging and rental cars).

- Job creation in both the construction and operation of the stadium.

- Additional mega-events a new stadium may attract to city—for example, Super Bowl, All-Star Game, or in extreme cases, global events such as World Soccer Cup or World Cup Rugby games.

- Enhanced city status resulting in a general increase in tourism, conventions, and so on.

- Community-building benefit of having a professional sports team.

Exhibit 9-5 illustrates one approach to highlighting the potential economic impact of a new stadium proposal. This exhibit is by Barrett Sports Group and was prepared for debate over public-sector financing of a stadium project for the San Diego Chargers of the NFL.

Opponents of the use of public funds for the construction or operation of sporting stadiums typically raise some or all of the following points:

- Owners of sporting clubs (typically already wealthy) capture an excessively high percentage of the value increase associated with the new stadium revenues.

- Total city revenue increases are overestimated. Some increased stadium revenues come at the expense of decreased city revenues elsewhere (i.e., it is a revenue substitution effect rather than a new revenue creation effect).

- Sporting stadiums rank low in terms of community priorities—for example, a preferred use of an increased sales tax to some is better schools, better hospitals, or better police and fire services.

Decision Making by Sporting Clubs

The level of public financing support for a new stadium project is the result of decisions by many groups. Some considerations for decisions by sporting clubs are:

1. Is 100% private funding feasible? In rare cases, 100% private funding of stadiums has occurred in recent years—for example, Staples Arena in 1999 (for Los Angeles Lakers and Los Angeles Clippers of the NBA and Los Angeles Kings of the NHL), Pacific Bell Park (now SBC Park) in 2000 for the San Francisco Giants of MLB, and Gillette Stadium in 2003 for New England Patriots of NFL. These three cases are the exception. In each case,

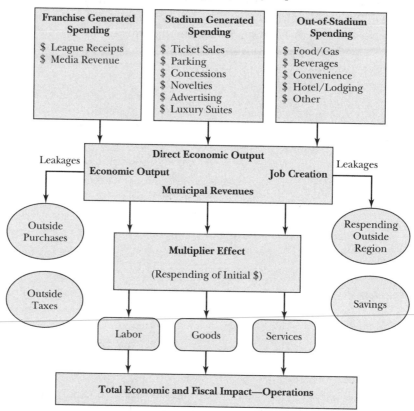

Economic and Fiscal Impact Summary—Operations

Source: Barrett Sports Group, "Task Force on Chargers Issues Final Report."

the revenue streams from the new stadium have dramatically increased over what occurred in their prior "home." Without such an increase, 100% private funding likely would not have been economically feasible. "Feasible" can also mean within the financial capability of the owner even if the projected revenues fall short of the projected costs?

2. What are the constraints and other costs (explicit or implicit) of public financing? Cities and counties can place constraints on stadium use—for example, constraints on naming rights or ticket price increases, and on alternate uses of the stadium. The costs of public financing can include sharing of revenue streams from a new stadium—for example, a 50/50 split of naming rights revenues between the sporting club and a city imposing extra taxes. There is a very high premium on a sporting club investing heavily in skillfully negotiating stadium contracts with cities or counties. A contract in which a club captures minimal stadium revenues can put that club at a severe economic disadvantage vis-à-vis other clubs with more favorable stadium contracts.

3. What is voter appetite for different levels of public financing? New taxes typically must pass voter approval at the ballot box. In some cases, voters may have little desire for public financing. In the 1980s and early 1990s, the San Francisco Giants were defeated four times in bids to seek public funding assistance to solve their stadium woes at the

"economically obsolete" Candlestick Park. In such cases, the existing team owners' options include (1) move the franchise to a city offering public finance assistance, (2) reduce their ownership by bringing in new investors to help privately fund a new stadium, or (3) stay in an existing stadium and accept a lower revenue base for the club. The Oakland Athletics of MLB have sizable stadium problems at Oakland Coliseum. It is unlikely they will be solved in the short run. The Athletics have decided to "cut their cloth" and operate at a player payroll level that is well below the average for other MLB clubs.

4. Upside from building strong community ties. A combination of private-sector and public-sector financing can lead to both sectors working productively together. This can lead to stronger ties between the sporting club, city officials and politicians, and the community.

5. Competitive situation in a league. If most clubs make heavy use of public funding, those few relying on private funding may have higher interest on debt payments that other clubs do not. This high-interest cost can place the club at a disadvantage as regards capacity to have a competitive payroll budget. The Percent of Public Funding column in Exhibit 9-4 illustrates how great the gap is between the 0% public financing by the San Francisco Giants and the level of public financing by many other clubs. The San Francisco Giants management team starts out each year with a $20 million interest cost item to cover from its revenue base that many other clubs do not have.

CASE 9.1   SAN FRANCISCO GIANTS AND PACBELL/SBC PARK[2]

Peter Magowan looked across a packed SBC Park in mid-season 2004. His mind was on the future of the organization he led. Prior to the 2004 season, SBC Park was known as PacBell or Pacific Bell Park. Since moving into PacBell in 2000, the Giants were blessed with a 60%+ surge in attendance—see **Exhibit 1.** In 2002, the Giants advanced all the way to the World Series, losing a heartbreaking final game seven to the Anaheim Angels. While the Giants had been quite profitable in 2000 and 2001, they were only marginally profitable in 2002.

There was no shortage of skeptics when the Giants launched their plans for a new downtown ballpark in 1995. After all, baseball's popularity was at an all-time low following a crippling strike. The Bay Area voters had already turned down four requests to provide public money for a new facility[3]. "People said, 'You'll never win an election, you'll never get financed, and even if you do, you won't field a competitive team and no one will come,'" recalled Magowan, President of the San Francisco Giants and Managing General Partner of the investor group that paid $100 million for the Giants in late 1992.[4] "We knew we couldn't have an economically viable franchise if we weren't playing in a new stadium," said Executive Vice President and Chief Operating Officer Larry Baer, who claimed that "the only time current ownership broke even at 3Com Park was in 1993, when the Giants won 103 games and drew 2.6 million fans."[5]

GIANTS' STADIUM HISTORY

The San Francisco Giants, previously the New York Giants, moved west for the start of the 1958 season (at the same time the Brooklyn Dodgers moved to Los Angeles). For the first

EXHIBIT 1   SAN FRANCISCO GIANTS ON-FIELD RECORD AND ATTENDANCE HISTORY: 1990–2003

Year	Ballpark	S.F. Giants Win/Loss Record	S.F. Giants Per Game Average Attendance	S.F. Giants Season Total Attendance	MLB League Average Total Attendance
1990	Candlestick Park	85–77	24,389	1,975,528	2,040,959
1991	Candlestick Park	75–87	21,450	1,737,478	2,058,014
1992	Candlestick Park	72–90	19,272	1,560,998	2,009,261
1993	Candlestick Park	103–59	32,177	2,606,354	2,637,470
1994	Candlestick Park	55–60	21,045	1,704,608	1,843,416
1995	Candlestick Park	67–77	15,327	1,241,500	1,793,589
1996	Candlestick Park	68–94	17,456	1,413,922	2,169,949
1997	3Com Park*	90–72	20,875	1,690,869	2,277,526
1998	3Com Park*	87–74	23,770	1,925,364	2,401,674
1999	3Com Park*	86–76	25,659	2,078,365	2,380,436
2000	PacBell Park	97–65	40,973	3,318,800	2,480,194
2001	PacBell Park	90–72	40,877	3,311,000	2,481,346
2002	PacBell Park	95–66	40,163	3,253,205	2,309,294
2003	PacBell Park	100–61	40,307	3,264,898	2,273,813

*Candlestick Park was renamed 3Com Park in 1997

Source: Baseball Almanac website at www.baseball-almanac.com.

two years, the Giants played in Seals Stadium, a former minor league ballpark. On April 12, 1960, the Giants first took the field at Candlestick Park. This was a 100% publicly financed stadium by the City of San Francisco that the Giants eventually shared with the NFL's San Francisco 49ers. By the mid 1970s, it was viewed as an average stadium for football and a sub-standard stadium for baseball. The notoriously cold winds made for both difficult playing conditions and difficult viewing conditions. Because the park was located approximately seven miles south of the San Francisco city center, the stadium did not take advantage of the vibrant business community in downtown San Francisco. Accessibility by public transportation was minimal. In the 10 years prior to the 1993 season, the Giants' attendance was only 80% of the average MLB attendance across all teams. This lack of attendance came despite some successes on the playing field, including a trip to the World Series in 1962 and 1989.

In 1992, then Giants owner, Bob Lurie, had become frustrated with the team's inability to pass a stadium financing measure and attempted to sell the Giants to Vince Naimoli for $115 million. Lurie led an investor group that purchased the team in 1976 for $8 million. Mr. Naimoli's intention was to move the Giants to St. Petersburg, Florida for the start of the 1993 season. However, National League[6] owners decided that they preferred a team in San Francisco and blocked the sale. MLB then turned to a syndicate of some of the wealthiest individuals in the Bay Area to purchase the team. The syndicate, which included among others Peter Magowan, Walter Shorenstein, Charles Schwab and Donald Fisher, purchased the team in late of 1992 for $100 million. With the purchase Peter Magowan became the Giants' President and Managing General Partner.

The next two years were difficult ones for MLB. In 1994 there was a players' strike, which angered fans and resulted in an average attendance drop across MLB of 20%. The Giants were especially hard hit with an attendance drop of over 40%. As the possibilities of major losses mounted, some members of the new syndicate became uncomfortable with their ownership positions. A portion of the new syndicate sold back to the other investors or new investors.

Faced with these challenges, the Giants began holding focus groups with the public to gain a better understanding of feeling towards financing a new stadium. The public showed minimal appetite for increasing local taxes to help finance a new stadium. The Giants started exploring the possibility of a privately financed stadium. Since they were losing at least $10 million per year at Candlestick, a facility that would at least allow them to break even would be an enormous improvement for their financial situation. The preferred site was on the waterfront at China Basin, a downtown location with sweeping views of the San Francisco Bay.

GAINING APPROVAL

Gaining approval for the new stadium required the Giants to work with the City, the public and numerous special interest groups. Those initially opposed to the new stadium proposal included residents in the China Basin community, environmentalists and recreational enthusiasts who preferred other uses for waterfront property, and industrial groups who did not like seeing a portion of the waterfront taken away from the shipping industry.

The first stage of the approval process was launched in December 1995, when the Giants introduced the Proposition B campaign to win voter approval to build the privately funded ballpark[7]. The campaign for Proposition B was marked by a merger of many parties who had been on opposite sides of the stadium issue when it involved sizable publicly financing. In March 1996, this merger of interests resulted in Proposition B passing with 67% of the vote. The next stage was to pass through the public entitlement process. Jack Bair, senior Vice President and General Counsel, played an important role in this process, which included dozens of public forums and numerous negotiations with public agencies and commissions. Among the agencies involved were the San Francisco Board of Supervisors, Planning Commission, Redevelopment Commission, Port Commission, Bay Conservation Commission, and California Transportation Commission. Specifically, the San Francisco Redevelopment Agency took a major role in serving as a catalyst between the Giants and the residents and special interest groups to develop a stadium that met the needs of all parties.

As part of the public entitlement process, a number of agreements were made to address the concerns of the public. One agreement involved the limiting of advertisements to the interior of the ballpark. The only advertising allowed on the ballpark exterior façade was that associated with the stadium's name. Additionally, all advertising within the ballpark was required to face inward towards the playing field. Further agreements involved provisions for public transportation such as city-provided traffic control officers and enhanced bus and ferry services. In September 1997, the Giants concluded the public entitlement process and were allowed to proceed with the plans for the ballpark.

DEVELOPING THE FINANCING PLAN

The private financing plan consisted of five primary parts, which were under the control of the China Basin Ballpark Corp. ("CBBC"). CBBC was a fully owned subsidiary of the San Francisco Giants, formed to finance and develop the stadium. **Exhibit 2** presents a breakdown of the financing sources used to cover the actual stadium costs.

Debt

John Yee, the Giants' Senior Vice President and Chief Financial Officer, spent a significant amount of his time during 1996 trying to secure favorable bank financing. While the mid- to late-1990s was a relatively friendly capital-raising environment, the Giants situation differed from most borrowing companies. This was a MLB team which had failed to obtain public financing for a stadium on four separate occasions. It was now attempting to privately finance a new stadium in one of the most expensive cities in the country. From a bank's perspective, this would be a project financing deal with a significantly different risk profile than most of

EXHIBIT 2   PACBELL PARK SOURCES OF FINANCING ($ MILLIONS)

Debt (led by Chase Securities)	$170
Stadium Naming Rights	50
Advertising and Concessions	75
Charter Seat Licenses	70
Tax Incremental Financing Deal	15
Total	**$380**

its loan customers. MLB teams in general have traditionally not been highly profitable businesses, with breaking even or losing money in a given year not uncommon. Moreover, past strikes and lockouts at the league level increased the risk profile for a lender. An MLB team had not successfully attempted a privately funded stadium deal since the early 1960s (Los Angeles Dodgers with Dodger Stadium).

The Giants secured a $140 million bank loan in September of 1996. The contract was structured as a construction project-financing loan with a provision allowing it to be refinanced before the end of the fifth year. The syndicate of banks was led by Chase Securities. During 1997, the Giants continued to push ahead and signed some major sponsors, including Anheuser-Busch, Coca-Cola and Chevron, finalized the lease agreement, concluding the public entitlement process, and began pre-construction work on the site. Additionally, the economy was booming and the interest rate environment had become even more favorable. As a result of the team's progress and the more favorable macroeconomic situation, the Giants went back to Chase and negotiated a better contract. In November 1997, Chase offered a new loan package, which consisted of a 20-year (expires 2017), 8% fixed-rate, $170 million face value construction project financing loan. The current yearly payment on this loan is approximately $20 million including both principal and interest payments.

Stadium Naming Rights

Over the past decade, professional sports teams have been selling corporations the naming rights to their stadiums. **Exhibit 3** provides a summary of the naming rights deals struck for new baseball stadiums in the past ten years. The Giants wanted to have a naming sponsor in place when they announced the stadium plans to the public.

To initiate the selection process, the team developed the following three criteria for a naming company: the corporation needed to (1) be national in focus, (2) have a strong Bay Area presence, and (3) be recognizable and respected by the general public. Approximately thirty local companies that met these criteria were identified. Peter Magowan wrote a letter to each company explaining the team's plans for a new stadium and inquiring on the company's interest in purchasing the naming rights. The letter stated that the team was looking to sell the rights for approximately $40 to $50 million. A number of companies responded and the Giants initiated serious discussions with about five of them. In the end, the Giants reached a 20-year, $56 million deal (with approximately $15 million coming up front) with the Pacific Bell telephone company[8].

Advertising and Concessions

After securing the stadium naming rights, the team turned its attention to acquiring advertising and concession sponsors. A benchmark of $15 million over 10 years with $3 million upfront was set for the Winners Circle Sponsorships, with the exception of beer and soda sponsorships which were set higher. Upfront meant a payment in 1997/1998, which was up to three years before the planned opening for the 2000 MLB season.

Sponsorship deals were signed with the Gap, Old Navy, Chevron, Webvan, Visa USA, Coca-Cola, Anheuser Busch and others. The team looked for creative ways to drive more revenue out of the deals such as a giant Coke bottle in leftfield that functions as a slide for children, cup holders at each seat sponsored by Webvan, unique outfield wall designs such as those created by Chevron and Old Navy, and a facilities management contract with Enron Energy

EXHIBIT 3 STADIUM NAMING RIGHTS DEALS AT SELECTED MLB STADIUMS

Year	Club	Name of Park (Capacity)	Total Price ($ Millions)	No. Of Years	Average Annual value ($ Millions)	Expiration Year
1994	Cleveland Indians	Jacobs Field (42,800)	$13.9	20	$0.695	2014
1995	Colorado Rockies	Coors Field (50,000)	15.0	—	—	—
1996	Oakland Athletics	Network Assoc. Coliseum (39,875)	10.8	9	1.20	2007
1997	Tampa Bay Devil Rays	Tropicana Field (45,000)	46.0	30	1.53	2026
1997	Anaheim Angels	Edison Field (45,050)	50.0	20	2.50	2018
1998	Arizona Diamondbacks	Bank One (48,500)	66.0	30	2.20	2028
1998	Seattle Mariners	Safeco Field (47,000)	40.0	20	2.00	2019
2000	Detroit Tigers	Comerica Park (40,000)	66.0	30	2.20	2030
2000	San Francisco Giants	PacBell Park (40,800)	50.0	24	2.08	2024
2001	Pittsburgh Pirates	PNC Park (38,000)	40.0	20	2.00	2021
2001	Milwaukee Brewers	Miller Park (42,500)	41.2	20	2.06	2020
2002	Houston Astros	Minute Maid Park (42,000)	170.0	28	6.07	2029
2003	Cincinnati Reds	Great America (45,000)	75.0	30	2.50	2033
2004	San Diego Padres	Petco Field (42,000)	60.0	22	2.73	2025

Source: Street & Smith's *Sports Business Journal* (December 28, 2003); *2004 Revenues From Sports Venues.*

Services. The team found that food and beverage concession companies preferred paying higher upfront fees to protect a lower operating commission rate. This was ideal for the team since it needed to raise money upfront to finance the stadium. The team ended up signing a concession deal for approximately $12 million for 20 years. In total the team received approximately $75 million upfront from the advertising and concession contracts.

Charter Seat Licenses

The Giants initially focused on raising approximately $40 million through the selling of charter seat licenses. A charter seat license is a one-time purchase of the underlying rights to a particular seat in the stadium, offering fans control over their tickets and seat location as well as future ownership of the seat. These seats are typically in premium locations. The Giants crafted their charter seat license program after witnessing the personal seat license program difficulties of the Oakland Raiders[9].

The Giants made three key decisions concerning its seat licenses. First, they decided to only sell about one-third of Pacific Bell Park's total seats through the program. Second, they decided to make them permanent and transferable, calling them "charter seats." Third, they made a commitment to the purchasers that season tickets would not increase more than 2% each year for the first ten years. The charter seat license was priced from $1,500 to $7,500 and gave purchasers the opportunity to invest in building the new stadium. The team set ambitious marketing and sales goals. They planned to raise $40 million from selling 13,700 licenses to a previous season-ticket fan base of 12,000 at Candlestick Park. Only former season-ticket holders were approached at first, and sales to that group reached close to 10,000. The seats licenses were then opened to the public, which increased the total sold to 14,600. The Giants ended up raising approximately $75 million, $30 million more than they had originally projected.

Tax Increment Financing Deal

The San Francisco Redevelopment Agency provided $15 million towards the Pacific Bell Park project. These funds went towards roads, infrastructure and a plaza that accommodates ferry landings and the public walkway located outside the stadium. The City agreed to lease to the Giants 13 acres of waterfront property located at 3rd and King Streets that is held in trust by the Port of San Francisco. The lease is for 66 years and is based on the fair market value of the property. The lease payment is approximately $1.2 million per year. It includes the ballpark land and land south of the park that is currently used as Parking Lot A. While the team collects parking revenue from this land, it is required to pay the City's parking tax. The City also agreed to provide traffic control officers and police to serve the area before, during and after games.

The Giants' investment syndicate did not purchase land surrounding PacBell Park. In part, this was due to financial constraints on the syndicate at the initial purchase date and at subsequent dates when the focus was on raising money for construction of the new ballpark.

Opening Day

The actual construction of the park commenced on December 11, 1997. Approximately two and one half years later, the stadium was ready for opening day on April 11, 2000. The final construction cost approached $350 million, including construction financing costs. The Giants were able to privately fund the project and get Pacific Bell Park built on the planned time schedule. The new ballpark exceeded even the high expectations of most fans. Relative to Candlestick Park, it was a move to "the promised land" for the fans.

The privately funding aspect is frequently raised in debates over new stadium proposals post 2000. Peter Magowan noted: "We've never tried to say our way is right for everyone. Our approach does not work for everyone. We simply had no choice at the time, and we were fortunate in that we built the stadium during a high time for the economy. Our timing was very good. If we had to do it now, I'm not sure we could."[10]

CLUB FINANCIALS

Exhibit 4 (Panels A to C) presents estimated revenues, operating income, and club valuations for the Giants from 1990 to 2003. These estimates are made by business journals— *Forbes* (1997 onwards) and prior to that *Financial World*. Clubs view their financials as confidential and rarely comment on estimates by third parties such as business journals. Exhibit 4 (Panel D) presents player total payroll information from 1990 to 2004. These data are taken from the *USA Today* MLB salary database, using information reported by individual teams. The highest paid player on the Giants payroll is Barry Bonds. Reported annual payroll from Bonds in recent selected years are 1996 ($8.266 million), 1998 ($8.916), 2000 ($10.700), 2002 ($15.000) and 2004 ($18.000).

EXHIBIT 4 SAN FRANCISCO GIANTS: ESTIMATED FINANCIALS ($ MILLIONS)*

Panel A: Revenues (Estimates By Financial World/Forbes)

Year (Season)	SF Giants	Rank in MLB	Highest	Lowest
1990	$ 50.0	11/26	$ 98.0 (N.Y. Yankees)	$34.0 (Seattle Mariners)
1991	48.9	15/26	91.1 (N.Y. Mets)	38.8 (Milw. Brewers)
1992	47.0	21/26	94.6 (N.Y. Yankees)	39.9 (Cleveland Indians)
1993	69.1	10/28	107.6 (N.Y. Yankees)	43.0 (Pittsburgh Pirates)
1994**	43.1	12/28	71.5 (N.Y. Yankees)	25.0 (San Diego Padres)
1995	46.4	15/28	93.9 (N.Y. Yankees)	24.9 (Pittsburgh Pirates)
1996	51.8	17/28	133.3 (N.Y. Yankees)	39.9 (Pittsburgh Pirates)
1997	69.8	15/28	144.7 (N.Y. Yankees)	43.6 (Montreal Expos)
1998	73.3	20/30	175.5 (N.Y. Yankees)	46.5 (Montreal Expos)
1999	71.9	20/30	195.6 (N.Y. Yankees)	47.1 (Montreal Expos)
2000	138.8	5/30	192.4 (N.Y. Yankees)	53.9 (Montreal Expos)
2001	142.0	8/30	215.0 (N.Y. Yankees)	63.0 (Montreal Expos)
2002	159.0	7/30	223.0 (N.Y. Yankees)	66.0 (Montreal Expos)
2003	153.0	8/30	238.0 (N.Y. Yankees)	81.0 (Montreal Expos)

Panel B: Operating Income (Estimates by Financial World/Forbes)

Year (Season)	SF Giants	Rank in MLB	Highest	Lowest
1990	$ 9.0	12/26	$24.5 (N.Y. Yankees)	−$ 9.8 (K.C. Royals)
1991	−4.4	21/26	30.4 (N.Y. Yankees)	−11.4 (Milw. Brewers)
1992	−11.1	23/26	25.0 (N.Y. Yankees)	−12.8 (Milwaukee/Oakland)
1993	−0.7	22/28	28.9 (Baltimore Orioles)	−6.3 (K.C. Royals)
1994**	−10.3	22/28	8.7 (N.Y. Yankees)	−17.4 (K.C. Royals)
1995	−6.0	26/28	38.3 (N.Y. Yankees)	−14.0 (Cincinnati Reds)
1996	−1.9	18/28	24.0 (N.Y. Yankees)	−11.8 (Cincinnati Reds)
1997	0.2	16/28	21.4 (N.Y. Yankees)	−20.5 (Toronto Blue Jays)
1998	−6.4	20/30	23.0 (N.Y. Yankees)	−11.7 (L.A. Dodgers)
1999	−9.0	27/30	17.5 (N.Y. Yankees)	−21.1 (L.A. Dodgers)
2000	27.4	1/30	27.4 (S.F. Giants)	−17.4 (L.A. Dodgers)
2001	16.8	3/30	18.7 (N.Y. Yankees)	−29.6 (L.A. Dodgers)
2002	13.9	3/30	23.3 (Seattle Mariners)	−25.0 (L.A. Dodgers)
2003	0.7	11/30	17.0 (Seattle Mariners)	−28.5 (Texas Rangers)

Panel C: Valuation (Estimates by Financial World/Forbes)

Year (Season)	SF Giants	Rank in MLB	Highest	Lowest
1990	$105	13/26	$225 (N.Y. Yankees)	$71 (Seattle Mariners)
1991	99	15/26	200 (N.Y. Yankees)	75 (Montreal Expos)
1992	103	13/26	160 (N.Y. Yankees)	81 (Cleveland Indians)
1993	93	19/28	166 (N.Y. Yankees)	75 (Montreal Expos)
1994**	102	14/28	185 (N.Y. Yankees)	70 (Pittsburgh Pirates)
1995	122	13/28	209 (N.Y. Yankees)	62 (Pittsburgh Pirates)
1996	128	14/28	241 (N.Y. Yankees)	71 (Pittsburgh Pirates)
1997	188	14/28	362 (N.Y. Yankees)	87 (Montreal Expos)

Panel C: Valuation (Estimates by Financial World/Forbes)

Year (Season)	SF Giants	Rank in MLB	Highest	Lowest
1998	213	15/30	491 (N.Y. Yankees)	84 (Montreal Expos)
1999	237	14/30	548 (N.Y. Yankees)	89 (Montreal Expos)
2000	333	10/30	635 (N.Y. Yankees)	92 (Montreal Expos)
2001	355	9/30	730 (N.Y. Yankees)	108 (Montreal Expos)
2002	382	7/30	849 (N.Y. Yankees)	113 (Montreal Expos)
2003	368	7/30	832 (N.Y. Yankees)	145 (Montreal Expos)

Panel D: Total Player Payroll (Club Information Reported by USA Today)

Year (Season)	SF Giants	Giants Rank in MLB	Highest	Lowest
1990	$20.942	7/26	$ 23.873 (K.C. Royals)	$ 9.496 (Chicago W. Sox)
1991	30.839	6/26	33.632 (Oakland A's)	11.546 (Houston Astros)
1992	33.126	10/26	44.352 (N.Y. Mets)	8.263 (Clev. Indians)
1993	45.747	14/26	45.747 (Toronto Blue Jays)	8.829 (Colorado Rockies)
1994**	40.747	5/26	44.785 (N.Y. Yankees)	13.529 (S.D. Padres)
1995	34.931	10/26	49.791 (Toronto Blue Jays)	12.031 (Montreal Expos)
1996	34.605	13/28	52.189 (N.Y. Yankees)	15.410 (Montreal Expos)
1997	33.469	19/28	59.148 (N.Y. Yankees)	9.071 (Pitts. Pirates)
1998	40.320	16/30	70.408 (Baltimore Orioles)	9.202 (Montreal Expos)
1999	46.059	16/30	88.130 (N.Y. Yankees)	15.150 (Florida Marlins)
2000	53.541	17/30	92.938 (N.Y. Yankees)	15.654 (Minn. Twins)
2001	63.280	16/30	112.287 (N.Y. Yankees)	24.130 (Minn. Twins)
2002	78.299	10/30	125.928 (N.Y. Yankees)	34.380 (T.B. Devil Rays)
2003	82.852	9/30	152.749 (N.Y. Yankees)	19.630 (T.B. Devil Rays)
2004	82.019	10/30	184.193 (N.Y. Yankees)	27.528 (Milw. Brewers)

Source: USA Today Website.

*These estimates are made by financial magazines: 1992–96 by *Financial World*, 1997 by *Forbes*. Neither the San Francisco Giants nor the MLB publicly release financial information on a regular basis.

**Strike shortened season.

In late 2001, the Commissioner of Baseball disclosed club financials in a congressional hearing. Exhibit 5 reports selected information from these disclosures for San Francisco Giants, the Oakland Athletics, and the highest and lowest for each line item in **Exhibit 5.** Oakland is the other MLB team in the San Francisco Bay Area and competes with the Giants in many off-the-field areas (such as fans attending, sponsors, and media rights fees).

The impact on revenues of the Giants' new stadium was dramatic. Using Forbes' estimates, revenues (after revenue sharing) increased from $71.9 million in 1999 at Candlestick to $138.8 million in 2000 at PacBell. Discrepancies exist among estimated information in Exhibit 4 and the 2001 disclosures by the MLB commissioner in Exhibit 5. Forbes estimates 2001 revenues for the Giants as $142.00 million while the MLB Commissioner disclosures report $170.295 million. These differences highlight the challenges in obtaining reliable financial information on individual teams. Forbes attributed much of the difference to their 2001 revenue estimate of $142.0 million being after deducting (a) approximately $20 million of annual debt interest cost tied to the new stadium, and (b) approximately $6 million

EXHIBIT 5

2001 Financial Disclosures of MLB Clubs Released by MLB Commissioner ($ Millions)

	S.F. Giants	Oakland Athletics	Highest	Lowest
Total Operating Revenues	$170.295	$75.469	$217.807 (N.Y. Yankees)	$34.171 (Montreal Expos)
Total Operating Expenses	151.295	82.582	201.349 (N.Y. Yankees)	72.690 (Montreal Expos)
Income from Operations	19.000	−7.113	40.859 (N.Y. Yankees)	−38.519 (Montreal Expos)
2001 Revenue Sharing	−6.308	10.520	28.517 (Montreal Expos)	−26.540 (N.Y. Yankees)
Income After Revenue Sharing	12.692	3.407	15.475 (Seattle Mariners)	−54.450 (L.A. Dodgers)
Income After Interest	−0.139	−0.532	14.793 (Seattle Mariners)	−68.887 (L.A. Dodgers)
Specific Revenue Items:				
Local Media	17.197	9.458	56.750 (N.Y. Yankees)	0.536 (Montreal Expos)
Other Local Revenue	61.524	13.932	56.211 (2nd - Seattle Mariners)	9.770 (Montreal Expos)
National Shared Revenue	24.401	24.401	24.401 (Equal)	24.401 (Equal)
Post Season Revenue	—	2.686	16.000 (N.Y. Yankees)	—
Specific Expenses:				
Players Salaries	72.185	43.821	118.471 (Boston Red Sox)	30.494 (Minn. Twins)
Other Local Expenses	79.110	38.761	84.222 (Seattle Mariners)	35.014 (Montreal Expos)

Source: *USA Today* (12/07/2001).

426

"revenue sharing" that the Giants make to smaller revenue-clubs as part of MLB's revenue redistribution plan. Forbes makes such adjustments to their estimates of gross revenues when reporting their revenue estimates for each club.

The Giants played to sell outs in most games in their first four seasons in the new park. Due to the large season ticket base, strong group ticket sales, and pre-season sales, the Giants have sold out over 80% of the tickets before the first pitch of opening day. The Giants have adopted variable pricing, charging more for weekend games than mid-week games. See Case 7.1 in this book for further information on variable pricing. *2004 Revenues From Sports Venues*[11] reports the following low price to high price range for the Giants and for the average across all 30 MLB teams in 2003:

	S.F. Giants	MLB Average
Luxury Suites	$65,000 to $115,000	$86,713 to $171,555
Club Seats	$ 4,500 to $ 7,500	$ 3,599 to $ 5,638
Season Tickets	$ 729 to $ 2,268	$ 747 to $ 3,638
Single Game Tickets	$ 10.00 to $ 70.00	$ 7.11 to $ 59.12

The 2003 capacity of PacBell was 40,800 which is below the MLB average of 46,278. The MLB range in 2003 was from 33,950 for the Boston Red Sox's Fenway Park to 56,521 at New York's Yankee Stadium.

Local media revenues of the Giants comprise local television and local radio. The primary source of local media revenues is the television contract with FOX Sports Bay Area, the local regional sports network (RSN). The current 10 year Giants contract expires in 2010. FOX Sports Bay Area carries five major professional teams—The San Francisco Giants (MLB), The Oakland Athletics (MLB), The Golden State Warriors (NBA), the Sacramento Kings (NBA), and the San Jose Sharks (NHL). Although the contract specifics are confidential, the San Francisco Giants receive the most money from FOX Sports Bay Area of the five professional teams it carries. Exhibit 5 reports local media revenues of $17.197 million in 2001.

PacBell Park brought a dramatic increase in other revenues, including concessions, suite rentals, and stadium advertising. Relative to some other stadiums, the Giants restricted the number of suites, believing that many corporations would struggle to effectively use 12 or 20 seats every single day of the 81 home games. Another source of revenues is the Double Play Ticket Website. This site allows season ticket holders to resell their unused tickets to the general public. The Giants facilitate the online sale, handle all transactions and collect a percentage of the sale from both the buyer and the seller. Buyers can pick up the tickets at the ballpark and be confident it is a "guaranteed real ticket." A key benefit of the Double Play website to the Giants is the increased renewal rate of season ticket holders. Most season ticket holders cannot use or share tickets to all 81 home games. "Unused tickets in the drawer" are a key reason for some season ticket holders not renewing for the next year.

Non-baseball related revenues include events such as annual college football bowl-games, concerts and soccer games. Pat Gallagher, President of Giants Enterprises, has the charge to make this revenue source a growing part of the total revenue mix. For example, in 2001 the San Francisco Demons of the XFL played home games at PacBell. The XFL was a high-profile new football league ("smash-grab" football) that was jointly owned by NBC and World Wrestling Entertainment. The Demons led the XFL in home attendance (averaging 35,005 per game). Unfortunately, the XFL survived only one year.

LOOKING FORWARD

The Giants management team has been juggling many balls since moving to PacBell/SBC Park. Uncertainty remains over the future direction of player payrolls. Some teams have adopted more aggressive positions than the Giants. The New York Yankees have increased total player payroll from $112.287 million in 2001 to $184.193 million in 2004. The Giants have tried to more modestly increase player payroll (from $63.280 million in 2001 to $82.019 million in 2004), make annual principal and interest payments on its private debt, and adopt a fiscally responsible management approach.

Many alternatives are open to the Giants. Should the player payroll be sizably increased in the hope of increasing the likelihood of playoff and World Series success? Will adding more superstars increase future local media and sponsor contracts when they are renewed? Can ticket prices be increased above their current levels? Can non-baseball revenues be dramatically increased? Do the members of the Giants investment syndicate have the appetite for the increased risks associated with some options being proposed? The Giants management team knew that both on-field and off-field challenges would continue. They also knew that any decisions they make would be analyzed and re-analyzed by many others. "Managing in the fish bowl" was something that Magowan, Baer, Bair, Gallagher, Sabean, Yee, and other members of the Giants' management team accepted came with the territory.

Questions

1. Outline the key events that prompted the Giants to conclude that a privately funded new stadium was the option to pursue in 1994/1995.

2. Critique and evaluate the individual financing sources adopted by the Giants with respect to PacBell. Include for each how the Giants can assess whether "any money is being left on the table" and the potential negatives for each source.

3. Stadium construction planning decisions include the total capacity and the mix of boxes/suites/premium seats, and so on. What factors should the Giants consider in deciding on these issues?

4. Giants Managing General Partner Peter Magowan recently stated: "We've never tried to say our way is right for everyone. Our approach does not work for everyone. We simply had no choice at the time, and we were fortunate in that we built the stadium during a high time for the economy. Our timing was very good. If we had to do it now, I'm not sure if we could." What factors will affect the viability of the private financing option for (a) Other baseball clubs? and (b) Sporting clubs in other sports?

5. While the Giants were successfully progressing during the 2002 playoff season, Managing General Partner Peter Magowan was reported to have said, "[A profit] will be realized only if the World Series goes its full seven games, and even then it's not a sure bet." Assume you are a founding investor in the syndicate (i.e., invested in 1994/95). How would you evaluate the "success" of your investment? Be specific where possible.

CASE 9.2   DALLAS COWBOYS: FINANCING A NEW STADIUM[12]

On May 28, 2003, Texas Governor Rick Perry signed Senate Bill 1111 into law. The legislation provided for the voters of Dallas County to decide whether to raise taxes to pay for a stadium complex for the Dallas Cowboys of the National Football League (NFL). At the time, the Dallas Cowboys were preparing to play their 32nd season in Texas Stadium. Only six NFL teams played in older stadiums. Of these, three had recent major stadium renovations (Chicago Bears, Green Bay Packers, and Oakland Raiders), while one (Arizona Cardinals) had a new stadium under construction. The San Diego Chargers and the San Francisco 49ers, along with the Cowboys, were still seeking a "solution" to the economic handicap of playing in a stadium that was more than 30 years old.

The Cowboys had long been one of the league's most successful, and highest profile teams. They had competed in eight Super Bowls, winning five, including three Super Bowl wins during the 1990s. The team was also financially successful, with the second highest estimated revenue of all NFL teams. The Cowboys' brand was rated the second highest in all of sports, behind the New York Yankees, and the highest in the NFL.

By 2003, however, the economics of football strongly favored a new stadium. The NFL's lucrative national television contract was divided evenly among all teams. The home team kept just 60 percent of ticket sales, with the balance shared with the other teams. This revenue sharing helped maintain competitive parity among teams, but inhibited financial results for the most successful teams. The most direct way to increase team income was to increase stadium-related revenue from luxury boxes, parking, and naming rights, which the team could keep to itself.

The Cowboys' owner Jerry Jones wanted a new stadium, which would hold approximately 100,000 spectators. The stadium was estimated to cost about $650 million, but was expected to provide substantial new revenue opportunity for the team—particularly if Dallas taxpayers picked up part of the cost to build the facility.

Despite success in the legislature, Jones knew that there was still work to be done. Although most recent stadium construction had been financed with large amounts of taxpayer money, many jurisdictions had recently resisted using taxpayer dollars to build sports stadiums. Lobbying groups opposed to public financing of stadiums had become increasingly well organized. The Cowboys would have to make the case to the voters in support of the stadium. They would also have to negotiate a lease agreement if the stadium were built. And, if the voters turned down the proposal, Jones would need to consider other options, some of which would require the Cowboys to take on sizable debt.

DALLAS COWBOYS

The Dallas Cowboys were formed as an NFL expansion team in 1960, becoming the 13th team in the league. The team lost all its games in the 1960 season, but by 1965, had became a competitive force, finishing second in their conference and making the playoffs for the first time. The following year they won their conference, with a 10–3–1 record before losing the NFL championship game to Green Bay. This was just the first of a string of division championships, leading to the team's participation in the Super Bowl V at the end of the 1970 season.[13] The

Cowboys won their first Super Bowl the following year. The team became a powerhouse in the league, appearing in three more Super Bowls in the 1970s (winning two), and winning the Super Bowl three times in the 1990s.[14] The team's on-field performance had suffered from 2000 to 2002, however. During each of these three seasons, the Cowboys posted records of just 5 wins and 11 losses, finishing last in their conference. The team hired a new coach, Bill Parcells for the 2003 season, raising hopes for return to their past dominance. Parcells was a long-time NFL coach, and had led the New York Giants to two Super Bowl victories.

The Cowboys initially played in the Cotton Bowl, located in the city of Dallas. On January 25, 1969, they broke ground in suburban Irving, nine miles from downtown Dallas, for the new Texas Stadium. They played their first game at the new stadium on October 3, 1971. The stadium had a capacity of 65,675, and was built at a cost of $35 million, financed with general obligation bonds. Part of the financing was in the form of personal seat licenses (PSLs), which were sold as bonds in 1968, priced from $1,000 to $15,000. The PSLs gave holders the right to buy season tickets, and expired at the end of the Cowboys' lease in 2008. The stadium was owned by the City of Irving.

Building from their on-field success in the 1970s, the Cowboys successfully developed an identity that transcended Dallas, becoming an American icon, known as "America's Team," and cultivating both a national and international following. One opposing player commented: "There's no way you can tell me anybody else is America's Team but the Cowboys. They've got the most beautiful cheerleaders in the world. They've got that star on their helmet. They've got that hole in the top of Texas Stadium so God can watch them play. It's America's Team."[15] Commentator and former coach John Madden said: "The America's Team thing is very real. It doesn't matter if it's the middle of nowhere or right there in another NFL city. Dallas fans are everywhere."[16]

The Cowboys on-field success, as well as the cultivation of the "America's Team" image, gave the team an extremely valuable brand. In a report entitled "The Most Valuable Brands in Sports," published in 2003, FutureBrand ranked the Cowboys' brand value second only to the New York Yankees. The Cowboys were by far the highest valued NFL brand, at $300.5 million. The second highest valued NFL brand was the Washington Redskins at $191.6 million, followed by the New York Giants ($167.4 million) and Green Bay Packers ($152.9 million).[17] A poll conducted in 2002–2003 by ESPN asked NFL fans to name their favorite team. The Cowboys ranked highest, at 10.8 percent, far ahead of the next team, the Green Bay Packers at 7.1 percent.[18]

Estimates of the Cowboys financial performance and team value for the 1995 to 2002 seasons, as published in business magazines (*Financial World* and *Forbes*), are presented in Exhibit 1. As a privately owned team, the Cowboys did not publicly release their financials, nor did they correct published estimates. However, the team was viewed by many as one of the league's most financially successful franchise, despite playing in an aging stadium. For the 2002 season, *Forbes* estimated team revenues at $198 million (second only to the Washington Redskins, with estimated revenue of $227 million), and operating income of $52.3 million (third in the league, behind the Washington Redskins at $87.8 million and New England Patriots at $67.3 million. *Forbes* estimated the value of the Cowboys at $851 million, second only to the Washington Redskins at $952 million.[19]

The Cowboys owner, Jerral ("Jerry") Jones, had made a fortune in the oil and gas business in Texas, part of which he used to purchase the Cowboys (and the right to operate the stadium) for $140 million in 1989. In 2002, Jones was listed as the 272nd wealthiest American by *Forbes*

EXHIBIT 1   DALLAS COWBOYS ESTIMATED FINANCIALS ($ MILLIONS)

Total Revenues

Year (Season)	Dallas Cowboys	Rank	Highest	Lowest
1995	$112.2	1/30	$112.1 (Dallas)	$42.9 (Carolina)
1996	121.3	1/30	121.3 (Dallas)	65.7 (Houston)
1997	118.0	1/30	118.0 (Dallas)	66.8 (Jacksonville)
1998*	161.7	1/30	161.7 (Dallas)	90.0 (Tennessee)
1999*	173.9	2/31	176.4 (Washington)	91.9 (Cincinnati)
2000*	181.0	2/31	194.0 (Washington)	107.0 (Arizona)
2001*	189.0	2/31	204.0 (Washington)	110.0 (Arizona)
2002*	198.0	2/32	227.0 (Washington)	126.0 (Arizona)

*1998–2002 revenues include the increased national television contract revenues.

Operating Income

Year (Season)	Dallas Cowboys	Rank	Highest	Lowest
1995	$16.4	2/30	$19.0 (S.F. 49ers)	–$18.9 (Carolina)
1996	30.2	1/30	30.2 (Dallas)	–8.0 (N.Y. Jets)
1997	41.3	1/30	41.3 (Dallas)	–20.9 (Detroit)
1998	56.7	1/30	56.7 (Dallas)	3.4 (Cincinnati)
1999	42.5	2/31	68.7 (Washington)	–1.0 (Green Bay)
2000	56.4	2/31	76.3 (Washington)	–16.4 (Seattle)
2001	75.4	2/31	79.4 (Washington)	2.7 (Green Bay)
2002	52.3	3/32	87.8 (Washington)	6.0 (Green Bay)

Valuation

Year (Season)	Dallas Cowboys	Rank	Highest	Lowest
1995	$272	1/30	$272 (Dallas)	$133 (Carolina)
1996	320	1/30	320 (Dallas)	170 (Indianapolis)
1997	413	1/30	413 (Dallas)	227 (Indianapolis)
1998	663	1/30	663 (Dallas)	293 (Detroit)
1999	713	2/31	741 (Washington)	305 (Arizona)
2000	743	2/31	796 (Washington)	338 (Atlanta)
2001	784	2/31	845 (Washington)	374 (Arizona)
2002	851	2/32	952 (Washington)	505 (Arizona)

Sources: 1995–1996 from *Financial World*. 1997–2002 from *Forbes Magazine.* Neither the teams nor the National Football League publicly release financial information or comment on estimates made by others.

Magazine, with a net worth of $875 million. Nine other NFL owners joined Jones on *Forbes'* list of the 400 wealthiest Americans.[20]

THE DALLAS COWBOYS' SITUATION IN MID-2003

Under their contract with the City of Irvine, the Cowboys controlled all Texas Stadium operations and retained all revenue except parking. The team paid rent of the greater of $950,000 per year or 8 percent of stadium revenue. Texas Stadium had 381 luxury suites, for which the Cowboys charged between $250,000 and 1.5 million for the term of the lease (which expired in 2009 with an option to renew for 25 years).[21]

EXHIBIT 2   Texas Stadium Information

Stadium Capacity: 65,846
Average Attendance: 63,141 (2000), 63,187 (2001), 63,090 (2002)

Average ticket price: $50.06 (2002), $53.06 (2003)

Ticket prices (2003):
Individual game ticket prices: $36, $37, $53, $60, $65, $78.
Season ticket prices: $360–680.

Season tickets included 2 preseason games and 8 regular season home games. Season ticket holders had the right to purchase tickets for home playoff games.

Luxury Suites

Suite Type	Annual Lease	Per Game Lease
8 seat Crown I	$30,000	$3,500
10 seat Crown I	35,000	4,500
12 seat Circle	45,000–75,000	5,500
14 seat Crown II	60,000	6,500
16 seat Crown I&II	65,000	8,000
20 seat Crown I&II	75,000–125,000	9,500
40 seat Circle/Crown	N/A	18,500

Suite prices included game tickets, parking passes. Up to five additional game tickets can be purchased for $80 each per suite. There were a total of 381 luxury suites.

Suites contain a refrigerator, counter seating, televisions, bar space, VIP parking, telephones, and room for mingling. Per-game suites include a fully stocked bar. Per-game lease prices are higher for premium games. Holders of annual leases can use their suite for any event held at Texas Stadium, such as concerts, although they must purchase event tickets.

Sources: Dallas Cowboys' website: http://www.dallascowboys.com. (See the website for a map showing seat prices at various locations in the stadium.) Attendance data from *2003 Revenues from Sports Ventures*, op.cit., p. 121. Average ticket prices from Fairbank, loc. cit.

The stadium capacity was 65,846, and average attendance for the previous three years had been just over 63,000. In 2002, the average Cowboys' ticket cost $50.06, and the team planned to increase ticket prices to an average of $53.06, slightly above the league average of $52.95.[22] The highest average price in the league, $75.33, was charged by the New England Patriots.[23] (See Exhibit 2 for information about Texas stadium tickets and seating.)

To replace the aging Texas Stadium, Jones proposed building a stadium, entertainment, and business complex that would cost up to $1 billion, of which $650 million would be needed to build a 100,000 seat stadium. Jones said that the team would be willing to pay an undisclosed portion of the money required.

The stadium that the Cowboys envisioned would have about 70,000 to 80,000 seats with open end zones that could house more people, bringing the total capacity to about 100,000. One of the open end zones would cater to people with families that wanted to play or picnic during the games rather than sit in seats. It would also feature attractions such as a half-pipe for skating. The other end would have attractions for adults, such as stores, bars, and restaurants. The stadium would have a retractable roof.[24] The complex would also include stores, facilities for hotels and conventions, and an athletic field for children, with the unifying theme of the Cowboys football team. The Cowboys said that the public subsidy, however, would only be used to build the stadium.[25] The team described the complex as:

> *Dallas Cowboys Park. Not just a stadium, but a destination attraction*
> *with a sports-themed town center offering shops, retail and entertainment,*
> *a branded hotel, community sports facilities including competition fields*
> *for local youth and adult leagues, and other Cowboys branded*
> *attractions.*[26]

The complex was envisioned as a five-pointed star, each point representing one element of the Park, with the stadium at the center, providing the unifying theme (see Exhibit 3 for a description of each element of Cowboys Park). The star theme for the Park recalled the team's star logo. The team cited five benefits of Dallas Cowboys Park:[27]

1. Economic growth and jobs: "a year-round destination attraction drawing millions of visitors, thousands of new jobs, and billions in economic impact,"

2. Revenue for roads, schools and police from new sales taxes paid by businesses in the park,

3. Convention and tourism revenue resulting from attracting new visitors to the Dallas-Fort Worth area,

4. Sports fields for local youth, and

5. Hosting Super Bowls and international events.

The two likely sites for the complex were quite different. One was in an industrial area of downtown Dallas known as "South Industrial." While an environmental cleanup of the site would likely be necessary due to a long history of polluting industry in the area, this was not seen as an insurmountable problem. Locating the stadium complex at South Industrial would bring new vitality to the downtown industrial area. The second site was Las Colinas in Irving, the suburb that was home to Texas Stadium.[28]

The bill Governor Perry signed into law on May 28, 2003 proposed that voters authorize an increased Dallas County hotel tax and rental car tax. Imposing the tax on the county rather than the city of Dallas increased the amount that could be collected, as it spread the tax over a larger population. The population of the city of Dallas was 1.2 million in 2000, while the county population was over 2.2 million, including cities such as Carrollton, Garland, and Irving, the home of Texas Stadium (Exhibit 4).[29] A countywide sports authority would issue debt, to be repaid by the new taxes. The hotel occupancy tax would increase by 3 percent, from 15 to 18 percent. The rental car tax would be increased from 5 to 6 percent. The Legislative Budget Board estimated that the new taxes would raise approximately $36.4 million in 2004, increasing to $41.9 million in 2008. The tax money would be used to service bond debt of up to $400 million issued to pay for stadium construction.[30]

Gaining taxpayer approval was not something that could be taken for granted. Dallas mayor Laura Miller, a vocal opponent of the plan, made the following comment after the legislature had turned down the city's top priority (a new convention center hotel) but passed the stadium bill, "I find it ironic that some of the legislators I talked to said they had problems with using tax money to fund a hotel, but now they have used much more tax money to fund a stadium that we don't need."[31]

EXHIBIT 3   THE FIVE POINTS OF DALLAS COWBOYS PARK

"A grand, mixed-use development, Cowboys Place will consist of corporate office and executive space, upscale residential developments of condominiums, and high-end apartments, each drawing in life and vitality from residents and the business community, and all within walking distance of the retail, dining, office, sports, parks and entertainment amenities offered at Legends Park."

Cowboys Place
Residential/Business
Mixed-Use Development

"In the shadows of the stadium will rest the heart of the Park—Legends Square. Designed with a town center environment, Legends Square will feature high-energy retail stores, many with a sports theme, plus restaurants and fine dining."

"Cowboys Fields will serve as an outdoor sports field complex for youth and adult league competition for football, lacrosse, soccer, baseball, field hockey, and many other field sports. Sports clinics, camps and competitions throughout the year will further enhance the fields as an invaluable and lasting community resource for families looking for safe recreational opportunities."

Legends Square
Retail, Dining, &
Family Entertainment

Cowboys Stadium
State-of-the-Art,
Retractable Domed Stadium

Cowboys Fields
Public-Use Sports
Field Complex

"... a domed, air-conditioned, 75,000-seat facility with a retractable roof and open end zones linked to fan decks that could increase seating capacity to 100,000 with reduced-cost tickets. A technologically enhanced stadium designed to flexibly adapt to a variety of sports and entertainment events—from Super Bowls to the Pan Am games, from the Cotton Bowl to major concerts."

Cowboys Hotel
Convention Hotel
& Conference Center

Cowboys Field House
Cowboys-themed,
Interactive Sports Entertainment

"... a destination hotel to support the region's tourist and convention trade. A Dallas Cowboys branded convention hotel will attract new convention business with state-of-the-art corporate meeting facilities, promote economic growth, and make the region more competitive for lucrative corporate gatherings and civic events."

"An innovative recreation center for family entertainment, featuring live-action, extreme, and participation sports like rock climbing, bowling, basketball, volleyball, virtual sports, inline skating, ice skating, and an exciting themed outdoor challenge course for team building experiences. The Sports Performance Studio, a state-of-the-art fitness center manned by Cowboys' trainers, will offer the health conscious the ability to train where the team trains. Anchoring the Field House will be a Cowboys-themed, interactive hall of fame."

Source (including quotations): Dallas Cowboys promotional package, "Five Points of Dallas Cowboys Park."

In general, cities in 2003 were struggling in an economic environment dramatically different from that of the 1990s. Citizens were not as receptive as they had previously been to taxpayer financing of sports facilities. Los Angeles, which lost both its NFL teams in 1995 (the Raiders returning to Oakland, and the Rams relocating to St. Louis), was believed by many to be reluctant to use taxpayer money to build a stadium or otherwise attract a new team.

EXHIBIT 4   DALLAS COUNTY

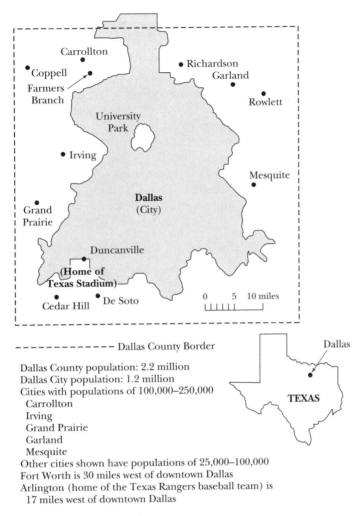

------------- Dallas County Border

Dallas County population: 2.2 million
Dallas City population: 1.2 million
Cities with populations of 100,000–250,000
  Carrollton
  Irving
  Grand Prairie
  Garland
  Mesquite
Other cities shown have populations of 25,000–100,000
Fort Worth is 30 miles west of downtown Dallas
Arlington (home of the Texas Rangers baseball team) is
  17 miles west of downtown Dallas

Source: *Rand McNally*, op. cit, p. 229, 524, 525. Populations as of 2000.

Los Angeles had many professional teams in other sports, two major college sports power-houses, and a wide range of other entertainment options for its residents. How different was the Dallas community from Los Angeles? The Cowboys believed that many people associated Dallas with the team, and that the Cowboys were the most recognized NFL franchise internationally—factors that bound the team and the city together, and that argued for taxpayer support of the team.

The proposal to tax hotel visitors and rental car customers had the appeal of not directly taxing the people who would vote on the measure. Cowboys political consultant and spokesman Allyn, commented, "That's the great wisdom of this [plan]. It will draw millions of visitors every year without any burden on local taxpayers."[32] This financing approach had been used successfully in 1998, when Dallas increased its hotel room tax by 2 percent, and imposed a 5 percent tax on rental cars in order to finance $125 million in bonds to help pay for the $435 million American Airlines Center used by the Dallas Mavericks NBA basketball team and Dallas Stars NHL hockey team.[33]

However, there were indications of local resistance beyond that expressed by the mayor. Rental car companies were already struggling. Hotel occupancy was only 52 percent in 2002, lower than in other Texas cities. One columnist cited a study of a projected increase in hotel bed tax from 14 percent to 16 percent in Atlanta, a city similar in size to Dallas. The study concluded that such an increase would lead to a 5 percent reduction in hotel revenue and visitor spending, leading to the loss of more than 8,000 jobs. A hotel occupancy tax of 18 percent would be one of the highest such rates in the country.[34] A survey of Dallas County voters conducted in early April 2003 showed overwhelming opposition, with 87 percent stating that providing funding for the stadium was not "the proper role for government," 61 percent disagreeing with the assertion that a stadium would stimulate the economy, and 83 percent saying that the County should not build a football stadium with public tax dollars.[35] A website—NoJonesTax.com—was set up to provide a forum for opponents of public financing of a new Cowboys stadium. Exhibit 5 has selected comments from this website.

EXHIBIT 5   **COMMENT ON DALLAS TAX PROPOSAL FOR FINANCING COWBOYS STADIUM**

The following is a selection of comments regarding the proposal to fund a stadium by increasing hotel and rental car taxes:

"It's an improper role for government to even consider doing this. If Mr. Jones wants a new stadium, he should tax his own ticket holders, his parking lots, and locker rooms." Dave Capps, owner of a rental car company, and founder of a website opposing the tax (NoJonesTax.com)*

Comments posted on the NoJonesTax.com website guestbook:**

- Since the only larger markets in the world would be London, Mexico City or Tokyo, the chance of the Cowboys moving on is nil, so don't try that threat.

- I guess y'all would be happier if the Cowboys left Dallas? Then we could be just like Los Angeles and like Houston was a couple a years ago . . . without an NFL team!

- Don't y'all have anything else to do? Dallas' needs this stadium to keep up with the other competitive markets out there. Where's your civc [sic] pride? I'm for this stadium to get Dallas back on the map!

- Go Jerry. Lets just get that out of the way first. I saw this site and thought what stupid people y'all are. Example: there was [a] guy saying, "If this tax is approved, we're moving outta Dallas."

- Why don't we ask the Cowboys to give up part of their money, they are highly overpaid, and let them build the dang place if they want it.

- The people in Dallas County buy every fairy tale Jerry Jones comes up with.

- The concept of using public tax dollars to fund or subsidize private enterprise is very, very wrong. How can our elected public officials not understand this?

- I just can't believe that we the people have been duped to believe that these sports facilities are going to benifit [sic] us. Back in days past owners payed [sic] to have these stadiums built and have prospered well. My question is to what did it benefit the tax payer?

- There should be a huge public outcry against this thing. Crime is soaring, money is needed for education, businesses are failing right and left, the city can't even meet the demands of its own budget, families are struggling, and this egomaniac wants to fritter our money away on such an unnecessary endeavor? I think not!

*Dave Michaels. "Signing Signals Stadium Kickoff." *Dallas Morning News* (May 29, 2003).

**http://www.nojonestax.com/mod.php?mod=guestbook (September 4, 2003).

Would Dallas voters support the tax increase to build a new home for the team? If not, what should the team do? The available options included: staying at Texas Stadium, renovating Texas Stadium to meet the Cowboys' future needs, building a new stadium without public funding, or relocating to a city that would provide the kind of facility that Jones wanted.

Questions

1. The Dallas Cowboys have one of the highest *Forbes* valuations and yet have one of the older stadiums in the NFL. Explain this situation.

2. The Dallas Cowboys have several options for refinancing for a new stadium, including 100% private or a mixture of public and private. What factors should the Cowboys consider when choosing their preferred financing option?

3. Assume the mixture of public and private financing option is chosen. What can the Cowboys do to maximize the likelihood of a favorable electoral vote on a hotel tax and rental car tax?

4. What debt capacity can the Cowboys sustain in order to raise private funds (as part of a mixture of public and private) for a new stadium?

5. How might the new stadium help the Cowboys be competitive "on-the-field" in the NFL?

Footnotes

[1]   This section was written by George Foster.

[2]   Stanford Class of 2004 GSB students Jason Harkness, John Hebert, and Patrick Molloy prepared this case under the supervision of George Foster.

[3]   The first initiative was led by former mayor Dianne Feinstein in the mid-eighties. The initiative, which was to build a new stadium near the Candlestick Park site, was not strategically crafted or well received by the public. This measure was voted down by the public by a large margin. The second initiative, led by then mayor Art Agnos in 1989, called for a stadium at the same site in China Basin that would eventually become home to Pacific Bell Park. The park would be built by a developer in exchange for the rights to build an arena in downtown San Francisco. The initiative lost by a narrow margin of approximately 1,100 votes. Two additional initiatives were attempted outside of San Francisco, one for a stadium in Santa Clara (1990) and one in San Jose (1992). Both of these initiatives failed as well.

[4]   "Giants Field Top Execs to Land Pac Bell Stadium." *Sacramento Business Journal* (March 31, 2000).

[5]   Ibid.

[6]   Major League Baseball, in its current form, is made up of two leagues, the American League and the National League. The Giants are a member of the National League.

[7]   Technically, Proposition B was only required to provide the stadium a variance from the city's existing waterfront height restrictions. This variance was specifically required for the stadium's lights.

[8]   Subsequent to the signing of the stadium naming rights contract, Pacific Bell was acquired by SBC. The contract provided for a change in name to the acquiring company in this situation.

[9]   The Oakland Raiders moved (back) to the Oakland Coliseum from Los Angeles in 1995. To finance renovation of the Coliseum, Alameda County proposed a personal seat license (PSL) plan that gave purchasers property rights to a seat for only 10 years at relatively high prices; for example, the best seats were

$4,000 for the PSL and the first-year annual fee of $610 for eight regular-season games. This PSL plan failed to deliver the sellouts that were hoped for in order to make the Raiders' move to Oakland a financial winner.

10 *Washington Times* (October 20, 2002).

11 *2004 Revenues From Sports Venues* (Milwaukee, WI: Media Ventures, 2004).

12 David Hoyt prepared this case under the supervision of George Foster.

13 The NFL merged with the rival American Football League (AFL) in 1966, taking effect with the 1967 season. The Super Bowl had begun as a competition between the NFL and AFL champions and evolved into the NFL championship game, played between the winners of the National Football Conference (NFC) and American Football Conference (AFC).

14 Team history from Dallas Cowboy website: http://lb.dallascowboys.com/history_main.cfm (July 31, 2003).

15 Tampa Bay defensive tackle Warren Sapp, quoted in the Dallas Cowboys' promotional publication *The Dallas Cowboys*, p. 5.

16 Ibid., p. 1.

17 FutureBrand, "The Most Valuable Brands in Sports: The 2002 Report," 2003, p. 2. Valuations were based on team financials, fan base, stadium operations, on-field performance, and a global survey of sports fans.

18 "The Back of the Book: You're a Shining Star: NFL's Five Points are Fans Favorites." SportsBusinessDaily.com (September 5, 2003).

19 Kurt Badenhausen et al. "Showing You the Money." *Forbes* (September 15, 2003), p. 82. Operating income was earnings before interest, taxes, and depreciation.

20 Forbes.com: (September 15, 2003).

21 Roger G. Noll and Andrew Zimbalist. "Build the Stadium—Create the Jobs!" in Roger G. Noll and Andrew Zimbalist, eds., *Sports, Jobs & Taxes: The Economic Impact of Sports Teams and Stadiums* (Washington, DC: Brookings Institution Press, 1997), p. 44.

22 Katie Fairbank. "Cowboys Rush for Sales: Tickets are Moving, But Not as Quickly as Some Might Expect." *Dallas Morning News* (September 6, 2003), p. 1D. Average ticket prices were determined by Team Marketing Report and published as an annual Fan Cost Index.

23 "Ticket Prices Up Around League." *San Jose Mercury News* (September 5, 2003), p. 5D.

24 "Cowboys' Planned $650M Stadium Part of Entertainment Complex." *SportsBusiness Daily* (March 24, 2003).

25 John Moritz. "Dallas Cowboys Stadium Bill Goes to Texas Governor." *Fort Worth Star-Telegram* (May 9, 2003).

26 "Five Points of Dallas Cowboys Park." *Dallas Cowboys*, p. 3.

27 Ibid.

28 Randy Lee Loftis. "Potential Dallas Cowboys Site Has Gritty Industrial Past." *Dallas Morning News* (May 27, 2003).

29 *Rand McNally 2003 Commercial Atlas & Marketing Guide* (Rand McNally & Company, 2003), pp. 524, 525.

30 Gott, loc. cit.

31 Gromer Jeffers, Jr. "Dallas Cowboys Stadium Plan Gets Legislature's Approval, But New Hotel Sacked." *Dallas Morning News* (May 27, 2003).

32 Michael Schurman. "Gilding Visitors Could Backfire on Us All, Mr. Jones." *Fort Worth Star-Telegram* (March 12, 2003).

33 Richard Alm. "City Ahead of the Game in Collections for AAC." *Dallas Morning News* (May 17, 2003), p. 3D. Tax receipts exceeded those required to pay off the debt as of May 2003. If the trend continued, the debt would be retired ahead of its 2008 due date. The arena tax was passed by less than 1,700 votes.

34 Schurman, loc. cit.

35 Survey of 1,000 voters conducted by Wilson Research Strategies, April 9, 2003.

SECTION 10...Financial Valuation and Profitability[1]

Key Issues

- The drivers of sporting club valuation include league strength/viability, current club strength, club brand/heritage strength, club stadium strength, city strength, and owner attributes.

- The underlying economics and chosen business model of each sport matter. The lowest valued NFL club is over double the value of the highest valued NHL club!!!

- Sources of evidence about the current market value of sporting clubs include the public equity market, the acquisition market, financial statement information, and discounted cash flow analysis.

- Allegations that leagues or clubs understate their profitability are made frequently. They typically involve one or more of: revenues inappropriately excluded, revenues inappropriately backended, costs inappropriately included, and costs inappropriately frontended.

Cases

Financial valuation creation is a key goal of many parties in the business of sports. This section examines topics related to how owners and investors have been able to capture part of that value creation:

Issue One: What are the drivers of the financial valuations of sporting clubs?

Issue Two: How should sporting clubs be valued and what are relevant information sources for this task?

Issue Three: What issues arise in disputes over sporting club profitability measurement?

Financial Valuation Drivers

Financial valuations of sporting clubs are required in multiple contexts. The following are illustrative. Clubs are bought or sold on a regular basis in many leagues. Buyers and sellers on such transactions likely will be making preliminary estimates of the current market price. Where clubs are owned by investment syndicates, an up-to-date valuation of the club will facilitate changes in ownership interests of individual syndicate members being made at current market values. Clubs that seek to borrow often find financial valuations are required by potential lenders. Decisions by leagues on the expansion fee that new clubs must pay take into account the market values of existing clubs.

Rankings of the most valuable sporting clubs are published on a regular basis. *Forbes* each year publishes its financial valuations of all clubs in the NFL, MLB, NBA, and NHL. Exhibit 10-1 presents the distribution across clubs, as well as the three highest and three lowest valued clubs in 2003–04 for the NFL, MLB, NBA, and NHL. *Forbes* also reports valuations for leading soccer clubs in the world. The highest five in 2004 were Manchester United—England ($1,186 million), Juventus—Italy ($828 million), AC Milan—Italy ($759 million), Real Madrid—Spain ($751 million), and Bayern Munich—Germany ($617 million). *Forbes* does not use a mechanical formula in its valuations. It takes account of multiple factors including revenues, profitability, and the stadium situation of the sporting club. In most cases, *Forbes* has to rely on its own estimates of club financials. Many clubs are privately held and some do not release the same level of detailed financials that publicly traded companies are required to do.

Why do sporting clubs differ in their financial valuations? What can management do to affect such valuations? Exhibit 10-2 outlines six categories of valuation drivers. These drivers highlight how decisions by key parties affect individual club valuations. These include decisions by leagues, players' associations, clubs, sponsors, fans, media companies, cities, and legislative (e.g., taxation) bodies. The topic of club valuation integrates many of the issues covered in prior sections of this book.

League Strength and Viability: Section 2 on leagues outlines key areas where league-related factors affect both (1) the level of total revenues and total costs and (2) how those revenues and costs are distributed across the individual clubs. These factors in turn influence the level of club valuations and the dispersion across clubs in those valuations.

EXHIBIT 10-1   *FORBES'* 2003–2004 VALUATION OF SPORTING CLUBS IN THE
NFL, MLB, NBA, AND NHL ($ MILLIONS)

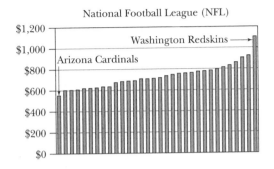

National Football League (NFL)

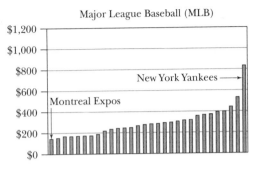

Major League Baseball (MLB)

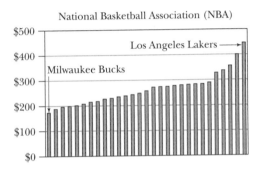

National Basketball Association (NBA)

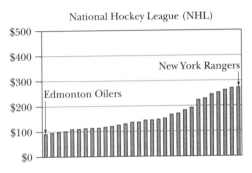

National Hockey League (NHL)

National Football League (NFL)

1. Washington Redskins	$1,104
2. Dallas Cowboys	923
3. Houston Texans	905
30. Minnesota Vikings	604
31. Atlanta Falcons	603
32. Arizona Cardinals	552

Major League Baseball (MLB)

1. New York Yankees	$832
2. Boston Red Sox	533
3. New York Mets	442
28. Minnesota Twins	168
29. Tampa Bay Devil Rays	152
30. Montreal Expos	145

National Basketball League (NBA)

1. Los Angeles Lakers	$447
2. New York Knicks	401
3. Chicago Bulls	356
27. Seattle SuperSonics	196
28. Golden State Warriors	188
29. Milwaukee Bucks	174

National Hockey League (NHL)

1. New York Rangers	$272
2. Dallas Stars	270
3. Toronto Maple Leafs	263
28. Calgary Flames	97
29. Buffalo Sabres	95
30. Edmonton Oilers	91

Source: *Forbes* (9/15/2003; 4/26/2004; 2/9/2004; 12/8/2003).

There are major differences in the average valuations across the four leagues (also shown in Exhibit 10-1):

	Average	Range
NFL	$733 million	$1,104–$552
MLB	$295 million	$ 832–$145
NBA	$265 million	$ 447–$174
NHL	$159 million	$ 272–$ 91

EXHIBIT 10-2   SPORTING CLUB FINANCIAL VALUATION DRIVERS

1. League Strength/Viability	**2. Current Club Strength**
• Media ratings/attendance	• Current attendance/season ticket holder support
• Fan avidity	• Existing sponsorship portfolio
• Revenue sharing upside	• Current on-field success
• "Cost certainty" (salary cap, etc.)	• Current "marquee" players
• Playoff revenue upside	• Quality of playing/coaching squad
• Extra tournament revenue upside	• Quality of scouting/player personnel
	• Level of "behaving badly" problems

3. Club Brand/Heritage Strength	**4. Club Stadium/Arena Strength**
• Club on-field success tradition	• Club stadium/arena strength
• Club "marquee" player tradition	• Revenue generating capacity
• Club fan loyalty tradition	• Ownership vs. tenant
• Club sponsor attractiveness tradition	• Attractiveness of contracts
• City vs. regional vs. national vs. global brand	

5. City Strength	**6. Owner Attributes**
• Market size/demographics	• Trophy status desire
• Affinity to sports	• Financial capacity
• Local economy health/diversification	• Taxation considerations
• Competitor in market for "share of wallet/eyeballs"	

Consider the NFL versus the NHL. The NFL has an agreed cost-to-revenue relationship at the league level, high total league revenues, a high central revenue to total revenues ratio, equal sharing by clubs of centrally distributed revenues, and a salary cap. The result is both a high average club valuation and a low ratio of the highest valuation to the lowest valuation. The NHL has low total league revenues, a low central revenue to total revenue ratio, and no salary cap. NHL clubs have lower average valuations than the NFL and the ratio of the highest to lowest valued clubs is 2.99 (2.00 for the NFL). One striking indicator of the importance of the league strength factor in NFL versus NHL valuations is that the lowest valued NFL club (Arizona Cardinals at $552 million) is more than twice the highest valued NHL club (New York Rangers at $272 million)!

Current Club Strength: Important revenue streams are promoted by strong current club strengths both on and off the field. High on-field success helps attract higher attendance and higher merchandising. High-profile players who have a low risk of "behaving badly" typically enhance the valuation of a club.

Club Brand/Heritage Strength: Section 7 illustrates steps that clubs have taken to promote their brand. Increasingly efforts here are focused on promoting club brands beyond their local area. The Dallas Cowboys of the NFL have long attracted fans from areas beyond Dallas and even beyond the United States. Similarly, Manchester United has a major fan base outside of England. Being a global sports brand enhances a club's financial valuation in part because of the extra revenues associated with merchandising and sponsorship.

Club Stadium/Arena Strength: Section 9 examines stadium economics. Two key aspects here are the total revenues the stadium/arena generates and the percentage of those revenues the club is able to capture.

City Strength: City size and its sports affinity help determine club financial valuation. A sports club based in New York has multiple benefits over those based in smaller cities that lead to higher financial valuations—for example, higher demand for tickets, higher average ticket prices, and higher media revenues where local media contracts are negotiated (as in MLB, NBA, and NHL).

Owner Dimension: Owners of sporting teams can have diverse motives. In some cases, the desire to own a "trophy asset" (such as ownership of an elite sporting club) can lead hard-nosed businesspeople to bid more than they would for other assets with similar revenue/cost characteristics. Taxation deductions available to owners and investors can also influence assessed valuations.

The Exhibit 10-2 classification is one approach. John Waldron at Goldman Sachs covers many of these categories in his five-part classification of "Drivers of Sports Franchise Valuation":[2]

- Strategic Position—for example, (1) historic team performance and (2) brand equity and fan loyalty.

- Economics—for example, (1) team operating performance, (2) league economics, and (3) upside opportunities.

- Comparable Entity Valuations—for example, (1) recent transactions and (2) expansion franchises.

- Ownership Issues—for example, (1) potential buyer universe, (2) league rules and restrictions, (3) tax consideration, and (4) rights of first refusal.

- Trophy Status—for example, (1) limited opportunity to acquire a professional sports franchise and (2) community standing.

Goldman Sachs is one of several investment banks with extensive experience in sporting club transactions and sports financing.

Forbes has long provided the most extensive coverage of sporting club valuations. Other sources of valuation numbers include Kagan (see www.kagan.com) and Shaw's Sports Business (see www.shawsportsbusiness.com).

Estimating Current Market Value of a Sporting Club

Many books and articles have been written on business valuation. Each year, multiple court cases involving valuation disputes are reported.[3] This section highlights some key issues in this area.

The Internal Revenue Service definition of "fair market value" captures what many interpret "market value" to mean:[4]

> *The price at which the property would change hands between a willing buyer and a willing seller when the former is not under any compulsion to buy and the latter is not under any compulsion to sell, both parties having reasonable knowledge of relevant facts. Court decisions sometimes state in*

addition that the hypothetical buyer and seller are assumed to be able, as well as willing, to trade and to be well informed about the property and concerning the market for such property.

The sources of evidence about current market value include:

(a) **Public Equity Markets.** Where a publicly traded market exists for a company, the prices at which its securities are traded are an important indicator of market value. Very few sporting clubs in the United States have publicly traded securities. In other countries, the position is different. Many of the major European soccer clubs are publicly traded. The prices at which these securities are traded are a direct indicator of the market value of those clubs and an indirect indicator of the market value of other soccer clubs in the same league that are not traded.

The most frequent way public equity market prices are used to estimate the market value of a privately held company is via market multiples—these include the market value to revenue multiple and the market value to operating income multiple. For example, the market value to operating income (profit) of publicly traded English soccer clubs may be used to estimate the value of privately held soccer clubs using the operating income of those privately held clubs.

(b) **Acquisition Market.** In each of the major sporting leagues, there are often one or more changes in ownership in recent transactions. The acquisition price in these transactions (or multiples based on this acquisition price—such as transaction price to revenue) can be used to infer the value of other sporting clubs. Exhibit 10-3 illustrates recent transactions and the acquisition price to revenue multiples for more than 28 exchanges of ownership.

A key challenge in using acquisition multiples is obtaining reliable information on the acquisition price. Sporting transactions are often complex, and can include components related to stadiums or media contracts that have to be debundled. For example, the "full" transaction price of $700 million in 2002 for the Boston Red Sox included an 80% interest in NESN (New England Sports Network). Goldman Sachs reported the acquisition price for the Red Sox franchise alone was $375 million after subtracting an estimate of the market value of NESN at that time.

(c) **Financial Statement Information.** The financial statements of most professional sporting clubs are typically audited. This is often a requirement of the league in which the club plays. The amount shown for shareholders' funds is a possible indicator of current market value. However, for most sporting clubs, this amount is a very "noisy" indicator of market value. A key "asset" to a sporting club is its players. Yet, under generally accepted accounting principles, not all these players are always included on the balance sheet and rarely at updated estimates of their "market values."

English Premier League clubs since 1999 have included financial amounts relating to a subset of their players on their balance sheet. Where a contract for an athlete playing elsewhere is purchased by an EPL club, that contract is included on the balance sheet as an "intangible asset." Thus, when Manchester United in 2003 purchased the player contract of Rio Ferdinand from Leeds United, the £30 million transfer fee was reported as an intangible asset on Manchester United's balance sheet. This £30 million

EXHIBIT 10-3   RECENT SPORTING CLUB TRANSACTIONS SINCE 2000

Sporting Club	Reported Acquisition Price ($ Millions)	Transaction Year	Acquisition Price to Revenue Multiple
NFL			
Atlanta Falcons	$545	2001	4.5
Baltimore Ravens	584	2000	3.9
Washington Redskins	800	2000	4.1
New York Jets	635	2000	5.2
MLB			
Los Angeles Dodgers	$330	2004	2.2
Anaheim Angels	185	2003	1.6
New York Mets	400	2002	2.3
Arizona Diamondbacks	219	2002	1.7
Montreal Expos	120	2002	1.9
Florida Marlins	159	2002	2.0
Boston Red Sox	375	2002	2.3
Toronto Blue Jays	140	2000	1.9
Kansas City Royals	96	2000	1.9
NBA			
Charlotte Bobcats (Expansion)	$300	2002	N/A
Boston Celtics	360	2002	4.4
Seattle SuperSonics	200	2001	2.5
Dallas Mavericks	280	2000	4.1
Denver Nuggets	202	2000	2.8
NHL			
Buffalo Sabres	$ 92	2003	1.8
Washington Capitals	92	2003	1.6
San Jose Sharks	147	2002	2.2
Montreal Canadiens	200	2001	2.5
Phoenix Coyotes	91	2001	1.7
Buffalo Sabres	145	2001	2.7
Colorado Avalanche	128	2001	1.6
Colorado Avalanche	120	2000	1.5
New Jersey Devils	175	2000	3.3
New York Islanders	188	2000	3.7

Source: John Waldron, *The Business of Sports*, Goldman Sachs (2003).

figure would be written down over the life of the Ferdinand contract. One limitation of such "intangible asset" disclosures for English soccer clubs is that only the player contracts of transferred-in players are recognized. Where a player is developed in the club's own "farm system" (youth academies), there is no transaction for an accountant to place a value on the player contract. Thus, David Beckham's player contract (a Manchester United player until 2003) was not reported on Manchester's balance sheet as he was an "internally developed" prospect. Beckham, the English captain and probably the most recognized player in the EPL, clearly was highly valued, but this value was not reflected in Manchester's financial statements. This approach to intangible assets by accountants is not unique to sporting clubs. Accountants adopt a similar restrictive approach when accounting for brand-related and similar intangible assets.

(d) **Discounted Cash Flow (DCF).** Finance courses place great emphasis on the conceptual validity of the DCF approach to estimate value-in-use of an asset. This involves:

- **Step One:** forecasting the expected future net cash flows from holding the asset.

- **Step Two:** discounting those future cash flows using a discount factor that takes into account the time value of money and the risk associated with the asset.[5]

Each of the above-mentioned sources of information should be used and combined. Each can act as a cross-check on the other information sources. A key principle in valuation analysis is to combine diverse approaches to develop a more reliable estimate of current market value (sometimes called triangulation).

Financial Profitability Disputes

Exhibit 10-4 presents the distribution of 2003 operating income of clubs in the NFL, MLB, NBA, NHL, and EPL. The numbers for the first four leagues are estimates by *Forbes*. The EPL numbers are based on each club's published financial statements (as summarized in Deloitte's *Annual Review of Football Finance, 2004*). The differences across clubs in estimated profitability are stunning!

Financial profitability of clubs is a key aspect of many negotiations in the sports business area. Three examples illustrate this point. The profitability of clubs (in aggregate or individually) is an issue in the negotiations of leagues with player associations or clubs with players (or their agents). Negotiations between teams and cities over the need for public financing assistance for a new stadium development invariably include debate over the profitability of the club with different levels of private debt. Fans criticizing ticket price increases announced by clubs often cite club profitability in their arguments.

Given the central role that the "profit" number plays in sports business negotiations, it is not surprising that disputes over profitability measurement arise. The major claim is that clubs understate their profitability (and by implication, profitability at the league level is underestimated). The major ways that the current year's profitability can be underestimated are:

- Revenues inappropriately excluded
- Revenues included, but inappropriately underattributed to sporting club
- Revenues inappropriately back-ended to subsequent years
- Costs inappropriately included
- Costs inappropriately front-ended from subsequent years

Revenue disputes often arise when the sporting club owner is also an owner or joint tenant of a stadium/arena or an owner of a media network showing the sporting club games. The argument is that revenues that should be assigned to the sporting club are inappropriately assigned to the stadium/arena or the media network.

EXHIBIT 10-4 *FORBES'* ESTIMATES OF 2003 PROFITABILITY OF NFL, MLB, NBA, AND NHL CLUBS ($ MILLIONS) AND REPORTED 2002 PROFITABILITY OF EPL CLUBS (£ MILLIONS)

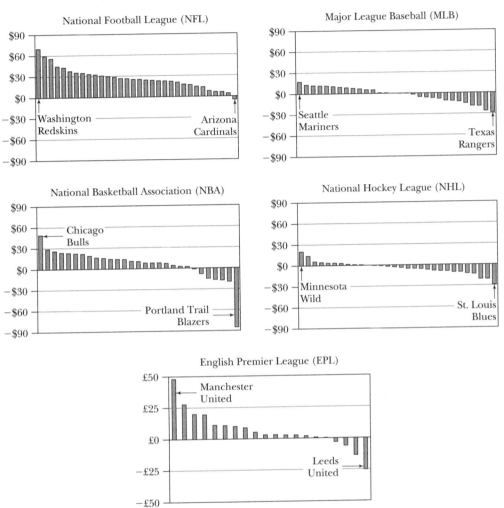

Source: *Forbes* magazine and club documents; Deloitte, *Annual Review of Football Finance* (August 2004).

Cost disputes often arise when costs that should be assigned to other activities are assigned to the sporting club—for example, the reported costs of a sporting team could inappropriately include the costs of media production of games by a media company the sporting club owns. Overstatement of costs can also arise when costs are inappropriately front-ended—for example, when costs that should be capitalized and spread over multiple years are fully expensed in the year they are incurred. Disputes also arise over the question of operating gains versus capital gains. Suppose a sporting club makes zero operating profits each year of a 5-year period, but that the valuation of the club increases from $100 million to $200 million in that same period. Using a broader definition of profits than that used in most income statements, this increase in sporting club value would be classified as a gain. This asset build motive is important to many investors in sporting clubs. However, accountants would not recognize this gain in their computation of the reported profitability of the club.

Case Study of Profitability in the NHL

The NHL operates with no salary cap and no salary tax. Many NHL owners claim they are losing sizable amounts of money and cite excessive player payments as the main cause. The *Forbes* data underlying Exhibit 10-4 highlights the NHL as having the highest percentage of clubs estimated to be losing money (20 out of 30 clubs in 2003). Not surprisingly, the NHL Players' Association disputes both the lack of profitability of NHL clubs and the claim that player salaries are the cause of profitability problems.

On February 5, 2004, Arthur Levitt, Jr. (former chairman of the Securities Exchange Commission) released a report titled "Independent Review of the Combined Financial Results of the National Hockey League 2002–2003 Season." The costs of this review were borne by the NHL. The review examined the finances and financial relationships of each NHL club. The aim was to compute the profitability of the hockey activities and exclude the nonhockey activities from each club. Levitt's financial estimates, as well as the *Forbes'* NHL estimates, are shown in Exhibit 10-5. Levitt's major conclusions included:

- "For the 2002–03 season, the NHL has reported combined operating revenues of $1.996 billion and a combined operating loss of $273 million before accounting for interest and depreciation expenses.

- The current relationship between leaguewide player costs and leaguewide revenues is inconsistent with reasonable and sound business practices. Player costs of $1.494 billion, or 75% of revenues, substantially exceeded such relationships in both the NBA and NFL as those relationships are set forth in their collective bargaining agreements."[6]

Levitt's operating income number is before interest on debt and depreciation. Adding these costs would further add to the magnitude of the NHL operating losses. Although *Forbes* adopts a broader definition of hockey activities[7] than Levitt, it likewise reports widespread losses for many NHL clubs. Both Levitt and *Forbes* estimated that the majority of NHL clubs had operating losses.

The NHL Players Association (NHLPA) has taken strong issue with the Levitt Review. It disputes the narrow definitions of how Levitt defines hockey activities. Detroit Red Wings Captain Steve Yzerman was quoted as saying: "The league chooses to not include some significant revenues in the business of hockey (that) the players' association feels there are.

EXHIBIT 10-5 PROFITABILITY OF NHL CLUBS (AGGREGATE OF 30 CLUBS) IN 2002–2003: COMPARISON OF LEVITT REVIEW AND *FORBES* ($ IN MILLIONS)

	Levitt Review	Forbes
Revenues		
Gate Revenues	$ 1,047	$ 965
Other Revenues	949	1,129
Total	1,996	2,094
Expenses		
Player Expenses	1,494	1,389
Other Expenses	775	829
Total	2,269	2,218
Operating Income	$ (273)	$ (124)

Source: "CBA: A Different Set of Numbers," http://www.andrewsstarspage.com (August 1, 2004).

There's your big discrepancy." The NHLPA also disputed the independence of Levitt. Anaheim Ducks defenseman Keith Carney commented: "We all know that there are ways to be creative in accounting. This guy was hired by the league. That just makes it hard for the players to buy."[8]

Individual clubs have reported results consistent with the Levitt Review. For example, the Tampa Bay Lightning reported in September 2004 that "over the past 5 years, the team, and the St. Pete Times Forum, which is also used for concerts and other events have accumulated operating losses of $53.9 million. Adding noncash losses from depreciation, amortization, and interest expense increased the 5-year loss to $141 million." The one bright light in the Tampa Bay disclosures was that in 2004, the team had its first operating profit of $3.6 million. This was fueled by $14.1 million of postseason revenues from its successful trip to winning the Stanley Cup. One motivation for these disclosures by the Tampa Bay Lightning was to negotiate better contracts with the city as regards property taxes and better revenue sharing of arena-related revenue (such as parking revenues).[9]

CASE 10.1   LOS ANGELES KINGS: WHAT'S THE FINANCIAL SCORE?[10]

The December 23, 2002 issue of Forbes included their annual estimates for the revenues, operating income, and current financial valuation of the 30 teams in the National Hockey League (NHL). Forbes estimated that the Los Angeles Kings had revenues of $81.0 million, an operating profit of $7.1 million and a valuation of $205 million in 2001–2002.—see Exhibit 1 for a five-year summary of Forbes' estimates. Tim Leiweke, President of the Los Angeles Kings and of Anschutz Entertainment Group (AEG), was less than impressed by Forbes' estimates, which he saw as overstating the team's profitability. In response, Leiweke released audited financial statements to the *Los Angeles Times* in December 2002, a highly unusual move. In doing so, he commented: "For the record, I've never talked to Forbes, they've never talked to our chief financial officer, they don't have our [financial] numbers because we're a private company and they're guessing."[11]

In early 2003, Phil Propper, an investment portfolio manager and media security analyst, offered to make an independent review of the Kings' finances. Propper, a Kings fan, received the green-light from Leiweke to conduct the study and publicly release his findings. He released the results over the Internet on April 8, 2003.[12] In a world where most sporting owners treasure their privacy, the Propper study offered rarely available insights into the detailed finances of an NHL club and a leading sporting arena. This case highlights issues raised in the Propper study.

The study brought to light issues of both the team economics as well as issues arising from the shared tenancy of the team's home arena, the Staples Center, located in downtown Los Angeles. The Kings shared the Staples Center with four other anchor tenants—Los Angeles Lakers (NBA), Los Angeles Clippers (NBA), Los Angeles Sparks (WNBA) and Los Angeles Avengers (AFL). Five anchor tenants are the most of any major indoor arena in North America.

Los Angeles Kings

The Los Angeles Kings entered the NHL as an expansion franchise in 1967 under the ownership of Jack Kent Cooke. Cooke, a Canadian, was also the owner of the Los Angeles Lakers. Up to 1999, the Kings and Lakers played at the Great Western Forum in Inglewood, which

EXHIBIT 1   FORBES ESTIMATES OF LA KINGS FINANCIAL RESULTS AND VALUATION (ALL VALUES IN MILLIONS)

	Revenues	Operating Income	Valuation
1997–1998	$38.5	$ (1.0)	$104
1998–1999	33.9	(14.5)	109
1999–2000	63.9	8.4	160
2000–2001	73.0	3.4	189
2001–2002	81.0	7.1	205

Source: Forbes Annual Issues reporting NHL financial estimates.

is 10 miles from downtown Los Angeles. The Forum had capacity of approximately 16,000 but limited suite space. During the 1978–79 season, Cooke sold the Kings, Lakers and Forum to Dr. Jerry Buss. This $67 million transaction was reportedly the largest business transaction in sport at that time.

Buss soon sold the Kings to Bruce McNall, who had accumulated wealth, first from trading in rare coins, and then through trading in thoroughbred racehorses and movie making. Before the 1988–89 NHL season, McNall made the blockbuster announcement that Wayne Gretzky—the leading NHL player in the game and a true sports icon ("The Great One")—was joining the Kings. The Kings with Gretzky had improved success and better attendance. During the 1994–95 season, however, McNall ran into financial and legal problems and was forced to sell his franchise. The new owners were Philip Anschutz and Edward Roski Jr. Anschutz was a Denver based billionaire with multiple successful business ventures in oil, railroads, and communications. Roski was a Los Angeles based commercial real estate developer. Anschutz and Roski paid $114 million to buy the Kings "out of bankruptcy."

During 1996 and 1997 Anschutz and Roski explored with the City of Los Angeles building a sports arena in downtown Los Angeles, near the convention center. In February 1997, plans for a new $300+ million arena were unveiled. Seating capacity was to be approximately 19,000. In October 1997, an arena naming rights deal with Staples (an office-supply firm) was announced. *Los Angeles Magazine* referred to the arena project as "development heaven" in November 1998, noting multiple revenue sources, including:

- Naming rights. Staples would pay $100 million over 20 years.

- Founding sponsors. A number of corporations, including United Airlines and Pacific Bell were expected to pay nearly $200 million for advertising and other promotional rights.

- Luxury Suites. Gross annual revenues of more than $37 million from160 suites priced at $197,500 and $300,000 per year.

- Premier Seating. The arena would contain2,500 premium seats, selling for prices ranging from $12,800 to $14,800 annually.

The article also noted that the $305 million Bank of America loan to finance the arena construction would require debt service of $24 million (at 8 percent interest) for interest payments before any repayment of principal.[13] The actual total construction and development cost of Staples was later estimated to be approximately $415 million. In April 1999, News Corp.'s FOX Broadcasting Group agreed to acquire a 40 percent share in the Staples Center (for an undisclosed amount). FOX also secured options for stakes in the Los Angeles Lakers and the Los Angeles Kings. In early 1999, the debt facility was refinanced with a $315 million private placement bond offering.

Staples was predominantly privately financed by a mixture of bank debt and cash infusion by Anschutz and Roski. The use of public financing was minimal. A 2003 study for the City of Los Angeles noted that "taxpayer exposure was limited through the guarantee from the Developer [Anschutz and Roski] that the debt reserve on the $38.5 million the city borrowed for the project and the interest lost on use of the $20 million the City provided from the Convention Center Debt Service Reserve Fund would be covered through a dedication of a portion of event parking fees and a tax imposed on tickets." The study also documented the additional revenue streams the City of Los Angeles received from Staples: (1) lease payments on "the Staples Center site at $302,737 per year; (2) taxes from ticket sales; (3) the

City's share of parking revenues; (4) net additional property taxes garnered from the operation of the Staples Center, which equal $3,399,033; and (5) incremental sales taxes, business license taxes, and utility taxes.[14] Leiweke of AEG noted: "Not one taxpayer dollar is involved in the construction, the development and the operation of Staples Center, the building. And I'm very proud of that."[15]

The Staples Center was the first stage of a larger development plan for the region surrounding the downtown convention center. Anschutz and Roski's L.A. Arena Company acquired in the 1990s sizable land holdings surrounding the Staples Center to play a key role in any such development. In September 2001, the Los Angeles City Council approved the LA Arena Company's development plan. Their plan included a 1,200 room hotel, a 7,000 seat theater, a 800-unit apartment building and an expansion of the convention center.

Staples Center Anchor Tenants

In 2004, there were five anchor sporting team tenants of the Staples Center. The Los Angeles Kings and the Los Angeles Lakers signed identical 25-year leases to play at Staples when they moved from the Forum to the Staples Center for the start of their 1999–2000 seasons.[16] Each played approximately 41 home games per year plus any playoff games. The Los Angeles Kings had made the NHL playoffs three of the five seasons in the 1999–2004 period, but had not made it to the Stanley Cup finals. The Kings were mid-ranked by Forbes in its annual valuations of the 30 NHL clubs.

The Los Angeles Lakers were the most highly valued NBA franchise. Since moving to the Staples Center in 1999, they had won the NBA Championship Series three times and made the playoffs every year. The Lakers took the mix of sports and entertainment to an intoxicating level. Laker games at Staples Center combined high-profile players with Hollywood celebrities at courtside.

The Clippers of the NBA were owned by Donald Sterling. Sterling purchased the Clippers in June 1981 when they were the San Diego Clippers. In 1984, they became the Los Angeles Clippers playing out of the Los Angeles Sports Arena. They moved to the Staples Center for the start of the 1999–2000 NBA season, signing a six-year lease. The Clippers played approximately 41 home games per season. They had not been a major force in NBA playoff games.

The Los Angeles Sparks were a foundation team in the WNBA, which was started in 1997. Ownership of the Sparks was initially held by the NBA, and its operations managed by Jerry Buss and the Los Angeles Lakers. They played at the Buss-owned Forum in their early years. Starting with the 2001 season, the team moved to the Staples Center. Over time, the Lakers acquired greater ownership in the Sparks, as the NBA sought to increase economic incentives at the WNBA club level. The Sparks were WNBA Champions in 2001.

The Los Angeles Avengers were an expansion franchise in the Arena Football League (AFL). Owned by Casey Wasserman, the Avengers played their first home game in April 2000 at the Staples Center. There were 8 home games in the AFL season plus any playoff games. The Avengers made the playoffs in 2002, 2003, and 2004.

Exhibit 2 presents 2002–2003 details on the ticket price range (H = High; L = Low) and average attendance for each of the five anchor tenants.

Anchor Tenant	Number of Home Games	2003 Season Tickets	2003 Single Game Tickets	Staples Capacity	Average Home Attendance: 2003 Season 2002 Season
Lakers (NBA)	41	$6,880 (H)*	$188 (H)	18,997	18,973
		903 (L)	24 (L)		18,997
Kings (NHL)	41	$4,435 (H)	$367 (H)	19,000	17,569
		877 (L)	10 (L)		16,756
Clippers (NBA)	41	$3,960 (H)	$125 (H)	18,997	17,231
		440 (L)	10 (L)		18,053
Sparks (WNBA)	17	$1,950 (H)	$130 (H)	18,997	9,290
		90 (L)	5 (L)		11,651
Avengers (AFL)	8	$1,260 (H)	$160 (H)	18,000	13,220
		72 (L)	10 (L)		12,398

*H = High Price; L = Low Price.

Source: *2004 Revenues From Sports Venues* (Milwaukee, Wisconsin: Mediaventures, 2004).

AEG and Staples Center

The Staples Center was managed and operated by AEG (Anschutz Entertainment Group). AEG owned or managed multiple sports and entertainment companies throughout the world. In addition to the Kings, it owns or had equity in multiple Major League Soccer (MLS) clubs including the Los Angeles Galaxy. It also owned and managed the $150 million Home Depot Center in Carson, California that included a 27,000-seat soccer stadium and a 13,000-seat tennis stadium.

Staples Center hosted many events beyond those of its five anchor sporting tenants, including NBA and NHL All-Star Games, Grammy Award Shows, numerous concert acts, and the 2000 Democratic National Convention. On average, in recent years there have been approximately 210 events at Staples each year—165 by the five anchor tenants (including playoffs) and 45 events by non-anchor tenants.

Extracts from Propper Study

Propper had access to all the financial records and related documents that he needed to conduct a thorough evaluation. He was also able to question the team's chief financial officer, Dan Beckerman. The following extracts are from section III (Findings of Fact):

> *The LA Kings lost $6.5 million in operating cash over the 2001–2002 season. When one adds losses from financing such as interest payments and deferred compensation, the losses escalate to $11.3 million last season. With the failure of the team to reach the playoffs this season as well as the constant stream of injuries which necessitated an unexpected number of minor league call-ups, total cash losses will approach $12.5 million in 2002/03. These losses are computed on a cash only basis and do not include any depreciation or amortization of previous capital*

expenditures. Total cash operating losses for the Kings during the AEG ownership era are $108 million. Looking at other portions of the AEG business empire, Staples Center is profitable, but only marginally so after making a significant debt service payment on the $315 million in debt held against the facility. Given that AEG ownership percentage of Staples Center is lower than that of the Kings, these profits are insufficient to cover the cash losses of the hockey team. Anschutz Entertainment Group does not earn any income from the Kings.

As to transfer payments between the entities, the Kings pay 8% of gross ticket receipts or $1.9 million to Staples Center for rent. This is the same rent paid by the Lakers and puts the Kings squarely in the middle of the league in terms of its lease payment. In return, Staples contributes 25% of the premier seat and luxury suite license and ticket revenues to the Kings. Again, this is the same amount of money that the Lakers receive. [Staples retains the 50% remaining after the 25% each to the Kings and the Lakers. The other anchor sporting tenants receive none of this revenue stream.] In addition, Staples Center and all its facilities are made available to the Kings that use them to sell their merchandise and place their sponsorships. The Kings do not make any material payments to AEG but do receive parking revenues on land owned by the parent company. In addition, AEG subsidizes the cost of the Kings' financial, legal and IT staff. These are expenses the Kings would have to incur themselves if they did not have a parent organization.

In terms of growing their revenue base, the Kings have had great success under the current ownership. Total revenues have grown 15.3% compounded annually (CAGR) over the seven full seasons the team has been owned by AEG. Total revenues now approach $67 million. Particularly impressive is the 18.2% CAGR in total gate receipts achieved over this period. The main reason for this impressive growth is the move to Staples Center. Gate receipts jumped from $19.6 million in 1998–1999 to $33.4 million in 1999–2000. This was due to a combination of greater attendance and higher average ticket prices, but the main stimulus came from the premier seats and luxury boxes as the Kings enjoy a much higher split of these revenues than they earned while playing at the Forum. Total admission revenues in 2001–2002 were $39.9 million based on average paid (not announced) attendance of 15,000 per game and an average ticket price of $48.12. This ticket price is comfortably below the league average to attend a regular season game.

In terms of broadcasting, the Kings share equally in the NHL's national television deals with the American and Canadian broadcast and cable networks as well as the Center Ice premium package. The local TV contract with FOX Sportsnet is in the top ten in the league in the high seven figures per season and contains an automatic escalator higher than inflation despite "dismal" ratings that sometimes are worse than soccer locally. FOX is also required to broadcast at least 65 games a season, and the contract goes through 2015. For radio, the Kings purchase airtime on local stations *and sell the advertising, a less than ideal arrangement that reflects the lack of interest on the part of any programmer to purchase the audio broadcast rights. The third largest revenue source is sponsorships, primarily advertising on the boards and on the video screens during games. Kings' management has grown advertising revenue to close to $7 million by requesting that the core sponsors of Staples Center also buy time and space during Kings' games.*

Gate, broadcasting and sponsorships make up 95% of total team revenues. Parking revenues are close to $800 thousand and are barely growing. Finally, concession revenues are only $1.3 million per season, a number that I did not at first believe. To verify this number, the Kings provided me with invoices given to them by the two outside vendors that run the concessions. The average fan purchases only $6.50 per game in concessions, a reflection of the fact than many people buy no food and drinks whatsoever. Aramark, the vendor keeps a certain amount to pay for food and labor, and the remainder is split equally between the Kings and Staples Center. At an average attendance of 15,000 and 41 home games, anyone can do the math and realize concessions are not a huge source of revenues. At the suite level, the average expenditure is higher but gross margins on the food and drink are much lower.

Operating expenses can be divided into two categories. The first includes all non-player salary costs. In these segments, the Kings have done an effective job in controlling the growth of these line items. Non-player expenses have grown at a 6.4% CAGR during the AEG era, 8.9% slower than revenues, and now total $25.5 million. The main contributors are game expenses which is the rent paid to Staples Center as well as the cost of producing each game ($5.4 million) and team expenses which include player per diem, travel, equipment, coaching and staff ($8.3 million). Team expenses are growing in low single digits while games expenses have grown at a double-digit pace as Staples Center is 2.5 times larger than the Forum and requires more staff to operate. Higher gate revenue also means higher rent that is computed as a percentage of paid attendance. In addition, the City of Los Angeles imposes a 3.5% ticket tax for games played at that facility. The Kings pay $1.2 million to broadcast games on the radio, $690 thousand for training camp, $643 thousand for public relations, $1.1 million for client relations and community affairs and $1.75 million for marketing. General and Administrative (overhead) is at $1.73 million. Each of these line items is barely showing any growth, and the Kings can legitimately make the claim that they run a tight ship.

Three non-player expense lines have grown at double digits compounded over the past seven years. The team has invested significant resources in scouting which is now at $1.7 million per season, a 16.2% annual growth rate. League dues have averaged 16.6% growth and are a material percentage of revenues, a matter that will be discussed later in this report. The main contributor to this is the Canadian Currency Equalization Program whereby, according the Associated Press, the strongest franchises in the U.S. subsidize teams north of the border that are handicapped by a weaker currency. In the absence of these payments, league assessments would have grown in the low single digits. Finally, season ticket sales expenses have jumped 12.1% a year to $1.4 million in an effort to broaden and deepen the fan base.

The second major category and by far the largest expense facing the franchise is player compensation. During the 2001/02 season this totaled $45.4 million. While the budget for this year forecast a similar number, the team will exceed this figure due to the numerous injuries that forced the premature call-up of several minor leaguers who are paid the front end of their two-way contracts while they are with the big club. In terms of player salaries, the Kings are in the top half of the league. Player salary growth for the Kings has been 18.9% compounded in the seven years that I am examining. If salaries had escalated at just 10% a year from when AEG purchased the franchise, the Kings would have generated a cash operating profit of $7 million in 2001–2002. In other words, the additional revenues captured by the move to Staples Center have been entirely consumed by the growth in player salaries.

Below the operating line, the Kings also receive and pay out cash for various financing requirements. The Playoffs are a significant source of free cash flow, generating approximately $4 million in revenues and $2 million in expenses per round. Failure to make the playoffs this season will add $2 million to the Kings' cash losses. The franchise owes $54 million in debt and the annual payment is $2.9 million in cash. Debt owed to the owners for paying for the team's losses accrues but there are no current cash payments. In addition, deferred compensation left over from the previous owner's era still amounts to $2.5 million a year in cash payments. Total deferred compensation inherited at the time of acquisition totaled $34 million with a balance of $8 million remaining after this season. This particularly hurts in that the Kings are still forced to pay players who are now competing against them on other teams. The current ownership had the choice of eliminating these payments through a bankruptcy filing yet volunteered to assume these obligations at a real cost to the team's bottom line.

After examining all the data and reconciling the official income statements with the annual free cash flows, **I can state definitively that the Kings have lost $108 million in cash since AEG has owned the team**. The greatest loss, which occurred in 1998–1999, was $31.7 million and the best year was 1999–2000 where the cash loss was $8.2 million. This year, the cash loss will be $12.5 million. Staples Center barely earns its cost of capital and does not generate nearly enough profits to offset these losses. These operating shortfalls are being absorbed by ownership and are almost equal to the original purchase price of the team. Philip Anschutz can put the team into insolvency at any time given the debt the Kings now owe him personally. Anschutz is permitted to write these losses off to shield income from other sources from taxes, but the *important point to remember is that these are cash, not paper, losses, and cannot be classified as a "tax shield." In the interest of full disclosure, Anschutz is legally permitted to deduct 50% of the team's purchase price from his personal taxes according to an IRS-approved schedule, but this benefit has been almost entirely consumed. These numbers are indisputable unless someone can prove criminal malfeasance on the part of the team and its management and auditors.*[17]

Levitt Report on NHL Profitability

In 2003, Arthur Levitt Jr. (former Chairman of the Securities Exchange Commission) released the results of a systematic study of NHL profitability at both the club level and at the league level (the aggregate of the 30 clubs). Levitt reported that "for the 2002–2003 season, the NHL has reported combined operating revenues of $1,996 million and a combined operating loss of $273 million before accounting for interest and depreciation expenses."[18] Levitt went to much effort to put the financials of each club on an "apples-to-apples" basis as regards their hockey activities. The majority of NHL clubs (19 out of 30) were reported by Levitt to have operating losses; only 6 NHL clubs had operating profits of $5 million or higher.

Issues Raised

The Propper Study raised a number of contentious issues. These included:

(a) Related Party Transactions. AEG had equity in both Staples Center and the Kings. It also had a 30 percent interest in the Lakers. AEG is on both sides of multiple transactions such as:

- Kings payment to Staples of 8 percent of gross ticket receipts

- Staples payment to Kings of 25 percent of premier seat and luxury suite license and ticket revenues

Kurt Badenhausen, statistics senior editor for *Forbes* observed: "The Kings have a complicated situation because they have a lot of money that goes to the company that operates the arena [AEG]. How you assign revenues that go to that company, the Kings or the Lakers, is up to their discretion. If all the revenues go to the arena company, then they can say the Kings lost money."[19] The current sharing rules were negotiated before the Kings and Lakers started playing at Staples in 1999 and before AEG took any equity stake in the Los Angeles Lakers. Both the Kings and the Lakers have identical leases.

(b) Operating Cost Responsibility. Arenas differed in how operating costs were shared. Consider the revenue stream associated with a premier seat and luxury suite license and ticket revenues. AEG used a "gross revenue" approach—25 percent each of "gross revenues" went to the Kings and the Lakers. AEG kept 50 percent of this "gross revenue" stream. However, this was not all profit to AEG. AEG incurred costs to market/sell the suites, to maintain the suites, and to have hospitality people in the suites at each event. An alternative approach would be use a sharing rule based on "net revenues" ("gross revenues" minus attributable costs). Here, each user would be assigned a percent of total operating costs based on the ratio of its net revenues to the total net revenues at the Staples Center (including concerts and other shows as well as games of anchor tenants).

(c) Debt Servicing Costs of Staples Arena. Given the $415 million cost of constructing the Staples Center and the minimal use of public financing, there was a high interest cost payment each year ($20+ million) to be paid by the owners of Staples. How should this high interest cost affect either the payments made to/charges made by the Kings and AEG? Many other NHL clubs either played in older arenas that had no debt or played in newer arenas where public financing covered most of the construction cost.[20]

(d) Responsibility to Pay Deferred Compensation of Kings Players (including former Kings players). When the Kings changed ownership in 1995, the new owners could have declared bankruptcy and avoided paying up to $34 million of deferred compensation contracted by the prior owner. Should any such payment be included when determining the current profitability of the Kings?

(e) Player-Related Costs of Current Kings Players. NHL player contracts are complex. A player's contract may have payments deferred beyond the length of his current contract (or even beyond his likely playing career). How should the Kings compute annual player costs in such situations?

Questions

1. Owners of clubs are typically alleged to understate their profits if profitable or overstate their losses if unprofitable. What pressures might lead clubs to adopt this approach?

2. The Propper study of the LA Kings concludes that "the Kings have lost $108 million in cash since AEG has owned the team. . . . This year the cash loss will be $12.5 million." Outline and critique the approach adopted by Propper and its key assumptions.

3. Assume you are hired by the NHL Players Association to dispute the Propper conclusion. What areas would you examine and target for attack?

4. Evaluate the "sharing rules" at the Staples Center for the five anchor tenants. Why might such sharing rules differ across arenas?

CASE 10.2 LIVERPOOL FOOTBALL CLUB: WHAT IS ITS CURRENT MARKET VALUE?[21]

Friday August 13th 2004 was a black day for Liverpool Football Club fans. It was confirmed that Michael Owen, one of its two home-grown superstars, had been traded to Real Madrid for £8 million. It was one day before the start of the 2004–2005 English Premier League (EPL) season. This was not the way new Manager Rafael Benitez envisioned opening his campaign to add to the impressive amount of "silverware" (championship trophies) the club had accumulated over many years.

That night a three-person private group met and formed Redfans Capital[22] to explore a potential equity investment in (or even takeover bid for) Liverpool. The largest current shareholder of Liverpool was the John Moores family (associated with Littlewood Pools), who held a controlling 51 percent of the equity. While Redfans had sizable financial capacity, they were concerned about over-bidding. They thought the risk of ownership of an EPL club had increased greatly since Roman Abramovich, a Russian businessman, purchased a controlling stake in Chelsea, another leading EPL team, in July 2003. Abramovich had very, very deep pockets and was operating with an "open check book." *The Wall Street Journal* reported in November 2003 that "during soccer's summer transfer period, he [Abramovich] spent $190 million on players [for Chelsea]—nearly as much as the other 19 Premier League Clubs spent combined." One challenge facing the Redfans Group was estimating the current market value of the Liverpool club.

Shares in Liverpool Football Club were not publicly traded, unlike shares of several other leading soccer clubs. Transactions in the shares of Manchester United, Arsenal and several other EPL clubs were regularly reported in the financial media. Market prices of these shares could be used to estimate the market value of these clubs. Estimating the current market value of privately-held Liverpool would require economic analysis of the EPL and of the on-field and off-field strengths of Liverpool.

European Soccer Leagues and the English Premier League

Europe had five major soccer leagues in 2004, in which 18 to 20 clubs within a single country competed against each other. Exhibit 1 presents summary information on the English, Italian, German, Spanish and French competitions. Smaller leagues (in terms of financial measures) were also found in other countries, often with one or two clubs in each country being dominant.

The English Premier League (EPL) was the elite club level competition for English soccer, with twenty teams competing. The league champion was decided based on points accumulated during the season, with 3 points for a win, 1 for a draw, and none for a loss. There was no post-season playoff. The EPL's 38 game season starts in August and ends in early May. There was a promotion and relegation aspect to the EPL that was also found in many soccer club leagues around the globe. The bottom three EPL clubs were downgraded to Division One of the Football League while the top three Division One clubs are promoted to the EPL. The Division One League was one of several leagues managed by the Football Association (FA), which is the governing body for English soccer.

EXHIBIT 1   KEY FINANCIAL OVERVIEW OF 5 MAJOR EUROPEAN SOCCER LEAGUES

	England	Italy	Germany	Spain	France
Teams in League	20	18	18	20	20
Top 4 Teams in 2003/2004	Arsenal Chelsea Man. United Liverpool	AC Milan Roma Juventus Inter Milan	Werder Bremen Bayern Munich Stuttgart Bayer Leverkusen	Valencia Barcelona D.Coruna Real Madrid	Lyon Paris SG Monaco Auxerre
Average Match Attendance 2003/2004	35,000	25,500	35,000	28,800	20,100
Total League Revenues (£millions) 2002/2003	£ 1,790	£ 1,162	£ 1,108	£ 847	£689
Total League Players Payments (£millions) 2002/2003	1,093	884	504	607	467
Player Salaries/Total Revenues % 2002/2003	61%	76%	72%	45%	68%
Total League Operating Profits (£millions) 2002/2003	£ 175	£ (381)	£ 115	N/A	£(61)
Revenue Composition					
Match Day	29%	18%	17%	N/A	15%
Broadcast	44	55	33	N/A	52
Sponsorship & Commercial	27	27	50	N/A	33

Source: Deloitte, *Annual Review of Football Finance* (August 2004).

Economics of EPL Clubs

Exhibit 2 presents ten years of summary financial data for Liverpool Football Club. The Annual Report for the Year ended July 31, 2003 was the most recent one available to Redfans. There were four major sources of revenue for individual EPL clubs:

1. EPL Media/Broadcast Revenues. The Football League on behalf of all EPL clubs negotiated with broadcast partners to cover EPL games. Individual clubs did not have separate television contracts with broadcast networks. The most important broadcast partner was BSKYB, which carried EPL games on a satellite television basis. For 2003/2004, £457 million of domestic television revenue was distributed to individual EPL clubs. The distribution formula had three components:

(a) 50 percent equally shared—£10.178 per club

(b) 25 percent merit fees, based on league position in the prior year. The higher the rank, the higher the fee.

(c) 25 percent facility fee, based on television appearances. The higher the number of television appearances, the higher the fee. The television broadcasters had a strong preference for carrying high profile winning clubs in their prime-time slots. BSKYB carried 132 games in the 2003–2004 season—the teams with the most games shown were Arsenal (15), Manchester United (14), Chelsea (12), Newcastle (9), and Liverpool (8). All clubs had a minimum number of games BSKYB must broadcast.

The five highest television payments to individual clubs in 2003/2004 were Arsenal (£32.754 million), Manchester United (£31.290 million), Chelsea (£30.487 million),

EXHIBIT 2   LIVERPOOL FOOTBALL CLUB—FINANCIALS 1994–2003 (AS REPORTED: £ MILLIONS) AND EPL SEASON RANK

A. SELECTED INCOME ITEMS

| | 12 MONTHS TO MAY 2 | | | | 15 MONTHS TO JULY 31 | 12 MONTHS TO JULY 31 | | | | |
	1994	1995	1996	1997	1998	1999	2000	2001	2002	2003
Revenues										
Broadcast/Media	10.785*	12.755*	17.325*	21.950*	26.868*	29.599*	29.606*	32.965	42.638	44.254
Matchday								28.235	30.616	28.662
Commercial (including Sponsorship)	5.988	6.327	9.104	16.317	17.521	14.589	15.897	20.061	24.131	28.403
Other	0.511	0.796	0.969	0.886	1.068	1.077	1.106	0.894	1.283	1.185
Total Revenues	17.284	19.878	27.396	39.153	45.457	45.265	46.609	82.155	98.668	102.504
Player Payments	9.789	10.384	13.234	14.599	30.128	36.273	40.107	48.880	56.031	54.431
Operating Profit	3.014	3.845	7.696	15.233	4.828	(10.175)	(17.936)	(4.341)	(2.766)	2.797
Net Transfer Activity	N.D.	N.D.	N.D.	N.D.	N.D.	(28.758)	(4.542)	(18.531)	(16.657)	(15.981)
Profit (After Tax)	1.080	(1.965)	(4.646)	4.655	1.872	(5.109)	0.758	(0.371)	6.041	2.304

B. SELECTED BALANCE SHEET ITEMS

| | YEAR ENDED MAY 2 | | | | | YEAR ENDED JULY 31 | | | | |
	1994	1995	1996	1997	1998	1999	2000	2001	2002	2003
Current Assets	3.763	12.755	7.539	18.769	12.455	15.517	22.472	16.546	23.695	14.363
Fixed Assets—Intangible	—	—	—	—	—	35.385	43.603	41.237	61.232	58.757
Tangible	12.209	18.747	22.366	23.177	33.989	38.986	40.008	41.217	40.937	41.933
Investments	0.001	0.001	0.001	0.002	0.002	0.002	0.003	0.003	0.003	0.003
Total Assets	15.973	31.503	29.906	41.948	46.446	89.890	106.086	99.003	125.867	115.056
Current Liabilities	6.618	6.992	8.985	17.439	20.159	21.944	40.321	37.323	52.245	45.211
Long Term Liabilities	1.427	9.022	9.998	8.767	4.200	17.300	15.614	11.769	17.657	12.045
Provision For Liabilities	—	—	—	—	—	1.972	0.777	0.380	2.177	1.820
Deferred Credits	2.227	2.438	2.545	2.628	2.633	2.527	2.469	2.349	2.266	2.154
Shareholders' Funds	5.701	13.051	8.405	13.060	19.454	46.147	46.905	47.182	51.522	53.826
Total Liabilities + Shareholder's Funds	15.973	31.503	29.906	41.948	46.446	89.890	106.086	99.003	125.867	115.056

C. EPL SEASON RANK

	1994	1995	1996	1997	1998	1999	2000	2001	2002	2003
EPL Season Rank (out of 20)	8	4	3	4	3	7	4	3	2	5

*Up to 2001, Media Revenues and Matchday Revenues were reported as a combined single figure.

Source: Financial Statements of Liverpool Football Club.

Liverpool (£26.607) and Newcastle (£26.419 million). The two lowest were Tottenham (£19.035 million) and Wolverhampton (£13.449 million).

This distribution formula created strong economic incentives to remain in the top tier of EPL teams. The EPL broadcasting contracts (in aggregate) were expected to remain at about the current level for at least the next 5 years. Any possible decrease in U.K.-based rights was expected to be offset by an increase in global revenues—"The global appeal of the Premiership is illustrated by the broadcast of 31,000 hours of Premiership football to 159 countries with a worldwide audience of 5.7 billion for the 2002/03 season."[23]

2. EPL Game-Day Revenues. These included ticket sales, food, drink, and other game-day concessions. Liverpool plays at Anfield Road, which had a capacity of 45,362. This was a relatively old stadium, having been opened in 1884. In recent years they had been negotiating to build a new 60,000 state-of-the-art stadium close to the current stadium site. Plans for a new stadium had been drawn, but financing was not yet in place. The EPL clubs with the highest stadium capacities and attendance percentages in 2002/2003 were Manchester United (67,721 capacity, with 99 percent attendance), Newcastle (52,181 capacity with 99 percent attendance), Sunderland (47,586 capacity and 82 percent attendance), Liverpool (45,362 capacity with 95 percent attendance), Chelsea (41,436 capacity with 94 attendance), Everton (40,168 capacity with 96 percent attendance), and Arsenal (38,040 capacity with 99 percent attendance).

The home club in the EPL kept all game-day revenues. Demand for tickets in the EPL was very strong, with the average stadium holding 37,784 and selling 94% of the seats available.

3. Sponsorship/Commercial Revenues. This included sponsorship, advertising, conference, catering, and merchandising income. One high profile sponsor was Carlsberg (a premium Danish lager brewed in the United Kingdom), which had signage on the playing jerseys. Other sponsors were Reebok, MNBA, Ladbrokes and Lucqzade.

4. European/Cup Revenue Sources. The top three or four teams in the EPL qualified to play in the UEFA Champions League for the following year. Liverpool finished second in the EPL in 2001/02 and qualified for 2002/03. In 2002/03, Liverpool came fifth in the EPL and did not qualify. UEFA Champions League is a 32-team pan-European competition to determine the leading club in Europe. In 2002/2003, £468.2 million in revenues were distributed to the 32 clubs participating. AC Milan was the winner. The four competing EPL teams and their Champions League revenue distributions were Arsenal (£20.9 million), Manchester United (£20.4 million), Newcastle (£15.6 million) and Liverpool (£13.2 million). Liverpool received the lowest distribution due to being eliminated early from the competition.

English soccer clubs also competed in several high-profile domestic tournaments. The most prestigious tournament was the FA Cup. This was a season-long competition, with the final game held in Mid-May after the EPL season has finished. Prize money for the FA Cup in 2004 was £2 million for the winner, £1 million for the runner-up, and reduced amounts for teams eliminated earlier. Recent winners had been Liverpool in 2001, Arsenal in 2002 and 2003, and Manchester United in 2004.

Player Payments

Player payments were the most significant cost item for EPL teams, comprising an average of 61 percent of total EPL revenues (Exhibit 2 reports Liverpool player payments for each year of the 1993/1994 to 2002/2003 seasons). The EPL had no salary cap, and clubs were able to spend whatever they decide on player payroll. Each year there were wide differences in both player payments and in player costs as a percentage of club revenues. For instance, for the 2002/2003 season, Manchester United paid 45.5 percent of revenues in player costs, Liverpool paid 53.1 percent, Leeds United paid 88.4 percent and Fulham paid 104.5 percent.

Manchester United's strong revenue base of £174.936 million illustrated how a well-managed club could have high player payments and still have a below average player payments/revenue ratio. Clubs could not sustain very high player payroll to revenue ratios over extended periods without continued cash infusions from an owner (such as from Fulham's owner Mohamed Al Fayed) or without experiencing financial solvency/bankruptcy problems (such as faced by Leeds United).

Summary Financials

Exhibit 3 presents summary financial data for a selected set of EPL football clubs with stocks publicly traded, drawn from two authoritative information sources on the Economics of EPL—Deloitte's *Annual Review of Football Finance* and *Soccer Investor Weekly*. (Deloitte's adjusted the line-items of individual clubs to present a standard comparable reporting format, which results in differences between the Exhibits 2 and 3 data for Liverpool.)

Three clubs in Exhibit 3 (Leeds, Chelsea, and Liverpool), did not have market capitalization amounts reported for August 6, 2004. Leeds United, previously publicly traded, was delisted in 2004. Leeds had spent large amounts on player acquisitions/salaries in the five years up to 2004 in an effort to move into the elite status and revenue generating league of tier one EPL clubs. Unfortunately, the highest place in the EPL ladder it attained was third in 1999/2000. It was placed into "administration" in March 2004 with negative shareholder equity of £44.268 million. At the end of the 2003/2004 season Leeds was one of the three lowest ranked EPL clubs and was relegated to Division One for the 2004/2005 season. Chelsea was publicly traded prior to the Abramovich investment in July 2003. Liverpool is privately held.

Alternative Approaches to Estimating Current Market Value

Redfans Capital considered several approaches in estimating the market value of Liverpool Football Club. Most experts agreed that using information from multiple approaches yields more reliable estimates of market value than sole reliance on any one approach.

Shareholders Funds Book Value Approach: Liverpool reported Shareholders Funds of £53.826 million for the year ended July 31, 2003 in the most recent annual report available to Redfans. In some contexts, this approach was a pivotal indicator of market value. For example, investment funds holding publicly traded equities were frequently valued using the market value of the underlying equities in the fund. Two aspects make this approach appealing in this investment fund context: (a) the underlying assets of the investment fund were highly liquid and frequently traded, and (b) market prices of the trades were readily observable.

However, in using this approach for the Liverpool Football Club, many of the key "assets" of Liverpool were neither highly liquid nor frequently traded (such as its stadium), and market prices for trades were not always available. A companion case discusses Liverpool's inclusion of player contracts of transferred-in players on its Balance Sheet (see Case 10.3: Liverpool Football Club: Putting Players on the Balance Sheet). Not all player contracts

EXHIBIT 3

SELECTED FINANCIAL STATEMENT INFORMATION (2002/2003 FISCAL YEAR: £ MILLIONS) AND MARKET CAPITALIZATION (AUGUST 6, 2004: £ MILLIONS) FOR PUBLICLY TRADED ENGLISH FOOTBALL CLUBS

Club/Fiscal Year End (1)	Revenues (2)	Player Payments/Wages and Salaries (3)	Operating Profit (4)	Pre-Tax Profit (5)	Shareholders Funds Book Value (6)	Market Capitalization (Aug 6, 2004) (7)	Premiership Rank in 2000/01; 2001/02; 2002/03; 2003/04
Arsenal	£103.801	£61.453	£19.497	£4.529	£76.211	£92.84	2; 1; 2; 1
May 03							
Aston Villa	45.447	30.872	(0.200)	(11.552)	50.679	33.89	8; 8; 16; 6
May 03							
Birmingham City	36.480	19.737	10.730	3.341	4.313	11.60	N/A; N/A; 13; 10
Aug 03							
Charlton Athletic	35.141	23.576	2.831	(0.464)	16.727	12.56	9; 14; 12; 7
June 03							
Chelsea	92.882	54.365	2.563	(26.290)	55.013	N/A	6; 6; 4; 2
June 03							
Leeds United	64.005	56.595	(25.446)	(49.505)	(44.268)	Delisted	4; 5; 15; 19
June 03							
Liverpool	103.981	54.431	19.765	3.641	53.826	N/A	3; 2; 5; 4
July 03							
Manchester United	174.936	79.517	47.789	39.345	156.833	667.25	1; 3; 1; 3
July 03							
Newcastle United	96.689	45.195	27.595	4.369	36.644	58.11	11; 4; 3; 5
July 03							
Southampton	48.875	26.666	8.700	(0.484)	10.624	17.88	10; 11; 8; 12
May 03							
Tottenham	66.506	38.024	11.028	(7.118)	31.238	26.92	12; 9; 10; 14
June 03							

Sources: (a) Deloitte, *Annual Review of Football Finance* (2004)
(b) *Soccer Investor Weekly* (August 10, 2004).

were included on Liverpool's 2003 balance sheet. Players "internally" developed through its own Liverpool Youth Academy were excluded. Moreover, the transfer payment at the time a player contract was acquired (acquisition cost) was the maximum that would show on the balance sheet as the value of the player contract. Liverpool did not increase the reported value of player contracts for players who attained national status after joining Liverpool. That is, Liverpool did not revalue upwards its player contracts even when the underlying asset had increased in value. However, it did reduce the value of player contracts over time using a systematic amortization schedule.

Market Multiple Approach: A frequently used valuation approach was using multiples from publicly traded companies to infer the market value of a privately-held company. Exhibit 3 presents information on eight EPL clubs with publicly traded securities. At least four different market multiples could be computed using the Exhibit 3 data:

1. Market Capitalization/Revenue
2. Market Capitalization/Operating Profit
3. Market Capitalization/Pre-tax Profit
4. Market Capitalization/Shareholder Funds

Exhibit 4 illustrates this approach using Manchester United as the benchmark.

Issues that arise in using a market multiple approach included: (a) which company or set of companies was the "best" benchmark?, and (b) which variable or set of variables (revenues vs. operating profit vs. .... etc) is the "best" way to infer value of the privately held company? The leading publicly-traded clubs that Liverpool viewed as either comparable or an aspiration-target were Arsenal, Manchester United and maybe Newcastle:

> Arsenal: London-based club with strong on-field performance. Had a large English and European fan base. Had plans to move to new stadium, but financing of it would strain the balance sheet.

> Manchester United: One of the elite sporting clubs in the world. It owned its own modern stadium and had global brand recognition.

EXHIBIT 4   USING MARKET MULTIPLES OF MANCHESTER UNITED TO ESTIMATE MARKET VALUE OF LIVERPOOL

Variable (1)	Manchester United Market Multiple (2)		Liverpool Amount (3)	Implied Market Value of Liverpool (4) = (2)×(3)
Market Capitalization / **Revenues**	£667.25 / 147.936	= 3.81	£103.981 mill	£396 mill
Market Capitalization / **Operating Profit**	£667.25 / £47.789	=13.96	£ 19.765 mill	£275 mill
Market Capitalization / **Pre-Tax Profit**	£667.25 / 39.345	=16.96	£ 3.641 mill	£ 62 mill
Market Capitalization / **Shareholders' Funds**	£667.25 / 156.833	= 4.25	£ 53.826 mill	£229 mill

Newcastle: Strong on-field club in recent years, with willingness to spend to acquire leading talent. Excellent stadium. Brand name had limited recognition outside England.

The other five publicly traded football clubs in Exhibit 3—Aston Villa, Birmingham City, Charlton, Southhampton and Tottenham—were at least a tier below Liverpool in both on-field achievement and global brand recognition.

Acquisition-Based Valuation Approach: When valuing a company for a potential acquisition or significant equity investment, it was useful to consider prior similar type transactions. Prior transactions relating to the specific private company being valued is highly relevant. In July 1999 Granada acquired a 9.9 percent equity stake in Liverpool Football Club for £22 million. This implied a valuation for Liverpool after infusion of the £22 million of £222 million (£22 million ÷ 0.099) in July 1999. Note, however, that as part of the transaction Granada also acquired the "right to manage a wide range of commercial issues for Liverpool F.C., including publishing, electronic media rights, and merchandising."[24] The Granada investment was for new shares. The largest shareholder's stake, held by Sir John Moores' family, was reduced to 51%.

In the March to May 2004 period, two groups submitted proposals to the Board of Liverpool Football Club. The Bridgemere Proposal was from Steve Morgan, a millionaire builder and lifetime fan of Liverpool. The Thai Investment Proposal was associated with the Prime Minister of Thailand (Thaksin Shinawatra). On May 13, 2004 the Liverpool Board of Directors released a statement through www.liverpoolfc.tv.

> *Liverpool Football Club confirms that it has received two indicative proposals for investment in the club, the Thai Investment Proposal and the Bridgemere Proposal backed by Mr. Steve Morgan.*
>
> *The board of Liverpool Football Club have today met with their financial advisors, Hawkpoint Partners, to consider these proposals.*
>
> *The board note that the Bridgemere Proposal, at £1.750 per share, current value of £61m for the entire club, which is a substantial discount to the value placed on the club by the board.*
>
> *The board have therefore concluded that the Bridgemere Proposal as currently constituted is not attractive.*[25]

The Bridgemere Proposal was relatively complex. It was estimated by the financial press to value Liverpool at £61 million prior to a cash infusion of £73 million. The Thai Proposal was more straightforward, reportedly seeking a 30% stake for approximately £56 million. This proposal valued Liverpool at £130 million prior to the £56 million cash infusion. The Thai Proposal was the subject of much debate (mostly negative) in Thailand and did not proceed to a binding agreement.

The July 2003 transaction for Chelsea shares also was a possible acquisition-related information item for valuing Liverpool. In July 2003, Roman Abramovich purchased the controlling stake in Chelsea Village PLC, held by Ken Bates. There was some ambiguity as to the specifics of the transaction. *Media World* (July 2, 2003) reported Abramovich paid £59.3 million in cash for the 50.1% stake. The *New York Times* (July 3, 2003) reported, "Roman

Abramovich, one of Russia's richest men, bought 50 percent of Chelsea Village, the holding company that owns the Chelsea soccer team and stadium. He paid about $100 million." *Sports Business Daily* (August 11, 2003) reported Abramovich made an initial payment of "more than $U.S. 300 million to gain control of the Chelsea soccer club." (The US/UK exchange rate in July 2003 was approximately £UK 1.00 = $US 1.60.) (Summary financials on Chelsea are in Exhibit 3.)

Questions

1. What are the major factors that affect the profitability and viability of Liverpool Football Club?

2. The playing squad is viewed as a key asset of Liverpool Football Club. Evaluate how its balance sheet represents this asset. How might this representation be "improved"?

3. Using each of the following approaches, estimate the value of Liverpool Football Club as of August 2004.

   • Shareholders' funds book value approach

   • Market multiple approach

   • Acquisition-based valuation approach

   What are the pros and cons of each of the three approaches?

4. An important valuation principle is triangulation: using information from multiple approaches/multiple sources to gain a more reliable estimate of firm value. How would you use this approach in valuing Liverpool Football Club?

5. Why might the current owners of Liverpool be reluctant to sell even if they perceive the bid price to be above "current market value"?

CASE 10.3 LIVERPOOL FOOTBALL CLUB: PUTTING PLAYERS ON THE BALANCE SHEET[26]

Financial reporting rules have been relatively slow to recognize that players are an asset to a sporting club. Changes in financial reporting rules in the United Kingdom provide insight into some financial dimensions of player value.

Liverpool Football Club was a leading soccer club in the English Premier League (EPL). Each year it publicly released its Annual Report, including an audited set of financial statements.

Sources of Current Liverpool Playing Squad

Liverpool's squad of Premier League players came from two main sources:

(A) Home-Grown Talent. These were players who started in the Liverpool Youth Academy (a "youth farm system"). Steven Gerrard, an English international player, was the highest profile home-grown talent on its 2004–2005 squad, first playing in the Premier League in 1998 at the age of 18. Michael Owen, who transferred to Real Madrid at the start of the 2004–2005 season, was also a high profile home-grown talent who started with the Liverpool Youth Academy. Owen played with Liverpool from 1997, when he was 17, to 2003. Home-grown player contracts could have two components:

Sign-On Bonus agreed to when a contract was signed.

Match fees (often a fixed amount per season, or in some cases a per game fee).

(B) Transferred-in Talent. These were players previously contracted to other clubs or contracted to other country federations. Harry Kewell, who joined Liverpool from Leeds United in July 2003, was a recent high profile acquisition. Liverpool paid Leeds United a transfer fee of £5 million for the right to register Kewell as a Liverpool player. Kewell had moved from Sydney, Australia to Leeds United when 17 years old and played his first game in February 1996. Liverpool's contract with Kewell could have the same two components as those for home-grown talent, a sign-on bonus, and match fees.

Liverpool's financial agreements included the payment of transfer fees to acquire new outside talent and the receipt of transfer fees from selling player contracts. For instance, Liverpool received a £8 million transfer fee from the sale of Michael Owen's player contract to Real Madrid.

Accounting for Player-Related Payments

There were three major categories of costs pertaining to Liverpool's playing squad: match fees, sign-on bonus, and transfer fees.

Match Fees: Liverpool consistently reported match fees as a player cost in the season to which they pertained (and were typically paid). Thus, Kewell's

2004–2005 season salary of approximately £3 million would be recorded as a £3 million cost for the 2004–2005 fiscal year.

Sign-On Bonus: Up to 1997, Liverpool reported the full amount of the sign-on bonus in the year in which the contract was signed. From 1998 onwards, the bonus was charged as a cost "to the profit and loss account in the accounting period(s) in which they are paid." To illustrate, assume a player signed for a £2 million bonus, payable in four equal yearly installments from the start of the contract. Up to 1997, Liverpool would have reported the full £4 million as a cost in the year the contract was signed. After 1997, Liverpool would report £500,000 as a cost each year that it is paid.

Transfer Fees: Up to and including 1998, Liverpool did not capitalize transfer fees paid to acquire player contracts from other clubs. No intangible asset for player contracts was shown on the balance sheet. Each year up to 1998, Liverpool reported as a line item in the income statement the net difference between transfer fees paid to other clubs for player contracts acquired and transfer fees received from other clubs for player contracts sold. Up to 1998, the £5 million transfer price Liverpool paid to register Kewell would have been included as an outgoing in the amounts used to compute the line item "Profit on Players Sold." Where the payments made to acquire players exceeded the payments received for Liverpool players whose contracts were sold to other clubs, Liverpool would report a "Loss on Players Sold."

Starting in 1999, Liverpool reported an intangible asset line item on its balance sheet and an associated "amortization of players' registrations" expense line item on its income statement. Footnote 2 to the 1999 Annual Report noted that it was now reporting intangible assets on its balance sheet (as required by The United Kingdom's Financial Reporting Standard 10— Accounting for Goodwill and Intangible Assets):

> *The company has changed its accounting policy in relation to the cost of player registrations following the issue of Financial Reporting Standard 10 "Goodwill and Intangible Assets." In adopting the change in accounting policy that element of a player's transfer fee, which relates to his registration together with any related costs is capitalized as an intangible asset. Provision is made for amortization of the amount so capitalized over the period of the respective player's initial contract with the company. Financial Reporting Standard 10 makes no provision for the value of players developed within the company.*

Assume Kewell signed a 5-year contract in July 2003. The £5 million transfer fee would be immediately shown as an intangible asset on the balance sheet. This asset would then be written down by £1 million each year of the 5-year contract period.

To facilitate comparability with its 1998 Annual Report, Liverpool also restated its 1998 profit before taxation for the accounting change. These disclosures were as follows:

	31 July 1998 £ millions
As previously stated	7.979
Prior period adjustment - intangible assets	14.812
- deferred taxation (note 17)	(4.581)
As restated	**18.210**

The effect on the prior period profit before taxation is as below:

	15 months ended 31 July 1998 £ 'millions
As previously stated	0.654
Players' registration costs now capitalized	12.402
Amortisation of players' registration costs	(10.753)
Net book value of players sold	(6.056)
As restated	**(3.753)**

The effect of the change in accounting policy for the period ended 31 July 1998 was to reduce profits both before and after taxation by £4,407,000.

Reported Intangible Assets

The result of these financial reporting changes was that Liverpool now showed amounts pertaining to the "transfer prices" of its transferred-in players among its balance sheet assets. The amounts Liverpool reported from 1999 to 2002 as an intangible asset for these player contracts were (in £millions):

1999	2000	2001	2002	2003
£35.385	£43.603	£41.237	£61.232	£58.757

These amounts pertained only to players whose contracts were purchased from other clubs. No costs were capitalized for players developed through the Liverpool Youth Academy. Exhibits 1 and 2 present financial information Liverpool reported over the 1997 to 2003 period. Up to 1997, Liverpool had a fiscal year that ended on May 2nd. In 1998, it chose July 31 as the end of the fiscal year. This meant the first year after this change had a 15-month fiscal year. Thereafter, the fiscal year was from August 1 to July 31.

Overview

Prior to its 1999 Annual Report, Liverpool reported one major asset on its balance sheet: "Fixed Assets—Tangible." This fixed asset line item was primarily its stadium (Anfield Road), which has capacity for 45,362, one of the largest in the EPL. Readers of Liverpool's balance sheet prior to 1999 would not find any recognition of the players' contracts as an asset. Was this an important omission? Since 1999, the transfer fees for transferred-in players have been reported as an "Intangible Asset," initially at cost and subsequently at amortized cost. Was this an important addition? What other improvements could be made to better represent on Liverpool's financial statements the value of their player contracts?

EXHIBIT 1   LIVERPOOL FOOTBALL CLUB-FINANCIALS 1997–2003 (AS REPORTED: £ 'MILLIONS)

A. SELECTED INCOME ITEMS

	12 MONTHS TO MAY 2	15 MONTHS TO JULY 31	12 MONTHS TO JULY 31				
	1997	1998	1999	2000	2001	2002	2003
Total Revenues	39.153	45.457	45.265	46.609	82.155	98.668	102.504
Operating Profit	15.233	4.828	(10.175)	(17.936)	(4.341)	(2.766)	2.797
Profit on Players Sold	N.D.	N.D.	2,805	3,209	5,668	13.229	2.328
Profit (After Tax)	4.655	1.872	(5.109)	0.758	(0.371)	6.041	2.304

B. SELECTED BALANCE SHEET ITEMS

	YEAR ENDED MAY 2	YEAR ENDED JULY 31					
	1997	1998	1999	2000	2001	2002	2003
Current Assets	18.769	12.455	15.517	22.472	16.546	23.695	14.363
Fixed Assets- Intangible	—	—	35.385	43.603	41.237	61.232	58.757
Tangible	23.177	33.989	38.986	40.008	41.217	40.937	41.933
Investments	0.002	0.002	0.002	0.003	0.003	0.003	0.003
Total Assets	41.948	46.446	89.890	106.086	99.003	125.867	115.056
Current Liabilities	17.439	20.159	21.944	40.321	37.323	52.245	45.211
Long Term Liabilities	8.767	4.200	17.300	15.614	11.769	17.657	12.045
Provision For Liabilities	—	—	1.972	0.777	0.380	2.177	1.820
Deferred Credits	2.628	2.633	2.527	2.469	2.349	2.266	2.154
Shareholders' Funds (SFs)	13.060	19.454	46.147	46.905	47.182	51.522	53.826
Total Liabilities + SFs	41.948	46.446	89.890	106.086	99.003	125.867	115.056

Source: Financials Statements of Liverpool Football Club.

EXHIBIT 2   LIVERPOOL FOOTBALL CLUB INTANGIBLE FIXED ASSET FOOTNOTE INFORMATION (£ 'MILLIONS)

Intangible Fixed Assets	2000	2001	2002	2003
Cost				
At 31st July, Year t-1	44.719	59.299	66.738	100.152
Additions in Year	20.088	20.463	38.824	16.851
Disposals in Year	(5.508)	(13.024)	(5.410)	(16.200)
At 31st July, t	59.299	66.738	100.152	100.803
Amortization				
At 31st July, Year t-1	9.334	15.696	25.501	38.920
Charge for Year	10.109	14.764	15.471	16.421
Impairments in Year	—	—	1.137	0.547
Disposals in Year	(3.747)	(4.959)	(3.189)	(13.842)
At 31st July, Year t	15.696	25.501	38.920	42.046
Net Book Amount				
At 31st July, Year t	43.603	41.237	61.232	58.757
At 31st July, Year t-1	35.385	43.603	41.237	61.232

Source: Financials Statements of Liverpool Football Club.

Questions

1. What changes occurred over the 1997 to 2003 period in the way Liverpool Football Club accounted for players as "assets" and player costs as "expenses"?

2. What factors might have motivated the changes you identify in requirement 1? Do the changes materially change the representations on the financial statements?

3. Briefly summarize the different accounting for the costs of acquiring the player-contracts of

   a. Home-grown talent such as Steven Gerrard

   b. Transferred-in talent such as Harry Kewell

   Why might (a) and (b) have different accounting treatments? What is the limitation of this different treatment? What might be done to have all players consistently reported in the financial statements?

4. For some publicly traded soccer clubs in the United Kingdom, the reported total net book value of player contracts exceeds the total stock market capitalization of the club itself. What alternate explanations might exist for this finding? Why might in other cases the total stock market capitalization of the club exceed the reported total net book value of player contracts?

Footnotes

1   This section was written by George Foster

2   John Waldron, Presentation at Stanford University (2004).

3   Examples include: K.G. Palepu, P.M. Healy, V.L. Bernard, *Business Analysis and Valuation: Using Financial Statements, Text and Cases* (South Western College Publishing, 2004), and S.P. Pratt, R.R. Reilly, and R.P. Schweihs, *Valuing a Business* (McGraw-Hill: 2000, 4th edition).

4   See P.B. Frank, M.J. Wagner, and R.L. Weil, *Litigation Services Handbook* (John Wiley,1990), Chapter 26 on "Business Valuations."

5   Examples of finance textbooks outlining the DCF approach include R.A. Brealey and S.C. Myers, *Principles of Corporate Finance* (McGraw-Hill: 2003, 7th edition) and J.C. Van Horne, *Financial Management Policy* (Prentice-Hall: 2002, 12th edition).

6   Arthur Levitt Jr., "Independent Review of the Combined Financial Results of the National Hockey League 2002–2003 Season," February 5, 2004.

7   "CBA: A different set of numbers," www.andrewsstarspage.com (August 1, 2004).

8   "CBA: The Levitt Report," www.andrewsstarspage.com (February 15, 2004).

9   J. Harrington, "Lightening Peek at Books," *St. Petersburg Times* (September 10, 2004).

10 This case was written by George Foster. The cooperation of Dan Beckerman and Phil Propper is gratefully acknowledged.

11 P. Lebrun, "Kings Prez Says Club in Red Ink," *Slam! Sports* (January 16, 2003).

[12] P. Propper De Callejon, C.T. Kugler, D. Tolen, P.S. Perry, and R. Gotcher, "Financial Analysis of the LA Kings," on http://www.letsgokings.com/kings/index.htm (April 4, 2003).

[13] J. Regardie, "Development Heaven—Development of Staples Center," *Los Angeles Magazine* (November 1998).

[14] R.A. Baade, "Los Angeles City Controllers Report on Economic Impact: Staples Center," July 21, 2003, p. 5, p. 11.

[15] B. Murray, "Shall We Gather at the Staples?" *Los Angeles Magazine* (October 2000).

[16] The Great Western Forum was put up for sale in October 1999. In June 2000 it was sold for $22.5 million to the Faithful Central Bible Church. R.A. Baade, "Los Angeles City Controllers Report on Economic Impact: Staples Center," July 21, 2003, p. 33 (from web search).

[17] Propper, loc. cit. Reprinted with permission of the author.

[18] Arthur Levitt Jr., "Independent Review of the Combined Financial Results of the National Hockey League 2002–2003 Season," February 5, 2004. The Levitt Study, discussed further in Section 10 of this book, was funded by the NHL.

[19] P. Lebrun, loc.cit.

[20] For example, American Airlines Arena in Dallas was built in 2001 for an estimated cost of $325 million. Public funds contributed approximately 50% of the cost. R.A. Baade, "Los Angeles City Controller Report on Economic Impact: Staples Center," July 21, 2003, p. 9 (from web search).

[21] This case was written by Susan Mackenzie and George Foster.

[22] Redfans Capital is a fictitious investor group created to facilitate discussion of the issues raised in the case. Liverpool fans are frequently called the "Redfans" because of the color of the club's home-field playing strip.

[23] Deloitte, "Football Finance: Improving Finances at Premiership Clubs," Deloitte Public Relations: Manchester, U.K., 04/06/2004.

[24] BBC News, July 13, 1999.

[25] Breaking.tcm, "Morgan bid 'unattractive' to reds," May 13, 2004.

[26] This case was written by George Foster.

APPENDIX   Information Sources Used

The sports industry is one of the most extensively reported industries. This book draws on multiple sources. The following were sources of key information and exhibits used in this book:

Barrett Sports Group. Based in Manhattan Beach, California, this group "provides strategic consulting services to the sports and entertainment industry." Areas of expertise include economic and fiscal impact studies, strategic planning, and valuation.

Address: 1219 Morningside Drive, Suite 101, Manhattan Beach, California 90266, U.S.A.
Website: http://www.barrettsports.com

Deloitte Sports Business Group. Based in Manchester, United Kingdom, this group publishes highly respected and authoritative reviews of the sports industry. A major area of expertise is football (soccer). Examples of publications are:

- *Deloitte Annual Review of Football Finance* (detailed survey of English soccer clubs and European soccer)
- *Deloitte Football Rich List*

Address: 201 Dansgate, Manchester, United Kingdom, M60 2AT
Website: http://www.sportsconsulting.co.uk

ESPN The Magazine. A recent addition (launched in March 1998) to the sports magazine category, it is now the second largest based on total advertising revenue. It draws on the resources of ESPN and has a target focus on the 18–34 ("MTV generation") demographic. It includes innovative survey results in its annual "Fan Satisfaction Ratings."

Address: 19 East 34th Street, New York, New York 10016, U.S.A.
Website: http://www.espn.go.com/magazine. See also its sister site: http://www.espn.go.com

Forbes. This leading business publication provides the most systematic estimates on club financial aspects. Each year sports/entertainment journalists at *Forbes* (led by Kurt Badenhausen and Michael Ozanian) estimate revenue, profits, player payroll, debt, and valuation for every club in the MLB, NBA, NFL, and NHL. These estimates are made using publicly available information sources. Estimates are also made for selected European soccer clubs.

Address: 60 Fifth Avenue, New York, New York 10011, U.S.A.
Website: http://www.forbes.com

FutureBrand. A marketing company (within the McCann-Erickson World Group) that focuses on brand development strategies and brand valuation. It provides studies on the most valuable sporting brands.

Address: 300 Park Avenue South, 7th Floor, New York, New York 10010, U.S.A.
Website: http://www.futurebrand.com

Goldman Sachs. A major global investment banking, securities, and investment management firm. It represents professional sporting teams in their acquisition, sale, valuation, or financing, and also provides advice and transaction assistance in stadium financing.

Address: 85 Broad Street, New York, New York 10004, U.S.A.
Website: http://www.gs.com

IEG. A Chicago-based leading sponsorship industry expert on "sports, arts, cause and entertainment marketing." It has multiple publications to facilitate up-to-date knowledge on sponsorship, including:

- *IEG Sponsorship Report*—biweekly newsletter delivered by mail and online
- *IEG's Guide to Sponsorship*
- *IEG's Sponsorship Sourcebook*

Address: 640 North LaSalle, Suite 600, Chicago, Illinois 60610, U.S.A.
Website: http://www.sponsorship.com

IMG. A global sports marketing company focused on "the marketing and management of sport, leisure, and lifestyle." It covers all major areas such as athlete representation, consultancy, event management, and licensing and merchandising. TWI, IMG's television division, is the largest independent distributor and producer of televised sports.

Address: 1360 East 9th Street, Suite 100, Cleveland, Ohio 44114, U.S.A.
Website: http://www.imgworld.com

Joyce Julius and Associates. A widely used "sports, special event and entertainment program evaluation" source. Provides customized products measuring media exposure—such as *Sponsors Report*® and *National Television Impression Value (NTIV*®*) Analysis*.

Address: 1050 Highland Drive, Suite E, Ann Arbor, Michigan 48108, U.S.A.
Website: http://www.joycejulius.com

Nielsen Media Research. A widely cited TV ratings company. It provides television audience estimates for broadcast and cable networks (as well as other areas such as for advertisers and advertising agencies). The Nielsen Sports Marketing Service provides custom reports for specific sports programming.

Address: 770 Broadway, New York, New York 10003, U.S.A.
Website: http://www.nielsenmedia.com

Octagon. A global sports marketing company that offers broad-based coverage of business areas of sports—athlete representation, consultancy, event management, property representation and sales, TV rights sales and distribution, TV production and archive, new media, and licensing and merchandising.

Address: 1270 Avenue of the Americas, 7th Floor, New York, New York 10020, U.S.A.
Website: http://www.octagon.com

Revenues from Sports Ventures (RSV). A weekly newsletter by Mediaventures that is available online on a subscription basis. It provides coverage of many aspects related to stadium financing, construction, and management. There is also an annual publication that reports financial and other information for North American sports venues for baseball, basketball, football, hockey, and soccer.

Address: Mediaventures, P.O. Box 240854, Milwaukee, Wisconsin 53224, U.S.A.
E-mail: rsv@sportsventures.com

Soccer Investor. A leading online information source for the business side of soccer. Covers all parts of the globe, with deep coverage of the English and Scottish soccer leagues. Two online newsletters are *Soccer Investor Daily* and *Soccer Investor Weekly.*

Address: Elizabeth House, 6th Floor, 39 York Road, London SE1 7NQ, United Kingdom
Website: http://www.soccerinvestor.com

Sports Illustrated. The sports magazine category leader in both paid circulation and advertising revenue. Provides broad coverage across multiple sports. Winner of multiple awards for investigative journalism as well as photography. Includes highly respected surveys, such as "SI's Fortunate 50" that lists the top 50 income-earning athletes (broken down by salary/winnings and endorsements/appearance fees).

Address: Time and Life Building, Rockefeller Center, New York, New York 10020, U.S.A.
Website: http://www.si.com

Street and Smith's Sports Group. The leading general source of up-to-date comprehensive information on the business of sports. It has multiple superb publications, including:

- *Sports Business Journal*—weekly publication in hard copy
- *Sports Business Daily*—three online editions (morning, regular, afternoon) each day summarizing sports issues in all areas of the media
- *By the Numbers*—annual edition that summarizes many key financial aspects of sports

Address: 120 West Morehead Street, Suite 310, Charlotte, North Carolina 28202, U.S.A.
Website: http://www.sportsbusinessjournal.com (See the "About Us" and "Company History" pages for an overview of publications available.)

Team Marketing Report. A leading publisher of sports marketing and sponsorship information. Products include:

- *Team Marketing Report Newsletter*—monthly newsletter on sports marketing
- *Sports Sponsor Fact Book*
- *Inside the Ownership of Pro Sports*

Address: 900 North Michigan Avenue, Suite 2100, Chicago, Illinois 60611, U.S.A.
Website: http://www.teammarketing.com

The Sporting News. A longtime sports weekly publication. It produces annual features including the "Power 100," profiling the most powerful people in sports.

Address: 10176 Corporate Square Drive, Suite 200, St. Louis, MO 63132, U.S.A.
Website: http://www.sportingnews.com

Sporting websites. There are numerous high-quality general sporting websites. These include:

http://www.espn.go.com

http://www.foxsports.com

http://www.si.com

http://www.sportinglife.com

http://www.sportingnews.com

http://www.sports.yahoo.com

Several of the above websites are linked to leading sports magazines. These include (in order of circulation) *Sports Illustrated, ESPN the Magazine,* and *The Sporting News.*

Each individual sport typically has its own set of websites and magazines. A good first pass is to examine the websites of the respective leagues, players' associations, and individual clubs in each sporting league.

NAME INDEX

COMPANY INDEX

Philips, 413
Phoenix Home Life Mutual Insurance, 78, 86
Pilot Pen, 260
Pittsburgh Gladiators, 114
Pittsburgh Pirates, 29
Players, 68
Players/Forsythe Racing, 67
Pop Warner, 165
Portland Sea Dogs, 124
ProServ, 162–164
Puma, 51
PWR Championship Racing, 67

Q

Qantas, 40
Quaker Oats, 74

R

Rabbitohs (Australian rugby), 58
Raiders (Australian rugby), 58
Rangers, 95
RCA Championships, 253
Real Madrid, 4, 43
Real Sports magazine, 402
Red Bull, 44
Reebok, 22, 44, 49, 51, 77, 78, 86, 166
Reliant, 413
Reliant Resources, 413
Revenues from Sports Ventures (RSV), 476
Rice University, 76, 225
The Richmond Times Dispatch, 91
R.J. Reynolds Tobacco Company, 242, 244–246
Roma, 95
Roosters (Australian rugby), 58
Rugby Union, 58

S

Sacramento Bee, 88, 89
Sacramento Kings, 42, 43
The San Francisco Chronicle, 91
San Francisco 49ers, 105–112
San Francisco Giants, 416–428
San Jose Clash, 49, 55
San Jose Mercury News, 222
San Jose Spartans, 53
San Jose State University (SJSU), 222–228
SBC Park, 416 et seq.
Scottish Premier Soccer League, 29
Sea Eagles (Australian rugby), 58
Sears, 87
Seattle Mariners, 34, 154–163
Seattle Reign, 87
SFX, 151
si.com, 478
Snickers, 51
Soccer Industry Council of America, 53
soccerinvestor.com, 477
Soccer Investor Daily, 477
Soccer Investor Weekly, 477
Southeastern Conference (SEC), 214, 215
Southern Methodist University, 225
Southwest Conference, 216
Spalding, 87
Spanish-Language Univision, 51

Spartan Foundation, 227
Speed Channel, 353
sponsorship.com, 476
Sponsors Report and National Television Impression Value (NTIV) Analysis, 476
Sporting Goods Business, 91
sportinglife.com, 478
The Sporting News, 22, 477, 478
sportingnews.com, 477, 478
Sports Business Daily, 477
Sports Business Journal, 477
sportsbusinessjournal.com, 477
SportsChannel, 78
sportsconsulting.co.uk, 475
Sports Illustrated, 22, 91, 477, 478
Sports Illustrated for Women, 399, 400
Sports Management Consulting Group (SMCG), 38, 40–45, 105
Sports Net, 345
Sports Sponsor Fact Book, 477
sports.yahoo.com, 478
St. George club, 29
St. Helens rugby, 28
Stadium Commitee of NFL, 28
Stanford University, 74, 87
Staples Center in Los Angeles, 20
Starbucks, 42
Storm (Australian rugby), 58
Street & Smith, 234, 477
Street & Smith's SportsBusiness Journal, 90
Sunday Telegraph, 89
Sun-Herald, 89
Sunshine Network, 352
Sydney Morning Herald, 89

T

Tampa Bay Devil Rays, 42
Tampa Bay Mutiny, 52
The Tampa Tribune, 90
Target, 67, 69, 70
Team Kool Green, 67
teammarketing.com, 477
Team Marketing Report, 477
Team Motorola, 67
Team Penske, 69, 70
Team Players racing team, 68
Team Rahal, 67
TelCel, 44
Telemundo, 73, 394
The Temptations, 334
Texas A & M, 216
Texas Rangers, 154–164
Texas Tech, 216
Tigers (Australian rugby), 58
TIME Magazine, 192
Time Warner, 97
Tommy Hilfiger, 201
Tora Takagi, 67
Toronto Blue Jays, 29
Toronto Maple Leafs, 17
Tostitos Fiesta Bowl, 215
Townsend Bell, 67
Toyota, 65, 67, 70
TSI Soccer, 51
Tulsa World, 90

U

Umbro, 51
United States Auto Club (USAC), 66

United System of Independent Soccer Leagues (USISL), 49
University of Arkansas, 216
University of California, Irvine, 225
University of California, Riverside, 225
University of California, Santa Barbara, 225
University of Chicago, 220
University of Colorado, 201–205
University of Connecticut, 73–77
University of Florida, 228
University of Hawaii, 225
University of Idaho, 225
University of Kentucky, 74
University of Miami, 200, 214
University of Michigan, 193–196, 219
University of Nevada, 225
University of North Carolina, 214, 220
University of Notre Dame, 214–221
University of Oregon, 40
University of Pacific, 225
University of Southern California, 27
University of Tennessee, 77
University of Texas, 216
University of Texas at El Paso, 225
University of Tulsa, 225
USA, 394
USA Today, 89
Utah Jazz, 43
Utah State, 225

V

Verizon, 18
Virginia Tech, 200, 214
Visa, 19, 74, 234, 263
Volvo, 251

W

Wake Forest University, 221
Walker Racing, 67
Walt Disney Company, 355
Warriors (New Zealand rugby), 58
Warsaw Sports Marketing Program, 40
Washington Commandos, 114
The Washington Post, 91
Western Athletic Conference (WAC), 225, 227
Women's National Basketball League (WNBA), 26, 27, 73–87
Women's Professional Basketball League, 76
Women's Professional Fastpitch, 79
Women's Sports and Fitness, 399
Women's Sports Foundation, 79, 211
Working Woman, 91
World Sporting Congress, 105
World Wrestling Entertainment, 4
World Wrestling Entertainment (WWE), 27
WUSA (women's pro soccer league), 73

Y

Yahoo, 44, 478
Yale, 18
Yale University, 251
Yawkey Trust, 323 et seq
YES Network, 4, 13, 352, 368

SUBJECT INDEX